# Chartism

## A new history

*Malcolm Chase*

Manchester University Press

Manchester and New York

*distributed exclusively in the USA by Palgrave*

*Published by* Manchester University Press
Oxford Road, Manchester M13 9NR, UK
*and* Room 400, 175 Fifth Avenue, New York, NY 10010, USA
www.manchesteruniversitypress.co.uk

*Distributed exclusively in the USA by*
Palgrave, 175 Fifth Avenue, New York,
NY 10010, USA

*Distributed exclusively in Canada by*
UBC Press, University of British Columbia, 2029 West Mall,
Vancouver, BC, Canada V6T 1Z2

*British Library Cataloguing-in-Publication Data*
A catalogue record for this book is available from the British Library

*Library of Congress Cataloging-in-Publication Data applied for*

ISBN  978 0 7190 6087 8   *paperback*

First published 2007

16 15 14 13 12 11 10 09 08   10 9 8 7 6 5 4 3 2

Typeset by
Carnegie Book Production, Lancaster
Printed in Great Britain
by Cromwell Press Ltd, Trowbridge, Wiltshire

# Contents

# Acknowledgments

This book has drawn on research accumulated over an unusually lengthy period. However, it would have remained unwritten but for Research Leave funding from the Arts and Humanities Research Council and study leave from the University of Leeds. I am grateful to both institutions for their support, likewise to the Marc Fitch Fund for a generous grant in aid of publication. The support of my colleagues at Leeds, in both the School of Continuing Education and the School of History, has been very important.

My profound thanks are due to the many institutions on whose holdings I have drawn, and to their staff who have so cheerfully assisted me. Among London repositories I owe thanks to Bishopsgate Institute, the British Library (St Pancras), the British Newspaper Library (Colindale), the Goldsmiths Library of Economic Literature (University of London, Senate House), the London School of Economics and the National Archives at Kew. In Manchester I should like to thank the archivists at the Co-operative College and the Labour History Archive & Study Centre at the National Museum of Labour History. I acknowledge also the assistance of staff at the museums' services of Ayrshire and Newport, at Wilton Lodge Museum, Hawick, at York Minster Library, the libraries of Staffordshire University and the University of York, and that of the library volunteers at the incomparable Whitby Literary and Philosophical Society. For over two decades I have been a voracious user of the Brotherton Library of the University of Leeds, an exceptional resource with an exceptional staff. My grateful thanks go to them all.

I am particularly indebted to the staff of the following municipal libraries, archives and local studies' centres: Barnsley, Birmingham, Bolton, Bradford, Dartford, Derby, Leeds, Manchester, Middlesbrough, Newcastle upon Tyne, Newport, Oldham, Stockport, Sunderland, Tameside (Ashton-under-Lyne and Stalybridge), Warwick, York and the West Yorkshire Archives Service in Bradford and Leeds.

My approach to trying to read the *Northern Star* 'innocently' was, over the space of several years, to browse through issues in chronological order, recording impressions and quotations into a dictation machine as I went along.

This would have been impossible, however, without the help of Sheila Salvin and, especially, Joan Winpenny (both of the School of Continuing Education, University of Leeds) who painstakingly transcribed the tapes that emerged each Monday morning from this exercise.

Presenting papers to a wide range of seminars and conferences on different aspects of Chartism has helped focus my thoughts, provided bracing scrutiny of the same and corrected countless misapprehensions. It would be invidious to mention some of these and not others, so I thank them all. I do wish to place on record, though, my appreciation of successive groups of students whose enthusiasm and informed participation in courses related to Chartism has done so much to enhance my understanding of the movement.

Debts of a more personal nature are legion. None of the following bears any responsibility for the defects of this work, but in different ways each has helped with its progress: Owen Ashton, John Baxter, Fabrice Bensimon, my parents Sherwin and Elizabeth Chase, Chris Close, Sean Creighton, Dodford Independent Electors, Stephen Duncombe, Richard Floyd, James Gregory, Robert Hall, Julian Harber, John Harrison, Ian Haywood, Ronald Morris, Ian Packer, Mike Sanders, Dorothy Thompson, William Turner, Roy Vickers and an anonymous reader. My colleague David Goodway was an important and unflagging source of encouragement. I am especially indebted to Eduardo Trigo O'Connor d'Arlach for allowing me to quote from the correspondence of Feargus and Francisco Burdett O'Connor (and to James Dunkerley for facilitating this) and to Angela Killick for her enthusiastic response to my request to make use of Ann Dawson's sampler.

'I know no person living', wrote Thomas Cooper in his autobiography, 'who could write a History of Chartism without making mistakes. I am sure that I could not.' There would be many more mistakes in the pages that follow were it not for Shirley Chase. She has nurtured this book, read successive drafts and her considered advice has enhanced it all. As always, our daughter Sarah helped keep everything in the most cheerful of perspectives. This book is theirs too.

*Osbaldwick, July 2006*

# Abbreviations

| | |
|---|---|
| ACLL | Anti-Corn Law League |
| Add. MSS | Additional Manuscripts |
| BCL | Birmingham Central Library |
| BL | British Library |
| BPU | Birmingham Political Union |
| Burland | J. H. Burland, 'Annals of Barnsley and its Environs', unpublished MS in Barnsley Central Library, Archives & Local Studies Section |
| CA | Charter Association |
| CNA | Central National Association |
| *DLB* | *Dictionary of Labour Biography*, vols 1–10, J. Bellamy and J. Saville (eds) (London, Macmillan, 1972–2000); vol. 11, K. Gildart, D. Howell and N. Kirk (eds) (London, Palgrave, 2003); volume 12, K. Gildart and D. Howell (eds) (London, Palgrave, 2005) |
| *ECC* | *English Chartist Circular and Temperance Record* |
| FPU | Female Political Union |
| FRA | Female Radical Association |
| GNCTU | Grand National Consolidated Trades' Union |
| GNU | Great Northern Union |
| *Hansard* | *Hansard's Parliamentary Debates*, 3rd series |
| HO | National Archives, Kew, Home Office papers |
| IUSA | Irish Universal Suffrage Association |
| LDA | London Democratic Association |
| LHASC | Labour History Archive & Study Centre, Manchester |

| | |
|---|---|
| LPRA | Leeds Parliamentary Reform Association |
| LWMA | London Working Men's Association |
| MAGBI | Miners' Association of Great Britain and Ireland |
| MEPO | National Archives, Kew, Metropolitan Police Papers |
| NAUT | National Association of United Trades for the Protection of Labour |
| NCA | National Charter Association |
| NCSU | National Complete Suffrage Union |
| NCREC | National Central Registration and Election Committee |
| NPFRA | National Parliamentary & Financial Reform Association |
| NPU | National Political Union for the Obtainment of the People's Charter |
| *NS* | *Northern Star* |
| NUWC | National Union of the Working Classes |
| *ODNB* | H.C.G. Matthew and B. Harrison (eds), *Oxford Dictionary of National Biography* (Oxford, Oxford University Press, 2004) |
| PRL | Political Reform League |
| PU | Political Union |
| RA | Radical Association |
| TS | National Archives, Kew, Treasury Solicitor's Papers |
| USCCS | United Suffrage Central Committee for Scotland |
| WMA | Working Men's Association |
| WYAS | West Yorkshire Archives Service |

# CHAPTER ONE

# May–September 1838:
# 'I hold in my hand a charter –
# the people's charter'

## Prologue: Glasgow Green, 21 May 1838

By general consent, continuous rain in Glasgow on Monday, 21 May 1838, subdued the extraordinary spectacle hardly at all.[1] All morning, the throng swelled on Glasgow Green preparing to welcome a delegation of the Birmingham Political Union (BPU). No other English organisation could have so galvanised Scotland. Equally, none but Glasgow's combined trades could have organised an event on this scale. At 11.00 a.m., marching to the strains of 43 bands, a procession began winding its way across Glasgow towards Parkhead. Here the delegation from the midlands, which had already addressed a meeting there earlier that morning, was waiting for them. At its head was Thomas Attwood, a banker, MP for Birmingham and the architect of the BPU, perhaps the most pivotal parliamentary pressure group of the early nineteenth century.

From Parkhead the assembly returned to the Green. All public work was suspended. Spectators crammed around windows along the route; new marchers fell in where gaps arose. Marching briskly, 4 or 6 abreast, the procession was 2 miles long and took an hour-and-a-half to pass. Over 300 banners were carried by the marchers. 'No Stone and Mortar Qualification' read one (a reference to the property ownership necessary to the right to vote).[2] Many banners referred to the iniquitous Corn Laws: 'Taxation without Representation is Tyranny and ought to be resisted' declaimed one, recalling a fundamental tenet of the American Revolution. On the flag carried by marchers from Strathaven, only the words 'Religion' and 'Covenant' were legible. Yet its appearance was a powerful statement linking the day's events to a long tradition of popular resistance to oppressive government. In the later seventeenth century, many Scottish Presbyterians had forcibly resisted the imposition of Crown control of the Church of Scotland. Strathaven's flag had been carried in 1679 at the Battle of Drumclog, at which untrained Covenanters had rescued prisoners from a cavalry force led by the notorious government commander the future Viscount Dundee.[3]

It was past 2.00 p.m. before the crowd, now numbering around 150,000, reassembled on the Green to listen to Attwood's speech. But first, as at all political gatherings of this nature, there were constitutional niceties to be observed. James Turner, tobacconist and local magistrate, was voted to the chair. He reminded his audience of the need for good order before introducing Thomas Gillespie. The crowd cheered as he declared that 'the wealth of the country, the product of industry, was grasped by tyrannical men, whose tables groaned under the weight of their feasts, while thousands were perishing for want'. The solution was 'to demand those rights which they believed heaven granted to man – to sweep away oligarchical oppression'. Those rights ('which the law rulers of our country had grasped from them') were to participate fully and fairly in parliamentary elections.

The rostrum then passed to William Pattison, secretary of the local branch of the Steam Engine Makers' Society and a member of the standing committee of Glasgow's trades. He observed with satisfaction 'that the demonstration that day had been got up by the working classes alone, without the least assistance of the monied aristocracy – (great cheering)'. To Pattison fell the duty of moving the adoption of a petition, brought from Birmingham. At its heart lay a profound grievance about the parliamentary Reform Act of 1832: though it had significantly extended the right to vote, it had done little to dent the landed classes' domination of politics, while working men went unenfranchised as before. A vote of thanks followed to the men from Birmingham: 'they now as well as we have found that the Reform Bill does not answer the purposes for which it was obtained'.

Only then, firmly reminded who it was that had invited him and organised this reception, was Attwood invited to speak. He began, predictably enough, by flattering his audience, whom he greeted as the 'unconquered men of Scotland'. He described how he had led the BPU in the agitation that culminated in the 1832 Reform Act and how the organisation had then lapsed, its supporters confident that the reformed Parliament would legislate in the interests of the whole people. But the Act had changed nothing and therefore, 'through the power of the people, it shall be cast onto the fire'. The BPU had been revived to achieve this. Universal male suffrage, voting in secrecy by ballot, and annual Parliaments had to replace the provisions of 1832. These were the principles at the heart of the petition that had just been proposed; they must now 'be united in order to command the Government, and thus to obtain the justice they claim'.

Attwood strongly hinted that petitioning alone might not suffice. 'We have to contend against the numerous blood-suckers of a place-holding and a pensioned aristocracy – (hear, hear.)' The whole political establishment was corrupt. How would the House of Commons be persuaded to act on their petition, if the moral force of their argument did not prevail? Attwood's answers displayed a subtle gradation of pressure. The people should be prepared to petition again and again; mass meetings should each elect a delegate to be sent to London to form an alternative Parliament.

> I would like to see the House of Commons that would set them at defiance – (tremendous applause.) But if they should be mad enough to despise your petitions – the petitions of two million brave men – (hear, hear) – then I would have you to proclaim a solemn, a sacred, and an universal Strike, not of master against man, or of man against master, but of all combined against the common enemy – (immense cheers.) ... a sacred week in which no work shall be done in Britain.

Again Attwood declared 'I should like to see the Government that would dare to face us', a statement greeted with '[t]remendous cheering, waving of hats, beating of drums, and other demonstrations of applause'. Whatever the strategy, unanimity of purpose and action across the whole country was needed. 'Peace, law, order, loyalty, and union are inscribed on your banners. (Cheers.) On these principles, the men of Birmingham will follow you to the death.'

Other midland delegates then spoke: George Edmonds, Robert Douglas (editor of the liberal *Birmingham Journal*) and two manufacturers, Philip Muntz and Thomas Salt. A few weeks earlier, Salt had convened a meeting in Birmingham of some 12,000 women to launch a Female Political Union. The relative absence of women from the Glasgow meeting was later remarked upon. In respect of gender politics, at least for the moment, Glasgow and Birmingham were marching in different steps. Finally, in a coda to the afternoon's proceedings, two delegates from the London Working Men's Association (LWMA) addressed the assembly. The first, St Pancras coal merchant Thomas Murphy, provided the only Irish voice in the afternoon's proceedings. More attention, however, was paid to the commanding figure beside him, Dr Arthur Wade, an Anglican clergyman from Warwick. Wade had been expelled from the BPU in 1833 for criticising its lukewarm attitude to further reform. The following year he had achieved national eminence as a leader in the campaign to defend six farm workers from Tolpuddle, near Dorchester, sentenced to transportation for trade union activities.[4] It was largely Wade's influence that had made it possible for the LWMA to associate itself with the demonstration. He followed Attwood in emphasising the moral weight of the reformers' cause while alluding to the physical momentum that could be placed behind it. He suggested a mass demonstration in London: 'I would say to you Scotsmen, Bluebonnets, come over the border.'

It had been a long day and the rain had been relentless. The speed with which the assembly dispersed suggests not everyone stayed to hear Murphy and Wade. Some papers failed even to report their speeches. Thus their references to the latest LWMA publication went largely unregarded. It extended the elements of the BPU petition by calling for three additional measures of parliamentary reform: payment for MPs; the abolition of the property qualification to become an MP; and the standardisation of constituency sizes to create equal electoral districts. So new was this pamphlet that no copies were available to distribute. Wade could only flourish a set of proofs in front of the crowd. 'I hold in my hand', he told them, 'a charter – the people's charter.'

The political culture of early Victorian Britain was primarily an oral one. Though literacy rates had increased steadily for some years, outdoor mass meetings like this were a primary vector of communication. People would walk considerable distances to attend: the Strathaven contingent, for example, made a round-trip of thirty miles. The functions of such a meeting were wider than just imparting information. Rituals of assembly created and affirmed identity. It was not the platform speakers alone who made grand statements on such occasions: audience participation was highly vocal (and not always as positive as these speakers enjoyed); and the theatrical spectacle of such a monster meeting – with the elaborate choreography of its gathering – was a profound statement about the mood and opinions of those assembled.

In any account of such a meeting, however, a note of caution must be entered. Few newspapers presented events of this kind dispassionately, even if their reporters heard and recorded every word spoken, which was highly unlikely at a meeting on this scale. Attendance figures particularly were an issue of contention. Given what is known about Glasgow and its environs, the Green and the general tone of reportage, the widely claimed turn out of 150,000 seems plausible; but the reader should be aware that newspaper estimates ranged between 30,000 and 100,000 in Whig and Tory papers, and between 100,000 and 200,000 in radical ones. Furthermore, reporters of political speeches routinely used a free, indirect style. This smoothed over what the reporter missed or needed to compress, while conveying (especially if heard read aloud, as radical newspapers generally were) the excitement of hearing first hand the events described.[5] Reports of the same speech often varied widely, with the scope for difference increasing as newspapers (as was common at the time) lifted and adapted others' coverage. Seasoned politicians might present selected reporters with their text, but few could then resist the temptation to amend or embellish it; occasionally one would explicitly acknowledge having done so.[6] In some versions of Attwood's speech, a reference to the 'blood-suckers of a place-holding and a pensioned aristocracy' was extended to embrace 'nine-tenths of the gentry' and 'the great body of the Clergy'.[7] It is well to be aware from the inception of any historical study that what one reads there is unavoidably provisional.

Nor can we understand gatherings like that of 21 May simply by describing them. Context is important, along with an understanding of the unspoken messages (clear to contemporaries but not us) which such events conveyed. Mounting frustration at the failure of the Reform Act to introduce meaningful change is clear; but Attwood's public avowal that this was so considerably intensified popular determination for further reform. Attwood epitomised the beneficiaries of 1832, the vast majority of whom seemed at best indifferent to extending the suffrage further. The local context, moreover, was pregnant with significance. Early in 1838, five Glasgow cotton-spinners had been found guilty of conspiring 'to keep up wages' and instigating 'intimidation, molestation and threats'.[8] Charged also with (though acquitted of) the murder of a strike-breaker, their trial seemed at times to extend to the whole principle of trade unionism. Public opinion was unsettled by abundant evidence of overt violence being used to secure trade unionist ends. In consequence, trade unionists were inclining to political rather than direct industrial action. It was therefore signif-icant that Glasgow's seventy trade unions organised this meeting, and were first to speak that afternoon. Gillespie was secretary of the defence committee for the spinners, now incarcerated in a prison hulk awaiting transportation. The warm promise of support from the men of Birmingham therefore had profound symbolic value. Regardless of recent history, it suggested that labour did not face the political establishment alone. A political campaign that tran-scended social class and individual interests was seemingly within sight.

Within sight, too, were some subtler messages. In a society where urban squalor was rife and casually accepted as normal, Glasgow still astonished observers. It was 'the worst of any we had seen in any part of Great Britain', according to one authority on the sanitary condition of industrial towns. 'For undisguised profligacy, offensive brutality, squalid wretchedness, and unbear-able filth, Glasgow to my mind excels all', wrote another; 'penury, dirt, misery, drunkenness, disease and crime culminate in Glasgow to a pitch unparal-leled in Great Britain', declared a third.[9] Yet here were tens of thousands of Glaswegians, shrugging this aside in an orderly but spectacular assertion that their circumstances should and could be different. The very paths on which they marched across Glasgow Green had been laid by unemployed workers in 1820, during a programme to alleviate distress and unrest in a year of general strike and rebellion in Scotland.[10] That so many working people paraded on the Green on their own terms was itself a politically charged statement. So too was Strathaven's Drumclog flag, kept not by any religious group but by the Strathaven Weavers' Friendly Society. Strathaven had been a significant contributory current to the failed Scottish rising of 1820.[11] The presence of radicals from the town was a visible reminder of a tradition of armed, radical mobilisation and their flag even more so.[12] The idea that the politically excluded were, in an almost religious sense, a chosen people covenanted to God in the pursuit of justice had wide currency. This extended far beyond Scotland, as will become clear later in this study. Furthermore, Strathaven and its flag (quartered with the saltire of St Andrew) reinforced the occasion's nationalist undertones. We need to be cautious not to read back modern nationalist attitudes into early Victorian contexts; but in Scotland and Wales, as well as Ireland, radical reformism was fuelled by resentment that political power lay with a propertied elite, ruling through institutions based in England. The BPU delegates signalled their recognition of this the next day, with a pilgrimage to 'the sacred field of Elderslie', near Paisley, birthplace of William Wallace. (The latter's sensational defiance of English authority at the turn of the thirteenth century was then, as it remains, a touchstone of Scottish nationalism.)

The identity of the speakers themselves also had symbolic significance. We have highlighted Attwood and Wade in this respect, but they were not alone. James Turner had provided the land on which the first mass radical meeting in Scotland had been held in 1816; in 1832 he had given the site for a memorial to the leaders of the 1820 rising. Thomas Murphy, like Wade, had cut his political teeth as an active participant in the 1820 campaign supporting Queen Caroline (the wife whom George IV sought to divorce). George Edmonds had led the Birmingham reform agitation during the Regency and in 1819 had been indicted for his part in electing a 'Legislatorial Attorney and Representative' for the town, almost exactly as Attwood was now suggesting that mass meetings across the country should do.[13]

Finally we should take stock of what was missing from the great gathering on Glasgow Green. First, Attwood did not refer to currency reform. 'He is a man of one idea', wrote one jaundiced observer, 'I never yet knew him make a speech since his admission into Parliament, in which the staple matter was not a paper currency.'[14] The extent to which Attwood was a currency reform monomaniac has been exaggerated by historians, although there is no doubt that his commitment to parliamentary reform was considerably strengthened by the belief that only a reformed House of Commons would pass the monetary measures he believed were crucial to economic prosperity. This was not necessarily a view that all his audience would have shared (or, indeed, fully understood). A judicious silence was clearly helpful here. A second and more significant silence, however, concerned the BPU delegates' almost unanimous suspicion of democracy. For them, universal male suffrage was a tactical necessity, not a principled objective. 'The masses of the people constituted the only engine through which it was possible to obtain reform', Attwood had told the BPU a few months earlier, 'and that mighty engine could not be roused into efficient action without the agency of universal suffrage. It was in vain to attempt to move the middle classes.'[15] Local government, not currency, was the BPU's immediate target for reform. Pragmatically, an inclusive reform movement appeared necessary to secure it. Even so, the limit of the BPU's vision was representative rather than direct democracy. The BPU's programme omitted the three additional points in the charter that Wade presented to the crowd (equal electoral districts, paid MPs and the abolition of the property qualification) precisely because its ruling council wished to circumscribe any extension to political power.[16] Underlining this ideology at Glasgow Green, there was neither a speech from nor a vote of thanks to John Collins, a Birmingham toolmaker and BPU emissary to Scotland. More than anyone, Collins had brought about the convergence of the Glasgow and Birmingham radical campaigns during an exhaustive tour of major Scottish industrial centres in the preceding weeks: 'A very plain, very sensible, very earnest, very colloquial orator, with a magazine of facts in the shelves of his memory. The workers crowded everywhere to hear the new evangel', one contemporary recollected.[17] Though Collins was thanked at dinner that night, one is left with the impression that this indefatigable but self-effacing activist was marginal to the controlling interests of the organisation.

## The People's Charter

With hindsight, the most significant missing element at Glasgow Green was copies of *The People's Charter*. The LWMA had resolved only six days previously to send Murphy and Wade there, to present 'our pamphlet entitled the "People's Charter"'.[18] As long ago as July 1837 it had pledged that 'in the course of a few weeks' this pamphlet would 'be prepared and printed for circulation, under the title of "The People's Charter"'.[19] The following year the LWMA's secretary, William Lovett, insisted on adding a lengthy introductory address. Further delays ensued when the printer (who was not being paid) had to prioritise other work. It finally appeared a few days after Glasgow Green.[20] It is difficult to suppress the thought that, had the initiation of a new phase in British radical politics been left to the LWMA alone, the cause would have been lost from the start.

Why then did *The People's Charter* so soon lend its name to the first (and arguably still the greatest) mass political movement in industrialised Britain? To answer this we need to examine three interlocking issues: the history of the ideas it contained, the process by which it was drafted and the nature of the association that produced it. There was nothing new about the publication except – and this perhaps crucially – its title. The six points for parliamentary reform that it contained had been proposed as a package as far back as 1777 in John Cartwright's *The Legislative Rights of the Commonalty Vindicated, or Take Your Choice!* This was itself an extended reworking of an edition of the previous year, *Take Your Choice! Representation and Respect; Imposition and Contempt; Annual Parliaments and Liberty; Long Parliaments and Slavery.* As the ponderous original title conveys, Cartwright was strongly committed to annual Parliaments. These he envisaged would offer a genuinely representative democracy in which MPs would be the mandated delegates of their constituents, rather than effectively unaccountable and subject only to re-election as infrequently as every seven years. To the 1777 edition Cartwright added payment for MPs and the abolition of the property qualification. Opinion would differ as to the relative merits of the six points, but thereafter universal male suffrage, shorter Parliaments (some advocated triennial elections) and, to a slightly lesser extent, the ballot occupied every radical agenda for parliamentary reform.

The LWMA was emphatic that all six reforms were needed. This had been a staple of ultra-radical thought since 1816, but *The People's Charter* did more than merely reassert established demands. The punchy title was itself significant: one only has to contrast it with earlier political pamphlets (Cartwright's, for example) to appreciate this. The allusion to Magna Charta of 1215 was one which all politically aware contemporaries would have understood. Indeed, radical interest in 'the Great Charter of Liberties' had grown over the previous quarter of a century, fuelled by an explosion of radical publishing in the Regency years.[21] At the French Revolution of 1830, the Declaration of Rights was widely referred to in English as 'the new Charter'. Taking a cue from this, a leading London radical publisher issued *The New Charter*, proposed '*as a Substitute for the Reform Bill*' in 1831. In 1832 the Metropolitan Political Union (London's pale equivalent of the BPU) issued *The People's Charter ... giving a Condensed View of the Great Principles of Representative Government, and the Chief Objects of Reform.*[22] Magna Charta constituted the foundation stone of English liberties and the People's Charter would complete the edifice. Since its inception, the LWMA had corresponded with some 150 like-minded provincial societies, and the purpose of this new publication was to form the focal point of a national agitation. The specific suggestion it be titled *The People's Charter* apparently came from the Colchester WMA.[23]

It was also distinguished by the manner in which it encapsulated the six points in, to quote its subtitle, *an outline of an act to provide the just representation of the people of Great Britain and Ireland in the Commons House of Parliament.* The result makes dry reading for modern tastes, but a key objective of the tract was to initiate 'some practicable step in favour of Radicalism'. The introduction actually asserted: 'we need not reiterate the facts and unrefuted arguments which have so often been stated and urged in their support'. Instead the need was 'to test the sincerity' of reforming MPs 'by proposing that something shall be done in favour of those principles they profess to admire'.[24] To that end the LWMA had not worked in isolation but had convened a public meeting in February 1837 to initiate a petition for the six points to Parliament.[25] This paved the way for a further meeting three months later which resolved to draw up a parliamentary bill based on these six points, and which appointed a committee comprising 6 members of the LWMA (Lovett; 2 renowned radical newspaper promoters, John Cleave and Henry Hetherington; 2 printers, Henry

Vincent and James Watson; and a wood-carver, Richard Moore) along with 6 sympathetic MPs. This committee has become part of the received wisdom of Chartist history, so it is worth stressing here that it was an utter shambles.

The full committee never met. Three MPs were defeated in the general election that summer, and drafting the bill was left to Lovett. The 38-year-old cabinetmaker was highly respected in London radical circles as a diligent committeeman, but he repeatedly postponed the task. 'Having my bread to turn and little time to my disposal it necessarily took some time.' On the one occasion Lovett did convene the committee not everyone was invited and only one MP, charismatic Irish nationalist Daniel O'Connell, actually turned up. He had to leave hurriedly for the Commons but not before making a series of suggestions which those who remained promptly ignored. Of the 6 nominated MPs only John Roebuck (unseated in 1837) had any input to the text – a preamble of less than 150 words. Effectively, then, Lovett wrote *The People's Charter*. A claim that the veteran radical Francis Place had a hand in it was only ever made by Place alone.[26]

Much more grievous than these delays, however, was the opening of a profound rift between O'Connell and English radicals. As the leader of those Irish MPs who demanded the reinstatement of home rule for Ireland, O'Connell's policy in the Commons was essentially opportunistic.[27] During 1837 he reversed his earlier support for factory reform and, in the wake of the Glasgow spinners' affair, became a high-profile parliamentary critic of trade unionism. In February 1838 O'Connell called for a parliamentary enquiry on workers' combinations. In the event nothing came of this, but at the time it appeared to many workers (especially those in textile industries) to be another repressive move against trade unionism. Lovett, an active member of the London Society of Cabinetmakers, was one of them. When the London trades set up a group to monitor the parliamentary enquiry, he became its secretary (just as he had of the Tolpuddle labourers' defence committee four years earlier).

It was at this point, when *The People's Charter* should have been nearing publication, that the complex inter-personal politics of British and Irish radicalism came into play. The former MP for County Cork, Feargus O'Connor, accused Lovett and the LWMA of complicity in the establishment of the parliamentary enquiry.[28] This 44-year-old barrister had broken from O'Connell in 1836 over Irish issues, since when he had assiduously cultivated English radicals. An instinctive rather than intellectual politician, and emotive where Lovett was understated, O'Connor was the antithesis of much that characterised the LWMA. The latter's preferred medium was the printed page, O'Connor's the platform. The wire-pulling micro-politics favoured by Lovett was completely at odds with the mass political mobilisation that O'Connor espoused. In February 1838 this would have mattered little had O'Connor's behaviour not been so blatantly opportunistic. He was still smarting at the reversal in 1835 of his electoral victory in Cork (when a parliamentary committee ruled he did not meet the £600 freehold property qualification). Though it would be exaggerating to describe him as a leader without a cause, O'Connor clearly calculated that outspoken support for the Glasgow spinners would cement his growing popularity in Scotland and northern England. Lovett and the LWMA executive replied with a scorching condemnation: 'You carry your fame about with you on all occasions to sink all other topics in the shade – you are the great "I AM" of politics, the great personification of Radicalism.'[29] Internal conflict thus bedevilled the Chartist movement even before *The People's Charter* was published or the concept of Chartism had emerged.

In O'Connor's defence it should be stressed that the LWMA on its own was incapable of creating a mass movement. This becomes clearer if we consider the Association in the broader context of metropolitan radicalism. Despite its title, the LWMA was an elitist organisation. Membership cost a shilling a month and was restricted to 'persons of good moral character among the industrious classes'. In all, the LWMA numbered only 291 full members, though it sought to extend its influence by admitting 'honorary members not of the working classes'. These included O'Connell, O'Connor, Murphy, Salt and Wade.[30] By far the greater part of the capital's radicals, however, belonged to the dozen or so district associations, of which the Radical Association (RA) in Marylebone, founded in September 1835, a year earlier than the LWMA, was the most influential. Marylebone parish was a sprawling, populous town within a city. O'Connor had played a large part in the formation of the Marylebone RA, the character of which was shaped through incorporating the remnants of the once-influential National Union of the Working Classes. The latter had mobilised those London radicals during the Reform Crisis who opposed piecemeal reform and were therefore critical of the Political Union movement, the BPU included.

The Marylebone RA, like other district associations, was decidedly different in tone from the LWMA: subscriptions were lower and its meetings were usually held on licensed premises. Whereas the LWMA devoted much energy to an extensive correspondence with reform organisations outside London, the Marylebone RA concentrated on establishing similar groups within it. Neither these RAs nor the LWMA, however, were notably long-lived, and none approached in importance the East London Democratic Association, founded in January 1837. The LDA ('East' was dropped in August 1838) espoused muscular republicanism, 'the principles propagated by that great philosopher and redeemer of mankind, the Immortal "THOMAS PAINE"'.[31] Nor was it shy of demanding the redistribution of private property. The LDA attracted the largest membership of any early metropolitan Chartist organisation. Even so this was still barely more than 3,000. As a newspaper closely linked to it observed, the capital was 'too huge a place to carry out the details of organization in a business-like and or satisfactory manner; and besides, the people are not sufficiently known to, nor have they the necessary confidence in, each other'.[32]

The volatile and fissiparous tendencies of London popular politics were the product of geography and social structure, exacerbated by the variety of associational cultures that flourished in a metropolis of 2 million people. Furthermore, although poverty was endemic in many parts of London, its economy did not share the vicissitudes of the industrial midlands, the north, south Wales or Scotland. As a result it was largely out of step with national trends, 'always the last to stir, or when it takes the initiative, such is its over-whelming bulk, and the consequent segregation of its parts, that no powerful and well compacted concentration of energy is produced … How different all this is in a provincial town!'[33] Although the LWMA's achievement in revital-ising interest in the six points has properly commanded posterity's respect, historians have almost habitually exaggerated its importance to the Chartist movement.[34] To understand why *The People's Charter* captured the popular imagination we have to look elsewhere than London.

## Feargus O'Connor

Both the BPU and the LWMA financed what they termed 'missionaries' to raise political awareness beyond their respective cities. Cleave visited Brighton for the LWMA as early as March 1837; from May its main targets were Yorkshire and the east midlands (and, in the autumn, mid-Wales), where Hetherington, Cleave and Vincent each made considerable headway. Collins was highly effec-tive in Scotland, but Salt's impact on Lancashire was muted. However, the real problem with these initiatives was that they were inevitably atomised: Britain was as yet without a national railway network; regional differences mattered immensely and were reflected and intensified by a newspaper press that was overwhelmingly provincial in character; public meetings (often called at short notice) were the dominant mode of popular political discourse. It needed a person of very distinctive qualities to overcome these difficulties. That person was Feargus O'Connor.

When he attacked the LWMA in February 1838, Feargus O'Connor had already done much to establish a reputation as an effective radical campaigner in northern England. Ireland and Britain were not hermetically sealed and there was nothing unusual in an Irish landowner seeking election to an English parliamentary seat. This O'Connor did at Oldham in 1835. He had just been unseated at Cork, and Oldham, a two-member constituency with a highly organised radical caucus and a significant number of artisan voters, was a natural choice as a location from which to re-launch a parliamentary

career. There were obvious attractions, too, in seeking to succeed the deceased
MP, the great agitator William Cobbett. Like O'Connor, Cobbett had had no
connection with Oldham but secured his election on the basis of a formidable
reputation. O'Connor had little reputation to trade on and the borough's other
MP, the radical mill-owner John Fielden, was pledged to support Cobbett's
son. John Cobbett was but a shadow of his father and was flaky concerning
the disestablishment of the Church of England (consistently one of the core
political issues of the nineteenth century). While the name of Cobbett was
enough to secure more votes than O'Connor, the thirty-five votes the latter
obtained split opposition to the Tories and lost the election for Cobbett.[35]

The Oldham result saddled O'Connor with a reputation as a political adventurer, at least in middle-class liberal circles.[36] This was unfair: constituency
politics in nineteenth-century England were highly fluid and John Cobbett
himself had similarly denied a Liberal candidate victory six months earlier
at Chichester. For O'Connor, who cared little for liberal opinion, the episode
brought distinct advantages. It introduced him to the industrial north. He
would later describe the encounter as a personal epiphany: 'I then for the first
time saw the Rattle Boxes and their victims ... the pallid face, the emaciated
frame, and the twisted limbs, wending their way to the earthly hell. I saw
the exhausted frame staggering home more ghastly still by candle light, after
fourteen hours' toil ... From that moment I became the unpaid advocate of
my fellow man.' No less crucially, Lancashire introduced him to the northern
audiences who proved warmly responsive to his highly individual style of political rhetoric. If O'Connor had been hazy about the character of radicalism
in England's industrial heartlands, then 'Lancashire College, at Oldham' (as
he described the experience) educated him.[37] In particular he came quickly
to appreciate the enduring importance of Henry Hunt. One cannot understand O'Connor outside of this context. Hunt had been the dominant figure
within popular politics after the Napoleonic Wars, decisively shaping a strategy
of open constitutional agitation. But this derived its force from the massive
numbers of working people Hunt's leadership mobilised. His scathing rejection
of piecemeal reform (including the 1832 Reform Act) and contemporary political economy made him an iconic figure among working-class radicals. Hunt
linked the two by consistently arguing that 'all that the radicals required was
a reformed parliament which would act for the benefit of the people ... It was
said that property should be represented: so he said [too], for labour was the
property of the people'.[38]

It was Hunt whom a huge crowd gathered to hear at St Peter's Fields,
Manchester, on 16 August 1819, only to be forcibly dispersed by yeomanry
acting on local magistrates' orders. The incident was immediately and universally named 'Peterloo'. Massive popular indignation, however, did nothing to
prevent the exoneration of those responsible for some 17 deaths and over 650

injuries, nor in their wake the introduction of repressive legislation and the imprisonment of Hunt. Peterloo became an iconic event in nineteenth-century domestic politics. As late as 1874, Liberal election literature still cited it as an example of 'Tory justice': in the 1830s and 1840s its memory was yet more potent. Each anniversary was marked by a rally on 'the blood stained fields of Peterloo', and also more widely, while Peterloo relics and veterans were vener-ated in their communities.[39] Ill-health removed Hunt from the public eye in the final years of his life. Yet his death in 1835 (broken hearted, it was widely believed, by working people's failure to protest *en masse* against the 1832 Reform Act) left a void in English popular politics. Feargus O'Connor had arrived in Lancashire intending to replace William Cobbett; he departed declaring that 'he would fill up the vacancy caused by the death of Henry Hunt'.[40]

O'Connor certainly had the physical qualities – a prodigious appetite for hard work, an imposing demeanour, and 'lungs of brass and a voice like a trumpet' – to imitate 'Orator' Hunt.[41] Talent as a platform speaker alone, however, would never be enough to reinvigorate, still less extend, the mass movement once led by Hunt. We have already seen how O'Connor had established a presence in London's radical circles through the Marylebone RA (founded two months after the Oldham election). At the end of the same year, at the Association's urging, he embarked on an intensive lecture tour of the industrial north, setting up RAs on the London model as he went. His visit coincided with growing disquiet at the impending implementation of the New Poor Law, against which his voting record while an MP was impeccable. His personal impact was immense, as he fully intended it should be. The recollections of one Barnsley handloom linen weaver provide a vivid portrait of Feargus at this time:

> His figure was tall and well proportioned, and his bearing decidedly aristo-cratic. He wore a blue frock coat and a buff waistcoat, and had rings on the fingers of each hand. In a graceful manner, and in emphatic language, he told the Radicals of Barnsley that he had sold off his horses and dogs, had greatly reduced his establishment, and come weal come woe, he would henceforth devote his whole life to promote the well-being of the working classes. It was even whispered among his admirers that he was descended from the ancient kings of Ireland. This made him an immense favourite; for the working classes, in spite of their democracy and republicanism, have a predilection for high blood in their leaders. The language of O'Connor, to ears accustomed to little else than the Barnsley dialect, as spoken by pale-faced weavers and swart cobblers, sounded like rich music.[42]

These observations about O'Connor's aristocratic demeanour were acute. Like Henry Hunt, he stood consciously in the tradition of the gentleman radical leader, a tradition traceable back through Hunt's precursor (and O'Connor's godfather) Sir Francis Burdett and Major Cartwright to John Wilkes, whose campaigning caused acute discomfort to governments in the 1760s and 1770s.

Renouncing wealth and breeding in the cause of democracy was politically potent and sharpened popular appreciation of the evils of old corruption. In practical terms, such figures were skilled in the language and etiquette of high politics; in modern parlance, they had good networking skills. It mattered not if breeding and wealth were exaggerated (though it helped to retain some of the latter to finance an appropriate lifestyle and a reputation for generosity). O'Connor positively encouraged the idea that he was descended from the ancient royal house of Ireland, while admitting only in private that gambling had cost him much of his personal wealth, a swingeing loss of £750 in 1834 forcing him to sell his race horses and curing the habit.[43]

All this would seem to confirm O'Connor's reputation as a political adventurer. Yet the path he chose in 1835 was neither easy nor calculated to restore his fortune. Had this been his motivation he would have fared far better practising as a barrister. Nor was life as a professional orator comfortable. For example O'Connor spent 123 days on the road between June 1838 and August 1839, during which he made 147 major speeches and participated in innumerable conferences, committees and court hearings.[44] This pattern of activity had been established in his northern tour of December 1835: bursts of intensive activity maximised public awareness and coverage in the regional press. It served him well, though by 1837, 'the first blush of curiosity having faded, I found that the press was entirely mute, while I was working myself to death'.[45] O'Connor alternated time spent seeking to influence radicalism in London with provincial speaking tours (notably in the winter of 1836–37 when he extended his activities to Nottingham, Newcastle and across central Scotland, before returning to Yorkshire).[46] London, however, was less receptive to his appeal and an attempt in 1836 to establish a Universal Suffrage Club, speaking for the whole city as the LWMA claimed to do but without the latter's elitist character, came to nothing.

The following year O'Connor and his close ally Bronterre O'Brien, the unstamped press journalist, became involved in the Central National Association (CNA), an organisation considerably less impressive than its title but a significant precursor to the politics of later years. It brought together a broad spectrum of ultra-tories, notably its leader James Bernard, a farmer and fellow of King's College, Cambridge. Bernard's economic and political thought had interested socialist circles for some time, while his opposition to the New Poor Laws and pro-manhood suffrage and anti-middle-class views were a combination attractive to O'Connor. Furthermore the CNA provided a platform from which to expose the workings of the allegedly reformed parliamentary system. At the general election of July 1837, three leading CNA figures – John Bell, editor of the radical *London Mercury* at Coventry, O'Connor at Preston and O'Brien at Manchester – exploited election proceedings to expose their intrinsically undemocratic nature. O'Brien was not even permitted to speak at the Manchester hustings (the forum where, prior to any poll, the returning officer asked for a show of hands from all present for each candidate); O'Connor won Preston's hustings but declined to go to the poll where he knew he would lose; Bell polled a mere forty-four votes. The episode highlighted the case for manhood suffrage. However, the narrow defeat of Richard Oastler, the leading Yorkshire figure in the factory reform and anti-Poor Law movements and the CNA-endorsed candidate at Huddersfield, suggested that even unreformed elections might be open to radical influence.[47]

Bernard's ultra-Toryism found limited political resonance in London, and the CNA rapidly declined from the summer of 1837; but O'Connor's involvement consolidated his growing reputation. In particular, participation in the CNA underscored O'Connor's status as an opponent of the so-called New Poor Law, i.e. the Poor Law Amendment Act of 1834. This Act sought to abolish relief of poverty from public funds except for those prepared to enter a workhouse and submit to a work, leisure and dietary regime considerably less attractive than that of the lowest-paid labourer outside it. Each workhouse served a union of many parishes, and this abolition of communal responsibility for the relief of the poor, combined with their punitive loss of freedom, was massively resented. Furthermore, workhouses seemed an insensitive and inappropriate mechanism through which to deal with cyclical unemployment and short-time working, both seemingly endemic in the northern factory districts. On the other hand, the 'Old Poor Law' was frequently inequitable and inefficient in its administration, and there were many (at least among those least likely to need poor relief) who supported the 1834 Act on the grounds of financial and administrative efficiency. The CNA was the only London body consistently opposed to the legislation. To many northern radicals, even the LWMA reeked of Malthusianism. Malthus was the political economist who argued that, over time, population growth would inevitably outstrip the land's capacity to support it. This irrevocably linked his name to criticism of the Old Poor Law (on the grounds that readily available poor relief encouraged profligacy and large families), and hence to arguments for the postponement of marriage and contraception.

For O'Connor, opposition to the New Poor Law attracted warm praise from Oastler,[48] while the CNA brought him closer to Oastler's Lancashire counterpart, the mercurial Methodist minister J. R. Stephens, as well as to key local leaders like Barnsley's Joseph Crabtree. In May 1837 these four appeared together on the platform at a mass meeting on Hartshead Moor, between Bradford and Huddersfield. With them were Bell, Bernard, O'Brien and John Fielden. The language they used gives a vivid indication of the hatred conceived for the New Poor Law, and of how closely O'Connor fitted in with their line of thinking:

Crabtree spoke of the New Poor Law as accursed; O'Brien as Malthusian;

O'Connor as necessarily meeting with the execration of every human being; Fielden as infamous; Bell as fatal and damnable ... Stephens as abominable; and Oastler as damnable, infernal, detestable, despotic, unchristian, unconstitutional, and unnatural.[49]

The audience may have exceeded 250,000. It was certainly the largest O'Connor had yet encountered, and it left him with an overwhelming sense of the pent-up political energies of the Pennine industrial communities. Later that day he fell into conversation with Joshua Hobson, the Leeds printer who had published *Voice of the West Riding*, the greatest of the provincial radical papers of the early 1830s. These journals were collectively called the 'unstamped' due to their publication in defiance of the heavy newspaper tax (designated by an official stamp on the masthead of legal newspapers) exacted by the Government. Those associated with them often earned punitive fines and prison sentences, but also enduring reputations as radicals of courage and integrity. Hobson, O'Brien, Cleave and Hetherington were all veterans of the unstamped. A substantial reduction in the Stamp Duty in 1836 all but killed off unstamped papers; but outside London there had yet to appear any new paper that embodied their spirit and political purpose. O'Connor was growing frustrated at press indifference to his speaking tours. Now he discussed with Hobson the logistics of producing a quality, radical, stamped weekly newspaper.[50]

A few weeks earlier, O'Connor had contemplated producing just such a paper from Barnsley, specifically from a spare room at Crabtree's pub, The Freedom Inn. However, Hobson's counsels prevailed and the paper, when it finally appeared on 18 November 1837, did so from the lofty address of Briggate, Leeds, and not Dog Lane, Barnsley (though the editor O'Connor appointed, William Hill, was Barnsley-born and a handloom weaver prior to becoming a minister in the Swedenborgian Church). For the next seven years, Hobson's print works turned out one of the greatest publishing phenomena of the nineteenth century. But its origins were chaotic: O'Connor had to make a last-minute dash to Manchester to purchase the requisite official stamps and only 3,000 copies were printed. Hobson was not equipped to print on the scale required by O'Connor: a new press and type had to be ordered, to pay for which O'Connor had quickly to raise substantial share capital. This at least had the merit of ensuring for the paper a wide network of interested supporters: some share capital was raised from Ashton-under-Lyne, Barnsley, Keighley, Oldham and Rochdale, but the greater part came from Bradford, Hull, Leeds, Halifax and Huddersfield. In all, £690 was raised, nearly all from £1 shares; but this was still insufficient to meet all the set-up costs, the remainder of which O'Connor met himself.

It was as well, therefore, that the *Northern Star* quickly became a major force in radical journalism. O'Connor's reputation helped. So, too, did his novel idea of presenting gifts of engravings to regular subscribers.[51] By January

1838 it was selling around 10,000 copies weekly. By the summer, although the geographical distribution of its shareholders reflected its Pennine heartland, its circulation extended across most of Britain. The paper balanced local advertising and information such as market prices, essential to maintain its Yorkshire circulation, with lively news reportage; but its key features were incisive, well-written editorials, a weekly declamatory letter from O'Connor, a poetry column, to which readers could submit their own verse, and extensive coverage of political activities from any locality that cared to send reports. These appeared, 'accompanied by all the flourishes calculated to excite an interest in the reader's mind, and to inflate the vanity of the speakers', recollected one who was many times thus noticed, 'dressed up with as much care as though they were parliamentary harangues fashioned to the columns of the daily press'.[52] In doing so the paper was boosting its circulation not merely by flattering its readers: rather it was promoting a sense of that seemingly boundless potential glimpsed by O'Connor on Hartshead Moor in May 1837. The accumulation of such reportage, column on column, week after week, imbued readers with a sense of belonging to a common crusade. The *Northern Star* gathered up news of local and regional activities, and steadily promoted the idea that all were part of a coherent and vital whole. And so in time they became.

## Into Chartism

So when O'Connor assailed the LWMA in February 1838 for its mishandling – as he saw it – of Parliament's enquiry into trade unionism, he did so from a position of strength. He was the owner of a weekly newspaper of rapidly increasing popularity. He had appeared on public platforms all over northern England, central Scotland, Nottingham and Tyneside. He was a familiar figure in London radicalism, while in the north of England he was closely identified with the anti-Poor Law agitation and its two leading figures, Oastler and Stephens.

In all this activity he consistently advocated radical reform centred on manhood suffrage and made swingeing attacks on the Whig Government – not just the 1834 Poor Law, but its handling of the recent Canadian rebellion, its restriction of civil liberties in Ireland, its connivance at the prosecution of trade unionists and its lukewarm attitude to factory reform. His capacity to fuse support for radical and ultra-tory objectives made him a commanding figure, as Oastler observed to a Huddersfield audience: 'It is perfectly true, and you all know it, that there is a wide difference, in our abstract principles, between Mr. O'CONNOR, and myself; but our ultimate object is one and the same. We both seek for the happiness, the contentment, and the security of all: and, for that very reason, we are neither of us Whigs.'[53] O'Connor's command of the burgeoning radical movement was not total (his absence from Glasgow Green on 21 May 1838 indicates that), but as that movement began to cohere around the BPU petition and *The People's Charter*, so O'Connor and the *Northern Star* were increasingly at its centre. As early as June his name was invoked by the influential Scottish *Monthly Liberator* as a potential source of assistance to elect an 'out-and-out radical' candidate in an anticipated Glasgow parliamentary by-election.[54]

The arguments expounded on Glasgow Green quickly took hold in other radical centres. For example, within three weeks a committee of Barnsley workmen drew up an address that amplified Attwood's dissatisfaction with the Reform Act, praised the Birmingham petitioning initiative and observed that these 'will, if they are assisted by the people, most assuredly obtain a great Charter, namely the right to vote for Members of Parliament'.[55] Indirectly, O'Connor had a hand in this address, for it was presented to the foundation meeting of the Barnsley branch of the Great Northern Union (GNU), a new initiative he had launched a week earlier at a mass meeting on Hunslet Moor, near Leeds. This loose affiliation (even 'federation' would be too strong a term) of mainly extant local organisations reinforced O'Connor's personal authority. His overriding objective, though, was to move the regional movement forward. Once Parliament, in February 1838, had rejected a motion (proposed by Fielden and supported by several hundred petitions, totalling over 250,000 signatures) that the 1834 Act should be repealed, the constitutional road pursued by the anti-Poor Law movement was seemingly at an end, unless the fight was extended to reform the Constitution itself. The sense that the agitation had reached an impasse increased a few months later when Richard Oastler's health broke down, closely followed by a collapse in relations with his employer (events which led to his partial withdrawal from public life and, ultimately, his imprisonment for debt, 1840–44).[56] What was necessary, O'Connor told a Dewsbury meeting in April, was 'a union based on such principles as would not only enable Radicals to think alike, but, also to *know* that they did think alike. Nothing, he said was so necessary as that they should know how each other thought and with that knowledge they might almost attain any object upon which they set their wishes.'[57]

The influence of the GNU, O'Connor and the *Northern Star* were therefore mutually reinforcing. Local declarations to affiliate to the Union were in effect endorsements of O'Connor, while the *Star* was the medium through which constituent elements were kept in contact. The GNU had no central co-ordinating committee nor a fund-raising capability. Tellingly, members received not a card but a medal – 'bought up with an avidity seldom equalled' – bearing O'Connor's likeness and listing five points of radical reform (the Charter but without equal electoral districts).[58] The GNU, its leader and the paper were a powerful combination but in themselves insufficient to secure that accelerating pace of popular political organisation which distinguished the second half of 1838. Similarly, neither were the BPU and its national petition nor the LWMA and *The People's Charter*. The convergence of all three, however, was potent.

The *Star* facilitated coherence and communication, while O'Connor provided a charismatic focal figure. The Glasgow meeting had established the principle of a single, national, mass petition (in place of an accumulation of local ones), while *The People's Charter* gave the movement a vivid and compelling identity. Initially, it was the petition (the full text of which the *Northern Star* published on 16 June) that most captured the popular imagination. Parliament's persistent failure to heed workers' petitions, exemplified in its attitude to Poor Law protest but traceable back at least to the deregulation of apprenticeship in 1814, actually increased popular commitment to petitioning as a political tactic, but with this crucial difference: a single national petition would carry a moral weight greater than the sum of its parts. Thus John Collins was warmly received at the launch of the GNU, and the tactics of the BPU were as warmly endorsed. This was but one of countless similar meetings that summer. In the northern textile districts, 'joining the men of Birmingham' was often linked to 'likewise becoming a branch of the "Great Northern Union"'. Passing references to the Charter, such as that in Barnsley early in June, were displaced by detailed discussions. Thus on 16 July the Dewsbury RA (a GNU affiliate) gathered at the home of Thomas Wharton 'to examine the "People's Charter", published by the Working Men's Association, the whole of which met the approval of the generality of its members'. Very soon meetings were making an integral link between 'the propriety of adopting the National Petition and People's Charter'.[59] By October the term was beginning to be used as shorthand for a whole new political order, as in 'a different class of justice would be appointed under the People's Charter'. Soon the term 'Chartist' was coined, shortly followed by 'Chartism'. The alternatives 'Charterism' and 'Charterists' had some currency, while tellingly Daniel O'Connell referred to 'Fergises'.[60] But the now-familiar terminology soon prevailed.

## 'Overwhelmed with public and private suffering'

Chartism was a profoundly politicised response to recent political history, but it did not develop in an economic vacuum. Indeed, in the later nineteenth century it became commonplace for those who had been Chartists or who sympathised with them to explain the movement and excuse its militancy exclusively as the politics of hunger. 'It might now be said we were fools', 63-year-old Ben Wilson of Halifax wrote in 1887, 'but I answer young people now have no idea of what we had to endure.'

I have been a woollen weaver, a comber, a navvy on the railway, and a barer in the delph [quarryman] that I claim to know some little of the state of the working classes. I well remember a few years ago having some talk with a friend who told me he was moulding bullets in the cellar in 1848; he had a wife and five children dependent upon him, but was unable to get work, trade being so bad ... Many a time in winter have I known what it was to be short of the commonest of food, and thousands in this parish were in the same condition. A great many tales of sorrow could be told ... these were times to make men desperate.[61]

The extraordinary outbursts of popular militancy in the years after the publication of *The People's Charter* cannot be explained without reference to economic conditions at the time. In particular, depressions in 1839–40, 1842 and 1847–48 were at times marked by frenetic political mobilisation. Hunger, however, does not readily translate into a sustained political movement, supported by a dedicated press and its own professional agents and lecturers, and for the most part distinguished by self-restraint and discipline. Yet this exactly is what Chartism was. Furthermore, as events in 1837 and 1838 showed, it was gathering momentum well before the economic downturn in 1839. Economic cycles help to explain no more than the timing of the peaks of Chartist activity.

Economic stimuli of a subtly different kind derived from the nature of British industrialisation and its widely varying impact on workers' employment and living conditions. Industrialisation cannot be crudely equated with mechanisation: its successive phases saw burgeoning demand for domestic producers such as handloom weavers and framework knitters in, respectively, the Pennine and midlands textile industries; millwrights and engine-makers to make mechanisation possible; handicraft trades catering for expanding consumer markets in clothing, footwear, furniture and fancy goods; and construction workers, initially as urbanisation drove forward on a scale unprecedented in history and then as the railway network developed from the early 1840s. However, many craft-based occupations, swollen by increasing demand for the goods they supplied, subsequently contracted as mechanisation extended its reach into their industries. In both cotton and woollens, handloom weaving was thus afflicted in the 1830s and 1840s (and was almost extinct by 1860). The long-term trend of income and employment opportunities for these workers was bleak; they were also the first thrown out of work if their trade faced recession and the last to be re-employed as it recovered. Bleak for different reasons were the fortunes of those in sectors where (though mechanisation was not itself a pressing issue) piecework, sub-contracting, the employment of unskilled labour and sweating were increasing as commercial operators eroded workers' traditional workplace autonomy (and incomes). This phenomenon was particularly acute in London, though its impact was felt more generally in artisan trades

like shoemaking and tailoring. Labour's share of the rewards of industrialisation was therefore highly uneven. There were winners and there were losers.
Viewed even in the aggregate, the modest gains in real incomes experienced in
the mid-1830s were lost between 1838 and 1842, and the recovery that followed
was gradual and critically punctuated in 1847–48.[62]

Three other factors accentuated workers' feelings of discontent. Firstly,
although the extent of factory-based production in Britain was actually modest,
even as late as the 1840s, those involved were required to submit to intrusive
discipline and long working hours, with minimal intervals for rest. 'The cruel
and tyrannical arrangements under which they perform their daily toil', to
quote an influential Chartist, was hugely resented.[63] Furthermore, the extensive
employment of women in textile mills was widely seen as corroding family life.
Given the high degree of regional specialisation in the British economy, these
issues loomed large in the discontents of some regions (especially Lancashire
and West Yorkshire) and hardly at all in others.

Secondly, and this perception was not regionally specific, workers enjoyed a
slender share of the benefits of economic growth (and for many there was no
material benefit whatsoever), while the disparity between wealth and poverty
appeared to be widening. 'In no country in the world', wrote a German visitor
in 1841, 'is there such a striking contrast, so defined a partition, so easy and
fearful a comparison between rich and poor, as in England.' In 1848 Florence
Nightingale wrote: 'England is surely the country where luxury has reached
its height and poverty its depth.'[64] Six years earlier, a decidedly more radical
commentator from the Manchester region summarised the situation thus:

> The country has undergone a change scarcely to be credited, except by those
> who have witnessed it. Villages have sprung into towns, and ordinary sized
> towns have become rivals in population and wealth of the great capitals of
> nations; gigantic factories, vomiting their dense clouds of poisonous smoke,
> have obliterated from the face of a large part of the kingdom every vestige
> of nature's beauty, while the plastered, tinselled, and gaudy palaces of the
> princes of commerce have sprung up, left and right, as if at the beck of an
> enchanter's wand.[65]

This degradation of the lived environment was the third key factor, impossible to quantify, though references to it in contemporary sources are legion.
The pace of urbanisation meant that much of the housing stock was poor:
new buildings were often hastily erected in a form inadequate for their site or
purpose; dilapidated older buildings were pressed into accommodating more
residents as the streets in which they were situated slid down the social scale;
and infilling of what had hitherto been open spaces, gardens or courtyards
was rife. Inevitably, the lowest-income families lived in the poorest housing.
Cotton handloom weavers in Ashton-under-Lyne lived 'almost to a man in the

old, filthy, and undrained parts of the town', reported the *Morning Chronicle* in 1849, 'the streets thereabouts were filthy and mean, the houses crumbling, crazy, and dirty'.[66] Environmental degradation accentuated consciousness of the disparity between wealth and poverty and was a recurrent feature of Chartist thinking. George Flinn, a leading conspirator in the Bradford Chartist rising of 1840, explained it thus:

> He was charged by his mill-master with having a little more knowledge than most of his fellow workmen; and in the eyes of a mill-master that is a crime of no small degree. Well, how was he situated in order to get this knowledge? He lived in a cellar, nine feet by seven. *This dwelling was his workshop, his bed-room, his kitchen, his study*; AND NOT UNFREQUENTLY HIS HOSPITAL. Could any man live thus and not 'acquire knowledge'. Was he to close his eyes to the fact, that while he was obliged to toil in such a position, the fruit of his labour was filched from him, and splendid mansions arose in every direction around him, inhabited by those that mock him with expressions of sympathy?[67]

The National Petition reflected such concerns as these exactly: 'With all these elements of national prosperity, and with every disposition and capacity to take advantage of them, we find ourselves overwhelmed with public and private suffering.'[68]

# Chartist lives:
# Abram and Elizabeth Hanson

Among those on the platform when the Great Northern Union was launched in 1838 was Abram Hanson, a shoemaker. 'They were slaves in the land called free, and starving in the land of plenty', Hanson told the audience. He welcomed the GNU, for although there were 'numerous associations' within 20 miles of Leeds, they lacked co-ordination and were 'awaiting opportunity to redress their wrongs'. In Hanson's view, there was no mistaking the main force for cohesion among northern radicals – 'the best friend the working classes ever had': Feargus O'Connor. Abram Hanson's politics was rooted in a forceful Christian ethic with strong anti-clerical overtones. At a Whitsuntide mass-meeting in 1839, for example, he launched into an attack on clergy of every denomination:

> They preached Christ and a crust, passive obedience and non-resistance. Let the people keep from those churches and chapels. (We will!) Let them go to those men who preached Christ and a full belly, Christ and a well-clothed back – Christ and a good house to live in – Christ and Universal Suffrage.[*]

Abram Hanson never sought attention beyond what he described as his 'little village', Elland, near Halifax, in West Yorkshire.[†] He had been born there in 1796 or 1797. He had no formal education to speak of, joking that he had been schooled in 'the College of Nature'.[‡] Yet, Hanson occupied a position of some prominence in this textile-producing village (its population in 1841 was less than 6,500). He was a respected source of medical advice, an actor in local theatricals and secretary of the local RA. He, and his wife Elizabeth especially, took a leading part in Elland's mobilisation against the 1834 Poor Law Amendment Act. The postponement of its introduction in northern England was an important factor in the form and timing of early Chartist activity. The Hansons were typical of local Poor Law activists who found through Chartism a place on a wider political stage. For Elizabeth this meant presenting the concerns of local women to a national audience through the Chartist press. For Abram it meant invitations from beyond Elland to speak at radical meetings, including the most important in the early phase of Yorkshire Chartism.

Very little of the micro-politics of communities as small as Elland found coverage even in local papers; but occasionally the Hansons can be glimpsed at work. Abram caused a stir at a parish meeting when he described himself as a republican and tried to thwart plans to celebrate Victoria's coronation at the ratepayers' expense. More dramatically, in February 1838 Elizabeth and other Elland women ambushed several Assistant Poor Law Commissioners outside the local workhouse. These civil servants were charged with ensuring that the much-hated new legislation was enforced, so the Elland women 'treat them with a roll in the snow'. On another occasion, when a local cloth merchant reduced the prices he paid to Elland weavers, 200 women success-fully prevented a cart-and-donkey train leaving the village to take work to weavers elsewhere.[§] Community politics in places like this could certainly be robust, but it was not without intellectual thrust. Elizabeth's opposition to the

---

[*]  *NS*, 9 June 1838; *Halifax Guardian*, 25 May 1839.

[†]  *NS*, 9 June 1838.

[‡]  'Reminiscences of notable shoemakers', *Boot and Shoemaker*, 8 February 1879; all unattributed quoted matter in the remainder of this section is from this article.

[§]  *NS*, 3 March 1838 ('treat' – pronounced *tret* – is past tense in West Riding dialect); *Leeds Times*, 16 June 1838.

New Poor Law, for example, was grounded in an informed understanding of the nature of the early Victorian economy. Taken to task on one occasion for ignoring predictions that economic expansion would alleviate poverty, she retaliated:

> You say, extend our commerce. We have ransacked the whole habitable globe. If you can find out a way to the moon, we may, with the aid of paper, carry on our competition a little longer; but if you want to better the condition of the working classes, let our government legislate so as to make machinery go hand in hand with labour, and act as an auxiliary or helpmate, not a competitor.[*]

Her remarks are indicative of 'grassroots' Chartism in such communities. There is scant faith in Attwood's advocacy of paper money. Machinery is the focal point of many grievances or, rather, government refusal to cushion handicraft labour from its effects.

The Hansons had the cause of Elland's handloom weavers very much at heart, and some newspaper reports assumed that Abram was himself a weaver. However, a number of prominent Chartists worked at the 'gentle craft'. Across Europe there was a long tradition of shoemakers leading radical or religious activities in their local communities. They were skilled craftsmen whose work lay outside the control of dominant local employers and landowners. Demand for shoemakers' services reflected fluctuations in local economies, and very few could survive by making new footwear alone, despite their status as independent artisans. Furthermore by the late 1830s highly capitalised midland shoe-manufacturing was beginning to squeeze provincial shoemakers. Much of their time was therefore spent cobbling, low-paid work but bringing with it a steady numbers of customers – men, women and all ages – to their workshops, which thus became natural places for gossip while the job was done. Many shoemakers therefore assumed leadership roles of one kind or another in their local communities.[†]

Abram Hanson was a prominent member of the Elland RA, founded in March 1837 amid the gathering political momentum that culminated in Chartism. Hanson's views on the 1832 Reform Act were typical: workers 'were nothing in a political sense but the mean slaves and serfs of the aristocracy of the land, and the aristocracy of the spindle'. 'Did the law require electors to be grammarians or classical scholars, or even honest men? No, but it asked "Do you pay £10 rent?"' In such circumstances 'there was but one course which could safely be depended upon – they must rely upon their own united exertions

---

[*]    *London Dispatch*, 1 April 1838.

[†]    E. Hobsbawm and J.W. Scott, 'Political shoemakers', in E. Hobsbawm, *Worlds of Labour: Further Studies in the History of Labour* (London, Weidenfeld & Nicholson, 1984), pp.103–30; D. Thompson, *Chartists* (London, Temple Smith, 1984), pp.179–86.

– they must think well of themselves, for hitherto they had been taught to think that money was everything in society and that poverty was a crime.' Hanson's prescription was clear: 'imitate the example of the Canadians, and be united in their demands for their rights'.[*]

Although Chartism drew from Hanson his greatest political efforts, his commitment to radicalism predated the movement. He appears first in reports in 1830 of public meetings in the area. Subsequently he was secretary, and then chairman, of the Elland RA, in which capacity William Lovett enlisted him as a signatory in October 1838 to the LWMA's pamphlet *The Radical Reformers of England, Scotland, & Wales, to the Irish People*.[†] He may at some point have been a Methodist lay-preacher and, as his call for 'Christ and Universal Suffrage' conveys, he clearly saw politics as an extension of the religious realm. One anecdote about Hanson, which illustrates the continuing importance of dreams in popular belief at this time, recounted how he fell into a reverie at his work. Reflecting on Oliver Cromwell and the parliamentarian cause, Hanson jolted awake. He rushed to find Elizabeth: 'I say, lass, thah mun find me a white hand-kerchief for my neck ready for next Sunday; I am going to praech.' To this she replied 'What ar' ta going to turn Methody na?' 'Noa', said Abram, 'but I am going to praech for all that. I've just fun aght that t'Charter is to be gotten by praeching and praying.'

One can never be fully confident about the authenticity of tales of this nature, but this one underlines that Hanson's style as a politician was rooted in the chapel culture and camp meetings of dissenting religion. His was not sophisticated rhetoric, but it was passionate and expressed in a manner immediately familiar to his audience. Yet it was Elizabeth's capabilities as a public speaker that were the more notable: she 'melted the hearts and drew forth floods of tears', concluded one report of a meeting addressed by Elizabeth.[‡]

Abram's education was certainly not confined to the chapel (or, for that matter, the pot house). The medical knowledge that led him to be frequently consulted by Elland's poor was rooted in a largely oral tradition concerning natural remedies. The professionalisation of medicine was very uneven in the early nineteenth century and bone-setters and herbalists continued to play an important role, especially in smaller communities. However, much of Hanson's 'knowledge in politics, the drama, metaphysics, and general literature' could have been acquired only from books. We have an insight into the world of the

---

[*]    *NS*, 27 January 1838; *Halifax Guardian*, 23 January 1838.

[†]    E. Webster, 'Chartism in the Calder Valley, 1838–50', *Transactions of the Halifax Antiquarian Society*, new series, 2 (1994), pp. 73–4; (W. Lovett) *Radical Reformers of England, Scotland, & Wales, to the Irish People* (London, Cleave, [1838]), p. 8.

[‡]    *Leeds Times*, 17 February 1838.

autodidact artisan in a deft portrait of an anonymous shoemaker (a generation older than Hanson) from nearby Halifax. His treasured personal library included (alongside a dog-eared Bible) a variety of religious works (mainly by seventeenth-century writers), but also Paine's *Age of Reason*, William Howitt's anti-clerical *History of Priestcraft* and *Labour's Wrongs and Labour's Remedy* by the Leeds socialist J. F. Bray. A popular novel, *The Gentleman in Black*, sat together with the magazine of a local building society and Cobbett's *Twopenny Trash, or Politics for the Poor*. Like Hanson, this shoemaker was passionately eloquent about contemporary politics; and as for Peterloo, 'woe be to the leather that is under his hammer when he is telling that tale'.*

Hanson's ebullience and appetite for learning made him a natural actor. He relished the cameo part of a shoemaker in *Ali Baba and the Forty Thieves*. Another part for which he was a natural choice was that of Last, the shoemaker in William Cobbett's political comedy *Surplus Population*. Last comes closest to articulating Cobbett's own opinions on the New Poor Law, triumphantly refuting 'a great Anti-Population Philosopher'. One can imagine the relish which Abram Hanson would have brought to an exchange such as this:

> LAST   It is your idlers that eat up the country: it is they that make the working-people so poor that they are obliged to come to the parish or starve.
>
> SQUIRE THIMBLE   Obliged to come and demand other people's property to live on!
>
> LAST   It is not other people's property: it is their own property: they inherit a right, both by nature and by law, to subsistence out of the land, in exchange for their labour, and if they be unable to labour, or can get no labour, they have the right without the labour.†

Although he never joined the ranks of professional Chartist missionaries, Hanson spoke frequently alongside the movement's leadership, for example O'Connor, Stephens and Collins on Hartshead Moor in October 1838. The conviction that universal male suffrage would secure comprehensive social and economic reform shone through the attack Hanson made on Chartism's opponents:

> They knew that having the Suffrage the people would speedily undo all the corrupt practices – that legislation would no longer regard party, but universal interests. That having to labour for the expense, they would sweep away the unmerited pensions – they would examine into that thing called the National Debt, and abolish the taxes that press upon the necessaries of

---

*   E. Sloane, *Essays, Tales and Sketches* (Halifax, Leyland, 1849), pp. 61 and 65.
†   W. Cobbett, *Surplus Population and the Poor Law Bill: A Comedy in Three Acts*, ed. S. Bushell, (Leeds, Pelagian Press, 1994), p. 45.

life. These things the factions desired not to have done, and therefore they laboured to keep the franchise from the people.[*]

Both Abram and Elizabeth articulated that growing consciousness among industrial workers in the mid-1830s of the gulf between poverty and wealth, of 'starving in the land of plenty', as Abram termed it; but, as the extract above shows, theirs was not knee-jerk hunger politics; nor was it simply a commitment to manhood suffrage as an abstract right. There was a growing awareness across the main industrial regions of converging economic, social and political interests. 'Union is progressing; it is rising under a new modification', declared Elland's female radicals in an address greeting the pardon of the Tolpuddle labourers.[†] For the women of Elland, led by Elizabeth Hanson and Mary Grassby, the wife of another active Chartist, the New Poor Law caused greatest alarm. It cast women in the role of dependants on their husbands' incomes rather than as contributors to the family income in their own right. They were more likely than men to need to claim poor relief, especially in widowhood or when raising a family. Such issues must have weighed heavily on 41-year-old Elizabeth in the winter of 1838–39. She was pregnant with her fourth child; the three others, girls aged 4, 9 and 11, were not yet contributing to the family's income. The new legislation, especially before its most draconian implications had been tempered by resistance and local defiance, was widely regarded as a major assault on the integrity of the family, the dignity of old age and the powerful popular ideology that held relief from poverty to be a legal and moral right.

In March 1838 Elizabeth and her neighbours constituted themselves as a Female Radical Association. Their opposition to the 1834 reforms centred on a female perspective: 'women had more to fear from the bill than men', Mary Grassby declared. As Elizabeth told a meeting, not only were women forced to wear shoddy (low-grade cloth made from recycled material) and their hair cropped on entry to 'the bastilles', but their children could be taken from them, especially if sick.[‡] This state-sponsored assault on femininity and the status of motherhood angered women and underscored the calamitous separation of married couples on entry to the workhouse. Dignified relief from the consequences of irregular employment and the spectre of the workhouse were the issues that most exercised women. Their political involvement would change decisively as opposition to the New Poor Law became increasingly absorbed into a wider political agenda, and also as the worst fears concerning it went unrealised (though the workhouse was a spectre that continued to haunt working-class homes well into the following century).

---

[*]   *NS*, 16 October 1838.
[†]   Ibid., 14 April, 9 June 1838.
[‡]   Ibid., 17 and 24 February 1838.

Female suffrage itself was not an objective Elizabeth or Elland's FRA prioritised: 'it is our duty, both as wives and mothers, to form a Female Association, in
order to give and receive instruction in political knowledge, and to co-operate
with our husbands and sons in their great work of regeneration'.* Chartism was
certainly not antagonistic to female suffrage, but the prevailing view was pragmatic, as the preface to *The People's Charter* conceded: 'against this reasonable
proposition we have no just argument to adduce but only to express our fears
of entertaining it, lest the false estimate man entertains for this half of the
human family may cause his ignorance and prejudice to be enlisted to retard
the progress of his own freedom'.[†] Once universal male suffrage was won it
was widely assumed female suffrage would eventually follow. Pending this,
most Chartist women concentrated on immediate practical issues concerning
the security and quality of family life. Thus Elizabeth and her friends joined
evening classes offered at the Elland RA's Dog Lane rooms. 'The Ellanders seem
determined not to wait the time of government appointments for national
education, but to begin and educate themselves', commented the *Leeds Times*.
They also wrote to – and doubtless avidly perused – the *Northern Star*. Given
how closely knit small textile townships like Elland were, we can be sure they
also had a hand in the donation to Chartist funds made by the local female
lodge of the Druids' friendly society.[‡]

As ever in the realm of the intimate and the personal, the exact relationship between the Hansons is something on which in the main we can only
speculate. For reasons that are unclear, Mary Grassby separated from her
husband James for a time in early 1838, but Elizabeth and Abram seem to have
sustained a close and affectionate relationship.[§] The anonymous Huddersfield
ex-Chartist who wrote the *Boot and Shoemaker's* tribute to Abram shortly after
his death in 1878, observed of the two that 'he generally contrived to have
his own way in the end'. He also quoted Abram jocularly likening himself and
Elizabeth to Socrates and his querulous wife Xanthippe, a remark redolent
of habitual chauvinism as well as an autodidact's pride in classical learning.
According to the same source, Abram frequented 'the public house too much',
(but this comment may reflect late-1870s' notions of working-class respectability as much as it did Hanson's character). Yet still the couple 'managed to
bring a family up in decency, considering his station in life'. And if, as seems
likely, Elizabeth belonged to Elland's Druids' female friendly society then she
will have attended its meetings in the Waggon and Horses pub. For his part,

---

*    Ibid., 24 March 1838.
†    *The People's Charter*, p.9.
‡    *NS*, 3 and 17 March 1838; *Leeds Times*, 3 March 1838; for female Chartism see espe-
cially Thompson, *Chartists*, pp.120–51.
§    *NS*, 17 March, *London Dispatch*, 1 April 1838; *Southern Star*, 2 February 1840.

Abram was quick (maybe more so than other Yorkshire Chartists) to praise 'the women [who] are the best politicians, the best revolutionists, and the best political economists'. 'Should the men fail in their allegiance', he told the inaugural meeting of the GNU, 'the women of Elland, who had sworn not to breed slaves, had registered a vow to do the work of men and women.'* This, then, was very much a Chartist marriage, made vividly so when Elizabeth gave birth to their son Feargus O'Connor Hanson in 1839.

From the summer of that year onwards, recorded instances of both Hansons' participating in politics rapidly diminished. Little Feargus was doubtless the main reason for this, but there may have been other contributory factors. There was a sharp decline in reports from Elland itself in *Northern Star*, an incidental consequence of the latter's evolution from a mainly regional to a truly national newspaper. Second, the New Poor Law, while remaining a perpetual grievance, receded somewhat as an immediate issue of contention. Third, early Chartism derived much of its strength from communities, like Elland, where political activity waned in step with the fortunes of domestic industry. The decline of handloom-weaving subdued the political temperament of the village. Though its Chartists formed themselves into a branch of the National Charter Association in 1840 and later supported the Chartist land plan, autonomous political activity in the village appears to have lessened. Furthermore, after 1840 outdoor mass-meetings, to which Abram's demotic style was ideally suited, were less frequent. All the Hanson children were raised in Elland but when their father warmed to familiar themes during the 1840s it tended to be in nearby Halifax, not Elland, that he spoke. Abram still represented Elland's Chartists at West Yorkshire delegate meetings as late as 1852, and Elizabeth continued sending small donations to Chartist causes.†

---

\*    *NS*, 10 February, 9 June 1838.

†    Ibid., 8 April 1843, 1 and 29 January 1848, 21 December 1850, 19 June 1852; Webster, 'Chartism in the Calder Valley', p.74.

# CHAPTER TWO

# October–December 1838:
# 'The people are up'

## An emerging movement

Abram Hanson addressed the great West Riding Meeting on Hartshead Moor, 15 October 1838, organised by the GNU. 'They were the serfs and slaves of those who, possessing the power of law-making, had always the power of extracting the fruits of their industry for the promoting of their own selfish purposes', he declared. 'He would tell them as Oastler, the people's friend, had told them – and he was a constitutional tory – he would tell them arm, arm, in defence of their rights ("we have done that lad"). Why did he say this? Because it was constitutional.'[1] Hanson was one of several speakers that day who referred to the constitutional right to carry arms and inferred that it might be necessary to use them. The most vehement was Joseph Rayner Stephens, who proudly claimed the mantle of Jack Cade. (In 1450 Cade had led a serious uprising which had begun as a mass petition to Henry VI against corrupt administration.) Stephens added for good measure:

> The Lord Jesus Christ … was the prince of Jack Cades! (Tremendous cheering.) … We will meet unarmed – (cheers) – unarmed, unless threatened; unarmed, until there be fear or danger; but if there be fear, – no, there can't be fear, only for our enemies, but if there be danger, why then Englishmen know their rights, and are ready to do their duty (cheers).[2]

More striking than such rhetoric, however, was the sheer array of individuals – twenty-one in all – who spoke that afternoon. John Fielden, O'Connor and Stephens were educated, middle-class and well-versed in the ways of the public platform; there were a handful of other middle-class speakers (a solicitor, a surgeon, a dissenting preacher), but the majority were workmen. They included a carpenter, a hatter, a leathercutter (in the chair), a shoemaker, a toolmaker, a woolcomber and both linen and woollen handloom weavers. Arguably the most remarkable contributor was not actually present: John Powlett. That was the signature to a letter read out on behalf of millworkers 'threatened with dismissal if they attended your glorious demonstration'. John Powlett was the fictitious name of the once-mighty Leeds cloth-workers' trade union. In the early 1830s it had been a driving force behind general unionism, not just in Yorkshire but nationally.[3] Powlett's name needed no explaining to the crowds on Hartshead Moor and was a vivid indicator of trade unionism's emotional investment in the Chartist movement at this time.

It is important to keep the GNU in proportion. It was short-lived and a precursor to something inestimably greater. The LWMA and the BPU developed the ideas of a *national* petition and *The People's Charter* and each continued to sponsor significant speaking tours to consolidate and extend the rapidly evolving movement. For the BPU, the indefatigable John Collins was the main link between the midlands and the north. For the LWMA, Henry Vincent was consistently the most successful missionary. From May 1838 he was based mainly in Bath, whence he worked the adjacent English counties and, increasingly successfully, south Wales. He was also in extensive demand elsewhere: 'my friends', he told a Manchester audience that August, 'I feel somewhat fatigued, having spoken every day for the last fortnight'.[4] Closely associated with Collins and Vincent in these endeavours were their immediate colleagues – Salt and Douglas for the BPU, Wade, Hetherington, Cleave and another London printer, Robert Hartwell, for the LWMA.

To this upper tier of activists should be added six others who were affiliated to neither organisation. The first was Reginald Richardson, a Salford carpenter turned newsagent and the secretary of the South Lancashire Anti-Poor Law Association. The second was George Julian Harney of the LDA and the third Robert Lowery, a Newcastle tailor. The other three were the main architects of Scottish Chartism: the mercurial John Taylor, a surgeon from Ayr; Abram Duncan, a bobbin-maker and spokesman for Glasgow's trades; and the secretary of the Edinburgh radicals, John Fraser. When members of this upper tier spoke at meetings, one or more prominent local activists generally appeared alongside them. Yorkshire examples include Hanson and George White, an Irish-born woolcomber from Leeds; in the Potteries, John 'Daddy' Richards (another shoemaker); in the western counties, William Prowting Roberts, a Bath solicitor; and in Durham, 'the Castor and Pollux of Northern Chartism' George Binns and James Williams, partners in a Sunderland booksellers and newsagency.

This combination of local talent and visiting speakers of wider renown ensured Chartism's success in many centres. Although local networks were crucial, time and again grassroots activists would plead for a visiting luminary to maximise interest. Vincent 'would draw 10,000 where a local orator would not draw 10', argued one Gloucestershire Chartist.[5] This placed a huge burden on Chartist orators of truly stellar quality, like Collins, O'Connor and Vincent; it would also leave the movement vulnerable if such figures temporarily withdrew from public life. For the moment, however, meetings occurred with escalating frequency.

Caveats about estimated attendances notwithstanding, the size of the greatest of these inspired participants and unnerved authority: at Newcastle on 28 June ('one of the most magnificent arrays of moral and numerical power ever exhibited by the masses of this country'); at Holloway Head, Birmingham (6 August, 200,000); Westminster Palace Yard, London (17 September, 15,000); Kersal Moor, Manchester (24 September, 300,000); Sheffield (25 September, 20,000); Trowle Common, Wiltshire (30 September, 30,000); and, as we have seen, on Hartshead Moor (15 October, 500,000 – a contentious estimate by O'Connor, as others ranged from 50,000 to 70,000).

Of these rallies, Birmingham and Kersal Moor were the most significant from a national perspective, the former because it extended the movement's tactics beyond petitioning and the latter because of the sheer scale of the gathering and the sentiments expressed. That attendance was around the quarter of a million mark was not generally disputed: the organisers, led by Richardson, had shrewdly chosen the day of the Manchester races, held on the moor later that afternoon. This was the occasion of a much-quoted speech by the Reverend Stephens: 'This question of Universal Suffrage was a knife and fork question after all; this question was a bread and cheese question, notwithstanding all that had been said against it.'[6]

The least impressive of the 1838 meetings, even disappointing, was London's Palace Yard meeting, given that the overall population of the capital was around 2 million. Palace Yard was notable, though, for assembling a truly national platform party, thanks to the LWMA which invited radical localities from across the country to send a delegate. Fraternal greetings 'in the great struggle for democracy and independence' were even received from France, brought by Arthur Wade (just returned from an LWMA promotional visit to Paris), accompanied by 'Mr Coulier, of Paris' – an early harbinger of Chartist internationalism.[7]

These massive demonstrations formed a backdrop to hundreds of smaller events, each significant in its local context and duly reported in tones varying from euphoria to disgust in the local press. At Newtown, Montgomeryshire, a crowd of 4,000–5,000 received the Welsh translation of the National Petition. The *Carlisle Journal* estimated that a quarter of the town's population heard O'Connor speak from the Town Hall steps. In north Essex a meeting, 'the largest remembered in Colchester for many years', heard a delegate from Ipswich call for a general strike if the Charter was not granted. At Hanley, a 'numerous and respectable' gathering, addressed by Collins and Richards, launched the Potteries Political Union. At Coatbridge Duncan berated his audience for being 'too supine, too much occupied with piping, dancing, and drinking, while government had been ruling them with a rod of iron'. At Bolton a wealthy manufacturer, Charles Darbishire, recalled a promise to agitate for manhood suffrage in 1832 and 'he was exceedingly happy to have the present opportunity of redeeming that pledge'. The *Norfolk Chronicle* reported with 'unspeakable feelings of distaste' how a Norwich meeting, 'packed to suffocation', was urged by Cleave and Julian Harney 'to read the National Petition and arm themselves with that'.[8]

A striking feature of these gatherings was the frequency with which they brought to the public eye veterans of earlier agitations. One Elland octogenarian recalled how 'in 1792 we held such meetings as the present … but when war commenced between this country and France our meetings were put down, and we were persecuted as disaffected persons'. A similar pedigree could be traced by Richards of north Staffordshire, 'Citizen' John George of south London (in the 1790s a member of the London Corresponding Society and subsequently of the revolutionary Spencean circle), John Knight of Oldham (an old Jacobin who had stood beside Hunt at Peterloo) and T. R. Smart of Leicester. When the National Petition was adopted at Stratford-upon-Avon, the linen draper chairing the meeting 'was one of the old Hampden club members of twenty years ago'. At Barnsley William Ashton, transported to Australia in 1829 for taking a leading role in a weavers' riotous strike, returned in May 1838 and immediately resumed a leading role in local radical politics. Salford's leading Chartist Reginald Richardson had attended Peterloo as a child.[9]

A middle-class presence was evident at many of these meetings but was no guarantee peaceable sentiments would prevail. Attwood made much of the running here: at Holloway Head 'he talked about the Legislature being unable to resist the demand of two millions of men, which, if not speedily complied with, would result in the two millions being increased to five, and he threatened the House of Commons that this immense body of people would exercise upon them a little gentle compulsion'. Specifying the use of a general strike as a possible tactic, Attwood observed that while 'he would be opposed to the employment of any violence, if the people were attacked the consequences must fall upon the heads of the aggressors'. At radical gatherings marking Hunt's birthday or 'the never-to-be-forgotten 16th of August 1819', speakers predicted 'the calamities brought on innocent people by those inhuman butchers' would now be avenged.[10]

By September 1838 Chartists were increasingly convinced of the righteousness of their cause and confident, too, of carrying it. In *The People's Charter* that cause had an appealing and intelligible focal point: 'set heart and soul and life upon all it contains; be resolved to have that all', a *Northern Star* editorial entreated, but 'be prepared to receive a denial; and be prepared to reiterate and enforce the claim'.[11] All this, combined with a strong historical awareness of the outcome of earlier agitations, and a profound sense of contemporary social bifurcation, inevitably infused speeches with a confrontational tone. The 33-year-old Stephens was consistently the most bellicose, his speeches suffused with the declamatory style of an Old Testament prophet.

The son of a distinguished Methodist family, Stephens had been received into the ministry in 1829 and from his appointment to the Ashton-under-Lyne circuit in 1832 proved a constant irritation to the Wesleyan authorities. 'Stephens's Ashton doings fill me with indignation', wrote Jabez Bunting, the predominant force in Wesleyan Methodism; 'it is plain he wants us to exclude him'.[12] That November Stephens resigned rather than be expelled, taking a sizeable portion of the circuit with him. Soon known as 'Stephenites', he led them from the 'Great Meeting House' in Charlestown, on the outskirts of Ashton. The disestablishment of the Church of England first drew Stephens into politics. From 1834, however, the leitmotif of his religious and political career was furious hostility to the New Poor Law, laced with a highly sentimentalised view of the working-class family. All this he expressed with rhetoric awash with wide generalisation and stark intimations of violence. At Bradford he predicted, 'there was no doubt that the New Poor Law Bastilles were intended to be a chain of barracks round the country, each capable of holding 500 to 1,000 men and each intended to be garrisoned by regular military'. Stephens told a Norwich audience: 'England stands on a mine; a volcano is beneath her ... and unless the distress and misery of the poor be met by good feeling and speedy remedy, no man can tell what a day, what an hour may bring forth', urging them to 'fight with your swords, pistols, daggers, torches. Women, fight with your nails and teeth; nothing else will do.' It was hatred of the Poor Law, not passion for parliamentary reform, that motivated Stephens. 'What care I about universal suffrage?' he asked a Wigan meeting. 'I don't care two straws about the question – I never think about it. I am arrayed on the side of right against wrong ... on the side of God against the wicked man'.[13]

For Stephens 'the side of right' included the *Northern Star*, in which he was a shareholder. O'Connor reciprocated by giving prominence to Stephens's speeches and including him in the paper's series of presentation engravings. O'Connor himself, though, was a subtler and more circumspect speaker, adept at playing on his audience's sense of alienation from the political establishment without explicitly endorsing the use of violence. At Carlisle, for example, he

> addressed them as the ill-paid but hard-working men of Carlisle, telling them that it was because they had been denied the fair fruits of their labour that so many had gathered to hear an entire stranger. All could see that they carried no bloody axe; they held out no threats. They left those things to those who wanted not to give the people Reform but to line their own coffers. These men now had got their Corporations, their Town Halls and their billiard rooms, whilst the working people had their gaols and their Bastilles.[14]

The purpose of these meetings, however, was neither simply to demand reform nor to roar defiance if it was denied. In the spring and early summer of 1838 Chartism was a *mood* rather than a movement. Even the name had yet to emerge. With the great Birmingham demonstration of 6 August, however, the nascent Chartist movement assumed more definite shape around a cluster of practical measures. Discussion about a National Petition had until this point been largely abstract: even though a text had been prepared the practical business of collecting signatures, ensuring national coverage and co-ordinating its presentation, had been largely ignored. A petition on the scale anticipated would need an organisational focus and a co-ordinating body to sustain the movement should Parliament ignore it. This in turn raised the issue of financial support.

The solution proposed by the council of the BPU, and received with acclaim at the Birmingham meeting, was a General Convention which would promote and manage the National Petition. Legislation from the French revolutionary period severely curtailed the capacity for such an initiative. To stay within the law it would need to comprise no more than forty-nine members, each elected by a public meeting (advertised in advance) and not by any specific organisation. The Convention, it was suggested, should be financed by a small voluntary levy paid by its supporters. A name for this – the National Rent – was borrowed from the similar method used to finance O'Connell's campaign for Irish home rule. O'Connor caught Birmingham's mood perfectly with the declaration that 'he recognised this meeting as signing, sealing and delivering the great moral covenant which had this day been ratified by the people'. 'THE PEOPLE ARE UP' declared a *Star* editorial the following Saturday.

A group of eight delegates to represent Birmingham at the Convention was elected at the Holloway Head meeting. Five had been present at Glasgow Green: Collins, Douglas, Edmonds, Philip Muntz and Salt. They were joined by three others, among whom was Muntz's brother George. Predictably the LWMA, whose relation with the BPU was frequently edgy, then claimed that eight delegates should represent the capital. At the Palace Yard meeting all those elected were Association members: Cleave, Hartwell, Hetherington, Lovett, O'Brien and Vincent were joined by two stop-gap candidates, proposed when Place and Roebuck declined nomination.[15] In the event the BPU's contingent fell to four and the LWMA's to seven (Vincent chose to represent Hull and Cheltenham instead), but two other LWMA activists (Wade and William Carpenter) were chosen to represent localities outside the capital. The preponderance of delegates from the two organisations would have implications for the Convention once it assembled, as well as leaving an enduring but exaggerated impression of the significance of the LWMA.

Such was the optimism with which plans for the Convention swung into action, however, that there was very little critical comment on matters of internal governance. Meetings to elect delegates were among the very largest that autumn and included the mass demonstrations on Kersal Moor and Hartshead Moor. Elections and the collection of National Rent and signatures proceeded in parallel against a background of mounting assertiveness. 'One feeling prevails in every town – or rather I should say *two* feelings', wrote Vincent from Huddersfield in August 1838,

> the *first* a general and almost universal radical opinion – resolved to aid in *one more attempt* to obtain by peaceful means a full recognition of the Universal Rights of the people – the *second* an apparent fixed resolution to appeal to *arms* should this *last* moral effort fail – I regret the prevalence of opinions of a physical nature – but we cannot wonder at them. Ever since the year 1818 – the Yorkshire and Lancashire people have been peacefully struggling for Universal Suffrage. They were the only two counties in which the principle existed to any extent – and the choicest spirits have become almost worn-out by their continuous exertions. However they will nobly do their duty now – they see *now*, for the *first time*, a corresponding energy in other parts of the nation.[16]

Given the economic situation and restiveness concerning the Whig Government's policies, it would (as Vincent suggested) have been surprising if the political mood of the industrial north was not hardening. More striking in late 1838 was emerging radical activity in areas where commitment to reform politics had hitherto been sporadic or non-existent. Vincent himself had extensively toured western England, where the latent energies he awakened were considerable. The scene that September, as cheering columns of Chartists from Trowbridge and Bradford-upon-Avon converged on Trowle Common, surpassed anything Wiltshire had witnessed, even during the 'outrages' three decades earlier. Then, workers in the county's woollen industry, reacting against the introduction of machinery, had conducted an extensive campaign of selective violence against property. Its objective was to reinforce their protests that legislation regulating mechanisation was no longer enforced. Now they looked to a reformed Parliament as the only means of arresting the steep decline of their industry. This was a community-wide response, symbolised by a presentation of silk scarves by the women of Trowbridge to Vincent and the town's leading activist, William Carrier, before the march to the common. Once there Carrier was elected a Convention delegate.[17]

Vincent was the pivotal figure, too, in Dorset, another county of sporadic political mobilisation and one still feeling the aftershock of the treatment of the Tolpuddle labourers. On 14 November a crowd estimated between 5,000 and 6,000 gathered on the downs outside Blandford Forum. Some had travelled over 20 miles to attend, drawn by placards – 'The People's Charter', 'Vote by Ballot' and 'Annual Parliaments' – and a 'great number of highly respectable females were present'. Vincent was accompanied by Hartwell and

W. P. Roberts. In the words of a local poet, writing subsequently in the *Dorset County Chronicle*:

> Why *Mr Vincen* miade it clear.
> Why vust-tha'd zen up members ev'ry year
> To Parli'ment, an ev'ry man 'o'd vote.
> *Though è mid be as poor as a church mouse*
> Still 'e'd be fit to vote, and fit to goo
> To miake the la's at Lunnen too
> [ … ]
> An' when the poor vo'ke got a shiare
> In miaken o' the la's, tha'll tiake good kiare
> To miake some good oones var the poor.[18]

Roberts, however, captured the mood of the meeting when, supporting resolutions both to adopt the Charter and for 'an immediate advance … in the Wages paid to Agricultural Labourers', he stated that the ultimate aim was 'to elevate the labourer in the social scale. The time was come when some great moral blow would be struck to emancipate the working classes of England from the chains of oppression under which they laboured.' These comments can hardly have been welcomed by the local magistrates and farmers who circled the meeting on horseback, nor the election that followed of the Tolpuddle labourers' leader, George Loveless, as a Convention delegate. For local officialdom, the meeting was merely trade unionism in a new guise. 'The men for miles around received notice that if they dared attend the Meeting they would be immediately discharged and several of them were discharged', while local clergy had preached against the event the previous Sunday.[19] To some extent this reading was accurate. Chartism was developing a capacity to adopt and adapt local political issues, as well as sweeping up the scattered remnants of the general trade unionism from earlier in the decade.

At many – perhaps most – meetings, significant numbers attending were armed with sticks or pikes. When Stephens opened the Hyde Working Men's Institute in September, 'firearms, swords and pikes' were glimpsed among the audience. As autumn turned to winter, the crowds became bolder. The discharge of firearms was reported at a number of meetings. Sunday gatherings were unusual and because most Chartists worked 10-hour days, 6 days a week, nocturnal meetings became the norm. But this was not just expediency: 'One grand phalanx, under the red glare of torch light', John Taylor wrote in proposing the first such gathering on Glasgow Green, 'would present a scene truly graphic, awful and commanding … it would be one of the most striking and imposing scenes ever witnessed in the annals of public meetings'. When Vincent and Hartwell returned to Trowbridge on 10 November they were greeted by a torchlight procession, accompanied by a band, banners and four men carrying on their shoulders a large box, mounted on poles and illuminated from within to reveal painted glass sides inscribed 'LIBERTY'. The general consensus of critics and supporters alike was that the size and, even more, the appearance of these gatherings were unprecedented. 'Never was there witnessed such a concourse of people together at Oldham, in the memory of the oldest man. It has far out-stripped all that have gone before.' 'Certainly it was a scene such as had never been seen in this neighbourhood before, since I knew anything', wrote one of the 'many hundreds' who attended Hyde's Convention delegate election. He recollected 'hundreds of flaming torches borne aloft with lantern transparencies bearing the inscriptions of the people's rights and wrongs'.[20]

'It is almost impossible to imagine the excitement caused by these manifestations', recalled Robert Gammage, a Northampton coach trimmer (and, from 1840, full-time itinerant Chartist lecturer) in 1854:

> The people did not go singly to the place of meeting, but met in a body at a starting point, from whence, at a given time, they issued in huge numbers, formed into procession, traversing the principal streets, making the heavens echo with the loud thunder of their cheers on recognizing the idols of their worship in the men who were to address them, and sending forth volleys of the most hideous groans on passing the office of some hostile newspaper. The banners containing the more formidable devices, viewed by the red light of the glaring torches, presented a scene of awful grandeur. The death's heads represented on some of them grinned like ghostly spectres, and served to remind many a mammon-worshipper of his expected doom. The uncouth appearance of thousands of artizans who had not time on leaving the factory to go home and ... whose faces were therefore begrimed with sweat and dirt, added to the strange aspect of the scene. The processions were frequently of immense length, sometimes containing as many as fifty thousand people; and along the whole line there blazed a stream of light, illuminating the lofty sky, like the reflection from a large city in a general conflagration.[21]

Gammage added to his account that the 'very appearance of such a vast number of blazing torches only seemed more effectually to inflame the minds alike of speaker and hearers'. Contemporary reports bear this out: 'England shall blaze from end to end', declared Harney at Carlisle, dressed in a toga and brandishing a stiletto, 'the firebrand is our weapon and we will weave no more for tyrants but their winding sheets.' Vincent proclaimed at Trowbridge: 'The Tocsin shall sound and the Bonfires shall be lighted on the tops of the Hills – they would meet with Torches every night'; 'they must make a grand strike together and the Bonfires on the Hills would be the signal'. At Rochdale O'Connor, pointing to a flaming torch, exclaimed: 'Look!! at that!!! it speaks a language so intelligible that no one can misunderstand, and those who are not within the hearing of my voice can comprehend the meaning of that silent monitor.' On 8 December at Bury, Stephens asserted that to kill anyone implementing the New Poor Law was 'justified by the law of God ... and know you, that *we may be ever ready to fight it out, and fight it out we will*'.[22]

The spectacle of torchlight meetings called to mind Captain Swing, the agricultural labourers' rising of 1830, in which arson was a central element. Though Swing was essentially a movement of the rural south, whereas torchlight Chartist meetings were held mainly in the industrial north, the collective memory of the political establishment elided the two. Perhaps this was inevitable in a world with very limited artificial lighting (and it was an axiom of English law that diverse criminal offences were treated more harshly if perpetrated under cover of darkness). These meetings profoundly unnerved polite society and, as a contemporary remarked, in the torches' glare 'the timid saw all the apparatus of rebellion and incendiarism'. Echoes of this appeared, just over two years later, in Dickens's novels *Barnaby Rudge* and *The Old Curiosity Shop*, both of which vividly evoked the terrifying appearance of flame-lit crowds, especially so the latter which was set in the near present and at one point flung its heroine into the midst of a nocturnal gathering of 'unemployed labourers'.[23] Yet, remarkably, the incidence of arson in connection with Chartist meetings was virtually nil. At Colchester it was alleged that Chartists obstructed a fire-engine en route to a blaze. More seriously, on 8 December a crowd prevented engines from attending a suspicious fire in Ashton-under-Lyne that wrecked an entire mill. Stephens was widely blamed for the attack, even though he was 11 miles away in Bury that night. No direct connection was established (though two weeks earlier he had bitterly criticised the mill's owner in a sermon at his chapel). However, the incident augmented a growing case against him which Henry Goddard, a detective from London's Bow Street police office, sent by the Home Office to trail Stephens, was gathering.[24]

Also accumulating in correspondence to the Home Secretary was abundant evidence that provincial authorities were increasingly unsettled by torchlight demonstrations. Serious daylight Poor Law riots in the Pennine textile town of Todmorden on 16 and 21 November reinforced that anxiety.[25] On 22 November, for the first time since Chartism had begun to take shape, the Home Office issued a direct instruction to magistrates: torchlight meetings should be suppressed. Local responses to this were initially hesitant, through fear perhaps of the consequences, and the measure had to be reinforced through a Royal Proclamation, banning all open-air nocturnal meetings, on 14 December. Two weeks later, on Thursday 27th, Stephens became the first notable Chartist to be arrested. This was an acid test of the mood in the restless northern textile region.

The enterprising Goddard apprehended Stephens in Ashton early that afternoon, without the military support that the magistrates who signed the warrant thought necessary. He did so before adequate preparations had been made to deal with his prisoner. There followed several hours of near farce. First Goddard had to sprint to an inn to hire a post-chaise in which to take Stephens to the home of Lord Francis Egerton (Lancashire's leading landowner and a senior magistrate) 12 miles distant on the other side of Manchester. When a stop was made at Manchester's Royal Hotel, 'for refreshment', a crowd immediately gathered round the carriage. News of the arrest spread rapidly – and in time for Richardson to distribute an announcement that 'the blood-hounds have laid hold of Stephens … the time has come'.

Vocal supporters of Stephens began to arrive at Egerton's gates almost simultaneously with Goddard and the prisoner. Egerton, who was meant to conduct the committal proceedings, chose that moment to exempt himself on the spurious grounds that he had yet to swear an oath of allegiance specifically to Queen Victoria. He therefore sent Goddard away while a full bench of magistrates, including those who had signed the arrest warrant, was assembled. After a 30-mile round trip on horseback, Goddard returned to Egerton's home at 9.00 p.m. to find magistrates gathering, protected by cavalry personally commanded by the army's Assistant Adjutant General for the north. It took until midnight for the bench to decide to commit Stephens, then another hour to ride back (with cavalry escort) to Manchester. Stephens was finally committed to the New Bailey Prison in the early hours of Friday morning.[26]

That no attempt was made to rescue Stephens, stage a major demonstration in his support or intimidate either magistrates or potential witnesses exposed the Lancashire authorities to some criticism. Though fears for his safety and property were primarily what prompted Egerton's refusal to conduct the committal hearing alone, the legal case against Stephens for instigating violence was far from clear-cut. Although Stephens's congregation shunned those who had informed against him (and three informers were subsequently compensated for damage to their property), the popular reaction to the arrest was characterised mainly by discipline and restraint. John Deegan, a prominent Lancashire trade unionist and Chartist, hastily arranged a public meeting in Ashton at which he appealed for calm. O'Connor declared that the Government intended to provoke 'an ill-concerted display of physical violence', the better to oppress the movement, adding with a characteristically theatrical flourish, 'Beware of the trap! THE TIME FOR FIGHTING HAS NOT YET COME.' All this doubtless facilitated Stephens's release on bail on the Sunday, Richardson being one of his sureties. Stephens arrived back in Ashton to preach in the freezing marketplace to a massive congregation, their heads uncovered and 'preserving the most reverential silence':

> It has been my practice – and has been charged upon me as a crime – to apply the rules of God's commandments to various institutions of the social system, in my own immediate neighbourhood, and in the country at large – to bring the principles and operations of the manufactures, the commerce and the legislation of this professedly Christian land to the standard of God's Holy Word.[27]

## Culture

Clearly something remarkable was taking place as 1838 drew to a close. Seldom had the constitutional right to bear arms been so loudly asserted or the language of physical force so widely used. It was one of the hardest winters in recent memory and the economy was in depression. Yet a highly politicised movement had emerged, distinguished first and foremost by its self-possession. Eight months previously, few radicals (even O'Connor) aspired to anything more than universal male suffrage; now they actively anticipated the imminent achievement of the six points of the Charter.[28] Chartism had yet to percolate into Cornwall, north Wales or north-west Scotland, but elsewhere almost all counties had registered the movement; and in most major centres, and many minor ones, committees were being formed to collect the National Rent and petition signatures, and elections held for delegates to the General Convention.

Nor was this all. In hundreds of localities a distinctive Chartist culture was emerging, at once earnest, celebratory and often laced with humour. Scottish Chartism tended to greater seriousness and was generally both more closely associated with temperance and overtly religious in tone. Proceedings at the meeting to elect a delegate from Stirling and Clackmannan opened with a prayer. The *True Scotsman*'s reporter was vividly reminded of 'the Covenanters of old, [who] proclaimed the doctrines of the Reformation from the hill sides, the mountain sides and the covert glens'. Local trade societies would attend with their banners ('We will tread down corruption', declaimed that of the Stirling weavers), as sometimes would local friendly societies. The procession to Nottingham Forest, where the petition was formally adopted on 5 November and Arthur Wade elected a Convention delegate, was led by a mounted marshal and accompanied by three brass bands. Prominent throughout the procession were the Chartist colours, in green and purple silk, plus the flags of the smiths' union and the tailors' association, the banner of the Hyson Green Friendly Society, the white lace banner of the Nottingham Female PU, tricolours, Union Jacks, the death's head and cross bones and – mounted on poles – a cap of liberty and a bundle of sticks (the fasces, usually tied round an axe, the Roman republican icon symbolising 'Unity is Strength').[29]

Female participation was a crucially important factor in shaping Chartism. The Nottingham FPU was one of well-over 100 women's Chartist groups formed during 1838–39. To contextualise this, however, at least 430 non-gender-specific (and therefore predominantly male) Chartist organisations can be identified in the same period. Chartist activity short of formal organisation has been noted in over 200 further localities. In all, therefore, around 640 communities in England, south and mid-Wales and Lowland Scotland witnessed some form of Chartist activity in the 18 months following the publication of *The People's*

*Charter.* This compares impressively with the 120 PUs (a third of them ephemeral) extant in the years 1830–32.[30] In addition, this vigorous growth markedly exceeded the 133 associations allegedly comprising 'the radical reformers of England, Scotland, & Wales', according to the LWMA in October 1838.[31]

Female societies emerged early in 1838 from the anti-poor law agitation, Elland's FRA being a good example. The major period of growth, however, followed the formation of the Birmingham FPU in the spring of 1838, at the initiative of Thomas Salt.[32] Some female associations were very large; Birmingham FPU, for example, boasted 3,000 members. More typical, though, were community-based societies: Elland mustered twenty-nine when its FRA was founded; Bradford boasted several based around particular streets and, in one case, a single courtyard. In a few instances women's groups constituted the only recorded Chartist activity in their community, for example in the corset-linen weaving burgh of Kirriemuir. It is inconceivable that at least some of Kirriemuir's men were not involved in Chartism, in all likelihood through the Forfarshire CA.[33]

Equally, women's societies did not encompass all female involvement in Chartism. Political discussion was a prominent component at meetings of many female friendly societies, but it was largely hidden from view.[34] The public life of Chartism extended beyond processions and rallies to include house-to-house collections and canvassing, and in all of these women were prominent and, as we shall see in chapter 3, probably took a leadership role in organising and enforcing exclusive dealing. In some localities FRAs organised the collection of women's signatures to the 1839 petition as a separate initiative. Where figures are recorded, the most successful of these (at Ashton-under-Lyne, Carlisle and Wednesbury in the Black Country) constituted around 20 per cent of all signatures collected in their locality. Birmingham and Monmouth managed 15 and 13 per cent respectively.[35] As a guide to the proportion of women among the 1.28 million signatures, these figures can be only approximate. However, they are broadly consistent with the ratio of specifically female to the otherwise 'male' Chartist associations.

The activities of women's Chartist groups were not confined to parades and petitioning. Most followed the format of local WMAs, i.e. regular, formally chaired meetings for lectures and discussions. Chartist men were often the lecturers, but women were seldom reported speaking at 'male' groups' meetings, and hardly any were nominated to Chartism's delegate bodies.[36] However, women fully participated at open-air rallies, often enthusiastically so: for example, Vincent was astonished that when he was pelted with stones at 'Toryfied and Whigified Cirencester', it was women who gave one of the culprits 'a good thrashing'; a similar incident involving an anti-Chartist heckler occurred at Stockton-upon-Tees, and women also occasionally featured among Chartists charged with public order offences.[37]

It is clear that the majority of male Chartists saw women as fulfilling a subaltern role in the movement: 'Go on, Radical females, as ye are called, in the good work', the *True Scotsman* urged; '*we need *your* aid to *assist us*.'[38] In the increasingly gendered world of organised labour the very idea of women signing parliamentary petitions was innovatory. When the United Framework Knitters organised a mass petition to Parliament in 1812 its instructions were unambiguous: 'All the Males in the Trade may sign but no Women.'[39] Women had, though, been a powerful force in the anti-slavery movement, a precedent often cited by Chartists defending female activism. The ideological issues at work here were more complex than mere unconscious chauvinism.[40] An important part of the rhetorical strategy of Chartism was to conjure up a domestic ideal in which the male was the breadwinner and the woman a wife and mother 'whose household duties ought to be her only employment'. Men 'felt the degradation to which their wives and children had been subjected', opined Salt, 'by being compelled to associate in factories, and toil at work which was in no way adapted to their sex or their constitution'. John Deegan declared: 'Women and tender babes are polluted by lickspittles' and 'sacrificed at the shrine of Moloch [by] ... the rich, the capitalists'.[41]

To a considerable extent these arguments could be sustained only by appealing to a mythical golden age (women's labour had been crucial to the 'pre-industrial' economy). But militant domesticity was deployed by Chartists as a powerful critique of middle-class social exclusiveness and of the implicit dismissal of political equality that it entailed.[42] Defending the domestic ideal in itself also justified women mobilising for Chartism, while the broad assimilation of Owenite socialist ideas (concerning the power of nurture over nature in decisively shaping personality) meant women were accorded a powerful, albeit of course gender-specific, role in shaping society. '*What have women to do with Politics?*' demanded Vincent: 'All – everything! ... as in a family ... so in a nation, the feelings, habits, desires, and patriotism of its people spring from the influence of the majority of the mothers of that people'.[43] As the movement grew in stature and extent, so an abiding concern of Chartists became to influence all dimensions of human existence, rather than merely achieve political reform. Thus mass mobilisation of women for the Charter was not incompatible with its explicit restriction of the concept of 'universal' suffrage to men alone.

Ostensibly, women activists accepted the patronising stance of their male counterparts. 'Sisters and Fellow countrywomen', the Nottingham FPU appealed,

> your important energies are recruited in aid of those measures in which our husbands, fathers, brothers, and children are now so actively and zealously engaged, headed by the first men and patriots of the day ... [behold] the tattered garments of your children ... their poor, pallid faces ... the care-worn

looks of your husbands, who, with their many hours of slavish toil, cannot provide food and raiment for them to satisfy Nature's cravings.[44]

Yet a close reading of this address 'to the Patriotic Women of England' reveals the consistent invocation of women's 'power', several invocations 'to fight' and a robust argument that withdrawing custom from unsympathetic shopkeepers would bring the middle classes 'to their senses … you, sisters … are the most fit and proper persons to deal out the blow and most effectually too'. Female members of the Dunfermline PU similarly contrasted domestic distress to their 'oppressors … rioting in luxury and debauchery'. They declared: 'If there is a woman in Britain [who] can tamely submit to such usage, she deserves not the name of woman'. The Birmingham FPU stated unambiguously: 'we aim at the possession of power for the purpose of abolishing all unjust laws'. Though such addresses sought to rally women to an essentially masculine cause, they did so in terms that were distinctly the women's own.[45]

Another striking feature of Chartist culture at this time was the burgeoning place within it of print. Chartism sustained not only the *Northern Star* but a plethora of other newspapers. Some were established publications with radical leanings that took up the Chartist cause – the *Sheffield Iris*, Glasgow's *Scots Times* and *Scotch Reformers' Gazette*, the *Dundee Chronicle*, *Aberdeen Herald*, *Brighton Patriot*, Hetherington's *London Dispatch*, the *Perthshire Chronicle* and the metropolitan *Weekly True Sun*. Pre-eminent among these titles was the spirited *Northern Liberator* which had commenced publication in Newcastle in October 1837. Published in three separate editions and with weekly sales exceeding 4,000, the *Liberator* was the only paper other than the *Northern Star* (and north of the border the *True Scotsman*) to develop a significant circulation beyond its area of publication. During 1838 three new Scottish Chartist papers were established – the *Ayrshire Examiner*, the Glasgow *Monthly Liberator* and the Edinburgh-based *True Scotsman* (pointedly titled to oppose the Whig *Scotsman*), along with Bronterre O'Brien's London-based *Operative*. Early in 1839 these were joined by two significant English titles, Vincent's *Western Vindicator* (Bristol-based but especially influential in south Wales) and the LWMA's *Charter*, along with the latter's rivals *Chartist* and *London Democrat*.[46] *Northern Star*, however, towered above every one of these papers. Average weekly sales of 11,000 during 1838 gave it a circulation larger than any other paper published outside of London. Its dominance is nicely demonstrated in a survey conducted in the Ayrshire town of Old Cumnock, where a total of 110 Chartists between them subscribed each week to 1 *Charter*, 1 *Operative*, 2 *Ayr Examiner*, 2 *True Scotsman* but 6 copies of *Northern Star*.[47]

A total of just 12 newspapers among 110 Chartists inevitably poses questions about how influential newspapers were. Fortunately there exists abundant evidence for newspaper consumption patterns, especially for *Northern Star*. 'A man lent me his paper when it was a week old for a penny', recalled a 16-year-old apprentice from Bingley, West Yorkshire, 'I giving him the paper back when I had had it a week.' Another youngster, Ben Grime of Oldham, purchased the paper every Saturday to read aloud to his father and neighbours over 'a tot of whoam-brewed'. A teenage handloom velvet weaver from Failsworth, Lancashire, recollected that the *Star* was 'subscribed for by my father and five others. Every Sunday morning these subscribers met at our house to hear what prospect there was of the expected "smash-up" taking place. It was my task to read aloud so that all could hear at the same time.' At nearby Mossley, the local WMA reported: 'we read the news of the week, and discuss it paragraph by paragraph as it is read'. In Middlesbrough *Northern Star* and other radical papers were 'generally read amidst loud applause'. Similar collective arrangements were reported at Nantwich, Cheshire, in woolcombers' workshops at Great Horton, Bradford (in each of which 'the *Northern Star* was always subscribed for'), in the knitting shops of Leicestershire and villages around Halifax. The typography of the *Northern Star*, with its abundant use of capitals, italics and exclamation marks, coupled with its practice of reporting speeches verbatim, helped turn these readings into almost theatrical events.[48] In retrospect, Chartism may be discerned as situated on the cusp of the transition from a largely oral to a mainly print-based popular culture. Through the *Northern Star*, O'Connor especially was able to thrive in both worlds. It was this, combined with formidable energy and a certain recklessness, that made him impossible to ignore.

## Controversy

O'Connor's increasing stature was abundantly evident, as 1838 drew to a close, in confrontations between him and the BPU and key Scottish reformers. With hindsight, faultlines may be discerned here that would damage Chartism. Yet what was most striking at the time was how O'Connor's personal authority prevailed.

Although O'Connor had been careful to cultivate Scotland, he was far from the leading figure as Chartism emerged there. Conspicuously absent from Glasgow Green in May 1838, his appearances both before and after had been sporadic. Probably the greatest integrating influences in Scotland were Abram Duncan and John Fraser, editor of the *True Scotsman*. The two pursued an effective campaign of publicity on behalf of the nascent movement in eastern and lowland Scotland and the Borders over the summer and autumn. Neither were moderates yet both were struck forcibly by the reluctance, at least beyond Glasgow, to endorse violence. Convention delegates elected by these regions tended to be moderate. They included Patrick Matthew, a landowner and grain dealer, for the counties of Perth and Fife, and the academic William Villiers Sankey. The forceful John Taylor, on the other hand, failed to secure nomination for his native Ayrshire. Memories of the momentous events of the Regency were more raw in Scotland than in England. English radicals looked to Peterloo, plausibly claiming it was an unjustified assault by the state upon a defenceless people, rather than to the revolutionary conspiracies of these years. Indeed, the Cato Street conspiracy of 1820 was largely suppressed in the popular mind (even though a handful of London Chartists, notably John George and Thomas Preston, had been implicated in it). In Scotland, on the other hand, the common reference point was the fiasco of the 1820 'insurrection', following which 3 working men were hanged, 16 others transported and many more – among them Fraser – imprisoned.[49] The sentences passed on the Glasgow cotton spinners in 1838 likewise increased apprehension.

Given also growing unease in the mainstream press about the violent temperament of English Chartist meetings, it is therefore not surprising that Duncan and Fraser should have moved closer to the 'moral force' position of the audiences they encountered. In a series of letters to O'Connor and Stephens, prominently placed on the *True Scotsman's* front page, Duncan argued that 'physical force revolution never yet benefited the great mass of the people'. How to enforce Chartism's overall aim if its constitutional and moral arguments were ignored was a question that would dominate internal debate over the coming year. A clear majority of Chartists adhered to the view summed up in the slogan 'Peaceably if we may, forcibly if we must'. Duncan and Fraser, however, adopted a more purist stance: 'You know that moral means, to be effective for the accomplishment of any purpose, must be faithfully, perseveringly and patiently prosecuted to ensure success', wrote Duncan. 'In even whispering that they may not succeed, you make the means to paralyse, if not destroy their influence.'[50]

Duncan's letters were followed up by draft resolutions affirming Scottish Chartists' attachment to constitutional means of reform, which Duncan and Fraser circulated to each Scottish locality with an invitation to send delegates to meet in Edinburgh and debate the issue. This initiative was far from universally welcome. The Ayr WMA, for example, replied with a question that neatly encapsulated the tactical (and for later historians interpretive) quandary underlying moral and physical force. Its members could not

> view the proposed national resolution to use nothing but moral means in any other light than an unconditional surrender; for if we cannot speak to the fears of our oppressors ... we shall never be able to speak with any good effect to their feelings, and we would ask you what good you can calculate upon obtaining, after having proclaimed to them that they have nothing to fear from physical force?[51]

The assembly at Johnstone's Temperance Coffee House, Edinburgh, on 4 and 5 December was thinly attended – some 50 delegates representing 19 (of approximately 80) localities. Fraser claimed to have received 60 written responses, 53 of them supporting the stance he and Duncan took. The general mood of the meeting decidedly favoured restraint from intimating physical force. In this it was persuasively abetted by the Reverend Patrick Brewster, a major dissident figure in the Church of Scotland. This mood was embodied in the series of resolutions passed, with Brewster in the chair, at an ostentatiously peaceful, torch-lit meeting on Calton Hill on 5 December – peaceful, that is, except for the vehemence with which 'the physical forcemen, the Stephenses and the Oastlers' were attacked. Brewster himself exempted O'Connor from criticism, but the Calton Hill resolutions ran completely contrary to O'Connor's strategy of seeking to hold Chartism together, as well as the strategy (one shared by the overwhelming majority of those calling themselves Chartists) to hold physical force as an explicit reserve should moral persuasion fail.[52]

Furthermore the accession of a prominent middle-class recruit like Brewster to the Chartist cause could be construed as strengthening the case for a renewed Whig–radical alliance for reform. This was O'Connell's consistent objective and the return to Britain of Lord Durham, former Governor General of Canada and critic of the Government's handling of the rebellion there, promised a further high-profile recruit to this cause. O'Connell, however, was an opportunist who had forfeited the respect of organised labour, while Durham was an irascible dilettante whose radical reputation reflected past postures rather than present efforts. O'Connor knew this; but he knew too that such a development, even if superficial and ephemeral, might damage the emerging Chartist movement. The extent to which Brewster supported O'Connell was undoubtedly exaggerated by O'Connor, but there were prominent Scottish Chartists who thought along these lines – notably the Kilmarnock bailie (councillor and magistrate) Hugh Craig. A draper, Craig chaired the local PU, funded the Chartist *Ayr Examiner*, and defeated Taylor in the contest to be Ayrshire's Convention delegate. Elements in the LWMA were also not averse to forging some kind of alliance with sympathetic Whigs, though that probably troubled O'Connor less.[53]

O'Connor's response was to rush to Scotland for six frenetic days' agitation. Broader issues than his personal authority were at stake. He was concerned to sharpen the distinction between Chartism and 'sham radicalism', eliminate a potentially damaging fissure in Scottish Chartism and clarify his strategic stance. 'I have told you to get Universal Suffrage by moral force if possible', he told a public meeting in Edinburgh's Freemasons' Hall, 'and moral means are sufficiently adequate to that end: but if moral means fail in obtaining Universal Suffrage, get it or die in the attempt.'[54] Feargus very nearly did die in the attempt. The pace of constant campaigning suddenly overcame him and in early February rumours circulated that he was dying of a ruptured blood vessel. Even Daniel O'Connell was moved: 'Poor unhappy man! I am, after all, sincerely sorry for his premature fate.'[55] Feargus, however, bounced back.

A similar controversy had beset the relationship between the BPU council and O'Connor. Although Attwood continued to hint of a resort to physical force if peaceable agitation failed, just as in Scotland Joseph Rayner Stephens's apparent readiness to adopt violence as an immediate, rather than final, route to reform unnerved Attwood's associates. When the BPU council debated the matter in October, Thomas Salt had been particularly vocal in censuring Stephens and O'Connor on the grounds that, by declaring the Charter would be obtained by a specific date, they were explicitly threatening violence. At its regular Tuesday meeting on 13 November, the council was brought to a sudden halt when O'Connor strode in, unannounced and unapologetic. Salt was absent, but a heated exchange nevertheless followed. Only John Collins established any middle ground, though he forcibly told O'Connor that setting a target date was an issue only the Convention should decide. O'Connor conceded the latter point but insisted on returning the following week to debate the broader principle.

The BPU council always met publicly and when it reassembled on 20 November the room was swamped with spectators. Many others were excluded and complained so loudly that proceedings were several times halted. By mutual agreement, what was now widely regarded as a gladiatorial contest between Salt and O'Connor was postponed for yet another week and the Town Hall hired for the occasion. Like many keenly anticipated encounters the occasion was something of a let-down. At a private meeting the day before, apparently brokered by Collins, Salt and O'Connor agreed to debate only the principles of their own positions; and Salt, who even so probably foresaw a public drubbing, apologised to O'Connor: 'there never was the least personal difference between Mr O'Connor and himself', he told a packed Town Hall, and 'he considered him one of the best friends of reform'. For his part, O'Connor, supported a resolution condemning the *exhortation* to violence, the search for cohesion ever to the fore. His moral authority appeared almost unimpeachable, while he used the fortnight's delay in resolving the BPU dispute to publicise his position in the *Star*, presenting himself as the defender of the people's rights.[56]

As 1839 began Chartism occupied a position of some strength. Exceptionally severe January weather and eager anticipation of the Convention softened whatever impact the government ban on torch-lit meetings might otherwise have had. Stephens was at least at liberty. Some well-placed Chartists even thought he had deliberately sought arrest to secure an opportunity to contest the legality of the New Poor Law in court.[57] On 12 January the *Northern Star* appeared with a new masthead. It featured the fasces, a leek, shamrocks, a thistle, a rose, oak leaves and, at the centre, a printing press radiating light like the sun. The inclusion of the printing press evoked the simpler machine that, with the legend 'Knowledge is power', had appeared on each issue of the great unstamped paper *Poor Man's Guardian* (1831–35). Chartism was developing cultural dimensions that took it beyond being merely a protest movement. At the same time, against the background of an economic depression of unusual severity, it was mobilising ever-increasing numbers. Without any overarching organisational structure it was successfully raising funds, collecting petition signatures and electing delegates to its National Convention. Two months previously, Stephens had urged a Wigan audience 'go to work like *"good 'uns,"* and get it done'.[58] With the New Year, the Chartists gave every impression of doing exactly that.

# Chartist lives:
# Patrick Brewster

When he first learnt of the Calton Hill meeting O'Connor affected to believe that proven radicals would never desert the cause. 'FRASER, I love you', he declared, 'DUNCAN, I thank you'; but his response to Brewster was dismissive: 'BREWSTER, I don't know you.'[*] This was not unreasonable. Hitherto Patrick Brewster had played no part in Scottish Chartism and as a minister of the Church of Scotland he was unequivocally a member of the establishment. Lord Aberdeen, a future prime minister, had presented him to his position at Paisley Abbey in 1818, on behalf of the Marquis of Abercorn. His first wife (who died in 1831) was the daughter of a colonel. Mary, his second, whom he married in 1834, was the daughter of Brewster's predecessor at Paisley, an unswerving loyalist. Patrick's brother Sir David Brewster was a college principal at St Andrews University, a distinguished scientist and a leading Scottish intellectual.[†]

---

[*]   *NS*, 29 December 1838.
[†]   H. Scott, *Fasti Ecclesiae Scoticanae*, vol. 8 (Edinburgh, Oliver & Boyd, 1920), pp.169–70; entries for David Brewster and Patrick Brewster: *The Oxford Dictionary of National Biography* (*ODNB*).

However, the 50-year-old Patrick Brewster did have a record of outspokenness on social and political issues. He had defended those involved in the Scottish disturbances of 1820 and was a prominent campaigner for the abolition of slavery. Unlike most middle-class abolitionists, however, Brewster also argued that the condition of many British workers was one of 'WHITE SLAVERY', with 'the British Operative ... as much at the mercy of his Master, as if he was a Negro Slave'. In this he was clearly influenced by one of Chartism's inspirational figures, Richard Oastler. At the same time – also in contrast to many abolitionists – Brewster deplored the continuing economic and political subjugation of emancipated slaves to their former owners.* He also supported Roman Catholic emancipation and Irish home rule. His appearance on public platforms with Daniel O'Connell in 1835 was officially censured by the Church, an act he fought vociferously (and unsuccessfully) right up to an appeal to the General Assembly of the Church of Scotland.†

Brewster's interpretation of the role of the Christian minister in political matters was similar to J. R. Stephens's, applying 'the rules of God's commandments' to social and political institutions. 'Our politics are the politics of the Bible – the religion of the Bible', he told a Paisley audience in November 1838: 'their politics are the politics of the state; and, let me add, the religion of the state.'‡ Brewster was unique among the clergy of Scotland's established Church in outspokenly supporting Chartism. There were few cognate figures in the Church of England either, the closest being Arthur Wade. Yet none of this (especially his association with O'Connell) recommended Brewster to O'Connor, who was deeply suspicious of the political and religious establishment. He was also apt to make snap judgements of character which, combined with a habitual tendency to exaggeration, sometimes led him to pronouncements that in hindsight he possibly regretted. Thus O'Connor – who once had embraced a Methodist lay-preacher for opening a Chartist rally with a prayer, promising that 'when we get the People's Charter I will see that you are made the Archbishop of York' – decided on the basis of a handful of newspaper stories about meetings 200 miles away that Brewster was a 'serpent' with whom he should deal personally and immediately. Meanwhile the *Northern Star* report of Brewster's failed attempt to block Taylor's election as delegate

---

\*    P. Brewster, *Duties of the Present Crisis, with a Special Reference to the Liberated Negroes in the British Colonies* (Paisley, Murray, 1838), and *Seven Chartist and Military Discourses* (Paisley, self-published, 1843), pp. 48 and 75; B. Fladeland, *Abolitionists and Working-Class Problems in the Age of Industrialization* (London, Macmillan, 1984), pp. 106–31.

†    S. Mechie, *The Church and Scottish Social Development, 1780–1870* (London, Oxford University Press, 1960), pp. 105–6; P. Brewster, *Reply to the Attacks Made on Mr Brewster in the Synod of Glasgow and Ayr for Attending the O'Connell Dinner* (Paisley, Gardner, 1835).

‡    *NS*, 29 December 1838; *Report of a Soirée in Honour of the Rev. Patrick Brewster* (Paisley, Caldwell, 1838), p. 6.

for Paisley and Renfrewshire referred in lurid terms to the 'sham radicals and government spies, headed by the Rev. Patrick Brewster'.[*]

Brewster for his part totally lacked the BPU's inclination to compromise with O'Connor. 'A fiery furious Blockhead', according to one contemporary, though principled and eloquent (albeit sometimes to the point of tedium), Brewster knew his own mind too well to be swayed by negotiation.[†] O'Connor thought him 'one of the most confident, insolent, bullying men in existence'. Unfortunately for Brewster, packed Chartist meetings were nothing like church services and he performed markedly less well on the platform than he did in the pulpit. Twice in January 1839, at Paisley and Glasgow, Brewster accepted invitations to debate with O'Connor and each time found the mood of the meeting totally against him. O'Connor defended his and Stephens's more extreme statements as isolated occurrences made in the heat of the moment. He emphasised his consistent adherence to the slogan 'Peaceably if we may, forcibly if we must'. Arguing that the Calton Hill resolutions made Chartism appear divided, which in turn encouraged moves to suppress it, O'Connor emotively asserted that 'BREWSTER and his moral cheats were the cause of STEPHENS's arrest'. Feargus was conciliatory to Fraser, but less so to Duncan, whom he accused of opportunism and hypocrisy. Repeatedly he cited a speech by Duncan, three months earlier, wherein he referred pointedly to the Battle of Bannockburn and to the willingness of 'the blue bonnets' to march into England and 'to destroy more abomination than their ancestors sallied from their hills to crush'.[‡] 'Mr Moral Philosopher Brewster' O'Connor largely brushed aside.

The cracks in Scottish Chartism had been papered over rather than repaired. There were two essential reasons for this. First, nationalist sentiment might be suspicious of government based in England, but it could also assert for Scottish Chartism the right to be self-determining. In May Brewster initiated the call for a separate Scottish Convention. When a 'Scottish Delegate Conference' finally convened on 14 August it was far from being under Brewster's tutelage; but his influence at the formative stage of what was to prove a significant event in Scottish Chartism's history was clear.[§] Second, religious ideals were seldom far from the surface of Chartism. In Scotland especially there were emerging Chartist churches, overtly combining political solidarity with a radical social

---

[*]  B. Wilson, 'The struggles of an old Chartist' (1887), in D. Vincent (ed.), *Testaments of Radicalism: Memoirs of Working-Class Politicians, 1790–1885* (London, Europa, 1977), p.198; *NS*, 12 January 1839.

[†]  Marginalia in Paisley Museum's copy of a local directory for 1841–42, quoted in T.C. Smout (ed.), *The Search for Wealth and Stability* (London, Macmillan, 1979), p.222.

[‡]  *NS*, 19 January 1839 and 29 December 1838.

[§]  For the conference, see chapter 5, this book, and A. Wilson, *The Chartist Movement in Scotland* (Manchester, Manchester University Press, 1970), pp.82–8.

gospel. The *Northern Star* claimed that 'a Chartist place of worship is to be found on the Lord's Day in almost every town of note from Aberdeen to Ayr', though in fact there were around thirty congregations. Strikingly, most were in west Scotland in what had been the seventeenth-century covenanters' heartland. There were approximately twenty English Chartist churches too, but many were ephemeral. These English congregations also tended towards religious humanism whereas the Scottish churches were more theologically orthodox: the *Constitution of the Greenock Christian Chartist Congregation*, for example, affirmed Christ's divinity and resurrection, and declared that the Bible constituted the complete revelation of God's will.* Chartist churches of every complexion, though, stressed the validity of full lay ministry: 'Baptism is as sacred when performed by a Chartist missionary as by any clergyman in the kingdom', argued the Scottish *Chartist Circular*. 'The holy sacrament of the Lord's Supper is also as sacred when dispensed by a lay preacher as by a bishop ... This was the practice of the Primitive Churches.'[†]

There was, then, a substantial and growing element within Scottish Chartism from whom Patrick Brewster commanded respect. His reputation was sustained both by his preaching a highly politicised social gospel, his practical responses to the problems of Paisley's workers and his frequent conflicts with Church authorities. And while Brewster was a powerful advocate of the religious duty of passive obedience,[‡] his version of it did not entail dumb acquiescence:

> A mighty crisis ... is not far distant. There are two great parties in motion, the friends of freedom and its enemies. There are two great and opposing interests standing forth in fixed and irreconcilable hostility. The struggle is between liberty and despotism ... What then is your duty, on which side will you stand[?] Every individual member of the community ... participates ... in the guilt of every oppressive enactment, while he ceases to raise his voice against the usurped power, or to demand the repeal of the unjust law.[§]

This was the philosophy Brewster put into effect in November 1839 when, on behalf of the unemployed of Paisley, he wrote the text of a petition to the Provost, the magistrates, the town council, 'the manufacturers and other wealthy inhabitants thereof'. While acknowledging measures taken to relieve distress, Brewster demanded 'the comfortable supply of present necessities ... not as a donation of charity, but as a right of property, vested in us by the

---

*    *NS*, 16 January 1841; *Constitution of the Greenock Christian Chartist Congregation* (Greenock, 1841), quoted in D.C. Smith, *Passive Obedience and Prophetic Protest* (New York, Lang, 1987), pp.171–2; Wilson, *Chartist Movement in Scotland*, pp.124–5, 142–50.

†    *Chartist Circular*, 28 March 1840.

‡    See particularly his *Essay on Passive Obedience*, 2nd edn (Paisley, Cuthbertson, 1836), and *Seven Chartist and Military Discourses*, pp.45–6.

§    Brewster, *Seven Chartist and Military Discourses*, pp.42 and 44.

laws of God and this kingdom'.* This was an argument derived from Cobbett and widely repeated among English anti-Poor Law campaigners: there existed a legal as well as moral right to poor relief at a level equivalent to that of the independent labourer tilling his own plot of land. Cobbett linked this to the effects of enclosure, the misappropriation of commons and the loss at the Reformation of monastic land formerly used for charitable purposes. Brewster himself specifically developed this argument in the third of his 'Chartist sermons' and one of his 'military sermons' on a text from Ecclesiastes: 'The profit of the earth is for all.'†

The 'military sermons' derived their title from another dispute in which Brewster became embroiled in 1842, when the officer commanding Paisley's garrison withdrew his troops from church parade because of Brewster's preaching. (One sermon was against enlisting in the army, arguing that the soldier sold 'his moral as well as his physical liberty'.) This case came before the Church authorities, where it was linked to complaints that Brewster had also preached in one of Glasgow's Chartist churches. The committee of enquiry was 'unanimously of the opinion that such conduct is highly censurable in any minister of the Gospel, involving a violation of ecclesiastical order, a contempt of decency, a profanation of the Lord's Day, a desecration of the Christian ministry as appointed by God to evangelize the poor and the mischievous encouragement of a system of disorganization and misrule both in the Church and in the State'.‡ Brewster was set to be suspended and, in February 1843, a ninety-three page 'libel' (an indictment in Scottish law) was served against him.

It is difficult for a modern secular readership to comprehend the gravity of the issues Brewster stirred up. As another clergyman recalled, 'a Radical like Patrick Brewster of Paisley was looked on as little better than an infidel'. Furthermore, these events were played out against a background of growing turmoil in the Church concerning the rights of major landowners (heritors) to make Church appointments to which parishioners objected. This culminated in May 1843 in 'the Disruption', an irrevocable split in which a third of clergy and half the laity left the Church of Scotland to form the Free Church. Brewster signalled his sympathy with the secession in the full title to the sermons he published that year: *Seven Chartist and Military Discourses Libelled by the Marquis of Abercorn, and Other Heritors of Paisley Abbey.* He might have joined the Free

---

\*    Poster, 'Petition of the Unemployed Operatives of Paisley', 20 November 1839, Renfrewshire County Council, Local Studies Section, Central Library, Paisley (accessed through SCRAN – www.scran.ac.uk – 10 October 2005).

†    Brewster, *Seven Chartist and Military Discourses*, pp.79f. and 201–21.

‡    Paisley Presbytery Minutes, quoted in Mechie, *The Church and Scottish Social Development*, p.106.

Church himself (as his brother did) but his social conservatism restrained him.*
However, the timing of the Disruption, just three months after Brewster was
served with the libel, saved him from suspension, the General Assembly being
swamped by more pressing issues and eager to minimise dissent within the
remnants of the established Church. In December he was formally acquitted
of all charges.

While the case against him was pending, and in defiance of charges that
he was neglecting official duties, Brewster had continued to devote himself
to a wide range of secular activities. He was a driving force behind the Paisley
Society for the Protection of the Destitute Poor and held various offices in the
town's Total Abstinence Society. Brewster, though, was clear on where his first
loyalties lay: 'Chartism was indestructible', he told a regional Church Synod,
'and would continue its onward march till it was enshrined in the Constitution
of Britain.' In 1840 he declared: 'I never will devote my time or money to any
purpose other than Chartism.' He made repeated attempts to purge the
movement of 'physical force', but although some separatist 'New Moral Force
Associations' were founded in 1839, they numbered merely 8 out of the 100 or
so Scottish localities in which there were Chartist associations of some kind.
Some other localities which agreed with Brewster in principle nonetheless
declined to secede from the main Chartist body.†

Undeterred, in September 1840, assisted by John Fraser, he campaigned to
establish a General National Association for Moral Force Chartists, an initiative
which drew from the *Scottish Patriot* the acidic observation that wherever the
pair agitated in favour of Chartism, 'there the cause is sure to recede or stand
still'.‡ Yet Brewster was far from marginalised: it is tempting to view Chartism
as divided into two irreconcilable factions, 'moral force' and 'physical force',
and to equate these with political moderation and extremism. But the reality
was far more fluid: even someone as militant in his attachment to moral force
as Brewster could sometimes seize the respect of those he opposed. In April
1841, for example, he led the rout of middle-class influence in the Glasgow
Emancipation Society that resulted in the election of seventeen Chartists to
its executive. The context of this was a visit to Britain by the radical American
abolitionist John Anderson Collins, who argued that Americans had a duty
to support Chartism just as Britons should support abolition, for the English
establishment was 'exercising the same prejudice against poverty, that we do

---

*    Brewster, *Seven Chartist and Military Discourses*, pp. 420–3; W.C. Smith, 1872, quoted
in Smith, *Passive Obedience*, p. 182; Wilson, *Chartism in Scotland*, p. 142.
    †    Thomas Johnston, 'Introduction' to P. Brewster, *Chartist and Socialist Sermons*
(Glasgow, Forward, ?1924), p. iv; *True Scotsman*, 6 and 13 July 1839; Wilson, *Chartism in
Scotland*, pp. 84–5, 155.
    ‡    Quoted in Wilson, *Chartism in Scotland*, p. 120.

against color'.* Brewster as much as anyone should be credited for establishing links between Chartism and radical American abolitionists. Towards the end of his life, he developed his personal vision of the social gospel to argue against racism: 'God hath made of one blood the whole family of man.' In 1857 he stringently attacked as racist British policy in India.†

A curious relationship developed between Brewster and O'Connor when the latter returned to Scotland on a speaking tour in 1841. The clergyman dogged O'Connor's steps to the point where both agreed to appear together at a number of venues and formally debate the issues dividing them. Though he performed considerably better than in their 1839 encounters, Brewster still commanded only a minority at each meeting. From O'Connor's perspective these debates publicised both his command of the platform and his carefully nuanced views about political violence. Most Chartists depended for their information on the *Northern Star*, wherein each encounter was reported at length, variously dressed up as a trial, a duel or a sporting occasion. O'Connor always emerged victorious in the paper's coverage, his opponent 'compelled to writhe under the lash of insulted pride and manly indignation'. It is unlikely that Brewster faired quite as badly as the *Star* claimed; but he lost heavily in votes of confidence at Aberdeen, Glasgow and, surprisingly, Paisley.‡ Unwittingly, Brewster was consolidating O'Connor's hold on Chartism, not weakening it.

The two clashed again at the Scottish delegate conference of January 1842. After that Brewster never confronted O'Connor again; indeed at a meeting in March called to forge an alliance between Paisley Chartism and middle-class reformers, he disarmed Chartists intent on wrecking the event with a vigorous speech in favour of 'the Charter, the whole Charter, and nothing but the Charter'.§ However, as chapter 7 shows, he effectively abandoned the movement at the end of 1842 to concentrate on local affairs. He regarded the 1843 publication of his *Chartist and Military Discourses* as a final statement and did not take up his pen again until the 1850s. By then the nature of Chartism had changed and Brewster's position was far less distinctive (and less stridently stated). A new book in 1853 appeared to signal a rethink on the moral legiti-macy of physical force. 'Resistance to tyranny is obedience to God, and slavery is but the curse of God upon cowardice.'¶ In practice his intellectual position

---

\* Fladeland, *Abolitionists*, p.118; see *Chartist Circular*, 29 May 1841, for a detailed article on Brewsterite arguments concerning American slavery and British abolitionists.

† P. Brewster, *The Perils and Duties of the War* (Paisley, 1858), quoted in E.G. Lyon, *Politicians in the Pulpit* (Aldershot, Ashgate, 1999), pp. 235–6; P. Brewster, *The India Revolt: Its Duties and Dangers* (Paisley, Parlane, 1857).

‡ *NS*, 23 and 30 October, 6 and 13 November 1841.

§ Ibid., 12 March 1842.

¶ P. Brewster, *Wellington 'Weighed in the Balance'; or, War a Crime, Self-Defence a Duty* (Paisley, Caldwell, 1853), p.16.

had changed little: it was his emphasis on circumstances that might negate the duty of obedience which had shifted. Even in 1841 Brewster had been prepared to approve theft of food by the unemployed. In 1844 both he and the *Northern Star* trenchantly denounced the Robert Burns Festival in an effort to reclaim the poet for radicalism. Brewster returned to a similar theme in 1845, when he led a counter-demonstration to the Whig-dominated dedication of the Scottish political 'Martyrs' Monument' in Edinburgh.* In 1848, when Paisley held a public meeting to welcome the French Revolution, Brewster took the chair.†

There was, then, scope for compromise between Brewster and O'Connor, though both were too abrasive and self-important to recognise it. However, the passionate commitment of both men and their supporters to their respective positions has to be recognised. Chartism mattered intensely: personal belief in it was not something to toss lightly aside. Brewster's intellectual convictions illuminate an important strand within Chartist thought. And it was Brewster, rather than Lovett and his circle, who did most to foreground 'moral force' arguments in the years 1838–42. Ironically, in this he was assisted by O'Connor, who exploited their personal enmity to publicise his own position.

After 1842 Brewster was a figure marginal to Chartism, albeit remaining committed to radical reform. Three months before he died, in March 1859, the 70-year-old led Paisley's delegation to Glasgow to hear John Bright speak in what was to be one of several stuttering stages on the road to a post-Chartist reform movement in western Scotland. A generous public subscription funded a statue in Paisley in Brewster's memory.‡

---

\* A. Tyrell, 'Bearding the Tories: the commemoration of the Scottish political martyrs of 1793–94', in P. A. Pickering and A. Tyrell (eds), *Contested Sites: Commemoration, Memorial and Popular Politics in Nineteenth-Century Britain* (Aldershot, Ashgate, 2004), pp. 40–2, and 'Paternalism, public memory and national identity in early Victorian Scotland', *History*, 90:1 (2005), p. 46.

† J. Parkhill, *The History of Paisley* (Paisley, Stewart, 1857), p. 89.

‡ A. R. Howell, *Paisley Abbey: Its History, Architecture and Art* (Paisley, Gardner, c. 1929), p. 38.

# CHAPTER THREE

# January–July 1839:
# 'The People's Parliament'

### 'The life-boat of Democracy'

Chartism was buoyant as the New Year began. For example, on 26 January sales of *Northern Star* reached a new peak of 17,640. Further underlining the importance of the press to Chartism, a new paper appeared the following day: *The Charter*. Published by Robert Hartwell on behalf of a committee of working men (all LWMA members), it was edited by William Carpenter. Carpenter was yet another radical pressman who had entered politics (and suffered imprisonment) through the unstamped press.[1] *The Charter* enjoyed initial sales around 6,000 an issue, highly encouraging given its implicit objective of counterbalancing the influence of the *Northern Star* and O'Connor. Yet its vision of contemporary Britain was no less bleak than its mighty rival's:

> Society everywhere exhibits phenomena as startling as they are novel ... who, indeed, can look abroad upon the present face of things, identifying himself with the fortunes of his country and his kind, and not be moved by a sense of the critical and insecure position of all that constitutes social happiness? The elements of society are thrown into a state of unnatural excitement and of violent conflict ... nothing is to be seen but the contentions of faction, the conflict of opposing interests, the bitter complainings of poverty, and the clamorous outcries of discontent. The poorest class of labourers – and they include no small number – are groaning beneath an accumulation of physical suffering unparalleled in history, and almost beyond the capacity of human endurance; the more prosperous and intelligent class of artisans and manufacturers are restless, discontented, and upon the very verge of turbulence, from a bitter sense of their political proscription and degradation.[2]

All elements within Chartism agreed that the General Convention, soon to convene in London, was central to resolving this situation. There was no lack of commitment to the National Petition, though its rejection by Parliament was widely predicted. All over Britain local leaders warned against excessive optimism. Addressing the Putney WMA, Edmund Stallwood, leader of the gardeners' trade society during the explosion of interest in general unionism five years previously, 'showed the misery and distress the people have been reduced to by exclusive legislation, and urged the necessity of subscribing to the National Rent'. Stallwood 'implored them not to have too much faith in the present parliament ... their petition might not be received'. In such a situation the role of the Convention in steering the movement through the confrontation with Parliament would be critical: 'Fear not', Stallwood assured his audience to loud cheers, 'let but the people be firm and stand together, and we must eventually succeed despite of all opposition.'[3] There were Chartists who believed that the Convention's function would be to manage the petition's collection and presentation, and nothing more, but the vast majority looked to it to set the course by which Chartism would face down the establishment. The National Rent was therefore needed not only to pay delegates' expenses but to finance widespread campaigning.

There was an element of risk to the Convention strategy. None could be sure what the Government's reaction would be to an elected body, sitting in London, that presumed to speak for the country. Care was taken to elect delegates in open, public meetings, and to limit the total to forty-nine, to conform with the Seditious Meetings Act of 1817. Technically 62 delegates were elected but 9 failed to attend even once. Todmorden Chartists found the cost of defending those involved in the anti-Poor Law riots there the previous November prohibited sending a delegate. George Loveless had been elected for Dorset without his knowledge: a public subscription had installed him on a smallholding when he returned from Australia, but to attend 'I must Hire a man to supply my place which at present I cannot afford'. Similarly, Manchester publican Edward Nightingale could not neglect his business. But a far more significant absence was that of three Birmingham delegates, including both Muntz brothers. The frailty of the rapprochement O'Connor had secured with the BPU the previous December was now exposed. Yet it is hard to escape the conclusion that, having just secured borough status for Birmingham and election to its first council, the interest of these leading middle-class reformers in Chartism had cooled. Brummagem distaste for emerging Chartist tactics, language and leadership was little more than a convenient smokescreen. As Dr John Taylor tartly commented, incorporation was 'the grave of Radicalism' in Birmingham.[4]

Despite these defections, much has been made of the preponderance of middle-class over working-class delegates. However, when allowance is made for non-attendees and early resignations, workmen (plus several journalists and others from the print trade who were former workmen) constituted just under two-thirds of the membership. Furthermore the middle-class members of the effective Convention included a number of proven ultra-radicals. We have already encountered Arthur Wade and John Taylor. Peter McDouall, a Scottish surgeon living in Lancashire, was a factory reformer who had taken J. R. Stephens's place as Ashton-under-Lyne delegate on the latter's recommendation. Lawrence Pitkethly, a Huddersfield draper, was one of Oastler's keenest supporters and a close associate of O'Connor. Another draper, John Frost of Newport, Monmouthshire, had been a leading figure in local politics since the late 1820s. His outspokenness had already resulted in the Home Secretary attempting to remove him from the magistracy.

The title 'General Convention of the Industrious Classes' was therefore no misnomer. Detailed rules and regulations were adopted, underlining the seriousness with which the assembly took itself.[5] The *Northern Star* and *The Charter* presented its proceedings with a gravity comparable to Parliament's, while the inauguration date, 4 February, pointedly coincided with the opening of the new parliamentary session. Chartists' emotional investment in the Convention was immense.

At Bradford, a daily report from local delegate Peter Bussey was read out by his wife at the beershop kept by the couple. Each night 'was like a theatre; there was a rush for early places, and all paid for admission'. The Convention, declared Abram Duncan to loud cheers at Tyneside's 'Female Democratic Festival', was 'the life-boat of Democracy'. 'A faint glimmering of hope has kept them from desperation', declared Barnsley Chartists, 'and this hope is now fixed upon you and your colleagues.' Henry Vincent asked '*What are our rulers about?*' in the opening address of yet another new Chartist paper, his *Western Vindicator.*

> Where are the statesmen with minds sufficient to comprehend the present alarming state of affairs? Most assuredly not in the present administration ... BRITAIN IS WITHOUT A GOVERNMENT! ... *there must be a Conventional Delegation of the people's will*; and that conventional delegation is to be found in the 'National Convention' now assembled in London.[6]

The early days of the Convention were not, however, untroubled. In a moment of near farce, delegates who arrived, as directed, at Brown's Hotel in Westminster Palace Yard found the hall was double booked and already occupied by the inaugural conference of the Anti-Corn Law League (ACLL). The collision of these two reforming movements, as unwelcome as it was unexpected, had a certain symbolic significance.[7] An uncomfortable few days were spent in a coffee house. Then, on 6 February, the delegates decamped to what the French feminist Flora Tristan (one of the Convention's many visitors) described as 'a shabby tavern in one of the dirty narrow little alleys just off Fleet Street'. Their new host was the 'Honourable and Ancient Lumber Troop', a drinking club with radical leanings which numbered the artist William

Hogarth among its past and Arthur Wade among its current members. This too was richly symbolic, for it located the Convention within London's rich but declining culture of radical debating clubs, where burlesque ritual and conviviality were almost as prominent as political discussion. In the Troop Hall, 'beautifully fitted up with a variety of military trappings', the delegates finally settled down to business.[8]

Observers were impressed by the general conduct of the Convention. Tristan was struck how 'there was not a single interruption, no whispering, no private conversations – quite unlike the House of Lords! Everybody gave his undivided attention and followed the debate with interest.' An otherwise scathing critic of the delegates' 'playing at parliament' conceded that these 'grim and sombre-looking men' demonstrated that 'the working classes in this country were as well qualified to elect representatives to parliament, as many who possess the privilege ... for the Chartist delegates had many among them vastly superior in intelligence and ability ... [and] vastly more *business*-like' than numerous MPs. Matthew Fletcher, subsequently estranged from Chartism, nonetheless recalled of his fellow delegates: 'No one need be ashamed at having been associated with them.'[9]

They were, however, far from being of one mind. This was hardly surprising in a body of diverse social background, representing localities as far apart as Wiltshire and Aberdeenshire. There was also a preponderance of Londoners: along with 10 members of the LWMA, 3 prominent members of the LDA sat in the Convention – Harney, for Derby, Newcastle and Norwich; Charles Neesom for Bristol; and shoemaker William Cardo for Marylebone. Despite the LWMA's reputation, its men were far from being the most cautious. That accolade belonged to James Cobbett. Having failed to circumscribe the remit of the Convention as early as its second day, Cobbett forced the issue back on to the agenda the following week. His motion proposed that the only function of the Convention was to manage the compilation and presentation of the National Petition. This precisely echoed the view of the Home Secretary, Lord John Russell, in the House of Commons three days before.[10] It was a comforting mythology for delegates who were nervous of being arrested, as it was for a Government trying to calm an alarmed Parliament. But Cobbett was in a distinct minority (the resolution was defeated 36 to 6) and promptly resigned.

## Ulterior measures

Russell, for his part, was being economical with the truth when he unwittingly anticipated Cobbett's motion. 'The elements of society', as *The Charter* claimed, were indeed 'thrown into a state of unnatural excitement': one consequence of this was that overt statements of opposition to parliamentary government were commonplace and calls forcibly to oppose it far from unusual. Discussion of what were termed 'ulterior measures', including arming, to be implemented if the petition failed was frequent and public. Both non-Chartist newspapers and extensive correspondence to the Home Office from provincial authorities reported them. In addition, the Home Office systematically accessed news and opinion from a variety of spies and informers: the details of the hall-booking shambles on 4 February are known mainly from a private letter sent by James Mills, the Oldham delegate, to a friend in Lancashire who promptly forwarded it to the Home Secretary.[11] From 8 February the Government directly intercepted the mail of selected delegates.

Rumours of insurrection abounded in certain urban centres. 'Their object in the dead of night is to fire the town at one end', wrote a Bolton informer, 'take possession of the town and burn the barracks.' Another wrote to a local justice: 'you as well as some of the Borough Magistrates are marked out as Wigs [sic] and your lives threatened besides property to be destroyed'. Chartism's leadership continually insisted that its strategy would not stop at petitioning. O'Connor was very far from alone in using language loaded with ill-omen for the establishment. Thomas Attwood, in one of several statements that give the lie to the notion that the BPU was consistently peaceable, had opened the new year by sharing with a Birmingham Town Hall audience his vision of 'two millions of men, acting under cautious and prudent leaders, with one heart and mind, and if dire necessity should make it imperative, with one hand'. On the same day George Harney told a Carlisle rally that 'three months will bring about the change we seek; and 1839 will be as memorable in the annals of England as 1793 in the annals of France'. A few days earlier, Bussey had urged the purchase of firearms and the formation of 'target societies'. When northern Convention delegates held a preliminary meeting on 7 January, Sheffield's William Gill, a scale cutter by trade, observed that 'a resort to force would be required to relieve the sufferings of the working classes ... nothing else than a demonstration of this description would operate upon their hard-hearted relentless tyrants'. 'Do as the gentlefolks do', urged the Leicester shoemaker and Primitive Methodist preacher John Markham, 'ornament your mantel-pieces with ARMS, ARMS, ARMS.'[12]

Such talk may have been bluster, but this is clearer in retrospect than it was at the time. Informed opinion in Whitehall tended to the gloomy: 'there is no military force in the country at all adequate to meet these menacing demon-strations', wrote Charles Greville, Clerk to the Privy Council, in his diary for New Year's Day, adding that 'the Magistracy are worse than useless, without consideration, resolution, or judgment'. Major-General Sir Charles Napier, the Army's Commanding Officer designate for the Northern District, noted that 'the government seem to be alarmed'. And, having met the Home Secretary and senior civil servants to discuss his new post, Napier observed that 'by their account the magistrates must be a poor set, on whom no reliance can be placed'. Once in post, from 4 April, Napier's assessment of the northern magistracy was more succinct: '*Funk* is the order of the day.' He added, though, that 'there is some excuse, for the people seem ferocious enough'.[13]

It would be a mistake, however, to suppose that an appearance of ferocity necessarily indicated concerted insurrectionary intent. This Napier realised, and it underscored his shrewd and humane handling of events in midland and northern England during 1839. While the Convention sat, acquisition of arms, and training in their use, were clear enough in many localities. Cutlasses and pikes were openly traded in the street markets of industrial Lancashire. Intelligence from Ashton-under-Lyne, Leigh, Middleton and Rochdale reached the Home Office as early as December 1838. The concentration of activity was greatest in Lancashire, but far from confined to there. Nocturnal walkers around Bradford would sometimes disturb groups armed with pikes. Spears, pikes, hand grenades and craa's feet (or caltrops – spiked iron balls which, thrown on the ground, disabled cavalry) were clandestinely produced in their hundreds at Winlaton ironworks on Tyneside. In Norfolk, blacksmiths in Norwich and Little Snoring were discovered making pike heads in early March, about the same time that Staffordshire Chartists were buying guns at 10 shillings a piece, apparently from Sheffield.[14] Such evidence cannot be lightly dismissed (indeed, it accumulated as the year progressed). At this stage, however, the central strategic thrust was ulterior measures and not insurrection. The assertion of the right to bear arms and its public demonstration were designed to increase pressure on Parliament as the presentation of the National Petition drew closer.

If James Cobbett's claim that they had no place in Chartism is discounted, then there were broadly speaking two positions about ulterior measures: whether to apply them immediately to reinforce petitioning or reserve them for the next stage of the contest. Some of the measures proposed would clearly be of limited efficacy. Abstention from taxed goods (alcohol, sugar, tea, coffee) was a moral statement rather than a practical measure to cut government revenue, attractive principally because of its resonance with the aims of the American Revolution. A 'run on gold', i.e. a mass withdrawal of savings from banks to precipitate a financial crisis, was even less plausible, unless trade unions and friendly societies could be persuaded to participate. Smaller local societies were often supportive, but larger unions and the nationwide affiliated orders (principally the Oddfellows) were necessarily financially cautious even if politically sympathetic.

Exclusive dealing, the collective refusal of Chartist customers to buy from unsupportive retailers, had rather more potential. It could be targeted at specific civic leaders or, more typically, at retailers and tradesmen who had the vote. Already a well-established practice in some communities, it had come close to winning the Huddersfield parliamentary seat for Oastler in 1837. 'The *way* to their brains is through their pockets – FIND IT', declared Joshua Hobson, calling for the campaign against those who had not voted for Oastler to be intensified. In November, Colne Chartists delivered a printed handbill to each shopkeeper stating that they 'require your kind attention to the National Rent, which is to support the delegates which the Nation have appointed to meet in the convention in London, to require at the hands of the Government JUSTICE FOR THE MILLIONS!' From January, Barnsley Chartists began every meeting with 'an index to exclusive dealing', in which the names of shopkeepers who had contributed to Stephens's defence fund and the National Rent were read out.[15]

The fourth measure, canvassed in the Convention from mid-February, was a general strike. Usually, Chartists spoke in term of a national holiday, sacred or holy month or week, or universal strike (as Attwood had at Glasgow the previous May). Like exclusive dealing, the notion of the sacred month was part of the Chartists' radical inheritance. William Benbow, a London Chartist and long-standing ultra-radical first developed the argument in his *Grand National Holiday and Congress of the Productive Classes* (1832), arguing for a simultaneous general strike and convention 'to reform society'. Benbow leant heavily on Spencean thinking and on that same tradition of anti-Parliament that underpinned the General Convention; but his anti-establishment invective and cogency were remarkable, and his book went through three substantial editions.[16] The idea of general strike was closely associated with arming, not necessarily offensively but certainly in defence against coercion to resume work. From mid-February few Chartists opposed a national holiday, but there were varying opinions about the timing of a strike and how soon to announce it. Bronterre O'Brien, for example, believed it would require 2–3 million signatures to the National Petition before a strike, or indeed any ulterior measure, could have real authority. O'Connor, by contrast, thought measures short of striking should run in parallel to the collection of signatures. Richard Marsden, a Preston handloom weaver, went farthest, calling on the Convention to commit the movement to a general strike and immediately name the date it would commence:

> The working men of the north signed the petition for the Charter, under the impression that the men who spoke for them of the holy week were sincere. None of the industrious classes, who signed the petition in this belief, ever thought for one moment that the legislature would grant the Charter. The people expected nothing at the hands of the government – they looked to the determination of this Convention ... all they had to do, was to let the country know when the sacred week was to commence.[17]

O'Brien's position was logical given the tardiness with which both the Petition signatures and the National Rent were accumulating. On 9 February the *Northern Star* reported that only £967 had been raised, together with half a million signatures. To focus minds, the Convention excluded delegates whose constituencies had yet to remit Rent or signatures: both Harney and Taylor found themselves barred from early sessions for this reason. The problem was administrative as well as political – the Convention had also to fulfil the functions of Chartism's secretariat. The burdens of this fell mainly on the indefatigable William Lovett, who received signatures, dealt with all correspondence and banking, and acted as the Convention's recorder and secretary. Within a week a further 100,000 signatures arrived, but there was clearly no room for complacency. 'We can no longer call it a National Petition', wrote an alarmed Thomas Salt to Lovett, 'the assumption upon which we have proceeded proved false.' O'Connor's response to the situation was to reinforce his oft-stated emphasis on the totemic status of the petition: '*It is the last, the very last* ... silence them, give it to them: let every man, woman and child sign the Petition; disarm all your enemies at once'.[18]

O'Connor's spirited optimism was an essential quality in a national leader. Nonetheless it had to be balanced with logistical effectiveness. Presentation of the Petition by the end of February, formerly the favoured option, was clearly inadvisable. Collecting signatures, even in centres with a strong record of supporting radical causes, was difficult to manage in the limited hours of daylight outside of work. Furthermore, committed Chartists took seriously the task of maximising signatures, linked the invitation to sign with a request to donate to the National Rent and were reluctant to return sheets until confident they had exhausted every possible source of support.

Tavistock in Devon provides a good example of this process at work. Its WMA canvassed the whole town with petition sheets and subscription lists, 'without missing scarcely a door'. Even so they collected only 1,366 signatures – about 22 per cent of the borough's population – though this compared well with the number of parliamentary electors (247 in 1832). 'Many professed liberal men', reported the secretary, 'found their right hands so stiff they could not write their own name and all their breeches pockets closely buttoned up.' The sheets were then delayed until someone was able to take them to Plymouth and book them on a London-bound coach.

In localities without a sustained tradition of radical organisation the obstacles could be considerable. 'Such is the enslaved state of the county of Gloucester that the people dare not sign a Petition', wrote one frustrated Chartist from the Forest of Dean to 'the Speaker of the National Convention'. Boston Chartists believed 'many more [signatures] would have been obtained but for the opposition of what is termed the religious world, particularly the Wesleyites'. Even in Warwickshire, Salt calculated that – excluding Birmingham – less than 6,000 signatures had been collected from a population of 77,000. 'I am quite unequal to the task', he wrote despondently to Lovett, detailing failures to get up public meetings in major centres such as Bromwich and Kenilworth.[19]

The Convention systematically gathered intelligence from each Chartist organisation about the state of its locality, distributing lengthy printed questionnaires to assist the process.[20] In consequence the Convention was well-informed and far from insulated from the outside world. In late February it sent out 'missionaries' in response to a recommendation from a sub-committee 'for extending political information' that Convention members be given leave of absence to tour areas 'not sufficiently instructed in the Chartist movement'. Those identified were initially all in southern England, but it was soon realised that insufficient instruction was a generic problem. Furthermore, strong Chartist centres had to be nurtured in the light of the decision to postpone the petition. Without a Convention member, the secretary of the Sheffield WMA wrote: 'it is useless for us to attempt to rouse the Working Classes here'. A similar request for a delegate to visit Darlington explained: 'Our town requires a mighty effort to stir it up to action.'[21]

The Convention's ranks were thus depleted as many members embarked on provincial tours. There was little at this point to detain them in London and, given the reputation of the Convention and the very real talents of many of its members, these were the most effective steps to take at this stage. Spring 1839 produced a remarkable flowering of popular political awareness unparalleled in any previous radical agitation. 'There is now more of a political feeling in this country than ever existed, perhaps, in any nation in the world', declared the *Western Vindicator*; 'it would seem that every man has become a politician'. In the Welsh industrial counties of Glamorganshire and Monmouthshire perhaps one in five of the population were committed Chartists.[22] In Scotland more than fifty new local organisations were formed during this spring campaign. The diffusion of Chartism into areas hitherto largely or totally bereft of any radical political presence was especially notable. Peter Bussey returned to his native North Riding to speak in the Tory backwater of Whitby and the stagnant borough of Thirsk, and to the handloom linen weavers of Cleveland and the Vale of York (a constituency similar to Pennine textile communities, but in an even greater state of decline). 'The People here have never heard Politics nor had any agitation on that Question', wrote Abram Duncan and Robert Lowery from west Cornwall. 'I found the Inhabitants fully Convinced that every thing was wrong and yet Ignorant of the means to cure the evil', reported John Richards from Sandbach and Leek. 'I pointed out that the privations of the Sons of Labour lay in want of the *Franchise*. This was news to them and never have I witnessed more enthusiasm.' In December 'not one Chartist association existed here', wrote a County Durham correspondent, but by March there were eighteen district societies in Sunderland alone. He added, significantly, that 'the Soil is good but the Labourers to cultivate are *few – too few*'.[23]

Henry Vincent returned to the west and an intensive itinerary, crossing and re-crossing south Wales, Herefordshire, Gloucestershire, north Wiltshire and north Somerset.[24] He revisited well-established Chartist centres – Bath, Bristol, Newport, Pontypool, Trowbridge – but also smaller communities like the Wiltshire textiles villages of Bromham and Holt. In the Herefordshire glove-making town of Ledbury, he 'could not find anyone who understood the principles of the Charter, but ... the name of Joseph Rayner Stephens is idolised by the people, who, though they seldom see a newspaper, appear to be thoroughly acquainted with his persecution'. Vincent left behind him a lively, if small, WMA, but the dramatic contrast between the town's deeply impoverished character and the ostensible ease with which he politicised it fuelled a reckless optimism in Vincent, common among the Convention's missionaries that heady spring:

> I then spoke to the people – simplified and explained to them the subject of government – told them of the Convention – and asked them if they approved of what we said, and if they would join with us – they shouted their assent, and swore they would fight for us if Government attacked us. We had a most determined display of popular enthusiasm. When the meeting concluded the people cheered us to our inn ... One thing I am now convinced of, that if we do not have an almost immediate *political* and *social* change, A BLOODY REVOLUTION MUST TAKE PLACE. The people will not starve much longer. Let their tyrant rulers beware![25]

Revealingly, Vincent was similarly enthused by the response of Holt where, he claimed, 'the National Petition was signed a few weeks ago by nearly every person in the village'. In fact, as the *Northern Star* would later report, 180 signatures were received from Holt, a little over 17 per cent of the village's population. This was an impressive figure (projected across England as a whole, it would have produced around 2.7 million signatures), but Vincent's over-enthusiasm risked fatal miscalculation of support.[26]

This almost habitual inflation of support for Chartism was having two deleterious effects. First it stoked the optimism of those Convention delegates who sought a swift and effective triumph for the movement. Second, it exacerbated the fears of the more cautious that the mood of the country was potential spiralling out of control and their belief that it was the Convention's responsibility to restrain it. Within the Convention this stance prevailed among most of the BPU members, along with Arthur Wade who (though London-based and representing Nottinghamshire) was an ex-BPU councillor. Paradoxically, they were also exercised by evidence from the west midlands that support for Chartism was apparently diminishing. Arguably, this revealed more about the Birmingham contingent's dissolving commitment than it did about the political potential of the region, a factor O'Connor overlooked when he upbraided the working people of Birmingham for being 'supine, dead, and careless'.[27]

On 4 March arguments about violence and ulterior measures swept through the Convention, in the wake of resolutions passed at an LDA meeting the week before. Wade especially took exception to these: 'He would not be party to any line of conduct which would only precipitate measures', he told the Convention, 'and end in the destruction of all.' The resolutions in question were: 'it is essentially just and indispensably necessary to meet all acts of oppression with immediate resistance'; and 'we hold it to be the duty of the Convention to impress upon the people the necessity of an immediate preparation for ulterior measures'.

Harney had chaired, and Marsden and William Rider (of Leeds WMA) had addressed, the meeting that passed these resolutions. Now the three, supported by Neesom and Sankey of Edinburgh, argued vehemently that the Convention should endorse them. It was a defining moment in the Convention's history. The LDA circle was defeated. O'Connor, fortuitously 'in bad health' and unable to attend the debate, kept his own counsel. Subsequently, through the *Star*, he attempted to shore-up the appearance of unity: 'Everything is going on well in the Convention. Rider, Marsden, and Harney are as good men as we have, and pray allow us the privilege of man and wife, to fall out among ourselves, so long as we are ready to join against the intruders and meddlers.'[28]

On the same day, 16 March, that O'Connor's emollient words appeared the whole question flared up again at a public meeting organised by the Convention to justify its decision to postpone the presentation of the National Petition (it had finally agreed on 6 May). This time O'Connor was present and he developed in detail the strategy that was to be followed. His opening statement reiterated the familiar Chartist slogan 'Peaceably if we may, forcibly if we must'. But he then proceeded effectively to commit the Convention to implementing a policy of active resistance:

They were determined by moral force if they could, but at all events, to have Universal Suffrage. (The cheers which succeeded this declaration continued for several minutes.) ... [But] if the people expected their petition, in consequence of being signed by one, or two, or three, or ten millions, would obtain Universal Suffrage, they were mistaken; and he would tell the members of the Convention ... that the people would impose a duty on them very soon after the presentation of the petition (cheers) ... there must be martyrs before Universal Suffrage would be attained. It was now out of the nature of things that the convention should break up without making some attempt for securing the Charter; or, if they should, the people would know how to deal with them ... They should present such a phalanx as would compel those who would refuse the Charter to their petitions to grant it to something else. The people should recollect that a million of petitions would not dislodge a single troop of dragoons.

Several delegates who had voted against the LDA resolutions the previous week now expressed sentiments very similar to those they had censured. Harney encapsulated the prevailing mood in a concluding speech which reiterated the prediction that Parliament would reject the Charter, adding that 'the people should then set about asserting their rights in earnest, and should have before the end of the year universal suffrage or death. (Loud cheers.)' This was all too much for Wade who immediately wrote in a non-Chartist newspaper: 'the cry of arms, without antecedent moral opinion and union of the middle classes with you, would only cause misery, blood and ruin'. Arguments rumbled on and, when delegates returned to the issue of physical force the following week, Wade narrowly escaped a motion of censure proposed by O'Connor.[29]

Consensus was irretrievable. It was now the Wednesday before Easter and the Convention agreed to adjourn, ostensibly to allow delegates time to return to their localities and attend meetings over the Easter weekend. Wade, together with three BPU councilmen, Douglas, Hadley and Salt, resigned the following day. These were far more significant than the previous BPU resignations. Only Hadley lacked stature within Chartism. Douglas, editor of the *Birmingham Journal*, had drafted the National Petition and chaired the Convention's opening session (at which Wade had led dedicatory prayers). Salt was important in encouraging female Chartism. Wade linked Chartism back to the general trade unionist movement of the early 1830s and beyond. All three had spoken at the Glasgow Green meeting in May 1838, Wade of course to present the People's Charter for the first time in a public forum.

Nor was this the only trouble to beset Chartism in March 1839. In Wigan on the ninth, Edward Nightingale had become the first person to contest a parliamentary election hustings expressly as the Chartist candidate. Had he been able to proceed to the poll (potentially a costly matter even for a conventional candidate) Nightingale might decisively have affected the outcome of the election, for the Liberals retained the seat by only three votes. Such episodes quickly became commonplace: Hugh Craig contested both hustings and poll in the Ayrshire by-election the following month, while O'Connor contested the hustings at Glasgow three months later. Chartists, however, welcomed these contests as theatrical opportunities to demonstrate the hugely undemocratic nature of the 1832 political settlement: Craig for example won the show of hands at the Ayrshire hustings on 27 April, only to be overwhelmingly defeated at the poll four days later.[30]

Far less welcome was the first major incident of anti-Chartist violence. On 22 March at Devizes, Vincent, Roberts and Wiltshire's Convention delegate Carrier were assailed by stones and other missiles in a concerted attack by, to quote *The Times*, a 'riotous body of destructives, who rejoice in the name of Conservatives', led by the county's Under-Sheriff. The Chartists and their audience were driven from the marketplace and barricaded themselves inside an inn which the rioters, some of whom carried firearms, threatened to set ablaze, until police and magistrates arrived. Worse followed when, on Easter Monday, eight days later, they returned to the town intent on avenging the indignity. Despite the presence of four troops of yeomanry and one of regular cavalry, Vincent was driven from the platform and, in a series of running battles, repeatedly knocked to the ground and seriously beaten. It took him a fortnight fully to recover.[31]

## The spectre of insurrection

The Devizes episode received wide publicity. It was not a decisive moment in Chartism's history, but it added to the unease of local authorities across the country at the growth of Chartist activity. It also strengthened the Chartist resolve to assert a right to resort, if necessary, to physical force. William Edwards, the mainstay of Chartism in Newport, allegedly threw down his newspaper on reading about Devizes, declaring that 'every Whig and Tory ought to have a nail driven through his b———y heart', adding that he could not answer for the consequences 'if the Charter was not granted on the 6th of May'. Feargus O'Connor immediately called for an army of defence, 'quick to return an assault; and the wadding of the first cannon which might be fired upon the people would ignite suddenly all the property of the country'. The public sale of arms in Chartist centres, hitherto largely confined to the cotton districts, spread. A vendor of steel pikes was reported providing a sample to, and securing a bulk order from, the council of the LDA. Loughborough Chartists, applying the principles of self-help that had long distinguished British industrial workers, started a penny-a-week arms club. From locations as far apart as Preston, Trowbridge and Truro came reports of significant withdrawals from friendly societies and savings banks to finance arming. South Wales Chartists established clubs to facilitate instalment payments for firearms, hawkers of which toured the valleys.[32] Soon copies of Francis Macerone's *Defensive Instructions for the People* were reported to be circulating. This cheap booklet on street warfare had first appeared during the reform crisis and had also been largely reprinted in a special issue of the *Poor Man's Guardian*.[33]

Reconvening after Easter, the Convention held a lengthy debate on the constitutional right to bear arms. This was political theatre and its outcome was never in doubt, but it served to reassure Chartist localities of the legality of the principle. Richardson, who had an unbounded appetite for legal research, supplied the detail, which was reprinted in pamphlet form to maximise its circulation.[34] Only Sankey, hitherto among the more militant delegates, expressed strong doubts.

There was a realistic possibility of armed social conflict in the late spring and summer of 1839, but the danger was far from uniformly spread. It was

all but non-existent in Scotland, a situation soon reflected both in the incidence of resignations from the Convention and in the concerted attempt of
the latter in July to send to Scotland many of its most forceful figures – not
to promote insurrection but to stiffen the resolve to resort to arms if necessary. Where violent conflict was distinctly possible it was often due to nervous
officialdom as much as directly to the Chartists themselves. The poor quality
of local magistrates and their fondness for requesting the protection of troops
(sometimes explicitly for their own homes) are recurring refrains in General
Napier's correspondence and journal.[35] He criticised the frequency with which
the Government acceded to such requests, and was particularly exercised by
the common – but militarily nonsensical – practice of dispersing these troops
in billets across a town. For example, in Halifax, 42 cavalry were billeted in 21
separate premises: 'Fifty resolute Chartists might disarm and destroy the whole
in ten minutes', Napier pointed out to local magistrates.[36] In this instance,
Napier succeeded in concentrating the detachment, but his wish to relocate it
altogether to Leeds or Sheffield, where he judged the military advantage to lie,
was blocked by the Home Secretary.

As we have already seen, by the spring of 1839 the purchase of arms had
become commonplace among English and Welsh Chartists. Drilling, typically
under the instruction of old soldiers, was similarly widespread. At several points
during the early weeks of his command Napier speculated that 'we shall have
a rough time', possibly even a concerted rising, in the near future. Three regi-
ments were recalled from Ireland at his request in anticipation of this. At the
beginning of May, as the Convention made its final preparations to present the
Petition, Napier was sufficiently apprehensive to write in his journal: 'things look
black enough ... Heaven defend my family!'; and 'how full of events next week
may be'. However, as it passed without incident, he concluded that 'all information now speaks of a rising on Whit-Monday [20 May]'. Contingency plans
were made to intercept any march on London from the north, with Derbyshire
selected as offering the best terrain for infantry and artillery to effect this.
However, as Whitsun approached Napier formed the view that the Chartists
were contemplating not a concerted insurrection, but a large-scale outbreak of
violence at a mass meeting, probably in Manchester, over Whit week.[37]

While Napier was confident that the army's superior fire-power and
discipline would rapidly overwhelm Chartist insurgents, he was fearful that
an isolated success against a small detachment of troops could encourage
widespread insurrection, with disastrous consequences:

> If only a corporal's guard was cut off it would be 'total defeat of the troops'
> ere it reached London, Edinburgh and Dublin; and before the contradiction
> arrived the disaffected, in the moral exaltation of supposed victory, would be
> in arms. This is more especially to be apprehended in Ireland, where rivers
> of blood would flow.[38]

In such circumstances, even in England, large-scale civilian casualties were very likely, a prospect Napier, though he was perfectly prepared to countenance them if necessary, found abhorrent. This was partly for humanitarian reasons and partly because he was genuinely sympathetic to the core objectives of the Charter. To his artillery commander he wrote of attending a Chartist meeting incognito and hearing 'orderly, legal opinions, pretty much – don't tell this – my own!' Privately, he noted: 'that the people of England have been, and are, ill-treated and ill-governed is my fixed opinion'.[39] Napier also knew, however, that the 4,700 troops under his command (required to cover an area extending from the Scottish border down to Nottinghamshire) might be severely stretched if simultaneous outbreaks – closely co-ordinated or not – were sufficiently wide-spread. His actions leading up to Whitsun's mass meetings therefore involved some subterfuge, ostentatiously marching troops through town centres in large numbers. Napier also met discretely with local Chartist sympathisers, assuring them of his support for peaceable agitation, but pointedly demonstrating the potency of the forces under his command.

The coercive resources of the State were never put to the test and, in hindsight, Napier's confidence that his troops would prevail seems obvious. The risk of failure would have been greatest early in the year. Although official nerves were raw, especially in late summer, once Napier settled into his command (reforming billeting and establishing effective working arrangements with local authorities) and the northern division was reinforced from Ireland, the prospect of failure was slender. How justified, though, was Napier's conviction that violence in some form was contemplated? The issue concerns the evidence not of Chartist arming – which is considerable – but of concerted quasi-military action, whether planned covertly or overtly. Most Chartist arms were procured by individuals. But several examples of large-scale manufacture (as we have already seen at Winlaton on Tyneside) and purchases came to light. In early May Peter McDouall ordered twenty muskets from a Birmingham dealer, to be delivered to an Ashton Chartist publican. '[T]here would be from five hundred to a thousand more wanted', he said, if the first order was satisfactory.[40]

Understandably, the Convention was cautious. When it received a letter from a purported London Chartist, urging a systematic campaign to promote the use of 'force against force', Lovett wrote cryptically on it 'A police spy'. (And so this correspondent later proved.)[41] In his autobiography, Lovett related how Convention delegates gathered privately at the Arundel Coffee House to discuss matters considered too sensitive to be aired in open session. Towards the end of April he compiled a document based on these *in camera* sessions, devoted to the question of ulterior measures. These were then re-drafted to form the *Manifesto of the General Convention of the Industrious Classes*, the publication of which the Convention authorised on 14 May, by which time (see below) it had relocated to Birmingham. The *Manifesto* duly appeared in a run of 10,000 copies complete with a woodcut portrait of Lovett on its cover. Its language was uncompromising:

> Shall it be said, fellow countrymen, that *four millions of men capable of bearing arms*, and defending their country against every foreign assailant, *allowed a few domestic oppressors to enslave and degrade them?* ... We have sworn, with your aid, to achieve our liberties or die ... [B]e assured, the joyful hope of freedom, which now inspires the millions, if not speedily realized, will turn into wild revenge ... *the once boasted manufactories of England will perish by an agent soldiers cannot cope with nor policemen avert* ... [A]t least, we trust, you will not COMMENCE the conflict. We have resolved to obtain our rights, '*peaceably, if we may – forcibly if we must:*' but woe to those who begin the warfare with the millions, or who forcibly restrain their peaceful agitation for justice – at one signal they will be enlightened to their error, and in one brief contest their power will be destroyed.[42]

The *Manifesto* then printed eight questions to be placed before simultaneous public meetings before 1 July. O'Connor had already publicised the need for such meetings in the *Star*, predicting one-and-a-half-million would assemble. These were not, however, to be the occasion of an uprising but were intended as a last dramatic demonstration of the extent of support for the Charter. Were those attending prepared to run on the banks, making all withdrawals in gold? Would they 'DEAL EXCLUSIVELY WITH CHARTISTS'? Support a sacred month, abstaining from alcohol for its duration? Had they armed themselves? Were they resolved to oppose any counter agitation for less than the Charter? And, finally, would they 'OBEY THE JUST AND CONSTITUTIONAL REQUESTS OF THE MAJORITY OF THE CONVENTION?'[43]

The *Manifesto* positioned the Convention as endorsing only defensive violence, but the distinction was slender. After weeks of debate, disagreement and prevarication the 'People's Parliament' had openly endorsed a policy that it knew would take it to the brink of conflict with the State, if not beyond. Its mood was confident: the decision to send delegates into the country to promote the Charter had paid off and the National Petition was ready, as planned, for 6 May. Circumstances, however, had combined to wrong-foot the Convention. It apparently supposed, naively, that the Petition, once prepared, could be presented immediately to the House of Commons. Unfortunately, the week commencing Monday 6 May which it had chosen for the purpose coincided with one of the more absurd episodes in British high politics, the 'Bedchamber Crisis'.

On Monday the Whig Government's Commons' majority was slashed in a vote on the Jamaica Bill. The following day it resigned. It was a potentially perilous moment for the country to be without a government. Almost the final act of Lord Russell as Home Secretary was to approve instructions for those towns judged most volatile, offering to arm special constables, suggesting the

formation of voluntary associations to keep the peace and encouraging for the
first time the immediate arrest of Chartist speakers 'at the time of committing
the offence' at any illegal meeting. A Royal Proclamation prohibiting arming
and drilling accompanied the letter, the circulation of which effectively mapped
the centres of Chartism's greatest strength.[44]

On Wednesday the Queen invited Sir Robert Peel, leader of the Conservative
Party, to form a government. This he began to do, only to discover on the
Thursday that Victoria would permit him no influence over the appointment
of her 'Ladies of the Bedchamber', women from aristocratic families who were
in theory capable of swaying the young Queen's judgement. More critically,
Peel believed, the denial of government influence over such positions would be
construed as a lack of royal confidence in his administration. Accordingly he
withdrew from forming a new government. On the Friday the Whigs were rein-
stated and the following Wednesday Parliament rose for its Whitsun recess.

The day the Whigs were defeated in the Commons, members of the
Convention had visited Attwood at his London home to discuss the National
Petition's presentation to Parliament and request him to announce simultaneously his intention to introduce a bill based on the Charter. Attwood demurred:
rumours were already rife that the Government was on the brink of resigning.
To the Chartists' further dismay, Attwood also stated that he did not agree
with all the demands of the petition, especially that for equal electoral districts,
and would not sponsor any bill related to it. Oldham's MP John Fielden was
more accommodating, though like Attwood he insisted the presentation of the
Petition should be accompanied by an explicit assurance that the Convention
had not endorsed '"ulterior measures" of a violent nature'.[45]

Strictly speaking it had not, for the secretive deliberations Lovett described
were still in train. So it was that on Tuesday 7 May the petition was loaded onto
a waggon, draped with Union Jacks, and decorated with flags and banners,
and (escorted by fifty-two delegates 'distinguished by ribbands' and marching
in pairs) delivered not to the Houses of Parliament but to Fielden's home in
Panton Square, off Piccadilly. There, from the window of a first-floor bedroom,
Attwood made a short, anodyne speech. The delegates then returned to Fleet
Street, leaving in Fielden's charge around three miles of paper, weighing a
third of a ton and rolled into a cylinder the size of a cart wheel. On it were
1,280,959 signatures.[46]

The quantity of signatures was rather less than the 2 million commonly
anticipated; on the other hand it significantly exceeded any previous single petition. The indefinite postponement of its presentation to Parliament, however,
presented the Convention with a quandary. Yet again the morale of the movement had to be maintained during a delay in bringing to a resolution the
focal point of the Chartist campaign. Even more than in February and March,
expectations – and governmental apprehensions – were running high.

A number of events around the time the petition was finally collated added to fears of confrontation. The first were disturbances, closely linked to local Chartists, in the Montgomeryshire flannel-weaving town of Llanidloes. Rioting on Tuesday 30 April seriously damaged a local hotel in which five policemen from outside of Llanidloes (three of them from London) were lodging. These had been sent to arrest local Chartist leaders in response to fears about arming in the district. A complete breakdown of local authority followed; yet the town was remarkably peaceable, the worst incident of lawlessness being the seizure of barrels from the hotel cellar, most of the contents of which were then tipped into the gutter. The situation was resolved only when troops arrived on the Saturday. Although the original incident was an anti-police riot rather than a Chartist disturbance, with a local opponent of Chartism taking a leading part (possibly to discredit the movement), the mud stuck to the Chartists. 'Llanidloes in Possession of the Revolutionists' and 'Ferocious proceedings and robbery by the Montgomeryshire Chartists', declaimed *The Times*. The 30 convictions that followed resulted in sentences ranging from 2 months' hard labour to 15 years' transportation. Montgomeryshire's leading Chartist Thomas Powell was sentenced to a year's imprisonment for seditious language, even though it was he who had rescued two of the constables trapped in the hotel.[47]

A further civil disturbance that increased apprehension occurred on the same day the Petition was conveyed to Fielden's home. Extensive violence – with barricades at one point erected in the streets – occurred at Longton, in the Potteries. These riots also appear to have originated in strong anti-police sentiment and were even more tangential to Chartism than those at Llanidloes, but the prevailing tone of reporting conjured them into a Chartist disturbance. Even the usually well-informed Napier believed them to be so, writing to his brother that the Chartists 'attacked the yeomanry who killed and wounded several' when there were just two fatalities, a soldier who had accidentally shot himself and an elderly bystander knocked down in a police charge.[48] That Napier of all people should have been misled (he also thought the riots had occurred 6 miles away at Stone) is indicative of the Government's deficient command of the intelligence resources needed to police Chartism.

Tuesday 7 May was also the occasion of serious rioting in Paris, resulting in 100 fatalities. This too impacted on British opinion, for past and current events in France were a near-constant subtext to the contemporary discussion of Chartism. When, a few days later, O'Connor announced over-optimistically to a Birmingham audience that revolution had broken out in France he was greeted by prolonged cheering. Only the week before Sankey and Collins had introduced to the Convention a motion condemning any mention of the 1789 Revolution in its proceedings, a move designed to discomfort Harney and his circle and to affirm the constitutional character of the Chartist agitation. Uncomfortably closer than France, the LDA's hall in Ship Yard, near

Temple Bar, was raided by the police on 10 May . There were 13 arrests, and banners, papers and 2 pikes were seized. Unlike at Llanidloes, the magistrates' response was lenient, the accused simply being bound over on security to keep the peace.[49]

The most significant incident to affect the mood of the Convention was the arrest of Vincent in London (he had briefly returned to the Convention). In Newport the previous month, Vincent had dared local magistrates to arrest him during the course of a two-and–a-half-hour speech at a meeting they had declared illegal. They did not oblige but subsequently issued the warrant on which he was arrested on 7 May. His was the first high-profile arrest since Stephens's. Thomas Powell, arrested after Llanidloes, was purely a local leader. None of those arrested at Ship Yard were notable Chartists, indeed most were not even LDA members, while those arrested at Longton had no apparent links to Chartism at all. Vincent on the other hand was both the first Convention delegate taken into custody and a Chartist of national renown. On 10 May he arrived back at Newport. A pitched battle ensued outside the committal hearings between special constables and Vincent's supporters (who included miners from as far away as 10 miles). It took a personal appeal by John Frost to restore order. Vincent was bound over to the next assize and offered bail with the sureties set at £1,000 (approximately nine years' wages for a skilled craftsman). Unable to locate anyone sufficiently wealthy to act as his guarantor, Vincent was committed to Monmouth Prison.[50]

## The Convention in Birmingham

Vincent had been arrested at midnight outside his own house, seconds after bidding goodnight to Frost with whom he had dined that evening. The news hardened the mood of the Convention when it resumed the next morning to debate its policy now that the Petition was complete. For several weeks the Convention had discussed physically relocating to the provinces, O'Connor at one point suggesting that it should itinerate. Relocation was intimately bound up with arguments about its future role, which in turn related closely to Chartist strategy.

The arguments unsuccessfully advanced by James Cobbett back in February resurfaced. Was the Convention merely a petitioning body, or did it have a more intimate relationship with those who had sent and financed its members? Was it even, as O'Connor argued, 'the only constitutional representative body of the people'? Probably most Chartists saw it in that light. Correspondents to it used language appropriate to addressing a legislative assembly. Some specifically requested 'the People's Parliament' to intervene in personal matters, just as they might a MP. 'The people were very anxious', O'Brien concluded, 'that the Convention should meet in Birmingham under the shelter of the guns made by the people there, especially when the time came for ulterior measures'. Yet when the matter was put to a vote in the first week of May, the prevailing mood – shared even by O'Brien – was that the Convention should remain in London. Vincent's arrest altered perceptions. With the National Petition now assembled, the Convention voted on 8 May to adjourn to Birmingham from 13 May.[51]

That Monday Convention delegates reassembled at the Chapel of the Birmingham Owenites. The contrast between a backstreet tavern in a metropolis largely indifferent to Chartism and a socialist hall in a large manufacturing centre could hardly have been greater. The Birmingham air was heavy with expectation. Since its inception, large crowds had gathered almost daily in the Bull Ring to hear news from the Convention. Latterly, interest in the National Petition had become acute, nurtured by the oratory of John Fussell (a journeyman jeweller and one of three working men who had replaced BPU delegates in the Convention following their resignation). Fussell was of a different stamp from those whom he replaced. He had no doubts about the direction Chartist strategy should take. As he told a Chartist meeting in early April, Attwood's and the BPU's espousal of 'moral power' was 'sophistry',

> lulling all into a state of stupor, which would inevitably prove their ruin
> and the ruin of their cause ... did the men who met John at Runnymede
> obtain their charter by moral power? No; and they should never obtain theirs
> unless they adopted the same mode of action as they did. First they must
> petition; secondly, demand; and while they demanded they must ... demand
> with arms in their hands, and then they should have some attention paid
> to them.[52]

Central though it had been in the formation of Chartism, the BPU had never reflected the bulk of Chartist support in the town; the criticisms of the Convention expressed by Salt and his colleagues when they resigned were completely atypical of the mood in Birmingham. Praying for 'the blessings of that Providence at whose breath every oppressor shall be swept from the land', one Birmingham locality hailed 'with heartfelt and boundless joy the auspicious hour which has given to the millions of our brethren in political bondage a mighty Congress, solemnly elected by the people, to assist and win our natural and imprescriptable rights and franchises'.[53]

The Convention's publication, the day after it arrived in Birmingham, of its *Manifesto* was a defining moment. None seriously doubted that the Whitsuntide mass meetings would endorse it. But equivocation about its content and publication, plus the three working days lost on transferring from London, meant time to organise those meetings was perilously short. It was impossible to organise at four days' notice the *simultaneous* assemblies for which the delegates, especially O'Connor, had hoped. If an intention to foment some kind of rising over Whitsun had ever been serious – and almost every indicator contradicts that supposition – then the final timing of events rendered it impossible. Nonetheless, an air of apprehension surrounded the coming weekend. The past ten days had seen the first arrests for drilling in south Lancashire,[54] while in Birmingham itself Fussell and his close colleague Edward Brown were arrested on the Thursday and charged with incitement to violence in speeches made at earlier Bull Ring meetings. Russell's circular to magistrates the previous week was stiffening municipal sinews.

This was especially true of BPU activists now occupying civic offices, who had good reason for wanting to distance themselves from Chartism. That afternoon, 14 May, the Convention agreed to adjourn once more, to permit delegates to attend the weekend's demonstrations and then report back on the mood of the country. Delegates wondered, only half-jokingly, if they ever would come back. Marsden's was the sole voice calling for a mass display of arms, though it was agreed that if there were wholesale arrests of Convention delegates then ulterior measures should be implemented immediately. That weekend, the *Northern Star* carried an editorial strongly advising those attending the demonstrations to leave their weapons at home, along with an address from the Convention warning 'give your oppressors no excuse for invading your inviolable right to meet and discuss your grievances by needlessly carrying arms to public places'.

Napier, on the basis of Home Office and his own intelligence, believed that the demonstrations would be peaceable, with the possible exception of Manchester's rally on Kersal Moor. ('What are five hundred constables and specials in a town which would turn out fifty thousand people to see a dog fight?', he pondered.) However Napier's assessment of the meeting, which he attended in disguise, was that at most 35,000 were present, of whom no more than 500 were 'wanting bloodshed and pillage'.[55] Napier was keen to extol his shrewd handling of Chartism and his estimated attendance cannot be taken at its face value. Equally the *Northern Star's* estimate of half a million is also unlikely. Whitsuntide was a customary holiday but there were no paid public holidays prior to 1871. This was one reason why Manchester's demonstration took place the following Saturday (25 May), the others being that it would coincide with horseracing on Kersal Moor and that O'Connor would be able to attend both this and other important rallies.

A more impressive statistic, not least because it can be verified against official newspaper taxation returns, is the circulation of the *Northern Star* for this period. In its 1 June edition the paper claimed average weekly sales for April and May of 32,692 (Stamp Returns suggest a weekly average of 36,000 for 1839 as a whole).[56] All over Britain a climate of opinion had been created that was highly attuned to the case for reform. Regardless of their ability or their willingness to attend mass demonstrations, therefore, hundreds of thousands were regularly exposed to the arguments of the *Star* and other Chartist newspapers, using the arguments of the Charter as a tool to think with.

This was abundantly evident during Whitsun week. In his 'Chartist life' (pp. 22–9), we glimpsed shoemaker Abram Hanson preaching 'Christ and a full belly ... Christ and Universal Suffrage' at the meeting on Hartshead Moor. On Newcastle Town Moor, Abram Duncan returned to the theme of righteous resistance to tyranny: 'The next time you meet in such numbers here', he told a crowd estimated at 100,000, 'your conduct will be that of a people united in one solid determination either to see their country free, or perish in one common conflagration.' Similar sentiments were expressed across the country, the largest gatherings being at Bath, Birmingham, Blackwood (Monmouthshire), Bradford, Carlisle, Glasgow Green, Hull, Liverpool, Newcastle, Northampton, Nottingham, Preston, Sheffield, Sutton-in-Ashfield, South Shields and Sunderland.[57]

In all these places local authority prepared for the worst. The Home Office undertaking to arm special constables had predictably met an enthusiastic response. To the modest Lancashire town of Leigh alone the Royal Armouries dispatched 150 swords, 300 long sea pistols, 300 flintlock pistols and 6,000 rounds of ammunition.[58] While the Chartists of Leigh had certainly been drilling, the provision of 650 weapons, in relation to a total population of 22,000, is somewhat startling (similarly the 1,800 special constables sworn in at Bradford). Hindsight, however, is a wonderful thing and subsequent generations have not always appreciated how well-founded the fears of the establishment appeared to be in the early summer of 1839, any more than they have comprehended why the Chartists were so sanguine of carrying the day. In a host of smaller centres over Whitsuntide the pattern of the monster meetings was repeated on a smaller scale: for example at Brighton, Dalston, Dudley, Heywood, Kendal, Leicester, Penrith, the Potteries, Southampton, Stockport, Wigton, and on Kennington Common in south London.

Violence, where it occurred, was small scale and incidental rather than calculated and strategic. The worst incident was in Manchester on 2 June when O'Connor led a large Chartist contingent in disrupting an open-air meeting 'of the working classes' organised by the Anti-Corn Law League. When they manoeuvred a giant banner inscribed 'Down with the Whigs', so as totally to obscure from view the League's platform, flailing fists and sticks were suddenly much in evidence. However, by the standards of early Victorian popular politics, as evidenced for example at Devizes a few weeks earlier and at countless election hustings, this was small beer.[59] For the time being, anticipation of the National Petition's presentation to Parliament, plus the dampening effect of arrests, constrained tendencies to violence. For its part, the Government maintained its policy of guarded surveillance and selective arrests, the most significant of them McDouall's. That these arrests were beginning to tell on the movement was evident in the launch in mid-June of the 'National Defence Fund', administered by a sub-committee of the Convention and promoted by O'Connor (he also headed the donors' list with a gift of £20). Few Chartists (assuming they even noticed) were likely to have been impressed by a relaxation of one of the penalties for anonymous political publications, a move designed to appease radical MPs ahead of the National Petition rather than to draw support from Chartism.[60]

The Petition was finally presented to the House of Commons on Friday 14 June 1839. Few Chartists had expected it to make a difference to parliamentary attitudes and in this respect 14 June did not disappoint. No indication was given whether MPs would formally debate it, and when Attwood and Fielden, with a theatrical flourish, rolled the giant cylinder into the Commons chamber it was greeted by laughter. The *Northern Star* pointed to this as evidence to persuade 'all the noodles who hope for favour or amelioration from the wretches who at present rule us ... if there be yet living one working man who is dolt enough to hope for help from these, this must undeceive him'. The whole exercise, concluded the paper, proved the necessity of 'the grand struggle for UNIVERSAL SUFFRAGE which *shall come* and that quickly'.[61]

The mood among committed Chartists was tellingly caught at Newcastle the week before, when Duncan asked an audience of female Chartists 'were they ready to make a sacred month of it, and take to the hillside?' and was met with repeated shouts of 'We will.' It was an exhilarating image: a chosen people gathered in the assurance of divine dispensation. '"The cattle upon the thousand hills"', declaimed Benbow in his 1832 *Grand National Holiday*, 'they are the Lord's, that is the people's, and when the people want them, the guardians who have kept them so long, will deliver them unto the people.' Benbow's allusion here was to Psalm 50, which also speaks of gathering 'those that have made a covenant with me'. Significantly, it was repeated almost word for word by Harney at a crowded Birmingham meeting one night in May. For Robert Lowery, taking to the hills evoked 'retiring from labour, like the Roman plebeians of old to the Aventine-hill'. O'Connor used the same trope; if denied their just demands, then the Chartists 'would light their torches and repair to the hill-side, and there remain until the prayer of their petition was granted'.[62]

Yet as the Convention delegates completed their fact-finding tours over the last fortnight of June some doubts crept in. O'Connor for one returned to Birmingham on 1 July wary of committing Chartism to a sacred month and preferring to try the other ulterior measures first. So did John Taylor. More thoughtful members of the Chartist leadership recognised that the general strike strategy was heavily dependent on the organised trades for its success. Not only did they have the authority to enforce strike action in critical areas of the economy, many also had the financial resources necessary to sustain a stoppage. In 1838 trade societies had been a key factor behind the take-off of Chartism. To quote O'Connor, it was 'the assertion of their political rights by which alone their [trade unions'] social and class regulations can be protected'. Joining Chartism was a matter of general commitment rather than taking out a formal subscription and many trade societies supported it *en bloc*. A 'declaration of adhesion in bodies' was made by the united trades of Birmingham, Bury, Newcastle and Oldham, for example. The trades were conspicuous participants at all the great mass meetings. But judging from press reports, they were less evident at Easter and Whitsun 1839 than they had been the previous year: perhaps memories of the Tolpuddle labourers' return from transportation and of the treatment of the Glasgow spinners were receding. There were many localities where the united trades did not adhere in bodies and the concerted support of individual trades was uneven: shoemakers were in general very sympathetic, the better-paid and apprentice-trained trades much less so. 'The people', the *Northern Star* observed,

> have not now even the Aristocratic portion of the shabby trades with them. We look with disgust and contempt upon those trades which refuse to join the people, from the sordid notion that their own laws are strong enough to defend their own rights. We shall soon see. The dirty fellows should take example from the joiners and carpenters of Birmingham, and from the whole body of the trades of Newcastle; their power makes the move irresistible. The people must *drill* the trades into line.[63]

Yet had all the organised trades actively supported Chartism, around 90 per cent of male workers would still have had to become involved via other routes, for trade union membership was slender in early Victorian Britain; and those excluded from trade unionism generally had slender financial resources to sustain strike action. A fundamental question hung over the viability of the sacred month and on Wednesday 3 July the reassembled delegates, now meeting in the Golden Lion Hotel, debated it in detail. That so few workers could turn to a union to support them if on strike troubled the Convention less than it might. Firstly, it was a reasonable supposition, given the community-wide response to Chartism evident in countless localities, that any strike action could be sustained communally. Secondly, there was a near-universal conviction that the State would swiftly force strikers back to work. 'By retiring from labour', Lowery for example believed, 'they would so derange the whole country that the authorities would endeavour to coerce them back ... they would resist the authorities unless their rights were conceded, and thus bring the struggle to an issue'.

The sacred month was therefore not an action short of outright insurrection, it *was* insurrection. In the intervening period since the *Manifesto* had been published, Taylor had discussed its recommendations at twenty-six Chartist gatherings in Scotland: 'with respect to the sacred month, they felt it would be

nothing short of physical revolution that would be caused by it'. For some delegates (notably Bussey, Brown, Cardo, McDouall, Marsden and Neesom) this
was a positive attraction. The majority, however, were more cautious, believing
with O'Connor and Lovett that while, to quote the latter, 'a holiday or sacred
month would be found to be the only effectual remedy for the sufferings of
the people', the cause should not be prematurely risked against a powerful
Government.[64]

This rather begged the question of why the Petition had been submitted (a
petition moreover O'Connor, for one, had always said would be rejected) if
the means to carry it by ulterior measures were not in place. Possibly a view
was forming inside the Convention that covert, rather than overt, measures
were required. Publicly, the Convention agreed to postpone any decision about
calling a general strike until after 12 July, when Parliament's response to the
National Petition would be formally agreed. Richardson alone made it a resignation issue, arguing that the sacred month should be ruled out completely and
other ulterior measures preferred, especially the run on banks. However, he was
also in dispute with the council of the Manchester PU about the non-payment
of expenses, so he may have welcomed a face-saving reason to resign.

Within a day of this debate events in Birmingham took a dramatic turn, with
an irreversible impact on the way contemporaries (not to mention posterity)
would view Chartism. The arrests of Brown and Fussell in May had failed to
quieten the exuberance of Birmingham Chartists: the case against Fussell was
wafer-thin, and he had resumed his nightly orations in the Bull Ring. Thursday
4 July was the first occasion, however, on which London Metropolitan Police
were used in policing Birmingham. More accurately, they were deployed with
the specific instruction to arrest any Chartist in the act of addressing a crowd.
The sixty-strong force had arrived only at 8.00 p.m. Hurriedly sworn-in as local
special constables while still at the railway station, the sixty marched straight
to the Bull Ring.

As events at Llanidloes and Longton recently demonstrated, anti-police
feelings ran high in 1839. At Birmingham, where almost any move against
Chartist activity was likely to be construed as an assault on the Convention
itself, the consequences of the Metropolitan Police's intervention were cata-
strophic. Deployed by magistrates without the support of local constables,
specials or the military, the Londoners were routed in a pitched battle lasting
twenty minutes. Several were injured, three seriously with stab wounds. It took
the intervention of the army to restore order and rescue bewildered constables
from the buildings and yards where they had fled for shelter. John Taylor acted
swiftly to urge the angry crowd massing outside the Golden Lion to go home
peacefully, Fussell having told him that he suspected 'it was the object of the
magistrates to excite the people into an outbreak, by the introduction of the
London police, rather than to protect the peace of the town'.[65]

That was, and remains, a plausible view, though we need to bear in mind the jaundiced view local Chartists had of their erstwhile Convention delegates, especially Philip Muntz who was now a Birmingham magistrate. BPU councillors in positions of municipal authority and influence did, however, stand to benefit from distancing themselves from the movement whose inception they had assisted. They were beholden to an electorate not of Chartists but of the prosperous and propertied, while Birmingham's Corporation was subject to the critical eye of the Government, likewise any future plans to extend it (and few Victorian municipalities were not local imperialists).[66]

Quietly, more than a few Chartist activists welcomed the Bull Ring riot. It lent authority to their argument that the establishment was unsympathetic not only to the claims of democracy but even to the merest public expression of those claims. To reinforce this case they could point to Peterloo and the Cold Bath Fields incident of 1833 in London (also involving the Metropolitan Police) when a coroner's jury had recorded verdicts of justifiable homicide on the deaths of two policemen involved in the tumultuous dispersal of a radical meeting. 'There seemed to be a disposition to murder the people, as at Peterloo', claimed one Bolton Chartist.

The *Northern Star* claimed that the Convention 'had now been wantonly, violently, and illegally attacked'. A north-east Chartist likened Birmingham on 4 July to the Boston Tea Party: both were defining moments that misled government into supposing it had justification for suppression. At least Boston in 1776 had been spontaneous; Birmingham in 1839 was engineered by 'the ministry of the present day' which needed an excuse 'for commencing that reign of terror, in which lay their only hope for escape from the growing knowledge and accumulating indignation of the people'.[67]

Inside the Convention the reaction was predictably indignant. Eighty arrests during the night had included those of Taylor and McDouall (the only other delegate in the Golden Lion during the rioting). This was enough to persuade delegates that the previous night had been a pre-meditated attack not only on a defenceless crowd but on the Convention itself. Though McDouall had been released without charge, Taylor had been remanded to Warwick Prison, accompanied by an extraordinary military procession 'with all the pomp and appearance of war'.[68] Three resolutions, hurriedly written by Lovett, were unanimously adopted and rushed by Collins to a local printer to produce posters with which to placard the town:

> *1st.* That this Convention is of the opinion that a wanton, flagrant, and unjust outrage has been made upon the people of Birmingham by a bloodthirsty and unconstitutional force from London, acting under the authority of men who, when out of office, sanctioned and took part in the meetings of the people, and now, when they share in the public plunder, seek to keep the people in their social and political degradation.

*2nd.* That the people of Birmingham are the best judges of their own right to meet in the Bull Ring or elsewhere, have their own feelings to consult respecting the outrage given, and are the best judges of their own power and resources to obtain justice.

*3rd.* That the summary and despotic arrest of Dr. Taylor, our respected colleague, affords another convincing proof of the absence of all justice in England, and clearly shows that there is no security for life, liberty, or property, till the people have some control over the laws they are called upon to obey.

By order, W. Lovett, Secretary. Friday, July 5, 1839 [69]

A public protest that evening was dispersed peaceably with the aid of Irish dragoons, backed by a large cannon, but street scuffles with the police (reinforced by forty further London policemen) led to many arrests. Next morning Lovett was seized at the Golden Lion, and soon joined in custody by Collins. Both were charged with inciting violence, Lovett by signing the resolutions and Collins by causing them to be printed. It seems clear the authorities would have taken the entire Convention if they could: at the committal proceedings late that night, Lovett was asked several times to state which delegates were present when the resolutions were passed. 'I refuse to answer that question', he responded. Similarly, Collins declined to identify who else had accompanied him to the printers. But Lovett went further, stressing he alone had written the resolutions and proposed their adoption:

I thought the people were justified in repelling such blood-thirsty and despotic power by every and any means at their disposal because I believe the institution of the police force is an infringement on the constitutional liberties possessed by our ancestors ... if the people submit to one injustice after another, imposed by self-constituted authorities, they will eventually be ground down to the dust without any means of resistance.[70]

In his 1876 autobiography Lovett referred only to 'feeling most strongly ... that a great injustice had been afflicted'. Ironically, in seeking to portray himself as a life-time political moderate, he had to suppress the strength of conviction and courage with which he confronted the Birmingham magistracy. Gammage (on what authority is unclear) even claimed the delegates had collectively wanted to sign the resolutions, but that Lovett had insisted 'that they could not spare victims ... he would alone sign'. Bail was set at the customarily punitive £1,000: it was nine days before sureties could be found that satisfied local magistrates of both their probity and ability to pay.[71]

O'Connor's comment to the Convention, a few days previously, that 'they were in the last stage of the agitation' now took on a vivid and unsettling aspect. 'If the English people be not sunk below the level of the meanest reptile that crawls in God's creation – such a state of things cannot, and will not, endure', claimed one Newcastle Chartist. The Bull Ring outrage 'exasperated the democracy all over the country', recalled another, 'then commenced the work of "preparation"'. The commander of Manchester's garrison observed on 15 July: 'There have been more Pikes made and sold within the last 10 days, than at any former period.' Henry Vincent, sureties for his bail having been secured, declared: 'A crisis is now at hand ... Fellow slaves! Rattle your chains!' Privately he confided his sense that 'a desperate feeling is now abroad – you can have no conception of the intensity – even in this aristocratic town of Cheltenham the people are *ripe* and *ready*'.[72]

The seriousness of the situation was reinforced the following Tuesday when Harney returned to Birmingham in police custody, having been arrested in Newcastle for remarks earlier in July about campaigning with a 'musket in one hand and a petition in another'. The Convention had returned to London for the parliamentary debate on the National Petition by the time Harney's case came up. He sought to persuade the Birmingham magistrates (whose members included a very uncomfortable Thomas Salt) that, extolling the value of oatcakes to sustain the Chartists during the sacred month, he had said not 'musket' but 'biscuit' – an isolated glimmer of humour to lighten the darkening mood.[73] Harney was remanded on bail to await the next Warwick assize.

## Hope deferred

On the evening of Friday 12 July Parliament finally debated a proposal from Thomas Attwood that a committee of the whole House take into consideration the National Petition. The Convention had prepared for the occasion as thoroughly as it could. Every MP likely to be sympathetic had been sent a personal letter 'in the anxious hope that you will think it your duty to support the motion', and reiterating that the petitioners attributed their 'grievous distress ... entirely to the misrepresentation of their Interests in the House of Commons'. The thirty-odd delegates who had neither resigned nor were in prison gathered in the Public Gallery to hear the debate. In contrast to its initial reception, the Petition was treated respectfully but the House was less than half-full and the quality of debate underwhelming. Lowery later recalled the 'want of fluency and facility of expression' in Russell's contribution, while Sir Robert Peel 'would not have commanded the attention of a working man's meeting'. Disraeli's 'was the most miserable deliverance I had ever heard', thought the Geordie tailor, punctuated by frequent hesitation, shuffling of papers and intermittent pauses to suck oranges.[74] The Petition was largely ignored: Disraeli used the occasion to attack the Whigs for introducing the New Poor Law, and Russell to ridicule Attwood's currency theories. When the House divided, Attwood's motion was defeated by 235 votes to 46.

The Convention resumed its business on Monday 15 July with yet another debate about the sacred month. But it was severely depleted: Collins, Harney, Lovett, Taylor and Vincent were either remanded on bail or in custody; Frost was in Newport defending himself against financial misconduct charges, a mischievous action brought against him by the borough council; O'Connor was in York to face criminal libel charges against the *Star*, concerning criticisms of the Poor Law; O'Brien was touring Tyneside. McDouall was present, but bailed on charges of seditious speech at Hyde in April. Since the Convention had relocated to Birmingham, seven delegates had resigned, culminating with Hugh Craig who, exasperated, had simply returned to his Kilmarnock drapery business.

Absenteeism, for whatever reason, began to attract acerbic comment. Events of the past few weeks were also taking a toll on the movement generally. John Fussell was not among those arrested in Birmingham on 4 July and as a result now found himself suspected of being a spy or *agent provocateur*. The evidence was conjectural, but suspicions lingered, even after he moved to London in the early 1840s. Across the country arrests continued, part of a tacit policy to tie-up as many activists as possible in time-consuming and morale-sapping legal proceedings, regardless of the likelihood of securing convictions. Notable cases included those of W. P. Roberts, William Carrier and William Potts at Trowbridge (for conspiracy); Timothy Higgins, secretary of the Ashton RA for possessing arms (a copy of Macerone's *Defensive Instructions* was also found when his home was raided); Sam Cook of Dudley, for sedition; Binns and Williams of Sunderland, again for sedition; and in Leeds two Chartists, one of them George White, secretary of the GNU, for extortion (they had been canvassing for National Rent).[75]

Undaunted, Lowery proposed a resolution that the sacred month be implemented from 12 August. Though his 1856–57 autobiography largely drew a veil over it, Lowery was among the most militant delegates, buoyed up by close knowledge of his native Tyneside where arming was extensive and enthusiasm for striking manifest.[76] A few were even more combative. Neesom, for example, moved an amendment to bring the strike forward to 5 August, though the mood in east London hardly justified his supporting a strike at all. This was seconded by James Osbourne, a currier from Brighton, who believed the strike should be called immediately. Only three others, however, supported Neesom's amendment. A significant source of dissent from Lowery's resolution was led by Bussey, firmly committed to the strike but wishing to establish a sub-committee to verify the extent of support and then recommend a starting date. An amendment to this effect was lost on the casting vote of the chair, Richard Tilley, a bricklayer, LDA member and delegate for Lambeth who had earlier supported Neesom's amendment. The Convention filled its chair on the basis of daily rotation, and at most other points in the calendar the casting vote would have fallen the other way. We cannot be sure what conclusion Bussey's proposed sub-committee would have drawn, but it could hardly have been more damaging than the final conclusion of this debate, late on Tuesday 16 July, that the country was ready to commence the sacred month on 12 August.

The sequence of events that followed did nothing to retrieve the Convention's reputation for strategic thinking and leadership. On 22 July the delegates reassembled, this time with both O'Brien and O'Connor present. O'Brien, despite recent exposure to the electric mood among Tyneside Chartists, did not believe the Convention was in a position to dictate the timing of a general strike. His solution was that an address reaffirming its necessity should be issued, which mass meetings would then be asked to endorse. McDouall, on the other hand, was all for pressing ahead: 'nearly a million of people would act on the recommendation of a strike'. Lowery condemned the timidity and cowardice of those who lacked the stomach for the strike. Neesom, declared 'the people were better prepared for the holiday than their leaders'. O'Connor was equivocal: 'if we played the card and lost it' he now asked, 'should [we] have any other card to play'? But he lacked sufficient personal authority within the Convention to carry a clear majority in favour of revoking the 16 July resolution, while at the same time being opposed to O'Brien's suggestion on the grounds that it abrogated Convention's authority. O'Connor's preference was to send delegates back to their constituencies to assess the situation and then reconvene at the end of the month to make an informed decision. O'Connor lost this argument and O'Brien's resolution was carried, though not by an overall majority.

Thus it was totally unclear whether the sacred month would commence on 12 August (just three weeks away) or not. The following day O'Connor steered through a resolution that was a hotchpotch of almost everything debated over the past eight days; and 12 August was now confirmed as 'provisionally appointed ... as the day for the general cessation from Labour'. A council of Convention would receive reports from delegates who were to return to their constituencies and assess the readiness to strike; the Convention would then reconvene and review the situation on Monday 5 August. All except Harney agreed to O'Connor's resolution: it appeared decisive, provided one overlooked the unrealistic time frame stipulated; and it preserved a veneer of continuing authority for the Convention.

This appearance was signally undermined, however, by the *Northern Star* of Saturday 3 August, in which O'Connor powerfully argued that the sacred month should be abandoned and three days of strikes and demonstrations held in its place. An editorial argued that 'the country is not for it; there is no state of adequate preparation; there is no proper organisation among the people; they are not able to act in concert with each other; they are not a tenth part of them in possession of the means of self-defence; they are not agreed in their opinions, either as to the practicality or the necessity of the measure'. By way of reinforcing the point, Chartist affairs were kept off the front page in favour of general news. On the Monday the Convention resumed, yet again, to debate the sacred month. The following day it finally decided to abandon the measure and instead 'cease work on the 12th inst., for one, two, or three days, in order to devote the whole of that time to solemn processions and meetings'.

It was now Tuesday 6 August: the view from the hillsides, so enthusiastically evoked a few months previously, was clouding over.

# Chartist lives:
# Thomas Powell

It is unlikely that Thomas Powell knew anything of the events unfolding in early August 1839 because he was 3 weeks into a 12-month prison sentence. His role in the Llanidloes riots, as we saw in the previous chapter, was entirely peaceable but it was Powell's misfortune to be readily identifiable as the region's leading Chartist by local magistrates bent on the suppression of the movement. Indeed they all but neutralised Chartism in the upper Severn Valley, setting Powell on a course that ultimately brought him, twenty years later, to a lonely death in a landscape as far removed from the Welsh hills as it is possible to imagine.

Thomas Powell was born (probably in 1802) in the Montgomeryshire flannel-weaving centre of Newtown, birthplace of the better known Robert Owen, socialist and educationist. After some schooling he was apprenticed to a Shrewsbury ironmonger. On completing his apprenticeship he moved to London to work as a shopman in an ironmonger's. It was there that Powell's political apprenticeship began, as one of a trio of skilled artisans and tradesmen, all newcomers to London, particularly interested in the rapidly emerging idea of co-operative trading.

Other notable members of this group were William Lovett, who had arrived from west Cornwall in 1821 and worked for a cabinetmaker a short walk from Powell's employer, and James Watson, a printer. Watson had arrived from Yorkshire in 1822, straight into the employment of the renowned republican and disciple of Thomas Paine, Richard Carlile. The three were largely self-educated, earnest and idealistic. All became members of the London Co-operative Trading Association, founded in November 1827, which aimed to use profits from its retail co-operative to employ members and ultimately to generate sufficient funds to purchase land where all members would settle. 'Why should poverty exist?' one of the Association's advertisements asked; 'should anyone, able and willing to work, be in want? The earth is large enough.' It maintained a library and organised regular classes on 'mental and moral improvement'. Both Lovett and Watson served the Association as storekeepers.[*]

The three were even more involved from the spring of 1829 as founder members in the British Association for the Promotion of Co-operative Knowledge. Lovett was storekeeper and Powell, from October 1830, secretary. This too ultimately hoped to settle its members on the land, but it also operated a 'labour exchange' (more accurately a product exchange), using as a currency notes representing the labour input involved in producing the items members traded.[†] Powell had become a citizen of an exhilarating world in which organised labour seemed poised not to overturn the capitalist economy but rather to leap outside it into an alternative of its own creation. He was, however, no idealistic utopian. He clashed publicly with Robert Owen over both the feasibility of labour notes as a general currency medium and Owen's lofty disdain for democratic principles. For the National Union of the Working Classes (the focal point of popular opposition to the 1832 Reform Act) Powell worked quietly in 'backroom' roles, for example collecting subscriptions and auditing accounts. He also lectured on currency issues to radical groups in the capital.[‡]

In the autumn of 1832, however, Powell forsook both London and co-operation for his native Montgomeryshire. In partnership with his brother he bought an ironmonger's business in Welshpool. The contrast with the world he had left could not have been greater. Welshpool was a market town of some 3,000 souls. It was dominated – politically and physically – by Powis Castle and its owner, an East India proprietor, Tory magnate and Lord Lieutenant of the County, Viscount Clive. For electoral purposes Welshpool was combined with five other towns to form the Montgomeryshire District parliamentary constituency. Welshpool was, by general consent, the most conservative of them all, but, undeterred, Powell played a leading role in the committee that brought a Liberal candidate – Colonel John Edwards – to within fourteen votes of

---

[*]    *Weekly Free Press*, 14 March 1829; see also *Lion*, 16 October 1829; W. Lovett, *Life and Struggles of William Lovett* (London, Trübner, 1876), pp. 40–2; I. J. Prothero, *Artisans and Politics in Early Nineteenth-Century London* (Folkestone, Dawson, 1979), pp. 241 and 379, n 8.

[†]    BL, Add. MSS 27,822, fol. 17; *Magazine of Useful Knowledge and Co-operative Miscellany*, 30 October 1830; Prothero, *Artisans*, p. 242.

[‡]    *Crisis*, 25 August 1835; *Poor Man's Guardian*, 11 February, 21 April, 14 July and 15 September 1832.

victory at the general election of December 1832. After successfully petitioning against the result on the grounds of corruption, Edwards was returned as MP the following April.

It is clear from Powell's sole recorded election speech that immersion in small-town politics had been something of a shock to the co-operator who had cut his political teeth among London artisans: 'I greatly lament the small-ness of our number', he told an audience in Newtown which, he thought, could 'form no idea of the difficulties our voters had to contend with. Threats in all shapes were tried and when these failed other stronger measures were resorted to – ruin and loss of all that was dear to us was to be the consequence if we acted contrary to their desire.' He concluded with a passionate call for the secret ballot and 'freedom for the expression of our opinions without which we can never be happy'.[*]

Powell was not long content to remain in the political goldfish-bowl of Welshpool. His reputation as an articulate and independent speaker soon spread countywide. The Llanidloes PU wrote of there being 'plenty of fire in the town and Mr. Powell is the man who is best able to set it ablaze'.[†] Powell concentrated his political energies on Llanidloes and Newtown (both with a mixture of domestic and mill-based workers). He also resumed his acquaintance with Henry Hetherington (whom he had known in the British Association for Promotion of Co-operative Knowledge), speaking alongside him when he visited mid-Wales as an LWMA missionary in November 1837.

Powell's personal life, however, was in turmoil. His brother had died in 1835, and Thomas was an indifferent businessman without him. It is also conceivable that his politics cost him customers; and this may also explain why he was struck out of the will of a wealthy elderly cousin that same year. In June 1838 he was declared bankrupt and his house and shop sold, followed soon after by his ironmongery stock.

It may therefore have been with a *frisson* of personal apprehension, as well as righteous indignation, that Powell led Montgomeryshire's Chartists, on Christmas Day 1838, to meet near the site on which Caersws workhouse was being erected. The *Shrewsbury Chronicle* described Powell's speech as 'decent and orderly', but not one of the speakers was 'respectable in property or character', according to the local clergyman who sent to the Home Office a close paraphrase of all that was said.[‡] Powell was now a marked man, like dozens of

---

[*] Quoted in E. R. Morris, 'Thomas Powell – Chartist', *Montgomeryshire Collections*, 80:2 (1992), pp.104–5.

[†] National Library of Wales, Aberystwyth, Powis Papers, letter, 3 December 1838, quoted in Morris, 'Powell', p.106.

[‡] *Shrewsbury Chronicle*, 4 January 1839; HO, 40/40, J. Davies to HO, 29 December 1838.

Chartist activists across Britain, his public political pronouncements subject to clandestine report and, not infrequently, distortion. On 9 April 1839, the same day that the General Convention in London finally debated arming, Powell allegedly told a crowd of more than 2,000 in Newtown:

> I have at all times stood forth as your leader in the warfare and I hope you will not now forsake me if called upon, but oppose force to force if necessary – some of your members want us to employ moral force – what will moral force do for us, what has it done for us? You have groaned enough under tyranny already and know it will not avail you. Be determined and your opponents will not withstand you – your number is sufficient. Be close together and you will march thro' every town and city in the kingdom.*

Again Powell was speaking in tandem with Hetherington, and the two proceeded to address Chartist meetings in Llanidloes, Rhayader and Welshpool over the following few days. The mood in mid-Wales was febrile, though Chartism was not alone responsible for this. As we saw in chapter 3, rioting on 30 April seriously damaged a hotel in Llanidloes; 5 policemen from outside the town were effectively held prisoner and the breakdown of law and order lasted 4 days.

The incident that sparked off the episode was an anti-police riot rather than a Chartist disturbance, and it was Powell, arriving in Llanidloes some time after rioting started, who actually rescued two of the police concerned, even though they were there in the first place to arrest the local Chartist leadership. Powell was taken up at his lodgings in Welshpool the following Sunday.† His arrest broke Powell financially if not psychologically. Within two weeks all his furniture and personal effects were sold by auction, while Powell struggled to meet the conditions of his bail. It took nearly eight weeks before sureties acceptable to the magistrates were found, a particularly blatant example of the manipulation of bail procedures, a tactic commonly used to detain Chartists without trial. One of the sureties was provided by Powell's old friend James Watson, an LWMA member and now one of London's leading radical publishers and printers.‡

Brought to trial at the summer assize on 18 July, Powell was charged with using seditious language at Newtown on 9 April. The case heard immediately prior to Powell's concerned a teenage Llanidloes weaver who was sentenced to fifteen years transportation for stabbing a special constable. By scheduling

---

* HO, 40/46, 6 May 1839, prosecution brief for *R. v. Powell*; Morris, 'Powell', p.113; see also *NS*, 20 April 1839; O.Ashton, 'Chartism in mid-Wales', *Montgomeryshire Collections*, 62:1 (1971), pp.23–4.

† *The Times*, 3 and 6 May 1839; D.Williams, *John Frost* (Cardiff, University of Wales Press, 1939), pp.158–9; Ashton, 'Chartism in mid-Wales', pp.25–33.

‡ HO, 40/46, 25 May 1839; Morris, 'Powell', p.111.

Powell's trial immediately after the Llanidloes rioters', the Attorney-General appears to have hoped to persuade the jury that he had played a significant contributory role in the riots. The actual evidence of seditious language was highly tenuous. There was also uncontested testimony that, soon after arriving in Llanidloes, Powell had publicly urged no resistance to the police and a return to work. However, he was found guilty, sentenced to a year's imprisonment and bound over to keep the peace for five further years on sureties totalling £800 – half of which he had to provide himself. Powell had committed, Chartists quipped grimly, a new crime, 'seditious staying of action'. The release terms were unusually punitive and through the intervention of Colonel Edwards at the Home Office they were quietly dropped at the expiry of the sentence.*

To Edwards's alarm, once released from prison Powell went direct to Newtown and the local Chartists. For Powell, however, small-town Wales was suffocating: he was homeless, in debt and estranged from his remaining family. He therefore returned to London to work as a shopman on the retail side of Hetherington's publishing business. He still carried some political weight in Montgomeryshire, though as he pointed out in a letter to Edwards at the time of the 1841 general election, 'those with whom I am most likely to have influence ... have no votes'. Edwards had asked Powell to write to his contacts back home and urge them to support his re-election. Powell's response is a good illustration that Chartists, for all their idealism, fully understood the *realpolitik* of electioneering: 'a little liberality must be displayed, men when excited are very dry and a glass of ale occasionally effects miracles ... A little violence if necessary must be used. Indeed, if I was there I would not be delicate on this subject.' Powell's sentiments are an instructive contrast to the mood two years later when he briefly returned to Newtown for a public dinner in his honour: 'Several speeches were made, and democratic toasts, songs, and recitations given. The evening was spent in joyous and rational hilarity.'†

Powell was an indispensable member of Hetherington's team, for example becoming the legal owner of the business to prevent its distraint in lieu of fines during one of Hetherington's periodic brushes with the law. He was also secretary of the London Atheistical Society and assisted George Holyoake – an energetic figure bridging Chartism, freethought and co-operation – in running the Anti-Persecution Union.‡ From October 1844, however, Powell devoted

---

* W. J. Linton, 'Who were the Chartists?', *Century Magazine*, November 1881–April 1882, reproduced at www.gerald-massey.org.uk/dop_linton_the_century_1882.htm; Ashton, 'Chartism in mid-Wales', p. 29; Morris, 'Powell', pp. 114–15.

† National Library of Wales, Aberystwyth, Glansevern Collection, no. 7702, Powell to Edwards, 26 June 1841, quoted in Morris, 'Powell', p. 115; *NS*, 28 October 1843.

‡ W. J. Linton, *Memories* (London, Lawrence, 1895), pp. 85–7; E. Royle, *Victorian Infidels* (Manchester, Manchester University Press, 1974), pp. 87–8, 315.

most of his political energies to one of the lesser-known radical initiatives of the
early Victorian years, the Tropical Emigration Society. Powell was its founding
secretary and edited its journal, entitled – imitation being the sincerest form
of flattery – *Morning Star*. The Society enthusiastically subscribed to the back-
to-the-land ideal, so vital a component of popular politics in the 1840s; but the
land to which it aspired was in the Venezuelan republic rather than the cold
clays of Britain. Lured by the prospect of easy cultivation in the tropics, some
1,600 people across 48 branches subscribed to its shares. An additional attraction was the active involvement of John Etzler, an extraordinary figure from
the fringe of London socialism and Chartism. Etzler was an inventor, visionary
and prophet of a mechanised utopia.* What his inventions lacked in a capacity
for practicable realisation was compensated for by vision and novelty (wind
and solar energy were central to Etzler's technological utopia).†

At the end of 1845 the first of two groups left for Trinidad, where a temporary base was to be established prior to the final short journey across the Gulf
of Paria to Venezuela.‡ Powell led the second party of 193 settlers, leaving
Britain in March 1846 and arriving at Port of Spain, Trinidad, two months later.
Only on arrival did they learn that the advance party had mostly died from
tropical fevers or heat exhaustion. Not without irony, their supposedly temporary home was named 'Erthig', an anglicisation of 'Erdigg', a palatial Georgian
house and estate in north Wales.

The periodic reports Powell sent back to Britain were an almost unmiti-
gated chronicle of death, dissension and despair. There were 30 deaths in the
first year and at least 75 desertions, including the community's doctor who
decamped with all its medical equipment. The remainder were irrevocably
divided between those who wanted to move on to the western United States
and those determined to tough things out; their sloop was unseaworthy; there
was a complete breakdown of communication with the Society in Britain; and,
most bitterly, 'Our leader, Mr. Etzler, has ran away to America, afraid to meet his
dupes. His accounts unsettled, no cause given, no explanation entered into.'§
There was a short flurry of optimism in August when a large group finally set
out for Venezuela. Powell visited them briefly and wrote with amazement of
his 'truly delightful' voyage, 'surrounded by aquatic birds of all colours and

---

\*    *English Chartist Circular and Temperance Record* (*ECC*), 128 (nd, July 1843); Etzler wrote
regularly for *NS* between August 1843 and December 1844.
†    G.Claeys, 'John Adolphus Etzler, technological determinism and British socialism',
*English Historical Review*, 101 (1986), pp.351–75; W.H.G.Armytage, *Heavens Below* (London,
RKP, 1961), pp.184–94.
‡    *New Moral World*, 26 October, 30 November, 14 December 1844, 3 May 1845; *Morning
Star*, 11 October 1845, 10 January 1846.
§    *Morning Star*, 28 March, 20 June, 1 August and 12 September 1846; *National Reformer*,
13 and 20 March, 10 April, 29 May 1847.

sizes and fish ... sporting in hundreds around you'. But by December only five settlers remained alive at the Venezuelan site. The remnants of the Tropical Emigration Society therefore regrouped at Erthig.*

Though the despairing tone of Powell's reports was seldom muted, his writings were occasionally distinguished by a nobility and optimism that belied the disasters that had befallen him in Wales and then Trinidad. Relating that a discontented member of the fractious community had informed Trinidad's Governor about Powell's prison record, he commented simply: 'It is at the animus displayed that I grieve and grumble, not that I care who knows, as I glory in the deed that sent me there, which was simply defending the rights of my fellow men.' He repeatedly appealed for aid from the Society's British supporters, but in May 1847 it was wound up without the Trinidad community being informed.† Lacking trades or professions through which to earn the price of a passage to a kinder climate, the remaining colonists were effectively stranded. Thomas Powell scratched a living at Erthig for another eleven years and then worked for Trinidad's only newsagent and bookseller. 'If my circumstances would allow me I would again try London for a living', he wrote to Holyoake in 1862; but, he added, 'unfortunately I have been foolish enough to beget a family and am tied to the Island unless I could leave behind sufficient for these poor creatures to live.'‡

We may surmise that it was not poverty alone that prevented Powell from bringing his family to Britain (though by 1862 he had fathered 5 children, all under 12 years of age, and it must have been a major consideration). Though Powell in this letter was silent on the matter, on a different document Holyoake scribbled cryptically against his name 'Married a coloured Wife.'§ Powell's dismissal of his 'poor creatures' is indicative of a casual racism typical of white West Indian males (many of whom fathered black families, not all recognising a continuing personal responsibility as at least Powell clearly did). A degree of self-loathing is evident in Powell's brief allusion to his family, sadly in keeping with the tone of this, his last ever, letter. He complains of the cost of food in Trinidad, the high taxation, the politically supine and rootless white population, the effects of African, Indian and Chinese immigration on 'native' (i.e. former slave) labour, and of how all his British friends had deserted him: 'not a letter has reached me in 6 or 7 years although I wrote several letters but

---

*   *Morning Star*, 26 September 1846, 27 January 1847.

†   Quotation from *Morning Star*, 20 June and 12 September 1846; *National Reformer*, 19 May 1847.

‡   Co-operative College, Manchester, Holyoake Papers, no 1415, Powell to Holyoake, 24 March 1862; *Secular World*, 1 February 1863.

§   Bishopsgate Institute, London, G. J. Holyoake Collection, Powell to Holyoake, 24 March 1862, account book of the London Atheistical Society (within 1845–48 letter book).

no answers arriving after repeated attempts to hear from them I gave up in despair'. Having walked out on his employer in disgust at his laziness, Powell was getting by on odd jobs as a bookkeeper. Less than eight months later he was dead.

In his collection *An Acre of Land*, the great Welsh poet R.S.Thomas wrote of the Welsh diaspora, 'we were a people wasting ourselves/ In fruitless battles … in lands to which we had no claim'.[*] Thomas had in mind Wales' human contribution to Britain's imperial expansion, but it is hard not to visualise Powell, too, on reading his lines. The land on which Powell battled for a living now sleeps beneath the runway of Trinidad's airport, Earthrigg.

Alone of those whose brief lives punctuate this book, Powell has a memorial: a plaque, erected in 1992 in Old St Mary's churchyard, Newtown. Robert Owen is buried nearby. Occasional pilgrims and the curious pause at Owen's grave; few, one suspects, give thought to Thomas Powell.

---

[*] R.S.Thomas, *Welsh History*, in *Collected Poems, 1945–1990* (London, Phoenix, 1998), p.36.

# CHAPTER FOUR

# July–November 1839: 'Extreme excitement and apprehension'

## The approach to 12 August

The cancellation of the sacred month and its substitution by three days of protest meetings was a climb-down of great significance for Chartism. Yet this was not entirely evident at the time, especially to opponents of the movement. The weeks since Lovett's arrest had seen escalating disturbance, not only in Birmingham (with its most serious night of rioting on 15 July), but at Bury, Newcastle, Monmouth and Stockport. Tension was exacerbated by a series of church occupations by Chartists, some of the most confrontational of all Chartist publications and the passage through Parliament of legislation that briefly came close to rivalling the New Poor Law in popular loathing, the Constabulary Bill. An understanding of these factors is necessary to put the events of 12–14 August into context.

Local circumstances explain each of the riotous outbreaks; but the overall effect was to increase apprehension that Chartists were intent upon fomenting major upheaval. Popular discontent had subsided in Birmingham but then reasserted itself on Monday 15 July when a crowd assembling to greet John Collins (finally released on bail) heard of a fight involving police officers. A chain of events was triggered, culminating in arson attacks on several shops in the Bull Ring and a ceremonial bonfire of their contents at the Chartists' customary meeting place, in front of Nelson's statue in the street outside. The targeted premises belonged to shopkeepers rumoured to be strongly anti-Chartist; before they were attacked the angry crowd besieged the police who had barricaded themselves into the Public Office. But satisfying though this episode seemed in the short term, humiliating police and magistrates and paying-off scores against an unsympathetic shopocracy, its real effect was to throw Birmingham Chartism into stark, unsympathetic relief. It was widely reported in exaggeratedly lurid terms, so lurid that Wellington declared in Parliament 'he had never known a town taken by storm, so treated as the accounts from Birmingham stated'. So apoplectic was Wellington that one well-informed observer thought his manner 'alarmingly indicative of a decay of mental power'. Three of the rioters were sentenced to death (subsequently commuted to transportation) for the capital offence of destroying a house. Yet outsiders who overcame their trepidation and actually visited Birmingham left almost disappointed at the modest extent of the damage.[1]

The other riots were less consequential, but served similarly to aggravate tensions as 12 August approached. At Bury on 17 July, responding to rumours that police were about to raid the Radical Hall, 'great numbers of men, women and stout lads poured into the town'; many were armed and fired guns repeatedly into the air. Three days later in Newcastle, police struggled to impose order when the rescue of a prisoner (arrested for an offence unconnected to Chartism) led to running battles and damage to a bank and the offices of the anti-Chartist *Tyne Mercury*. Ten days later the 'Battle of the Forth' saw large-scale military intervention to prevent a Chartist open-air meeting in central Newcastle. Then, on Friday 2 August, the Riot Act had to be read outside Monmouth assize court as Vincent prepared to stand trial. At Stockport on 7 August, after magistrates sought to stop all meetings and impose a curfew on beershops, troops were used to search a popular Chartist pub for arms. A night of street skirmishes ensued.[2]

These events occurred against the background noise, to quote a correspondent to *The Charter*, of 'extreme excitement and apprehension' elsewhere. The Birmingham death sentences were greeted with widespread dismay. At Lye in the Black Country, the yeomanry was stoned as it passed through en route to Birmingham. Evidence of arming was accumulating and the manufacture of arms often brazen. At Bolton 'there is no attempt to conceal the making of them for two of the workshops are at the front of the street and the men are seen at work by all passers by'. Near Stourbridge 'even children' were employed to make craws' feet. Rumours circulated round Manchester of machines being built to throw shells and fire. In Stockport raids on six houses recovered pistols, muskets, fowling guns, pikes, bayonets, swords, daggers, bullet moulds and percussion caps.[3] 'Applications to me have become more numerous within the last fortnight than they ever were before', a Bradford gunsmith told magistrates on 26 July, and included 'almost daily applications for Soldiery Guns', and for alterations 'to place the sight of the Musquet further from the end of the Barrel in order that the Bayonet might have better hold'. At nearby Shipley a blacksmith and his two assistants worked full-time 'Manufacturing Spears for the use of Charterists'. These followed a distinctive design (with hooks for cutting cavalry bridle reins) recommended by Macerone and favoured by Chartists in a number of centres.[4]

A new development was mass attendance at church services by Chartists. This tactic was developed in response to local authorities' growing willingness to declare Chartist meetings illegal.[5] Not to be confused with Chartist churches, mass attendances occurred mainly in towns whose civic elites were most suspicious of the movement. Birmingham Chartists were the first to use the tactic, the day after Lovett and Collins were arrested. Overwhelmingly, however, church demonstrations were linked to 12 August and the Sundays either side of it. Demonstrations of this kind were held in less than a tenth of the 400-odd centres with formally constituted Chartist associations. None were in Scotland and only three in Wales.[6] Where they occurred, however, the social tensions generated were extraordinary.

Sometimes the Chartists gave advanced notice of their intentions, combined with a request for a sermon on a specific text (commonly the Epistle of James 5:1, 'Go to now, ye rich men, weep and howl for your miseries that shall be upon you'). Chartists would gather nearby and march *en masse* into the church, crowding to the front and into the private pews (often a majority of the seating in Anglican churches). The customary occupants would be crowded out or refused access, and occasionally scuffles broke out in consequence. Most Chartists made a point of attending in their working clothes, sometimes donning aprons for the purpose or, as at Merthyr Tydfil, 'the Chartist uniform – a peculiar design in Welsh flannel', woven at a local mill. This met with complaints, as did the relatively few alleged instances of smoking and drunkenness. However, no incidents were reported of services actually disrupted: the nearest to this was a mass walkout at Ashton-under-Lyne when the preacher announced his text as Luke 19:46, 'My house is the house of prayer: but ye have made it a den of thieves.' But the church occupations were avowedly confrontational, not with religious worship itself but with the social elitism of the Church of England (symbolised in private pews, assize services and the social class of the clergy) and its integral relationship with the political establishment.[7]

A few church occupations elicited from the clergy concerned a sympathetic response (though never unconditional approbation). Dr Whittaker of Blackburn agreed to preach on James 5:1 but advised that 'no nation ever attained civil liberty by mere charters and acts of legislation ... brethren be patient in the Lord'. In the one recorded instance of the occupation of a Roman Catholic church, the priest elaborated an argument familiar from Cobbett, namely that humane poor relief was a casualty of the Reformation. But when 'he asserted that the poor in this country now have no protection in the laws, and that divine charity left the land when the catholic religion was changed for protestantism', his 1,500-strong congregation jeered and hissed. Most preachers, however, used the occasion for leaden homilies on duty and obedience, or to attack Chartism

at what they believed to be its source, namely the envy of wealth and the disregard of the world to come. Several chose Philippians 4:11, 'For I have learnt in
whatsoever state I am, therewith to be content.' 'Deluded persons', declaimed
the Reverend Close of Cheltenham, 'CHARTISM is *rebellion against man*.' At
Preston the vicar rounded on the Chartists for failing to ascribe 'the evils of
their condition to their own misconduct', adding that 'they were too apt to lay
them at the door of the virtuous and the Godly'.[8]

Church demonstrations took Chartism into the very heart of the local
establishment. Members of local elites were unnerved by the sudden proximity
of 'persons who wore anything but a Sabbath aspect, either as regards cleanli-
ness or dress', conversing in 'rough' dialect. 'There is much alarm in the town
about this matter', Napier noted at Nottingham, 'among a certain class.'[9] The
atmosphere of such demonstrations was one of disciplined truculence rather
than rebelliousness.

As 12 August grew nearer, however, Chartist publications increasingly
assumed an openly insurrectionary tone. The *Northern Star*'s circulation
now exceeded 40,000 copies each week, outselling even *The Times* and being
among the largest – probably the largest – sales ever achieved by a newspaper
at that time.[10] As a measure of O'Connor's influence and of the importance
of print media in helping Chartism to cohere as a national movement, this
figure is eloquent. However, posters and printed addresses, aimed beyond the
movement, momentarily had the greatest impact. From its Newcastle base the
Northern PU was particularly active. Its *Address to the Middle Classes of the
North of England* was among the most uncompromising statements of social
hostility ever published by Chartists:

> We address you in the Language of Brotherhood probably for the very last
> Time ... It is your intense and BLIND Selfishness that is rendering almost
> inevitable a Civil Convulsion. This Fact will be remembered in the Day of
> Trial. You have not been with us and therefore you are against us. Should the
> People (and it were folly to doubt it) succeed, they will owe you no gratitude
> – should they fall you will be involved in their ruin ... they will "DISPERSE
> IN A MILLION OF INCENDIARIES", your Warehouses – your Homes – will
> be given to the Flames, and one black Ruin will overwhelm England![11]

It was for the Durham CA edition of the *Address* that Williams and Binns
were arrested and charged with sedition. Yet this had little impact on north-
eastern Chartism as a similarly bellicose address *To the Middle Classes of
Darlington, and its Neighbourhood*, issued a few days later, indicates. 'You
ARE now on the brink of a CIVIL WAR at HOME ... oh FOOLISH AND
INFATUATED MEN!'[12] Bradford Chartists circulated a printed appeal 'for the
Defence Fund' among local shopkeepers warning that 'in all cases of refusal to
this reasonable request we shall know how to discriminate between our Friends

and our Enemies'.[13] Other circulars were directed at trade societies: Richardson invoked Magna Charta and the seventeenth-century radical heroes Hampden and Sydney; Bolton Chartists warned of increasingly 'tyrannical interference' from a Government intent on suppressing trade unionism.[14]

All these publications emphasised a new element in the broader political context, the County and District Constabulary Bill introduced in the House of Commons on 24 July. This was not particularly an anti-Chartist measure: it originated in mounting unease at the incidence of crimes against property which, it was believed, the uneven policing of the time encouraged. Borough forces allegedly led petty criminals to migrate into the adjacent counties where regular policing was limited to the ancient office of parish constable. The Home Secretary hinted that concern about Chartism had influenced his decision to introduce the Bill; but equally the climate of anxiety at the end of July made it an opportune moment to bring to Parliament a measure that was likely to meet stiff opposition from MPs hostile to the growth of central government at the expense of local autonomy.

This debate had rumbled on since a Royal Commission at the beginning of the year (fuelling the anti-police sentiment which was a powerful element in disturbances at Birmingham, Longton and Llanidloes).[15] The Bill's introduction added urgency to calls for the Charter, fuelling appetite for the sacred month and increasing apprehension lest it should fail. Bolton Chartists argued that 'the FINALITY LORD' was introducing a force 'professedly intended to put down "Trade Strikes"'. O'Connor declared: 'All law was now at an end in this country'; while Richardson claimed: 'The little gilded staff of the antiquated constable is grown into a murderous bludgeon.'[16] A poster issued by the Northern PU on 8 August, calling for a general strike, exclaimed: 'Englishmen! You asked for a Redress of Grievances, and your answer is a Bourbon Police.'[17]

The spectre of a government-controlled 'immense Constabulary force' in rural areas helped push Chartism even further into rural England in July and early August, for example to the hitherto politically inert North Riding market towns of Thirsk and Northallerton.[18] In its final form the Rural Constabulary Act of 1839 was a pale affair, permissive not compulsory, and bereft of central-ised control except for a small and largely powerless inspectorate. But this was not immediately apparent, while the continuing accretion of local *ad hoc* measures in anticipation of 12 August further stoked Chartist fears. The south Durham town of Stockton-on-Tees provides a good illustration of how, as summer wore on, Chartist activity met with escalating official alarm.

A team from the Durham CA had first visited Stockton at Easter and a local association was set up immediately. Local Chartists repeatedly clashed with the borough authorities. Publicans and others who offered them meeting places were threatened. Chartists' mail was delayed and tampered with. When, on 17 July, an informer reported a meeting, 'chiefly of mechanics and the labouring classes, [although] some females were also present', had openly discussed arming, Stockton's Mayor immediately pleaded to the Home Office that 'a military force ... be stationed in this Town' (which it was, contrary to Napier's advice). From nearby Hartlepool another correspondent predicted that 'every House will be pillaged and even human life sacrificed'. Stockton magistrates swore-in 235 special constables – professionals, retailers, tradesmen, 22 'gentlemen', the Tees customs men and the local Poor Law Relieving Officer. A central core of a 100 then formed a quasi-military 'association for protection of the lives and property of Her Majesty's Subjects', which the Stockton Corporation sought to equip with rifles and cutlasses. Just over the Tees in North Yorkshire rumours circulated that 'there were 11,000 Chartists' in Stockton (its population barely totalled 9,000), and at Yarm bridge public-spirited citizens tried to dissuade travellers from crossing the Tees to reach it. These responses to Chartism in the summer of 1839 speak volumes for the extent to which across northern England local authority and polite society were unnerved by the threat of a general strike. Why then was the sacred month called off?[19]

## A grand moral demonstration

Stockton illustrates how fragile, even illusory, the sacred month was as a political strategy. Only one derisory arms' cache ever came to light there. O'Connor's substitute for the sacred month, the 'grand moral demonstration' of 12–14 August passed with barely a catcall on its streets. Yet two weeks before, the *Northern Liberator* had boasted that 'the people of Stockton are ready to do their part, and if many hands make light work, there will be little difficulty in the work of national regeneration'. Within days the Durham CA executive concluded that outside of Sunderland the county was inadequately prepared for the sacred month. It was not that local authority was so efficient that support was stifled: on the contrary, Stockton's uniformed association rapidly acquired a reputation bordering on the clownish, while infantrymen sent to Teesside spent most of their time disconsolately packed into goods wagons, rattling along the Stockton & Darlington Railway in an effort to protect the two towns simultaneously.[20] Rather, the whole notion of a general strike, even for one or two days – and still more an entire month – called both for mass support and detailed preparation.

Some responsibility for the lack of preparedness lay with the Convention, which failed to give a timely or clear enough lead. On the other hand its indecision was understandable, confronted by incomplete information as to the state of the country. The mass circulation of the *Northern Star* and the shoal of other papers swimming in its wake can easily mislead: internal communication was a recurring problem for the Chartist leadership at every level. Chartism's history was littered with meetings which failed because of short notice, or whose speakers were prevented from attending by double-bookings, misdirected correspondence or the vagaries of road conditions, early railway time-tabling and (in coastal communities) tides and weather.

It was partly to overcome such challenges to effective communication that stellar orators like O'Connor and Vincent maintained such punishing speaking schedules. Furthermore, sustained political activism requires relentless optimism. When local organisers like Bussey claimed that 'the work is progressing gloriously here' and 'there was no doubt of success', a thin line, visible chiefly with hindsight, separated encouraging leadership from irresponsible bellicosity.

Finally, of course, the Convention was involved in a game of bluff with the political establishment. Few delegates expected Parliament to concede anything in response to the National Petition, and it is unlikely that many thought a strike would achieve much more. There was, however, a widespread feeling that repressive action by the Government would stimulate a general crisis: the Bull Ring riot of 4 July seemed an early harbinger of exactly this. When the Convention departed from Birmingham for the parliamentary debate on the Petition, delegates left assuming they would shortly be arrested. Some even travelled 'in the full hope that Govnt will take them into custody', as one observer wrote of Bussey.[21]

As we saw in chapter 3, however, the Convention lost numbers not through mass arrests but by slow attrition, a process wherein resignations played a large part. It was a depleted and demoralised body that finally gripped the nettle on 6 August. Evidence was mounting that the sacred month would fail. Doncaster, Rotherham and Sheffield were not sufficiently 'up to the mark'. Belper Chartists demanded that 'some other plan might be adopted', Derby was 'not ready' and Loughborough was disappointed 'that other places of larger note' would not take the lead. Hyde was 'fully prepared, yet we believe the whole country is not', and instructed its delegate to withdraw the vote against strike action. Most trades in Preston were 'decidedly against'. In Middleton, 'those decidedly for the Holiday are in the minority'. Richards reported from the Potteries: 'I find but very little provision [is] made to carry it out ... My opinion therefore is that the Sacred Month cannot in common prudence be attempted here.' Lowery later claimed McDouall conceded that 'if he named 400 armed men for his neighbourhood [Ashton-under-Lyne] he would probably overstate the number'. Delegates' understanding of the situation in Scotland (now seriously under-represented in the Convention) was poor but, to judge from reports made to a Scottish delegate conference the following week, it was little different – limited opposition to the *notion* of the sacred month but a concerted feeling that its immediate implementation would be disastrously premature.[22]

There were some isolated claims of readiness: the Colne Valley was 'ready at any time'; in Bath 'the biggest fear is that a strike will not take place'. In

Shepshed 'seventeen in every twenty' would strike. Preparations were well advanced in Bradford, argued Bussey, though the *Northern Star* had 'done infinite mischief'. Across the Pennines, some east-Lancashire Chartists even suggested burning the paper.[23] Thus it is conceivable that, had a decision been reached sooner to stage a short demonstrative stoppage, support for it would have been more widespread. Instead, perhaps the most notable feature of the stoppage was the church demonstrations preceding it. However, an attenuated general strike was achieved, principally in and around Manchester but also in Barnsley, Carlisle, the Dewsbury district, Macclesfield, Mansfield, Nottingham, Sheffield, south Wales, the Durham coalfield and to a limited extent on Tyneside.

Elsewhere Chartist activities were largely confined to evening marches and meetings of relatively little significance. Bristol's was 'thinly attended'; 2,000–3,000 gathered for a peaceable rally in Norwich, and only 200–400 in Halifax. At Dukestown, Monmouthshire, Chartists met 'for the purpose of petitioning the Queen to dismiss the present Ministry; to call to her Council better and wiser men, and to dissolve Parliament', adding a menacing coda that 'in the present excited and alarming state of the country, when no man can say what a day can bring forth, it will be enough to tell the men of the hills, that Wales expects every man to do his duty'. Oldham Chartists pointedly passed a resolution declaring the national holiday unnecessary. 'There has been no procession, no gathering, and no striking here', reported *The Charter*'s correspondent from Birmingham; there as elsewhere the sentencing of Lovett and Collins to a year's imprisonment the week before may have subdued activity. Yeomanry dispersed a crowd estimated at 150 on Trowbridge Common. In London meetings convened at four different venues marched to Kennington Common, south of the Thames, where a crowd of some 12,000 heard O'Brien, O'Connor and Taylor speaking mainly to a resolution to petition the Queen to reverse the death sentences passed on the Bull Ring rioters.[24] That these three (especially O'Connor) were there at all, and not in the north, suggests they had almost lost interest in the events of the day or were embarrassed by them.

Where significant stoppages occurred, disturbances were commonplace as local authorities moved with varying effectiveness to impose order. In Lancashire social relations were further strained by the twentieth anniversary of Peterloo on 16 August. In Charlestown, Ashton-under-Lyne, police backed by troops raided the home of the Claytons, both of whom were wounded in 1819. Their objective was to prevent 'Owd Nancy' publicly displaying the black petticoat she had worn at Peterloo, alongside a green cap of liberty in the French revolutionary style. They seized the petticoat but the cap of liberty evaded them ('it wur where thou durstna go for it', Nancy later told Ashton's Chief Constable).[25] In Newcastle, where the Northern PU issued a call for a general strike on 12 August, there was a feeble demonstration in the afternoon, partly reflecting a feeling Tyneside had been abandoned by the Convention Harney awaited trial in Warwick, O'Brien was in London and Lowery had been dispatched to Ireland on a futile mission to win support from the O'Connellites and secure a Dublin delegation to the Convention.[26]

Outside of Newcastle, however, there were minor confrontations between soldiers and strikers in several industrial villages, including Winlaton. The strike on the Durham coalfield was almost total. While this stemmed from a festering dispute with the mine owners, gaining the Charter was incorporated into the strike objectives of many collieries. What James Williams described as a 'colliery war of extermination' followed, sackings of politically active miners extending, it was claimed, even to those found merely carrying Chartist literature.[27] There was street fighting, and seventy arrests, in Sheffield following the dispersal (assisted by dragoons) of a nocturnal rally involving perhaps 7,000 outside the Town Hall. At Dewsbury (where a cap of liberty was planted on top of the market cross) parades assembled at 5.00 a.m. and toured the communities of the Spen Valley to the north over the next three days. Here, however, magistrates' intervention was confined to ordering pubs and beershops to close. In south Wales acts of industrial sabotage and ill-discipline preceded 12 August, but the authorities forbore to enforce a return to work. In Nottingham the Riot Act was read at a rally which then dispersed peacefully. Rather more tumult greeted attempts to disperse turn-outs in Bury, a situation exacerbated by the presence of Metropolitan Police. Manchester's Chartists fanned out along the main roads in the early hours of 12 August, visiting each factory in turn and successfully calling out their workers, in defiance of police and military intervention.[28]

In most of Lancashire, including Manchester, strike action was confined to the Monday alone. In Bury and Heywood, however, 9 out of 10 mills were still out on Wednesday, likewise at Bolton. It was here that the gravest disturbance of the 'holiday' occurred.[29] As at Birmingham in July, much of the responsibility lay with inexperienced local officialdom, anxious to distance itself from a movement with which it had hitherto sympathised (the Mayor, for example, was a former committeeman of the Bolton RA). The situation was further complicated by local Tories' refusal to recognise the authority of the Liberal council (Bolton had been incorporated in 1838), claiming that the pre-incorporation office of the Boroughreeve was still paramount. It was the latter, assisted by township constables, who attempted to police Chartist church attendances, not the newly formed corporation and its constabulary force. But hatchets were buried in anticipation of 12 August and 1,500 special constables were sworn-in in readiness. Shops closed and all normal business was suspended as, throughout the day, marches and open-air meetings occupied the town centre. Next morning the Mayor and aldermen (all, as was common in this period, magistrates) ordered the arrest of the principal speakers from the day before, including John Warden, Bolton's Convention delegate. Soon after their arrest, however, they were rescued by an angry crowd. Serious fighting ensued before they were re-arrested. When crowds rushed the courthouse during the committal proceedings, the Riot Act was read and church bells tolled as a signal for the special constables to assemble.

It was now 4.00 p.m. Prolonged chaos ensued. Shortly after 6.00 a large crowd chased around thirty specials through the streets, forcing them to take refuge in Little Bolton Town Hall. Having smashed all the windows, demonstrators uprooted a lamp post and used it to smash open the main doors. Defending themselves with iron supports wrenched from the ground-floor concert room seats, the specials retreated to an upstairs room and barricaded themselves in. According to one account, moves were made to fire the building. After an extraordinary delay (due to a breakdown in relationships, as much as communication, between the corporation and the military) troops finally arrived at nearly 9.00 p.m. They rescued the specials, but only after firing into the concert room which was thronged with demonstrators and again as the panicking crowd dispersed.

Remarkably, there were no fatalities and only one demonstrator was wounded. But a comfortable Chartist assumption about 'the men of the Army, our brethren, whose interests are the same as ours', was exploded. It had generally been assumed that 'the soldiers would not fight against the people' or if they did that the power of the people would be such that 'soldiers and all would but give us a snack'.[30] Both Newcastle and south Wales Chartists successfully encouraged desertions from the army, but the numbers involved (allegedly 'more than a dozen' at Newport) were small.[31] Furthermore, the strikes coincided with another flurry of arrests, some of which we have already noted. Others included O'Brien on his way home from the Kennington Common meeting, 14 activists in Stockport, 5 members of the Manchester Chartist council, several Chartists for arms' possession in Norwich, local leaders from Ashton and Stalybridge, and the original architect of the grand national holiday himself, William Benbow. After three arrests in Barnsley, the GNU branch seriously considered burning its membership and minute books to avoid incriminating anyone (instead it hid them – it was March 1840 before it was considered safe to retrieve them).[32] In addition Joseph Rayner Stephens's long-delayed trial began as the truncated sacred month ended, while Collins, Lovett and Vincent were each starting a year's imprisonment.

Morale was slipping and with it, for the very first time, Feargus O'Connor's personal authority among the Chartist grassroots. Bradford shoemaker John Jackson, hitherto, he said, one of O'Connor's 'most ardent admirers', spoke for many when he described the 10 August *Star* (reporting the Convention's cancellation of the strike) as 'a sickener' that had come on those 'anxiously awaiting the arrival of the day of deliverance' like a sour and sudden storm.

At Carlisle in late August, Taylor pointedly addressed a rally on the same night O'Connor visited the town, denouncing him for the sacred month fiasco in terms so strident local magistrates sought his arrest.[33] Unsurprisingly, criticism was loudest from Bolton, and O'Connor's response to it was noticeably self-protective. He ducked the charge that he himself had argued that 'the resistance of the people should consist in their abstinence from labour', instead claiming to have taken it on himself to persuade the Convention to pull back from the sacred month as a means of saving the faces of fellow-delegates:

> No man has so many enemies as I have; and in doing my duty, I calculated upon the opportunity which I afforded many of creeping out of a hole ... I am ever among you, and will remain among you until the work is done; but no hunting for false popularity will ever make me place you in a wrong position. For seven long years I have been at my post, not seeking for leadership, but doing duty; for every act I claim credit, but above all, for that which you would hastily condemn, and for which I shall live to receive your thanks. Suppose I was wrong, in your opinion, do you think that so old a friend should not be allowed a fault?[34]

'Whining, wriggling cant', Jackson called this.[35] It was four months before O'Connor went to Bolton and faced his critics. By then the context in which Chartism operated had drastically changed. For the moment, disappointment was palpable. Before even August was over the Prime Minister, Melbourne, felt relaxed enough to appoint Russell Colonial Secretary. His replacement at the Home Office was the flashy but shallow Lord Normanby: the appointment indicated the crisis was over, for even Melbourne doubted Normanby's competence. Soon another Cabinet member, the Attorney-General, would openly boast that Chartism was as good as extinct.[36]

The final days of the Convention, which reconvened in London on 2 September, were unremarkable and sombre. The mood was reinforced by the passing of the Rural Constabulary Act the week before, together with three other bills extending the police forces of Birmingham, Bolton and Manchester. The first of these had been introduced after the Bull Ring riots, the other two following August's 'grand moral demonstration'. Delegates also digested the news from Chester assizes, where sentences had been passed on 6 Chartists, including 18 months' imprisonment for Stephens and 12 for McDouall. Heightening the air of confusion, and even betrayal, Stephens had vociferously rejected Chartism in court. Though he had become attached to Chartism as much through O'Connor's agency as his own volition, most Chartists understandably agreed with the Attorney-General (prosecuting for the Government) that Stephens was desperately 'trying to shake off the Chartists'.[37]

On the third day Taylor pressed for the Convention's immediate dissolution. He was opposed by O'Connor, who suggested a delay until 7 September. Both

were defeated and the assembly staggered on until 14 September, preoccupied mainly by an unedifying squabble about members' expenses. There was
a further defeat for O'Connor when he failed to block a proposal that the
Convention adopt a 'Declaration of the Rights of the People'. (O'Connor argued
that it overthrew established liberties accumulated since Magna Charta.) Its
adoption committed the Convention to – among other things – an elected
magistracy, a non-hereditary House of Lords, the power of Parliament to take
into public ownership any land that had once been 'appropriated to public and
general use' and the abolition of the standing army. (Interestingly, it proposed
no interference in the powers of the monarchy.) It is an eloquent measure of
the nadir in the Convention's reputation by September 1839 that its endorsement of so far-reaching a programme was consistently ignored ever after. It
was indicative also of O'Connor's own waning influence.[38]

Similarly eloquent, and more immediately significant, was the cool reception for O'Connor's argument that a different kind of organisation was needed
'to watch over and carry forward the cause of the people'. O'Connor was clearly
influenced here by the Scottish delegate conference he had attended in mid-
August at which nearly all major Scottish centres had been represented. While
much of the conference had been devoted to the discussion of ulterior measures (repudiating the sacred month as impracticable), the central achievement
was to establish a United Suffrage Central Committee for Scotland (USCCS),
funded in proportion to their memberships by each locality and charged with
promoting and organising Chartism across the country.[39]

Any predilection O'Connor had towards forcing a direct confrontation with
the establishment had evaporated. Recognising that Chartism was in for a long
haul, he wanted the Convention to lay the basis for a similar structure to
Scotland's. By contrast Taylor (conspicuously involved in neither the Scottish
conference nor USCCS) and his principal allies, Harney and Bussey, were
impatient to leave London to go into 'the country where the struggle must
finally take place ... rather than remain here and do nothing'.[40] How far-off that
struggle remained was widely pondered. The events of mid-August suggested
that it was a long way. It was now, and only now, that significant elements
within Chartism took a conspiratorial turn.

## Insurrection

Of its very nature, conspiracy leaves limited evidence. For all the sophistication of its intelligence-gathering about *current* Chartist activities, the State was
conspicuously less successful in accumulating hard information about *intentions*. It is also difficult to distinguish loose talk from firm planning. When
Vincent observed back in March (speaking near Blackwood, Chartism's great
south Wales gathering place) that 'a few thousand of armed men on the hills

could successfully defend them. Wales would make an excellent republic', this was clearly loose talk. Similarly, in April, he suggested taking magistrates and even cabinet ministers hostage. But the advocacy of similar tactics by John Frost a few weeks later – at a meeting also involving Bussey, Lowery and O'Brien – should perhaps prompt pause for thought; so too a poster Frost published after Vincent's arrest, which observed that 'a coal-pit is quite as safe a place for a tyrannical persecutor as a gaol for an innocent Chartist'. Subsequent statements by rank-and-file Chartists, that local worthies should be held underground until they 'got what they wanted', reinforce a sense that more was afoot than empty threats. Yet we can still only speculate.[41]

As the Convention drew to a close surer signs of firm planning can be discerned. The principal evidence, though, emerged well after the event. Prominent were the allegations of William Ashton, the veteran Barnsley radical encountered in chapter 2. In March 1840 he was sentenced to two years' imprisonment for his part in events in Barnsley around 12 August. Once released, Ashton made several allegations concerning O'Connor at a meeting in Barnsley, but was howled down. However, in March 1845 he detailed his charges in private correspondence that found its way into the Chartist press. Central to Ashton's narrative was the claim that a secret meeting, on the day the Convention dissolved, had fixed on the night of 3 November for a co-ordinated rising. Several Convention delegates had been present, including Frost, Taylor, Bussey and Cardo. The focal points for the insurrection were to be south Wales and West Yorkshire, led by Frost and Bussey respectively. Ashton and Bussey then returned to Yorkshire together. During the journey Ashton concluded that Bussey was unable or unwilling to fulfil his role. Soon after, Ashton hurriedly visited France, for reasons that remain opaque; but just before his departure he shared his suspicions about Bussey with the *Star*'s editor William Hill, who undertook to apprise O'Connor and urge him to warn Frost. But O'Connor was in Ireland from 6 October to 2 November, and Hill informed him only on his return, far too late to influence the unfolding tragedy.[42]

What other evidence supports Ashton's assertion that the timing of a general rising was fixed about the time the Convention dispersed? Firstly, in December 1840 Joseph Crabtree of Barnsley told a prison inspector: 'I heard of the expected rise at Newport and that there was to be a rise elsewhere. I got out of the way and went to Glasgow.' In his autobiography, published 1889, a Carlisle weaver recollected that events in November 1839 'were not the isolated and insignificant affairs which many supposed. They were certainly well known beforehand in Carlisle, and if successful might have been imitated in a fashion, but more extensively along the banks of the Tyne and the Wear.'[43] In 1856, Robert Lowery recollected how 'shortly after the Convention dissolved' Dundee's Convention delegate Burns told him that 'some of our leading men … had met to concoct a rising' under the cover of a supper party (ostensibly to honour the Bury delegate Matthew Fletcher). 'I observed that I supposed it was F.O'Connor's scheme, and that he would leave them in the lurch. He answered that they had not let him into their secret, for they did not think he was to be trusted.'[44]

Secondly, a decade later Alexander Somerville, a self-serving patriotic journalist with a knack of getting things half-right, claimed to have been introduced to a Chartist 'Secret Committee of War' in the summer of 1839. Somerville, who had served with the British Legion in the Spanish Civil War of 1835–37, was asked to advise on military matters, but declined. He claimed that his subsequent anti-physical force writings were decisive in averting revolution. Later still, Somerville specified that the secret committee comprised McDouall, Richardson, Taylor and the Polish émigré and LDA member Bartolomiej Beniowski.[45] Taylor and Beniowski (an officer in the Polish rebel army of 1831) were linked as plotters by intelligence reports in August 1839, but the plot had a purely metropolitan dimension and, like much LDA activity, appears stronger on sound than substance.[46]

Thirdly, and more reliable than Somerville because partly corroborated, there are the claims made in 1856 on behalf of the Tory and Russophobe David Urquhart. In the late summer of 1839 Urquhart was seeking to become Tory parliamentary candidate for Marylebone. Following Chartist interruptions at his public meetings, Urquhart met Marylebone's Convention delegate William Cardo. The latter was hugely impressed by Urquhart and introduced him to certain other delegates (one was Warden from Bolton; Lowery and O'Brien may also have been involved). They shared with Urquhart 'a plan for a simultaneous outbreak in the long nights before Christmas' in which 'a Polish emigrant' directed 'military organization … and was to have command in the mountains of Wales'.[47] Though these claims surfaced only in the mid-1850s, a meeting between unnamed Chartists and Urquhart is referred to in a letter of 22 September 1839, written by his friend Pringle Taylor.[48] Urquhart claimed that he, plus a handful of confidants, hurriedly toured the main Chartist centres, successfully dissuading local leaders from participating in the venture. 'I have gone forth single-handed among the towns of England against the Chartist insurrection, and subdued it', he proudly boasted, but 'Frost was missed by half-an-hour'.[49] It seems more probable that these local meetings were primarily to promote Urquhart's distinctive ideas about foreign policy (these achieved some popularity among Chartists in 1839) and that any reference to insurrectionary plans would have been sketchy post-sacred month speculation. Insurrection and foreign-policy issues merged in Urquhart's mind due to his conviction that Russian agents (among whom he claimed Beniowski was prominent) were constantly at work undermining Britain.[50]

Fourthly, we have the account of William Lovett, published in 1876 but pieced together shortly after his release from prison in August 1840 from several unnamed sources (one of them Taylor). In Lovett's version Frost and 'two or three other members of the Convention' agreed on co-ordinated risings in Wales and the north. The Welsh would rescue the imprisoned Vincent and the English would rise for the Charter. This plan was shared with about forty West Yorkshire leaders at a meeting in Heckmondwike, between Huddersfield and Bradford. Someone present agreed, the week before the rising would commence, to enlist O'Connor to lead it. According to Lovett's anonymous source, O'Connor gave the impression that he would readily do so. However, soon afterwards he dispatched George White (the GNU secretary) to dissuade northern localities from rising because Wales would not act; and O'Connor sent the Montgomeryshire delegate Charles Jones 'to assure the Welsh that there would be no rising in Yorkshire, and that it was all a Government plot'.

This account has proved popular with some historians, but it is severely flawed: O'Connor was out of the country, and, while the precision regarding the Heckmondwike meeting seems persuasive, the town was a popular location for regular meetings of West Yorkshire delegates, usually held on the third or fourth Monday of each month. The gathering on 21 October was just such a meeting (and attended by 13 delegates, not 40).[51] Perhaps a decision was made there to send a copy of an unspecified resolution to Blakey of Newcastle and this hints at secret correspondence: Robert Blakey was the proprietor and co-editor of the *Northern Liberator* and Taylor was then on Tyneside (lecturing, he archly said, 'on Chemistry, explaining the nature of explosive forces'). Moreover, a readiness to rise in concert with Wales is clear in the 1882 memoirs of Thomas Devyr, a staff reporter on the *Liberator*. But, equally, the correspondence may have been completely innocent.[52]

The best that can be said for the evidence of an intended *general* rising in November 1839 is this: it was discussed by a small, self-appointed group, mainly Convention delegates, during the late summer, but how detailed their plans were is unclear. There was wide awareness in West Yorkshire, and to a lesser extent in Tyneside and Carlisle (and perhaps Lancashire), of an intended Welsh insurrection and some agreement to act in concert with events there. But most of this evidence is entirely retrospective and much of it shot-through with the settling of personal scores (one of the less attractive features of Chartism from 1840). Chartist arming and the rhetoric of resistance were extensive, but neither in itself constitutes sufficient evidence of insurrectionary intent. More significant was perhaps the sub-divisional reorganisation of Chartist localities, documented on Tyneside, in Lancashire and south Wales, a development that facilitated secrecy and could provide the structure for waging the guerrilla warfare that would follow a successful rising. It was in Wales that this develop-ment was most striking and was most pertinent, for insurrectionary intentions were abundantly and unequivocally in evidence in Newport on 4 November. Events there tragically culminated in the largest number of fatalities of any civil disturbance in modern British history. For that reason, and because of its pivotal place in the history of Chartism, the Newport Rising deserves close attention.[53]

## Newport, 3–4 November 1839

Throughout the autumn, south Wales bubbled with Chartist activity. In early October delegates from across the region appointed seven 'missionaries' to promote the Charter; throughout September and October, influential figures were criss-crossing the region, and making unexplained trips beyond it. Isaac Tippins, for example, a Nantyglo tailor, was absent from work for much of October; Dr William Price of Pontypridd was rumoured to be in Staffordshire and northern England, though he said he would be in London; Frost left Newport for the hills, 3–8 October, was in Lancashire 6 days later, back in Monmouthshire by 19 October and was advertised as speaking in Halifax 2 days after (he failed to appear). The final week of October he mainly spent in Blackwood, closeted for some time with an unknown visitor, 'a tall working man' from northern England. It is possible that this visitor was arguing the need of additional time to prepare for an English rising. According to Lovett, Frost told this visitor that the Welsh would not tolerate delay and he 'might as well blow his own brains out as try to oppose them or shrink back'.[54] We have already noted talk of taking hostages and rescuing Vincent; and even if there was no nationwide plan, many Chartists clearly knew something extraordinary was planned for Newport. Within forty-eight hours of the Newport tragedy, a disaffected employee of Henry Hetherington informed the Home Office of what Charles Jones had told him weeks before: 'it was generally known among the Chartist leaders that an outbreak would take place'. An unknown London Chartist wrote to Taylor: 'The failure there is beyond the comprehension of all here, success seemed so certain.'[55] What happened at Newport was no spontaneous outburst of fury or despair, nor a peaceable demonstration that went tragically wrong: it was the culmination of careful preparation.

Geography is significant to understanding events in Newport on 3 and 4 November. The town was an important port serving the ironworks and coalfield of the Monmouthshire valleys. Early industrialisation in south-east Wales developed mainly in the Glamorganshire towns of Merthyr Tydfil and Dowlais, near the head of the Taff which flows south to Cardiff. Soon after, industry developed in the Monmouthshire valleys to the east: the Rhymney, Sirhowy and Ebbw (which merge at Risca and join the sea just south of Newport), and the Afon Lwyd, which meets the Usk just outside Newport and flows through the town. The valleys imposed a hard logic on the region, dictating the layout of roads, canals and tramways – all converging on Newport – serving the 'black domain' of collieries and ironworks. These valleys and the sides of the hills between them were strung with rapidly expanding communities. An estimated 29,000 were dependent on coal and iron along the Afon Lwyd and the adjoining Clydach; 27,000 in Ebbw Vale (divided into the Ebbw Fach and Fawr at its northern end); at least 20,000 along the Sirhowy; and 11,000 people in the Rhymney Valley. The Taff Valley and its tributaries accounted for around 60,000. Of this total of around 150,000 people, roughly a quarter were industrial wage-earners, of whom around 9,000 set off on the rain-drenched Sunday of 3 November for Newport.[56]

The vast majority came from Monmouthshire rather than Glamorganshire. Not all did so eagerly or even voluntarily: there was extensive coercion. Others joined because not to do so risked being ostracised, regardless of the outcome. The precise objective was known only to a small group. At its heart were Frost, the only national figure involved and until recently a magistrate (the Home Office having revoked his commission for his outspoken Chartism); Zephaniah Williams, a bankrupt former owner of a small colliery, who kept a beershop near Blaina in the vale of the Ebbw Fach; and William Jones, landlord of The Bristol House pub in Pontypool, the main town in the valley of the Afon Lwyd. Closely associated with them were a score or so local leaders. They included Frost's son Henry; Dr Price of Pontypridd in Glamorganshire; John Rees, alias Jack the Fifer, a rootless stone mason from Tredegar near the head of the Sirhowy Valley, who had fought at the Alamo with the Texan People's Army in 1835; and four styled 'captains' – the brothers Edward and Isaac Tippins, Pontypool master shoemaker William Shellard and George Shell, also of Pontypool, an apprentice cabinetmaker whose father was one of the founders of the WMA there.[57]

The full ramifications of the conspiracy and its command chain will never be known but the events of late October and early November are fairly clear. The original plan appears to have been for three co-ordinated marches: one from the Monmouthshire valley heads to capture the market and communication centre of Abergavenny, 25 miles north of Newport; another from the Merthyr area, over the Beacons to capture Brecon; and a third from the remainder of the region on Newport. Had these succeeded, Chartist armies would have been in a position to inflict massive damage on one of the heartlands of the British economy, controlling communications between south Wales and England, and an inspiration to English Chartists to commence local risings of their own.

This ambitious project, however, was abandoned around the last weekend in October, apparently on Frost's personal initiative. At this point Price and most Glamorgan participants dropped out. Williams and Jones redoubled their efforts to stir up the Chartist lodges of Monmouthshire, while Frost stationed himself at Blackwood, halfway up the Sirhowy Valley. Here he received messages and visitors from the region and beyond, including, as we have seen, an agent from northern England who may have been Charles Jones. A meeting of coalfield delegates at Dukestown, at the head of the Sirhowy, on Monday 28 October appears to have refined the plan to march on Newport. However, the thousands of furtive conversations in workplaces, pubs and beershops during the ensuing week were couched in generalised terms of 'Frost's policy' and his promise to secure the Charter within a month.

At a lodge meeting in the Coach & Horses, Blackwood, on Wednesday 29 October, Jones told the assembly to bring torches and candles for a great meeting on the hills the following Sunday; then, a few hours later at Crumlin's Navigation Inn he talked of liberating Vincent and putting Lord John Russell in his place. On the Thursday miners flocked to The Colliers Arms, Nelson, near the Rhymney, to hear from Williams that Frost promised the Charter within three weeks if they accepted his orders. Supporters would be issued a card, recording their number and division: hundreds were sold in pits, iron-works and the now nightly Chartist lodge meetings that week. Not everyone purchased willingly: Richard Arnold, a Blaina puddler was told that 'if any man was at home and could not show his card after they returned from Newport ... they would destroy them like killing toads'. Guns and pikes were brazenly sold in pubs and Chartist lodges, and makeshift pike manufactories were hurriedly set up in Beaufort on the Ebbw Fawr, at the Pillgwenlly marshalling yard in Newport and in at least one cave in the mountains that loomed over the valley heads.[58]

That Wednesday the Superintendent of Police at Tredegar shared with magistrates the intelligence he had gleaned of arming and 'a simultaneous rise throughout the kingdom this week' but it had little impact. 'Here's a triumph to Radical boys!' proclaimed a poem by the Newport WMA's secretary in the *Western Vindicator* of Saturday 2 November: 'may right soon prevail – may wrong ever fail ... Here's working men's Radical cause!/ Here's a triumph to those – who all wrong will oppose,/ In spite of all power and LAWS!' The same issue carried an article, 'The question of resistance to a Government', which detailed 'the right to and the means of resisting oppression to consti-tuted authorities'. A local ironmaster noted uneasily that 'respectable people around ... are completely frightened', pubs and the market were eerily quiet, absenteeism from work was rife, a local business family had fled the district and, he added in a postscript, he had just learnt 'tomorrow evening or Monday is to be the day'. This almost certainly reflected the decisions of a delegate meeting at Blackwood the previous day, which apparently finalised matters. There were to be musters on Sunday night at Blackwood, Dukestown and on Pontypool racecourse. Their objective was Newport. The Chartists would enter under cover of darkness in the early hours of Monday. The soldiery, said Frost, would be asleep or either too frightened or too sympathetic to confront them. Messages to expect dramatic developments were sent on to England, possibly to the north and certainly to Gloucestershire, Somerset and Wiltshire. Then the delegates took tea and went their separate ways. There was now no turning back.[59]

Visiting Newport that weekend was the Sanger family, fairground showmen touring Welsh market towns with an exhibition of comic and topical peep-shows. They intended to stay a week but Newport on Sunday night was awash with rumour and anxiety. James Sanger, a Trafalgar veteran, had seen enough excitement for one lifetime. Hurriedly he hitched up the family's caravan and left, pitching by the roadside some miles out of Newport for what was left of the night. But rest was impossible, so dense were the crowds that milled past the van. For his son George, 14 at the time, the next two hours remained among his most vivid experiences: while his father blocked the doorway, armed with a blunderbuss, his wife huddled the children around her. 'On they came, many of them half drunk, yelling, swearing, and waving great cudgels, a terrifying mass of men.'

Up the valleys the migration had started early on the Sunday. In Tredegar young Henry Hughes was being carried home on his father's back from church: 'it was a dark night with mist and rain and we were meeting troop after troop of Chartists with pikes and rifles on their shoulders and one troop after another would be asking my father if he had met troops ahead ... On that Monday morning there was not a young man or an old man to be seen in the place, only girls and women and they were in great fears and tears.' Blackwood collier's wife Mary Ferriday noticed that her husband William was unusually quiet. Two men called for him about 6.30 p.m. William told his wife he knew neither where he was going nor when he would return. 'I cried aloud and the children as well. Some of them went out after him. He kissed them in the road and then said Goodbye.'[60] William Ferriday had just fifteen hours to live.

So too had 19-year-old George Shell, who left his lodgings in Pontypool around 4.00 p.m. 'I shall this night be engaged in a struggle for freedom', he wrote to his parents, 'and should it please God to spare my life, I shall see you soon; but if not, grieve not for me. I shall fall in a noble cause.' The Lwyd valley contingent was to mass on Pontypool racecourse where over 1,000 pikes were stacked in readiness. An advance party, including Shell, left for Newport early, but some 2,000 were still assembling when William Jones appeared on horseback at 10 p.m. and led them off. There was (and remains) a lack of clarity about the objective of the Lwyd valley men. Were they all to march into Newport from the north? If so their departure was perilously late. Or were some to march north on Abergavenny and, even, Monmouth to release Vincent? Certainly there was widespread intimidation and industrial sabo-tage late on Sunday night and into the early hours of Monday, the timing of which meant that the perpetrators could not possibly be in Newport by dawn. Most dramatically, the huge blast furnaces up the valley were forcibly stopped, enveloping their communities in unaccustomed darkness and causing massive structural damage to the plant as the contents cooled. Those responsible then made their way towards Pontypool, many arriving only after sunrise. There was talk of storming the police station and the home of the Lord Lieutenant to take him hostage, and of marching up to Monmouth once it was confirmed Newport had been taken. Both William Jones and Zephaniah Williams had previously spoken of placards being prepared, to announce the setting up of an 'executive government', with Frost as its president. Clearly, something of the original vision from mid-October had survived: those who directed the rising had considerably more ambitious intentions than simply storming Newport.[61]

The major rendezvous that night was Welsh Oak, downriver from where the Sirhowy and Ebbw meet. As early as 1.00 a.m. some 2,000 were waiting, their numbers constantly augmented by further crowds moving down from other assembly points up the valleys. Chief of these was the mountain that separated Nantyglo and the town of Ebbw Vale, where perhaps 4,000 had assembled under Williams's personal supervision late on Sunday night. Unsurprisingly, many took drink along the way to stiffen resolve and shut out the driving rain. As news of their real objective spread many must have felt massively unprepared.

As the night wore on a sodden army gathered at Welsh Oak. Some were numb with cold and nervousness, some hyper-actively discharged firearms into the air; others were doubtless at prayer. They waited for Frost who was surveying Newport from Cefn, two miles nearer the town. He in turn was apparently waiting for Jones and a sizeable contingent from Pontypool. Some time before 6.00 a.m. he turned back to Welsh Oak and met with Williams. Hazarding that they could take the town without assistance from a Pontypool force, Frost finally led his army, now some 5,000 strong, onto the Newport road around 7.00 a.m.

It was already getting light when they stopped an hour later at the Waterloo pub on the western side of the town. Inside, Frost hurriedly conferred with his lieutenants. Emerging to cheers, 'Jack the Fifer' assembled the marchers into military formation, half-a-dozen or so abreast, a man with a gun at the end of each line. At Malpas on the north side, Jones was waiting with a force of around 2,000. Smaller advance parties from Pontypool, among them George Shell, had joined the main force at Cefn.

It was Frost's column that bore the brunt of the fighting that followed. The original intention had been to enter Newport from the west, sacking the Newport workhouse along the way. The western approach, though, had been selected since both the Welsh Oak and Pontypool columns could meet there. Without the latter it made sense for Frost to enter Newport from the south, for the workhouse had been pressed into use as a barrack for a detachment of the 45th Infantry. Frost's aim was to confront the local authorities and their special constables, a sentiment quite likely hardened by the personal animosity he bore the Mayor and corporation over their treatment of him earlier in the year. It certainly made tactical sense once news had reached him that a number of Newport Chartists had been arrested the previous night and were being held in custody at one of the town's main hotels.

Sunday in Newport had been extraordinary. For every family – like the Sangers – who fled, another arrived in a state of equal alarm from a mining community nearby. That night Mayor Thomas Phillips, having dispatched requests for help to London and Bristol and sent word to neighbouring towns of the impending dangers, selected the Westgate Hotel as a temporary headquarters. All 500 of Newport's special constables were on alert and some raiding parties successfully apprehended known Chartists, either in their homes or heading out of town to join Frost. Phillips, the Riot Act to hand in his pocket, gathered his deputy, Newport's small regular police force and some of the specials at the hotel, where all the arrested Chartists were held. To his credit, Phillips was not looking for violent confrontation and seems to have thought the Chartists were intent only on demonstrating. Only around 8.00 a.m., when the gathering presence of thousands of armed men was at last apparent on the outskirts of the town, did Philips send to the workhouse for an armed attachment to join him.

Thus most of the Chartists who marched into the town-centre shortly before 9.00 may not have known that the Westgate Hotel contained an attachment of thirty-one infantrymen. Conventionally these soldiers have always been presented as young and inexperienced; but it was the 45th Infantry that had savagely suppressed a small-scale rising of agricultural labourers in Kent the previous year – 'the Battle of Bosenden Wood'. While we do not know if these were the same soldiers, Lieutenant Basil Gray, commanding the troops inside the hotel, doubtless recalled that a brother-officer had been killed in the Kentish rising.[62]

Frost's column approached the Westgate Hotel down the hill to its rear. After an unsuccessful attempt to force open the gates into the back yard, the head of the column marched round to the front in the high street. As they did so several specials were seen fleeing away. Gun butts and pikes were used to smash windows and shuttering. Chartists continued to pour into the street as the leading group massed by the entrance portico. There was shouting and chanting. The release of the prisoners and surrender of the Mayor were demanded. A shot was fired, possibly at the retreating specials; but another special who remained inside the building later said that, as he tried to shut the front door on the angry crowd, it knocked into a Chartists' firearm which accidentally discharged.

The exact truth will never be known; but the sound of gunfire and the simultaneous realisation that armed Chartists were pouring into the entrance hall of the hotel (and from there into the rear passage linking the main rooms) prompted the command to load and fire. Phillips and the troops had locked themselves inside the public room at the far-left end of the hotel. Its projecting bay window offered a raised and unhindered view of the high street. As they opened its internal shutters, both the Mayor and a sergeant were wounded by gunshot. But then the soldiers stepped up to the window 2–3 at a time, fired into the crowd, retired and reloaded as others took their places. Chartists from the middle and rear of the column, uncertain what was happening, were still streaming downhill into the high street where they met the continuing fire. As the crowd at last began to flee, the firing stopped, but enraged Chartists inside the now smoke-filled building were wrecking it. So the soldiers opened the door onto the rear passageway. Systematically and repeatedly they fired into the smoke.

'*There* was a dreadful scene', wrote a special constable who remained inside the hotel, 'dreadful beyond expression – the groans of the dying, the shrieks of the wounded, the pallid, ghostly countenances and the bloodshot eyes of the dead, in addition to the shattered windows and passageways ankle-deep in gore.' Outside, those at the rear of the Chartist column fled into the countryside; the rest sought shelter where they could. The streets were littered with abandoned arms: 'Many who suffered in the fight, crawled away, some exhibiting frightful wounds, and glaring eyes, wildly crying for mercy', wrote the editor of the local paper, 'others, desperately maimed, were carried in the arms of the humane for medical aid; and a few of the miserable objects that were helplessly and mortally wounded, continued for some minutes to writhe in tortures, crying for water.'[63]

Around 50 Chartists were seriously wounded and upwards of 22 killed. The exact numbers are unclear, for many endured an uncomfortable journey home to nurse their wounds in private. A number of the dead were privately buried by their families; but 3 days later, under cover of darkness, the authorities buried 10 bodies in unmarked graves. They included William Ferriday, whose wife Mary arrived later 'with an infant in her arms, and in an agony of distress', trying to reclaim or at least see his body; George Shell, who had managed to confront Phillips inside the hotel, was shot several times and took three hours to die; Williams, a deserter from the 29th Infantry (which the 45th had replaced a few weeks previously); and a fourth, William Griffiths, in whose pockets were found a card reading 'No. 5 of H Division' along with a membership card of the Aberdare WMA.[64]

# Chartist lives: John Watkins

Who fought for freedom, more than life?
Who gave up all, to die in strife?
The young, the brave, no more a slave,
Immortal Shell!
That died so well, –
He fell, and sleeps in honour's grave.

They shot him, shot the father's son –
Too soon his honest race was run.
The 'red-coat' fired – poor Shell expir'd.
Freedom! he cried,
He spoke, and died.
He gain'd the freedom he required.

[ ... ]

They laid him in his timeless tomb.
Oh, weep not for his happy doom:
But, on the sod, let's kneel to God,
And may his spirit
Our hearts inherit,
That we may break the despot's rod.

(John Watkins, 'Lines on Shell, killed at Newport',
*Northern Star*, 26 September 1840)

The fate of the leading figures in the Newport rising produced immense outpourings of anger, indignation and emotion from Chartists. Not the least of these were poetic: laments for the dead, tributes to the transported and eulogies to the incarcerated. In 1840 the *Northern Star* published a series of eight 'Sonnets devoted to Chartism' by 'Iota', an alias for one of the Newport rebels. One anticipated the poem above:

Some future bard shall sing thy triumph, SHELL!
And all thy virtues, all thy worth shall tell.
Thy countrymen shall glory in thy name,

> Thy fall reflects upon thy foes a shame
> Which ages shall not wipe away.

Defiance was a common element in all these tributes. Of none was this more true than those, accompanying a mass of flowers, placed anonymously on the rebel graves in Newport churchyard on Palm Sunday, 1840:

> May the rose of England never blow,
> The Clyde of Scotland cease to flow,
> The harp of Ireland never play,
> Until the Chartists gain their day.

Palm Sunday 1841's verse was more defiant:

> Here lie the valiant and the brave,
> They fought a nation's rights to save;
> They tried to set the captives free
> But fell a prey to tyranny!
>
> Yet shall they never be forgot,
> Though in their grave their bodies rot;
> *The Charter* shall our watchword be
> Come death or glorious liberty!*

Poetry mattered to the Chartists, especially after November 1839. Verse, rather than the speakers' platform or journalism, was the safest public space wherein to proclaim revolutionary sentiment. To write, read (especially aloud) or sing verse was also to confront polite culture. It located Chartism within an intellectual and political tradition that extended back to the English Revolution: Milton and Marvell were among the most popular models for Chartist poets (pointedly Andrew Marvell was the only historical subject in the *Northern Star*'s pantheon of portraits). It also located the movement in a vital present. 'It is the workers', one contemporary declared, 'who are most familiar with the poetry of Shelley and Byron.' Chartist poetry consoled, but it also avowedly educated and enervated. To quote the Manchester Chartist Benjamin Stott (a bookbinder):

> Its burden shall cheer the oppress'd and forlorn,
> With the hopes of a happier day.
> It shall waken the slave to a sense of his wrongs,
> And his soul shall delight in the strain;

---

* *NS*, 27 June 1840; placards quoted in (W. Johns) *The Chartist Riots at Newport* (Newport, Johns, second edn, 1889), pp.68–9, and *Midland Counties Illuminator*, 1 May 1841. (It was a Welsh custom to decorate graves on Palm, or 'Flowering', Sunday.)

> It shall tell the poor bondsman what to him belongs,
> And teach him to burst from his chain.*

Chartist poets aspired to greater sophistication than the street balladeers of the time, successfully so. Where broadside ballads stressed pathos and sensationalism,[†] Chartist poetry was a critical vehicle for 'Knowledge, the great Enfranchiser' (the phrase is Thomas Cooper's, Chartism's most significant poet), less a consolatory retreat than a place for debating and representing what the Chartist future could be.[‡] The movement produced a large number of poets, nearly eighty contributing to the weekly poetry column of the *Northern Star* alone,[§] some of whom (Cooper, Allen Davenport, Ernest Jones, J. B. Leno, W. J. Linton, Gerald Massey) continue to command attention.[¶]

John Watkins, who wrote the eulogy to Shell that heads this chapter, is not of this select group. His efforts were more obviously emulative of established poetic forms and authors, and less supple and adroit than the best writing of his peers. But no poet wrote more prolifically in the service of Chartism before 1845. Watkins was also responsible for extensive prose writing (over the signatures 'Junius Rusticus' and 'Chartius', as well as his own) and very likely the *Northern Star*'s 'Chartist Shakespeare' column.[**] He also wrote *John Frost, a Political Play*, a five-act drama in muscular iambic pentameter. For dramatic effect Watkins had Frost's wife oppose Chartism – which was very far from the truth – and Henry Vincent fall in love with one of Frost's daughters, another imaginative, but more plausible, touch. There are passages of striking anger and bitterness in the drama, in which Watkins articulated sentiments as close

---

* F. Engels, *The Condition of the Working Class in England*, ed. W. O. Henderson and W. H. Chaloner (Oxford, Blackwell, 1958 [1845]), p. 273; B. Stott, *A Song of Freedom*, in *Songs for the Millions and Other Poems* (Middleton, Horsman, 1843), p. 83.

† See, for example, *The Last Farewell to England of Frost, Williams and Jones* (Shrewsbury, France, 1840): 'Many a heart will beat in sorrow,/ Many an eye will shed a tear,/ Many an orphan and its mother/ Will lament in Monmouthshire;/ For the third of last November,/ When their fathers went astray,/ Tens of thousands will remember/ The sad disasters of that day.' Quoted in full in R. Palmer, *A Ballad History of England* (London, Batsford 1979), p. 118.

‡ T. Cooper, *Purgatory of Suicides* (London, How, 1845), Book 2, stanza 74, p. 75.

§ See S. Roberts, 'Who wrote to the *Northern Star*?', in O. Ashton et al. (eds), *The Duty of Discontent* (London, Mansell, 1995), pp. 68–70.

¶ For all, except Davenport, see for example I. Armstrong, *Victorian Poetry* (London, Routledge, 1993; and for all, except Leno, see A. Janowitz, *Lyric and Labour in the Romantic Tradition* (Cambridge, Cambridge University Press, 1998). Also T. Randall, 'Chartist poetry and song', in O. Ashton et al., *The Chartist Legacy* (Woodbridge, Merlin, 1999), and 'Poetics of the working classes', of *Victorian Poetry*, special issue, 39:2 (summer 2001).

** Detailed biography and bibliography in *DLB*, vol. 12; also Roberts, 'Who wrote to the *Northern Star*?', pp. 57–8, and Janowitz, *Lyric and Labour*, p. 155.

to open advocacy of revolution in print as any Chartist at this time. Again, it was George Shell who captured his imagination:

> All foes are conquered when we conquer fear,
> As did bold Shell, who braved a bloody bier.
> To gain his rights he took the manliest course –
> The plain straightforward argument of force!
> Vengeance is now our cry. Remember Shell!
> We'll live like him – at least we'll die as well.[*]

All the principal Chartist poets (Jones excepted) were working men. Watkins was not. He took up Chartism at its inception, finding in it the means to give some political coherence to the frustrations he felt about life in the small, conservative, coastal town of Whitby where he lived. Subsequently, he joined the trade of agitation as a full-time Chartist lecturer, author and newsagent in London. This was a radicalised version of the literary career Watkins craved from his late-teens.

He had been born in 1808, the eldest son of the Lord of the Manor of Aislaby, near Whitby, on the North Yorkshire coast. Details of his education are unclear, as are the reasons that persuaded him to abandon a legal career. He scratched a living with his father's support and from publications such as *A Stranger's Guide through Whitby and the Vicinity* (1828). In 1838 Watkins published two *Letters* to the residents of Whitby, 'calling upon them to Release the Town from the Tyranny of Toryism'. 'Nothing is so antichristian as Toryism', opined Watkins, who also compared it to 'devilism'. He was drawn to the radical import of Christianity but it was *The People's Charter* that crystallised his political outlook, remarkably so, given his isolation from the movement's heartlands. Watkins seized on the Charter in a *Third Letter*, published in the late summer of 1838:

> There are about 10,000 inhabitants in Whitby – about 350 of these possess the elective franchise, and an oligarchy, consisting of some 70, rule the rest against their will; that is, make slaves of them ... Labour depends upon capital for employment, and the capitalist will not employ the labourer unless he renounce his birthright – the poor man must choose between slavery and starvation ... Reformers should unite and form a separate communion ... Submit to the laws; but be not slaves of the Tory tyrants that make such laws. Form a branch association with the working men of other towns – procure the People's Charter to be granted, and you can repeal bad laws, and make good ones in their stead.[†]

---

[*]   *NS*, 2 January 1841.
[†]   *Letter to the Inhabitants of Whitby* (Whitby, Forth, 1838); *Second Letter to the Inhabitants of Whitby* (Whitby, Forth, 1838), quotations from pp. 28 and 45; *Third Letter to the Inhabitants of Whitby* (Whitby, Forth, 1838), pp. 10 and 27.

Watkins extended his argument early the following spring in *Five Cardinal Points of the People's Charter*, a forty-page pamphlet of striking force and clarity. Watkins martialled all the arguments in favour of the Charter circulating at this time, with the commonplace exception of equal electoral districts. This was, perhaps, less because he feared that these would swamp Westminster with Irish members than because small parliamentary boroughs like Whitby would almost certainly have been disfranchised. Watkins presented the Charter as completing a political process begun with Magna Charta, creating a democratic, accountable parliament that would cleanse the country of corruption and eliminate 'factious government or class legislation'. Furthermore labour, argued Watkins, is the source of all wealth; it is thus a form of property just like land, with which it should enjoy equal rights. On this ethical and social argument, as much as an abstract one of innate political rights, universal suffrage rests. There was also, however, a religious imperative: 'Charterism is a secondary christianity – Christians must be Charterists.'[*]

There was no tradition of political radicalism in Whitby, and Watkins was only ever a minority voice there. Only thirteen attended the first meeting of its WMA, established by Watkins in February 1839. Undaunted he persevered and by June the Association had a permanent base on the pier which doubled as a Working Men's Chapel. There Watkins preached each Sunday and directed worship with the aid of a booklet of hymns he wrote for the purpose. Services were 'conducted with as much decency and decorum as though the congregation had been in the habit of assembling there for a number of years', reported the *Northern Star*. But in Whitby the appeal of Chartism dimmed with its novelty: by mid-September Watkins was writing bitterly that 'the working men of Whitby are very backward in their own interests, and forward in the interests of their foes. The association here is likely to be suspended for want of support.'[†] Instead, he focused his efforts 30 miles away on Teesside and was almost immediately arrested for a speech at Stockton in which he had called on his audience to fight for the Charter 'like heroes [and] die for it like martyrs'. We saw in the previous chapter how apprehensive Stockton's local establishment was in the face of Chartism: 'The fact is', Watkins told a friend, 'the Stockton Magistrates ... were in a panic and violently prejudiced against all chartists'.

The incident sealed his reputation and was extensively reported. On his acquittal he entered into a public correspondence with Lord Normanby (recently appointed Home Secretary), demanding that he intervene to return property confiscated from Watkins at his arrest. It greatly helped Watkins that

---

[*]  J. Watkins, *Five Cardinal Points of the People's Charter* (Whitby, Forth, 1839), pp. 3 and 30.

[†]  *Yorkshire Gazette*, 2 February 1839; *NS*, 1 June and 14 September 1839.

Normanby, whose seat was near Whitby, could be cast almost as a social equal. Much of Watkins' popular appeal stemmed from his self-presentation as a gentleman 'friend of the people', converted by force of argument to their cause and ready to suffer with them. 'Born the heir of class distinctions', Watkins told readers of *Northern Star*, 'I nevertheless cast off all un-won privileges and flung myself into the ranks to fight my way up with the people.' There were of course several precedents for this, pre-eminently that of Feargus O'Connor (to whom Watkins dedicated *Five Cardinal Points*); and, like O'Connor, there was a strong element of self-promotion in Watkins's political activities. His imprisonment, despite its brevity, was the subject of a five-part account printed in both the *Northern Star* and the *Northern Liberator*. Readers were also treated to poetic 'Lines Written in Prison'.*

Personal ambition motivated Watkins considerably:

> You seem to wonder that I should be a chartist [he wrote to a close friend in January 1840], but if you were in the north we would soon teach you to be one too. Is it not natural that men who do their best to deserve success, and yet find all their efforts frustrated by a cursed system that rewards the undeserving alone – is it not reasonable that such men should be discontented and desire a change? It is this that has made me a chartist.

Subsequent moves in his Chartist career were directly instrumental. He took up the temperance cause, the relevance of which to Chartism he had touched on in *Five Cardinal Points*, and was among the sixty-eight original signatories to an address on teetotal Chartism in the *English Chartist Circular* in March 1842.† When this attracted the wrath of O'Connor (for whom teetotal Chartism implicitly conceded that not all men, in their present condition, were fit to exercise the vote), Watkins trimmed smartly. He moved to London in 1841 to establish a 'depot for the vend of true Chartism'. Watkins had been a large fish in the small pool of North Riding and Teesside Chartism, milking his brief imprisonment to promote a national reputation. But in the capital there was no shortage of more plausible Chartist martyrs, some with radical political careers stretching back to the French Revolution, many of whom had endured substantial periods of imprisonment. Watkins quickly decided that the only route to political eminence lay in promoting O'Connor's vision of Chartism: 'To injure O'Connor is to injure the people', Watkins declared. But he also went much further, as William Lovett later recalled:

> Among the most prominent of our assailants in London was a Mr J.Watkins, a person of some talent … who preached and published a *sermon* to show

---

\*    Watkins to Chambers, 1 April 1840, quoted in J.Watkins, *Life and Career of George Chambers* (London, Watkins, 1841), p.147; *NS*, 25 April 1840 and 5 June 1841.

†    Watkins, *Life and Career*, pp.146–7; *ECC*, 9 (March 1841).

the justice of assassinating us. An extract from this very popular discourse (for it was preached many times in different parts of London) will serve to convey its spirit ... 'Shall traitors to the people – the worst of traitors – be tenderly dealt with, nay courted, caressed? No, let them be denounced and renounced to face the guillotine ... We are in a warfare, and must have martial law – *short shrift, and a sharp cord.'*

The language Watkins used was not merely gratuitously violent; it clearly associated him with 'jacobin' principles. Yet he never fully comprehended that O'Connor was not one of Chartism's jacobins, even though Watkins's career now hinged on his support for the Chartist leader. For the time being all was well.

Watkins married the daughter of a London stonemason and supported his father-in-law's trade union both financially and through his regular column in *Northern Star*. Such was his reputation as a combative O'Connorite speaker that in August 1841 he was appointed full-time lecturer for London by the capital's Chartist delegates. His lectures were the basis of both his almost weekly *Star* column and intermittent political sermons. O'Connor paid Watkins handsomely for this work, although the paper denied rumours that he received as much as £1 per week. Intellectually, Watkins's greatest impact was made with his *Address to the Women of England*, a very full statement of the prevalent male Chartist view of gender relations, which first appeared in the *English Chartist Circular*. Only a man committed to Chartism was worthy of a woman's love. Her natural sphere was the home, not the world of work outside it, creating a place of contentment wherein her husband would find solace and refreshment from the rigours of earning a wage to support his family. Few Chartists were prepared to concede that women as well as men should receive the right to vote. Watkins's view was that the vote should be given to single adult women but not to any wife, for she and her husband were one. (In *Five Cardinal Points* he had argued that wives were their husband's property.) Although attacked by female Chartists for condescension, the *Address* was influential and was quickly reprinted in pamphlet form. A clear measure of the esteem in which it was held came in 1842 when Sheffield Chartists collected pamphlets to send to the Irish Universal Suffrage Association: they sent 250 copies of *What Is a Chartist?* and *Hints about the Army*, but no fewer than 1,000 of Watkins's *Address*.†

Other indicators of Watkins's popularity were his election by London Chartists as secretary to the appeal committee (1841–42), to aid the imprisoned Bronterre O'Brien, and the testimonial organised in July 1842 by City of London

---

*    W. Lovett, *Life and Struggles of William Lovett, in His Pursuit of Bread, Knowledge, and Freedom* (London, Trübner, 1876), p. 251; *NS*, 1 May 1841.

†    *NS*, 21 August 1841, 29 January, 9 July, 17 and 24 September 1842; *ECC*, 1:13 (April 1841).

Chartists when Watkins was ill (Feargus O'Connor headed subscriptions with a donation of 10 shillings). However, Watkins lacked a personal following where it mattered most, among the Chartists of the industrial north, and his next course of action – which was publicly to oppose O'Connor – was a disaster. We shall see in chapter 8 that the years 1842–43 were beset with difficulties for the National Charter Association (NCA), founded in 1840 to place Chartism on a more secure organisational footing. Watkins's opposition began tentatively in November 1842 with the pronouncement that the temporary executive appointed to manage the NCA was undemocratic. Early the following year he 'earnestly entreated' O'Connor 'not to give pain to the Chartists by calling them "his party"' and strongly criticised O'Connorite members of the executive, even calling Peter McDouall 'a swindler'.

That the accounts of the NCA were in disarray was never disputed. O'Connor, however, was swift to exempt the executive from personal culpability and atypically (for his policy as proprietor was seldom to interfere in editorial decisions) criticised the editor of the *Northern Star* for publishing Watkins's attack. O'Connor reserved his strongest words for Watkins's attitude to the Manchester Chartist John Leach, president of the NCA. A former handloom weaver, Leach had been a factory operative until sacked for resisting wage cuts in 1839. Despite persistent poverty, O'Connor emphasised that Leach had repeatedly donated to Chartist funds 'money freely given to him'. The implication was clear: Watkins was carping unfairly against Chartists less fortunate, economically and socially, than himself.[*]

Watkins was far from alone in attacking O'Connor. A central segment of the evidence for the Newport Rising being part of a national conspiracy derives from allegations first made public in 1845, that O'Connor was complicit in the affair. If Watkins knew anything that might have compromised O'Connor, uncharacteristically he made nothing of it. His allegations centred on issues of personal trust and debts, moral and financial, he claimed O'Connor owed him. Watkins soon learnt the hard way that no one within Chartism was bigger than O'Connor. He was compromised by his earlier exaggerated attacks on O'Connor's critics, in defence of which he could only plead he had 'regarded him as a personification of the Cause'.[†]

Cut off by his earlier behaviour from Lovett, the natural focus of non-O'Connorite Chartism in the capital, Watkins was forced to make his own way. The medium he chose was a journal, the *London Chartist Monthly Magazine*, the first issue of which appeared in June 1843. However, it was not a propitious time to launch a new Chartist journal, while the monthly magazine was

---

[*]  *NS*, 12 November 1842, 28 January and 4 February 1843.

[†]  *John Watkins to the People, in Answer to Feargus O'Connor* (London, Watkins, 1844), p. 4.

a relatively untried format in radical publishing. It failed after four issues. Elsewhere, Watkins characterised O'Connor as 'the chief stumbling-block in our way to the Charter', adding that he 'retreats under cover of the *N——S——*, where, like the cuttle fish, he hides himself under a cloud of ink'. Two pamphlets followed, *The Impeachment of Feargus O'Connor* (1843) and then *John Watkins to the People* (1844), its title page adorned with a quotation from *Macbeth*: 'This tyrant, whose sole name blisters our tongue, was once thought honest.' Watkins followed these with a steady stream of articles for *Lloyd's Weekly Newspaper*, denouncing the Chartist leadership in general and O'Connor in particular. His appearances at political meetings were now sporadic, the last of them in April 1848 when he turned his venom on O'Brien.[*]

It was an unedifying end to a Chartist career that had begun with such engaging enthusiasm ten years before. Watkins continued to move in radical and literary circles but, in keeping with his status as a man of independent means, shifted towards the political centre. In 1849, his first wife having died, he married the daughter of Ebenezer Elliott, a Sheffield businessman who had been an early supporter of Chartism but had broken away over its stance on the Corn Laws. Watkins's biography of his new father-in-law was dedicated to the Tory statesman Robert Peel. The couple enjoyed a comfortable home in Clapham Rise, from where, describing himself as a 'Gentleman', Watkins made a will in August 1850. He died in 1858.[†]

John Watkins is not an appealing figure. An exaggerated taste for controversy and self-aggrandisement, not to mention his intolerance of those with whom he disagreed, so detracted from his reputation as a capable and, occasionally, even gifted writer that histories of Chartism have paid scant attention to him. Even Gammage, who passed-up few opportunities to discredit O'Connor, barely glanced at Watkins.[‡] Chartism, however, was a broad church, embracing schemers and careerists as well as idealists and romantics. Watkins is significant for the intellectual contribution he made to Chartism up to the early 1840s, especially through his poetry. *Lines to Shell, Killed at Newport* typifies the reactions of committed Chartists to the events of November 1839. And Watkins's criticisms of O'Connor helped prepare a wider hearing for others with more serious charges to lay.

---

[*]  *Lifeboat*, 16 Dec 1843; *NS*, 15 April 1848; *DLB*, vol.12.

[†]  J.Watkins, *Life, Poetry, and Letters of Ebenezer Elliott, the Corn-Law Rhymer* (London, Mortimer, 1850); National Archives, Kew, PROB, 11/2263/228, John Watkins.

[‡]  R.G.Gammage, *History of the Chartist Movement, 1837–54* (Newcastle upon Tyne, Browne, 1894), pp.261 and 267.

# CHAPTER FIVE

# November 1839–January 1840: After Newport

## Reaping the whirlwind

In Newport the full enormity of events was quickly apparent to all concerned. The *Monmouthshire Merlin* spoke for many when it speculated that, but for the torrential rain late on Sunday, 'the attack would have been made in the night, instead of the morning: it must have been successful, and flaming houses would have proclaimed the town's doom'. No air of triumphalism greeted the insurgents' dispersal. It was universally feared that Chartist bands would regroup in the hills and attack again. Around noon that fateful Monday, the wounded Mayor sent a hurried dispatch to Bristol, predicting a renewed assault the town would be unable to repulse. On Tuesday night, and several times more in the ensuing weeks, large numbers assembled up Ebbw Vale, threatening to descend on Newport. 'I am glad and thankful to let you know we are all alive. I did not expect we should have been alive here now', wrote one resident on Wednesday, 'we did not dare go out, nor try to make our escape, for the whole town was expected to come down.'[1] It was Tuesday before news from Newport reached the region's other major centres, where large groups of workmen hung around the streets or were glimpsed ominously in the surrounding hills. On Saturday the *Western Vindicator*, under the headline 'REVOLUTION IN WALES!', glossed over what had happened in Newport; its reporter claimed 'by this time, I doubt not, Brecon is besieged' and that Monmouth was now 'the principal object'. Across south Wales fear was palpable. It took weeks to disappear.

But the leading figures in the rising knew all too well the scale of their defeat. The fighting had not long subsided when the agitated figure of Frost was glimpsed, his face engulfed in tears, rushing away from Newport. He was arrested that night at the home of a Chartist printer where he had crept to get food and a change of clothing, sodden and exhausted after a day spent hiding in a coal truck. He and the printer had with them seven pistols, powder flasks 'and an immense quantity of bullets'. In the fields around Newport and up the valleys disconsolate marchers, some wounded, made their way home. The more fortunate hitched rides on the trams, the tracks for which they had used as roadways into Newport just twelve hours before. William Jones was arrested, brandishing a pistol, in woodland in Ebbw Vale several days later. In his pocket was a pamphlet celebrating the Llanidloes rioters. Zephaniah Williams was discovered in Cardiff Bay on 23 November, aboard a ship about to sail for Portugal. He was unarmed but was carrying over £100, mostly in gold sovereigns. In all 125 were arraigned for trial; but the total initially arrested, though unclear, was far higher. Large numbers were detained a few days and then released without being charged. These arrests were partly precautionary and partly intimidatory: many rumoured to have been involved or merely away from home on 4 November were arrested. William Roberts, the Chartist solicitor from Bath (and Frost's legal adviser), was arrested and detained for forty-eight hours on being seen in Blackwood in the company of Frost's daughters.[2]

The authorities, however, faced a severe shortage of accommodation for prisoners. The Newport workhouse was pressed into use as a makeshift prison, the symbolism of which was not lost on Chartist supporters. The situation was eased by a government decision to try all serious cases within weeks by a special commission, rather than wait until the spring assizes. Once informal and summary justice had run its course and a number of sentences for public order offences handed out, the actual number of prisoners committed to appear before the commission was whittled down to some sixty. At Monmouth Courthouse on 11 December 'true bills' (cases to answer) for high treason were found against 16 prisoners and, for a range of other offences (sedition, riotous assembly, conspiracy, burglary), against 24 more. Trials were to begin on 31 December, the first for high treason since 1820 when the Cato Street conspirators had been sentenced to death by hanging and their bodies thereafter decapitated (a vestige of the prescribed punishment of hanging, drawing and quartering).[3]

A feeling of numbed incredulity assailed Chartists on learning the news from Newport. For most it was totally unexpected, for the few aware of the wider conspiracy, 'most extraordinary and unaccountable', to quote one London Chartist, 'beyond the comprehension of all here, success seemed so certain'.[4] Few newspapers were in a position to report the tragedy quickly: at least one that did claimed the Chartists had captured Newport. O'Connor, whose boat from Dublin had docked in Liverpool on 3 November, spent the following two days in, first, Manchester and then Oldham, where he heard the news from Wales. On arriving in Leeds the day after, O'Connor went straight to the *Northern Star* offices. Only then did he discover the calamitous truth: the editor William Hill had known something of the conspiracy for several weeks but had failed to do anything about it. Despair, incredulity and panic ensued.

One indicator of this was the *Star* of 9 November, notable for a roaring silence. The front page led with three stories: O'Connor's visit to Oldham; plans to establish a trades' hall in London; and a 'radical tea drinking' in Manchester to celebrate Henry Hunt's birthday. Inside, reference to Newport was relegated to the second editorial, blaming the Government for 'the fierce yell of men rendered desperate by tyranny', and to a short report on page 6 concocted from other newspapers. On the back page further second-hand reports appeared beneath a terse announcement that they were 'accounts of some seemingly mad and ill-concerted hostile movement in Wales'. O'Connor was floundering and the paper with him. Coverage in the *True Scotsman* and *The Charter* was noticeably more extensive. The following Saturday, the *Northern Star* played down the extent of events in Newport, claiming them to have been no more than a riot involving at most 2,000 protesters, while O'Connor resumed his regular column with an appeal for funds to secure the best possible lawyers to defend those involved.[5]

To make sense of the wider ramifications of Newport and the events that followed, it is necessary to unravel what Hill actually knew. The south Wales insurrection was originally to have coincided with at least two other risings, in Yorkshire and on Tyneside. However, a failure of nerve in Yorkshire led to the Welsh acting alone. As we saw in chapter 4, this Hill knew from Ashton of Barnsley, who had been party to conspiratorial discussions among certain Convention members in late September. Hill may not have known of the Tyneside dimension. However Dr John Taylor subsequently told Lovett that he was in Newcastle at the time, 'preparing my men for some move without telling them what'. Taylor also asked William Burns, a Scottish Convention delegate privy to the wider conspiracy, to join him on Tyneside where several hundred armed Chartists waited on a signal from Newport. On the Tuesday morning, enraptured by erroneous reports in *The Times* that Frost was 'in possession of South Wales at the head of 30,000 men', Newcastle Chartists 'met in exultant groups' and posted the proclamation: 'The hour of British freedom has struck.' A woman very close to Taylor wrote to him the following week of her house 'being besieged by persons enquiring for you – and they all express their surprise that your name was not more prominently forward in the late movement'.[6]

When he spoke to Hill, Ashton had been *en route* to France, suspecting (correctly) that the designated Yorkshire co-ordinator Peter Bussey would fail to act. Ashton urged Hill to warn O'Connor and tell him to alert Frost. Bussey may have lost the stomach for a fight (Ashton's view) or believed that insufficient time was available to act effectively. In 1845 Ashton claimed that a jealous O'Connor deliberately engineered Frost's humiliation by failing to warn him of Bussey's perfidy, instead sending George White round the West Riding to halt preparations. By 1876, when Lovett published his third-hand account of the affair, the tale was so garbled that he blamed O'Connor for both encouraging the conspiracy and backing out, sending White into Yorkshire and Charles Jones into Wales to cancel everything. Lovett was no friend of O'Connor and little confidence can be placed in this: Jones was almost certainly in London and O'Connor most definitely in Ireland.[7]

Nonetheless, O'Connor's absence at this crucial time looked suspicious and needs explanation. He may well have anticipated that, following the failure of the sacred month and the slide in the Convention's reputation, Chartist frustration would boil over into confrontation with authority somewhere; if so he may have judged it expedient to absent himself. However, in July he had been found guilty of publishing in the *Star* a criminal libel against certain Poor Law authorities, but sentencing had been postponed. One reason for his visit to Ireland (where he maintained a home on what remained of the ancestral estate) was to arrange his financial affairs, in anticipation of a severe fine. O'Connor was impetuously generous (and had to be to maintain the gentlemanly reputation on which his leadership of Chartism partly depended), but he was far from wealthy. He also owed money to a banker. A complex arrangement of secured loans and remortgaging was needed. The visit was necessarily at short notice because until 20 September he could not predict when the Convention would close. It was logical, once in Ireland (for the first time since 1836), to make the visit a lengthy one. O'Connor was a curiously sensitive man, acutely aware of status and reputation. Apart from consolidating his precarious finances, he felt keenly the need to confront O'Connell, who had recently claimed that O'Connor so lacked influence in his native Ireland he dared not return.[8]

O'Connor's absence from Britain in October 1839 intensified the vacuum created by extensive arrests and the demise of the Convention. Chartism's most effective communicator and unifying force was absent precisely when his personal authority was most needed to hold the movement together. Burns' story, that the Convention's conspiratorial circle did not trust O'Connor, has the ring of truth: plans for concerted risings would probably have been laid even had he remained in England.[9] It is inconceivable, though, that O'Connor would have sat on the knowledge – as Hill did – that Frost would be isolated and exposed in leading a Welsh rising. Henceforward, O'Connor's relationship with Frost would always be tinged with the poignant knowledge that he had unwittingly abetted the disastrous outcome at Newport; and he could never explain the situation without jeopardising colleagues and exposing Chartism to the damaging charge that it was an insurrectionary movement.

The situation called for all O'Connor's reserves of energy and resilience. His interpretation, and the *Northern Star*'s, was that the Whig Government was complicit in the Newport Rising. At the very least it had ignored warnings that continued obduracy in the face of Chartism's legitimate demands would end in violence. Additionally, it was darkly hinted, the Whigs were 'the proximate as well as the remote authors ... the unsuspecting confidence of patriotic men has been abused to their destruction by the practised, hired, bloodhounds of a murderous faction'.[10] There is absolutely no evidence to suggest that Newport was the result of a government plot; but paid informers had overstepped the murky line separating spy from *agent provocateur* before. O'Connor's position, perfectly compatible with condemning the use of violence for political ends, was widely shared. The *True Scotsman* set out the argument for 'remote authorship' especially cogently:

> We have to look below the heaving surface to discover the cause of the late convulsion. We tell the Whigs and Tories they are its cause. They were deaf to the voice of the people; and, as they sowed the wind, they must now reap the whirlwind. They have set justice at defiance, and its attendant avengers are now at their door ... Whilst we admit that the people do not act wisely in breaking out into civil convulsion, they would never be guilty of such conduct were they justly treated, and, therefore, on Whig and Tory, the foes of freedom, do we directly charge the high crime of maddening the people into a revolution, whose fault is but secondary, whilst that of their foes is primary.[11]

The Newport trials therefore assumed huge significance: 'look upon the approaching Welsh trials as a contest between the Government and the people', Chartists were told. O'Connor knew that defence counsel of the very highest calibre was required. Swiftly he organised an appeal to meet the costs, donating the profits from the *Star* of 21 December (its price increased to 5½d) to the fund. Without the Convention, the paper was the only medium through which a national campaign could be managed. After the difficult editions of 9 and 16 November, the *Northern Star* regained its stride. O'Connor raced round northern England raising funds, an experience which reinforced his conviction that a permanent secretariat was needed to maintain Chartism. The immediate objective, however, was a co-ordinated mass agitation if (or rather, it appeared, when) Frost and his colleagues were found guilty. In the *Star* of 23 December O'Connor argued passionately for 'the absolute necessity of immediately calling a new convention', a call echoed in Scotland.[12] Realistic Chartists knew they needed to sway public as well as official opinion if appeals for clemency were to prevail.

In Wales, as an anxious November subsided into dark winter, the mood of the political establishment brightened. Thomas Phillips, Mayor of Newport, having recovered from the wounds sustained in the fighting inside the Westgate Hotel, was widely lauded: he was presented with a purse of 2,000 sovereigns by the grateful citizenry while nationally the State drew him to its heart, being made a freeman of the City of London and on 9 December knighted by the Queen. Almost as significant, the rigid etiquette of the Court was overturned and Phillips was invited to dine privately with Victoria and her Privy Councillors.[13]

O'Connor's call for a new convention was ostensibly heeded when just such a body assembled in London on 19 December, prefaced by a Borders Convention (with delegates from Wales, Edinburgh and West Yorkshire) earlier that month. The London convention lacked both status and authority, and its remit was simply to organise a campaign to support the Welsh prisoners. Its membership was haphazardly assembled from Bolton, Bradford, Hull, Newcastle, Nottingham, Surrey, Sheffield and Marylebone.[14] O'Connor initially agreed to be Dewsbury's delegate but, though in London for the first of the three weeks it sat, never attended. For this new convention was not what it seemed. This was the point at which Beniowski, hitherto 'particularly anxious to know when his services will be required', figured prominently in Chartist conspiracy as Marylebone's delegate, underlining that Ashton's, Urquhart's and Lovett's accounts of Newport's evolution confused their narratives with subsequent events in December and January.[15]

## The January risings

Not all Chartists accepted O'Connor's approach to the trials of the Newport rebels. 'What for did they no tak t' th' hills and stand it out like men?' was the sentiment Lowery recalled among pot-room strategists at the time. In the week after the rising, a covert meeting in the home of a Halifax Chartist elected a delegate to liaise with other localities with a view to 'going to work, and to do it in a better fashion than it had been done in Wales'. On 15 November William Cardo, a central figure in Urquhart's narrative, was arrested in Newport, outside the Westgate Hotel. He claimed simply to be trying to 'get the whole transaction and truth about the late Riots'. He told the landlord: 'No reliance can be placed on the reports in the lying newspapers.' Supposed sightings of Beniowski and Taylor in Newport about the same time fuelled suspicions. Officials could prove no intention to make mischief, however, so Cardo was simply put onto the London mail coach next day. (Within days he was at Taylor's side in Cumberland.)

Beniowski's presence in Wales is supported by intelligence received in London on 16 November, that 'Major Beniwisk went down to survey the country'. Its main thrust, though, was that a Brick Lane baker named Joseph Williams was receiving provincial mail on behalf of a 'council of three', directing a conspiracy whose aim 'is to fire property, the shipping in the River and Docks, to kidnap the principal men of the State'. The report continued that Williams, Cardo, Beniowski and Charles Neesom had recently addressed a meeting at Bethnal Green Trades' Hall, a regular LDA meeting place. A simultaneous rising in London, Manchester and Newcastle on the eve of whatever day Frost might be

executed was openly discussed and funds collected for the purpose. Shortly afterwards Neesom visited Yorkshire, ostensibly to ascertain 'how far the working
classes are disposed as regards numbers to unite for the *People's Charter*'.[16]

O'Connor had more than an inkling of what was going on, for he publicly
challenged Neesom's intentions. He also inserted a cryptic announcement
in the 'To Readers and Correspondents' column of the *Northern Star* on 23
November:

> To the Dewsbury people – I know no more of the matter than the man in
> the moon. I never even heard of it till Monday last. I had not seen George
> White for more than two months. I had neither hand, act, nor part in the
> foul trick played upon the people. They will have no difficulty in putting the
> saddle upon the right horse.

The reference to White echoes Ashton's later erroneous claims about O'Connor's
role in Newport. It was actually Bussey who had sent White out to cancel the
Yorkshire insurrection planned to coincide with Newport's. 'The right horse'
could only indicate Bussey, by then bound for America and the subject of
a ribald ballad sung on Bradford's streets, alleging for good measure that
'Equality Peter' had decamped with local Chartists' funds.[17] Evidence implicating O'Connor in conspiratorial networks is thin and unreliable (he was said
to have promised £500 to a Chartist 'Council of War' according to an anonymous London informer); but he was certainly aware of them and therefore kept
a discrete distance from the Newcastle, Manchester and Yorkshire delegate
meetings in early December where plans were discussed. But there was some
dialogue between O'Connor and leading conspirators, for on 8 December John
Taylor wrote to a close female friend:

> Matters are coming to a crisis, and that in a short space ... It is said your
> Irish Friend O'Connor, has proved himself the coward his enemies always
> called him, and having before betrayed the men of England in the matter of
> the strikes has now refused to take part with the men of his own country
> (Yorkshire) – he is agitating for money to pay lawyers, as if money could
> save Frost when he knows every Lawyer would give ten years Briefs to hang
> him, if it is to be done at all, other means must be used and the Chartists
> are not worth the name of men if they don't try them.[18]

Taylor added that 'the Pole has not gone to Wales' and hinted that a date
around Christmas would be selected for the rising. This was plausible. Bradford
magistrates received information on 17 December that the rising was planned
for the 27th and that the London convention would give the final signal. Textile
mills would be set alight at strategic points to divert troops. A Manchester
source suggested Yorkshire and Lancashire would rise at the end of the month,
a situation Napier considered sufficiently serious to warrant visiting Bradford
personally just before Christmas.[19]

A steady background noise of belligerent restiveness accompanied all this. A new edition of Macerone's *Defensive Instructions* appeared. A purported plan to fire Nottingham barracks arrived anonymously in Napier's post ('a trick to make us fidgety', he concluded). Caltrops and fireballs were manufactured in Sheffield, the latter tested on a church in Bramhall Lane on 25 November; fireballs were also made in Nottingham where gunpowder was openly on sale. Newport had done nothing for the nerves of English JPs and Napier observed that in Birmingham, Bolton, Bradford and Carlisle 'magistrates ... settled that their town was the head-quarters of Chartism, which was not true. Manchester is the place.' The latter is highly doubtful, but it was where northern delegates held a secret meeting during the second week of December. Taylor detailed the preparations he was making in Cumberland: he 'had 900 men ready to rise well-armed and well fit up in every respect and that he had bought 1000 shirts for his men at 2/6d each, with 2 pockets for ammunition at the breast and a belt for pistols or sword'. In early January there were several incidents in which lone sentries and soldiers were fired on. There were rumours that London Chartists were acting in league with French radicals and that the judges would be assassinated on their way to Frost's trial.[20]

O'Connor had difficulty living quietly with the knowledge an English Newport might materialise. When he wrote the above, Taylor may well have just seen the previous day's *Star*, containing O'Connor's caution 'against those who give exaggerated accounts of the spirit of one locality to the people of another locality ... Our enemies cannot openly beat us, but our friends may secretly do it.'[21] However, sometime around Christmas a deputation from the London convention called at the hotel where O'Connor was staying preparing Frost's defence. They chided him for his non-attendance and asked outright what he would do if Frost was convicted. Allegedly O'Connor replied that 'he would place himself at the head of the people of England, and have a b——y r——n' to save Frost. Four years later, when all this became a matter of uncomfortably public debate, O'Connor claimed only to have said he'd risk his own life sooner than see Frost hanged.

Whatever he said, the deputation left with the distinct impression that he was ready to fight: this was the information given to West Yorkshire emissaries at the end of the month, when the rising was fixed for 12 January. By then O'Connor was in Monmouth (he attended the Newport trials throughout). So an LWMA member, Henry Ross, well-known to O'Connor from their time in the CNA, was sent to apprise him of arrangements. Ross told him that Beniowski would be the Chartists' 'commander-in-chief', on account of his experience and skill as an officer in the field; but, once the rising was over, he would be shot since his colleagues considered him 'a dangerous and ambitious man'. O'Connor subsequently denied giving Ross any impression that he was committed to joining the venture; Lowery, Newcastle's delegate to the

December convention, later claimed Ross's visit was simply to ask O'Connor to pay delegates' travel expenses.[22]

Tuesday 31 December, the date set for Frost's trial, was fast approaching. If O'Connor had indicated that he would lead a rising, this may have been because he calculated that Frost would actually be acquitted. High treason, a contentious and seldom-tested area of the law, is a shorthand for a cluster of legislation. There were four counts in the indictment against Frost: two for 'levying war against her Majesty in her realm', one for 'compassing to depose the Queen from her royal state and dignity'; and one for 'compassing to levy war against the Queen with intent to compel her to change her measures'. This left considerable margin for reasonable doubt, an issue pursued relentlessly by Frost's lawyers during the nine-day trial. Privately, they told O'Connor their belief was that Frost would not be convicted. They discredited some Crown witnesses, forced the prosecution to abandon others, and constructed an important technical argument concerning the communication of details about prosecution witnesses to the defence team. The Government's senior legal officer, Attorney-General Sir John Campbell, was unimpressive. When, on Wednesday 8 January, the Chief Justice finally summed up the case he was widely understood as directing the jury to return a 'not guilty' verdict. 'To my utter astonishment and dismay', Campbell wrote that night, 'Tindal summed up for an acquittal.' As the jury retired, Campbell held a hurried meeting of his team 'to consider what was to be done upon the acquittal, and we agreed that there was no use in prosecuting the others for treason'. Suddenly they were interrupted by a messenger. The jury had needed scarcely thirty minutes to reach a unanimous verdict.[23]

Their verdict was 'guilty', with a recommendation for clemency. Sentencing was postponed until all trials were concluded. In subsequent days the trials of Williams and Jones reached the same conclusion. Other insurgents changed their pleas to 'guilty' in the hope of less severe sentencing. Lesser cases of riot and conspiracy were briskly despatched by the court in a few hours while in several cases Campbell unexpectedly dropped all charges. Inevitably this led to suspicions that, having obtained the verdicts it wanted in the key cases, the Government was content to temper severity with lenience and that this was a tacit admission of the overall ambiguity of the evidence. There were thus good grounds for hoping clemency would prevail when the court reassembled to sentence the prisoners. All over Britain Chartists leapt into action to secure their liberty. The majority, co-ordinated by O'Connor and the *Northern Star*, chose petitioning.

A minority, however, chose that moment to implement the hitherto inchoate plans for an English insurrection. The plans for a rising on 12 January were apparently confirmed when delegates from northern England met in Dewsbury on 28 December. O'Connor later claimed that soon afterwards James Arran of Bradford and Richardson from Manchester asked him to prepare to travel to Dewsbury and 'take command': but it is impossible to square this with O'Connor's movements, unless they travelled to Monmouth to do so. (For what it is worth, O'Connor claimed his reply was that he would never 'command troops that I did not marshal myself'.) Another near-contemporary account refers to O'Connor's 'betrayal of the Dewsbury Chartists' but then locates this in the days immediately before Newport – further evidence of how inextricably muddled the evolution of the Welsh and subsequent English risings became in the minds of contemporaries.[24]

O'Connor stayed in Monmouth for the trials of the other Newport prisoners. Nevertheless, there was a widespread expectation in Yorkshire that the *Northern Star* would, on Saturday 11 January, appear with a section printed in red type as a signal that the uprising should commence. It did not, but it *did* carry an editorial denouncing all plots and a call to 'beware of damaging the cause of Frost and his associates ... by any outbreak of physical violence'. This helps explain why the risings in England in the early hours of 12 January were singularly limp affairs. However, there were also sharp differences between the willingness to contemplate insurrection in England and south Wales. In Lancashire there was no more than a mere flicker, evident mainly in the actions of influential local moderates to ensure the region remained quiescent. In Nottingham, Napier stepped up patrols in response to rumours and encountered armed 'Chartist sentinels' on the streets though they 'offered no violence'. In Newcastle barely a tenth of an intended muster of 700 armed Chartists turned up. They were immediately sent home by the *Northern Liberator's* staff reporter Thomas Devyr, who, however, had to face down a death threat from one of their number who wanted to carry out an arson attack on Alnwick Castle instead.

This hothead was Robert Peddie, an Edinburgh staymaker who had recently arrived on Tyneside in the course of a brief and mercurial career as a Chartist agitator. In Dewsbury there was gunfire and signal balloons were sent up and answered from two nearby villages. The disturbance petered out when one balloon caught fire. Gunfire was heard in Bradford and, according to one account, the road between Bradford and Halifax was 'completely filled with men having torches and spears with them'. Bradford magistrates fully expected a rising that night but nothing untoward happened. In Barnsley a large crowd of armed Chartists did gather but, finding the Yorkshire Yeomanry on patrol and hearing nothing of any rising in Sheffield, they dispersed.[25]

However, Sheffield was the location of a serious disturbance that night. Its leading militant Chartist, Samuel Holberry, had been in close contact with various centres during the preceding weeks, including Barnsley, Bradford, Dewsbury and Nottingham. Closely guarded class meetings were held in various houses across the town. If the testimony of arrested Chartists who subsequently turned Crown evidence was true, then the Sheffield element of the West Riding conspiracy was relatively well equipped. In addition to the ubiquitous caltrops, daggers and pikes, 'Boardman said he had a thousand rounds of Ball Cartridges – James Marshall said he had about 400 rounds – I said I had about 400 rounds, Birks said he had but a few, Holberry said he had a deal [of] Hand Grenades and if I am not mistaken he said 12 dozen and a quantity of fire balls', recollected iron-turner Samuel Thompson of a conversation among leading conspirators the previous Friday.

Thompson, Boardman, Marshall and Birks were leaders of four of the eight sections into which the Sheffield conspirators were divided, with Holberry at their head. (In addition there were Attercliffe and Rotherham contingents.) Five section leaders claimed to be able to muster 224 insurgents between them, a figure which if both accurate and indicative of the size of the other groups (bold suppositions) would imply a total strength of around 450. Broadly similar figures are mentioned for Dewsbury, Bradford and Barnsley. On even the most sanguine estimates, had it gone to plan the West Riding mobilisation of 12 January 1840 would never have matched Newport's.[26]

The instrument of the conspirators' downfall was James Allen, landlord of the Rotherham pub where the leaders met. They had taken Allen, 'an ardent Chartist', into their confidence, not suspecting his sympathies stopped short of insurrection. Allen shared what he knew of their plans with Rotherham's Chief Constable, who encouraged him to take a full part in the proposed rising. In the early afternoon of 11 January, Allen visited Sheffield to receive final instructions. On his return he passed them straight to a waiting magistrate. Holberry was arrested at his home around midnight. It was a prosaic end to the career of one of the few English Chartists who brought military experience to the movement. His objective was to control Paradise Square, an important open space in the centre of Sheffield, round which were grouped the Town Hall, police office, important commercial buildings and coaching inns. To facilitate this, detachments were to mount diversionary attacks on magistrates' houses, Sheffield barracks and in Rotherham. Holberry's failure to show up alerted most of the intended participants: fewer than fifty emerged from the shadows, fighting briefly with police and night-watchmen before disappearing. A handful of prominent Chartists were pursued and arrested. Among those evading capture was Ashton, back from France accompanied by an anonymous Frenchman. Perhaps the putative links between English Chartists and French revolutionaries had borne fruit; but just possibly this was Major Beniowski (who spoke poor English but, as an educated Pole, probably good French).[27]

The aborted Sheffield rising was initially overshadowed by the anticipated news from Monmouth, where sentencing was scheduled for Thursday 16 January. Likewise eclipsed was the sole evidence of any metropolitan dimension to a Chartist conspiracy. On Tuesday 14 January the East End was rife with rumours 'that the long contemplated rising of the chartists was to take place at 12 o'clock that night'. Arson attacks on the docks were particularly predicted. On Wednesday Londoners awoke to find mounted messengers constantly on the move between police stations and Whitehall; parish and insurance company fire-engines were on standby, as were 'floating engines' on the Thames. Troops were on the alert. Nothing happened. The following night, the LDA met in the Trades' Hall, Bethnal Green. There were 600 ('chiefly working men and mechanics') in the body of the Hall and around a further 100, mostly women, in the gallery. Beniowski, Charles Neesom and Joseph Williams were on the platform.

Proceedings began as usual with a Chartist hymn. According to police spies and witnesses, Beniowski then whipped up the audience with a passionate declaration that only 'blood, blood, blood; blood alone' would buy freedom. Then Williams predicted that freedom would be obtained within four weeks, whereupon Neesom promised 'we will wield the sword of freedom in four days'. Richard Spurr, an LWMA member, was just advising the audience to 'put your trust in God, and keep your powder dry' when police with drawn cutlasses burst into the Hall. In the ensuing commotion several LDA activists were arrested, among them Neesom. Beniowski was seen exiting sharply through a side door, leaving behind 'a formidable stick'. Police found two loaded pistols, a sword and a pike; bullets, cartridges and knives littered the floor.[28]

As we have seen, possession of weapons, even loaded firearms, was not unusual at Chartist meetings; nor at this time was possession in itself an offence. It seems likely this was a pre-emptive raid in case Frost's sentencing was accompanied by violent demonstrations in London. In any case we should be wary of over-emphasising conspiracy: the vast majority of Chartists awaited the news from Monmouth not with a weapon in their hand, but simply hoping the jury's call for clemency would be reflected in sentencing. That hope, however, was dashed on 16 January when Frost, Williams and Jones were sentenced. They were to be drawn on a hurdle to the place of their execution, hanged until they were dead, then their bodies publicly decapitated and torsos quartered. The Crown, not their families, would dispose of their remains. Simply reading the sentence can still induce nausea; in 1839 the effect was scarifying. An already extensive campaign for clemency was turned overnight into a mass movement demanding a Royal Pardon. Chartists' appetite for insurrection may have been uneven, but there was an implicit and near-universal endorsement of the principle of legitimate resistance to undemocratic rule which Frost now personified.

There was however one last insurrectionary flicker, timed for the day before an appeal against Frost's conviction was concluded. On the night of 26 January a few hundred Bradford Chartists staged a rising in the hope of precipitating a domino effect across the country. 'They would take all the places on their way to London', after which 'they would upset the government'. Robert Peddie, whose earlier eagerness, while in Newcastle, to push ahead despite the fiasco on 12 January was so noticeable, was the leading figure, along with one James Harrison. Harrison, allegedly a woolcomber but effectively a professional informer, was employed to spy on Chartism. He came close to acting the part of an *agent provocateur* in the episode, but it was Peddie who provided the catalysing effect with his seemingly authoritative knowledge of insurrectionary intentions at Carlisle and Newcastle. He had arrived in West Yorkshire as recently as 22 January – quite where and with whom he had spent the period since 12 January he never divulged – and made much of his acquaintance with John Taylor. It was about this time that Taylor published his extraordinary pamphlet *The Coming Revolution*, an almost apocalyptic vision of 'a mighty convulsion ... about to shake to their centre all the institutions of the world'; 'In the towns, fires raging in every quarter, and plunder going on in every street'. Five years later O'Connor recollected that, 'about the time of the Bradford rising', Taylor had visited him and revealed plans for rebellions in Carlisle, Durham, Edinburgh and Newcastle; for reasons that will become clear shortly, this could only have been after, and not before, 1 February. Through his association with Taylor, Peddie had tapped into a rich current of conspiratorial conjecture. Sadly he did not share O'Connor's realisation that Taylor was no longer in control of his mental faculties.[29]

The Bradford rising itself can be briefly summarised.[30] The intention was not to hold the town indefinitely but to seize control of the market area just long enough to pillage it in order to equip a baggage train to accompany the Chartist army. This would then proceed to Dewsbury, seizing cannon from Low Moor ironworks on its way. Reinforcements were expected from Halifax and perhaps Leeds. But the only reinforcements on the night were 300 or so, gathered on a cricket field outside Bradford. They melted away once the futile force in the town-centre was dispersed. Peddie escaped to Leeds where he was arrested four days later. The character of the night was summed up by an extremely contrite Emmanuel Hutton:

> I was called on about two o'clock [a.m.] by some person who came and tapped at the window ... I got up and a person told me to to come down the lane. I found a lot of people there when I got down, and I did not know for what purpose they were there assembled. They said, 'come, thou art going to the market with us, arn't thou' ... One fellow gave me a thick piece of wood as long as myself; he said 'carry that to the market for me'. He gave me a bundle of cartridges and I broke several of them up and put the loose powder in my pocket. They said 'come we are ready for moving off,' and they urged me to go with them, and I went with them. As soon as I got into the Market-place I saw them running about so that I did not know what they were doing. The first man that I saw that I knew was Briggs the constable. I set off towards home again as fast as I could run.[31]

The 'piece of wood', it emerged at Hutton's trial, was a gun. 'I don't know who gave it to me. I wish I had', he later told a prison inspector, 'there seemed no one appointed to lead.'[32]

On Tuesday 28 January, Frost's appeal was rejected. A majority of the fifteen appeal judges ruled that the Crown had failed in its duty to furnish the defence lawyers with a list of its witnesses in good time; but a further majority ruling held that the defence had not objected in time. The matter was now out of the court's hands, and firmly in those of the Government. For the first time O'Connor publicly expressed the view that Frost would be executed at the Government's insistence. The following day the Cabinet did indeed agree that Frost, Williams and Jones should be executed. The decision, though unanimous, was reached only after 'very painful deliberation', one participant recollected, with Macaulay and Palmerston somewhat hesitant. Melbourne, the Prime Minister, and Normanby, the Home Secretary, were more robust. Normanby wrote immediately to Monmouth Gaol stipulating that the sentence should be carried out the following Thursday, 6 February.[33]

Confirmation of the sentence served only to increase the overwhelming sympathy among Chartists for Frost. For example Arthur Wade, whose stand against physical force at the General Convention had led to his resignation and widespread condemnation, personally presented to the Queen 'seven voluminous petitions' for a pardon. This sympathy manifested itself in a massive programme of petitioning and meetings with the aim of securing the Newport prisoners' freedom. Its extent gives cause for thought, for it reveals the resilient appeal and durability of Chartism at a time when the movement might have withered in the face of events the previous year, or leached support as the January conspiracies were exposed. The fate of Frost especially became a rallying point that unified the movement, his sentence the symbolic embodiment of every reprehensible element of Whiggism. We saw in chapter 3 how the collection of signatures to the 1839 National Petition was sluggish. This was not the case now. Within days, tens of thousands of signatures were collected: 17,000 in Sunderland in 3 days, in Oldham 18,000 over the space of just 2, and 30,000 in Birmingham in 6 days. It was a similar picture in Scotland: Aberdeen Chartists collected 15,000 signatures and in Edinburgh, where 17,000 signed the 1839 petition, 22,000 signed for Frost. Dundee also accumulated over 20,000 signatures and in Paisley, where the organisational lead was taken by the Town Council, 14,784 signatures were collected in just 14 hours.[34]

The Queen's marriage to Albert, on 10 February, was close at hand and many Chartists expected a pardon, either as a magnanimous gesture to accompany the wedding or a pragmatic concession to head-off demonstrations. The Government was facing extensive criticism for its handling of Chartism. Back in October Campbell had openly boasted that Chartism was extinct. It was a statement that came to haunt both him and the Government, 'showing that the

Ministers were off their guard – to say nothing of its tone of triumph, which was anything but conciliatory', to quote one perceptive critic.[35]

The day Frost's appeal was quashed, criticism of the Government's handling of Chartism triggered a no-confidence debate in the House of Commons. This helps explain why the Cabinet was resolutely opposed to clemency when it discussed the Newport convictions next day. Equally the news from Bradford cannot have helped matters. However, pressure was mounting as petitions and memorials streamed in and Frost's defence counsel repeatedly lobbied the Government for a reprieve. Then, on 31 January, the Chief Justice told Normanby personally that the Government should consider sparing the lives of all three prisoners. 'This opinion produced a great effect; and even Lord Melbourne confessed that it would be difficult to execute the men after such a hint.'[36] The sentences on Frost, Williams and Jones were commuted to transportation for life.

It must have been shortly after this that Dr Taylor visited O'Connor, for he announced his intention to equip and crew a boat and sail it to intercept the transport ship that would be carrying the Newport prisoners. 'My answer was, "Taylor, I always thought you mad, but I'm sure of it now," and it ended in him laughing most lustily, and asking me for £10 to take him home.'[37] Though it may well be that Frost's life was ultimately spared through the intervention of the Chief Justice, all appearances were that a campaign of mass petitioning – with O'Connor at its head – had succeeded where insurrection had signally failed. To the culture and organisational ethic which made that campaign possible we now turn.

## Beyond conspiracy: activities in the Chartist localities

In any historical narrative built on key events, there is always a danger that the internal life and culture of what is being described are overlooked. The mass petitioning movement O'Connor led depended heavily on the culture and internal solidarity of Chartism. O'Connor's overarching influence, and the power of the *Northern Star* in a movement still without any central co-ordinating body, were important; but above all Chartism was sustained by the sense of solidarity its adherents shared through their commitment to a common political endeavour. Clearly economic insecurity was an important stimulus to political action; but as Chartism evolved there emerged too a collective impulse to self-improvement.

As we have observed in earlier chapters, Chartist localities often developed in a loose cluster with existing trade and friendly societies and anti-Poor Law campaigns. Within wide local variation, there was often an intimate overlap with particular workplaces, occupational groups, dissenting religious congregations, public houses or (in Scotland especially) temperance activity. By January

1840 most Chartist localities had been in existence at least eighteen months
– often longer where an existing association had taken up the Charter as soon
as it appeared: 'we felt we had a real bond or union', recollected John Bates of
Queensbury, West Yorkshire, 'and we transformed our Radical Associations
into local Chartist centres'.[38] But regardless of longevity, as localities evolved
they developed a spectrum of activities beyond the narrowly political.[39]

One already touched upon (see Brewster's 'Chartist life') was religious. This
was most apparent in the fifty-odd separately constituted Chartist churches,
mostly in Scotland. English Chartist congregations tended towards religious
humanism, the Scottish to theological orthodoxy. 'Orthodoxy' is, of course,
a relative term. There were close links between the two Glasgow Chartist
churches and the city's Unitarian congregation (which gave a whole Sunday's
collection in May 1840 to help establish the Glasgow Chartist Worshipping
Assembly), while the Glasgow Universalist Church played a prominent part
in the evolution of Scottish Chartism generally (it also hosted the August 1839
conference that established the USCCS).[40] More typically – at Bromsgrove and
Oldham for example – religious services were held in Chartist halls, without
a specifically Chartist church being formed.

Very few Chartist localities completely separated political ideals from a
radical social gospel. The 'genius of Christianity' propels Chartism, declared
the *True Scotsman*, 'The Charter springs from Zion's hill' sung South Yorkshire
Chartists. Many localities organised camp meetings on the Methodist model.
When O'Connor visited Sheffield in September 1839, Chartists from the region
prepared the previous day with a camp meeting at Hood Hall, 'a deep hollow,
in the shape of a crescent, the hills round which formed a romantic gallery,
on which the delighted assemblage sat', recollected a Barnsley Chartist. 'It was
a glorious sight to see from five to ten thousand persons joining in a song of
adoration to the Great Creator; and we could not help comparing it with the
brave Covenanters of old.' Hymns were sung evoking the idea of the Chartists
as a chosen, covenanted people and extolling legitimate resistance to tyranny,
along with a parody of the National Anthem ('O Lord our God arise,/ Scatter
our enemies,/ And make them fall').[41]

A close affinity with religious nonconformity was also evident among
the meeting places used for Chartist gatherings. Although Chartist relations
with nonconformist sects – especially Wesleyan Methodism – were sometimes prickly, overlapping adherents and a shared suspicion of the established
Church frequently brought Chartists and local dissenting congregations
together. Premises were loaned by a range of denominations – Independent
and Primitive Methodists, Baptists, Independents (i.e. Congregationalists),
Mormons and in Scotland the Secession Church – as well as free-standing
congregations (examples include the 'Revd Browning's Hall', Tillicoultry; 'Dr
Thorburn's Chapel', South Shields; and the several chapels allied to Joseph

Rayner Stephens). Symbolically, when Huddersfield Primitive Methodists moved to larger premises in 1840 their old chapel became the town's Chartist hall. Localities able to afford their own premises often designated them chapels without confining their use to worship (e.g. Reformers' chapels in Leeds and Middleton, Democratic chapels in Nottingham and Trowbridge, the Chartist chapel at Mansfield). However many Chartist-controlled premises went by secular titles: Hyde's lively Chartist Institute, Keighley's Working Men's Hall, Chartist halls in East Wemyss and Campsie (Fifeshire), the People's Hall in Edinburgh and Chartist, RA and WMA rooms too numerous to mention. A handful used local socialists' premises (Birmingham, Bradford, Leeds and notably the Manchester Hall of Science).

All this might suggest that Chartist meetings were predominantly polite, even pious, in tone. It must be stressed therefore that in England routine Chartist meetings were held mainly in public houses; in some instances the association was a close and enduring one, notably The Wellington Tavern at Dewsbury and The Brewers' Arms in Brighton (though both landlords were threatened with the loss of their licence by local magistrates if they persisted in hosting Chartist meetings). Other regular haunts included trade societies' halls (often with a beershop attached) and in Yorkshire the Oddfellows Friendly Society premises. In Scotland masonic halls were often used – not so in England (Hull conspicuously excepted) where freemasonry had become more socially conservative. A unique example underlining the rootedness of Chartism in local communities was the use by Sunderland Chartists of the town's lifeboat house. The political complexion of local authorities usually meant that town halls were denied to Chartists. There were occasional exceptions, mainly in Scotland (e.g. Pollockshaw, Bannockburn and Dunfermline's Guildhall); but in general the whole history of Chartist meeting places is a history of contested public space.[42]

It was not simply the size of Chartist assemblies that meant they were so often held outdoors. Examples of small outdoor meetings abound and include barns, beaches, waste land and (a whiff of undisguised pleasure here) 'the spot where Oliver Cromwell battered Stockton Castle down'.[43] Though overt support for the movement in Wales and rural England diminished, the wide appeal of Chartism continued to be clear: 1840 saw Chartist meetings in locations as far apart as Kirkwall in the Orkney Islands and Amiens in northern France (the latter comprising émigré Scottish linen workers and their families).[44]

Though Chartists took themselves seriously their associational culture was far from being staid or humourless. As support consolidated so there emerged a rich variety of recreational activities. These reinforced solidarity and had immense symbolic value in underscoring the historical roots and moral claims of the movement, especially shared meals and the practice of toasting Chartism's iconic figures. They were also clearly immense fun. Surrounded by evergreens, portraits and banners, speakers would formally propose each toast and another would be made in response, interspersed with recitations and songs. In 1839, when Ashton-under-Lyne Chartists commemorated Hunt's birthday, there were toasts to 'the Working Classes, the true and legitimate source of all power'; 'the immortal memory of Henry Hunt, the man that never deceived the people'; 'the Education of the People, and may the State speedily provide for their moral and intellectual improvement'; 'M'Douall, Higgins, Lovett, Collins, Stephens, and all true patriots who are suffering incarceration in the cause of freedom'; 'Feargus O'Connor, Esq., and the brightest luminary in the British hemisphere, the *Northern Star*'; 'Richard Carlile, Henry Hetherington, and the liberty of the press'; 'the immortal memory' of Paine, Cobbett, Cartwright, Emmet, Knight, Hibbert, Hampden, Tyler, Sidney, Hardy, Horne Tooke, Volney, Voltaire, Palmer, Mirabeau, Robespierre, Tell, Hofer, Washington, Wallace, Robert Burns; 'and all the illustrious dead of every nation, who by their acts and deeds have contributed to the cause of liberty'. Toasting was interspersed by songs, solemn and comic, and recitations (including 'the manifesto of the Convention, wrote by Mr. Lovett').[45]

Other events reported in the same issue of the *Northern Star* included Brighton's 'instrumental and vocal concert' in aid of the *Southern Star* newspaper, and at Kilbarchan (Renfrewshire) a Halloween 'dramatic entertainment' by 'young amateurs of the village' under the direction of the local WMA – raising £6 for the Glasgow Relief Fund. Amateur dramatics was a useful means of raising funds for prisoners and their families, having the advantage that sympathetic patrons might discretely support the cause without being directly identified with it. Examples included *The Patriotic Play of William Tell*, performed at Sutton-in-Ashfield, and numerous productions based on the trial and last days of the Irish rebel Robert Emmet. Others were devised as the occasion demanded, often blurring the line between performance and protest. In 1838 the officers of the Barnsley RA took the leading roles in the 'trial' of an effigy of a local baker, alleged to give customers short measure; the audience played the jury; found guilty, the effigy was hanged and then burnt on the steps of the subject's shop.[46] In 1840 Dundee Chartists hired a river steamer to attend an afternoon of entertainments, presented by their Perth compatriots, which included a spoof trial of the local Whig MP. The Chartist Institute in Hyde regularly staged plays. Keighley Chartists organised a 'radical entertainment' for presentation at the local fair.

Music was another staple element in Chartist recreational culture. While Aberdeen and Manchester Chartists obtained the services of, respectively, the local carpet weavers' and Foresters' friendly society bands to help celebrate the release of Lovett and Collins, Rochdale boasted its own uniformed 'Radical Band', Salford a Chartist Brass Band and, in West Yorkshire, Chickenley Chartists' 'Patriotic & Scientific Band'. Several localities organised their own choirs, among them the Sutton-in-Ashfield and the Bristol Democratic Harmonic Societies. Every locality enlivened social meetings with communal singing, comic singers and dancing.

Educational initiatives lent another dimension to Chartist associational life. We have seen how Elland Chartists were 'determined not to wait the time of government appointments for national education, but to begin and educate themselves'.[47] This was a typical response but the extent and formality of educational activity varied widely. Some localities ran reading or news rooms open to all, as at Derby, 'whether they belong to the Chartist Society or not'. In Nottingham, operatives' libraries operated in pubs that were also centres for Chartist localities.[48] Most localities offered regular discussion classes, such as Trowbridge WMA's twice-weekly 'political school', open to men and women. Its 6 teachers were appointed by the Association's committee for 6 months and could be fined for non-attendance. The curriculum appears to have been drawn entirely from the content of the Chartist press. But many localities ran more ambitious 'educational clubs', 'adult schools' and, for children particularly, Sunday schools. Reports uniformly stressed that such enterprises were autonomous: for example the 'Democratic Sunday School' in Thwaites, West Yorkshire, proclaimed itself 'the people's own', 'their little commonwealth' and 'entirely of the labouring class'.

This was a powerful attraction even in Scotland, where provision of publicly funded education was more generous. 'Let us, therefore, send all our juveniles to their schools', the *True Scotsman* argued, 'and not to any of the rotten old regime.'[49] Opportunities for self-directed improvement were seen as an important factor in the struggle to reform society. Such was the social and political gulf between Chartists and the upper classes, there was widespread suspicion of initiatives designed by others to improve workers. This attitude was summed up with acerbity by 'a Radical of the old school' writing in J. R. Stephens's *People's Magazine*:

> The 'Mechanics Institutions', with all other 'institutions' for the 'diffusion of knowledge', where rich and the poor are on committees *together*(!) are all so many traps to catch the people; and by lectures, experiments, papers, books, and all the mountebank exhibitions of pretended science mixed, perhaps, with a little coaxing and flattery, to pervert their understanding, and prevent their attaining a knowledge of the true cause of their miserable and degraded state. We warn the people to shun all this as a pest.[50]

In an editorial Stephens praised the above for its 'sound wisdom and good practical sense'. Such attitudes were most entrenched in the cotton-factory districts and the most ambitious Chartist institutes, mimicking the range of provision but not the management culture of Mechanics' Institutes, were located in this region. Chartists founded Stalybridge's People's Institute in 1839 as a direct rival to the town's Mechanics' Institute, and opened it every day, for political meetings, acts of worship, children's day and Sunday schools, adults' evening classes, dances and 'dramatic recitals'.[51]

Common to every locality was the practice of naming children after leading figures in the movement, Feargus O'Connor being strongly preferred – Abram and Elizabeth Hanson of Elland were among the very first to name their child Feargus. The naming of children after radical heroes was no novelty (in 1822 John and Mary Frost had christened a son Henry Hunt) but it often required nerve to ensure such a baptism. 'I suppose they want the child hanged', the Vicar of Selby told the congregation at the baptism of little Feargus O'Connor Mabbot. The Vicar of Sowerby, near Halifax, disputed the choice of Feargus O'Connor Vincent Bronterre for one child; when the parents held firm, he retained the baby after baptism to say additional prayers over it. Even civil registrars were not above arguing with parents who sought to register 'a young patriot'. Nor was life necessarily plain-sailing for the child afterwards: Feargus O'Connor Holmes, the son of Keighley woolcombers, went through school referred to only as 'F' by a master who refused to let such names pollute his lips.[52]

Such incidents reinforced Chartists' conviction that the established religious and civil institutions of society were not to be trusted. Early in 1838 O'Brien had written that 'the pulpit, the press, the stage, the universities and public seminaries, the literature of the country, in short, every avenue to knowledge, every channel and vehicle of information ... are all preoccupied and conducted in the interests of the upper and middle classes'. This perception extended to other areas of public life – self-evidently politics, of course, but the clash of social antagonism was evident in other arenas, pre-eminently statutory poor relief and its stigmatising alternative, charity. Hostility to the New Poor Law was a powerful stimulus to the further growth of an already well-established culture of working-class mutualism. Inevitably, very large numbers of Chartists were also friendly-society members and countless Chartist localities drew practical support from local branches of national orders such as the Druids, the Foresters and the Oddfellows. Direct financial support was less usual and, where it occurred, came mainly from small local societies. Dundee, unusually, had an Oddfellows Democratic Society which appointed missionaries 'delivering Chartist lectures' across Fife.

Direct Chartist involvement in providing sick, death and unemployment benefits was slight, reflecting how extensive and sophisticated friendly societies had become by the late 1830s. But a few Chartist localities did provide benefits of this nature. Hyde's Chartist Institute, for example, operated a 'Board of Health' through which members, for a weekly subscription of a halfpenny, could access medical assistance. Stockport had a 'Radical Chartist Burial Society' to keep its members from the ultimate indignity of a pauper's grave, and both Sunderland

and Newcastle for a time operated benefit societies. Cirencester WMA and the Manchester Christian Chartists both contemplated the launch of land companies to facilitate the acquisition of small-holdings by their members.[53]

In the early years of the movement, however, the means (religion and education aside) through which Chartists in the main sought to step outside 'the rotten old regime' was retail co-operation. Food represented by far the largest element in the spending of industrial workers' households and limited budgets left them vulnerable to poor-quality and adulterated goods, and to short measure. Retail co-ops pre-dated Chartism but were a natural extension of exclusive dealing, a central plank of Chartist tactics in 1839. Some existing co-ops assumed an intimate relationship with Chartism, as happened with the co-operative at Ripponden in the West Riding, founded in 1832 and later administered from the Chartist Hall, or the Huddersfield Co-operative Society, whose anniversaries celebrated Chartist heroes and which supported the cost of organising Chartist rallies. The first co-operative directly to emerge from Chartist activity was Hull's, in April 1839, promoted as 'the means of bringing the shopocrats to their senses.'[54]

Thereafter Chartist co-ops mushroomed. Their adoption would 'raise supporters to that independent position in society which will enable them to treat with contempt, all the malevolence of aristocratic and shopocratic tyranny', *The Charter* asserted. Hull's second retail store, opened in December, was greeted as evidence that 'the working classes are beginning to see they have the power in their hands to redeem themselves from the trammels of the shopocracy and the middle class men'. It is impossible to determine how many Chartist co-ops there were: in many localities an occasional collection would purchase a few sacks of flour at wholesale price for distribution to members. However, around forty localities in these early years established their own retail stores. The title usually adopted was 'Joint Stock Provision Company' or 'Store'. Their distribution was heavily weighted towards northern England. Perhaps four or five were Scottish; only two (Bristol and Bridgend, Glamorganshire) were south of the Pennines.

Joint stock provision stores had the additional advantages of providing an autonomous space for Chartist meetings and a further means of fundraising. The sums involved could be substantial. Stockport's 'Patriots' Store', for example, devoted half of its profits to prisoner relief (profits which would otherwise have been redistributed back to members as a dividend on purchases); and when the County Durham missionary George Binns faced imprisonment or a £5 fine for holding a meeting in the market place, the local co-op paid the whole. When Dewsbury magistrates intervened to deny Chartists the use of the Wellington Inn, the co-op became the base for a wide range of their activities, including West Riding delegate meetings. The 'large and commodious room' of Stockton's co-op was the scene of weekly dances to raise funds for prisoners throughout the summer of 1839 – at one 'testimonial tea', singing and dancing lasted until 4.30 a.m. Co-operation, like exclusive dealing, was also a sphere where female Chartists played a pivotal role. However, although leading Chartists lauded co-operation as 'the most practical form of exclusive dealing' and 'the speediest means of working out our political regeneration', participation was inevitably limited to those able to manage without credit (a minority of working-class households at this time). The initial outlay required to join was typically a ten-shilling share. Too much emphasis on co-operation risked alienating those many households whose existence was too precarious to join such ventures.[55] How to facilitate the participation of men who could afford no more than a copy of the *Northern Star* – or a pint to sup while they heard it read aloud – was a constant preoccupation of Chartist activists.

Many active Chartists saw that pint (and the several that might well follow) as a key cause of the problems confronting disenfranchised workers. Consumption of alcohol in Victorian Britain was prodigious. Many thoughtful Chartists advocated temperance (moderate alcohol consumption and abstinence from spirits) or teetotalism (complete abstinence). Most joint stock provision companies reflected this attitude: 'one of the standing rules' of the Edinburgh co-op was that 'no intoxicating drinks be kept in the store, nor any of the society's business be transacted where they are sold'. Limiting alcohol consumption was integral to the long-established radical tactic of abstaining from taxed goods and, as we saw in chapter 3, the General Convention had recommended complete abstinence from alcohol for the duration of the sacred month. Drink, especially beer, however, was an integral part of workers' culture, especially for those employed in the most physically strenuous occupations or hot or dusty environments. Beer also had a significant calorific content, while frequently contaminated water supplies in rapidly expanding urban centres meant it was often more prudent to drink beer. Pubs and beer-shops had long been the traditional resort of workers and their trade societies, and were often the only indoor meeting places available to Chartists, usually at no cost beyond the 'wet rent' of their purchases. Considerably fewer localities met at temperance hotels and coffee houses than did in pubs, not least because the latter were predominant and the temperance movement (which later became a conspicuous facet of Victorian society) was still in its emergent phase.[56]

Feargus O'Connor did not himself advocate temperance, a reflection perhaps of personal predilections and certainly of his intention to make Chartism inclusive. But teetotal Chartists in this early phase of the movement's history had no hesitation in placing themselves squarely under his leadership. The secretary of the Leeds Total Abstinence Charter Association, for example, wrote poetry eulogising O'Connor as well as deploring the demon drink. The *Northern Star* routinely reported temperance activities and carried letters and editorials on temperance. O'Connor seriously considered adding to its portrait gallery the great Irish temperance reformer Father Matthew, administering the teetotal pledge.[57] Like trade unionism and friendly societies, the temperance movement was closely woven into that culture of self-improvement which was also a central element of Chartism. A mutually supportive relationship was therefore common in many localities. 'The working classes, who meet for mutual instruction, are no longer influenced by intoxication', an optimistic Colchester Chartist declared in February 1838. The events of 1839 prompted a number of localities to form specifically temperance Chartist bodies. Among those to do so were Leeds (where the society also campaigned for Chartist candidates in local municipal elections), Burnley, Newcastle, Leicester, Bradford (a Chartist Temperance Co-operative Society large enough to elect its own delegate to regional meetings) and the East London Chartist Temperance Society, the latter boasting a parallel women's society. Among the many Scottish Chartist temperance associations were those in Alva, Cumnock, Strathaven, Tillicoultry and Glasgow (which ran a teetotal co-operative school).[58]

Other Chartist localities were effectively temperance in tone if not formal constitution: Bolton WMA met at the town's temperance hotel, which its secretary managed, and the Bolton Temperance Band regularly played at Charitst rallies; Wooton-under-Edge Chartists emphatically forbade the consumption of alcohol at their social events; Durham County CA required its full-time missionary to sign the teetotal pledge; at Paddock, near Huddersfield, the temperance hotel was run by local Chartists and the local CA met there. As was the case in many localities, Paddock's Chartists divided into classes, but they distinguished between classes of total abstainers from drink and tobacco and those of 'moderate' imbibers. East Manchester's Brown Street CA held regular weekend teetotal festivals of dancing and singing (admission 4d, women 2d). Brown Street's 'MERRY CHARTISTS' also held weekly dance classes.[59]

Diverse though these activities were, what united them was far more significant than what divided them. They were sustained by common commitment not merely to the political objectives of the Charter but to the overarching ethos it signified, and bound together by ties that were at once both broad and political but often also intimate and personal. 'Yours in Chartism', they might sign private correspondence, 'in the good cause', 'in the great cause', 'in the best of causes'; 'Your brother in the Cause of Right against Might', 'of truth and justice', 'of Real Democracy', 'in the cause till Death'.[60] Committed Chartists effectively *inhabited* Chartism: decorating their homes with *Northern Star* prints; purchasing their food from a Chartist store; educating themselves and their children in its schools, at its meetings and from its newspapers. Those without access to a Chartist store could mail-order Chartist shoe polish, ink, breakfast powder or fabrics advertised in the Chartist press.[61] The solidarity of the personal was also manifest in the way Chartist localities governed themselves.

By the autumn of 1839 the adoption of the Methodist class system was almost universal. In part this was a pragmatic response to the difficulty of obtaining premises in which to meet as well as to the possibility of official suppression. Classes, often focused on a particular street or workplace, could meet almost invisibly in a member's home or street-corner beershop, where none need be excluded from full participation as he or she might from large assemblies. Each class nominated a member to attend regular executive meetings for the locality, usually termed the 'Chartist council'. Large towns were often divided into districts (four in Newcastle's case) or would naturally develop a loosely federated range of localities (as many as twelve in Manchester).

Industrialised counties, notably Durham and the West Riding, also operated councils. Large and elaborate constitutions were frequently devised for their governance, to ensure that officers and members were rotated or at least subject to frequent re-election. For example, the constitution of the Tillicoultry Chartist Temperance Association stated that it was 'to be dissolved and reconstructed every three months'; half the Leeds executive had to be re-elected each month and in Brighton the officers and half the committee every quarter. It was the Chartist councils that mainly organised collections for prisoners and their families, appointed missionaries and arranged lecturers in a circuit (again, after Methodist practice); but in all matters of policy a general meeting (usually held quarterly) was sovereign, often chaired by a non-office holder elected for that meeting alone.[62]

## Counting the cost

It is necessary to speak in terms of localities rather than branches because at no time before August 1840 did Chartism enjoy central co-ordination beyond that which O'Connor and the *Northern Star* brought to it (though in Scotland the USCCS, through the medium of the *Chartist Circular*, did much to supply the deficiency). The demise of the General Convention in September 1839 made it imperative that a national structure be established, while the campaign to pardon the Newport prisoners helped provide a national focus that might otherwise have proved elusive, given the vicissitudes of 1839. Yet the distinctive culture they had created manifestly was a success; likewise the organisational infrastructure that sustained Chartism at the local, district and often regional level. This was especially important as one consequence of 1839 was significant personnel loss from the movement.

There were those – often veterans of earlier radical politics and frequently members of the relatively prosperous 'middling sort' – for whom the right of armed resistance was essentially an abstraction, central to moral suasion but not to be implemented in practice. Among Convention delegates, Matthew Fletcher, Sankey, Wade and the whole BPU contingent (with the important exception of John Collins, the sole wage-earner) were national figures who fell into this category. Almost every locality experienced similar losses. For example, Henry Heavisides of Stockton-upon-Tees, self-styled 'printer, radical and poet', prominent in the local defence of Queen Caroline and the reform movement of 1830–32, parted company with Chartism over the sacred month. In later life Fletcher wrote dismissively of the 'miserable knots of a dozen or two in each town, meeting generally in some beer-shop, and calling themselves branches of the National Charter Association'. This, as the foregoing survey of local Chartist culture makes clear, is a caricature, but it does underline the downward shift in the social composition of Chartism from late 1839.[63]

Emigration caused further attrition, with Tyneside and the West Riding particularly affected.[64] However, the most significant loss of personnel stemmed from the considerable number of active Chartists who were in prison, around 500 in all. A majority of these were 'rank and file', typified by Emmanuel Hutton of Bradford, 'a Chartist by reading the Star Newspaper'.[65] Of 476 arrested Chartists referred to in an official report, 160 were textiles workers, 120 craftsmen (a quarter of them shoemakers), 49 labourers and 39 miners.[66] A substantial number of the prisoners had been key local leaders, such as Timothy Higgins, secretary of the Ashton-under-Lyne RA, Binns and Williams, mainstays of the County Durham CA, White of Leeds (secretary of the GNU), Roberts of Bath and Carrier of Trowbridge. Chartism also suffered at the highest level of its leadership. Collins, Harney, Lovett, McDouall, O'Brien, Richardson, Stephens and Vincent were all in prison for most or all of 1840. Of this important group only Stephens repudiated Chartism, an action that (outside of his Ashton powerbase) earned him the undying contempt of almost all Chartists: 'in fact many felt pleased he got a heavier sentence than Dr. McDouall', a Cheshire Chartist recalled. Stephens' apostasy, reinforced by his refusal to share with other Chartist prisoners the considerable subscription raised by the movement, led to occasional public bonfires of copies of his *Star* portrait and also to murky allegations of sexual impropriety.[67]

With varying degrees of success, the remainder continued to pursue their political careers in some way. Collins and Lovett wrote their book *Chartism: A New Movement of the People* while imprisoned in Warwick, the impact of which will be assessed in chapter 6. His nine months' incarceration merely gave Richardson more time for writing, including his remarkable *Rights of Women*. In May 1840 jailed Chartists were joined by Feargus O'Connor himself; chapter 6 explains how O'Connor's fortunes while in prison waxed rather than waned.

Few prisoners shared O'Connor's good fortune, though Binns and Williams were well-treated, the latter making a good marriage to a friend of the prison governor. Working-class prisoners, unable to procure any comforts, faired at best indifferently, especially if sentenced to hard labour. The treatment of Samuel Holberry became a national *cause célèbre* (see pp. 152–7). At Beverley Gaol, Peddie spent six weeks in total silence, working a treadmill in full view of spectators outside the prison. This routine was then varied for three months by stone-breaking until reduced to half-time on health grounds. Finally, after sixteen months he was set to tailoring. At Chester Castle, Chartist prisoners were placed in cells below ground level; 'at the time we write, the water is actually running down the walls', they reported to the *Star* in September 1840. At Monmouth prisoners slept three to a bed; at Warwick Lovett and Collins were persistently ill due, they claimed, to prison soup and porridge; while conditions in York Castle cost Barnsley Chartist Peter Hoey the use of a leg.[68]

The efforts of Chartists to sustain these prisoners and their families were prodigious. Yet in the popular imagination none held the power that John Frost did. Once his sentence was commuted to transportation their campaign focused on securing his free pardon and return. But there was to be no further concession. On Monday, 24 February, Frost, Williams and Jones departed on the convict-ship *Mandarin*, without even the opportunity to bid their wives and children farewell. One last incident delayed their passage: on the Wednesday *Mandarin* lost her top and mizzen masts in a gale and was forced to put back to Falmouth harbour for repairs. While there, Barclay Fox, an impeccably respectable Quaker industrialist from the town, impetuously determined to see Frost. Disguising himself as 'a missionary & tract distributor', Fox secured permission to board the ship and address the convicts. He enquired 'if any tracts or religious books would be acceptable. Frost came forward and answered with the most consummate contempt for all children's & old women's books. He "would be obliged for a Pilgrim's Progress or some solid reading however".' That night in his journal Fox wrote:

> Frost's is a face one cannot easily forget, wan & haggard & indented with deep furrows, a small piercing grey eye & a beetling brow surmounted by a shock of grey hair. Much character without decided talents in his face. All the bold badness, without any of the sublimity of a Revolutionist.

Fox found a copy of *Pilgrim's Progress* and sent to it to the Welshman. Frost wrote a last, emotional letter to his 'dearest Mary'; then, on the Friday evening, *Mandarin* weighed anchor and transported him to Tasmania and an uncertain future.[69]

# Chartist lives:
# Samuel Holberry

Samuel Holberry was born in Nottinghamshire in 1814, the youngest of nine children of agricultural workers.* Samuel received some schooling but, destined for a life like that of his parents, while still a child worked on the land – typical jobs for his age would have included scaring birds, weeding, stone-picking and minding livestock. He worked for a short time at a cotton mill in his native Gamston but a life on the land seemed certain when, still in his early teens, he became a farm labourer. However, at 17 he took a decision that was to change his life: lying about his age, he enlisted in the 33rd Infantry. Holberry saw service in Ireland and Northampton. Northampton radicalised the young Holberry, for the town and surrounding villages comprised a major centre of radical political activity and one of several midland areas where Cleave and Hetherington established satellites of the NUWC in October 1833.

The NUWC during the Reform Crisis (as we saw in chapter 1) mobilised radicals who were opposed to piecemeal reform and therefore also to the 1832 Act. Northampton's shoemakers also forged close links with general unionism at this time, allying themselves to the GNCTU, the short-lived but remarkable union closely associated with Robert Owen, the 'Tolpuddle martyrs' and a host of subsequent Chartists. The offence for which the Tolpuddle trade unionists were transported in 1834 was that of swearing secret oaths. The sentence was extraordinary but the case far from unusual: there were prosecutions in at least five other places in 1834, Northampton among them. Holberry later told Sheffield Chartists that 'when he was a soldier the soldiers had been putting down secret meetings where they had taken oaths'.†

Holberry, however, established positive connections with Northampton's shoemakers and attended evening classes in the town. His decision to buy

---

*    The fullest accounts of Holberry's life appear in *ECC*, 118–22 (May–June 1843), 'communicated by a friend at Sheffield' and based partly on information from Holberry's wife, and in *DLB*, vol.4.

†    I. Prothero, *Artisans and Politics in Early Nineteenth-Century London* (Folkestone, Dawson, 1979), p.293. M. Chase, *Early Trade Unionism* (Aldershot, Ashgate, 2000), pp.149 and 165; TS, 11/816/2688, quotation from examination of Samuel Thompson, also reproduced in D. Thompson, *The Early Chartists* (London, Macmillan, 1971), pp.270–9.

himself out of the army in April 1835 was almost certainly connected to the Northampton experience. He moved to Sheffield where he worked first as a cooper and then as a rectifying distiller; and he met and fell in love with Mary Cooper, a labourer's daughter. Thrown out of work in 1837, he worked for a time in east London but returned the following October to marry 19-year-old Mary. Holberry joined the Sheffield WMA in late 1838 but emerged as an active Chartist only during mass church demonstrations the following autumn. In the organisation of these Holberry took a prominent role. 'A fine-looking man; in height he measured six feet one or two inches' and had 'jet black hair', a contemporary recalled. 'He was a leading speaker' at the Sheffield Chartists' Fig Tree Lane meeting rooms, recalled another.[*] But by November 1839 he was again unemployed, and Mary was pregnant.

In such circumstances and against the background of Newport and the onset of winter, Samuel Holberry might well have become involved in insurrectionary plans anyway; but his recent contacts with radicals in Northampton and (presumably) London made him an obvious emissary for Sheffield Chartists. He toured Nottinghamshire, Derbyshire and other West Riding centres (Barnsley, Bradford and Dewsbury) involved in the winter rising. As we have already seen, only the intervention of the publican, on whose premises Holberry and other leading conspirators met, prevented some form of insurrection in Yorkshire on the night of 11–12 January. Just prior to that Saturday night Holberry had inspected Chartists and their arms; 'he said every man must put two shirts on and whatever clothing they could to keep them warm he said they must get a 6d. Dram to keep out the cold'. As we have seen, the conspiracy at best mobilised numbers in the low hundreds. Even had it proceeded unhindered it would never have matched Newport. Holberry belatedly recognised how precarious their chances were. Late on Friday night he told the section leaders, 'now we have said nothing about what should be done if we are put off and he said he should say to begin to Moscow the Town'. Large-scale arson would be a last desperate attempt to inspire a reaction elsewhere: 'it might all end in smoke but there were plenty of other towns', his cousin recalled him saying.[†] His midnight arrest, Mary at his side, a dagger in his pocket and grenades lying on the floor, forestalled everything. (Mary too was arrested and detained for two days but no charges were brought against her.)

Holberry, however, was destined to occupy a similar place in the Chartist pantheon to Frost's. This was not because of the intrinsic significance of the attempted rising ('the stark staring mad proceedings of a knot of fools', the *Northern Star* initially commented) but because of the pathos of his situation. Young, idealistic, unemployed with a bride of fifteen months expecting their

---

[*] *ECC*, 122 (June 1843): examination of Thompson.
[†] HO, 20/10, W. J. Williams interview with William Wells.

first child, Holberry cut a sympathetic figure. Asked '[S]urely you would not take a life?' by the policeman who arrested him, he responded: 'But I would, in defence of liberty and the charter. Mind, I am no thief or robber, but I will fight for the charter and will not rest until we have got it, and to that I have made up my mind.'* He claimed to have been neither betrayed nor misled by any *agent provocateur*.

After the precarious verdict in Frost's trial and the popular response it evoked, the Government wisely brought only a lesser charge of seditious conspiracy against Holberry at the York spring assizes. It then took care to secure 'ample accommodation for all the Reporters', to help publicise the outcome. The prosecuting counsel shrewdly covered their table with hand-grenades, shells, bullets and cartridges brought from Sheffield. Holberry received a four-year sentence, eight other conspirators lesser terms. All were led away to the house of correction at Northallerton, county town of the North Riding, selected by the judge who had been discretely guided by John Bayly, one of the Crown's prosecution team. As Bayly told the senior Whitehall official overseeing Chartist prosecutions, of all the prisons within York's jurisdiction, Northallerton 'was farthest away from their own homes' and the one where prisoners 'are worse fed & hardest worked'.†

William Martin, an itinerant Chartist preacher arrested in Sheffield in September and charged with seditious libel, was jailed alongside Holberry. Both were placed on the 'silent system', liable to be punished if they spoke to other inmates during working hours. Martin described their first evening at Northallerton:

> At five o'clock one of the officers threw a black loaf on the bed and a prisoner placed a tin of skilly on the floor. It was the worst meal I ever had in the course of my life, and surely no individual can be a better judge of course food than an Irishman. The monster hunger compelled me to swallow the dose ... On the following morning the Governor came round to inform those who had not been sentenced with hard labour that they must work on the treadmill. I raised an objection, and told him that the judge said the law would not allow me to be put to hard labour but he told me he had the magistrates' orders to obey. I thought I would try it before I suffered any resistance. I did so but so great were my sufferings that I felt as I never felt before.‡

Holberry was treated in exactly the same way. Northallerton Prison was run in a spirit of parsimony unusual even by the standards of the time: all prisoners

---

*    Quoted in *DLB*.
†    *NS*, 15 January and 21 March 1840; *ECC*, 119 (May 1843); *DLB*; TS, 11/813, fo. 2, J. Bayly to G. Maule (21 March 1840).
‡    *NS*, 6 March 1841.

not sentenced to hard labour were required to work to pay for their meals. Four hours daily on the treadmill was the only employment offered. Holberry soon discovered that solitary confinement was the only alternative if he refused the treadmill. It was not uncommon for prisoners 'put to the wheel' to fall from it, 'stretched to all appearances lifeless on the floor', as another Chartist, 55-year-old William Brooke of Bradford, did. Yet their situation was at least better than that of 4 other Sheffield men (arrested in the act of rioting) sentenced with hard labour: the local interpretation of this entailed a daily total of 8 hours on the wheel. The oldest of these four was John Clayton, 52, and he was dead within ten months. Clayton was frequently sick and unable to work the treadmill: the inquest into his death established that he had 'laboured under a complication of diseases – rheumatism, gravel, and asthma from the time of his confinement'. But the regime at Northallerton cannot have helped matters. His death was announced by the *Northern Star* in a black-edged column on the front page and ever after was ascribed 'to the treatment he endured in Northallerton gaol'.[*]

Clayton's death prompted a review of the Chartist prisoners at Northallerton. None had been even remotely well-off prior to their arrest: 5 of the 9 had been unemployed. Clayton had lost his job as a cutler the previous year and, with his wife, was hawking greengrocery to evade the workhouse. Thomas Booker, another ex-cutler aged 55, had seen his earnings drop from 50 shillings a week to 7 over the previous 2 years. Thomas Penthorpe, a shoemaker, estimated his earnings at 5–9 shillings a week. Poor health had forced James Duffy to give up his handloom and eke a precarious living running a backstreet beershop. Following delays because visiting magistrates insisted Home Office approval was needed, a request from Holberry and Martin to be removed from the treadmill had been acted on the previous May. They were now 'employed in pulling old rope to pieces' for 9 hours daily, their free exercise limited to 30–60 minutes. Duffy, Booker and his son William were released part-way through their sentences a year later. 'My persecutors have not been able to obliterate from my heart and mind one single letter of the glorious Charter!' Duffy told his son, though his health was ruined and he died two years later. Others were transferred to alternative prisons but Holberry remained at Northallerton. His health was giving increasing cause for concern and finally in September he was transferred to York Castle. He was bilious and, according to the surgeon who examined him soon after his arrival, 'weak; his skin and eyes are still suffused with bile; his pulse is quick and his appetite bad'.[†]

---

[*] *York Courant*, 4 February 1841; *NS*, 6 February 1841; see also H.L.Fairburn, 'Chartist prisoners in Northallerton', *North Yorkshire County Record Office Review for 1999* (Northallerton, NYCC, 2000), pp. 41–7.

[†] *NS*, 13 June, 25 July 1840; C.Godfrey, 'The Chartist prisoners, 1839–41', *IRSH*, 24 (1979); *ECC*, 119 (May 1843).

At first Holberry refused a place in the prison hospital. Perhaps he was misled by the change of regime (he was now at last permitted to write letters and receive visitors) and possibly he was afflicted by the delusions and euphoria common in the later stages of tuberculosis. Edward Burley, a plasterer and York Chartist who often visited Holberry, found him unable to exercise or even walk. By March he could no longer hold a pen. York's Chartists led what soon became a national agitation for Holberry's release on compassionate grounds. On 17 June release was offered in return for 2 sureties, each of £100. His supporters were still desperately trying to secure these when, four days later, the 27-year-old Holberry died. A coroner's jury decided that the cause of death was tuberculosis. The York Chartists strenuously argued that prison conditions were to blame for his death but the court exonerated the authorities.

Mary Holberry – who had seen her husband only once while he was in prison – was both widowed and childless, their son Samuel having died in October 1840 aged 18 weeks.[*] Holberry's death was announced in the middle of a lecture at the Sheffield WMA rooms: there followed first a stunned silence, then sobbing and finally 'curses both loud and deep'. 'I was struck dumb', wrote the lecturer, 'I staggered, my head reeled to & fro like a drunken man's. I felt mad. I spoke on for upwards of two hours – the crowded meeting all seemed bursting – never such a feeling in the world did I see.' The Sheffield Association organised a funeral that made a vivid statement about both Holberry and Chartism. York Chartists commissioned a death mask from a local sculptor and an oak coffin for the body. All those attending the ceremony on 27 June were asked to refrain from drinking alcohol. The procession comprised a band, liveried undertakers, mutes, an elaborately decorated horse-drawn hearse and mourning carriages – all the trappings of a middle-class funeral. Several banners were made for the occasion: 'Vengeance is mine, and I will repay it, saith the Lord'; 'CLAYTON and HOLBERRY, the Martyrs to the People's Charter'; 'Thou shalt do no murder'; 'The Lord hateth the hands that shed innocent blood.' The assembled mourners were legion. Even the *Sheffield Iris*, a Whig paper implacably opposed to Chartism, put the attendance at 20,000, although the *Northern Star* thought it nearer 50,000. Harney's grave-side oration was audible only to a fraction of the crowd; but within days it was printed and swiftly became a staple recitation at meetings.[†]

Publicly, Chartists tended to blame Holberry's involvement in the Sheffield rising on 'mouthing fools, who afterwards cowered before the power they had

---

[*]   *NS*, 17 October 1840.

[†]   Ibid., 2 July 1842; *ECC*, 121 (June 1843); TS, 11/601, J. Bairstow to T. Cooper, 22 June 1842; see also T. Laqueur, 'Bodies, death and pauper funerals', *Representations*, 1 (1983), p.118. R. Fyson, 'Chartism in north Staffordshire', D.Phil thesis, University of Lancaster (1999), p.129.

evoked, and traitors who urged men to acts they took care not to participate in and who no doubt were well rewarded for their villainy'. But such was the extent of support for Chartism by the summer of 1842, and popular disgust at the treatment of prisoners in the Northallerton 'hell hole', that it is doubtful if this disingenuous defence was necessary. The notion that Holberry and other Chartists were political prisoners endured. As late as the 1860s Normanby, Home Secretary at the time of his imprisonment, was still being assailed for encouraging 'mean and servile-minded magistrates' to treat Chartists 'worse than thieves, burglars, and even murderers', allegations with some justification for, as a North Riding grandee, Normanby would have had local knowledge of Northallerton's regime.* Not only was the Home Office less than fastidious in checking the zeal of local prison government, Bayly's letter to Whitehall immediately after the Sheffield trials shows the Government to have been directly complicit in his mistreatment. Hardly less than John Frost, Samuel Holberry was held up as *the* martyred patriot, deference to whose memory became a defining characteristic of what it meant to be a Chartist. 'Father! Who are the Chartists?' a *Northern Star* poet asked:

> Millions who labour with skill, my child,
> On the land – at the loom – in the mill, my child
>
> [ ... ]
>
> And they've sworn at Holberry's grave, my child,
> (That martyr so noble and brave, my child)
> > That come weal or woe,
> > Still *onward* they'll go
> Till Freedom be won for the slave, my child!†

---

\*   *Reynolds's Newspaper*, 17 May 1863, quoted in Godfrey, 'Chartist prisoners', p. 215.
†   J. M. Owen, *Father! Who Are the Chartists?*, NS, 10 February 1844.

# CHAPTER SIX

# February 1840–December 1841: 'The Charter and nothing less'

## The National Charter Association

'Poor Frost is gone. Poor fellow!' wrote Henry Vincent from his prison cell in March 1840. 'He is one of the few really honest men that I have ever had the pleasure of knowing.'[1] John Frost faced an uncertain future in Tasmania, and so too did the Chartist movement he left behind. However, the local activities outlined in chapter 5 provided a resilient base, and from it a more-structured organisation emerged during 1840. Campaigning for Frost's return (and by association Williams's and Jones's) helped to consolidate Chartism during the early months of 1840 when it might have drifted or lost support.

A special convention was organised in Manchester in February to consider the best strategy to secure pardons, an event which was well-supported and served to reunite leading Chartists around a desire to take the movement forward. Simultaneously, a policy of packing the public meetings of other organisations, to swamp them with Chartist resolutions, served to re-focus attention on the core issues embodied in the Charter. Thus at Merthyr Tydfil 'the working men' swamped a meeting convened to congratulate the Queen on her marriage, elected a Chartist chairman and inserted their own demands into the loyal address. A similar address at Shoreditch, east London, was augmented by the wish 'that her reign may be the era of an improved condition of the people of England'. Carlisle Chartists completely subverted a meeting of the Lord's Day Observance Society, while in the east midlands promotional meetings of the Labourers' Friend Society were targeted.[2]

Invasions of ACLL meetings were always boisterous. Public meetings lay at the heart of Victorian civic discourse and Chartists aimed to foreground manhood suffrage at every opportunity such occasions presented. The direct threat to Chartism posed by the ACLL was slender: its appeal to working people was limited, though the two were rivals for the support of the middling sort. But the ACLL was an energetic organiser of public political meetings, and so was frequently the target for hostility which focused on its claim that Corn Law repeal was all that prevented popular penury being transformed into prosperity. (The laws prohibited the importation of foreign grain unless domestic prices rose above a prescribed level.)

The Chartist riposte was that repeal would benefit only 'the commercial interests, the men who speculate in the labour of the millions, the men who have thriven and now thrive out of the produce of industry ... the profit mongers'. By lowering bread prices repeal would encourage wage reductions, and by undermining agriculture rural migration to the towns would be accelerated and labour cheapened yet further. Chartists, for example the Salford powerloom weaver John Campbell, Irish by birth, painted a lurid picture of the 'wide-spreading ruin' that repeal would bring if enacted without the stabilising measures only a reformed parliament would pass.[3] Leaguers were also condemned for what Chartists judged their past political sins: 'consider who amongst them have done any thing for the Poor', demanded Stroud Chartists. 'Are they not all – aye every one of them – the zealous supporters of those who have passed the *odious* and *cruel Poor Laws?*'[4]

The ACLL also stood accused of distracting popular discontent from the real political issues of the day. So, when it called a public meeting in Dundee in May 1841, the Chartists' Democratic Council energetically placarded the town with details of the time and place and a reminder of the plight of Frost, 'the murdered Clayton', the extent of the National Debt, the compensation paid 'to the owners of Black Slaves' and the £70,000 recently spent on the royal stables. 'Crowd to the Thistle Hall on Wednesday', it concluded, 'to express your detestation of the most infamous government that ever ruled in Britain.' The ACLL deplored such behaviour: it placed Chartists 'out of the pale of political society', declared one bamboozled chairman, adding they 'ought to be excluded from all orderly public assemblies'. But Chartists argued that they were exercising the only form of democratic expression available to them. 'Public meetings are the parliaments of the working-men', one told an ACLL meeting, 'their speakers are their representatives, and in their name I come here to demand attention to the charter; I have a right to be here and to discuss with you our grievances.'[5]

However, pressing issues surrounded Chartism's own internal governance. Loose clusters of localities and an *ad hoc* Convention had seemed appropriate when sheer weight of numbers seemed sufficient to secure the People's Charter; but they were inadequate to sustain a movement that was now embarking on an indefinite agitation. There was an urgent need to widen the appeal of Chartism and reassert its core message in the wake of the public damage many, including dedicated supporters, felt had been done by events that winter. Even those most loyal to O'Connor and the *Northern Star* knew that he alone could not carry

the burden of creating and maintaining a nationwide organisation; furthermore sentencing, in the long-postponed case of seditious libel facing O'Connor,
was likely to be custodial. With so many of its key personnel imprisoned,
Chartism – especially in England – needed to reorganise itself. The first half of
1840 was increasingly dominated by discussion of a variety of plans to revive
and organise the movement.

The plans of the Newcastle-based Northern PU were a highly regarded
exemplar. They began from the premiss that the General Convention had failed
because too much had been expected of it. It had been elected haphazardly to
act as Chartism's deliberative assembly, its national secretariat and the main
organiser of its missionary effort. The Northern PU therefore addressed these
problems at a regional level with a new constitution adopted unanimously
in April 1840 by a meeting of nearly 2,000 members. Each locality elected a
representative to a twenty-six strong executive which deliberated in private but
published its proceedings. Officers were elected every six months at a general
meeting, the Northern PU's governing body. 'The principal feature is proposed
to be a system of missionary visitations in the various localities.' The Northern
PU was not the first in the field with a plan for reorganisation. The previous
December, LDA members had attempted to create a London Association of
United Chartists: but it was an unpropitious time and the association quickly
foundered. The Metropolitan Charter Union led by Henry Hetherington,
which replaced it the following spring, was more solid. Its ambitious objectives
included a network of co-operative stores and coffee-house reading rooms. The
aim was for all London's working men's and radical associations to merge into
it. Its secretary would be salaried and its governing council responsible for
appointing and deploying paid lecturers. But London continued to frustrate
Chartist aspirations. In practice the affiliated localities numbered only four and
the organisation was notable mainly for contributing to the mutual antipathy
that dominated relations between Chartists in the capital and the rest of the
country.[6]

That antipathy was much in evidence when a national conference convened
in Manchester in July to discuss plans for a national organisation. 'The
Chartists of the metropolis have decided, after the most mature deliberation,
that the best plan of organisation for the friends of liberty is that recommended and adopted by the Metropolitan Charter Union', the latter declared;
'it would be useless and impolitic to incur the expense of sending delegates to
Manchester.'[7] The arrogance of the statement is almost breathtaking (and the
Union subsequently thought better of it) but it should be noted that a similar
conference at Nottingham in April had been abandoned: only ten delegates
turned up and actual attendance fell to two at one session. Inevitably, the
Manchester conference was without key national personalities.

Though supportive, O'Connor absented himself because he was preoccupied with the on-going legal action against him. At least he could choose not to attend: many others were already in prison. Among them was Bronterre O'Brien, sensationally acquitted in March at Newcastle assizes (on charges of unlawful assembly, sedition and conspiracy) but sentenced to eighteen months imprisonment at Liverpool assizes in April, having been found guilty of similar charges. Before he was jailed, however, O'Brien called for a fundamental change of direction by proposing that Chartism should henceforth focus on contesting parliamentary elections.

In essence this was a revival of an earlier radical idea, 'legislative attorneys' (alternative MPs elected to an anti-parliament). Its similarity to the General Convention attracted and repelled Chartists in approximately equal measure.[8] But O'Brien argued that the elections should be at the hustings of the next general election, where Chartist candidates could be elected by the traditional show of hands and then constitute a genuinely alternative parliament. Its very mode of election would powerfully illustrate the undemocratic nature of the existing constitution. O'Brien believed that Chartist voters would outnumber the existing electorate by 5 or even 9 to 1. Could Westminster's 'mock parliament', he asked, 'take coercive measures to put down a real parliament, proved, by the same process, to represent five-sixths or nine-tenths of the empire?'[9]

There were doubts as to the legality of this procedure, however, and many Chartists lacked the stomach for further direct confrontation with authority. 'I heartily curse *Martyrdom*', Vincent told his cousin, 'and readily admit that we must adopt more *rational means* of proceeding than rushing headlong into the *fangs* of that law, which, as *Paine* says, it is always better to obey until we can effectually supersede it by better.'[10] Others doubted whether Chartism needed a new convention. 'What we want is men deputed to agitate and combine our party together', wrote Robert Lowery, 'if a district can pay a man to sit in a Convention, it can pay him to agitate, and he will do the cause ten times as much good.' Harney agreed: impressed by the USCCS, he urged English Chartists to adopt a similar organisation. This was necessary, he believed, to combat the ACLL whose Manchester-based central office impressed many Chartists even as they endeavoured to suppress its activities in their localities. Harney therefore suggested that Chartism, too, should maintain a central secretariat in Manchester, along with a network of county lecturers.[11]

Suspicious of anything that lay beyond his capacity to control, O'Connor was uneasy about developments during the spring of 1840. He preferred to build on the obvious success of the *Northern Star* by starting a daily newspaper, the *Morning Star*. He offered to part-fund this himself, but its central feature would be a network of 20,000 subscribers whose money would give the paper an assured income and maintain a London-based convention, a permanent secretariat and a team of lecturers. There was a paradox here: 'London ever has been, and ever will be, rotten', O'Connor declared and he would have nothing to do with any London-based association. The arithmetic behind his proposal was as haphazard as his prose was ebullient. Yet, as so often with O'Connor, these were combined with shrewd insight. 'Northern Star ... has made brothers and sisters of every working man and woman in the Empire,' he observed. 'Steam has annihilated space', yet repeatedly Chartism had been frustrated by inadequacy in its internal communications and the Northern Star had trailed behind the news. A daily paper offered a way out of this quandary and O'Connor knew how much easier its management might be, both editorially and in distribution terms, if it was located in the capital. (Leeds had only just been linked to the emerging national railway network, with a station still two miles from the centre.)[12] However, few shared O'Connor's conviction that the movement could sustain a daily paper. His contribution to the debate was notable mainly for presaging later issues in the management of Chartism, and for indicating that there were limits to his influence. The National Charter Association of Great Britain (NCA) that emerged from the deliberations of the twenty-three delegates at Manchester was an amalgam of elements from virtually all the plans that had been advanced over the preceding months, except O'Connor's.[13]

'Wherever possible, the members shall be formed into classes of ten persons', remitting a weekly subscription of a penny via their leader to the NCA. Each town was to have a Chartist council, entitled to half the subscriptions collected. In each region there was to be a county or district council; but the governing body was a national executive council, comprising a secretary, treasurer and five ordinary members. These were to be elected by the whole membership. The secretary would be salaried at £2 per week and members would be paid while the council was in session, and receive an allowance and expenses when employed as missionaries. O'Brien's plan to bring forward Chartist candidates at every possible election was warmly commended, but the selection of 'candidates who are legally qualified to sit in Parliament' was urged and there were no proposals for them to constitute an alternative parliament. It was 'urgently recommended that strict sobriety be observed by all members and officers of this Association', and the main medium of communication between executive and members would be 'the "Northern Star", "Scottish Patriot", and such other of the Chartist newspapers as may be selected by the Executive Council'. The formation of the NCA was a bold step, taken without O'Connor (who was finally gaoled in May) and indeed any of the leading Chartists of the previous two years. In fact only three members of the 1839 Convention – Deeghan (Stalybridge), Smart (Leicestershire) and James Taylor (Rochdale) – participated in its formation. A new generation of leaders were coming to the fore, notably James Leach, a Manchester mill worker whose position as president of the provisional Executive made him Britain's first, formally elected national political leader. Leach had lost his job in 1839 after leading resistance to wage cuts, after which he existed precariously on the proceeds of bookselling and printing. In April 1840 he escaped imprisonment by pleading guilty (to seditious conspiracy and possession of arms) and accepting an indefinitely deferred sentence which, however, the judge threatened to revoke 'if he attended any more of these meetings' (i.e. where arming was discussed). Leach brought to the NCA the administrative punctiliousness of an active trade unionist, but he was also a lucid public speaker and passionately opposed to any accommodation with middle-class opinion.[14] His claims to have devised the whole concept of the NCA were overstated, but it undoubtedly bore the imprint of his trade unionist perspective.

The NCA was also highly innovatory, the first national political party in history. It had a formal constitution with explicit aims and criteria for membership. Its nationwide coverage rested on individuals' subscriptions rather than, as was the case with parties in Parliament, the expression of 'interest' and the personal largesse of their most active supporters. Membership was open to all who were willing to subscribe and signify their agreement with its objective: 'to obtain a "Radical Reform" of the House of Commons, in other words, a full and faithful Representation of the entire people of the United Kingdom', on the principles of *The People's Charter*. The NCA sought to be inclusive. Almost the only moment of note at the aborted Nottingham conference was when a female observer interrupted a delegate's reference to working men and the Charter with the cry of 'Aye, and women too.' Along with the standard iconography of the fasces, cap of liberty, tricolour, a hive (indicating industry), shamrock, thistle and rose, the NCA membership card gave symbolic equal emphasis to images of a male and a female worker. While the position of women and men within the movement was far from one of complete equality, and the Charter called only for universal male suffrage, the NCA made no distinction between the membership rights they enjoyed.[15]

It is, however, necessary to be cautious in assessing the NCA. Its Scottish affiliates were few and a number of English localities were suspicious of it, especially in the midlands. (The Metropolitan Charter Union, though, overcame its disdain to become the NCA's London district council in September 1840.) Furthermore the NCA always appeared more coherent and comprehensive on paper than on the ground. It recruited only a fraction of the total supporters of the movement, peaking at some 400 branches and a total membership of around 50,000.[16] But this, it should be stressed, was a remarkable achievement for a pioneering organisation whose support was drawn overwhelmingly from those least able to pay a regular subscription. It provided an organisational focus within a movement hitherto without a formal structure. It signalled a determination to move forward, rather than dwell on the events of the previous year (the obvious problem in campaigning, however effectively, for Chartist prisoners); and it alone provided central co-ordination for Chartist agitation beyond that derived from the press. Moreover, while Scotland had, in the USCCS *Chartist Circular*, a lively journal enjoying a peak weekly circulation of over 20,000, other Chartist papers (*Northern Star* aside) endured uneven fortunes. *The Charter* closed in March and the *Northern Liberator* in December 1840; and there were fewer Chartist periodicals generally in 1840 than in 1839.[17] The NCA therefore added organisational ballast to the movement and to some extent diminished the appearance that Chartism was O'Connor's personal crusade.

However, it was certainly not independent of O'Connor's influence. The NCA became a means through which he strengthened his hold on the movement: acquiescence in the policies of the NCA was effectively expressed through loyalty to the newspaper. By turning over the *Northern Star* to promote the NCA and be the primary means of communication among its members, O'Connor signalled that the NCA was the movement's citadel, to be respected and defended even by those Chartists who were not paying members. Without the *Star*, the NCA and its executive would have been almost paralysed. Nowhere was this more obvious than in the executive's attempt to promote its own periodical in the autumn of 1841. Only four issues appeared before it closed, because the executive was too busy to get the journal out regularly.[18] The *Northern Star* on the other hand was reliable, its professional staff were able to act on NCA material at short notice and its circulation extended far beyond that of any other Chartist periodical. The fortunes of the *Star*, however, reflected those of the broader movement and its average circulation for 1840 was little more than half that for 1839. O'Connor and the NCA needed each other. Not the least of the NCA's achievements was that it helped to hold Chartism together, and indeed presided over the renewal of the movement at a time when its most influential leader was imprisoned in York. However, York was no Northallerton and O'Connor no Holberry. The circumstances of his imprisonment made possible his continued intervention in Chartism and helped shape the mythology of 'the lion of freedom'.

## The lion of freedom

The lion of freedom comes from his den,
We'll rally around him again and again,
We'll crown him with laurels our champion to be,
O'Connor, the patriot of sweet liberty.

The pride of the nation, he's noble and brave,
He's the terror of tyrants, the friend of the slave,
The bright star of freedom, the noblest of men,
We'll rally around him again and again.

Though proud daring tyrants his body confined,
They never could alter his generous mind;
We'll hail our caged lion, now free from his den,
And we'll rally around him again and again.

(*The Lion of Freedom, Northern Star*, 11 September 1841)

*The Lion of Freedom* was written by an unknown Welsh female Chartist to mark O'Connor's release from prison in August 1841. His reception on that occasion was among the most theatrical in the history of a movement never lacking in drama. But to understand its significance it is necessary to follow the train of events that led to it and examine the use to which O'Connor put his loss of liberty. The Government's legal pursuit of O'Connor was determined enough, but it knew a failed prosecution would present him with boundless propaganda opportunities. As we have seen, O'Connor had lived under the shadow of a trial since the previous autumn. Stephens's case was similarly delayed; but whereas that served to quieten, even demoralise, Stephens (as it was surely intended to), the effect on O'Connor was the opposite. His credentials as a victim of official persecution were being emphasised without the irksome necessity of going to prison. Even when he did stand trial and was found guilty, at York on 17 March 1840, he managed to negotiate a delay in sentencing until after the Liverpool assize where he was to have been a co-defendant in Chartist trials there (a prosecution that eventually did not proceed).

The ultimate outcome of O'Connor's trial, heard at the same assize as those of the Bradford and Sheffield conspirators, was never in doubt. However, O'Connor exploited the trial to make a bravura five-hour 'defence of Chartism'.[19] The Whig Government, not Chartism, was the real enemy of the constitution. Chartists (whom O'Connor equated throughout with 'the people') were exercising their legal rights in pursuit of the suffrage denied to them. As for physical force, O'Connor treated the jury to an anecdote about the findings of a 'Scotch gentleman' concerning Ireland:

His belief was, that the landlords, parsons, and magistrates were the promoters of all the conspiracies, seditions, and outbreaks. His remedy was, when insurrection broke out, forthwith to hang the nearest landlord, parson and magistrates, his assurance being that such a course would effectively tranquilise the country. (Laughter.)
Let us understand each other. We are of different politics. I neither court your sympathy, desire your pity, or ask for your compassion. I am a Chartist – a democrat to the fullest extent of the word; and if my life hung upon the abandonment of those principles, I would scorn to hold it upon so base a tenure. This avowal is not likely to serve me in your estimation.[20]

And so it proved. The jury took all of ten minutes to reach a unanimous guilty verdict that passages from the *Northern Star* of July 1839 were seditious libels (that is, their purpose was to incite insurrection). O'Connor's strategy had been to appeal to the country at large rather than the jury. He sought to take on himself the Government's general persecution of Chartism. His trial was unconnected to any specific riot or conspiracy and he was innocent of any act of violence. His demeanour was that of a noble martyr. 'This is my last letter for some time', he wrote in the *Star* shortly before he was sentenced:

> In a few hours after you shall have read this, I shall be consigned to a gloomy dungeon, not for any particular merit of my own, but in consequence of your disunion. Under these circumstances, you will suppose that I am about to scold and chide you; but no, my friends and companions, the last glimmer of my lamp shall be devoted to lighting you on the road to freedom.[21]

On 17 May 1840 O'Connor began an eighteen-month prison sentence at York Castle. Prison conditions varied widely according to local practice, and a prisoner's influence, status and ability to procure comforts. O'Connor fared pretty well. Reports in local papers that he had been given a guided tour of York Minster and other places of interest en route to the prison were probably mischievous; but within a short time of his arrival (and 'herding and feeding with convicted felons' according to the *Star*), O'Connor was given a cell of his own. 'His meals are, we understand, served up from one of the inns in the city', reported the *York Gazette*.[22]

A different picture was presented by the *Star*, which emphasised the routine and menial prison tasks, slopping out included, he was required to do. At the time of sentencing O'Connor had been sick with an undefined condition (consequent perhaps on rupturing blood vessels the year before) and he arrived at the Castle armed with medical opinion that 'the usual prison discipline, and being *deprived of exercise*, would lay the foundation of disease, which would ultimately SHORTEN LIFE'. Within a few weeks his cell included items of his own furniture, plus cage birds for company, and he was allowed books and newspapers. Privately he boasted: 'while I was in York Castle I read two-hundred of the best works and wrote a number myself'. This was typical Feargus flummery, though he may have sketched some of his *Practical Work on the Management of Small Farms* and probably did write one or two other pamphlets.[23] Far more importantly, he successfully circumvented restrictions on writing for the *Northern Star* and from the end of 1840 his weekly contributions resumed almost unabated.[24]

*Management of Small Farms* was not published until two years after his release (and much of it was not his own work); but O'Connor's sentence did coincide with a marked shift in his thinking, placing the provision of small-holdings at the heart of his social and political vision. Symbolically, O'Connor's last publication before his imprisonment had been an open letter to James Leach, developing an argument that the land should lie at the heart of revitalising Chartism. The paramount material advantage of manhood suffrage, he argued, would be 'the restoration of my fellow man from a too-artificial to a more natural state of life'. Such 'complete and entire independence' was possible only if man 'enjoys for the *whole* of his life a field whereon to exercise his labour'. From this O'Connor developed a case for 'Chartist Agricultural Associations – Five-Acre Associations – or Landed-Labour Associations', an idea to which, he promised, he would return on his release.[25]

At first sight O'Connor's agrarian proposals look little more than another contribution to contemporary debate about Chartism's future, an opportunistic linkage of the long-established popular interest in getting 'back to the land' to a political movement in a state of uncertainty. But land reform had always been integral to the social programme Chartists anticipated would follow the enactment of the Charter. This was due partly to the obvious and enduring place of landed property at the heart of the political establishment; it also reflected the long pedigree of agrarian agitation – from opposition to enclosure, through Thomas Spence, to early 1830s interest in communal land-holding – which ran like a red thread through English radicalism. The vocabulary used by O'Connor in his letter to Leach drew on the well-established radical agrarian trope of the *natural* versus the *artificial*. Spencean veterans like Allen Davenport, John George and Charles Neesom had played a formative part in London Chartism: at least one Spencean song enjoyed new life in the 1840s, with 'Chartist' simply substituted for 'Spencean' in its title. Young William Lovett had been an eloquent advocate of an allotment economy and the Chartist press ran frequent articles on land reform. Above all, perhaps, countless migrants to industrial towns brought with them a culture still rural at its heart.[26]

O'Connor refined his agrarian thinking while in prison. One letter, smuggled out to the *Northern Star* in July, argued for a co-ordinated exodus of urban workers to the land, to improve wages in the industrial labour market. A second urged the foundation conference of the NCA: '[T]hink of the only refuge for the destitute. THE LAND! THE LAND! THE LAND! THE ENGLISH LAND!'[27] Subsequent letters on the same theme were pointedly addressed to Leach, implying for the newly formed NCA a subaltern role to O'Connor. In late summer, amid the welter of co-ops, schools and temperance groups, came news of two Chartist localities about to establish land societies.[28] By the autumn Chartist lectures on land schemes of one kind or another were commonplace, even inducing from retirement the elderly and disabled Thomas Preston, in the 1790s a member of the London Corresponding Society and another former leading Spencean.[29] O'Connor reiterated the agrarian theme in letters from prison throughout 1841, culminating in the pamphlet *'The Land' the Only Remedy for National Poverty and Impending National Ruin*. This, though ostensibly addressed to Irish landlords, elaborated a vision of England prior to industrialisation. 'What was England then? A great national family, the several branches consisting of agricultural weavers and weaving agriculturalists.'[30]

It would be an exaggeration to claim that the land question dominated Chartist discourse as a result of O'Connor's interventions from prison. As the survey of local culture and activities in chapter 5 revealed, 1840 was a highly fertile year for the Chartist movement, not least in terms of redefining and expanding its activities and aspirations. Agrarianism simply took its place alongside co-operation, temperance, Chartist churches and schools. But its close association with O'Connor gave it a certain cachet. He was laying the ground for a potentially fundamental realignment of the movement, embracing dimensions hitherto secondary to its core political objective.

## New moves

O'Connor was not alone in contemplating a root and branch reconfiguration of Chartism: religious, educational and temperance initiatives, plus a movement for household suffrage looming on the movement's flanks, constituted far more significant challenges. From his cell O'Connor fulminated against all four, collectively dubbing them 'the new move'. The inclusion of 'church Chartism' was misleading, since Chartist churches, as we have seen, existed amicably alongside other activities in a wide range of localities, and Chartism generally was imbued with the vision of a radical social gospel. But 'Knowledge' and 'Teetotal Chartism', together with household suffrage, posed a different order of problem for those, especially Feargus O'Connor, who sought to maintain the unity of the movement around the central concept of *The People's Charter*.

Knowledge Chartism was incubated in Warwick Prison. As 'the lion of freedom' contemplated captivity, William Lovett and John Collins anticipated their liberation. They could have been released in May 1840, two months before their sentence concluded, had they agreed to the Home Secretary's condition that they be bound over for their good behaviour. All too familiar with squalid cells, a diet that failed to meet even the inadequate standards nominally laid down for it and the casual indifference of prison authorities, it would have been understandable had they accepted the offer. Lovett especially was in poor health. But they refused: 'we have been about the first political victims who have been classed and punished as misdemeanants and felons because we happened to be of *the working class*', they responded, 'to enter into a bond for our future good conduct would at once be an admission of guilt'.[31] Their principled stand meant they were not released until 25 July.

A deputation of Chartists, led by William Cardo, gathered at first light at the prison gates to greet them. Also waiting, discretely, were around a 100 troops drafted to Warwick the previous evening. All publicans had been forbidden to host any meeting associated with the release but the landlord of The Saracen's

Head defied the ban and offered his premises for both a celebratory breakfast and an evening celebration. Both were subdued affairs. After breakfast and a somewhat stiff exchange of formal pleasantries with Cardo and his colleagues, Lovett excused himself and hurried away to London. It was left to Collins to invest the proceedings with a sense of occasion commensurate with Cardo's prediction that their liberation would be 'the resurrection of the cause'.[32] Collins alone accepted the invitations that came from all over Britain to attend rallies to celebrate their release. Often accompanied by McDouall and White (newly liberated from Chester and Wakefield respectively), Collins returned to the stump oratory that had made him a central figure in 1838. His reception was warm and frequently overwhelming. Not for the first time, the self-effacing Birmingham toolmaker played a central role in invigorating Chartism. Lovett's understandable desire to be reunited with his wife, Mary, and subsequent convalescence in the seclusion of west Cornwall, command sympathy and respect; but his failure to recognise (or, if he did, care for) the popular acclaim prison had earned him, would soon marginalise him completely.

   In Lovett's bag as he travelled to London was the manuscript of a book written, with Collins's assistance, during their final months in Warwick. That September it appeared: *Chartism; A New Organization of the People, Embracing a Plan for the Education and Improvement of the People, Politically and Socially; Addressed to the Working-Classes of the United Kingdom, and more especially the Advocates of the Rights and Liberties of the Whole People as Set Forth in the 'People's Charter'*. It was a curious mixture of the grandiloquent and the mundane, betraying Lovett's earlier interest in Owenite socialism. On the one hand it included 'specimens of lesson cards' detailed enough, for example, to permit an accurate sketch of the course of the pulmonary artery; on the other hand it brimmed with confidence in a secular millennium:

> The spirit which has awakened, pervades, and moves the multitude, is that of intellectual inquiry. The light of thought is illuming the minds of the masses; kindled by cheap publications, the discussions, missionaries, and meetings of the last ten years: a light which no power can extinguish, nor control its vivifying influence. For the spark once struck is inextinguishable, and will go on extending and radiating with increasing power; thought will generate thought; and each illumined mind will become a centre for the enlightenment of thousands, till the effulgent blaze penetrates every cranny of corruption, and scare[s] selfishness and injustice from their seats of power. *Chartism* is an emanation of this spirit.[33]

*Chartism; A New Organization of the People* was suffused with the spirit of the Enlightenment, as filtered through the artisan intelligentsia of socialist London. The lesson cards which formed the appendices covered geology, mineralogy, 'Truth', 'Rights', 'Duties' and human anatomy. The bulk of the book comprised thoughtful evaluations of various educational systems and detailed proposals and plans for infant, preparatory, high and adult schools and circulating libraries. There was a strongly worded defence of workers' alcohol consumption, asserting that while 'drunkenness and dissipation' were 'daily diminishing', viciousness of working conditions encouraged excessive drinking. While committed to the creation of 'an enlightened public opinion in favour of the People's Charter, such as shall *peaceably* cause its enactment', Lovett and Collins still 'maintain[ed] that the people have the *same right* to employ similar means to regain their liberties, as have been used to enslave them'. There was a passing remark about 'a few individuals ... in different parts of the country, whose feelings or sympathies have at times got the better of their judgments and prompted them to talk violently or behave unjustly'; but this was as close to controversy as the authors ventured. Theirs was a sober tract for new times.[34]

Where they did court controversy, however, was in packaging their educational proposals as rules and regulations of an 'association to be entitled the National Association of the United Kingdom, for Promoting the Political and Social Improvement of the People'. It is unclear whether Collins had much say in this: Lovett claimed all the credit for writing *Chartism* and it is replete with arguments and even specific phraseology from LWMA addresses that he had written. Furthermore, the manuscript was edited and some textual changes made by Lovett's mentor Francis Place.[35] To claim the title 'National Association' within three months of the formation of the NCA was maladroit, even if not intentionally confrontational. But the book attracted little attention until the following March when Lovett issued an *Address* launching a National Association as outlined in the book. Collins, Hetherington, Cleave and Vincent also signed the document which they then circulated among sympathetic Chartists for signing. Although it stressed the urgency of attaining the Charter, the address called on working people to become their own 'social and political regenerators', structuring their associational life to achieve this. O'Connor promptly dismissed the proposal as 'Knowledge Chartism', the clear import of which was that 'a standard of learning was a necessary qualification to entitle a man to his political rights'.[36] A careful reading of Lovett and his associates shows they meant no such thing, but the mud stuck. A bitter Lovett ascribed the financial losses incurred by the second edition of *Chartism* to 'the clamour subsequently raised against us by the O'Connorites'.[37]

This ostensible challenge to the NCA might have seemed less serious had it not emerged almost simultaneously with a concerted move in support of teetotal Chartism. Less than two months after *Chartism* appeared Cleave, Hetherington, Vincent, William Hill and Charles Neesom sent an address to the *Northern Star* with the suggestion that all members of the NCA's foundation conference should sign it. The address opened with the observation that Chartists had endured 'one of the most fiery persecutions ever waged against truth and justice. But, at the same time', it continued, 'you have had to contend with an enemy in your own camp – an insidious and powerful enemy – an enemy continuously *weakening you, and adding to the strength of your profligate oppressors.* That enemy is THE LOVE OF INTOXICATING DRINKS.' The address concluded with a call to establish 'Chartist teetotal societies in every city, town and village'. As we saw in chapter 5, temperance was an integral part of Chartist culture but this address raised the drink question in a particularly acute form. It called not for temperance but for total abstention (teetotalism) which it sought to make a central, defining feature of Chartism; and it concluded with the contentious statement 'NO GOVERNMENT CAN LONG WITHSTAND THE JUST CLAIMS OF A PEOPLE WHO HAVE THE COURAGE TO CONQUER THEIR OWN VICES.'[38]

If 'Knowledge Chartism' could be construed as conceding the franchise should be earned through educational improvement, then 'Teetotal Chartism' apparently argued that large swathes of the unenfranchised did not deserve the vote because they drank. Vincent was the formative agent in this aspect of the new move. As his release from prison drew near, he underwent a profound conversion to teetotalism. His expectations of Chartism without alcohol mirrored Lovett and Collins's vision for it with education. '*Chartism in twelve months* time, will be growing into an enlightened and irresistible force', he wrote from prison in October, vowing to dedicate himself to the cause upon his release: 'The time *now* spent on drinking will then be spent on thinking – and ... *thought* is *Democracy!*'[39] Teetotal Chartism gathered more momentum than Lovett's educational proposals. Vincent was one of the movement's most popular and compelling orators and he made rapid strides towards his vision of a teetotal Chartist movement.

The four co-signatories were also significant: Cleave (the leading London radical publisher), Hetherington (the most respected veteran of the unstamped press), Neesom (until recently an authoritative advocate of physical force) and the editor of the *Northern Star*, William Hill. Soon their address was circulating in pamphlet form (supplemented with a diatribe against '*stupid, reckless, ruinous*' tobacco). In 1841 Cleave commenced a new periodical, *English Chartist Circular and Temperance Record*, which achieved a circulation second only to the *Star* and its Scottish namesake. That spring it published an expanded version of the original address, signed by 70 prominent figures in the movement; with supplementary signatures over the following weeks, the total soon reached 135. Its coverage was impressive. James Leach was there; so too were William Rider and John Watkins, two of O'Connor's warmest admirers; ten were – or had been – imprisoned for Chartist activities and another (Walsingham Martin) was the brother of a noted Northallerton prisoner. Other signatories included senior officers from NCA branches in Bradford, Burnley, Liverpool, Manchester, Northampton, the Potteries, Preston and Salford.[40]

This was a major tranch of opinion-formers within the movement, but O'Connor's opposition was implacable: 'I object to Teetotal Chartism, because all who do not join in, and I fear there are many, will be considered unworthy of their civil rights.'[41] Furthermore, by conjuring a spectre of 'Church Chartism, Teetotal Chartism, Knowledge Chartism and Household Chartism' as allied forces undermining the movement, O'Connor seemed poised to purge from Chartism's mainstream all who declined his leadership. Yet there was a compelling strategic logic to his actions, derived less from a desire for personal aggrandisement than from a shrewd grasp that Chartism's strength rested on presenting a united front that made no concession whatever to the right of universal male suffrage. Anything that diverted energies from that objective undermined the whole. Anything that implied that the right of some to vote was stronger than others undermined the whole. But O'Connor's inclusion – or, rather, invention – of 'Household Chartism' was disingenuous, for while a household suffrage movement had emerged in 1840, its relationship to Chartism (unlike the other three elements of the so-called new move) was tangential.

Household suffrage meant simply a right to vote granted to male heads of household, and therefore excluding lodgers, those living in multi-occupancy, furnished rooms or with their parents. The momentum behind it derived from middle-class liberals anxious to defuse Chartism and/or genuinely believing the vote should be entrusted only to those already expected to exercise good judgement, as ratepayers and heads of families, in broader society. It had originally been an objective of the BPU when it reformed in 1837 until, at Attwood's urging, replaced by universal male suffrage to consolidate popular support for the Union. Its appeal to middle-class liberals lay partly in its excluding those who were often seen as rootless (and, therefore, potentially threatening) members of society, a consideration that weighed heavily in rapidly expanding urban areas. Household suffrage also conformed to existing legal principles by tying the right to vote to property, in this case not outright ownership or substantive tenancy but at least occupancy, on formally defined terms, of premises suggestive of some status in society. Household suffrage was offensive to those claiming the franchise as of right, and it would have been difficult, even controversial, to define and therefore administer.

Some who espoused universal male suffrage might have accepted household suffrage as an interim position but in practice it was usually yoked to another compromise, namely triennial rather than annual parliaments. This affronted Chartism's fundamental conception of representative democracy. Not all six points of the Charter were sacrosanct: equal electoral districts prompted doubt and, even, outright opposition; and not infrequently the secret ballot was seen as unmanly. O'Connor himself was prepared to trim on that point, declaring that the ballot 'put a mask on an honest face'.[42] However, it is striking how

few Chartists were prepared, even temporarily or pragmatically, to compromise on the four core points of the Charter. There were a few exceptions,
conspicuously in Leeds where Chartists were making headway in local politics,
working alongside middle-class liberals and perhaps therefore more disposed
to compromise. Despite being the place of publication of the *Northern Star
& Leeds General Advertiser* (as its masthead proclaimed), Leeds was far from
typical of the northern textile towns where Chartism flourished. It had a
broader industrial base, less susceptible to the extremes of economic fluctuations, and fewer domestic textile workers whose predicament gave Chartism a
distinctive edge in many northern centres.

Faced with a less confrontational style of Chartism, middle-class radicals
in the town were more accommodating than in neighbouring towns. Their
focal point was the *Leeds Times*. Under the editorship of Samuel Smiles,
this happily joined Chartism in opposing the dominant journalistic force in
local politics, the *Leeds Mercury*, which defended the legitimacy of the 1832
settlement. But Smiles's view of Chartism was that it was 'a Knowledge agitation' and he was stringently critical of physical force. In September 1840 he
became the founding secretary of the Leeds Parliamentary Reform Association
(LPRA), which included several notable textiles magnates and ACLL activists.
Its suggestion that working men unite with middle-class reformers, under a
banner of household suffrage and triennial parliaments, created a stir in Leeds
NCA branch. Matters came to a head when the West Ward Chartists agreed
not to stand a candidate in a municipal election but support an LPRA member
instead. This was happening almost literally on the doorstep of the *Star*, and
the paper could hardly ignore it. William Hill dubbed the LPRA 'the Fox and
Goose Club' (wily manufacturer foxes swallowing credulous worker geese into
a political alliance) and treated it to a coruscating editorial.[43]

Here the matter might well have rested had not the LPRA invited several
radical MPs, and notably Daniel O'Connell, to speak at its 'Great Reform
Festival' on 21 January 1841. This was projected as a national event, to be held
in linen manufacturer James Garth Marshall's newly built Egyptian-style mill,
specially decorated and illuminated for the occasion. Marshall and Smiles were
avowedly seeking to outflank Chartism and make the LPRA the vanguard of a
national movement. The festival was promoted as 'the first grand Conference
which has been held between the middle and working classes, since the
passing of the Reform Bill'. This, combined with the personal enmity between
O'Connor and O'Connell, plus the wide attention that a visit from the latter
to the home of *Northern Star* would attract, made it imperative that the paper
destabilise the event. The LPRA told O'Connell that it anticipated no more
than 'some slight Chartist opposition' and 'a few discordant notes'. But the
Fox and Goose Club dominated the *Star* for weeks. One measure of its gravity
for Hill and O'Connor was that this was one of the rare occasions the paper

included an illustration: a cartoon, drawn in prison by O'Connor himself, depicting the festival as comprising an audience of geese and a platform party of smartly attired foxes (excepting O'Connell, portrayed as a fox dressed as a peacock).[44]

However, the audience was far from goose-like. Leeds NCA council organised a rival rally, timed to end just before the LPRA's commenced. In boisterous mood, everyone at the Chartist demonstration proceeded to Marshall's mill. Among them were delegates from across the country, including Collins who had refused Marshall's invitation to join the platform party. The non-arrival of O'Connell, due to an expedient delay on the road, offered the LPRA's council an escape route. In O'Connell's place Joseph Hume, MP, a staunch advocate of household suffrage, headed the platform. However, the resolution he proposed mentioned neither household suffrage nor triennial parliaments, instead pledging the assembly to support 'a further enlargement of the franchise, as should make the interests of the representatives identical with the whole country, and by this means secure a just government for all classes of the people'. This was ambiguous enough to secure Chartist support. Powerful speeches, welcoming class co-operation in principle but emphatically championing the Charter, were made by Collins, Robert Lowery, Scottish Chartist leader James Moir and Arthur O'Neill (a Christian Chartist of increasing prominence in Birmingham). Their argument was passionately summarised by Lowery, whose speech encapsulated why even 'moderate' Chartists were suspicious of the motives of middle-class reformers:

> I stand here as a working man, I stand here as a Chartist; as a man bred and born in the lap of poverty; as a man who claims nought from his riches; but from his existence as a man, who scorns that agitation that refers men back to musty parchments for the rights of the people. I stand here as a man who says that the rights of citizenship are written in Heaven, and not in the Courts of Kings and of Parliaments (cheers) ... I know you will tell me that as Chartists, we have been violent, we have uttered language no honest man could ever assent to – but middle men, I ask you, have you ever stepped into the huts of poverty? Have you ever seen your wives in rags and your children without food? If you have not, then I ask you to bear in mind the causes why those of whom you complain have been violent, to keep in mind that those who have been violent have drained degradation to its bitterest dregs ... What is the extent of representation that will truly represent the people, and secure to them their rights? I say no representation short of that which admits every man arrived at a mature age to a vote – that is to say Universal Suffrage.

Lowery had much fun at the expense of the absent O'Connell:

> I say shame that man (cheers from the Chartists and groans from others in the meeting). I cry cowardice upon that man for not being here (renewed

cheers from the Chartists and loud groans and hisses for the speaker, from others in the hall). I expected that it was arguments I was to hear – I expected gentlemen would listen to reason. I expected that the classes who are clad so bravely would have listened to me; but I am sorry that I have been so mistaken in them.

And, turning to the platform party, he concluded:

I am afraid that prejudice prevails so far with you, that you cannot forget and forgive; and I beg of you therefore not to think of me as an individual; but to think of our common country. I am willing to bear every insult; but when I do bear it, I hope you too will also shew your patience; and as you do plume yourselves upon your superiority, I shall sit down expecting to hear your better wisdom (cheers and hisses).[45]

Hume's resolution was carried and the meeting peacefully dispersed. 'No suffrage was just that was not universal' was the Chartists' concluding message. The *Leeds Times* and the *Northern Star* disputed whether the cheers with which the meeting closed were 'for Reform' or for O'Connor, Frost, Williams and Jones (plus groans for O'Connell). But, either way, the LPRA was humiliated. Assailed on its other flank by the *Leeds Mercury*, it stuttered on only until October.[46]

As winter ended, therefore, a united Chartist front had drowned out the call for household suffrage. Unwittingly, the LPRA had galvanised a defence of O'Connor's view of Chartism and from the isolation of his York cell Feargus saw his authority reasserted for him. This makes his lumping together of 'Household Chartism' with religious, educational and temperance strands, into a secretive and sinister 'New Move', disingenuous, even perverse. O'Connor's first salvo was a letter to the *Star* on 13 March. 'Church Chartism, Teetotal Chartism, Knowledge Chartism, and Household Chartism … I mean to denounce one and all as trick, farce, cheat or humbug'. Even before then the *Star* had showed scant regard for the part played by Chartist speakers at Marshall's mill (to which it had never sent a reporter of its own). Collins was pilloried even for being there. The paper's position was a mass of contradictions, underlined on 3 April when O'Connor fulminated against 'the new move' while, on an adjacent page, an editorial criticised his assault on Church Chartism. Furthermore he had no real quarrel with teetotal Chartists. Their activities continued to be covered extensively in *Northern Star*. Several of his closest associates, as we have seen, signed the address that appeared in *English Charter Circular*, with whose proprietor he remained on cordial terms, and to which he contributed regularly. It was a paper, declared the *Star*, 'filled with sound wisdom, and no trash'. O'Connor's real quarrel was with Lovett, and more specifically his presumption in calling his new venture the National Association.

As chapter 1 showed, the relationship between the two had long been cool. Although superficially cordial, O'Connor reciprocated Lovett's dislike. Indications of this are subtle. Shortly before Lovett left prison, the *Northern Star* omitted his name from its definitive list of Chartist prisoners. The cele-bratory verses O'Connor wrote, to be sung as Lovett and Collins left prison, were about their author (and the land) rather than their supposed subject. The history of the *Star's* presentation portrait of Lovett is especially revealing. It had been billed as 'in preparation' within a few weeks of his imprisonment, but in February 1840 the engraving was still 'in preparation'. Lovett left prison five months later but of the portrait there was no sign. Meanwhile Collins had been accorded a handsome full-length portrait. On 5 December Lovett's portrait was listed tersely as 'to follow', while a second engraving of O'Connor was announced for the following week. It appeared, but Lovett never did. It is even conceivable that this O'Connor portrait was adapted from an uncompleted engraving of Lovett.[47]

Once out of prison Lovett was a Chartist without an associational home: the LWMA was defunct and – quite apart from his antipathy to O'Connor – Lovett considered the NCA to be illegal. In this he was not alone, and its rules were subsequently recast to address points made by, among others, Place and Collins. Lovett was clearly sincere in wanting to create 'a new organization of the people' and probably indifferent to its implications for the NCA. His continued attachment to the Charter, however, was never in question except in the columns of *Northern Star*. It blatantly claimed Lovett's 'Knowledge Chartism' and the LPRA to be integrally linked, also that the National Association's political objectives comprised triennial parliaments and house-hold suffrage. In vain, first Vincent, then Cleave, Hetherington and Neesom, wrote to the paper refuting this and complaining of the language it had used: 'is it Democracy or Chartism to say a man is a spy, a traitor, one who has sold himself to the Government, because he appends his name to a document that has for its aim the attainment of the People's Charter?'[48]

Unfortunately, the proposal to establish the National Association in March 1841 was made in a manner certain to invite the suspicions of the uncharitable. It had often been Lovett's and the LWMA's method to circulate documents in a final draft form, inviting recipients to add their name. But the circulation of the 1841 proposal, with its challenge to the authority of the NCA, carried a warning that unauthorised publication would be deemed 'a breech of honour'. When the *Northern Star* (which was sent a copy by an unsympathetic recipient) exposed the 'secret move', there was a flurry of claims from some signatories that their names had been added without their knowledge or that they had misunderstood the address's purpose. Finally Lovett conceded that names had been included without specific permission.[49]

Thorough and sure-footed in the arena of the committee room, Lovett had bumbled on the wider stage. Moreover, while Lovett may have been convinced that his new Association would be truly national, organisation on that scale was not his forte; nor was *Chartism; A New Organization of the People* the publication best calculated to promote it. The Association, when it finally emerged in autumn 1841, was feeble. Including the wives and children (enrolled as 'auxiliaries') of its male membership, it still never exceeded 500, fully 300 of whom enrolled for its dancing classes.[50] There were just two branches, both in London, or three if one counts the imitative and short-lived 'National Association' at Hawick in the Scottish Borders.[51] Perhaps the most damning assessment came from William Linton, a member and warm admirer of Lovett: 'his new association, after attracting a few hundred members, dwindled into a debating club, and their hall became a dancing academy, let occasionally for unobjectionable public meetings'.[52] Ironically it was the *Northern Star* that secured nationwide awareness of the National Association. And it was O'Connor, abetted by Hill, who conjured the 'New Move' into an entity with substance and significance when it had neither.

In the spring of 1841, reading the *Northern Star* in his cell, Feargus cannot have been other than gratified by the response to the new move elicited by the paper. The LDA (on the brink of converting into a branch of the NCA) expelled Neesom, declaring: 'we consider the attempts of the New Move gentry to turn the minds of the Chartists from their present organisation, as impolitic, unwise, and unjust, believing it to be for their aggrandisement'. The Cardiff branch of the NCA passed a resolution declaring Collins 'unfit to be a representative ... we look upon him as a man who has sold himself'. And Derby NCA repudiated 'the new-fangled scheme propounded by Lovett, Collins and Co., feeling convinced that it is a Whig scheme for sowing strife and discord among the Chartists'. Motions expressing confidence in 'the caged lion' abounded.[53] The Middlesbrough NCA provided a pertinent illustration of how spurious the idea of the new move really was. This fledgling Chartist locality enjoyed significant support from local middle-class reformers. It was rooted in the town's temperance movement, under whose aegis it first met when unable to secure the right to hold meetings of its own. Its 'Working Men's Reading Rooms' and Library were the only freely available facilities of their kind in the town, anticipating by several years the establishment of a mechanics institute. Yet the Middlesbrough NCA implacably pursued the O'Connorite line, as a report it sent to the *Northern Star* illustrated:

A spirited meeting of the Chartists of this place was held in the Working Men's Reading Room, Newcastle Row, on Wednesday night week, when spirited addresses were delivered on the present state of the country and the prospects of the people, by Messrs Sutherland, Hollinshead and Maw. The different speakers advised their hearers to abstain from intoxicating liquors, and join the working men's Library, which is already established; and likewise for the people not to be led away by any new move, whether it was commended by real enemies or pretended friends, and as far as the Chartists of Middlesbro' are concerned they are determined to struggle for the Charter and nothing less.[54]

## People's candidates

The dispute O'Connor manufactured coincided with the first elections to the NCA council and of delegates to a Convention intended to initiate a new phase in the movement's history. O'Connor was, of course, unable to participate in either, but the new move furore ensured that those elected were steadfast for the Charter and opposed on principle to collaboration with the middle class. The movement they were shaping was in good heart. One of the main tasks of the Convention, which met in London in May, was to manage the continuing campaign for the pardon of Frost, Jones and Williams. On 25 May, Thomas Slingsby Duncombe, radical MP for Finsbury, presented to the House of Commons a petition for the pardon totalling 1,339,298 signatures. These had been accumulated quietly and efficiently with none of the delays and heart-searching that attended the 1839 National Petition (which was also fewer by 59,000 signatures). The petition was an astonishing achievement, logistically as well as politically. Furthermore, a vote to endorse the petition was tied and lost only on the Speaker's casting vote (he argued the motion interfered in the royal prerogative). With understandable acerbity, Chartists noted that Daniel O'Connell reneged on a promise to support the motion.[55]

Duncombe's importance in Chartism from this point is easily overlooked. The best-dressed man in the Commons, grandson of a bishop and nephew of Baron Feversham, this old-Harrovian ex-Guards officer was an unlikely champion of the Charter; but his tenacious pursuit of the Government on issues such as theatre licensing, the opening of Chartists' mail and church rates, plus a consistent record of supporting all resolutions for parliamentary reform, won the admiration of many Chartists even before he adopted the cause of Chartist prisoners in 1840. His aristocratic disdain for party politics, especially of the Whig variety, was also attractive in a context where style and presentation were powerful in cementing popular support. His gambling debts were the stuff of legend, but Duncombe certainly had style. Not the least contribution he made to Chartism in 1841 was to persuade the Commons to permit the petition to be carried into the chamber on the shoulders of a team of stonemasons, dressed in fustian (the coarse, dark cloth dominant in workmen's clothing). 'The uniform of labour has been seen at the bar of the House of Commons, for the first time in the history of agitation', McDouall commented, 'and the powerful arm of industry has rolled the complaint of one million and a half of people to the footstall of boasted justice and pretended mercy.'[56]

For all his swagger, Duncombe was no political dilettante. He was a persuasive model of what a Chartist MP might be, cultivating his constituency and carefully researching and preparing his speeches to the Commons (a trait remarked on as unusual at this time).[57] He also had the presence of mind to dismiss an invitation to the LPRA's reform festival. All of this was significant in 1841, for the mind of the NCA leadership was increasingly turning to how Parliament might be confronted through the electoral process itself. The main task of the 1841 Convention was to develop the proposition, enshrined in the NCA constitution, that Chartist candidates should stand in parliamentary elections. This, as we have seen, originated in O'Brien's proposal to swamp the hustings at the next general election with Chartist candidates who would then constitute an alternative Parliament. However the Convention was preoccupied with the politically possible and legally defensible, understandably so, given all that had happened over the previous two years (and nearly a fifth of Chartists, imprisoned or transported in 1839–40, were still serving their sentences).

The concluding address issued by the Convention's working party, of which McDouall and John Skevington of Loughborough were leading members, was therefore cautious and a useful counterpoint to the eternal optimism of O'Connor. 'Prepare yourselves for the approaching elections', it counselled. MPs voting against Duncombe's motion of 25 May should be targeted. 'Destroy your enemies, especially the bastile Whigs and Malthusian pack', it urged; 'aim at … the return of your friends', 'take up the dreaded weapon of exclusive dealing', 'put down Whiggery first and Toryism next'. Two-member constituencies especially should be targeted: 'we have received certain and infallible evidence that in severel [sic] places either of the factions will split votes with our candidates, that is to say, a Tory and a Chartist, or a Chartist and a Whig may be returned'.[58]

Melbourne's Government was fragile and its demise widely predicted. The ensuing general election would be the first since 1837 and therefore since Chartism emerged. An official NCA statement on the election had to be made – the Government's treatment of Chartist prisoners especially made untenable a policy of crying plague on both parties. Yet the decision to enter the election, rather than stand back and condemn that which Chartists of every complexion believed was patently absurd, was a bold one. However, the financial outlay and organisational input required would be prodigious. Moreover, the exact date of the general election could not be predicted (in theory it could be as late as spring 1844), making it additionally difficult to focus the efforts of a movement that was in its very essence that of the politically excluded. Chartism's cause would have been greatly helped had Melbourne's administration clung to power into the autumn. But the convention was still in session when, on 4 June, the Tories won a vote of no-confidence in the Government, triggering a general election. Whatever the timing, it was unlikely that Chartism would make much impression at the polls; but faced by a sudden election its efforts could be little more than tokenistic. Candidates were needed who were legally entitled to be MPs; enfranchised supporters had to be found in each contested constituency to move and second Chartist nominations; and 'the dreaded weapon of exclusive dealing' needed time to bite.

In few areas of early nineteenth-century life is the aphorism 'The past is a foreign country: they do things differently there' more applicable than in the conduct of parliamentary elections.[59] Inside Westminster, political parties were rolling coalitions of shifting interests; outside of it they did not exist in any formal sense. A multiplicity of two-member constituencies (where each voter had two votes and the highest and second-placed candidates were elected) complicated electoral arithmetic. General elections were spaced out over a week or more (one man could therefore contest two constituencies in a row). All residents of a constituency, enfranchised or not, were entitled to make their views known at the hustings where the election was decided by a show of hands. This might be all that was needed to select an MP, for only if a candidate who was defeated at the hustings demanded it would a poll be held. Polling was restricted to those who could prove they were legally enfranchised. Minimal restrictions on candidates' spending, an endemic culture of treating electors, and also in many seats bribery, made electioneering prodigiously expensive. (Duncombe, admittedly in exceptional circumstances, had spent around £40,000 on 5 contests at Hertford between 1823 and 1834.) Consequently large numbers of constituencies (a third in 1841) went uncontested, since the chances of ousting the sitting member or their anointed successor were hugely outweighed by the costs involved. Furthermore, candidates who proceeded to the poll were normally required to share the official costs involved.

Into this bear pit, under-resourced and under-prepared, strode a handful of Chartist candidates in the general election of June–July 1841.[60] All came bottom of their poll. Lowery successfully challenged Macaulay, a Whig minister, at the Edinburgh hustings and then overwhelmingly won the hustings at Aberdeen. However he then polled only thirty votes.[61] At Banbury, Henry Vincent faired rather better with 51 votes. William Villiers Sankey, Edinburgh's General Convention delegate, contested Marylebone but polled only 61 votes against the winning Liberal's 4,661. Local Chartists persuaded a noted Sussex anti-Poor Law campaigner, Charles Brooker, to contest Brighton (nineteen votes – an humiliating result but less-so than the zero votes secured by Thomason, Chartist candidate at Paisley).[62] Dr James Bedford, a maverick with no previous interest in Chartism, garnered nine votes at Reigate. Only at Northampton could a Chartist parliamentary candidate be said to have made a genuine impression at both hustings and poll. Helped by Tory failure to find a second candidate to contest the two-member constituency, McDouall polled 176 votes, almost all from voters supporting the Tory as well. No voter chose both McDouall and the highest-placed candidate, a Liberal, and very few paired him with the second Liberal elected, even though the latter described himself as a 'whole hog radical'. The message was clear: even in a constituency with a high proportion of relatively poor voters, a Chartist candidate would make headway only if clinging to the coat tails of a well-disposed Tory.[63]

These results were hardly surprising. They were a far cry, however, from the guarded optimism of the Convention, and even farther from McDouall's antic-ipation that twelve Chartist MPs would be returned who might then hold the Commons balance of power if the general election result was close. This calcu-lation had always depended on the additional return of certain middle-class radicals who supported the Charter. 'We claim them as Chartists!' declared the Star of Crawford (returned at Rochdale) and Fielden and Johnson (victors at Oldham). Perronet Thompson, defeated at Hull, was a similar case, and on the same argument the Dundee Chronicle (now edited by R. J. Richardson, who had moved to Scotland following his release from prison) claimed William Williams (re-elected at Coventry) and a defeated Liberal at Glasgow as Chartist candidates. Only Duncombe (re-elected unopposed for Finsbury), however, could be totally relied on to support Chartism in any and every eventuality. The remaining radicals were independents who leant mainly towards the position of the LPRA (which Thompson, Crawford and Williams actively supported).[64] Even on the most generous definition of 'Chartist', therefore, by the conven-tional yardstick of seats won and lost the 1841 general election was an abject failure for Chartism.

However, the conventional yardstick is hardly applicable. The Whigs were driven from office, and Chartist delight at that was almost palpable. The general consensus was summarised by an anonymous Birmingham Chartist: 'if they did not succeed in returning two Members of the Working Class, of two evils they would chose the least and support the Tories'.[65] Predictably, much credit was claimed for their having done so. In particular, the result of the West Riding election (a narrow Tory victory in a hitherto strong Whig seat) suggested exclusive dealing had played a contributory, perhaps even decisive, role. Similarly, in closely canvassed Rochdale Sharman Crawford snatched a single-vote majority over the sitting Liberal. However, there was never a blanket policy of supporting Tory candidates. Chartists were pragmatic: the test of a candidate was support for the Charter, the liberation of prisoners, a factory act and repeal of the New Poor Law and rural police. 'Wherever, by splitting with the Whigs, you can return your man do so', instructed a Star editorial, 'wherever, by splitting from the Tories, you can return your man do so.' Chartism's real challenge was to the electoral system itself, and some strikingly effective interventions were made at hustings across the country. Among the English constituencies were Bradford, Carlisle, Gateshead, Leeds, Leicester, Newcastle upon Tyne, North and South Leicestershire, Norwich,

Preston, Sheffield, Sunderland, Tynemouth and North Shields, the West Riding and Wigan; and in Scotland there were Chartist candidates at the hustings for the Ayr District, Clackmannan and Kinross, Dumfries, Edinburgh, Fifeshire, Glasgow, Paisley, Perth and Roxburghshire. 'Many had ridiculed the idea of the non-electors having candidates', observed Lowery, 'but the results in almost every instance were highly favourable to the extension of liberal views.'[66]

Not all Chartist candidates matched Lowery, whose attack on government foreign policy drew grudging acknowledgment from Macaulay. Richardson's verbal onslaught on another minister, Fox Maule at Perth, was described as 'real sledge hammer work'. 'If the Redeemer of the world was in Wigan, he would not have had a vote', cried the Chartist who nominated the 'People's Candidate' there. William Martin offered Derby the judgement of a Solomon on the matter of who to prefer between Whig and Tory: 'both Partys are Rogues ... take a Tory by the heels and nock down a wigg [sic] with him and destroy both factions'. But in general Chartist speakers and candidates prepared carefully for this unimpeachable opportunity to propound the Charter direct to the political establishment, exploiting the obvious theatrical nature of the hustings to the full. At the West Riding hustings, in Wakefield, Harney was initially denied a hearing; but a 600-strong Huddersfield contingent who had marched 13 miles to attend, all armed with staves, secured silence by raising their 'forest of oak saplings' into the air and striking them against each other.[67]

Each hustings triumph was held up as another example of the iniquities of current parliamentary government. In addition there were some blatant examples of election processes being applied specifically to disadvantage Chartist candidates. Lowery contemplated a legal challenge against the Sheriff of Edinburgh's handling of the election until advised that 'there was no doubt we might make out a case, but had we £2,000 to begin with?'[68] Gateshead's Mayor tried to prevent John Mason from speaking because he was not a resident of the borough, a spurious move given that his opponent was also from outside the constituency. Stockport's Chartist candidate was forced to withdraw after the Mayor demanded a £10 contribution to election costs even before admitting him to the hustings. At Norwich the Mayor demanded a surety of £200 before organising an election. The Monmouthshire District was a farce: the returning officer refused to accept a Chartist nomination because it was made too late, but accepted a spoof Chartist candidate put up by local Whigs as a spoiler against their opponent. Newport Chartists then spent the day canvassing against this so-called 'Chartist'. His shop-front was wrecked at the close of the poll, one of three incidents of violent behaviour (the others, more serious, were at Carlisle and Norwich). Violence was an ever-present threat at elections but generally the crowds who supported these 'people's candidates' were impressive both for their size and self-discipline, a fact remarked on – not without surprise – by a number of liberal papers and journals. 'I should say there were in that crowd nine non-electors for [every] one elector', recalled a musician whose band attended the West Riding hustings.[69]

## The lion of freedom comes from his den

O'Connor was freed from prison, on health grounds, before his sentence expired. On 30 August 1841 he was released into the embrace of a tumultuous reception organised by the York NCA, attended by delegates from across northern England and beyond. More correctly, he was actually released on 26 August into the embrace of a hansom cab which took him to Etridge's Hotel. There he kicked his heels until the elaborate event York's Chartists devised could proceed as advertised. A cab returned him the following Monday to the prison gates, helpfully open so that officials within could view the spectacle without. O'Connor was led to 'a splendid triumphant car', shaped like a horn of plenty and swathed in green velvet with pink upholstery. It had been specially commissioned by the York NCA (its finances were so stretched by the gesture it subsequently raffled the carriage to recoup the cost). 'Our procession made a Rout of the Principle [sic] streets of the city', recollected Thomas Rooke, one of the organising committee, six decades later, 'winding up on the Knavesmire where Mr O'Connor made a speech to the crowd outside – he spoke from the Balcony of the Grand Stand.'[70]

Rooke recalled nothing of O'Connor's speech, except that he gestured to the race course and declared: 'I would Rather see the Turf yield to the spade of the husbandman than to the hoof of the Racehorse.' This was understandable in an 80-year-old man, but in reality the content of the speech was almost incidental. It was the carefully orchestrated event itself that spoke volumes. First, it recalled the great Factory Reform 'Pilgrimage' to York Castle Yard in 1832: then as now hundreds of workmen and their families had walked as far even as 50 miles to attend; that meeting had sealed Richard Oastler's reputation as 'the Factory King', this one was to confirm O'Connor's place at the head of Chartism. Second, O'Connor was clad in a suit of fustian, specially made for him by Manchester Chartists, a gesture of obvious symbolism. It evoked the presentation of the Newport petition to Parliament.

Even more importantly, it communicated O'Connor's intransigent stance in the face of 'pretended friends and real enemies'. Fastidious and fashionably dressed, O'Connor had always struck an aristocratic bearing; but now his appearance was transformed into that of the very 'fustian jackets, blistered hands and unshorn chins' he addressed each week in the *Northern Star*. His attire was a timely statement. The general election had witnessed hustings victories for a number of working men. Among them, as a banner at York proclaimed, was

'William Martin MP, formerly an inmate of Northallerton Hell Hole, delegate for Bradford'. In his speech at the grandstand, Martin declared 'it was clear now that the people were determined to place confidence in men of their own order'. O'Connor's fustian suit showed how receptive he was to that mood. Four months previously he had sailed close to the wind in his personal attacks on the skilled artisans who supported the National Association, contemptuously dismissing Hetherington, for example, as middle class and a member of the 'shopocracy'. Then, O'Connor had stressed his own credentials as one 'promoted from the ranks of the aristocracy to a commission in the democracy'. Now that claim was vindicated in a moment of pure political theatre. Feargus O'Connor was closer to the heart of the Chartist movement than ever before.[71]

# Chartist lives:
# Elizabeth Neesom

Nothing, beyond the fact that she was born in Cheltenham, Gloucestershire, is known about Elizabeth Neesom's life before she married Charles Neesom, a tailor, in 1830.[*] She was his second wife and, at 31, five years his junior. In 1819 Charles had frequented The Mulberry Tree in London's Moorfields, the pub where the followers of Thomas Spence regularly met. The gentle Spence, radical polemicist, poet and agrarian visionary had died in 1814; the circle he left openly 'boasted that the Government had been more annoyed by Individuals belonging to them than by any other body'. Neesom considered himself fortunate not to have been implicated in the Cato Street conspiracy (to assassinate the Cabinet) in 1820.[†] There is, though, no other evidence for his involvement in politics of any kind until he married Elizabeth.

We may reasonably infer that Elizabeth shared Charles's political

---

[*]   HO, 107/1521/51/5, Census, 1851; Charles Neesom's obituary (based on an unpublished autobiography, now lost), *National Reformer*, 20 and 27 July 1861; also *DLB* entry, vol. 8.

[†]   HO, 40/8(3), fo.115, report of 'A', 13 November 1817; *National Reformer*, 20 July 1861.

commitments, not least because they included the National Union of the Working Classes and the Grand National Consolidated Trades Union which encouraged female participation. Between 1831 and 1833 the NUWC was the organisational focus for those who rejected the Reform Bill as irrelevant to working people. Elizabeth's first appearance in the radical press was as a contributor to the Victim Fund that NUWC organised to support those prosecuted for selling unstamped newspapers. The same donations list included a remittance from NUWC Class 40, sent by Charles. He was an unstamped vendor who narrowly escaped arrest.* The Neesoms knew the risks involved, not least because in 1833 Charles replaced as treasurer of the NUWC a man imprisoned for selling Hetherington's *Poor Man's Guardian*. Neesom's involvement in the GNCTU came through his union, the London tailors' trade society. Calls for one great union that would represent all labour had been growing since the late 1820s, reaching an ambitious peak in the GNCTU of 1833–34. A loose federation rather than a tight, formally constituted organisation, it involved the unskilled as well as the skilled, rural as well as urban workers, and women as well as men. In all these respects it anticipated Chartism or, perhaps more accurately, Chartism exhibited much of the character of general unionism by a different name.

In the mid-1830s Charles was increasingly dogged by defective sight (common in tailors), so the couple opened a newsagent's shop at 160 Brick Lane. There Elizabeth ran a school. Private working-class day-schools were an important force in nineteenth-century popular education: in the early 1830s at least a half of all children attending school were pupils at such establishments. There was little difference at this time between their education and that available in church schools.† We do not know what curriculum Elizabeth offered her pupils but, given the general standards of private working-class schools, and especially what can be gleaned about her own opinions, it is safe to conclude that it would have been far removed from that lazy historical cliché, the 'dame school'.‡

The Spenceans were a close-knit group whose influence extended across London radicalism long after their Mulberry Tree meetings ceased. In 1835 Elizabeth and Charles Neesom took into their home Allen Davenport, the biographer of Thomas Spence and a notable radical author and poet in his own right. Elizabeth nursed Davenport during his recovery from a near-fatal illness.

---

* *Poor Man's Guardian*, 20 April 1833; P. Hollis, *The Pauper Press* (Oxford, Oxford University Press, 1970), p. 191.

† W. B. Stephens, *Education Literacy and Society, 1830–70* (Manchester, Manchester University Press, 1987), pp. 25, 49, 204, 255.

‡ P. Gardner, *The Lost Elementary Schools of Victorian England* (Beckenham, Croom Helm, 1984).

When Davenport returned to public life it was at her husband's side, notably in January 1837 when the 2 men were among the 12 founder members of the East London Democratic Association.* As earlier chapters have indicated, the LDA (as it became) was an important force in metropolitan radicalism; it was also the locus of such conspiratorial currents as existed in early London Chartism. The reputation of Davenport, Neesom and their circle went before them and Home Office intelligence, matured in the surveillance of Spencean activity in the Regency years, moved seamlessly into reporting on the LDA. The sheer extent of records thus generated should not be allowed to distort the overall picture of the LDA. It was larger, longer-lived and of greater vitality than the LWMA; and, unlike the latter, it admitted women as members.

The development of a cognate female organisation was paralleled, as we have seen, in hundreds of other communities across the country. Elizabeth Neesom was secretary of the London Female Democratic Association, which shared its headquarters with the LDA at the Democratic Rooms, Temple Bar. As the Association's only named officer she was almost certainly responsible for writing its address to 'the women of England, and particularly the metropolis' in May 1839. This particularly stressed the lack of education as the main obstacle to women's full participation in political and social affairs, probably reflecting Elizabeth's personal beliefs and experience both as a woman and as a teacher. The Association urged its 'sisters and friends' to 'shake off that apathy and timidity which too generally pervades among our sex (arising from the prejudices of a false education)'; it also emphasised 'in accordance with the rights of all, and acknowledging the sovereignty of the people our right, as free women (or women determined to be free) to rule ourselves'. In practical terms this was reflected in the Association's practice of never admitting men to its meetings except by the majority agreement of women present; and if it was proposed that a man should *speak* to their meeting then both a majority and a week's notice was required. Thus in September 1839 the London delegate to the National Convention Robert Hartwell, and Elizabeth's husband, gave the requisite notice and addressed a special meeting of the Association at Bethnal Green Trades' Hall. Even so the report in *Northern Star* was more representative of the established order. 'Called to the chair Mrs Neesom opened the business in a neat and spirited address, and concluded by calling upon Mr Neesom to address the meeting.' It then reported only the speeches of Hartwell and her husband, on 'the necessity of women understanding political science', 'the progress of female associations' and 'the vicious education of women'.[†] In January 1841, when the LDA

---

  *  *Prospectus of the East London Democratic Association* (London, ELDA, 1837), reprinted in D.Thompson, *The Early Chartists* (London, Macmillan, 1971), pp.55–6.
  †  *NS*, 11 May and 14 September 1839. See also *Operative*, 14 April, 12 May and *Charter*,

reconstituted itself as a branch of the NCA, Elizabeth Neesom led its women's organisation into a new Female Patriotic RA. The earlier rules governing male participation were retained and there was an additional emphasis on practical mutual help. One half of the Association's funds were set aside to assist members during illness (the other to supporting Chartist prisoners and their wives); and during the hour before each of its meetings Elizabeth ran an adult school for members.[*]

The Neesoms were childless but marriage to a leading Chartist nonetheless placed burdens on Elizabeth. Charles spoke frequently at meetings across London, and was away for weeks when the 1839 Convention transferred to Birmingham. Throughout the Convention, Elizabeth had to run both the newsagent's and her school. Charles was away again in November and December 1839, ostensibly assessing the extent of popular support for the Charter in Yorkshire but almost certainly involved in the failed conspiracy intended to coincide with the Newport trials.[†] With rumours rife in London of a disturbance intended to coincide with the sentencing of the Newport prisoners, on 16 January 1840 police raided an LDA meeting. They burst through the doors at almost exactly the point Neesom declared from the chair: 'I tell you we will wield the sword of freedom in four days.' A quantity of arms was discovered and nine men were arrested on the spot. Elizabeth was almost certainly among the 100 or so women in the hall and a plainclothes policeman later reported: 'I saw Neesom leave the hall with a female beside him.' He was arrested at their home later that evening.[‡]

The consequences for the Neesoms were grave. After a night in the cells (spent singing *To Arms Ye Brave*) Charles appeared at Bow Street magistrates' court to be charged with sedition and conspiracy. Bail was set at a colossal £1,000 and he had no alternative but committal to Newgate Prison. Never the easiest of people when confronted by authority, Charles spent a day on bread and water in solitary confinement, for refusing to attend chapel. Eventually an anonymous sympathiser offered the required surety, and Charles and Elizabeth were reunited. The respite was brief. Neesom and his fellow-prisoners were required to appear regularly in court as a condition of bail. After missing one of these appearances the Neesoms' furniture was seized from their home in distraint and Charles was committed to the Queen's Bench prison. The newsagents declined drastically and Elizabeth depended largely

---

13 and 27 October 1839.

[*]  *NS*, 30 January 1841; see also J. Schwarzkopf, *Women in the Chartist Movement* (London, Macmillan, 1991), pp. 214–15.

[†]  Chapter 5 above and *NS*, 2 and 30 November, 7 and 14 December 1839.

[‡]  *Morning Herald* and *Morning Post*, 16 January 1840; *Charter*, 19 and 26 January 1840; *Northern Liberator*, 25 January 1840.

on the income from her school to survive. Then in July the Crown offered to postpone sentencing indefinitely if Charles would plead guilty. He refused. The case dragged on for months until eventually all charges were dropped.[*]

The affair profoundly unsettled Charles. Very few Chartist prisoners renounced their political convictions, but most left prison intent on pursuing a different strategy to secure them. Neesom concerned himself with education even more than he had previously, leading him to support Lovett's National Association. The Neesoms also turned to temperance. Their decision to do so stemmed initially from what might be termed dietary radicalism rather than a moral judgement about the mental and physiological effects of alcohol. In August 1840 Charles renounced sugar because it was taxed, 'determined that he would *never* take any more until the Charter be the law of England'. By October this commitment had evolved into fully fledged teetotalism. Shortly afterwards Neesom became the secretary of a new body, the East London Chartist Total Abstinence and Mutual Instruction Society.[†] Elizabeth became the guiding force of the East London Female Total Abstinence Chartist Association which met in her Brick Lane schoolroom.

The Association's inaugural address to its 'Sisters and Countrywomen' was no mere re-hash of the seminal documents whose authorship Charles Neesom shared. The women grounded their arguments for total abstention in a firmly feminist educational perspective. 'Perhaps at no former period of time has the female character exhibited so much zeal, or displayed so much brilliancy of talent, as in the present day', they declared:

> Sisters, we have hitherto been considered inferior to men in powers of intellect, and truly the want of proper education has made us appear so; but we much doubt whether this would have been the case had we possessed the same opportunities of acquiring a proper education which the other sex has enjoyed. Let us endeavour to remove this reproach, by embracing every opportunity of cultivating and improving our minds. We earnestly entreat you to this, that you might be able to impart a sound education to your offspring, and train their tender minds in the way of truth and virtue.

Their economic argument for abstinence was not rooted in a generalised case that the money saved would improve subsistence, but was rather 'because that portion of hard-earned wages which is now squandered away at the pot house and gin palace would enable us to secure a sound and proper education for our children, in accordance with our views and feelings'. One detects here the hand of both the politically sophisticated Chartist and the independent school teacher: 'A well-regulated mind disdains servility and cringing. Let us

---

[*]   *NS*, 16 May, 2 June and 11 July 1840; *National Reformer*, 20 and 27 July 1861.
[†]   *NS*, 10 October 1840; BL, Place Collection Set 56, p.29; *ECC*, 5 (February 1841).

reject their Church and State offers of education for our children, which is only calculated to debase the mind, and render it subservient to class interest.'*

The Neesoms were soon engulfed, however, by the dispute O'Connor manufactured with the 'new move'. Repeated raucous demonstrations and even vandalism by over-enthusiastic O'Connorites, usually in the early hours of the morning, forced Charles to close their shop and Elizabeth to shut down the school. It is doubtful that her ambitious Female Total Abstinence Chartist Association survived. Charles was forced to resign as one of London's delegates to the 1841 Convention and was expelled from the ex-LDA branch of the NCA.†

By 1845, the couple were eking out a haphazard living as newsagents and booksellers from a room in the Standard of Liberty beershop further up Brick Lane. The landlord, William Drake, was an ex-shoemaker and LDA member; he was also an NCA stalwart and a delegate to the London district council, and the Tower Hamlets NCA met at his pub. The East London Shoemakers' Mutual Protection Society, a friendly society-cum-land scheme, also met on the premises. All this underlines how artificial the divisions wrought by O'Connor within Chartism actually were. Here were two of the movement's leading teetotallers running a bookshop in a local NCA leader's pub, the headquarters of a friendly society so enamoured with O'Connor that in 1845 it dissolved itself and invested all its funds in Chartist land plan shares.‡

Charles Neesom's continued commitment to Chartism was fully evident in December 1842: like Lovett and O'Connor he withdrew from the Complete Suffrage Union because its promoters, while endorsing the six points, insisted it should disassociate itself from Chartism. But there was to be no reconciliation with O'Connor, whom Charles described as 'a mere vindictive demagogue'.§ In 1847 Charles took over from Lovett as the National Association's secretary, and he and Elizabeth were stalwart members of its sole ancillary branch in the City of London. However, their energies were increasingly devoted to the promotion of dietary radicalism. In 1848 they publicly converted to vegetarianism, committing themselves to a new phase of radical activity. Charles told a meeting of the Vegetarian Society that fellow-members 'might rest assured that their work would never be complete, until the carnivorous passions of men were subdued by the mild and peaceful principles of the Vegetarian

---

\*   *NS*, 30 January, 1841.

†   Ibid., 24 April and 1 May 1841; *National Reformer*, 27 July 1861; cf. W. Lovett, *The Life and Struggles of William Lovett* (London, Trübner, 1876), p. 252.

‡   J. Bennett, 'The LDA, 1837–41', in J. Epstein and D. Thompson (eds), *The Chartist Experience: Studies in Working-Class Radicalism and Culture, 1830–1860* (London, Macmillan, 1982), pp. 104, 109, 117–18; M. Chase, *'The People's Farm'* (Oxford, Clarendon, 1988), pp. 172–3; *NS*, 16 December 1843.

§   *National Reformer*, 20 July 1861.

system'.* They distributed tracts 'by the hundreds' and pasted copies of *Do You Eat Flesh?* and *Nature's Bill of Fare* to their front door:

> Sometimes a number of persons gather round, and eagerly read, while some knock at the door and ask for information. Our friend, if in the way, advances to the threshold, which is elevated from the pavement by two or three steps; a conversation, and sometimes a discussion ensues, and there you 'behold the man,' firm and erect, strong in the correctness of his prin- ciples, preaching and teaching, in truly apostolic style, with a sonorous and emphatic voice, the primitive, humanizing, elevating, and health-giving prin- ciples of Vegetarianism.†

No more than a poor living was to be earned advocating vegetarianism. In 1851 Charles Neesom recorded his occupation in the Census as 'tailor' and probably got by on casual work for east London sweating shops. A letter he wrote in 1850 about hydropathy (the treatment of disease by the application of water, internally and/or externally) gives some insight into life at the Neesoms' home in Baldwin Street, Bethnal Green. It extolled the benefits of the dietetic use of water which, he said, had improved his own physical and mental health and brought him sleep as restful as that of childhood.‡ Many Chartists, impa- tient in the pursuit of knowledge and suspicious of the social establishment (to which, increasingly, medical practitioners belonged), explored alternative medicine;§ and, like temperance and dietary radicalism, alternative medicine reinforced the perspective that a regimen of individual reform should be prior- itised since calls for legislative reform went unheeded. Another LDA couple with views similar to the Neesoms, Martha and Joseph Schell Vietinghoff, ran the Homeopathic and Mesmeric Medical Establishment, in Clerkenwell, which advertised in the Chartist press.¶ In 1861 Joseph Vietinghoff treated Charles when he became terminally ill. He died aged 77, on 8 June, in Elizabeth's arms. His last words were reportedly: 'Bessy, you have been a good wife to me.' William Lovett, 'with some emotion', delivered one of several graveside eulogies

---

\* *Vegetarian Messenger*, 1 (1849–50), p.14, quoted in J. Belchem, 'Temperance in all things: vegetarianism, the Manx press and the alternative agenda of reform', in M. Chase and I. Dyck (eds), *Living and Learning* (Aldershot, Scolar, 1996), p.154; see also *Spirit of the Age*, 25 November 1848.

† *Vegetarian Advocate*, 15 October 1848 (my thanks for this and the following refer- ence to James Gregory).

‡ *Water Cure Journal and Hygienic Magazine* (September 1850).

§ See J.F.C. Harrison, 'Early Victorian radicals and the medical fringe', in W.F. Bynum and R. Porter (eds), *The Medical Fringe and Medical Orthodoxy, 1750–1850* (London, Croom Helm, 1987), pp.198–215; and Belchem, 'Temperance in all things'.

¶ *Cooper's Journal*, 4 May 1850; *Operative*, 16 June 1839; Bennett, 'LDA', p.109.

and a memorial meeting at the City Road Hall of Science was organised, the proceeds of which were presented to Elizabeth.[*]

In its handsome obituary of Charles, the *National Reformer* said of Elizabeth: 'she has been of the same views as her husband, and has seconded his efforts throughout. She has been for a long period his right hand and main stay.'[†] Theirs had been a powerful political partnership, celebrated by the *National Reformer* which shared in the Chartist idealisation of marriage and the place within it of the 'good wife'.[‡] However, Elizabeth was not just a political partner. She had had a galvanising effect on her husband when they married; and though we can but guess at the content of her 'neat and spirited' speeches, her leadership of the key metropolitan female Chartist organisations reveals Elizabeth to have been a political activist in her own right.

[*]   *National Reformer*, 15 and 22 June 1861; *Reasoner*, 16 June 1861.
[†]   *National Reformer*, 27 July 1861.
[‡]   E. Yeo, 'Will the real Mary Lovett please stand up?', in Chase and Dyck (eds), *Living and Learning*, p.178; Schwarzkopf, *Women in the Chartist Movement*, p.145.

CHAPTER SEVEN

# 1842:
# 'Toasting muffins at a volcano'

## Introduction

In the autumn of 1841 Lord Francis Egerton (the Lancashire landowner glimpsed in chapter 2, gripped by indecision in the face of Stephens's arrest) surveyed the 'state of feeling in this fearful vicinity'. It was not Chartism alone that perturbed him, nor the onset of a further economic depression. The ACLL, determined in his opinion 'to excite positive disturbances if possible', leant a new dimension of menace to the disturbed state of industrial Lancashire. 'In living in it all, I always feel as if I were toasting muffins at a volcano', Egerton grimly observed. Volcanic similes were much favoured by Victorian social commentators. Twelve months later, an Anglican clergyman from the cotton district looked back on the events at the heart of this chapter, the strike wave of 1842, and concluded: 'it is the opinion of many of our soberest and soundest-minded men, that the storm, though hushed is not subdued; and that the late outbreaks will prove only as the flashings of the crater before the eruption of the volcano'.[1]

The cotton districts were not alone in presenting a picture of incipient insurgency. 'We are arrived at an awful crisis', a spy reported that an NCA lecturer had told Derby's post mortem on the 1841 election; 'the day and hour is at hand when there must be a mortally Bloody Revolution'.[2] Of course, such talk was hyperbole, and this particular example may have gained in the telling, but industrial England was unusually tense and apprehensive in 1841–42. Industry was in recession, short-time working and wage reductions were commonplace and bankruptcies were increasing. Across the textile districts resentment simmered at the Government's continued failure to reduce working hours, especially because Prime Minister Peel had given an incautiously sympathetic hearing to the West Riding Short Time Committee (including Hobson, printer of *Northern Star*) in October 1841.[3] By February 1842 Peel's effigy had been burnt in towns across England while his private secretary had been shot dead walking along Whitehall. His murderer had mistaken him for Peel himself and, while his plea of insanity was accepted at the time, circumstantial evidence discovered since links him to Glasgow Chartism. Attempts on the Queen's life in June 1841 and again in May and July 1842, had nothing to do with Chartists; but equally they did nothing to ease the political temperature. The moral climate, Scotland's leading Chartist paper commented, made such assassination attempts inevitable.[4]

Egerton's anxiety proved well-founded, and the ACLL did indeed help electrify the political atmosphere in 1842. However, this was also the year of the second national Chartist petition, a 'document' of unparalleled magnitude. With the strikes and disturbances that followed, the summer of 1842 was therefore a momentous phase in the history of Chartism. But it was framed by the complete suffrage initiative, which had the potential (or so it seemed) to synergise middle-class radicalism and Chartism. It is with the events around the complete suffrage conference that spring that any narrative of 1842 must begin.

## A middle-class embrace?

To sympathise with the poor oppressed Chartists is considered *vulgar* – but I *do most sincerely* – condemning of course *in them*, as I wd. in any, an appeal to physical force – but their transgressions in this way have been wondrously few – considering the oppression they are enduring, & their deprivation of rights as human beings, I am often filled with astonishment at their patience & forbearance.

Elizabeth Pease, of the north-east industrial dynasty, was unusual in expressing those sentiments in a letter sent to an American friend in June 1841. This was not, she explained, because Chartism was anathema in the Quaker circles in which she moved. Indeed, as far as the points of *The People's Charter* were concerned, 'it is thought *unaccountable* for a *gentleman* to say he sees nothing wrong in these – but for a lady to do so is almost outrageous'.[5] Among middle-class liberals with a nonconformist background, cautious support for at least the principles within *The People's Charter* was indeed gathering momentum in the second half of 1841. 'One of their principles is a denial of the right of property to confer franchise & possibly they are right, though I am not yet prepared to admit it', wrote the west-country Quaker Barclay Fox.[6] The influential journal *Nonconformist* was particularly supportive. Founded by the former Congregational minister Edward Miall in April that year, its main objective was to support the political campaign for the disestablishment of the Church of England (and thereby abolish all the political and fiscal

advantages Anglicanism enjoyed over other denominations). Miall was forth-
right in criticising the established Church: 'have they never looked into that
dark, polluted, inner chamber of which it is the door? Have they never caught
a glimpse of the loathsome things that live, and crawl, and gender there?'[7]

Locating Anglicanism, as he did, at the heart of the political establishment, Miall was also favourably disposed to other radical endeavours. The
*Nonconformist* was generally supportive of the ACLL, particularly those
Leaguers prepared 'to summon all classes to one mighty effort for freedom'.
The journal preceded the ACLL's conference of November 1841 with a series
of articles, 'Reconciliation between the middle and working classes', co-
authored by Miall and Joseph Sturge, a Quaker grain-importer and noted
anti-slavery campaigner.[8] A founder member of the ACLL, Sturge carried
sufficient weight at the conference to arrange a well-supported adjunct session
to consider proposals for a cross-class alliance to secure manhood suffrage.
Those present included several important friends of the Chartist movement:
Hamer Stansfield (a key figure in the now-defunct LPRA), Perronet Thompson,
Sharman Crawford (who, as we saw in chapter 6, probably owed his Rochdale
parliamentary seat to Chartist support) and, in the chair, Francis Place. It was
agreed that any alliance should be separate from the ACLL, but there was
enthusiastic support for Sturge's proposal and he and Crawford were delegated
to progress it. The title they chose for this alliance had first been used by Miall,
'complete suffrage', signifying a demand for all six points of the Charter while
(pointedly) avoiding any specific reference to it. By mid-December Sturge and
Crawford had circulated through ACLL networks an inaugural address for
the signature of all 'who are friendly to a reconciliation between the working
classes and those that move in a sphere above them'.[9]

This 'political mustard seed', to quote Miall, attracted close attention in
Chartist circles. There was general sympathy towards much for which the
*Nonconformist* stood. Chartists, too, were critical of the 'law-Established
Church' and its 'bloated priesthood'; and in the Chelmsford shoemaker John
Thorogood (imprisoned for non-payment of church rates in 1840) Chartism
had its own disestablishment martyr.[10] In Birmingham, his home town, Sturge
addressed the first anniversary celebrations of the Chartist Church, in which
Collins now played a prominent part. He was favourably received by large
meetings in both Edinburgh and Glasgow, that endorsed his proposals for a
'cordial union of the middle and working classes'. The NCA branch in Newtown,
Montgomeryshire, voted to purchase 100 copies of the collected *Nonconformist*
'reconciliation' articles which a leading Manchester Chartist had published.
The newly formed teetotal Chartist society in the Leicestershire framework-
knitting village of Earl Shilton agreed to subscribe to just two newspapers a
week, the *Northern Star* and the *Nonconformist*. In Bath Vincent, together with
W. P. Roberts and Robert Philp (both stalwart O'Connor supporters), addressed

a joint ACLL and Chartist meeting on Sturge's plan. The Scottish *Chartist Circular* ran several sympathetic articles, and there seemed a genuine prospect of unity between the new initiative and Chartism.[11]

But there were also less-sanguine signs. At a Paisley meeting promoting Sturge's plan, 'to the astonishment of all present' none other than Patrick Brewster 'read a severe and sarcastic lesson' to those who thought that this new development superseded Chartism. He concluded by proposing 'the Charter, the whole Charter and nothing but the Charter', predictably carried by 'a forest of blistered hands'. Cleave's *English Chartist Circular* practically ignored complete suffrage until it published the NCA executive's policy statement concerning 'the course we ought to pursue, for or against the middle class, and the Corn Law Repealers'. Each 'should make a public and unreserved declaration and attachment to the whole principle of the Charter, before he can take part with us in the agitation, or co-operate with us'. When Miall suggested to a London meeting of Chartists and Leaguers that it might be politic not to ask for all six points at once, William Lovett rounded on him: if the six points were not conceded *en bloc*, 'it would be like giving the right of the suffrage to the sparrows, and allowing them to elect only hawks'. Complete suffragists, Lovett insisted, 'must come out for the Charter as a whole'. Lancashire Chartists were split: James Taylor (Rochdale's delegate to both the 1839 Convention and the foundation conference of the NCA) felt able to support the initiative 'as it was a sign of a better feeling and better times'; but James Leach 'thought if Mr Sturge and his friends were sincere, they ought to go over to the chartists, and not ask the chartists to go to them'.[12]

Even to hint that incremental reform might be acceptable was seen as blatantly disregarding the political integrity of the Charter and the sufferings of the more than 500 Chartists imprisoned or transported in 1839–40. Chartist suspicions were further aroused when complete suffrage was espoused by the *Leeds Times* (a paper in search of a cause since the LPRA had collapsed) and by calls from the margin of Sturge's campaign for parliamentary reform significantly short of the six points. Chief of these was a proposed 'Midland Counties Charter', which substituted triennial for annual parliaments, and manhood suffrage limited to those aged over 25.[13] Nothing came of this but it hardly benefited the complete suffrage cause in the midlands. Then, in February 1842, the *Nonconformist* argued for the first time in favour of separate complete suffrage associations, a tacit admission that the goal of uniting middle-class reformers with Chartists was probably beyond reach.[14] Leach's insistence that Sturge and his followers should 'go over to the chartists', and not the other way round, was seemingly vindicated by the gathering momentum of the second mass petition for the Charter. With memories of O'Connor's almost royal progress around the country still fresh in their minds, most NCA supporters were in no mood for compromise. Week after week, O'Connor and the *Northern Star* poured scorn on the 'Complete Humbugs'. O'Connor exempted Sturge (a figure of considerable moral authority because of his anti-slavery campaigning) from charges of chicanery, but readily levelled them at Sturge's associates. O'Connor's fiercest invective was directed at complete suffragists who argued that the six points could be gained incrementally. The ballot without universal male suffrage was anathema, while the vote would mean nothing if working men could not themselves take seats at Westminster: MPs would simply continue to legislate to protect their selfish interests. 'We are the *Anti-Class Legislation Army of Chartists*', O'Connor reminded 'the working people', an army always on its guard against the blandishments of the middle-class embrace.[15]

Chartists who accepted the complete suffrage movement's overtures in good faith risked O'Connor's wrath, especially if judged shaky on similar issues in the past. O'Connor had a good memory. When James Williams, a lynchpin of Sunderland Chartism, stated that he was 'surprised and astonished' at the force of O'Connor's attack on 'the Sturge move', he received this rebuttal:

> We are threatened with a junction of all the routed forces under the most delusive form in which treachery has been as yet attempted. The Sturge move is to include the Whigs generally – the Attwoodites, the Corn Law Repealers, the Christian Chartists, the 'new movers,' and above all the waiters upon that 'new move' ... in 1838 you had a sly thrust at me, in consequence, as you stated, of my opposition to Wm. Lovett and the London Working Men's Association. In 1840, you took another dig on behalf of those with whose conduct at the memorable Fox and Goose meeting at Leeds the Editor of the *Star* found fault ... If YOU sign the Sturge Declaration I will surprise and astonish you, by moving a vote of censure upon you myself, as a member of the National Charter Association.[16]

Such disputes were not the product purely of O'Connor's egotism; nor were they indicative of an emerging divide between 'sensible' and 'unsensible' Chartists. They were, as much as anything else, a clash of spatial perspectives. O'Connor was devoted to maintaining a national mass movement, whose potency depended on its capacity to confront authority with a single undiluted programme, not the graduated series of priorities incremental reform implied. Williams's perspective, on the other hand, was focused on Sunderland, where Chartism's spirited election campaign in 1841 had ended in frustration. George Binns had been triumphant at the hustings but unable to proceed to the poll because of the cost involved. Furthermore Perronet Thompson, the sympathetic radical who had shared Binns's hustings victory, came bottom of the poll, if by a relatively small margin. Two Conservatives were returned in their stead.[17]

In seeking common ground with Chartism, complete suffragists suffered because of their close association with the ACLL, from which Sturge and his circle took care to distinguish themselves. Miall even dared to predict that 'the complete suffrage question is taking the place of the anti-corn law agitation'.

Chartists, however, tended not to discriminate, instead lumping together 'the fallacies of the Corn Law Repeal Sturge humbug'.[18] Since the Walsall by-election of February 1841 (where the League ascribed the victory of a protectionist candidate to Chartist support), the atmosphere between the two had deteriorated from largely boisterous rivalry to an at-times violent enmity. With the tacit encouragement of the League's leadership, Manchester's Operative Anti-Corn Law Association was turned into the fearsome physical defender of ACLL meetings from Chartist disruption. This was achieved mainly by recruiting migrant Irish O'Connellites, dubbed ironically 'lambs'. From there it was but a short step to returning the compliment of disrupting Chartists' meetings. This, from May 1841, the Association did.

The apogee of its success came in March 1842 when O'Connor lectured at the Manchester Hall of Science on the repeal of the Irish Union. O'Connor compiled the report that appeared in *Northern Star*. Fighting broke out even before he rose to speak when the 'League assassins' tried to force a chairman of their own on the meeting. Having defended the legitimate chairman (James Scholefield) and 'punched one rascal in the head, knocking him down', O'Connor wrote: 'I went in front, took off my hat, and cheered the Chartists on.' However several Chartists 'attempted to drag me back, saying "Feargus, they'll murder you"'. Already he had been hit by several stones, yet nonetheless he cried, 'for God's sake let me loose, I must jump down'. Just then he was hit 'by a large stone just above the right eye, which knocked me down, the blood gushing out copiously'. He was carried out for medical attention and his own protection. The *Manchester Guardian*, a staunch ACLL supporter, told it differently. While agreeing with the *Star* that almost all fixtures and fittings were torn up for use as missiles, 'Mr. O'Connor, it is said, made a prompt exit through a back door, on the beginning of the fray.'[19] In fairness to O'Connor, he did not make so sharp an exit: police arrested the Irishman whose stone had felled him and they both were charged with affray. The cases collapsed but, whatever the truth of the matter, O'Connor's self-esteem had been dented. As the organiser of the 'lambs' wrote gleefully to the League's leader Richard Cobden:

'The lion' – the king of Chartism – F.O'C. – knocked down 3 times – has he says 7 wounds – six he can tell the position of – the 7th. was I believe inflicted as he was running away – wh[ich] he did after fighting about two minutes. Christopher Doyle very much hurt – Bailey – confined to his bed – Murray – ditto – 4 others (Chartists) seriously hurt – Revd. Schofield – black eye – loose teeth – cut lip – contusions behind (got in following Feargus) – 4 of the 'lambs' badly hurt – 2 with their sculls fractured – they however *are used to it* & will soon be well. The damage is estimated at £40.[20]

O'Connor had been repaid in his own coin, and few of his critics could resist expressing satisfaction. 'Deeply as we regret this outburst of physical force', commented Edward Miall, 'we think Feargus O'Connor should be the last man to complain of it.'[21] For all its reputation as a tight, cohesive and somewhat sober organisation – the very epitome of early Victorian bourgeois politics – the ACLL was not at all shy of confrontation.[22] The Manchester episode provides an amusing opportunity to assess the reliability of *Northern Star* reporting; but it was a portent of tensions that would erupt later that year and immediately soured O'Connor's attitude to the emerging National Complete Suffrage Union (NCSU). Within a fortnight O'Connor was planning a counter demonstration to coincide with the launch of the NCSU at a conference in Birmingham in early April: 'every move of the enemy must be jealously watched, promptly met, and bravely encountered'.[23] However, despite his attitude and, as we have seen, the prickliness even of Lovett towards the initiative, a significant body of Chartists attended the NCSU launch. Collins, Lovett, Neesom, Vincent and Wade were among them; but they also included Bronterre O'Brien, R.J. Richardson and a dozen 'grassroots' activists of particular significance in their own localities, where at least eight of them were NCA officer holders.[24]

It was with something of a flourish that, early in the proceedings, Sturge drew from his pocket a letter from France, warmly supporting the NCSU. Its author was Feargus's uncle, Arthur O'Connor, whom Sturge had recently visited in Paris. Given the care Feargus always took to link himself with Arthur, it was a shrewd gesture; it also publicly located the NCSU in a tradition of radical mobilisation that long pre-dated Chartism. However, if the Chartist contingent thought this presaged the easy accommodation of the Charter by the NCSU, by day three of the conference they knew differently. One by one each of the 6 points embodied in *The People's Charter* was accepted as policy; but a clear majority of the 80-odd delegates voiced profound disquiet at any use of the terminology 'Charter', 'Chartism', 'Chartist'. Late that day Lovett led a charge in the name of 'the legislative textbook of the millions' that threatened to wreck the unanimity Sturge had carefully cultivated. Lovett sought to bind the next NCSU conference, first, to a fairer representation of working people among its delegates and, second, to consider the Charter in detail, 'in order to effect a cordial union of the middle and working classes'. If it approved the Charter, then the NCSU must 'use every just and peaceable means for creating a public opinion in its favour'.

Supporting Lovett, the Liverpool NCA activist Bernard McCartney entered a passionate plea to the conference to acknowledge,

> the justice and necessity of the people's charter … A name to which myriads of minds, enlightened and elevated, had clung through good report and evil report, through persecution unparalleled and privations unequalled; and which adoption would, in his opinion, do more towards healing the breach which unhappily existed, than any or all other courses which the conference could under any circumstance pursue.[25]

With hindsight, this Chartist resistance looked futile and the debate pointless: the six points had after all been adopted as NCSU policy. Robert Lowery, the only Chartist present to break rank over the issue, thought that Lovett's contingent was 'fighting for *names* when great principles had been recognised'. But against this heresy was put the argument that 'the name of the people's charter, like the baron's charter of old, has been widely recognised by the people as an epitome of their political rights'. This was not merely sentimental: there was a clear practical reason for the Chartist stance. The full title was *The People's Charter; Being the Outline of an Act to Provide the Just Representation of the People of Great Britain and Ireland in the Commons House of Parliament.* It was precisely in this form as a parliamentary bill that the Charter was continually circulated, in new editions and newspaper reprints. 'It was all very well they had adopted principles', Vincent told the conference, 'but if they did not take practical steps to carry them out, in the shape of a document to be hereafter presented to parliament, they would not do all they ought to do'. Lovett was yet more explicit: a 'simple declaration of abstract principles' would not do; 'these principles will eventually have to be defined, perhaps by our present corrupt House of Commons, who will assuredly seek to nullify their efficacy and mar them in detail, just as the boroughmongering parliament did the principles of the Reform bill'. The Chartists argued the integrity of the Charter transcended whatever excesses might have been perpetuated in its name; and, they emphasised, it originated from a committee involving respected MPs (as we saw in chapter 1, this was a fiction but it was not the moment for Lovett to remove his light from beneath the bushel).[26]

After a lengthy debate that forced the conference into an unplanned evening session, the Chartists withdrew to consider their position. When they emerged they proposed an amendment to preserve unanimity while leaving open a door to the future adoption of the Charter. The NCSU should pledge itself 'at some future period to call another conference in which the whole people may be fully represented for the purpose of considering any documents' that encompassed the individual principles the conference had adopted. Even then there was still opposition to this watered-down proposal, notably from John Bright a leading ACLL figure. After further haggling, the Chartists' amendment was adopted unanimously. Privately, Bright conceded, 'the Chartists were I think the best speakers'.[27]

It was doubtless with relief that Lovett stepped back from this controversy and busied himself with the finer details of the NCSU constitution and inaugural address. These documents he then moved at the final session the next day. But the Charter still cast its shadow over the proceedings when two of the Bradford Chartists present, Joseph Brook and James Dewhurst, proposed a final resolution thanking 'the working classes for the indomitable courage, steady perseverance, and Christian forbearance manifested by them as a body, in times of trying want and surpassing emergency, brought about by the misrule of class legislators'. McCartney tried to persuade them to withdraw the motion in order to preserve harmony, but 'they would not accede to it; the conference might either reject or adopt it'. Harmony of a kind was restored when Lovett successfully proposed an emollient amendment. However, Brook and Dewhurst had struck a discordant – and, as subsequent events proved, unfortunately enduring – note.[28]

There were now two national organisations promoting radical parliamentary reform on the basis of universal male suffrage, no property qualification for MPs, annual parliaments, equal representation, payment of members and the ballot: the NCA and the NCSU. The NCA's tactic was to disparage the NCSU at every turn. The *Northern Star* headlined the 'important proceedings' at Birmingham, but the news printed beneath was of a 'great public meeting' there, organised to coincide with the NCSU's, and of an NCA delegate meeting that followed it. Eight of these thirty delegates juggled their attendance with the NCSU conference to which they were also nominated.[29] While the *Star* diligently reported any occasion on which Chartists routed local NCSU meetings, it failed to report the NCSU conference, other than via an editorial on 'the wily ones assembled in consultation upon the best means of putting down Chartism'. This gave grudging praise to Lovett and predictably rather more to Brook and Dewhurst. Next, O'Connor slated O'Brien for attending the NCSU conference rather than the NCA delegate meeting, and for having adopted a more conciliatory stance than other NCA men present at the conference.[30] O'Brien's response was inflammatory: 'While I differ essentially from Mr. Lovett and his friends, as regards the practicability of a union with the middle classes *generally*, I differ still more from those heartless and factious politicians who ... confound the honest middle-class man, that would give me my rights, with the knave who would not'.[31]

Factious O'Connor may have been; heartless he was not. His irrepressible commitment and recklessness in controversy endeared him to, rather than repelled, popular audiences. As a German journalist, resident in Bradford at this time, wrote: 'in their O'Connor the English people see themselves. O'Connor is the people summed up in one man, endowed with all their virtues and afflicted with all their vices.'[32] A new national petition was nearing completion, sustained by a centrally co-ordinated national organisation in a way that the 1839 petition conspicuously had not been. Chartism seemed poised for an impressive advance. Conspiratorial voices, so tragically evident in 1839–40, were mute. In their place O'Connor – charismatic, energetic, egotistical – had led the way in forging a constitutional platform. Hard though it might be for so-called 'sensible Chartists' to swallow, he alone ensured that Chartism remained a genuinely mass movement.

The political career of Thomas Cooper illustrates this perfectly. The

Lincolnshire-born shoemaker embraced Chartism with an almost messianic fervour. Henry Vincent seethed with anger at the 'mad O'Connorite named Cooper' who led 200 Chartists in disrupting, 'by noise and oaths &c', an NCSU meeting Vincent addressed that July.[33] Cooper's retrospect on why he was 'O'Connor mad' is revealing:

> I do not controvert the phrase ... With midwinter, 1841–42, the severest distress commenced in Leicester. I had seen wretchedness enough before; but now, when employ ceased for thousands, and that for months, the distress was appalling ... The spring of 1842 was fearful. The lack of employ continued; and the people grew either despairing or threatening.

Cooper was no vacuous demagogue. Among the reams of poetry he had committed to memory as a young man were the first three books of Milton's *Paradise Lost*. He had also taught himself a good reading knowledge of French, Greek and Latin. His significant contribution to Leicester Chartism that winter had included running a popular political Sunday school. But Cooper's 'attachment to O'Connor' was absolute:

> The people taught me this attachment. I did not teach it to them. I was assured they had no hope in Chartism, but in him. He won me also, by his letters, and by his conversation, in the few interviews I had with him, during my Leicester chieftainship. I saw reason in the after time to alter my opinion of him; but during the period I am referring to, I held that *union* was the absolute requirement for Chartist success; and as the people cleaved to O'Connor as their leader, I became a foe to all who opposed him as the fomenters of *disunion* ... I was the people's instrument, rather than their director.[34]

## The 'leviathan petition'

The widening rifts between O'Connor and other leading Chartists would have been more prominent had not the movement been preoccupied with its second mass Petition. Agreed by the NCA in October 1841, preparations had been actively underway since November. Petition sheets, printed at the *Star*'s Leeds works, were dispatched all over the country. The aim was 4 million signatures and it was taken for granted that the well-established network of Chartist localities, backed by the regional and national infrastructure of the NCA, would rise cheerfully to the task. Yet the Petition was not without controversy, highlighting the difficult balancing act required of O'Connor as he attempted to broaden support for Chartism beyond the already remarkable extent mobilised in 1839.

Ireland was the movement's Achilles' heel. It was vastly different, economically, socially and culturally, from Britain. However, since the Act of Union of 1801 it had been united with Britain and governed from Westminster. Its popular politics were dominated by Daniel O'Connell's mission to secure the repeal of the Union, a cause he made synonymous with the political aspirations of Ireland's Roman Catholics. However, the disparity between the economies of the two countries led Irish migrants to flock to largely Protestant Britain. There were over 416,000 Irish-born residents in Britain in 1841 and they constituted a significant tranche of opinion in several major urban centres (75,000 in London, 50,000 in Liverpool, 44,000 in Glasgow, 33,000 in Manchester).[35] But O'Connell pursued repeal with the same single-mindedness that O'Connor did the Charter: the two men, as we have seen several times, were in no sense political bed-fellows. This partly reflected the circumstances of O'Connor's departure from Irish politics in 1836, but it also reflected O'Connell's propensities for personal invective and political opportunism, besides which Feargus paled by comparison. So hostile was the reception for Robert Lowery, the General Convention's missionary to Dublin in 1839, that he had to be physically carried from his first public meeting by a supporter, and prevented from entering his second, before wisely deciding to cut his losses and return.[36] A new feature of Chartism in 1842, however, was the emergence of support for the movement in Ireland in the form of the Irish Universal Suffrage Association. The Association, with a total membership of just over 1,000, was an effective presence in Belfast and Dublin, and boasted smaller clusters in fourteen other towns, notably Drogheda, Newry and Sligo. By 1842 Peter Brophy, the IUSA's first secretary, was selling around 400 copies of the Northern Star each week in Dublin.[37]

Brophy's sales were helped by the paper's generous coverage of IUSA activities. The Irish Association energetically argued the integral link between Chartism and repeal of the Union. Recalling that in 1800 the Irish House of Commons had voted for its own dissolution, the IUSA argued that repeal 'would in truth be of little benefit to Ireland, if it merely threw power into the hands of men who would take the first opportunity of selling the country again'. In any case, the IUSA argued, repeal could not realistically be expected of an unreformed Westminster Parliament. Equally, Chartism was uncertain of success without the massive additional political pressure the Irish could bring to bear. 'The Repealers of Ireland', wrote the IUSA's president Patrick O'Higgins, 'are the Prussians whose coming up will enable their English brethren to win the great moral Waterloo.'[38] To cement this relationship, O'Connor and the NCA committed Chartism to repeal, and the text of the 1842 Petition therefore included the formula 'that your Petitioners complain of the many grievances borne by the people of Ireland; and contend that they are fully entitled to a repeal of the Legislative Union'.[39]

Repeal of the Union had not been elevated to the status of a seventh point of the Charter, for it took its place alongside demands for the repeal of the New

Poor Law, freedom of assembly, the disestablishment of the Anglican Church, a pardon for the Newport prisoners, an end to taxation without representation, cuts in the cost of the monarchy, the standing army and the 'unconstitutional police force', reductions in working hours and complaints at 'a host of other evils, too numerous to mention, all arising from class legislation'. But the inclusion of repeal (and to a lesser extent the 1834 Poor Law, which did not apply in Scotland) troubled many Scottish Chartists. Their objections were partly on principle, for the Petition was drawn up by the NCA whose Scottish branches were minimal, and partly a means to take issue with O'Connor's dominance of the movement. There was also a religious dimension, for the entwining of repeal with Irish Catholicism repelled many Protestants. In January 1842 a Scottish delegate conference decided, albeit only on the chairman's casting vote, formally to 'disapprove the petition proposed by the English executive council, and recommend to the people of Scotland the adoption of a petition for the People's Charter, without embracing any question of detail'. O'Connor, who attended as the delegate for Rutherglen and Elderslie, was powerless to reverse the decision (he may even have missed that particular session). However, over the following weeks a steady flow of protest eroded confidence in it. Peter McDouall, the most prominent Scot in the NCA, criticised it on procedural grounds and questioned the motives behind it: Lovett's National Association was content with the Petition, why then should Scotland demur? Significant numbers of Scottish localities repudiated it, some having discovered their delegates ignored their earlier adoption of the Petition. Not implausibly, O'Connor blamed a small number of ministers (some from Chartist churches). He took pains to exempt from criticism the congregations led by those 'saints of the Glasgow Chartist Synod', however, and by mid-February Scotland was effectively behind the Petition.[40]

Effectively but not totally. The economic depression of 1841–42 was arguably harsher in the west of Scotland than anywhere else in Britain. In such circumstances the appeal of cheaper bread through abolishing the Corn Laws was considerable and it was a political objective to which all classes could subscribe. Some pointed to the conspicuous exclusion of Corn Law repeal from the 1842 Petition and claimed to detect O'Connorite humbug. Among those alienated by O'Connor in this particular round of controversy was William Pattison, the engineering trade unionist who had moved the adoption of the first Petition on Glasgow Green in May 1838. For Chartism to lose the active support of men like Pattison, or James Williams of Sunderland, was arguably more serious than the higher profile disputes between O'Connor and Lovett or O'Brien, for the intellects and energies of grassroots activists such as these were the force that sustained day-to-day organisation of Chartism at a local level.

Furthermore Chartism was permanently weakened in Wales, where it never fully recovered from the Newport disaster. In north Wales there never had been a Chartist presence outside Mold. In mid-Wales it was now confined to Newtown and, precariously, Llanidloes.[41] In south Wales Chartism prospered in Merthyr Tydfil, reinforced by the energetic publishing efforts of David John and Morgan Williams. Alongside Chartist tracts in Welsh, their newspaper *Udgorn Cymru* ('Trumpet of Wales') out-sold and out-lasted its English-language counterpart the *Advocate and Merthyr Free Press*.[42] Almost half of the 48,000 Welsh signatures to the 1842 Petition came from Merthyr and its vicinity. It was there, too, that active commitment to insurrection lingered, the central figure an itinerant haberdasher and NCA activist from Nottingham, George Black. From his base in Merthyr Black sold 'vast quantities' of arms, according to Glamorgan's Chief Constable, and co-ordinated shadowy preparations for a further rising timed, or so it seemed, for the second week of February 1842.[43] However, elsewhere in south Wales the movement was a shadow of its former self. Williams, the sole Welsh delegate to the 1842 Convention, exempted only Abergavenny from the picture of decay, frankly doubting (albeit mistakenly) if there even was a viable association in Newport.[44]

Viewed against the background of the state of Chartism in Ireland, Scotland and Wales, the achievement of the 1842 Petition was even more impressive. Mindful of Lowery's experience in 1839, the 1842 Convention missionary to Ireland, Christopher Doyle, concentrated on Belfast, which contributed 2,000 signatures (compared to, apparently, none in 1839). In Scotland the effect of the dispute earlier in the year was apparent in the total of 78,000 signatures collected from Glasgow and Lanarkshire combined, when 80,000 had signed in Glasgow alone three years earlier, and in the dramatic collapse of support in Paisley (2,000 signatures against 13,546 three years earlier). In England a pattern of diminished support is clear in East Anglia where Boston, Ipswich, King's Lynn and Norwich all submitted fewer signatures compared to 1839, and Colchester managed only a marginal increase.[45] All these centres, especially Norwich, campaigned in their surrounding villages in 1839, and the smaller totals suggest a diminution in active support for Chartism in rural England, an impression derived also from the evidence for rural southern England and North Yorkshire.[46]

Everywhere else, however, there was a massive leap in support for the 1842 National Petition. Few Chartists, especially since 1839, believed Parliament would hear their prayer, but that was hardly the point. Petitioning was a legitimate and time-honoured means of placing requests and grievances before Parliament. 'If it made no impression on that house', William Beesley of Blackburn told the Convention, 'it would make a great impression on the country.' The task of collecting signatures galvanised localities and provided an incentive to evangelise the Chartist case yet further. For example, the naval dockyard town of Sheerness, untouched by Chartism in 1839, yielded 800 signatures in 1842: over 4 consecutive evenings after they had finished work,

2 Chartists exhaustively canvassed the inhabitants, driving the 'real truth of Chartism into their heads'.[47]

Analysis of the Petition's returns can be only approximate. Figures for a particular locality often included satellite communities, but the extent of this was not clear, nor the practice consistent, between 1839 and 1842. In addition, specific local totals were often not recorded: this was particularly the case in 1842 when signature sheets flooded in up to the very day the Petition was presented to Parliament. It is clear though that English Chartist centres generally secured significant increases in signatories compared to 1839, in some cases being doubled.[48] In all 3,317,752 people signed the 1842 'National Petition of the Industrious Classes', more than two-and-a-half times the 1839 total of 1,280,000. To put this achievement into perspective, the population of England, Wales and Scotland in 1841 was only just over 18,500,000. Early Victorian society was overwhelmingly youthful compared to the twenty-first century and the population aged 20 and over was a little under 10,000,000 (and the population over 21, the legal minimum for voting, somewhat less than that). So the signatories to the 1842 Chartist Petition equated to around a third of the adult population. Put another way, those signing were over three-and-a-half times more numerous than the British electorate at the general election the year before.[49] Of course there was a modicum of signatures from Ireland and probably rather more from those aged under 21. But the extent of support for the 1842 Petition was, and remains, staggering.

The presentation of 'the Chartist leviathan petition' also created an impression commensurate with its size. The National Convention gathered in London on 12 April at the same haunt as its 1839 precursor. The twenty-five delegates devoted much of their time to systematically and intensively agitating the capital, recognising that for all its immense size London was under-represented in the movement but also seeking to maximise public interest in the presentation of the petition on Monday 2 May. Though not a delegate, Thomas Slingsby Duncombe effectively stage-managed the final phase of the Petition campaign. Chartists were asked to mail their completed signature sheets to Duncombe at his home in Albany, an elegant apartment building off Piccadilly. It almost beggars belief that the Petition's 6 miles of paper (weighing over 6 hundred-weight, or 305kg) was assembled at one of London's most exclusive addresses, where Duncombe's neighbours included the former Whig Cabinet Minister Macaulay.[50]

Duncombe secured permission for the Petition to be presented on a Monday, even though this was customarily reserved for government business, since a large accompanying procession could be guaranteed on 'Saint Monday' (commonly an unofficial holiday for working people). 'Unless it was a splendid one', Duncombe told McDouall, a procession 'would not benefit the cause.' It was indeed splendid. Seven bands (including, implausibly, one of Grenadier

Guardsmen), marshals on horseback, hundreds of banners and countless flags attracted a crowd estimated by *The Times* (no friend of Chartism) at 50,000. The centre of attention, however, was the Petition itself, a gigantic roll carried by relays of London tradesmen on a huge decorated box constructed for the purpose. As with the Newport prisoners' petition the previous year, Duncombe arranged for the bearers to bring their burden direct to the Commons' chamber while it was in session. But, neither he nor Parliament's officials had realised the physical problem this posed. The Petition became jammed tight in the Members' Entrance. Attempts were made to dismantle both its casing and part of the door frame; but eventually the Petition had to be disassembled and taken in pieces into the Commons by its bearers and accompanying Convention members. Heaped up on the floor of the chamber, it dwarfed the clerks' table on which, technically, it was supposed to be placed. Duncombe made a short, forceful speech of formal presentation and the clerk to the House then had to read out the text in its entirety. It was a deeply satisfying piece of political theatre.[51]

Predictably less satisfying was the Commons' debate next day, on a motion from Duncombe, that six representatives of the Chartists be allowed to speak to the Petition at the bar of the House. The wide range of issues contended in the Chartists' Petition unsettled MPs, but Duncombe told the Commons, 'you may think many of their arguments absurd, their schemes of redress wild and visionary, be it so; but do not decide against them without hearing them'. Both Peel and his Home Secretary Sir James Graham spoke to oppose the motion; but the most powerful speaker was Macaulay, who seized on the Petition's range of reference as indicative of the political programme that a Parliament elected by universal male suffrage would enact:

> The Government would rest upon spoliation ... What must be the effect of such a sweeping confiscation of property? No experience enables us to guess at it. All I can say is, that it seems to me to be something more horrid than can be imagined. A great community of human beings – a vast people would be called into existence in a new position; there would be a depression, if not an utter stoppage of trade, and of all of those vast engagements of the country by which our people were supported, and how is it possible to doubt that famine and pestilence would come before long to wind up the effects of such a state of things. The best thing which I can expect, and which I think everyone must see as a result, is, that in some of the desperate struggles which must take place in such a state of things, some strong military despot must arise, and give some sort of protection – some security to the property which may remain.[52]

Duncombe's attempt to finesse the House into permitting a second episode of political theatre failed. The motion was defeated by 287 to 49. The Convention was unsurprised and unperturbed. Parliament's reaction was only

to be expected and, unlike in 1839, delegates knew that their movement was
in for a long haul. Much of their deliberations were concerned with organisational and promotional matters. Bronterre O'Brien was unusual in adopting
an almost apocalyptic tone: 'We are on the verge of great changes. The present
system is worn out, and must give way.' O'Connor, in a *Northern Star* letter 'to
the imperial Chartists' the following Saturday, was more measured: Monday 2
May was a victory for the Chartists, for they alone could muster the forces on
display; they 'had paraded Chartism in open day, and brought us under the eye
of the heretofore blind. They ask what it was? And echo answers "LIBERTY"
... Be not intimidated! Be not down-hearted!! Be not influenced by the House
of Commons' defeat.'[53]

## 'Almost more than man'

O'Connor's letter was less ebullient than usual. The main reason was not hard to
find: lower down the same column, he was forced to address complaints made
in the Convention about 'denunciations' in the paper. The morning after the
procession to Westminster, William Thomason (a Scottish delegate), Bronterre
O'Brien and W. P. Roberts all rose to deplore internal strife. Thomason's and
O'Brien's interventions were predictable, but Roberts's less so. Roberts ('one of
the finest fellows I ever met', O'Connor once confided to a friend) was close to
O'Connor. However, the *Star's* 'denunciations ... were one of the most fruitful
sources of disunion it was possible to conceive', Roberts told the Convention.
'Eternity's last bell' would toll, 'ere Mr. O'Connor's fame would be forgotten',
he continued. 'No man had done more for the movement than Mr. O'Connor;
but such wholesale adulation was calculated to turn the head of any man; and
Mr. O'Connor must have been almost more than man, if he was not affected by
it.' These remarks attracted additional attention due to comments made by the
radical MP John Roebuck, during Parliament's debate on Duncombe's motion,
supporting the Petition's principles but denouncing the text as the work of 'a
cowardly and malignant demagogue' and a 'reptile beneath his contempt'.[54]

   O'Connor felt criticism keenly, but there may also have been a more personal
reason for the relatively subdued tone he adopted: his health. Periodically
O'Connor would fade away for a few days, 'very much knocked up', he occasionally explained.[55] His punishing schedule may have been the sole reason for
these occurrences (the most recent during the Scottish delegate conference). In
April he became a pledged teetotaller, an out-of-character action for which the
reasons (never given) were probably medical. The muted manner in which news
of this became known suggests that O'Connor genuinely regretted his earlier
strictures on temperance Chartism or, possibly, that he thought abstinence
incompatible with his popular persona. That he undertook to 'try it for twelve
months' implies that he knew he might not stick to it.[56]

For the moment at least the denunciations were stemmed. The shadow of complete suffragism, however, hung over the 1842 Convention. The NCSU was both an opportunity and a threat. In striving for unity, a policy of cautious pragmatism emerged from the Convention. Within a week of its conclusion, this was manifest in the Nottingham branch's decision to support Joseph Sturge at a forthcoming by-election for one of the two parliamentary seats in the constituency. The local political situation was a ripe one which Chartists were well placed to exploit. They had supported the victorious Conservative in an early 1841 by-election, then switched allegiance at the general election to the two victorious Whigs. Wholesale bribery was rife on that occasion, in the execution of which the Whigs were simply more blatant than the Tories. So, rather than force an official enquiry, the Tories accepted an undertaking that one of the Whig MPs would shortly resign, triggering a by-election they would not then contest. It was therefore generally assumed that a high-profile Tory (John Walter, editor of *The Times*) would soon be Nottingham's MP. Such blatant disregard for the parliamentary process offended Liberals and Chartists alike. When the by-election arrived in the first week of August, Sturge was a familiar figure in the constituency, and his Chartist supporters pledged to 'act upon the Principle of neither giving Bribes nor opening Swill Shops'. O'Connor was frequently at his side, backed by a non-electors' committee composed entirely of Chartists and funded from donations solicited in the *Northern Star*.[57]

These donations enabled several Chartists to devote themselves almost full time to the approaching contest. O'Connor, McDouall, Cooper and a minor galaxy of midland Chartists organised close canvassing, exclusive dealing and daily demonstrations. For the NCSU, Vincent and O'Neill were important bridging figures. Additional relish was provided by the sudden arrival of Joseph Rayner Stephens to support Walter. This was the first occasion he had appeared before any Chartist crowd since his trial and disavowal of the movement. A new contest, as heated as that between Sturge and Walter, suddenly gripped Nottingham. The night before the hustings each side simultaneously rallied its supporters in the marketplace. Large numbers of Chartists brought with them their *Northern Star* portraits of Stephens. Marshalled by McDouall, they assembled in front of Stephens and ceremonially ripped them to shreds, 'throwing the torn fragments at his face'. The Tories had assembled an impressive force of 'lambs' to protect their platform which immediately advanced on the Sturgeites. At this point Sturge and Vincent prudently bolted, leaving the field to O'Connor and the Chartists. The result was not edifying but it cemented O'Connor's popular reputation for fearlessness and, at the micro-political level, physical force. He leapt from the platform into the crowd, followed by McDouall and the Stockport Chartist Thomas Clark. 'It was no trifle to receive a blow from O'Connor's fists', Cooper recalled dryly in his autobiography; but the account he sent to his wife was rather more dramatic:

He fought like a dragon – flooring the fellows like ninepins – was thrown – forty men upon him – Sprang up again – seized a fellow by the leg who stood on the wagon – tore him down (Stephens and the rest had cut) and then mounted the Tory wagon! What a shout then rent the air, amidst throbbing hearts! I shall never forget it! McDouall and others then crowded the wagon and it was dragged alongside ours – we stepped on to it and, successively, addressed the meeting.[58]

Next day both Vincent and O'Connor were nominated as candidates at the hustings, alongside Sturge and the increasingly uncomfortable Walter. This was a ruse to enable them to address the crowd, which as non-residents of the constituency they could not otherwise do. Having done so they withdrew, leaving Sturge to trounce Walter on the show of hands. Immediately the Tory demanded a poll. As the crowds dispersed, Cooper and an Irish bagpiper led a large assembly round Nottingham, singing Chartist hymns, 'cheering at the friendly mansion and groaning at the foe's retreat', an activity that ceased only at 2.30 next morning. The final outcome was a moral victory for Sturge and the Chartists. Walter won by only eighty-four votes and was then unseated for bribery. The election was ordered to be re-run the following year.[59]

## 'The Charter or no return to labour'

The entry of an NCSU candidate, with Chartist backing, onto a political stage rendered febrile by wholesale corruption made this by-election extraordinary. But its final week unfolded against the background of something even more tumultuous and momentous, a wave of strikes so substantial as to merit perhaps the title of general strike.[60] The 1842 strike-wave was essentially spontaneous and beyond the control of the NCA executive, yet it was intimately bound-up with Chartism. It also constituted one of the most serious threats to social stability during the Chartist period. Graham, the Home Secretary, believed the threat was graver in 1842 than in 1839.[61]

We have seen that in 1839 'declarations of adhesion in bodies' were made by trades' meetings in a number of industrial centres. There was no formal means of joining Chartism: a person was a Chartist by personal conviction and an organisation, by public declaration. With the NCA's formation a mechanism became available through which to subscribe to the movement. Early in 1841 members of its Manchester-based executive began a concerted initiative to persuade the region's trade unions to affiliate. Leach and Doyle drew parallels with general unionism in a presentation to Manchester trades' delegates at the town's Carpenters' Hall; and Peter McDouall, in the journal he published from Ashton-under-Lyne, proposed that trades should constitute themselves as localities of the NCA, an idea based on Dundee's thriving Trades' Democratic Universal Suffrage Association. A Chartist trade locality was technically distinct from the equivalent local trade union (in any case trade unions were relatively scarce while bodies, organised with varying degrees of formality as 'a trade', were commonplace) but 'if a Trades' Union be unanimous to adopt the Charter', McDouall suggested, 'then form your Association out of the whole Union'.[62] In Bristol, like Dundee, there was a combined Trades' NCA, but generally individual occupational groups affiliated to the appropriate NCA district, for example shipwrights in Aberdeen, tailors in Birmingham and shoemakers in Stafford, Northampton and Nottingham. In 1841–43, a third of all the NCA localities in London were trade ones. Manchester trade localities included block printers, boilermakers, bricklayers, carpenters, fustian cutters, painters, powerloom weavers, shoemakers, tailors, hammermen (an aggregation of various metal trades), mechanics and smiths. The latter

> after maturely examining the subject, had found that the trades' unions had not accomplished that for which they had been formed, namely the protection of the labour of the working man; and, therefore, they had come to the conclusion that nothing short of a participation in the making of the laws by which they were governed, would effectually protect their labour. Having come to this conclusion, they had joined the National Charter Association.[63]

It has to be stressed, though, that the NCA's national membership had reached only 50,000 by April 1842: Chartists by conviction rather than enrolment remained the norm. Outside Manchester and London this largely applied also to trades' groups. Trades' unions were cautious bodies and Chartism was widely presented by a hostile press and establishment as an insurrectionary movement. 'Their Trade Union was illegal enough at present', commented a London shoemaker in 1842, 'and they were unpopular enough with the masters, without making them more so.'[64] Yet despite appearances few unions were politically disengaged, especially in periods of economic rupture and distress like 1842.

While it was common prudence to distance a union from political activity, it was typically Chartism that provided the intellectual tools with which trade unionists thought outside the parameters of their own immediate interests. Thus the Manchester Trades' Congress of August 1842 decided against recommending member societies to overturn their bans on political discussion; yet this same congress voted for a general strike until the Charter was won. David Morrison, the mechanics' leader and strongly for retaining the ban, was a delegate to the Chartist conference a few days later and subsequently prosecuted for his role in the strike wave. When Morrison picketed the Bridgewater Foundry, he told his workmates: 'though we might think we were well off, yet ultimately the distress would reach us also; that it was our duty to sympathize' with striking mill hands.[65]

Trades' support for Chartism was not unanimous. Members of the Operative Stonemasons' lodge at Canterbury, for example, criticised the Birmingham Chartist who was their national secretary for introducing political comment in union literature: 'I have, however, yet to learn', he replied, 'what difference it makes to the working-man whether his employer reduces his wages 6d. per day or the self constituted "authorities of the land" impose a political tax on his food ... or that there is more virtue in resisting the one than in resisting the other'.[66] A handful of trades explicitly rejecting association with Chartism were distinguished by consistently successful unionisation, for example the shipwrights, coopers, and typographers. Trades with less secure, but nonetheless active, unions were usually more committed both to inter-trade activity and to Chartism. These included all construction workers, the textiles industries (where even apparently strong unions were insecure in the face of new technology), shoemakers, tailors and also trades where unionisation was relatively recent, notably engineering. A final factor predisposing some workers to Chartism was the collapse or steep decline in effective trade organisation. This was noticeable in the north Staffordshire Potteries, an area where industrial disturbances were particularly serious in the summer of 1842 and where the 'plug riots' (as the strike wave was popularly known) began.

The year 1842 was seemingly one of unrelenting depression. Prices were high, unemployment increasing and the response of many employers to slackening trade was to cut wages. When London masons struck in March, the *English Chartist Circular* called for a generous show of solidarity to prove 'Chartism the friend and protector of Industry'. Birmingham Chartists helped sustain the midlands nail-making communities in May and June and (although 8 of them were imprisoned from 2 to 6 months for holding unlawful meetings) were active again on the strike-bound Black Country coalfield from late July to September.[67]

At the beginning of June colliers from north Staffordshire turned out in protest against a wage reduction, demonstrating in a time-honoured fashion by parading the Potteries with loaves of bread on poles. They received strong local support, and the following month, when there was a similar turn-out, a Committee of Operative Colliers was formed, its headquarters at a Hanley pub regularly used for Chartist meetings. Systematic stoppages commenced across the north Staffordshire coalfield as pickets halted work at each pit, raking out the fires of colliery engines and pulling out the plugs from the steam chambers. As boiling water cascaded onto engine-room floors, steam engines were rendered instantly inoperable – a dramatic form of protest but without risk of permanent damage to the plant. The dispute's aims widened from reversing wage reductions to demanding pay rises, a shorter working week and abolishing 'truck' (payment in kind rather than money). One by one most Staffordshire potteries closed for want of fuel, the potters showing (according to the main local newspaper) 'a quiet determination to endure anything, so that the rise of wages asked by the colliers may be gained'.[68] Coverage in the *Northern Star* ensured that the dispute was a matter of more than merely regional interest. Meanwhile demonstrations by the strikers widened out: sprawling columns several thousand strong marched westwards into Shropshire and north almost to Stockport, drawing plugs at collieries and demanding food from shops and houses along their way.[69]

All this activity had significant underpinning from Potteries' Chartists. At least 5 district NCA committeemen were miners, 2 of them the most prominent leaders of the Hanley colliers. Other leading Chartists addressed public meetings supporting the strikers. John 'Daddy' Richards, delegate to the 1839 Convention, was corresponding secretary to the Committee of Operative Colliers. Though the strike was neither Chartist inspired nor led, its resolve and effectiveness were clearly stiffened by Chartists. As the strike wave widened the same was apparent elsewhere. In the Black Country on 10 August, Cooper and O'Neill (fresh from the Nottingham election) addressed striking colliers at Wednesbury, 'counselling them to persevere with their strike; and ... on the necessity of uniting to win the People's Charter'. From the Chartist Chapel in Birmingham, O'Neill was promoting 'AN UNION OF THE WORKING MEN DESIROUS OF GETTING a Fair Day's wage for a Fair Day's work'.[70]

Cooper went on to speak to similar audiences in Bilston, Wolverhampton and Staffordshire. He was threading his way across the midland coalfields, and thence to Manchester for a meeting of the NCA executive, to which he had recently been elected. As he went he addressed public meetings and picked up money owed by newsagents for his paper the *Commonwealthman*. By the time Cooper arrived in the Potteries the miners had drifted back to work, but the strike and the economic dislocation it had caused had created an atmosphere of crisis. Local Chartists now directed their energies at paupers. The Burslem workhouse currently housed 850 in premises designed for 350, and 1,000 more were receiving 'outdoor' relief. On 9 August Richards 'spoke in a strain of the most fervid eloquence' to an open-air meeting of Burslem paupers which was dramatically augmented mid-way through by the arrival of 2,000 inmates and out-relief recipients from the conurbation's second 'Bastille'. The meeting culminated with a resolution that 'the distress which is gnawing the vitals of the British population can never be permanently removed until the People's Charter becomes law of the land'.[71]

Staffordshire had initiated a strike-wave that was beginning to surge across a huge swathe of Britain. Thirty-two counties were ultimately hit by strikes that summer. Although the extent of the disturbances was modest in most counties, Cheshire, Lancashire, Staffordshire, the West Riding of Yorkshire and Lanarkshire were crucial exceptions. As in 1839, London was out of step with the mood of the industrial north: there 1842 was a year with an exceptionally low level of documented strike action and serious disorder was limited to demonstrations around mainline stations against the dispatch of troops to the midlands and the north. Although the extent to which striking miners genuinely embraced Chartism as an objective widely varied, a close affinity between Chartism and other trades was nearly always manifest.[72] This was inevitable, Richard Otley of Sheffield pointed out at his subsequent trial:

> In the manufacturing districts there are, at least, four out of every five of the working classes, that either are actually Chartists, or hold Chartist principles. This being the case, it is quite impossible that there should be a turn-out for wages, without having a great number of Chartists among the turn-outs.[73]

Insofar as a case could be made that a hidden hand guided the 1842 stoppages, it was not Chartism but the ACLL that was most frequently identified. Stoppages were of limited consequence, and could be positively advantageous, to employers if occurring at a time of limited demand for their products and high prices for raw materials (in the summer of 1842, especially, coal). Workers, once re-employed could be paid less: the immediate local context of many 1842 strikes was where employers reduced wages. If, additionally, widespread stoppages and unrest persuaded the Government to change its economic policy, then potentially there could be wide and long-term political gains. A resolution precisely on these lines was considered by the ACLL's conference in July. Although it was defeated, suspicions lingered that ACLL members were happy to foment a strike-wave by imposing wage reductions they knew their employees would resist. O'Connor said exactly this at the end of July: for a while the Home Secretary ordered the interception of Richard Cobden's mail; and subsequently he and Peel devoted significant energy to proving the ACLL's complicity, publishing a substantial dossier to that effect in 1843.[74]

Some ACLL members probably did announce wage reductions on the assumption that there could be an advantageous political spin-off; rather more were content to accept a strike when their works were targeted. 'All the corn law repeal party left orders with their overlookers to stop the works as soon as the mob made its appearance', a Bolton correspondent told the Home Office; 'those firms whose owners are of a more conservative turn held out, however.'[75] This helps explain the speed with which the strike-wave spread. It is not, however, a sufficient explanation. Deepening economic distress that summer strengthened workers' resolve not to accept wage cuts. The commonest slogan that August was 'A fair day's wage for a fair day's work' (sometimes also expressed as a demand for the wage rates paid in 1839 or 1840). The strikes' overtly political dimension was the culmination of almost half a decade of Chartist activity and, more directly, of energetic support from local activists, partly principled, partly opportunistic. Hence the strike-wave became closely bound up with Chartism, not through official NCA policy but something far more profound, though more difficult to pin down: the involvement of local Chartists as advisers, advocates and participants in the strikes.

In contrast to 1839, Chartists were not waiting on their national leadership to announce its strategy. It was a logical initiative to add the call for the Charter to every strike resolution possible. Who first suggested that is unclear, for as early as March delegates from seven trades (including powerloom and handloom weavers) had told an ACLL meeting that 'they would come out for nothing short of the whole Charter.'[76] The suggestion had come almost certainly from a leading NCA activist from the Ashton-under-Lyne and Stalybridge area, closely associated with McDouall. Among the delegates Richard Pilling, an Ashton weaver, was particularly prominent. It was Pilling who put a resolution to a Stalybridge strike meeting, on 29 July, 'that a fair day's wages could not be obtained without the Charter being made the law of the land'. That is not quite the same as a resolution declaring a strike until the Charter became law, but on 1 August Hyde factory worker George Candelet, chairing a strike meeting, endorsed a resolution to turn out if employers imposed further wage reductions, with this comment: 'I hope you, men of Hyde, will be true to one another, and then we will soon have our rights; that will be the Charter and nothing but the Charter.' Only on 2 or 3 August at nearby Dukinfield, in a resolution moved by Pilling, was it explicitly declared 'that, if the masters continued in their abatements, the people should turn out, and stop out, till they got a fair day's wage for a fair day's work, and until the Charter became the law of the land'.[77]

Thereafter this formula, or a variant, became a commonplace in strike demands. In the face of continued 'abatements', a mass meeting of Lancashire and Cheshire textile workers was called for Sunday 7 August on Mottram Moor, a traditional site for Chartist meetings south of Stalybridge. It was resolved to proceed with 'this great national turn-out', and chairman William Muirhouse of Hyde, a prominent figure in the recent weeks, instructed all present to assemble at 5.00 a.m. next day, 'when we will proceed from factory to factory, and all hands that will not willingly come out we will turn them out. And friends, when we are out, we will remain out, until the Charter, which is the only guarantee you have for your wages, become the law of the land.'[78]

That morning 2,000–3,000 strikers fanned out from Stalybridge and turned out nearly every mill still working in the Ashton area. Reassembling in Ashton marketplace that afternoon and now augmented by as many as 10,000 more, the strikers split: one column marched on Hyde, the other on Oldham. The latter streamed into Oldham behind a black flag and a red cap of liberty mounted on a pole. Both columns drew boiler plugs and, excepting one mill at Oldham, neither met resistance. Strike meetings were held that evening in both towns and resolutions passed for total stoppages until the Charter was law. The pattern established was repeated throughout the week. 'The police and military were rather observers than anything else', Manchester magistrate Absalom Watkin noted in his diary.[79] A particular effort was made to prevent any fracturing of support along ethnic and sectarian lines: the Liverpool Irishman Bernard McCartney and the IUSA's secretary Peter Brophy from Dublin both travelled to Manchester to support the strikes.[80] Given the numbers involved, the incidence of violence was strikingly low. The mood was one of surging optimism, born of the wide support they received and the absence of effective resistance. This is vividly captured in a letter written by an unknown Ashton mill-worker, which fell into the hands of the authorities. Turned out on the Monday, the author joined the strikers next morning:

> Tuesday 9th Met at 5 o'clock went to Oldham, Hyde, Manchester, Stockport, & Newton lees – Hurst and all other places round about and stopt every Mill in them – Soldiers and police trying to stop us, took a sword from one of the Soldiers, broke it in pieces made bloody noses for the policemen. Wednesday 10th went to Glossop dale stopt every Mill there. Masters thought to stop *us* got knocked down ... the Shop keepers are going hand in hand with us giving £5, £4 & £2 a piece for men to go to preston, Hull & every Manufacturing town in Great Britain and Ireland to stop them – now is the time or never – lose this opportunity and we are lost! lost! Lost!!!! We get plenty of something to eat the Shops are open they give us what we want. Today Augt 11th to Stockport, they are stopt but we go a parading the Streets like Soldiers 6 a breast. News from Manchester Bloody fights Soldiers ready to fight for the people police the same Now's the time for Liberty we want the Wages paid 1840 if they wont give it us Revolution is the consequence. We have stopt every trade – Tailors, coblers – Brushmakers – Sweeps, Tinkers, Carters – Masons – Builders – Colliers &c and every other trade. Not a Cart is allowed to go through the Streets.[81]

Community support for the strike at this stage was considerable, but some shopkeepers were doubtless influenced by a wish for self-preservation. Oldham shopkeepers issued posters sympathising with the strikers and promising 'all pecuniary assistance', but also demanding that local manufacturers 'make an immediate arrangement with the workers in their employ, as the best means of preserving the peace and good order of the town'. Watkin wrote on Thursday 11 August: 'All is unquiet and unsafe', noting that violence had spread as the authorities belatedly sought to get a grip on events. 'The disturbances extend in every direction and become very alarming', he added the next day; then on Saturday the disturbances 'are now assuming a more determined political character. "The Charter or no return to labour" is now the general cry ... The man who delivered our coal today told Elizabeth that they should bring no more, and that they would now have the Charter.'[82] Public order was now seriously compromised. At Preston on 12 August two strikers were shot dead by soldiers. There were also serious casualties among a squad of Manchester police when supporting army pensioners ('a considerable number' of 'picked men') fled on sighting an approaching strike column.[83]

The strikes were now percolating southwards, extending 'to the pettiest of trades, and several miles into rural situations which adjoin the manufacturing districts' of Derby, according to a Chapel-en-le-Frith observer on 12 August. The crisis in Derbyshire had rapidly deepened, vividly apparent in the Home Secretary's personal plea that the county's leading landowner, the Duke of Devonshire, should abandon the new grouse season and immediately return from shooting on his Yorkshire estate.[84] In Stockport magistrates and military were locked in argument about how – or indeed whether – the courts could be protected, and it was widely supposed that the workhouse would be besieged. 'They now had an opportunity of obtaining Every Priviledge they were entitled to', a local Chartist leader told strikers that Saturday night, but he counselled restraint and 'insisted that the Charter would do away with class legislation and open a door of admission to all places and priviledges'. Only now was an element of direction from Chartism apparent at the higher level. On the Sunday, Leach and Doyle of the NCA executive visited Stockport and addressed camp meetings on the theme 'The CHARTER the PEOPLE'S HOPE'. They also arranged the election of a Stockport delegate to a NCA conference in Manchester the following Wednesday.[85]

That weekend Lancashire strikers entered West Yorkshire for the first time. A pathetic fallacy circulated among Yorkshire's middle class that the so-called 'plug rioters' were entirely from outside the county. Lancashire alone actively supported the strike, in contrast – to quote the Huddersfield postmaster in a report to the Home Office – to 'our own operatives who in fact do not appear to sympathise'. Within a day he had revised his opinions, but in doing so gave a revealing sketch of those who spoke at Huddersfield strike meetings: 'very moderate, all Strangers evidently in humble life – sensible, shrewd, determined, peaceable'. Meanwhile on Bradford Moor a journalist mingled with the crowd at a Chartist camp meeting where plans were laid to initiate the strike the next morning; 'we found a determined spirit of hostility to the existing system of things', he wrote, 'the Bible was often quoted'.[86]

As the 'great national turn-out' entered its second week, strikers swept through West Yorkshire. The cotton district was at a standstill. At noon on the Monday Bolton had 'the appearance of a deserted village', according to a local teacher. 'Do you not perceive', said a Chartist to him, 'a strong analogy between these doings and the ominous miasma that passed over France before the dreadful revolution?' The events of 1789 probably lurked in the minds of Leeds magistrates that same morning as they drew up a warning notice that 'a Large Number of Lawless Persons are expected to VISIT LEEDS in the course of a very short time, with the object of creating Terror'. Prosperous residents of industrial towns left, if they could afford to do so. The resort of Southport, for example, 'was quite full of company', wrote a Bolton mill-owner's sister, 'many most likely have come out of these disturbances, but [I] have been surprized to see so many men here at such a time as this'.[87]

Saturday's *Northern Star* had brought news of the strike to areas far beyond its epicentre. Scotland's copies were dispatched from Leeds on Thursday evening, so the news arrived in good time to stiffen the resolve of those striking against wage cuts at over 100 pits in Lanarkshire, Midlothian and Fife. On 13 August, Clackmannanshire miners determined to 'never again produce a pennyworth of wealth till the People's Charter be law', provided the rest of the country fell in with the same plan by 23 August. Airdrie and Fife collieries adopted the same objective, and Dunfermline Chartists immediately formed a 'Cessation-from-Labour Committee' to promote the plan on both sides of the border.[88]

That Monday resolutions to strike for the Charter were passed in places as far afield as Carlisle and the Leicestershire coalfield. In the Potteries the colliers' dispute of the previous month rapidly reignited. At a mass meeting in Hanley, chaired by Cooper, Richards and a local colliers' leader, proposed that 'all labour cease until the People's Charter becomes the law of the land'. It is unclear whether they predicted, and still less were capable of directing, the forces unleashed by that resolution. Plug-drawing escalated into widespread rioting, looting and attacks on the workhouse, police stations and homes of magistrates and Poor Law officials. In crowd actions charged with symbolism, women stormed pawnbrokers' shops and redeemed pledges without payment; fires were made of property deeds and police records. Richard Croxton, an unemployed potter and Chartist, led a gang extorting money from middle-class homes and was heard to say that 'he would rather walk up to his knees in blood than eat his breakfast'. After prolonged unemployment earlier that year, Croxton had swallowed his pride and applied for poor relief: he had spent the past five weeks stone-breaking for nine pence a day, an income on which Richard and his wife somehow fed themselves and their two children. After twenty-four hours during which local authority lost all control, special constables and dragoons finally managed to restore order just as a large body of turn-outs from Cheshire approached the Potteries.[89]

There was also serious violence in West Yorkshire. 'Not to work again until the charter was established' had been agreed at a rally outside Bradford's Oddfellows' Hall early Monday morning, whereupon two columns of demon-strators headed for Halifax, turning out mills along the way. Handloom weavers, who joined the strike as the processions passed, threw their shuttles into sacks and lodged them with sympathetic publicans, signifying that they would not resume work without a collective decision to do so. It was clear from the sheer press of people (plus the fact most made their way home again at night) that this was no Lancashire incursion but an indigenous movement. 'I had unusual opportunities of noticing them closely', wrote one eye-witness, 'and was surprised at the numbers whom I recognised as factory hands round about, and navvies also.' All Halifax, or so it seemed, was waiting to greet them. There was particular sympathy for 'thousands of female turnouts ... poorly clad and not a few marching barefoot' who refused to disperse when the Riot Act was read, daring the military to kill them and defiantly singing the 'Union Hymn'. Eventually cavalry cleared the streets, 'cutting down or riding over all who stood in their way'. Frank Peel had been a child when he watched the strikers as they passed along the Bradford to Halifax road:

> The sight was just one of those it is impossible to forget. They came pouring down the wide road in thousands, taking up its whole breadth – a gaunt, famished-looking desperate multitude, armed with huge bludgeons, flails, pitch-forks and pikes, many without coats and hats, and hundreds upon hundreds with their clothes in rags and tatters ... As the wild mob swept onward, terrified women brought out all their bread and eatables, and in the hope of purchasing their forbearance, handed them to the rough-looking men who crowded to the doors and windows. A famished wretch, after struggling feebly for a share of the provisions, fell down in a fainting condition in the doorway where I was standing. A doctor, who lived close at hand, was got to the spot as soon as possible, but the man died in his presence. One of his comrades told us that the poor fellow had eaten raw potatoes at Ovenden after being without food for two days.[90]

On Tuesday 16 August, a day heavy with symbolism as the anniversary of Peterloo, Halifax sought revenge on the cavalry who had violently dispersed the crowds the day before. Knowing that demonstrators arrested so far would be taken by train to Wakefield Prison, an ambush was organised at Salterhebble on the hillside road to the nearest station at Elland. The route looked more 'like a road to a fair or the races', a bystander recalled, 'all busy – women as well as men – in rushing along the various lanes over my head with arms and aprons full of stones'. As the cavalry returned from the station it was assailed by 'stones, bricks, boulders, like a close fall of hail'. Horses and soldiers were wounded in the struggle to escape down the narrow lane, and the equipment of eight men whose mounts had thrown them was ransacked as they lay semi-conscious on the road. The rest of Tuesday was punctuated by ugly confrontations in the constricted streets of central Halifax. At several times bayonets were used or shots fired to disperse crowds. A report sent by the Mayor to the Home Office, two days later, listed eight men 'severely' or 'dangerously' wounded with gunshot and bayonet injuries. In all there were at least three fatalities (one a soldier). In addition, 'many a tale of wounded men lying out in barns and under hedges was told'. Carpet weaver Charles Greenwood, one of the ambush party at Salterhebble, spent the night hiding in a drain. When he crept home he found that his 16-year-old son had died 'of tuberculosis and want of food' during his absence.[91]

As even this abbreviated account of events in Halifax makes clear, things had long since spiralled out of such central control as they had exhibited a week before. 'Those who attacked the soldiers at Salterhebble were neither Lancashire people or people from a distance, but principally young men from the surrounding districts', a leading Halifax Chartist emphatically recalled.[92] The day before these disturbances, a conference of trades' delegates assembled in Manchester's Carpenters' Hall to take stock of the situation and co-ordinate the strike action in the Manchester region. 'No sufficient guarantee is afforded to the producers of wealth, but from adoption and establishment of the people's political rights, as a safeguard for their lives, liberties and interests of the nation generally.' Delegates agreed that the support of 'shopkeepers, dissenting clergymen and the middle classes generally' was needed if the strike was to be effective 'in the struggle for the attainment of their political rights'; equally, there was no sense that support for the stoppage was weakening. The conference took two whole days 'calmly and coolly discussing which was the best remedy for the present state in which the country is now engaged', reported a Derbyshire delegate to his committee at Glossop, 'and, at the last a majority was, that all cease from their work till the People's Charter become the law of the land.' The majority exceeded 120 out of the 141 delegates present.[93] In almost every sense this was now a Chartist strike but it still lacked the NCA's endorsement. The executive was scheduled to meet in Manchester on the Tuesday, after attending the unveiling of a monument to Henry Hunt at the Peterloo commemoration that morning. We have already glimpsed its president James Leach at Stockport the previous Sunday, hastily arranging additional delegates to transform the meeting into an emergency convention; but most members arrived in Manchester only on Tuesday morning.

O'Connor had played no part in the strike-wave so far and arrived from Birmingham early on Tuesday. He was followed shortly after by John Campbell, secretary of the NCA executive, and Thomas Cooper (who had been smuggled out of the strife-torn Potteries). As their train weaved its way into Manchester, the two looked out of the windows with astonishment: 'so soon as the City of Long Chimneys came in sight, and every chimney was beheld smokeless, Campbell's face changed, and with an oath he said, "Not a single mill at work! something must come out of this, and something serious too!"'[94]

It is an illuminating anecdote: the entire executive was aware there were strikes, but those from outside the north (even Campbell who had moved away only a few months previously) were taken aback at their extent, solidity and politicisation. 'Their deliberations were', reported *Northern Star*, 'most anxious.' Six of the almost sixty delegates actually opposed giving official NCA support to the general strike. They were neither middle-class nor 'new movers', but included William Hill and both delegates from Sheffield, Richard Otley and George Harney. The latter, despite – or rather because of – his consistent espousal of French revolutionary ideals, spoke with authority, all too aware that Sheffield was almost totally untouched by the strike-wave. However the majority prevailed, as McDouall subsequently explained:

> The question of having or not having a strike was already decided, because the strike had taken place: the question of making that strike political was also decided, because the trades had resolved, almost unanimously, to cease labour for the charter alone ... What had we to do? To decide whether or not it was advisable to oppose and counteract that which the trades, the local leaders, and the people had already done? ... I reply that we were not.[95]

There was a fundamental gap between the perceptions of the movement's national leadership and those of the Lancashire labour activists. Trade unionists such as Pilling or the smiths' leader Alexander Hutchinson (who chaired the Manchester trades' conference) had been involved in Chartism since its inception and firmly established a link between the two. Yet even Pilling, who claimed with some justification to be 'father of this Movement', was not invited to attend the NCA conference; nor was Hutchinson.[96] The link between trades' organisations and Chartism was cultural and intellectual as much as structural. For the trade unionist seeking to make sense of workplace issues in a wider political context, Chartism provided tools 'to think with'. This applied also, to a significant extent, to leaders in the as yet largely non-unionised mining industries.

In Scotland, the picture that emerges is of the key role of a local leadership politicised through Chartism. The secretary to the Airdrie and Coatbridge miners, for example, had been a delegate to the Scottish Chartist convention in January 1842. The Sheriff of Lanarkshire, a seasoned observer of industrial relations in the Glasgow region, thought both its coal and ironstone miners were 'acting under Chartist direction'. In April he had told the Home Office, 'in all the conferences I have had with the deputations of the workman I could perceive the clearest evidence of a deep sense of wrong, real or imaginary on their part, which seemed to be the result of Chartist principles, and gives me reason to fear that these disturbances are at bottom ... for political purposes and will not be soon eradicated'. In August 1842, 10,000 Lanarkshire colliers were on strike.[97] The Chartist dimension to miners' militancy also had a more-basic educative function, as one Dudley ironstone-miner explained: 'The men did not follow the chartists for the chartist principle, but they fled to them for refuge, and were glad for anyone to come and instruct them about the prices of iron and so on.'[98]

In sharp contrast to the situation at local level, however, the conjunction of strike leaders and the NCA executive was haphazard. There was little its members could do other than 'express their deep sympathy with their constituents, the working men now on strike', and endorse an address McDouall had drafted 'To the People', hoping the strike would spread yet further:

Be firm, be courageous, be men. Peace, law and order are on our side – let them be revered until your brethren in Scotland, Wales, and Ireland are informed of your resolution; and when the universal holiday prevails, which will be the case in eight days, then of what use will bayonets be against public opinion?[99]

But since the fracas at Bolton, in August 1839, no one seriously believed that troops would never fire on the people. There was a disconcerting realisation that violence, especially directed at the military, was counter-productive. Furthermore, by the end of the week, for every new town whose trades agreed on a 'National Strike for the Charter', as in Dundee, there was another (as in Dunfermline) that imposed a deadline after which there would be a return to work if the strike had not become general. Others, for example Sheffield, Birmingham and Aberdeen, held only sympathy meetings and awaited developments.

NCA stalwarts did all they could to widen and intensify strike activity. The midlands lecturer John West had an electrifying impact in Belper and Derby. The latter was awash with rumour and anxiety on 22 August, when striking mill workers and framework knitters from across the region descended on it. 'The appearance in Friargate of long processions of ill-dressed, half-starved people, headed by men carrying upon poles loaves of bread dipped in blood obtained from the slaughter houses, struck me with horror', one onlooker recalled in later life.[100] James Arthur returned from Manchester to Carlisle where he told Chartists 'to expect positive encouragement in the Northern Star on Saturday'. The paper arrived on Saturday afternoon, 'and tho' it did not altogether please them, it determined them … to cease work'. William Beesley, 'a pest to Society', was spotted in Blackburn 'skulking about in disguise'.[101] In Birmingham George White issued animated calls to 'Work no More Until Liberty be Established … Now is the Time!!'[102]

The effect, however, was negligible. At Loughborough an imposing set of resolutions for 'our Holy Cause', a strike 'until the People's Charter becomes the Law of the Land', was adopted, but the area's NCA delegate John Skevington was arrested within twenty-four hours and strikes of quarrymen and knitters commencing that weekend collapsed within a few days.[103] The stoppage on the south Wales coalfield was confined mainly to Merthyr Tydfil, whose Chief Constable thought it 'a shadow of the Manchester affair and their object the Charter'.[104] London missionary Ruffy Ridley was sent by the executive to rouse the largely unaffected west country. He addressed striking lace-makers in the Somerset town of Chard, but his attempt to rouse Trowbridge was a failure: 'the men of this place are ready to strike, but they are in want of information as to whether those on strike intend to hold … the general complaint is that there is no public body sitting, either in London or Manchester, to direct the Movement'.[105]

There was much substance to this complaint, for the Manchester conference had dispersed promptly the day after it convened, so promptly that angry Oldham strikers publicly burnt the *Star* and portraits of O'Connor, and the paper's 20 August issue was 'kicked about the Chartist room in Manchester'. Cooper maintained that they dispersed because of police interest in the NCA address 'To the People' (all delegates' names were attached to it). O'Connor claimed that he was advised to tone down the *Northern Star*'s coverage of the conference to avoid prosecution and, even, the confiscation of its presses. It seems as likely that the executive dispersed so members could promote the strike-wave but restrain violence. Cooper himself arrived home in Leicester too late to stir up the town he later described as 'in a state of terror and discouragement', though strike action there was limited to around 3,000, chiefly glove makers.[106] O'Connor, on the other hand, was preoccupied with his new daily newspaper, the *Evening Star*. This, moreover, was London-based, and its first issue under his management and editorship appeared on 23 August. The need for a daily paper had long preoccupied O'Connor and the strike-wave certainly demonstrated the difficulties of communicating rapid and accurate political news; yet this precise moment was the least opportune for Chartism's most influential leader to decamp to London, leaving the *Northern Star* entirely in the hands of its editor William Hill, who opposed NCA support for the strikes.[107]

The strike-wave, however, was losing momentum, as became evident within days of the NCA conference's dispersal. The *Star* of 20 August dampened enthusiasm. The issue had always been intended as a special one to commemorate Peterloo and mark the unveiling of Manchester's memorial to Henry Hunt. None of this coverage was set aside: it occupied the entire front page and much of the second. Tension between reporting present turmoil and honouring a living past was evident throughout. It was resolved only in Hill's editorial, which reiterated that 'the League-men have caused all this hubbub', and concluded by hoping that 'the people will not be discouraged if, after all, having tried the strike as a means for obtaining the Charter, they find it to fail'.

As the news from Halifax sank in – the nearest that Chartism's English heartlands came to Newport's experience – Chartist activists repeatedly tried to restrain strike-related disturbances. In Nottingham the 'Battle of Maperley Hills' (22 August, in which 400 strikers and their supporters were arrested) concluded 2 days of violence that began when the NCA delegate, Thomas Clark, had left the town.[108] In Oldham Chartists opposed to the continuation of strike action enrolled as special constables. Bradford Chartist James Dewhurst, who worked as an NCA lecturer, was knocked unconscious in an altercation with strikers who marched into Cleckheaton on 18 August. Heckmondwike workers were now 'opposed to the continuance of the strike, as they consider it a plot of the League. They are only out on compulsion.'[109]

Similar sentiments were voiced by Chartist leaders elsewhere. Carlisle's Chartists split on the issue; Ridley told Trowbridge Chartists that the ACLL had deliberately set out to 'exasperate the People [and had] Driven them to despair'.[110] This perception was fuelled mainly by the line Hill and O'Connor pressed in the *Star*, but isolated incidents reinforced it. Manchester's Chief Constable had ascribed the bitterness of the strike there to 'the inflammatory speeches of the Paid Lecturers of the Anti-Corn Law League'; and in Derby the local executive of the League distributed house-to-house a leaflet praising 'the determination of the people' and advising 'you have a moral right to subsistence ... you receive misgovernment instead'.[111]

The most obvious indicator of a lessening of momentum, however, was a drift back to work. This began before the ambivalent 20 August issue of the *Northern Star* hit the streets. A sustained stoppage in West Yorkshire would always have been difficult if the pits did not turn out. Other than around Halifax, this was the case: on 15 August in Wakefield a coalfield general meeting specifically rejected strike action. Mills in the centre of Huddersfield and Leeds began to reopen as early as Thursday. Bradford factories generally returned on 19 August, and much of Halifax was at work again by the weekend.[112] On the Monday reports indicated a return to work in Bolton, Blackburn, Oldham and Wigan. Merthyr was reportedly 'much milder' by Wednesday, when, despite resolving to stay out until at least the arrival of that week's *Northern Star*, miners began drifting back.[113] Leicester glove hands resumed work during the following week, the last occupational group outside Lancashire and coalmining to do so. In south Lancashire and the adjacent part of Cheshire the strike remained solid beyond August, especially in Manchester. Workers returned 'gradually and some reluctantly' during September. Macclesfield mills reopened from 18 September. Manchester's powerloom weavers were the last to resume work, on 26 September. The September phase of strikes, however, was not attended by demonstrations as that in mid-August had been, and all claims that these were strikes for the Charter was abandoned.[114]

That events had turned decisively was, however, less-obvious at the time. This was partly a function of communication difficulties. Home Office disturbance papers suggest that a better organised system existed than in 1839. Graham's use of paid spies and informers (frequently an erratic source) was significantly less than Russell and Normanby's, and instead a wider provincial correspondence (including railway and Post Office officials, as well as local worthies and the military) was developed.[115] Nonetheless, there were significant time-lags before events could be reported to those authorities best able to respond to them, while (as the Mayor of Macclesfield told his Stockport counterpart) 'every occurrence is exaggerated by rumour and much is circulated without foundation'. The most dramatic example of this occurred on 15 August. Peel, spending a rare two days away from Whitehall with his family in the midlands, received a report that Queen Victoria had been assassinated and underwent an anxious wait pacing the local railway station for the next down train to hear if this was true.[116]

Most difficult of all, however, was the sheer weight of business that dealing with the strike-wave entailed for the Government. In an age with a slender Civil Service and generally relaxed attitudes to ministerial workloads, Sir James Graham had good grounds for complaint when he wrote on 21 August that he had been working 'without a spare moment' in the Home Office on 'the mad insurrection of the working classes' ever since Parliament had risen for the summer in mid-July. As yet Graham could not discern an end to the disturbances. He and Peel had worked into the early hours of Friday 19 August, personally supervising police and military protection for the capital in advance of what appeared to be a threatening Chartist mass meeting. After a snatched sleep, the two then held a lengthy meeting with stipendiary magistrates from the strike-hit regions, summoned to London to help them more accurately assess the situation. The meeting was interrupted with news of further disturbances in the Potteries and of the strikers' intention to march on Peel's Staffordshire family home. This too was only rumour, as a scribbled note from Lady Peel confirmed that night: her hastily improvised defences 'should have been equal to an attack from two or three hundred until assistance had come. But then', she added, 'we expected three or four thousand.' Not until a whole week later did Graham venture the view that 'the state of affairs is somewhat improved: at least the insurrection is overawed; but the rebellious spirit is unbroken'.[117]

The geographical extent, emotional intensity and political focus of the 1842 strike-wave presaged revolution in the minds of many contemporaries. Graham believed the strikers to have been defeated but not tamed. 'The spirit is still kept alive, which a little will easily inflame', wrote a Church of England minister; 'we are overrun with Chartism and disaffection', wrote another.[118] The view was widespread among Anglicans that the strikes were in large part ascribable to 'infidelity' and nonconformity, but thoughtful observers also pointed to secular issues. 'It is difficult for anyone not in the manufacturing districts to have any idea of the slender hold on the people of anything like allegiance to a faith in any way or shape of the existing Government and political institutions', wrote Marshall, the Leeds manufacturer who had been prominent in the LPRA. 'They look upon it as an Incubus to be removed, if possible without injury to Person or Property; but the belief is growing that it MUST fall to pieces.' On 16 August Marshall had witnessed a 'mob' he thought to be from outside the town 'closing round Leeds'. To his astonishment, most of the prisoners taken in the ensuing disturbances 'belonged to this neighbourhood & were not strangers ... Work-people here, though well disposed to protect person & property, sympathize strongly with their fellows, whom they think their own.'[119] The memory of the 1842 strike wave remained vivid in the minds of all who experienced it. In 1887, Joseph Lawson of Pudsey related how, incredulous, he had watched as a striker stood directly in front of a troop of cavalry and shouted that he was

> determined that no more work should be done till the 'People's Charter' was the law of the land. He bared his breast as he spoke, and told both the magistrates and soldiers, they might pierce his heart with bullets or lances, but the people were moved to no longer starve when there was an abundance in the land, kept from the producers of all wealth by bad and unjust laws.

Lawson commented: 'Being but a young man, and not having much experience of riots, from all I could hear and see it seemed to me that order and quiet would never be restored till the government was changed to pure Democracy. In this I was mistaken.'[120]

The year 1842 was a point at which history failed to turn.[121] 'He hoped every one of them would stand firm', a Manchester emissary told Leeds Chartists, 'for if they failed this time they might never have another opportunity.' The NCA's address 'To the People' captured an identical sense of providence: 'centuries may roll on as they have fleeted past, before such universal action may again be displayed ... Brethren, we rely upon your firmness; cowardice, treachery, or womanly fear would cast our cause back for half a century.'[122]

However, neither cowardice nor treachery defeated the 1842 strike-wave (and certainly not 'womanly fear', a spectre rooted in the sexist attitudes endemic to a male leadership and wholly at odds with the familial and communal dimension of Chartism). History failed to turn for a combination of reasons. First, with deaths occurring directly from hunger, political ideals understandably took second place to meeting basic subsistence needs. The New Poor Law, draconian in conceptualisation and initial execution, proved flexible. Widespread outdoor relief was available. Although conditions attached to it often caused resentment (as in the Potteries and Stockport) the system, viewed as a whole, worked well enough to help sustain the social fabric rather than tear into it further. Second, some major industrial centres were all but untouched by strikes, notably Birmingham, London, Monmouthshire and Tyneside. Third, the military mobilisation of August 1842 was at least as extensive as it had been in 1839 and was maintained with unparalleled intensity. Napier had left for a command in India in September 1841, pointedly telling Whitehall there remained 'a great deal of distress and wretchedness' in northern England; but he had also instilled considerable discipline in the troops garrisoned there. Furthermore, in the light of 1839–40, Napier had shrewdly reviewed the case for reforms in the army's establishment and barracks, benefits of which were apparent in 1842.[123] Special constables were also mobilised on a wide scale: 1,300 at Halifax and over 100 each even in locations, such as Doncaster and

Settle, largely untouched by the strike-wave. The overall impression is that these were more effective and disciplined in 1842 than in 1839–40.[124]

The fourth cluster of reasons why the strikes failed was logistical. Without extended credit from shopkeepers or donations from wealthy supporters, it was almost impossible to sustain a general strike. The situation echoed the predicament of the 1839 Convention. Once it became clear how little the middle classes 'were prepared to assist and support the people in the struggle for the attainment of their political rights', to quote the manifesto of the Manchester Trades' Congress, the only plausible strategy was a systematic and carefully co-ordinated escalation of strikes across the country. In greater Manchester, where trades' and Chartist organisations meshed effectively, this was achieved to an impressive extent. Elsewhere, even in West Yorkshire, its incidence was uneven, and at a national level it scarcely existed at all. Due to the diverse reasons alluded to above, the NCA was unable to achieve this. Its Conference dispersed just twenty-four hours after learning the full extent of the strike, without plans either to reconvene or for the executive to stay in touch with events. Its key personnel scattered (including, critically, O'Connor who went to London, which was completely untouched by the strike wave). The only force for cohesion was therefore the *Northern Star*, temporarily operating without O'Connor's involvement, under an editor whose opposition to Chartist involvement in the strikes was a matter of public record. It was futile simply to wait on the spread of spontaneous strike action in a society as intensely regionalised as Britain's, and in the face of a Government that combined – on the whole successfully – military decisiveness where needed and judicious licence where it was not. Finally, continued distress might have fuelled further disturbances over the following winter; but the recession abated. The English harvest of 1842 was the most abundant for a decade and grain prices fell sharply during the rest of the year. The order by the Queen in Privy Council that Sunday 2 October should be observed as a day of 'Prayer and Thanksgiving to Almighty God, for the late abundant Harvest' was both heartfelt and of profound symbolic importance.[125]

## Complete suffrage, complete humbug?

As in 1839–40, widespread arrests followed the 1842 disturbances. The bulk were for public-order offences or petty thefts executed in the heat of protesting. It is difficult to establish how many of those arrested (1,500 in the north-west alone) were eventually tried. However, 152 were sentenced at York assizes and in Stafford a Special Commission tried and sentenced 208 for their role in the Potteries disturbances, 54 of whom were transported. The arrests' impact on the Chartist leadership was considerable. Leach was arrested at home on 17 August. Two detachments of infantry and one of cavalry were sent to

Stephens' chapel in Charlestown, Ashton-under-Lyne, to arrest Pilling as he addressed a strike meeting on 12 September. The Mayor of Manchester had lithographic copies made of the *Northern Star*'s portrait of McDouall to accompany a wanted poster offering a reward of £100 (around 2 years' wages) for his capture.[126] Bairstow, Beesley, Campbell, Candelet, Cooper, Doyle, Harney, Hill, Leach, McCartney, O'Connor, O'Neill, Richards and Skevington were all arrested. McDouall fled to France.[127]

As the strike-wave receded, the authorities' position on bail sureties generally relaxed (Cooper and Richards were unfortunate exceptions, detained for eleven weeks). All those leaders who were to stand trial did so in the spring of 1843. The year 1842 therefore closed not with trials and prison sentences but, much as it had begun, with the NCSU occupying the centre of the political stage. In April the NCSU conference had concluded with the edgy compromise that 'at some future period' another conference would be convened, 'at which the whole people may be fully represented for the purpose of considering any documents' embodying the six points of the Charter. The Chartist contingent present always understood by this that *The People's Charter* would be fully debated at the next national NCSU conference. In September Lovett drafted an address for the NCSU central council, inviting representatives to be elected to a conference on 27 December, 'for the purpose of preparing a bill to be submitted to parliament, for securing the just representation of the whole people'.[128] Council approved it and paid a leading Birmingham Christian Chartist to print it for national distribution. There was widespread optimism that the conference would negotiate a *rapprochement* between Chartists and middle-class suffragists. Nottingham's June by-election seemed a good augury and even O'Connor's continued exhortations that Chartists should settle for nothing less than the whole Charter, 'name and all', was not necessarily incompatible with the middle-class embrace.[129] At the grassroots level, Joseph Sturge, the NCSU president, could be and was extolled as 'a thorough going Chartist'.[130] Merthyr Tydfil miner David Rees was clear: 'the Sturgeists are no other than Chartists they claim the 6 points of the Charter as we do. Only they tried to change the name from Chartists to Sturgeists after the name of that Honourable Gentlemen Mr Sturge and they see that nothing else will do but the Charter and only the Charter.'[131]

Rees's remarks were made when a Merthyr delegate was elected to the December conference. All over Britain Chartist localities participated enthusiastically in these elections. Some who participated did so from genuine conviction, others because the *Star* told them to ensure only through-going Chartists were elected. The two positions, in any case, were not incompatible. The NCSU believed it could ensure the conference was not swamped by O'Connorites by stipulating that each town could select 2, 4 or 6 delegates (according to size), half chosen in each case by registered parliamentary electors and the other half by non-electors. This was to reckon without Chartists' time-tested techniques of packing meetings, their powers of persuasion when addressing them, or the grounds for genuine collaboration that existed in a number of localities.

However, the council's greater error, or rather its middle-class members' error (for they kept its two Chartist members, Lovett and Neesom, in ignorance) was to draw up a 'new bill of rights' with the intention that this would be the document prioritised on the conference agenda. Lovett was furious, and told Sturge so: 'I believed that the majority of the working classes would not desert the document they had so long fought for.'[132] While Lovett consulted his London constituents about tactics to defeat the move at the conference, O'Connor and his supporters simply redoubled their efforts to pack it. 'They forced their way into the meetings called by the respectables; and the respectables disappeared', wrote Cooper about Leicester, which elected four working men as a result. Three of Bradford's four delegates were 'out and out' Chartists, and both of South Shields'. A significant number of smaller districts returned just one delegate, and these were uniformly non-electors' choices. NCSU branches themselves did not always disdain manipulating elections. Newcastle's called the election at only a day's notice, Sheffield's held it during a weekday dinner hour and Alnwick started with unprecedented promptness and dispatched the entire business in four minutes.[133]

The 374 delegates who assembled in the Birmingham Mechanics' Institute on 27 December were therefore split into three groups: complete suffragists intent upon manipulating the agenda; Chartists, led by O'Connor in person, intent on thwarting them; and a smaller group of Chartists, led by Lovett, situated uncomfortably between them.[134] Lovett had publicly pledged to propose the Charter as an amendment to the NCSU bill of rights, and the complete suffragists privately to walk out immediately if O'Connor was elected chairman. However, Sturge's election to the chair was unopposed; furthermore the O'Connorite Chartists sat back while Lovett, burning with indignation at the way he had been misled, argued unsuccessfully to have the bill of rights removed from the agenda.

That took up most of the first day. Finding Sturge and his allies immoveable, next morning Lovett proposed an amendment stating the 'prior claim over all other documents' of *The People's Charter*, 'having been before the public for the last five years, forming the basis for the present agitation in favour of the suffrage, and for seeking the legal enactment of which vast numbers have suffered imprisonment, transportation, and death'. O'Connor seconded the amendment with a short and understated speech (all that was needed). Cooper and James Williams proposed a compromise whereby the bill of rights and the People's Charter would have been debated side by side, but both camps were too entrenched to agree to that. 'It is not your principles we dislike, but your leaders', the complete suffragist Lawrence Heyworth yelled at the Chartists, 'we'll not have you, you tyrants.'[135]

The Lovett–O'Connor amendment was carried by 193 votes to 94. Sturge and his followers, desiring (as Lovett put it) 'no fellowship with Fergus O'Connor', walked out and concluded the conference to their own satisfaction in a temperance hotel down the street. Of the Chartists present, only Patrick Brewster and R. K. Philp voted with Sturge. O'Neill formally registered that he was neutral. Vincent and Williams, both of whom were absent, shortly afterwards made public their affiliation to the Sturgeites. All hopes of developing a nationwide, cross-class, parliamentary reform movement lay in tatters. For that reason, too, 1842 may be described as a point at which history failed to turn.

# Chartist lives:
# Richard Pilling

In December 1845, a Chartist Convention was held in the Carpenters' Hall, Manchester. Richard Pilling attended as delegate for Ashton-under-Lyne. Meeting just three years after the 1842 strikes, in the very building where the combined trades had voted to stay out until the Charter was the law of the land, thoughts of what had happened that momentous year were naturally uppermost in delegates' minds. Their business done, they gathered for supper in The Mosley Arms Hotel. No Chartist social gathering was complete without toasts, and after they had dined Feargus O'Connor rose and proposed a toast to the 'Plug Drawers of 1842'; he then called 'upon Mr. Pilling, the father of the movement, to speak for his children'. Pilling, reported the *Northern Star*, responded 'in his usual style of simple but effective eloquence'.[*]

---

[*]   *NS*, 27 December 1845. The main source of information about Pilling's life up to 1842 is his remarkable closing speech to the jury, 7 March 1843, which appeared in *The Trial of Feargus O'Connor, Esq. (Barrister-at-Law) and Fifty-Eight Others* (Manchester, Heywood, 1843), pp. 248–55; see also the excellent entry on Pilling by Naomi Reid in *DLB*, vol. 6; M. Jenkins, *General Strike of 1842* (London, Lawrence & Wishart, 1980), esp. pp. 106–27; D. Thompson, *The Chartists* (London, Temple Smith, 1984), pp. 214–16 and 285–7; and *ODNB*.

The Chartist movement was built by men like Pilling: simple but effective orators who seldom moved far beyond their home locality. Pilling was consistently identified with workers' interests in south Lancashire for almost half a century. He was a Bolton lad, the son of a handloom weaver. On trial at the Lancashire assize in 1843 (with fifty-eight others, for offences relating to the 1842 strikes), he told the jury how he was making his way to Manchester on 16 August 1819 to hear Henry Hunt speak when he heard of the tragedy unfolding at St Peter's Fields. He was 20 at the time but had already been working as a weaver for a decade. He was soon to be married (his wife, Elizabeth, bore their eldest son around 1824).

Of their life in the 1820s little else is known, but at some point they moved to Stockport. Richard was sufficiently well-established in the local community to have become both a leading figure in the Stockport PU (founded March 1831) and to have been involved in establishing a similar organisation in Rochdale seven months later.* He found work in a Stockport mill as a powerloom weaver, and 'I was not long in the factory until I saw the evil workings of the accursed system – it is a system, which, above all systems, will bring this country to ruin if it is not altered'. The choice for Pilling, however, had been a stark one. As a child aged 11 he had earned 16 shillings a week; at 30 and the father of three children, his wages – 'and I worked hard' – at the handloom had fallen to just 6 shillings and 6 pence. 'Sooner than become a pauper on the parish I submitted', he explained, this in a town described by one contemporary as 'notoriously one of the darkest and smokiest holes in the whole industrial area'.†

The PUs did not long survive the Reform Act of 1832; even the famous Birmingham PU was stood down in the mid-1830s until revived by Attwood in 1837. Richard Pilling now channelled his political energies into his trade union and the campaign for a ten-hour working day. He was profoundly influenced by 'that noble king of Yorkshire' Richard Oastler. Involvement in the Ten Hours Movement, along with the campaign to defend the Glasgow cotton-spinners, drew Pilling into Chartism. By December 1838 he was a member of the Stockport WMA, serving as its secretary for a time. Like Chartists across Britain, Pilling waited for news of Parliament's reaction to the 1839 Petition, and the General Convention's response, with a mixture of resignation and keen anticipation.

The weekend after the Petition was presented, Pilling addressed a 6,000-strong crowd in Stockport. His speech was scrambled by the police reporter taking notes but the thrust is still clear:

Had the working people been in the legislature by their Charter this Nation

---

* N. LoPatin, *Political Unions* (London, Macmillan, 1999), pp.107 and 176.
† *Trial*, p.249; F. Engels, *The Condition of the Working Class in England*, trans. W. Henderson and W. H. Chaloner (Oxford, Blackwell, 1958 [1845]), p.52.

would now have been the most prosperous nation in the World. The working people as the origin of the arts, improvements, ingenuity and wealth, of the empire are the only fit persons to govern this or any other nation. The people will never be happy until then and I hope the working people will stand by the convention to obtain the Charter morally if they can, but have it we will.*

When the news came that the Petition was rejected Pilling was quick to join in moving Stockport Chartism forward with a call to apply all the ulterior measures.

Stockport's authorities sought to pre-empt the sacred month by arresting local Chartist leaders at the end of July 1839. Pilling, though, was not among them and was thus in Stockport courthouse on 2 August to support his colleagues at their committal proceedings. During the hearing the magistrates decided that Pilling too should be arrested: he was taken into custody on the spot and charged with sedition, conspiracy and attendance at unlawful meetings. Typically punitive bail conditions – for £400 plus two £200 sureties – were demanded and, having predictably failed to find them, Pilling was remanded in custody. Fortunately he had to wait only ten days before appearing at the Chester assize (alongside McDouall and Stephens) where his case was held over to the next assize and Pilling released on bail. Conditions were attached to this which Pilling risked breaking when he threw himself back into Chartist activities on returning to Stockport. He organised collections for prisoners (becoming involved in a dispute with police about the legality of doing so), assisted in petitioning for the pardon of the Newport prisoners and was involved in the disruption of Anti-Corn Law League meetings.

These were risks worth taking, for at the following spring's assizes Pilling was discharged. Undaunted by this brush with the law, he almost immediately took a leading role in an eight-week mass strike by Stockport powerloom weavers against wage reductions. This time his luck broke. Although he remained on the right side of the law, he was blacklisted by local employers when the strike was over. So Richard, Elizabeth and their six children moved to Ashton, where their seventh child was born the following year. Richard and his two eldest sons found employment as weavers, and his eldest daughter, aged 11, as a silk-throwster (i.e. spinner). With four other children, one of them only a few months old, Elizabeth Pilling could not work outside the home and the family's economic position, even with four wages coming into the home, can never have been better than adequate. During the winter of 1841–42, Ashton's mill owners enforced wage reductions. Then in March the couple's 16-year-old son, James, was forced to give up weaving having developed chronic tuberculosis.

The loss of his earnings reduced the family's income to 16 shillings a week,

---

* HO, 40/41, fol.90, 11 May 1839.

3 of which were immediately paid out as rent. 'I have gone home and seen that son', a tearful Pilling told the jury at his 1843 trial, 'lying on a sick bed and dying pillow, and having nothing to eat but potatoes and salt.' There was no effective treatment for tuberculosis, other than good diet, warmth and fresh air (commodities in short supply to working families in industrial Lancashire), but it was common to give consumptive patients alcohol as a palliative. Pilling recounted how a family friend begged a bottle of wine for James from 'a gentleman's house in Ashton', but was rejected with the words: 'Oh, he is a chartist, he must have none.'

Even if this account gained in the telling, it explains much about Richard's militancy in the months that followed. 'Such usage from the rich will never convince the chartists that they are wrong', Pilling laconically observed. James died shortly before the strikes began. His father contemplated suicide. The almost maniacal energy he invested in the strike campaign was clearly in part a displacement of bitter grief. In the three weeks after Pilling proposed the Dukinfield resolution (to 'turn out, and stop out, till they got a fair day's wage for a fair day's work, and until the Charter became the law of the land') he spoke to meetings, sometimes of thousands, in Ashton, Blackburn, Bolton, Burnley, Chorley, Clitheroe, Colne, Droylsden, Hurst, Hyde, Manchester, Oldham, Padiham, Preston, Stalybridge, Stockport and Todmorden. He generally made his way between them all on foot, helping turn-out countless mills on the way, and in midst of it all he was the Ashton weavers' delegate to the Carpenters' Hall trades' conference on 15 August.[*]

Pilling concentrated on workplace issues rather than Chartism, but he was unequivocally supportive of O'Connor and the Northern Star, the instrument, he observed in 1840, 'of inflicting upon a base government the punishment they so richly deserve'. When, after his release from York Castle, O'Connor toured Lancashire it was Pilling who chaired the reception in the Charlestown Chartist Rooms, introducing the lion of freedom by saying that 'he had devoured the whigs and would, by the assistance of the people, eat the Tories'.[†] This rhetoric lacked polish but wanted nothing in passion: sentiments of this kind were routine among Chartism's lesser orators. However at his trial in 1843 Pilling dug deeply into his intellectual resources to make a speech in his defence that was shrewdly pitched, yet both noble and daring. 'It is stated by one of the witnesses', he began,

> that I was the father of this great movement – the father of this outbreak. If so, then punish me, and let all the rest go free. But I may say it is not me that is the father of this movement; but that house [i.e. Parliament]. Our

---

[*]   Trial, p.73.
[†]   NS, 6 June 1840 and 4 December 1841.

addresses have been laid before that house, and they have not redressed our grievances; and from there, and there alone, the cause comes.

He then detailed the remorseless impact (and, from an employer's point of view, financial imperative) of recurrent wage reductions, and depicted the squalor of cotton operatives' working conditions and the material poverty of their homes. With restrained emotion that nonetheless moved the court-room to tears, Pilling used his own family's experience to illustrate these. Contextualising the agitation in this way minimised the risk inherent in his opening gambit – 'punish me, and let all the rest go free'. He did not deny his commitment to Chartism: 'I want to see the people here well educated; and if a man has the means in his pocket he will get his children educated; and if the people are once well informed, then the Charter must be the law of the land.' But Pilling's emphasis on the inequality of workmen before Parliament, the law and 'the system' was meant to appeal unashamedly to jurors' emotions. Rhetorically he invited them to 'feel for us'; 'just put yourself in this situation'; and several times he paused to enquire 'How would you feel?'[*]

Feargus O'Connor frequently appealed to the ideal of the male breadwinner: indeed, the emphasis he placed on it was one of the elements of his thought that was most attractive to factory operatives. Pilling's defence speech, made of course to an all-male jury, drew on the same theme. He spoke of fathers carrying babies to the mills to be suckled by their wives at meal-times, of the sexual harassment of women workers on the factory floor, and above all he gave voice to his own feelings of helplessness and injured masculinity:

> I have a nervous wife – a good wife – a dear wife – a wife that I love and cherish, and I have done everything that I could in the way of resisting reduc-tions in wages, that I might keep her and my children from the workhouse, for I detest parish relief. It is wages that I want. I want to be independent of every man, and that is the principle of every honest Englishman; and I hope it is the principle of every man in this court.

Pilling concluded by saying that 'the masters conspired to kill me, and I combined to keep myself alive'.[†]

It is scarcely exaggerating to claim that Pilling's speech turned the whole trial. Certainly, O'Connor could not hope to match the moral authority with which Pilling had spoken. Especially for those defendants (48 of the 59) without defence counsel, Richard Pilling's speech marked a sea-change in the proceedings. The 59 were tried on 9 counts ranging from conspiracy and sedition to disturbing the peace. None was found guilty on more than one count (and those only of unlawful assembly or conspiring to incite workers to

---

[*]  *Trial*, pp. 250–5.
[†]  Ibid., pp. 254–5.

leave work unfinished, an offence under the Master and Servant Act). Twenty-seven were acquitted altogether, Pilling among them. The guilty were never called for sentencing: it was not unusual for this to be postponed indefinitely if the Crown was satisfied simply to secure a guilty verdict, but this may have been prompted by a wish to suppress awareness that a clumsily conceived prosecution, headed in person by the Attorney-General, had been trounced.

In the event of guilty verdicts on the major charges, sentencing would very likely have been grievous. O'Connor gleefully published the proceedings, with a preface ramming home the message that the ACLL was complicit in all that had happened. Pilling's stature within the movement was greatly enhanced. Few were troubled that he had downplayed the Charter as a strike objective, for his commitment to Chartism and his use of it to critique class legislation had been explicit. Pilling was a delegate to the 1844 Convention, at which he initiated campaigns against tightening the Master and Servant Act, calling for Chartists to become more involved in local politics. He was a Convention delegate again in 1845, supported the Land Plan in 1846–48 and organised Ashton Chartists in the municipal political arena. When in May 1848 a Chartist National Assembly was convened to reorganise the movement, Richard Pilling was one of twenty commissioners appointed to see its plans to fruition.

His economic situation, however, remained precarious and was not helped by his continuing commitment to trade union activities. He was a negotiator for the Ashton spinners in a successful 1843 strike, and involved in a similarly successful strike of the weavers that autumn. However, his son William was sacked when he returned to work, apparently for no other reason than being Pilling's child.[*] Richard too was apparently thrown out of employment around this time. In August 1848 he sailed to America, apparently in search of work, though the coincidence of his departure with the shooting of a local policeman for which several Ashton Chartists were arrested occasioned comment. There was no evidence implicating Pilling but, whatever his motives, his American venture was unsuccessful. By the autumn of 1850 he was back in Ashton. He never found factory work again and instead made a precarious living as a grocer, his family's income supplemented by the earnings of those children still living at home. The last of them, born in 1845 and named James after the older brother who died in 1842, still fulfilled this role at the time of the 1871 Census.

Like most Chartists who lived long enough, Richard Pilling supported the Liberal Party in old age and saw in municipal politics a forum where at least some measures could be secured to improve the quality of workers' lives. He was also involved, through local branches of the National Reform Union and the Reform League, in the agitation for parliamentary reform which culminated in

---

[*]		*NS*, 9 December 1843.

the second Reform Act of 1867. He died in 1874. The *Ashton Reporter*, mourning the death of 'one of the old landmarks of Ashton historic radicalism', suggested that 'if ever there was a time in his life that Mr Pilling looked back to with pleasure, it was 1842, and the part he played in the events of that year'. If that was so, it was pleasure tempered by an abiding sense of loss, both personal and political.*

---

\*    *Ashton Reporter*, 5 December 1874.

# CHAPTER EIGHT

# 1843–46:
# Doldrums years

### Fragmentation and tension

The tensions within Chartism concerning the NCSU remained more significant than they appeared, even though few Chartists had walked out with Joseph Sturge from the Birmingham conference. Although William Lovett stayed with the Chartist contingent, the episode did nothing to alleviate his distaste for O'Connor and he rapidly drifted to Chartism's margins with his beloved National Association. Bronterre O'Brien, too, was swiftly marginalised. George White was apprehensive that an 'O'Brienite party' was in the making.[1] In O'Brien's adopted home, Brighton, there had even been fist-fights in the NCA branch; then, when it met to elect a delegate to attend the NCSU conference, O'Brien and his opponents traded insults, 'each party grumbling at the others like … bears'. But O'Brien's political capital was rapidly diminishing. His paper the *British Statesman* was in decline throughout the last quarter of 1842 and folded in January. Its final issues were dominated by virulent criticism of O'Connor, to which the latter responded in kind in the *Northern Star*. Bronterre, too, drifted to the margins of Chartism and in October 1844 moved to the Isle of Man.[2]

Similar tensions were evident in Sunderland, though here complete suffragists were in the ascendancy: James Williams had been elected to the Birmingham conference despite refusing to pledge to retain the name of the Charter. On his return to Sunderland, having thrown his weight behind Sturge, his allegiance shifted to the ACLL: he assisted John Bright in the 1843 Durham by-elections. Meanwhile his close associate George Binns emigrated, disillusioned, to New Zealand. North-east Chartism never fully recovered from their loss. Williams' final appearance on a Chartist platform was in January 1843 in a set-piece debate with Samuel Kydd, an emerging Chartist orator who specialised in taking on ACLL and complete-suffrage opposition. Williams was treated so viciously by Kydd and his supporters that even the *Northern Star* reporter thought frankly that 'the whole hogmen' should have relented.[3]

Several NCA loyalists had been fearful that the NCSU would 'outgeneral us if we don't look out very sharp', to quote the Birmingham Chartist E. P. Mead.[4] Ultimately, however, only Henry Vincent made a high-profile showing as a complete suffragist. But he was too-much an individualist to attract a definite following and instead became something of a travelling political showman, entirely dependent on his earnings from itinerant lecturing. With poignant self-knowledge, Vincent pictured himself as 'a sort of ... Punch' performing before largely middle-class audiences. He regularly punctuated his career by contesting parliamentary elections, always as a Chartist candidate 'ultra enough to satisfy the most ravenous radical', as *The Times* commented on his performance in Kilmarnock in 1844. No Chartist appeared on more election platforms than Vincent: indeed, no one of any political persuasion had a more consistent losing record in parliamentary elections (eight in total) in all the years between the 1832 Reform Act and the First World War. Over each of these contests lingered the suspicion that Vincent had no wish to jeopardise his livelihood by winning, so cavalier was his attitude to campaigning. He disdained to canvass, made little effort to understand local issues and some-times arrived in the constituency only the day before the hustings.[5] More charitably, his actions may have stemmed from a belief that to take undemo-cratic elections too seriously was to concede a critical point of moral and political principle. Yet all this added little lustre to the reputation of Chartism, much though it gilded the lily of Vincent's reputation as one of the most remarkable public speakers of his age.

The impression that Chartism was fragmenting, in the different ways exem-plified by Lovett, O'Brien, Williams and Vincent, was reinforced by disputes at the highest level within the NCA. These concerned not political principle but administrative acumen and personal probity. Impressive though it was, the NCA never matched the aspirations its keenest supporters held for it. It never succeeded formally (or financially) in uniting under its aegis all who called themselves Chartists. Subscriptions, even for the 50,000 members it mustered in 1842, were only ever haphazardly remitted to the executive. *Northern Star* editor William Hill was regularly critical of the way in which it conducted its business. The secretary John Campbell reciprocated and as early as April 1842 had pointedly extolled the virtues of the *English Chartist Circular* while damning the *Star* with faint praise.

The situation was rendered more fraught by the private doubts which several leading figures had about Campbell's abilities as secretary: 'an honest Chartist but not fit or energetic enough in that role', thought George White.[6] In October 1842 an emergency executive had to be convened when Campbell and Leach were remanded in custody, having failed to raise bail after their arrest. NCA finances were revealed to be in a parlous state and the first act of the temporary executive was a penny levy on each member, so that prisoners could be supported. These were uncertain times for almost every senior figure in Chartism and tempers were fraying fast. O'Brien accused O'Connor of talking-up the ACLL's role in the strike-wave as a subterfuge to distract attention from his own desertion of it. Campbell claimed O'Brien's assaults on O'Connor to be motivated by disappointed ambition. Almost everyone attacked McDouall for fleeing to France until O'Connor admitted that he had advised him to do so.[7]

Then, in November 1842, Hill led a charge against Leach and Campbell in a swingeing critique of the latest NCA balance sheet, especially the amount spent on officers' travel expenses. His attack on Campbell for 'gross and plain jobbing' was little short of an allegation of theft. Hertfordshire, Leicestershire and Nottinghamshire Chartists wrote to the *Star* with accounts of organising collections to meet his expenses at meetings addressed by Campbell; yet now the balance sheet showed that he had claimed on central NCA funds for the same purpose. O'Brien, G. J. Harney and White made similar criticisms. Chartist localities were alarmed: 'the very unpleasant differences which now exist at headquarters', declared a north Lancashire delegate meeting, 'threaten to impair, if not destroy, our moral power and influence'.[8]

As so many prominent Chartists were already in Birmingham for the NCSU conference, a special meeting was held there on the night of 28 December to resolve the dispute. Mead proposed drawing a line under it all, arguing that no one had acted immorally. But Leach was determined to clear his name, understandably so since Campbell had just confounded everyone by resigning and, though present, remaining largely silent. Campbell also failed to produce the NCA's books. North Lancashire delegates made further claims against Campbell, while similar allegations emerged against McDouall and the NCA lecturer Bairstow. Leach countered that Hill had suppressed letters from localities supportive of the executive. With the account books elsewhere, and neither Hill nor McDouall present, the meeting had little alternative but to appoint a committee to look into the matter.

All this was reported on the front page of the first *Star* for 1843, alongside O'Connor's strongest attack yet on Vincent and Williams, 'who by private letter writing, by secret conspiracies, and by open denunciation, when they dare, would destroy FEARGUS O'CONNOR and the *Northern Star*'. On the same page were claims by McDouall that Hill had placed himself at the head of a plot to 'shake and assault' the executive. This sorry ensemble was rounded off with an account alleging that a well-known but anonymous Yorkshire Chartist (probably White) had deserted his wife and was 'leading a common prostitute about the country with him'. This originated from Leach who asserted that Hill had previously suppressed the story, explaining that 'in a short time a great number of the advocates would be in prison, and the movement would want all the assistance that could be got'. This account of Hill's reasoning at least had a ring of truth about it, for everyone who had attended the emergency 'meeting of delegates in conference' at Manchester in August 1842 was now awaiting trial. It was a wretched beginning to the New Year.[9]

And it got worse. Within a week John Watkins, one of those asked to serve on the enquiry committee, wrote declining to do so. Campbell was refusing to hand over any NCA records until paid a claim outstanding of over £16 for arrears of salary and expenses. Never able to resist using a dozen words where none would do, Watkins then observed that Chartists generally were pained at being described by O'Connor as 'his party'; he then dismissed McDouall as 'a swindler' and closed by demanding the election of a completely new executive. Watkins could not be ignored: he was one of the *Star's* most prolific contributors and Hill had allowed him considerable space for this latest effusion. It was his intervention that finally brought O'Connor off the fence, with a coruscating attack in the *Northern Star* on 4 February. O'Connor launched into Watkins for his polemic against the executive, and into Hill for publishing it. Both had argued the NCA should henceforward have an unpaid executive to prevent peculation by officials. Perhaps the prospect of an executive made up of the likes of Watkins was more than Feargus could bear (O'Connor himself had never served on the body). This was not, however, about personalities only: it was an important issue of political principle.

A central tenet of the Charter was that MPs should be paid, so that working men might take seats at Westminster; yet Hill and Watkins implied that working men should be excluded from Chartism's directing body and accused those who currently served on it of blatant dishonesty: 'If you have an unpaid Executive, you must have a purely middle-class executive,' O'Connor wrote. 'You cannot get working men to live without wages and the very moment you elected working men as your officials, that moment every door closed against them, and at once they were marked, and if in work dismissed.' O'Connor exonerated Leach, Bairstow and McDouall from any blame. Campbell, though, he accused of 'mal-practices', but still suggested that he should receive the money he claimed if, on handing over the NCA's books, it appeared that he was out of pocket. 'I have always said', O'Connor continued, 'that the difference between Whigs, Tories, and Chartists is this: that the two former magnify the virtues and throw a veil over the vices of their party; while the latter, in general, magnify the vices and throw a veil over the virtues of their friends.' It was an apt summary, albeit one from whose charge O'Connor himself was scarcely exempt. Though too late to retrieve matters completely in the executive's favour, O'Connor's intervention drew the heat from the dispute. Soon after, Campbell suddenly emigrated to America. The NCA account books were never retrieved.[10]

O'Connor had also crossed a personal Rubicon. He had for the first time, publicly and at length, criticised the editor of the *Northern Star*. Yet just as he had hesitated before throwing his authority behind Leach and the principle of a paid executive, Feargus now dithered before dispensing with Hill's services. This was hardly calculated to bolster confidence in the *Star*. It never again matched its achievements of 1839; nonetheless, weekly sales in 1842 maintained an impressive average of 12,500, though in 1843 sales fell sharply away to an average of around 8,700. The situation was not helped by O'Connor's other journalistic venture: the *Evening Star*. Experienced pressmen like Cleave told O'Connor that the *Northern Star* was being hit by sales of his London daily. Such was his conviction that Chartism needed a daily paper, however, that Feargus persevered with the project even when it failed to meet his expectations and began to cost him serious money. The latitude permitted to Hill back in Leeds, in order that O'Connor could concentrate on the London venture, was something which with hindsight he was beginning to regret. Of course O'Connor's closer involvement in the *Northern Star* would not have prevented Campbell's dishonesty, any more than it would have maintained the momentum of the 1842 strikes. It might, however, have diminished the public perception that the NCA leadership was seriously divided and (at best) of limited competence. It is noteworthy that O'Connor made this public assertion of authority over Hill exactly at the point when he gave up the *Evening Star*, trailing a loss of £3,500.[11]

It was another five months before O'Connor and Hill finally parted company, their mutual loathing so complete that one can but wonder how they ever had worked amicably.[12] This, indeed, was the most cogent criticism Hill levelled at his former employer: if he lacked competence and personal probity to the extent that O'Connor claimed, why had he not been dismissed sooner? Possibly O'Connor had been unable to secure anyone else he felt would conduct the paper efficiently. Hill had, after all, been a remarkably effective editor. Alongside Joshua Hobson as printer and production manager, Hill had presided over the rapid growth of the publishing phenomenon of its age. So total was O'Connor's involvement in Chartism as a whole, that he had no alternative but to delegate responsibility for the *Northern Star*, trading off personal political preferences against operational efficiency. This is what he had done in 1838–39 in order to build a mass platform for Chartism; it is what he did in 1840–41 while in prison and again in August 1842 when launching the *Evening Star*. Now, in February 1843, O'Connor left Hill in post to concentrate, first, on the forthcoming Lancaster trials and, second, on revitalising Chartism through a comprehensive programme of agrarian reform.

The outcome of the trials at least alleviated the gloom that swirled around the NCA executive. As we have seen, the result of the trial represented a triumph for the Chartists: 59 were collectively tried on 9 separate counts each, but out of a possible 531 guilty verdicts only 32 were obtained by the prosecution, all on lesser counts alone. In the event none of the guilty was called up for sentencing. The outcome had not been predicted. Harsh sentences, including fifty-six of transportation, had been handed down to the Staffordshire strikers and rioters the previous October, and when Cooper and John Richards were tried for sedition and conspiracy the following spring each received a prison sentence, Cooper two years and Richards one on account of his advanced age (he was 70).

Immediately after the strikes, the Government had seriously considered pressing charges of high treason but was dissuaded by the difficulty of finding sufficient evidence. Even so, it seemed likely that a trial before the full Court of Queen's Bench in London would be sought, in order to maximise the gravity and publicity of the proceedings and ensure that the jury was drawn from an area of minimal support for Chartism. The Government's overriding desire, however, was to secure the political advantage of trying these cases swiftly.[13] High among its objectives was to implicate O'Connor in every turn of the strike-wave, placing him at the centre of a tightly knit political conspiracy. The Attorney-General wrote to the Home Secretary:

> I propose to charge O'Connor as a general conspirator with the others and not to proceed against him for libel merely, or for acting as a Delegate, or taking part at the meeting of Delegates – I propose to try him in the same indictment with the worst of the defendants who headed mobs, made seditious speeches, and stopped mills and factories. I shall blend in one accusation the head and the hands – the bludgeon and the pen, and let the jury and the public see in one case the whole crime, its commencement and its consequences.[14]

'I am sorry that Fergus escaped', Prince Albert wrote to Sir Robert Peel; 'still the effect of the trial is satisfactory'.[15] Albert was mistaken in that O'Connor not only walked free but made considerable political capital from his acquittal. However, he was correct insofar as the prospect of the trial had dogged the entire Chartist leadership and imposed on the NCA a financial burden it was scarcely fit to maintain.

The conclusion that Chartism had touched a nadir in its fortunes is reinforced by briefly examining the state of its press. By the autumn of 1843 there were fewer Chartist periodicals than at any time since the movement's emergence. *Evening Star* and *British Statesman* were not the only casualties. Two short-lived ventures (Watkins's *London Chartist Magazine* and O'Brien's *Poor Man's Guardian and Repealer's Friend*) barely achieved the status of ephemera before folding. The really grievous loss was that of the *English Charter Circular*, which closed in January after losing on average £3 an issue over its final months. On the most generous of definitions, only five Chartist papers remained by the autumn of 1843: the *Aberdeen Review*, the *Carlisle Patriot*, the *Edinburgh Weekly Register*, the *Scotch Reformers' Gazette* and the *Northern Star*. Too few copies of the Scottish titles survive to be certain that they were consistently Chartist periodicals, while the *Carlisle Patriot* was purely a local paper with Chartist sympathies. So the *Northern Star* stood alone, the one journal, so the *English Charter Circular*'s valedictory editorial lamented, 'to give battle to the combined hosts of faction; and that one journal incapable of boasting such a circulation as might naturally be expected to be claimed by the only openly avowed organ of millions of men!'[16]

The picture of the movement that emerged from the *Star* during the second half of 1843 was uniformly discouraging. O'Connor finally sacked Hill on 8 July. Hobson assumed editorial responsibility until Feargus recruited Harney to assist him in September. This arrangement was mutually advantageous: it gave Harney an assured regular income, brought to the *Star*'s permanent staff one of Chartism's most impressive prose writers and provided the movement with a further salaried lecturer and organiser. Harney's recent experience, though, was that there was all too little to organise. He found Sunderland Chartism 'in anything but a thriving condition' on a visit in August. 'Chartism is shelved in Edinburgh', he reported, while in Glasgow it was 'all but assassinated by the preaching prigs, and political knaves ... since their defection to the Complete Suffrage ranks ... the worst enemies of Chartism'. Three months earlier the *Northern Star* ran an editorial on the Welsh Chartists: 'where are they? what are they doing? are they still alive?' The sole response came from Newport, detailing the first Chartist gathering there for some time. In mid-Wales there were no recorded Chartist activities of any kind during 1843. White observed that people were not 'content to waste their lives listening to speeches'. They 'no longer come out to hear lectures', Hill discovered during a visit to Scotland, 'because they know all that the lecturers can tell them. They have heard the old story over and over again, till they are tired of it.'[17]

The range of activities reported in the *Northern Star* was but a shadow of that of earlier years. As 1843 drew to a close, the NCA executive decided to put a dozen lecturers into the field to prepare for a new National Convention and a fund-raising initiative in 1844. Realising the seriousness of the fracture in Scottish Chartism, it decided to include Scotland's industrial districts, but was shocked when none of its letters seeking to make arrangements was answered. This was detailed in the executive's end of year address, which appeared in the *Star* of 16 December alongside 'Chartist Intelligence' from little more than 20 localities, 6 of them public-house meetings in London. Only Manchester, Preston and Salford were listed from Lancashire, and Hebden Bridge and Sheffield from Yorkshire. The north-east looked superficially healthy, due largely to reports from its energetic lecturer, Robert Gammage. There were no reports from Wales or the English midlands. The only item of Chartist news remotely deserving more than a column inch in a national newspaper was a visit to Hyde by O'Connor. Nor was this week atypical: it was wholly indicative of how the *Northern Star* and the movement it served bumped along for the next three years. Chartism did not collapse but it seldom gave the impression of great vitality. In the localities it ebbed and flowed. In any week there would be something to applaud: on 16 December the news from Glasgow concerned the formation of a NCA district council, only the fourth thus far in Scotland.

However, an attentive reader during the years 1843–46 would gradually become aware of some resounding silences – not a single item from Teesside, for example, throughout the years 1844 and 1845 (the region's press was simi-larly silent regarding Chartism), and only sporadic reports from once-thriving centres such as Aberdeen, Brighton, Elland, Hull, Rotherham, Sunderland and Wolverhampton. 'Time was when this district was considered one of the strong-holds of Chartism', reported Huddersfield in September 1843, hoping 'that the slumbering energies of Chartism in this neighbourhood will once more be raised'.[18] Even visits from O'Connor frequently failed to revive Chartism in the localities concerned. He always attracted bumper audiences; but there were frequent allegations that the numbers of new NCA members enrolled on such occasions were exaggerated.[19] Harney and Hobson were reduced to padding out the *Northern Star* with general and foreign news, book reviews and, in 1843–44 particularly, detailed coverage of 'the colliers' movement'. In the latter at least there was something dynamic to point to. Indeed, the contribution made by Chartists to the development of trade unionism in the mid-1840s was indicative that, even in retreat, Chartism was still a vital force.

## The 'United Trades' movement'

Formal Chartist organisation had only ever made limited headway on the coal-fields, and the extent to which it did varied between regions. However, the relative absence of Chartist branch life and NCA members does not mean the appeal of the Charter went unheeded. Mine owners exercised significant control, directly or through their managers or sub-contractors, of many aspects of miners' lives besides work: the provision of housing; the administration of local government and justice; and the availability of employment opportunities outside the mine. This may have made miners wary of overt political activity; it certainly encouraged occasional displays of deference, and it influenced the continued prevalence of violent and/or theatrical protest. However, the coal-field strikes of 1842, although the product of conditions in the pits themselves, were interleaved with Chartism, the influence of which was manifest in the formation of the Miners' Association of Great Britain and Ireland (MAGBI) in 1842–43.[20]

This, the first national miners' union, emerged from consultations between

leaders from different coalfields during the summer of 1842. Several strike
meetings called for a national congress of English and Welsh miners, but the
decisive lead came from West Yorkshire where county-wide meetings were
held during the strike-wave at Halifax, passing resolutions for the Charter, the
formation of a general union and 'a general strike so as to bring all machinery
and all power requiring coals to a stand'.[21] The *Northern Star* was the main
medium of communication between the coalfields and generously covered 'the
Pitmen's General Union', from the initial steps (taken by a miners' philanthropic
society at Wakefield in November 1842) through to the formal establishment of
the MAGBI the following year. Estimates place its peak membership between
30,000 and 40,000. Either of these figures would comfortably have made the
association the largest trade union of its day. It was comparatively weak in
Scotland and made no progress in Wales, so these figures suggest that at least
a third of English miners belonged.[22]

Throughout its relatively brief yet impressive life, the leadership of the
MAGBI was closely associated with Chartism: its draft constitution was
submitted to O'Connor for his legal opinion; William Prowting Roberts was
its national legal officer; its treasurer Martin Jude and at least two of its general
secretaries had been active Chartists; and its journal, the *Miners' Advocate*
(commenced in December 1843), was edited by William Beesley. Peter Brophy
(founding secretary of the Irish Universal Suffrage Association) was its full-
time organiser on the Cumberland coalfield, enlisting IUSA's assistance to stem
the flow of Irish blacklegs during a strike there in 1844.[23] Among the rank
and file of the MAGBI, however, attitudes were more ambivalent. In part this
may simply have been a consequence of 1842. O'Connor was not permitted to
address its 1844 conference; there was hostility to the circulation of Chartist
handbills at its assemblies and criticism of Roberts's influence. Roberts could
have made a comfortable living as a solicitor in his native Bath; instead, driven
by a highly politicised contempt for employers and landowners of every persuasion, he devoted himself to fighting industrial cases, earning the sobriquet of
'the miners' attorney general' by near-constant appearances in magistrates'
courts across the English coalfields. Roberts was indispensable to the MAGBI,
but this does not mean he was easy to get on with nor, even, politically adroit.
Much of the responsibility for initiating a protracted and bruising strike on
the Durham and Northumberland coalfields in 1844 lay with him, a move in
which he was opposed by Martin Jude. The great strike of 1844 was by turns
heroic, desperate and tragic.

Although the MAGBI lingered on, it was broken by the strike. It had
sustained the action inadequately and in the face of competing claims it could
not meet from countless other disputes in the British coalfields. These included
a three-month strike in Lanarkshire and turn-outs, some of similar duration,
in Yorkshire. There large numbers of blacklegs were employed; there were

mass evictions of miners from their homes and a flat refusal by employers to negotiate with the union, which they described as 'an unjust and uncalled for interference with the rights of masters and men'.[24] In Durham the attitude of the mine owner Lord Londonderry was even more vituperative. Whole families were evicted: 'Multitudes of them resort to the sea shore, living & sleeping amongst the rocks, where they exist on refuse, fish, and any other eatable matter they can collect.'[25]

The MAGBI survived the 1844 strike in only a vestigial form, with a central-ised structure that was little more than nominal.[26] A number of regional coalfield unions survived or were revived, however, and as late as 1863, when a national miners' conference was held at Leeds, the MAGBI was a key point of reference. Furthermore, Chartism continued to generate a nurturing climate for working-class culture and associational forms. Benefit, friendly and mutual instruction societies all prospered in the 1840s. This was the period in which life assurance and building societies took off as a truly popular form of mutual help, a development reflected in the *Northern Star* and in which many Chartists became involved. Trade unionism similarly benefited from this collectivist impulse. Trade unions typically experience growth during phases of economic expansion and the years 1843–47 saw an escalation of trade society activity. In London, registration of friendly societies, many actually trade societies, reached a peak between 1842 and 1844. In Leicestershire a trade union presence was reasserted in the hosiery industry, notably in the fine-glove trade where, under the leadership of the Chartist Thomas Winters, a society was formed that embraced more than 1,200 of the 1,400 workforce.[27]

A number of major urban centres saw the formation of new bodies for inter-trade co-operation. In Bradford an umbrella organisation, the United Trades, was formed in 1843 under Chartist auspices. Largely due to the energy of George White a Woolcombers' Protective Society was formed along with a union of female powerloom weavers. Similar bodies elsewhere included Bristol's United Trades' Association (1844) and the Birmingham Central Committee of Trades (1845), chaired by John Mason, a full-time Chartist lecturer in 1840 and dele-gate to the 1843 Convention.[28] In 1846, Aberdeen trades formed the Delegated Committee of Sympathy to 'support each other in the event of a strike of any of them, or when any general movement was required in support of trade unions'. This probably owed something to the extraordinary trades' demonstration that greeted O'Connor and Duncombe when they visited Aberdeen in the autumn of 1843. In Sheffield that same year a committee of trade societies proposed 'the formation of a union to embrace all the trades of Sheffield'.[29]

The mid-1840s also saw a growth in trade unionist networks nationally, and here again Chartist influences were at work. The Manchester engineers' United Trades' Association, led by Chartist Alexander Hutchinson, was extended in 1844 to become the Mechanics' Protective Society of Great Britain. The same year the General United Tailors' Trade Protection Society was formed. It too exhibited a distinct Chartist hue. It nominated the *Northern Star* as its official organ and the *soirée* concluding its first conference was presided over by Roberts and Duncombe. Its secretary was J. P. Whitaker, a temperance Chartist and National Association member who spoke alongside O'Connor when the 1842 Petition was formally adopted in London. The president of the Cordwainers' General Mutual Assistance Association was another Chartist. Founded in Birmingham in June 1844, by November it had 120 constituent societies nationwide. It is a reasonable supposition that most of them involved Chartists in leadership roles. This was definitely so at Colchester, for example, where closed shops were enforced across the city. In the spring of 1845 the Association merged with the Philanthropic Society of Boot and Shoemakers, Chartists in both organisations arguing that free-standing trade societies should give way to federated mutualism under a central executive.[30]

Chartists brought well-honed intellectual and organisational resources to trade unionism; but Chartism was also the repository for much of the idealism that had sustained the general unionist movement of the early 1830s. The argument that effective trades' organisation depended on nationwide affiliation and mutual assistance was increasingly asserted in Chartist circles in the mid-1840s. 'Unless the trades generally adopt the principles of a General Union, there is no hope of making a successful stand against the encroachments of the principal capitalists', observed a London tailors' branch in a report sent to the *Northern Star*.[31]

The benchmark to which such discussions generally referred was the Grand National Consolidated Trades' Union (GNCTU). 'The trades have long tried local societies and found them powerless for good', wrote Samuel Jacobs, NCA secretary in Bristol: 'they next tried general unions of particular trades and found that these could not successfully resist the encroachments of the task masters ... They then attempted to form a National Trades Union; but it was broken to pieces through mismanagement before it had grown into a "monster combination".' As we have seen, Chartism had yet to secure trades' affiliates on a scale to make it a 'monster combination', though it had come close in August 1842. But there were many within the movement who believed it had the potential to do so. Jacobs, an officer in Bristol's cabinetmakers' society, was one of them. Towards the end of 1842 he floated a proposal for a National Trade Benefit Society; then in 1843 he led his society into a Manchester-based federation in search of the 'one great society' that would 'maintain our wonted respectability and save our trade from that wretched fate that hath befallen too many of the hitherto flourishing and respectable occupations'. Soon he was the driving force behind the United Trades' Association of Bristol and then, in 1845, one of several Chartists instrumental in the formation of the National Association of United Trades for the Protection of Labour (NAUT). Imbued with the optimism that was an essential quality in any nineteenth-century labour leader, Jacobs pointed to the GNCTU's failure to grow into a 'monster combination', and declared, 'I thank God that the NAUT has arrived at that state.'[32]

The NAUT was not exactly the monster combination Jacobs anticipated but its title (a conscious echo of the National Association for the Protection of Labour of 1829–31) indicated its aspirations to be so. It was an autonomous organisation, unconnected to the NCA, which specifically emerged from a nationwide testimonial to Duncombe, in appreciation of his successful parliamentary opposition to tightening the Master and Servant Act. It is unlikely, however, the NAUT would have emerged without the *Northern Star's* enthusiasm for general unionism and trades' federation, or its willingness to promote the Association and be the principal vector for communication between its disparate membership. In November 1844 O'Connor actually changed the paper's subtitle from the *Leeds General Advertiser* to the *National Trades Journal.* The change coincided with moving the paper to London and the gathering momentum, encouraged by the paper, for 'a general conference of trades' delegates', 'A TRADES' PARLIAMENT'.[33] The NAUT emerged from a national trades' conference the following February and rapidly became the largest trades' organisation in Britain since the GNCTU, enlisting at its peak in 1846–47 at least 50,000 members.[34]

The cynical might suppose that the *Northern Star* was a paper in search of a circulation, but its change of emphasis was a principled as well as a pragmatic response to the circumstances in which Chartism operated in 1844, compared to the late 1830s when the paper began. With the possibility of a return to mass agitation and petitioning seemingly remote, the *Northern Star* sought to fuse the Charter, trade unionism and agrarianism to make Chartism vital and relevant once more. There was a closer overlap between these three than might at first seem apparent. Carving out a space within the industrialising economy where working people rather than their employers determined the kind of work they did – at what pace, at which times and in which environment – was an abiding preoccupation of the labour movement. It was one which O'Connor was simply reflecting in his calls for a land plan. The NAUT did the same when, at its founding conference in July 1845, it established an adjunct organisation 'for the Employment of Labour in Agriculture and Manufacture'.

## 'Our Last and Only Resource – the Land'

We saw in chapter 6 how on the eve of imprisonment in 1840 (and often thereafter) O'Connor had briefly advocated 'Chartist Agricultural Associations' and argued that the land should lie at the heart of a strategy for revitalising Chartism. He failed to persuade the NCA's foundation Conference to make the land central to its activities, but refined his agrarian thinking while in prison. Shortly after his release in 1841 he published a pamphlet, '*The Land' the Only Remedy for National Poverty and Impending National Ruin*. In this way O'Connor began to lay the ground for a fundamental realignment of the movement, embracing social dimensions hitherto secondary to its political objectives. He did little initially to develop this: the movement was absorbed in preparations for the 1842 Petition and then immersed in the strike-wave. However, in January 1843 the *Northern Star* began a series of editorials on the land, probably commissioned from the paper's London correspondent, Thomas Wheeler, who had leapt to national prominence as secretary of the NCA's temporary executive. Henceforward he was to be a major and stabilising figure in the movement, especially once elected general secretary of the NCA at the Chartist Convention of 1843.[35]

The constitution that emerged from the 1843 Convention marked a fundamental departure for the NCA. All mention of the Charter was expunged from its objectives, which instead were expressed as 'by peaceful and legal means alone to better the condition of man, by removing the causes which have produced moral and social degradation'; and, second, 'to provide for the unemployed, and [provide the] means of support for those who are desirous to locate upon the land'. The document was devised with the intention that the NCA should be eligible to register as a friendly society. This would confer legal status as well as some protection against defaulting officers (the spectre of Campbell clearly lingered here). The main benefit of registration, however, would be a new venture: the Chartist land plan. Once approved by the official Registrar of Friendly Societies, the NCA would be able directly to buy and sell land and buildings (unregistered organisations could acquire land and buildings only as tenants or through the cumbersome, expensive and not always foolproof means of trustees). The land plan was presented as an integral part of the NCA, though subscription would be an optional extra for members. As the land fund accumulated, country estates would be purchased and divided into small farms. These would then be allocated to land-fund subscribers via a lottery.[36]

The other major feature of the 1843 constitution was its revised provisions for internal governance. Henceforward a salaried executive would be responsible to the annual convention, which also became the electoral college for it. This secured closer scrutiny of the executive, but at the cost of members' direct participation, and it was not something with which all Chartists felt comfortable. The situation was clouded further, for this was the first occasion O'Connor stood for election to any NCA body. Among the unsympathetic this reinforced suspicions that he sought total control of the movement. When two Birmingham stalwarts wrote to William Lovett offering to nominate him as executive secretary they received a reply by return of post: 'I regard Feargus

O'Connor as the chief marplot of our movement in favor of the Charter; a man who, by his personal conduct, joined to his malignant influence in the "Northern Star," has been the blight of Democracy from the first moment he opened his mouth as its *professed advocate* ... my Chartist brethren will never redeem their Cause from the odium which he and his satelites have cast upon it, till they relinquish his pernicious councils'. For the avoidance of doubt Lovett immediately published this response in pamphlet form.[37]

Attendance at the 1843 Convention was thin, reflecting the near-exhausted state of Chartism. Only twelve English counties, plus London, Abergavenny and Coggeshall (a decayed Essex textiles centre) were represented. The Scots were conspicuously absent. Few of the movement's commanding figures attended. Indeed, few of the thirty delegates, Harney and O'Connor aside, had ever made an impression beyond their immediate locality. Some notable Chartist activists were serving sentences arising from 1842 – Cooper, O'Neill, Richards and White, for example; but it is highly doubtful that O'Neill would have sought involvement in the NCA, for others from the Birmingham Chartist Church of which he was pastor, notably John Collins, refused to do so. In previous years, prison had taken its toll and yet the movement's leadership had managed to renew itself. Now other factors were clearly at work: fragmentation and secession were having their effect. Not one former member of the LWMA was present, while Bairstow was the sole signatory to the 1841 teetotal Chartist address present. However, through the revisions it made to the NCA's internal governance, the 1843 Convention initiated a major reform. Henceforward, any financial problems related to securing sufficient income to operate effectively, but not to the personal honesty or competence of the executive.

The 1843 Convention was the first occasion on which Chartism's highest assembly debated land reform. Throughout 1843 the *Northern Star* extolled agrarian reform, giving lavish coverage to O'Connor's increasingly frequent lectures on the subject. In April he shared with readers a vision for a model agricultural community, a 1,000-acre estate divided into 4-acre plots, with a 100 acres set aside as common land and a village centre with a school, library and surgery. The following month he completed, with substantial help from Wheeler, *A Practical Work on the Management of Small Farms*, which appeared first in instalments and then as a book: no fewer than 7 editions appeared over the next 4 years.

O'Connor explicitly distinguished his vision from the communities envisaged by Robert Owen. This was a community but it was not communitarian: 'there should be nothing in common, save and except the public institutions and the 100 acres of land. Every man should be the master of his own house, his own time and his own earnings.' Just in case there was any doubt on the matter, he added for good measure: 'I tell you that my plan has as much to do with Socialism as it has with the Comet.'[38] However, O'Connor's burgeoning interest in agrarianism cannot fully be understood without reference to the Owenites. Since 1839 they had run a model community, 'Harmony', in Hampshire. All its members were meant to live, socialise and educate their children beneath the roof of Harmony Hall, which housed a communal kitchen, dining-room and laundry. All agricultural activities on the surrounding estate were similarly a collective responsibility.[39]

Any proposal to create a model community at this time inevitably invited comparison with Owen's, for Owenite communitarianism had been before the public in one form or another for over two decades. Moreover, thanks to Wheeler's influence, some of what appeared on agrarianism above O'Connor's name was suffused with Owenite phraseology.[40] The Owenite Universal Community Society of Rational Religionists was modest in size, but Owen himself could count among his supporters many Chartists, including Wheeler, Henry Hetherington, *Northern Star* printer Hobson and its business manager John Ardill, and O'Connor's staunch Huddersfield ally Lawrence Pitkethly. Lovett was more distant but was clearly influenced intellectually by Owen. Critics, moreover, sometimes failed to distinguish between Owenism and Chartism: in his 1841 election address Disraeli, for example, pledged to defeat 'Jesuits and Infidels' and 'Chartists and Socialists', who, he claimed, were 'banded together with revolutionary design'.[41] Owenism's most contentious feature was its rejection of conventional Christianity in favour of 'rational religion', a form of deism bordering on the atheistical and routinely stigmatised as 'infidelism' by opponents and by the majority of Chartists. The *Northern Star*, for example, regarded as 'a national evil ... the infidelity which Mr. OWEN and all the principal leaders of Socialism interlard their system'.[42]

Neither pragmatism nor religious sentiment, however, fully explains why O'Connor distanced his agrarian ideas from Owen's. There was a fundamental ideological difference. We have seen in Richard Pilling's trial speech that the male-breadwinner ideal was a powerful one, especially among factory operatives. It was one that the life-long bachelor O'Connor faithfully mirrored. Robert Owen, who fathered 8 children during 32 years of marriage, regarded the family as a corrosive institution, the central underpinning of private property, self-interest and individualism, to eliminate all of which his projects were designed.[43] O'Connor clung tenaciously to the ideal of the family as a socialising, educative and, where possible, economic force. For Chartists, the social upheavals of the 1830s and 1840s were as much a crisis for the family and male authority as for anything else. Feargus upheld the return to the land as a means of averting this crisis – even reversing it:

> There is no sight, however, which can be presented to my eyes so beautiful, so cheering, so natural and becoming, as that of the husbandman tilling the ground for his own and his family's sole use, behoof and benefit. When I see a man with his foot on his spade, I think I recognise the image of his God,

and see him in that character which even the Malthusian deigns to assign him – A MAN STANDING ON HIS OWN RESOURCES ... In his own little holding he recognises the miniature of nature. When he leaves his castle in peace, it is ever in his sight as the repository of all that is dear to him, and when he returns at noon, his eyes are gladdened, his feelings are excited, and his heart bounds, while receiving the welcome, the attentions, and caresses of his wife and darling children.[44]

It was doubtless no coincidence that his projected thousand-acre estate would be twice the size of Harmony. He thought on a grand scale, as did Owen; but unlike him, O'Connor had potentially far more material, human and financial, to work with. His objective was nothing short of grafting a land plan onto Chartism. It is indicative both of O'Connor's personal authority and of the extent to which agrarianism was already entwined with radicalism that the proposal was extensively and sympathetically regarded within the Chartist movement. When the *Northern Star* ran an editorial, during Convention week, entitled 'Our last and only resource – the land', it was framing an argument about labour and the industrial economy; but the title would have as aptly indicated how Chartism itself would be reinforced. 'Aye, this is something tangible!/ Yes! Just the ticket', Mead declared in his poem *On Reading the New Plan of Organisation*: 'we've play'd at bowling long enough,/ And never struck a wicket'. And White, who in 1840 opposed co-operative stores because they diverted energy away from politics, wrote from prison to extol the merits of the land plan: 'It is quite clear that something practicable ought to be commenced. People will not be content to waste their lives listening to speeches.' Even Bronterre O'Brien extolled 'O'Connor's four acres' as the most effective route to secure cheap bread: 'mind, I am no admirer of Feargus O'Connor – it's quite otherwise I assure you. But truth is truth, come from whom it may.'[45]

However, these ambitious plans began to unravel within weeks of the Convention, when the NCA was refused official registration as a friendly society. O'Connor hotly disputed this decision, so the NCA sought specialist legal opinion. This suggested that there were scant grounds for appeal. Denial of registration was no obstacle to the NCA continuing its established political and organisational activities (a plenitude of organisations flourished in the Victorian period without benefit of legal recognition). However, unable to deal in property, the land plan was cast into a state of limbo. A further Convention was therefore held in April 1844. O'Connor (somewhat disingenuously) recommended its deliberations to the wider movement on the grounds that it had replaced a 'long and inexplicable Plan of Organisation', including the land plan, with 'a short and easily understood one' that excluded it. The Chartist land plan was now to be free standing, without constitutional linkage to the NCA.

The exclusion of all mention of the Charter from the 1843 constitution had been extraordinary. Now the object of the NCA was affirmed as being 'to

secure the enactment of the "People's Charter" by peaceful, legal, and constitutional means'. The mood of this Convention, half as big again as the previous
September's, suggested that Chartism was re-establishing itself. McDouall
judged it safe to return from France and a public subscription was raised to
help him recommence his political career. With an eye to the next general
election, the Convention also initiated moves to register potentially sympathetic voters. O'Connor appeared on the platform at Lovett's National Hall to
chair a meeting in support of striking north-east miners, and with O'Brien
in Ipswich to debate Ireland. O'Connor also publicly reiterated his conviction
that Vincent remained a Chartist, and wrote an open letter apologising to the
Glasgow Chartist James Moir for overreacting to claims Moir had made about
Scottish Chartism.[46]

All was not, however, sweetness and light. Moir's original comments had
struck a raw nerve: he had pointed out that only two Scottish localities had
sent delegates to 1844 Convention; that financial remittances to the NCA from
north of the border were infrequent and never more than a few shillings; and
that claims for recruitment following O'Connor's tour of Scotland in the
autumn of 1843 had been exaggerated. This picture was consistent with the
situation elsewhere. White had headed back to Yorkshire in frustration at the
torpor of Birmingham; in July Doyle found that 'the poverty of the friends to
the cause' in Morpeth and Alnwick was so great that he could not organise
any meeting there, and he then encountered a similar situation in Liverpool;
in May O'Connor had to subsidise wages for the NCA executive from his
own pocket, so depleted were its finances.[47] The Oldham Chartist Hall, whose
foundation stone O'Connor had laid, closed within weeks of its opening and
reopened as a music hall.[48] O'Connor was also unwell, advised to rest by his
doctor on account of lameness in June.[49] Then, in August, he met Richard
Cobden, leader of the ACLL, for a set-piece debate in Northampton, the first
time the leading personalities of the two movements had ever met. O'Connor
was eloquent but scarcely fervent, and discursive rather than argumentative.
Even his own account, printed in the *Star*, conceded that Cobden 'has not been
over-rated. He is decidedly a man of genius, of reflection, of talent, of tact.' He
concluded 'I am not then astonished that a wily party should have selected so
apt and cunning a leader.'[50]

His decision to transfer publication of the *Northern* Star from Leeds to
London was designed to refresh both the paper and the movement it served.
Hobson continued as editor, an increasingly nominal arrangement since
Harney's had been the hand behind much of the paper since his arrival as
sub-editor. There were clear advantages in terms of distribution to publishing
from London; the move also had personal advantages for O'Connor (who lived
there) and for Harney, who was a Londoner and whose personal commitment
to continental radicals and nationalism was more easily pursued in the capital,

where continental exiles tended to gather. It also brought the paper closer to the NCA executive, which effectively operated from the capital because its secretary Wheeler lived there; and it anticipated the emergence of the NAUT the following year, to whose executive Hobson was elected. On 30 November 1844 the *Northern Star* appeared with a new masthead, typeface and sub-title from its London premises. O'Connor anticipated that the paper would now 'be the means of rallying the proper machinery for conducting the Registration Movement, the Land Movement, the National Trades' Movement, the Labour Movement, and the Charter Movement'.[51] A new agricultural column appeared alongside regular coverage of the American east-coast land movement.

In October O'Connor again took up his pen to write about how 'to get the land'. There followed a series in which he expounded a vision placing the land and *The People's Charter* side by side, the one being the essence of the democratic and equitable society the enactment of the Charter would secure:

> Patronage, which is a consequence of, and springs from, the Large Farm System, *withholds the land from you*; while the law of primogeniture, and the barbarous law of settlement and entail, prevents such are as able from buying small allotments of land. To break through these barriers is easy and simple, and should be the great national object. By its accomplishment alone can you now set up the principle of individualism against that of centralisation ... I admit that the land of a country belongs to society; and that society, according to its wants has the same right to impose fresh conditions on the lessees, that the landlord has to impose fresh conditions upon a tenant at the expiration of his tenure. Society is the landlord: and as society never dies, the existing government are the trustees ... Society looks on the performance of all requisite duties as the only condition on which its lessees can make good that title.[52]

This was a radical interpretation of the rights and responsibilities of private property and the State. O'Connor was not expounding the land plan to create a socially conservative alternative to, or deviation from, Chartism. He conceived its estates as demonstrating how society would be reconstituted under the Charter, and thus as recruiting more Chartists. In time he dared to hope that such estates might be so successful as to persuade even an unreformed Government of the desirability of a small-farm system.[53]

O'Connor's main priority now was to secure the movement's approval for his land plan. He did not lose sight of the central importance of securing a reformed Parliament: indeed, his 1844 Christmas letter rallied Chartism to contest the next general election even more fiercely than that of 1841 in order to secure the return of 20–30 'Duncombeites'. The immediate context of this was the growing prominence of Duncombe as a radical parliamentarian, not only with regard to the Master and Servant Act but also in harrying the Home Secretary about his use of the Post Office to open the mail of suspicious political figures. He linked this particularly to the surveillance of continental exiles resident in London. Duncombe's campaign 'lit a flame throughout the country'.[54] Though there was respect in Chartist circles for Sir Robert Peel (see chapter 9) on account of his taxation reforms, there was none for Home Secretary Graham who was personally identified with the suppression of the 1842 general strike. Duncombe's growing stature as – to quote Peel – 'the organ of the Chartist Party', was warmly admired by O'Connor and something the Irishman clearly wanted to emulate. Indeed, Feargus seriously considered making a by-election challenge at Edinburgh in 1846; later that year he carried the hustings at a Nottingham by-election but declined to poll.[55] But in 1845, the conjectured general election was still up to three years away. O'Connor's mission was the land.

## 1845–46

Popular agrarianism was a long-established strand within English radical politics and there was a spurt of interest in land schemes during 1845. In central London, interest in the 'Prestonian Plan' revived the political career of the veteran ultra-radical Thomas Preston: 'the old man's assertions were bold, but not new; they were but a smaller part of the grander scheme of Paine, in his Agrarian Justice, to which was attached some little of an old plan of the author's – the Spencean'. The East End Boot and Shoemakers' Mutual Protection Society discussed a plan of its own. In Manchester, Leach addressed a smallware weavers' meeting that resolved to form a mutual benefit society to rent land. A Staffordshire potters' society was accumulating funds for the purchase of land in America. The national trades conference, from which the NAUT emerged, heard calls from the masons and woolcombers of Bradford to take land on which to employ surplus labour. 'On all sides we hear the cry, "The land! the land!"', observed another radical paper: 'men are looking to this source of wealth, determined, if man may be doomed to "gain his bread by the sweat of his brow", that they will for the future with the *sweat* have the *bread!*'[56]

No proposal, however, approached in scope and ambition that of the 'Chartist Co-operative Land Society', approved by the 1845 Convention. It would demonstrate, according to its objects, 'to the working classes of the kingdom – firstly, the value of the land, as a means of making them independent of the grinding capitalists; and, secondly … the necessity of securing the speedy enactment of the "People's Charter", which would do for them nationally, what this society proposes to do sectionally: the accomplishment of the political and social emancipation of the enslaved and degraded working classes'.[57]

These were bold claims but Chartism needed boldness in the early months of 1845. The April Convention comprised merely 13 delegates, 6 of whom represented London; 3 provincial delegates were actually London-based executive members, while Lancashire was completely unrepresented.[58] Weekly sales of the *Northern Star*, having briefly rallied with the move to London, had bottomed out at around 6,500. Self-destructive strife ran through almost every issue. In February, following *Lloyd's Newspaper*'s publication of Watkins's charges against O'Connor, its editor William Carpenter (an 1839 Convention member) was pilloried in an unsigned *Star* article darkly hinting at his sexual peccadilloes and concluding: 'WHAT drove a wife into a mad house, and who is it that has been elevated to take her place in bed and board?'[59]

Claims and counter-claims swirled around Peter McDouall. These began with allegations that Leach had drawn money from the fund subscribed for McDouall on his return to Britain. When Leach responded by producing McDouall's signed receipts, the latter claimed this to have been an accounting ruse: NCA executive members, Leach included, had persuaded him that Leach was in distress and should therefore unobtrusively share donations. A Manchester-district NCA enquiry vindicated Leach, whereupon McDouall sent the *Star* a thirty-nine page letter of complaint. This it declined to print. Glasgow NCA secretary James Smith alleged that McDouall was plotting to establish a separate Scottish NCA. McDouall claimed that Smith was a spy. Leach claimed McDouall had spread rumours that O'Connor was in the pay of the government. McDouall asserted O'Connor had struck a deal with the Attorney-General to fix the outcome of the 1843 trials, giving in return information to help convict McDouall. And so the wearying cycle of disputes continued.[60]

Into the midst of all this O'Brien fired potentially the most damaging salvo of all by printing the allegations William Ashton of Barnsley had privately made about O'Connor's complicity in the Newport Rising. These and O'Connor's defence against them were detailed in chapter 4; here, we need merely note the domino effect of counter-claims that followed. William Hill, still bruised from his falling-out with O'Connor in 1843, corroborated Ashton; so O'Connor at last exposed his former editor as the one man, Ashton apart, who could have warned Frost that Yorkshire would not rise to support him; for good measure O'Connor claimed that Ashton had been paid by Barnsley Conservatives to spread his rumours.[61] By publishing Ashton's claims shortly before the 1845 Convention, O'Brien probably hoped to destabilise the land plan.

Even though he could muster a solid argument in his defence, O'Connor took a huge risk in reprinting Ashton's allegations in the same issue of the *Star* that finally launched the Chartist Co-operative Land Society. But the following week he overplayed his hand with a further assault on O'Brien which intensified the impression that Chartism was collapsing in on itself. O'Connor detailed O'Brien's extensive income from writing for the *Star* and the contributions he had made to keep Bronterre's *Operative* afloat in 1838–39; he accused O'Brien of personal and political cowardice; claimed that his Manx publishing business was subsidised by Tories; and concluded with the assertion that O'Brien had maliciously tried to destabilise south Lancashire Chartism in 1839–40. O'Brien did this, first, by concocting 'a most filthy and beastly story' about J. R. Stephens and 'a very amiable little girl'; and, second, by continuing to spread the allegation after O'Connor had begged him to suppress it in the interests of Chartism and Stephens had made 'a satisfactory explanation'. This, said O'Connor, was the real reason why Stephens had withdrawn from Chartism and then renounced it.[62] Even if all O'Connor's revelations were true, it is unclear what cause was being served other than diverting attention from attacks on himself.

Yet it is an indication of O'Connor's understanding of popular aspirations that the land plan, once finally launched, attracted prodigious support. Headlines such as 'Revival of Chartism', 'Resurrection of Chartism' and 'Return of the Good Old Times' began as hyperbole, but over the next two years Chartism was transformed. With at least 70,000 weekly subscribers at its peak and over 600 branches, the plan became considerably larger than the NCA.[63] Chartism was not converted into the land plan; but the latter filled the vacuum left by the decline of so much normal Chartist activity after 1842. Its officers effectively became the only centrally paid lecturers the movement could afford. Its branches were swiftly assimilated into local Chartist culture: officially, weekly meetings were held to collect instalment payments on shares; in practice they also provided opportunities for reading the *Star*, political debate and conviviality. Meetings were held in the usual range of pubs, temperance and friendly-society rooms, socialist halls and nonconformist premises.

Much of the plan's momentum derived from key local activists, often steeped in the radical agrarian tradition of the pre-Chartist years: in Manchester Leach; in Cheltenham Thomas Sidaway; in Bradford James Arran; in north Lancashire Beesley; and in east London Allen Davenport. Like Hobson and Wheeler, Davenport was also rooted in the Owenite socialist tradition. In different ways all three were instrumental to the success of the scheme. Hobson was a formative influence on the initiative right up until Harney finally replaced him in October 1845; and Davenport, Spence's biographer and one of the most thoughtful and prolific worker–writers on land reform, was enlisted by Harney to broaden the *Northern Star's* coverage of agrarian issues and remind its readers of the long pedigree of the concept of 'the People's Farm'.[64]

Popular commitment to the plan was sustained despite its prolonged and at times bewildering quest for legal recognition.[65] Although the aborted 1843 NCA constitution had been refused registration as a friendly society, it had been based closely on one the Owenites had successfully registered in 1839. The reasons for refusal given by John Tidd Pratt, the Registrar of Friendly Societies, were that the political purposes of the NCA put it in breach of the 1799 Unlawful Meetings Act and the 1817 Seditious Meetings Act: it therefore

fell outside the requirement of the 1834 Friendly Societies' Act that all the activities of a registered body must be 'not illegal'. Chartists had always operated
in the knowledge that aspects of their organisation, particularly any federated
structure with an elected governing body, were potentially vulnerable to prosecution under the 1799 and 1817 legislation (this consideration had governed
the size of successive National Conventions). It was therefore a reasonable
assumption that the land plan *would* be able to register, once decoupled from
the NCA.

A bullish O'Connor, still smarting from the rejection of the 1843 constitution, was prepared to proceed without registration. However, a special land plan
convention, in Manchester in December 1845, refined the constitution into a
form (it thought) eligible for registration. The assembly elected to register under
the Building Societies Act of 1836 (this modified friendly societies legislation
specifically to permit the transfer of shares between members without incurring
costly Stamp Duty). However, this set of rules was also rejected by Pratt on the
grounds that the avowed connection with Chartism still placed it in breach
of the law. A follow-up request to register as the National Co-operative Land
Society was refused on the grounds that the allocation by lottery of holdings
to shareholders contravened the Lotteries Acts. Yet large numbers of registered
land and building societies used raffles to determine the order in which properties should be allocated to members. For example, O'Brien's *National Reformer*
energetically promoted Bowkett Building Societies, all of them overt lotteries.
Bowkett Societies, however, imposed a low ceiling on membership.[66]

It was the scale of the Chartist enterprise that unnerved Pratt, along with its
political affiliations. When challenged that the NCA's objectives were to secure
the enactment of the Charter 'by peaceful, legal, and constitutional means',
Pratt pointed to the recent judicial ruling that the term 'not illegal' within
friendly society law did not encompass activities wider than the functions
of such bodies as defined in the legislation concerned. Duncombe therefore
proposed a parliamentary Bill that the formula 'not illegal' should be replaced
by 'any legal purpose whatsoever'. The Act that emerged duly broadened the
scope of what might be construed 'legal' under friendly society legislation, but
only if the Attorney-General certified it so. In July 1846 the Attorney-General
refused to certify the land society as legal on the grounds that it breached the
Lotteries Acts.

Undaunted, new members continued to join the society. O'Connor's next
tactic was to seek registration under the Joint Stock Companies Act, passed
earlier in 1846, as the Chartist Co-operative Land Company. There was a ten-
month delay while draft deeds were scrutinised by the Board of Trade, during
which the provisionally registered Company continued to operate. However,
just as the Friendly Societies Act had not been framed with political bodies
in mind, so this new Act had not been drawn up to accommodate a company

that had a mass, open-ended body of shareholders. It required registration to be accompanied by the names and addresses of those who held one-quarter of the shareholding, a few signatories in most capitalist undertakings, with the details of all shareholders to follow in due course. This had to be drawn up as a legal instrument, not a petition, with all names in alphabetical order and Stamp Duty payable at £3 15s per 100. Undaunted, the directors of the National Land Company (as they and it were now known) set about collecting the requisite details. There were 43,847 shareholders by August 1847, hardly any of whom owned more than one share.

Legal obstacles were stacked against the Chartist land plan at every conceivable turn, but the plan's progress within Chartism itself was also not entirely smooth. While it helped consolidate Chartism, it also intensified the misgivings of those already opposed to O'Connor. There was also understandable unease about its problematical legal status, the remuneration of its managers and their accountability. In November 1845 West Yorkshire delegates met at Dewsbury's Co-operative Hall in advance of the Manchester national conference to draw up a series of resolutions for consideration there. The identity of their suggested trustees indicated reservations about the plan's executive. This, they unanimously resolved, should be unsalaried.

The main thrust of the Dewsbury resolutions, however, was to demand several constitutional changes to secure legal registration. Unfortunately Harney (in his first month as sole editor of the *Star* and presumably at O'Connor's bidding) badly mishandled the issue by refusing to print the report sent to him from Dewsbury. The delegates therefore had it printed as a leaflet and distributed it themselves. There followed the familiar flurry of criticism and innuendo about 'underhand attacks', 'gentlemen, who would spitefully nibble at the details of this Land Plan' and 'THE DEVIL, attempting to pull his hoof or horn into plans which he cannot subdue for his own purpose'. O'Connor was suffering from another of the bouts of illness that periodically afflicted him. (At the beginning of 1845 he had been laid low for nearly a month due to lethargy and eye inflammation.) Now he claimed emotively that the Dewsbury resolutions made him 'tremble for the safety of my child. Otherwise I doubt whether I should have left my sick-bed to have periled my life in its defence.'[67]

It was consistent with the status of a gentleman radical leader, sacrificing all in the defence of the people, that O'Connor should make such a claim; but his reaction was transparently disproportionate and a potentially worrying portent. Could the management of a financial enterprise as complex as a national land company be entrusted essentially to one person? O'Connor had massive reserves of energy and tenacity, an engaging enthusiasm and an infectious optimism. It is no exaggeration to say that he loved 'the fustian jackets' and their families, or that his commitment to their needs (as he saw them) was without limits. But O'Connor resented even constructive criticism, while his head was easily turned by praise, He found delegation difficult, though his own eye for detail (particularly financial detail) was poor. Yet, paradoxically, as the land plan developed, criticism from within Chartism and official intransigence from without alike galvanised further support. Subscribing became a political act in itself, a gesture of defiance in the face of class legislation and government hostility, and a vote of confidence in O'Connor's leadership of Chartism as a whole.

## 'The People's First Estate!'

Come let us leave the murky gloom,
The narrow crowded street:
The bustle, noise, the smoke and din,
To breathe the air that's sweet.
We'll leave the gorgeous palaces
To those miscalled great;
To spend a day of pleasure on
The People's First Estate!

The banners waving in the breeze,
The bands shall cheerfully play,
Let all be mirth and holiday
On this our holy day.
Unto the farm – 'O'Connorville,'
That late was 'Herringsgate,'
We go to take possession of
The People's First Estate!

(John Arnott, *The People's First Estate*, *Northern Star*, 1 August 1846)

In March 1846 the Chartist Co-operative Land Society purchased its first estate at Heronsgate, near Rickmansworth, Hertfordshire. Legally the 103 acres were purchased in O'Connor's name because, as we have seen, the Society could not be registered. This was publicly acknowledged. Much less widely known, however, was that a substantial mortgage was immediately raised on the property to free-up capital. The pulse of Chartism was quickening. Duncombe had recently presented petitions totalling 3 million signatures for a free pardon for Frost, Jones and Williams. Predictably Parliament voted against acting on them, but Chartists made much capital at the expense of Cobden and Bright, 'who skulked out of the House of Commons just previous to the division'. The list of voters and abstentions was widely touted as defining the battle ground at the next general election. Huge interest was attracted by the 'first fustian landlords', whose names were determined by a draw in Manchester on Easter Monday. Success in the ballot provided 4, 3 or 2 acres (depending on whether 2, one-and-a-half or single shares were held by those whose names were drawn). Roads would be laid out, the land cleared for cultivation, drainage installed, and a cottage with outbuildings erected on each plot. In addition each allottee would receive a cash loan for the purchase of stock and equipment. Repayment of this was to be bound up with a rent (over £11 annually for a 4-acre plot), contrary to publicity suggesting that allottees would be freeholders.[68]

Work on 'O'Connorville' commenced almost at once, personally overseen by Feargus who moved into the existing farmhouse in Heronsgate and sent regular bulletins 'from Paradise' to the *Northern Star*: 'My pale face is turned into a good, sound, sun-burnt ruddy complexion. I can jump over the gates without opening them. I am up every morning at 6 o'clock, and when I look out of my window at the prospect, and think of the number my labours will make happy, I feel myself a giant.' By June the workforce on the estate numbered 200, all hired directly (O'Connor distrusted contractors) and managed by him and a single foreman. For most of the summer O'Connor spent only Wednesdays and Thursdays away from Heronsgate, working in London for the *Star* and on his personal affairs. Even for the Nottingham by-election in July he spared only a single day.[69]

On Monday 17 August the fruits of this labour were thrown open to inspection in 'the Chartist jubilee'. It was a term freighted with symbolism: Chartists knew their Old Testament and the Levitical institution of jubilee had long featured in the lexicon of English radical agrarianism.[70] At least 12,000 toured the estate, inspected the building work and petted Rebecca the cow (named after the Welsh tollgate protesters and clad in a tricolour especially for the occasion). Most came from London in a carnival of some 100 decorated vans and carts that had threaded its way from Oxford Street early that morning; but there were also contingents from Reading, Oxford, Devon, Lancashire and Yorkshire. Amid the dancing, recitations and speeches, the real star of the occasion was the people's first estate itself. The mood of the occasion was captured in a speech by a recent recruit to the cause, 27–year-old Ernest Jones, barrister, author and son of a former *aide de camp* to the Duke of Cumberland (since 1837 the King of Hanover). Two weeks earlier Jones for the first time had addressed a Chartist demonstration, 'the birthday of renewed Chartism', at Blackstone Edge on the high moors between Lancashire and Yorkshire. Looking around O'Connorville, Jones declared:

> I think we may call this its christening ... we baptise with *earth* instead of water – and this indeed is holier, since it is the land devoted to the purpose for which God designed it, the maintenance of those who till it by the sweat of their brow. (Cheers.) When I left London this morning I thought I was only going some seventeen or eighteen miles out of town: I now begin to

think I must have made a very long journey indeed, for I have come to a
land that at one time I scarcely ever expected to see. I have come from the
land of slavery to the land of liberty – from the land of poverty to the land
of plenty – from the land of the Whigs to the great land of the Charter! This
is the promised land, my friends![71]

# Chartist lives:
# Ann Dawson

It is one of the most affecting, and certainly most colourful, material remnants
of Chartism (see frontispiece). Naivety of execution combines with vibrancy of
colour to create an impression at once youthful and sunny, elegiac and optimistic. This needlework sampler, depicting the O'Connorville schoolhouse, is
a vivid reminder that Chartism embraced men, women and all ages, and at
its heart was a profound commitment to education and self-improvement.
These factors were integral to the so-called 'new move' from 1840; but they
had always been integral to Chartism. The handiwork of Ann Dawson, whoever
she was, confounds any simplistic division of Chartism into robust O'Connorite
'physical force', on the one hand, and peaceable Lovettite 'moral force', on the
other. Consider the sentiments Ann embroidered:

> Britannia's the land where fell slavery's chain
> Had bound fast its victims in hunger and pain,
> Where no eye would pity, when no hand would save.
> Then came forth to break it O'Connor the brave.
> A band of brave fellows, whose hearts caught the sound,
> Arose from their slumbers and rallied around
> Resolved in defiance of fool and of knave,
> For freedom to fight with O'Connor the brave.
> The Charter and No Surrender.

'The Charter and No Surrender' was a universal rallying cry in the movement,
especially after Parliament rejected the first Petition in July 1839. Immediately

below it Ann embroidered a book overlaying a ship's anchor, encircled by a wreath of roses, with the words 'bible and hanker' underneath. Below these is cross-stitched a two-dimensional representation, 'The chartist school at o[']connorville near London'. Reading Ann's handiwork, one can almost hear a child's voice breathlessly rushing the final lines of a recitation, for the presentation of the text loses its structure at this point. Overwhelmingly samplers were the work of girls, typically aged between 8 and 15, though examples by boys and older children are not uncommon. Thousands of nineteenth-century samplers survive, typically worked with exacting precision and often expressing sententious or religious sentiments that lead almost inevitably to the conclusion that these were accomplished only under close adult supervision. However, Ann Dawson's work has a subversive quality, for several reasons. The expression of overt political sentiment in samplers is extremely rare, and the use even of secular verse is atypical of the genre. Ann's work, however, is subversive in terms of technique as well as content. By the 1840s samplers worked by working-class children tended to be highly stylised. Broadly speaking, embroidered samplers had evolved from the late medieval and Tudor periods, when for female members of elite households embroidery was a recreational pursuit as much as a practical accomplishment. Sixteenth-century samplers were generally 'broad linen rectangles stitched with a collection of motifs often drawn from herbals and bestiaries'. Adding verses was a mainly eighteenth-century development, one which has been seen as inculcating profoundly patriarchal ideals of femininity. Teaching embroidery to the poor gathered momentum in the late eighteenth and the nineteenth century. Books were published setting out how this should be done and needlework became a major component of the curriculum of both secular and religiously organised schools. One consequence was a marked move away from both spontaneity and ornament, as samplers frequently comprised cross-stitched alphabetical and numerical sequences, the name and age of the child responsible and sometimes that of the school attended. Increasingly the canvas on which they worked was not linen but a woollen cloth, cheaper and easier to work, called 'tammy'. Prolific use of richly coloured silks or mercerised cottons, made possible by the manufacturing and retail revolutions of the eighteenth century, remained a hallmark of samplers worked in middle- and upper-class households. However, those produced by poorer needleworkers, especially in the institutional context of school or orphanage, tended to the monochromatic.[*]

Clearly, Ann's sampler does not fit the above generalisations. It is in the

---

[*]    R. Parker, *The Subversive Stitch* (London, Women's Press, 1984), pp. 85, 173–4; National Society for Promoting the Education of the Poor in the Principles of the Established Church, *Instructions on Needlework and Knitting* (London, The Society, 1847); J. Toller, *British Samplers* (Chichester, Phillimore, 1980).

nature of generalisations that there will always be exceptions, but her work is spectacularly exceptional. Visually arresting though it is, it decidedly does not exhibit the order and precision of most surviving samplers. This is suggestive of something natural and unforced rather than the regimented presentation of school work, based on a copybook or a teacher's worked example. Dawson's sampler is also riotously colourful and it is worked on linen. It incorporates both verse and stylised elements from an earlier period which were far less common in the Victorian period. The two diminutive figures in the bottom corners, for example, are 'boxers'. These were common motifs in seventeenth- and eighteenth-century samplers, probably derived from an even earlier Italian pattern depicting lovers exchanging gifts (and of course resonant with the biblical figures of Adam and Eve) and gradually simplified by successive generations.[*]

The other striking element is the depiction of O'Connorville's schoolhouse. This too is stylised, very much in the manner of the four-square Georgian-style dwellings depicted on many samplers. Dawson's rendering, though, is also strikingly accurate and can have been based only on close observation of the original or, perhaps more likely, its representation in land plan promotional material. It conforms very closely to the building as it was projected at the time the estate was acquired in 1846. An elaborate, coloured map produced then, and echoed in an engraving presented to *Northern Star* readers the following January, shows the building exactly as the sampler does, with 3 doors, 6 lower and 3 upper-floor windows and a central clock tower flanked by a chimney on either side. It is not clear if the school as built (it was completed in the spring of 1847) actually included the tower, which suggests that Ann Dawson copied either the original map (which toured the main Chartist localities) or the subsequent engraving. But she may have been among the throng at the 'People's Jubilee', celebrating the estate's acquisition in August 1846, or the crowds at Mayday and Whitsun 1847, celebrating the arrival of the first 'fustian freeholders'.[†]

Who then was Ann Dawson? It is impossible to say with certainty. From the inception of the civil registration of births in 1837 up to 1843, approximately 350 girls were registered in England and Wales with the name Ann Dawson.[‡] The sampler itself offers no clue, nor does its provenance.[§] It is tempting to

---

[*] S. Mayor and D. Fowle, *Samplers* (London, Studio, 1990), plate 6; L. Synge, *Antique Needlework* (London, Blandford, 1982), pp. 71–2.

[†] BL, MAPS, 162.S.1, 'O'Connorville' (1846); *NS*, 22 August 1846, 8 and 29 May 1847.

[‡] Calculation based on data available at the Free Births, Marriages and Deaths website: http://freebmd.rootsweb.com (accessed 11 June 2004).

[§] It was purchased in 1981 by the current owner, Angela Killick, from an antique shop in the Portobello Road, London, whose owner had in turn bought it from an antique market in the East End: after that the trail runs cold. I am grateful to Angela Killick for

suppose that Ann was a pupil at O'Connorville, although the settlers included none named Dawson. The inclusion of two stags, the Hertfordshire county emblem, suggests that Ann was a local girl: but stags like boxers were part of the stock imagery deployed on samplers, probably owing to the frequency with which they appeared in heraldry. Moreover, Dawson is not a name appearing in Census records for this part of Hertfordshire in 1851. The name is, though, not uncommon in the Chartist heartlands of the industrial north, and it may be here that some clues to the identity of Ann Dawson may be found. The dominance of male names in records of the Chartist movement necessarily means that identifying her is a conjectural process. She may have been the daughter of any one of several active Chartists with that surname: John Dawson of north Staffordshire (auditor of the Hanley and Shelton land plan branch); William Dawson of Holbrook, Derbyshire (contributor to the *Northern Star* Victims' Fund); or Isaac Dawson of Droylsden (an active member of his local NCA branch).[*]

There were at least 63 fully paid up land plan shareholders named Dawson: 16 were weavers, 11 labourers, 4 woolcombers, 3 tailors, 2 spinners, 2 bootclosers and 2 mechanics. Other textile-related occupations accounted for 4 Dawsons, engineering 3, while book-keeping, floristry, gardening, hawking, iron-moulding, joinery, mining, stonemasonry and school teaching each accounted for one. So too did the trades of brass polisher, glazier, potter, publican and warehouseman. This occupational spectrum is compatible with a systematic national sample of the membership, wherein weavers, then labourers, are the largest groups, followed at some distance by boot and shoemakers, tailors, stocking knitters, woolcombers and then spinners.[†]

A geographical breakdown reveals a similar distribution of Dawsons in Yorkshire (22), Lancashire (11) and Cheshire (7). Finally, the gender breakdown of the Dawsons is consistent with national trends: all are male except Sarah Ann Dawson (a weaver from Bacup in east Lancashire) and two sisters from Droylsden, described as 'too young' in the occupations' column of the share-holders' register: their names were Betty and Ann, and their father, according to the 1851 Census, was Isaac Dawson.[‡] It is a reasonable conjecture that this Ann Dawson was the young woman responsible for the remarkable O'Connorville sampler, though conjecture is all it can be, not least because she had been born only in 1842. If 1847 (embroidered in the top-right corner) is the date of

---

permission to reproduce the photograph that appears here and for sharing with me her thoughts about the sampler.

[*]   *NS*, 10 April 1841, 24 August and 7 September 1844, 11 March 1848.

[†]   National Archives, Kew, Board of Trade Papers (BT), 41/474/2819 and 41/476/2659, Shareholders' Registers for the National Land Company; D. J. V. Jones, *Chartism and the Chartists* (London, Allen Lane, 1975), pp.134–7.

[‡]   HO, 107/2234/37/15.

this work, then its completion by a 5-year-old would be exceptional, possibly explaining the deficiencies in its execution. It is, though, conceivable that 1847 is meant to indicate the date O'Connorville opened and therefore that the sampler was completed sometime after. The coincidence of a signed artefact, typically made by girls of school age, with a land plan member of the same name who was the daughter of a Chartist activist is intriguing. Its implications are worth pursuing further.

Ann, Betty and their brothers Benjamin and Joshua were all shareholders, listed at the same address, Ashton New Road in Droylsden. The enrolment of children in the plan was not uncommon, though few families' incomes stretched to enrolling four, which would have involved a sizeable financial investment. Significantly neither Isaac nor his wife Hannah enrolled. More typically parents might enrol just one child, as for example did Jonathan Dawson, a labourer from Attercliffe near Sheffield. Where three or more members of the same family owned shares most, if not all, were wage-earners, for example the Dawsons of Marcham, near Abingdon (Berkshire): Thomas, a hawker, labourers Jonathan and Job, and Jonathan junior, a gardener. The Droylsden Dawsons, then, made a substantial investment in the plan. Yet the 1851 Census makes clear that they were not among the middle-class supporters of Chartism, whose names occasionally appear as shareholders.[*] Isaac (aged 36 and originally from Huddersfield) was a baker. Because of his non-appearance in local trade directories it is probable that he was employed in a bakery, rather than running an establishment on his own account. Hannah, also 36, had been born in Lancashire, as had the eldest son Benjamin, in 1836. Mother, son and Ann's elder sister Betty were card room operatives, employed in the mills in the tedious, dust-ridden drudgery of preparing cotton fibres for spinning. Very likely they were afflicted by the respiratory illnesses endemic to carders.

Hannah had borne another son, Samuel, in 1848 and the resultant family of 7 supplemented its income by taking in 3 factory weavers as lodgers: Martha Dutton, aged 19 from Huddersfield; Catherine Litherland, aged 20, from 'Woolridge' (probably Woolwich, south London); and James Hartly, aged 19, from Colne, Lancashire. Underlining that theirs was a working-class neighbourhood, the Dawsons' neighbours comprised, on one side, a family of cotton spinners and, on the other, a hatter's felt maker and his stepson (again, a felt maker) and two daughters, aged 16 and 20, both of them factory weavers. A short walk up Ashton New Road lived another family named Dawson: Francis and Ellen, both born in Ireland, and keeping house for their 4 daughters (all employed as weavers), 2 grandchildren (the elder, aged 11, employed short-time in a mill) and 6 more weavers who lodged with them.

---

[*]    Analysis based on 1851 Census for Droylsden: HO, 107/2234/37/15.

Droylsden was a far from prosperous neighbourhood. Though described in 1841 as 'one of the rural portions of the parish of Manchester', its economy and character were intimately bound-up with its better-known neighbours Ashton-under-Lyne and Stalybridge. In February 1841 powerloom weavers at Droyslden's largest mill had been defeated in a bruising lock out for resisting a wage cut, and the village, according to *Northern Star*, was 'one scene of poverty, misery, distress, starvation and want'.[*] Intersected by 2 railway lines and 3 canals, Droyslden was far too small to have a varied industrial base: this was confined to cotton, silk, hats, calico printing and dyestuffs. Of its 1841 population of 2,996, almost everyone aged 11 and over was employed in some capacity in the textile industry. There were three nonconformist chapels but, until 1848, no Anglican church. Droylsden could also boast of as many beer-shops (15) as it had shopkeepers, plus 4 pubs.[†]

Ann lived on the main street. Ashton New Road had been laid out in 1826 to improve the route between Manchester and Ashton; its footpaths were made only of cinders and it was totally without lighting until 1848. The combination of textile mills and overwhelmingly working-class residence made Droylsden an almost archetypal Chartist centre. Nearly 3,000 signatures from the locality were claimed for the 1839 Petition, and 2,600 in 1842. Subsequently Droylsden formed its own branch of the NCA and, in 1846–47, of the land plan and its associated Land and Labour Bank. It is indicative of how tightly knit this community was that its burial society invested its funds in the bank, urging other societies to do likewise. Droyslden's Chartists met first in the Total Abstinence Rooms, but later opened their own premises in 'a cottage taken for the purpose', just off the Dawson's road, in Edward Street. Droyslden also acquired a reputation for truculence similar to the Chartists of Stalybridge and Ashton, the town's first historian noting how in the mid-1850s 'formidable looking pike heads' were regularly dug up on open land less than a mile from Ashton New Road.[‡]

Droylsden was too small to yield much documented material about Chartist activity. But in our search to understand the world inhabited by Ann Dawson, putative creator of the O'Connorville sampler, we can reasonably infer the existence of a spectrum of activities and opinions similar to neighbouring textile communities. In the smallest townships, Chartism and nonconformity were

---

[*]   E. Butterworth, *Statistical Sketch of the County Palatine of Lancaster* (London, Longman, 1841), p.90; M. Jenkins, *The General Strike of 1842* (London, Lawrence & Wishart, 1980), pp.54, 56.

[†]   *Pigot and Slater's General and Classified Directory of Manchester and Salford* (Manchester, Pigot & Slater, 1841); *Victoria County History*, vol.4: *Lancashire* (London, Constable, 1991), pp.282–7.

[‡]   D.Thompson, *The Chartists* (New York, Pantheon, 1984), p.348; *NS*, 1 April 1848; J.Higson, *Historical and Descriptive Notices of Droylsden, Past and Present* (Manchester, self-published, 1859), pp.154–5.

often the only cultural forces beyond pubs and beershops. At Crompton, north of Oldham, 'there was no mechanics' institute – no public library – no reading room except one supported by chartists – nor any bookseller's or stationer's shop in the place'. These were localities where communal support for Chartism reached near total levels at the movement's peaks; and where the political commitment of women – typically working in the carding rooms, spinning rooms and weaving sheds of the local mills – was commonplace and seldom remarked on except by outsiders. They might organise tea parties or collect donations for the dependants of Chartist prisoners, but equally they appeared in processions and rallies carrying their own banners. They assumed the role of radical teachers, and they confined their custom to shopkeepers who pledged to support the Charter; formally they might directly organise systematic exclusive dealing, as a meeting of more than 1,000 female operatives resolved to do at Ashton in May 1839. They also issued manifesto statements, sometimes of startling force: 'Tis better to be slain by the sword than die with hunger', declared Ashton's female Chartists in 1839. 'We are determined that no man shall ever enjoy our hands, our hearts, or share our beds, that will not stand forward as the advocate of the rights of man, and as the determined enemy of the damnable New Poor Law.' They looked forward to 'seeing intelligence the necessary qualification for voting, and then sisters, we shall be placed in our proper position in society, and enjoy the elective franchise as well as our kinsmen'.*

It was only to be expected, therefore, that children in these communities should in their own way share their parents' commitment to Chartism. The common practice of naming a child after a radical hero is the best-documented reflection of this. However, historians have allowed the humorous aspects of the practice to deflect attention from the substance of what it meant to be raised in a Chartist household (for who can resist smiling at the thought of Fanny Amelia Lucy Ann Rebecca Frost O'Connor McDouall Leach Holberry Duffy Oastler Hill Boden?).† The overwhelming majority of Chartist parents, however, resisted such adulatory gestures, the Dawsons being a case in point. Much more important was the participation of their children in Chartist activities. Few hostile press reports of Chartist meetings could resist diminishing their importance by stressing that youths were present in large numbers; but youthful support extended into other spheres. For example in the general strike of 1842, 'the first day the mills were stopped, a body of five-hundred

---

* S. Bamford, *Walks in South Lancashire* (Blackley, self-published, 1844), p.36; *NS*, 1 June 1839; P. Pickering, *Chartism and the Chartists in Manchester and Salford* (Manchester, Manchester University Press, 1995), p.214; quotation from *NS*, 2 February 1839.

† Birth registered in Birmingham, 1842: Jones, *Chartism*, p.24; Pickering, *Chartism*, pp.40–5 is the only serious consideration of Chartist youth.

girls, belonging to the dissenting Sunday-schools at Oldham, marched at the head of the rioters, singing their school-hymns'.[*]

The home itself was an environment with a Chartist dimension. Plates and cups decorated with images of Hunt and, later, Stephens were mass produced for sale in the industrial north. Tens of thousands of prints of leading Chartists and other radical heroes were distributed by the *Northern Star* to adorn walls in readers' homes. William Adams (born 1832) was raised in the home of his grand-mother, a washerwoman, where 'one of the pictures that I longest remember – it stood alongside samplers and stencilled drawings, and not far from a china statuette of George Washington – was a portrait of John Frost'. William Farish, a handloom weaver born above his father's weaving shop in Carlisle, recalled: 'I had one of these portraits myself. After being framed by my own hand, [it] served for years to adorn the wall of my bedroom.' Ann Dawson's sampler, clearly not an illustration of work suitable to show a prospective employer, was intended precisely for display in a domestic setting. We can readily imagine it taking pride of place alongside mass-produced artefacts of popular radical culture.[†]

Children, of course, were also expected directly to contribute to the family economy at an early date. Ann's elder sister Betty probably worked in a card room from the age of 11; she was certainly there at 13 when the 1851 Census was taken. Some time in the mid-1850s Ann followed Betty into the mills: in the 1861 Census she is listed as a cotton weaver.[‡] One of the great attractions of the land plan was that it appeared to offer both a practical means to end children's employment in factories and reinstate the mother at the heart of domestic life. If the Dawsons were among the Lancashire pilgrims to O'Connorville on Mayday 1847, they would have heard O'Connor warm to this theme in a speech delivered in the schoolhouse itself:

> I have brought you out of the land of Egypt, and out of the house of bondage. And must I not have a cold and flinty heart if I could survey the scene before me without emotion? Who can look upon those mothers, accustomed to be dragged by the waking light of morn from those little babes now nestling to their breasts? (Here the speaker was so overcome that he was obliged to sit down, his face covered with large tears, and we never beheld such a scene in our life; not an eye in the building that did not weep.) After a pause Mr. O'Connor resumed: Yes, this is a portion of the great feature of my plan to give the fond wife back to her husband, and the innocent babe back to its

---

[*]    J. Sinclair, *National Education and Church Extension* (London, Rivington, 1849), p.67.

[†]    W.E. Adams, *Memoirs of a Social Atom* (London, Hutcheson, 1903), pp.163–4; W. Farish, *Autobiography of William Farish* (1889), p.50.

[‡]    RG, 9/2989/62/27.

fond mother. (Here the speaker was again compelled to pause, and delivered the remainder of his address sitting down.)

See what a different race I will make – see what a noble edifice for the education of your children. (Cheers.) While a sectarian government is endeavouring to preserve its dominion, and fostering sectarian strife, I open the sanctuary of free instruction for the unbiased instruction of youth, and woe to the firebrand parson who shall dare to frighten the susceptible mind of infancy by the hobgoblin of religious preference. (Tremendous cheering and waving of hats.) Let the father nourish, and the fond mother nurture, their own offspring (cheers) and then we shall have a generation of FREE CHRISTIANS. (Loud cheers.)[*]

It was one of O'Connor's most bravura performances. Modern secularisation still does not blunt the opening biblical imagery, in which the audience is cast in the role of Israel, a chosen people against whom are contrasted (inverting the establishment view of Chartism) the firebrand parson and a narrow sectarian Government. Robust anti-clericalism of this kind was common in Chartism. The focus on familial relationships draws on another deep-seated popular emotion, identifying factories with the reversal of the natural order of labour and home life. O'Connor's sentiments on this occasion, as so often, show how powerful the idea of independence was among Chartists, independence from the caprice of undemocratic government and a State Church, and from industrialism's 'house of bondage'.

The key to his popularity as a Chartist leader, especially in the Pennine textile districts, was his capacity to reflect back to his audience and readers their own perceptions of their place in society and their aspirations to improve it. Though religion meant little to O'Connor, he well knew how close it lay to the heart of popular radical feeling. In the sampler this is vividly conveyed by the Bible and anchor, recalling the words both of St Paul ('hope we have as an anchor of the soul, both sure and steadfast') and for the Dawsons probably also those of local Chartist poet, Benjamin Stott:

> Lift up your faces from the dust,
> Your cause is holy, pure and just;
> In Freedom's God put all your trust,
> Be he your hope and anchor.[†]

In all likelihood the Dawsons were not at O'Connorville on Mayday 1847;

---

[*]   NS, 8 May 1847; for a detailed analysis of this speech see M. Chase, 'We wish only to work for ourselves', in M. Chase and I. Dyck (eds), *Living and Learning* (Aldershot, Scolar, 1996), pp. 136–7.

[†]   Hebrews 6:19; B. Stott, *Song for the Million*, NS, 24 September 1842, reprinted as *Friends of Freedom*, in his *Songs for the Millions* (Middleton, Horsman, 1843), p. 28; for Stott see *DLB* entry, vol. 6.

but they would have read the speech in the *Northern Star*. We can picture Ann embroidering by the window (maybe helped by sister Betty or the lodgers Catherine and Martha), then tidying her work away as the daylight fades. A carder's cough is heard in the unlit street outside. A mother slips to a neighbour's to share news about exclusive dealing. Men talk volubly of Feargus's latest letter 'to the fustian jackets' on their way to the Chartist rooms in nearby Edward Street. All too often the intimate and the personal evade the historian's gaze. We see through a glass, darkly; yet whoever Ann was, her sampler affords us a glimpse of Chartism at its 'grassroots'. And what we see is not mere hunger politics, but an endeavour to improve every dimension of human life.

# CHAPTER NINE

# July 1846–April 1848: 'A time to make politicians'

## Taking stock

The context of the 1847 May Day rally at O'Connorville differed considerably from the People's Jubilee nine months earlier, when the estate was first thrown open to inspection. At the most obvious and pressing level of human predicament, the full enormity of the Irish famine was becoming apparent, following the total failure of the 1846 potato harvest and a crisis of mortality over the winter. This had the incidental effect of making the land plan, which was regularly promoted as refuting Malthusianism, appear yet more timely and necessary. Second, within a fortnight of the May Day meeting, Daniel O'Connell had died, bringing to a close one of the most significant and turbulent careers in Irish politics but also opening up a real possibility of co-operation between Irish nationalists and British Chartists. Third, parliamentary politics had been transformed following the resignation of Sir Robert Peel on 29 June 1846 and his replacement by Lord Russell at the head of a Whig ministry. Chartism's, and especially O'Connor's, relationship with Peel was complex and needs to be teased out before the history of the movement in the years after his resignation can be fully understood.

Peel's resignation was occasioned by his Government's defeat on the Irish Coercion Bill (giving it special emergency powers in Ireland). This was not, however, the real reason for his defeat. Four days earlier Parliament had finally repealed the Corn Laws, an epoch-defining moment for England as significant as O'Connell's death would be for Ireland. Only a third of Conservative MPs voted for repeal and Peel had therefore relied on Whigs and Liberals to get the measure through. The price of his success however was to split the Conservatives and to lose office. Peel was admired in Chartist circles. His 1842 budget had been warmly commended by O'Connor and the *Northern Star* for reducing import tariffs and implementing income tax (for the first time in peacetime). His 1845 budget had reduced tariffs further and the equalisation of sugar duties in 1846 addressed what was popularly seen as an iniquitous tax to support West Indian planters. It mattered not that the collective achievement of Peel's fiscal management may have been less than was claimed for it (a conclusion, in any case, easiest reached in hindsight).[1] It was the overall impression that mattered and Peel's administration had passed other legislation that Chartists perforce had to concede was positive: the Mines Act of 1842 prohibited the employment of women and children below ground; and the 1844 Factory Act regulated for the first time the employment of adult women (and thus may have helped re-establish male control in the spinning sector).[2]

The complex interplay of gender, paternalism and state authority surrounding this legislation should not be allowed to obscure its significance. Though its enforcement may have left much to be desired, and the Act itself fell short of the factory movement's demands, it was nonetheless heralded as progressive legislation. Even the Joint Stock Companies Act and the Bank Charter Act were of some import: though remote from the daily lives of working people, they reinforced the sense (most readily apparent in the 1842 and 1845 budgets) that Peel's administration governed according to criteria other than its supporters' direct personal interest. In this respect, repealing the Corn Laws trumped everything. Chartist opposition to the ACLL had stemmed from the belief that it misdirected political energies to feather the nest of manufacturing employers. Although there were protectionists within Chartism (notably Bronterre O'Brien and James Leach) Chartism's generally consistent message was always that repeal was desirable, but the reform of Parliament had to precede it. Without the safeguard of democratic government, any reduction in the price of bread would simply be exploited by employers in lowering wages, even assuming that an unreformed Parliament would pass such a measure. Popular awareness of the developing subsistence crisis in Ireland sharpened perceptions that the repeal of corn import tariffs was unequivocally advantageous, regardless of the social complexion of the Parliament passing it. Repeal also drew from the NCA executive grudging admiration:

> The measures of the late cabinet, in our opinion, have nothing intrinsically valuable in themselves, to recommend them to the people – they have not a tendency to free labour from the merciless grasp of capital, nor in the slightest degree meliorate the condition of the operative and labouring classes, but, nevertheless, there was a boldness in their conception and an earnestness in their execution that challenge our admiration and bid us hope for the time when equal energy and talent will be employed within the walls of Parliament for the advancement of those great principles which alone can ensure the liberty and happiness of the people.

O'Connor was bolder, commenting that 'for five years Peel has led an incipient

Chartist Movement', the consequence of which was that Russell's Government would find it difficult to hold the line that the 1832 Reform Act was final. This perspective found its ultimate conclusion in a curious novel from the fringes of literary Chartism, Charles Henningsen's *Sixty Years Hence* (1847), which depicted, in the near future, Peel's political career being crowned by enacting the People's Charter. It was a vision that, following his untimely death in 1850, received graphic endorsement in the addition of Peel to the portraits the *Northern Star* presented to regular readers.[3]

However, in terms of accounting for the decline of Chartism, the impact of Peel's legislation is certainly not a sufficient explanation.[4] It does, though, help to explain shifts – apparent from 1845 – in the movement's trajectory, especially taken in conjunction with what can be discerned of O'Connor's private opinions of Peel. Towards the end of 1843 Feargus wrote at considerable length to his elder brother Frank, whom he had not seen since the latter emigrated to South America in 1819.[5] This was no ordinary letter, its intended recipient being no ordinary man. General Francisco Burdett O'Connor, as he now was, had fought with considerable distinction in the revolutionary army of Simon Bolivar, retiring from active service in 1838.[6] It is a revealing reflection of Feargus's character that he never publicly mentioned his brother's achievements, even after Frank contacted him after many years' silence in December 1842.

The account Feargus gave his brother of his own endeavours is equally revealing. Sweeping generalisation was punctuated with minutely detailed accounts of athletic feats, duels, courtroom dramas and victories against O'Connell. On Chartism Feargus was uncharacteristically brief: 'in 1835 I established an Association in London, the fruits of which was a petition to Parliament last year signed by 3,500,000 demanding the enactment of the principles of the Association. Nearly all London with countless bands and banners followed the gigantic roll in procession, which was carried by sixteen able-bodied men, relieved every two minutes, in to the very body of the house.' Feargus had little else to say about Chartism, a word, like *Charter* and *Chartist*, that he did not use in his letter. Rather than presenting himself as the leader of Chartism, he cast Chartism in a supporting role in the drama of Feargus O'Connor.

But he did write at greater length about Peel: 'You and I have been taught in early life to hold the name of Peel in execration', he reminded Frank (alluding to Peel's term as Secretary of State for Ireland, 1812–18). Now, however, Peel

is ... England's only great man. In their opposition they have nothing to stand before him. His first act comprehensively designated as his Tariff was the most statesmanlike, the most just, and the most comprehensive law ever proposed by a minister ... Peel is by no means the cruel man that we have been led to suppose. He attaches more importance to the character of the man than perhaps any statesman that ever lived before him, nor do I believe that he would hold office tomorrow at the expense of his personal character. True, I admit that a prime minister should be responsible for every act of his Cabinet. And that many bad ones have been committed during his administration, but in my opinion they have been forced upon him, by his less scrupulous colleagues.

Disraeli's memorable assessment of Peel's administration was that 'the Right Honourable Gentleman caught the Whigs bathing and walked away with their clothes'.[7] O'Connor similarly believed Peel's 1842 budget to have created jealousy and resentment among the Whig opposition; but he went much further, telling Frank that 'the master class under the Whig parliamentary influence' had tried to destabilise Peel's Government with 'an incipient revolution', the lock-outs that had led to the strike-wave that August. As we saw in chapter 7, the course and the causation of that phenomenon are too complex to be reduced to so simplistic and conspiratorial an explanation. That O'Connor believed this, however, is significant, particularly when read alongside his extraordinary encomium to Peel. His belief that the Government was led by a statesman of unparalleled integrity – almost a tacit ally in the struggle against the aristocracy, the master class and Whiggery – cannot but have influenced the direction and force of O'Connor's anti-establishment rhetoric.

Viewed alongside Peel's fiscal and other reforms, it is easier to understand why so many Chartists believed the land plan to represent the best way forward for Chartism – and, indeed, why O'Connor held out the hope that it might be something the Government would imitate. It is also noteworthy that insofar as Feargus revealed to Frank the tactics 'the people' under his leadership should now pursue, the focus was wholly on 'the next general election'. This would be 'a grand struggle between the Aristocracy and the unrepresented people. The aristocracy will endeavour to preserve the present limited franchise, while the people for their part will strain every nerve to share it with them, by the return to Parliament of a small number of their own friends, there to advocate their principles.' This had been Chartism's strategy at the 1841 election: its reiteration here reveals not only that O'Connor recognised that Chartism had little new to offer but that he was conceptualising the movement as, effectively, a pressure group. This term is thin and anachronistic when applied to Chartism in 1838–42, but rather less so in respect of the movement in the mid-1840s.

Another factor shaping Chartism in the late 1840s was the continuing saga of internal dissent, the unhappy escalation of which after 1842 was noted in chapter 8. The issues that swirled around the Dewsbury resolutions of December 1845 were resurrected in 1847 when Joshua Hobson came to a very public falling-out with O'Connor. Hobson's departure from the editorship of the *Northern Star* in November 1846 had not been marked by open enmity, but the following June he successfully sued O'Connor for breach of contract for dismissing him without notice. Then, towards the end of 1847, he took great exception to O'Connor criticising a land scheme developed by the NAUT. The Association had appointed Hobson and the Owenite George Fleming to draw up a plan for its agrarian operations and Hobson had emphasised its merits compared to (as he saw it) the Chartist land plan. Now, in letters to the *Manchester Examiner*, Hobson railed against O'Connor, claiming that he had siphoned-off £5,000 from the *Northern Star*, when it was based in Leeds, to support himself and was now taking land plan funds. Hobson concluded with a withering attack on the directors for failing to secure legal registration for the scheme.

This was the most sustained assault on the land plan from within Chartism thus far, and it attracted wide attention. A public meeting was organised in Manchester at which O'Connor faced his critics. Subscriptions were sent in from localities all over the country to fund a libel action against the *Examiner*, and the dispute was exhaustively covered for weeks, sometimes over more than a whole page, in the *Star*. William Lovett, not one suspects without a certain glee, had copies of the *Examiner* sent down from Manchester, carefully cutting out the relevant columns and making them up into a booklet.[8]

Hobson was not the first Chartist to criticise the scheme but he was the most prestigious. Others O'Connor mostly dismissed with a welter of detail about how he had subsidised Chartism since its inception and personally carried the burden of bad debts (of £3,400 he claimed) owed to the *Star* by defaulting newsagents. It is difficult to adjudicate on the veracity of these claims and counter claims. It was certainly the case that firm lines between the paper's, the land plan's and O'Connor's own finances were impossible to draw. Richard Oastler was probably close to the truth when he wrote that O'Connor 'is much more likely to spend his own money in *their* service, than to use *theirs* on his own account'; this certainly summed up the view of most Chartists. Private correspondence reinforces this conclusion: 'I am really in a pickle', O'Connor confessed privately in 1847, after receiving an unexpected demand for £167 Stamp Duty on land plan purchases.[9]

## Ernest Jones versus Thomas Cooper

The land plan's directors faced a recurrent problem in preventing critics from drawing lurid conclusions from the fact that purchases of estates were made in O'Connor's name. This legal stratagem was forced on them because, without official registration, the plan could not own real property. In 1846 Thomas Cooper had chided shareholders precisely because land purchases were made in O'Connor's 'own name, with your money and without asking your leave … Can you get this estate out of his hands when you choose? Echo answers, "Can you?"'[10] For good measure he added that the *Northern Star* was being secretly subsidised from land plan funds. For this, Cooper was summarily dismissed to the outer regions of Chartism, soundly defeated when he attempted to replace Wheeler as NCA general secretary and formally expelled from the NCA at its 1846 Convention. The expulsion motion was moved by a newcomer to Chartism, Ernest Jones, fresh from 'his maiden speech to his new allies' the previous day at the Blackstone Edge rally he described as 'the birthday of renewed Chartism'.[11]

Jones's role in the expulsion of Cooper had a symbolic quality, deriving from the status of the two as Chartist poets, Jones ascendant, Cooper in decline.[12] Many Chartists wrote poetry, but Cooper was one of a select group regularly contributing poems to the movement's papers. While in prison, 1843–45, he had written *The Purgatory of Suicides*. Although most Chartist poems prior to 1845 consisted of a few stanzas, typically ballads or another lyrical form, Cooper's 'Prison Rhyme' consisted of nearly 1,000 stanzas in the 9-line form used by the sixteenth-century poet Edmund Spenser for his epic *The Faerie Queene* and subsequently adopted by Keats, Byron and Shelley. Until 1843 Cooper was no more than a local leader within Chartism; but *Purgatory*, sprawling yet compelling, was a powerful claim to national status. Both within and beyond Chartism it was widely praised, not least by O'Connor and the *Northern Star*. Cooper was subsequently damning about O'Connor's role in helping the poem through to publication (alleging that though he facilitated its publication he failed to subsidise it as he had promised). However, Cooper conceded that O'Connor had 'made very intelligent criticisms' when *Purgatory* was in draft; and the *Star* ran lengthy extracts over twelve weeks when the poem was published in August 1845.[13]

Cooper, though, was a muscular intellectual with a sure sense of his own importance. He was happy to be lauded by the *Star* as 'the great poet of Chartism' but not at all prepared to yield to O'Connor's urging that he publicly support the land plan. *Purgatory* also represented a personal epiphany. It opened with a poetic rendering of Cooper's speech to the strike-torn Potteries on the night of 15 August 1842, and concluded with a resounding affirmation of 'the march of Thought', and 'the glorious power of Gentleness,/ Of Pity and Mercy, Goodness, Love, and Truth!', only to close with the poet still imprisoned and pondering 'when would come/ The day that goodness shall the earth renew … And when the Many cease their slavery to the Few.'

For O'Connor, despair was permissible in poetry but never in politics; when, early in 1846, Cooper developed a detailed philosophy of non-resistance (in, of all places, lectures to the National Association) a breach was inevitable. Cooper's opinions extended to denying any moral right to the use of violence in self-defence and attacking Chartist supporters of continental liberation movements as accessories to aggression. Dismissed by O'Connor as 'absolutely childish, if not idiotic', they were subjected by Harney to a lengthy and coruscating review in the *Star*: 'erroneous and absurd, we owe them no respect nor shall we pay them any'. Cooper demanded a printed retraction from Harney. When, predictably, this was denied, he turned to Feargus's old adversary *Lloyd's Weekly London Newspaper* and published a series of denunciations of O'Connor, 'his filthy *Star*' and the management of the land plan.

Fortuitously, the rapid tarnishing (in O'Connor's view) of Chartism's poet laureate overlapped the unheralded arrival of Ernest Jones. He appeared, literally proffering sheaves of poetry, in the *Northern Star*'s offices on 28 January 1846. Jones was a literary and political adventurer, with pretensions to aristocratic connection and aspirations to the wealth to match. There was some substance to the social pretensions (Jones's father had been *aide de camp* to Queen Victoria's uncle, the King of Hanover) but his financial aspirations were dashed with wearisome regularity. Too impatient to make a success of his career as a barrister, Jones had recently entertained hopes either of becoming a dramatist or of employment with the ACLL; but he then decided, whether on a whim or in desperation is unclear, to enlist in the Chartist cause.[14] He brought to Chartism an engaging blend of literary ability, charm and social cachet which he placed entirely at the service of the movement.

O'Connor warmly welcomed this unexpected infusion of talent and energy, and perhaps also the close comradeship of one who, uniquely within Chartism, he could regard as a social equal: by the end of 1846 they sometimes dined together 4 or 5 times a week. In May Jones was put forward for election to the NCA executive, the *Star* puffing his candidacy as that of a poet 'of talents which will make him a valuable acquisition to the democratic ranks. It is a glorious proof of the progress of democratic principles, that in spite of force and fraud, political and social persecution, such men as Mr Jones are avowing themselves as converts to Chartism.' His poetry was catapulted into the *Star* (and Cooper's as pointedly excluded) and soon after anthologised, first as *Chartist Poems* and then in a cheap edition as *Chartist Songs and Fugitive Pieces*. Jones himself, as we saw at the close of chapter 8, took centre-stage at the two most important Chartist meetings of summer 1846, at the traditional northern rallying ground of Blackstone Edge and at the People's First Estate, O'Connorville. In January 1847 he commenced editing, jointly with O'Connor, the *Labourer*, 'a Monthly Magazine of Politics, Literature, Poetry, &c', which was used to reinforce Chartism's claims to literary substance by publishing work of greater length than could be accommodated in a newspaper, and to promote both the NAUT and the land plan.[15]

Jones was again at O'Connorville in May 1847 as the first settlers arrived. The scheme appeared to be in good heart. Registration as a joint stock company had been initiated and a National Land and Labour Bank had been opened to attract further capital. A second estate, Lowbands in Worcestershire, had been purchased the previous October. Two more were purchased in June 1847, at Minster Lovell in Oxfordshire and Snigs End, Gloucestershire. Further ballots for allottees on these new estates had already been held. O'Connor spoke of locating 'some thousands' on the land within the next few years. Weekly income had just hit a new peak of £3,095, the list of subscribing localities filling two whole columns of the *Star*. Local branches celebrated 'England's May Day' with soirées, tea-parties, cricket matches, church bell-ringing and jubilant processions accompanying the first 'Chartist farmers' to O'Connorville and 'a happy home for honest industry'.[16]

The land plan had also enervated Chartism overall. Despite the movement's internal controversies, and the continuing buoyancy of the British economy, the momentum behind the land scheme was such that it pulled Chartism up with it. Even Cooper would soon concede that 'the wish to improve their condition by the possession of the land is taking root in the universal heart of the working classes'.[17] O'Connor enquired, with some justification,

> where Chartism would be but for the land? ... But for the land where would now be the Chartist executive or Chartist staff? The great advantage of the Land movement is this – that it supplies food for sensible agitation in good times and bad times. Good times have always been destructive of Chartism, but now assist it, because it is then that the working classes have the best opportunity of subscribing to the Land Plan; while bad times compel them to think about the land as the only means of escape.[18]

The nature of the plan also permitted the promulgation of some powerful messages. 'The National Land Company did not wish to carry the object by brute force, no', director Philip McGrath pointed out to a meeting in Bermondsey, 'they met in chapels to consult upon the best means of buying back the land, which had been unjustly taken from them.' The December 1846 land conference had decided that a schoolhouse would be built on every estate with masters and mistresses appointed by the directors but answerable to the colonists alone. The estates were also to be devoid of public houses and beershops, a situation to which land plan literature ostentatiously drew attention: 'LABOURERS BE SOBER. BUY LAND INSTEAD OF GIN; AND YOU WILL HAVE A GOVERNMENT OF YOUR OWN CHOICE', declaimed O'Connor in his 1846 Christmas message. The *Labourer*'s first foray into fiction was the story of a Chartist who had turned to drink after the failures of 1842, but then reformed so as to raise the subscription needed to join the land plan. 'That's not Charter', exclaims his wife, 'Charter was always getting thee into trouble.' ... 'Oh lass', rejoined Will, 'but it's Charter all the time, for only but for Charter the Land would never come up.'[19]

The land plan was also an opportunity to refute allegations that Chartism was indistinguishable from socialism. This was a point of some significance: as we saw in chapter 8, getting 'back to the land' had hitherto been most obviously associated with Owenism. 'Communism either destroys wholesome emulation and competition', O'Connor argued, or else it ends 'in the worst description of despotism – the despotism of self-surrender and non-reliance on self'. In terms of rebuilding links with middle-class radicals, this was shrewdly judged: an interesting reflection of this can be seen in the 1848 novel *Mary Barton*, in which Elizabeth Gaskell has a Chartist, John Barton, as the protagonist. Gaskell carefully and sympathetically contextualised Barton's resort to extreme violence, while she explicitly dissociated him from Owenism.[20]

## The general election of 1847

By emphasising education, temperance, political moderation and gradual constitutional change, it was almost as if the land plan was constructing a version of Chartism as it might have appeared had there been no fragmentation around 'the new move'. Furthermore, in the early months of 1847 the directors came close to espousing a version of 'household Chartism' through the claim that all male allottees would automatically be enfranchised. O'Connor painted a picture in which Worcestershire would be wrestled from Tory 'land-crabs' by 300 Chartist voters.[21] These claims were given additional relevance as it became increasingly apparent that a general election was likely. Six years before, a handful of Chartist candidates strode, determined but largely unprepared, into the general election (see Chapter 6). By common consent, the next time they would need to mount a concerted campaign.

The NCA executive had begun discussing the matter in early 1845, following an appeal from O'Connor to secure the return of 20–30 'Duncombeites' at the next election. Rapid urbanisation, and therefore increasing property values, were creating a situation in which registered voters could significantly expand. The system of confirming electoral rolls by a quasi-judicial process before a Revising Barrister also meant that the law was fluid and open to challenge and wide local variation. Though this could never enfranchise more than a handful of Chartists in any one place, since constituencies were generally small quite significant shifts in voting patterns could be effected through efficient registration.

Peel's brief resignation from office in December 1845–January 1846 prompted an emergency Convention, followed in the spring by plans to levy a special subscription on NCA members to meet the costs of an election campaign. In particular, the executive called for the ACLL and the Whigs 'to be met on the hustings, and unmasked in the presence of the people'. 'Hurrah! then for DUNCOMBE', commented *Northern Star*, 'for Labour and the Convention and D––n the expense.' A similar message was expounded following the repeal of the Corn Laws. The requirement that MPs, on appointment to the Cabinet, offer themselves for re-election made possible several by-election challenges when Russell formed his ministry in Peel's place. White in Leeds and O'Connor in Nottingham mounted spirited hustings challenges but, predictably, only Vincent proceeded to poll (at Plymouth, where he took just over a fifth of the votes cast in a straight fight against the Lord of the Treasury). O'Connor was emboldened to predict the election of at least twelve actual Chartist candidates at the next general election, 'with Mr. Duncombe as our leader'.[22]

Registration, however, was time consuming and costly. Up to the summer of 1846, the Revising Barrister for Manchester, for example, rejected 450 claims put forward by Chartists, 'and they were not prepared with the means to carry the question into a court of law'. A large proportion of the 3,000 claims put forward by Chartists in Birmingham were similarly disallowed. So in September 1846 the NCA established a National Central Registration and Election Committee (NCREC) under Duncombe's presidency. Chartism now had an active co-ordinating body preparing for the next election. Together with the NAUT, registration became an effective counterweight to the land plan in the columns of the *Northern Star*, though the same personnel tended to be active in more than one area, Duncombe in the NAUT and NCREC, and Thomas Clark and the London Chartists William Cuffay and Edmund Stallwood in the NCREC and the land plan. Thomas Clark, the Irish-born cotton weaver who was an energetic member of both the NCA executive and the land plan directors, thought that 200,000 might be added to the electorate 'if the working classes exerted themselves with judgment'. This, however, was hardly a realistic figure when the combined British electorate was 973,000.[23]

The pattern of NCREC activities was quickly established. Its weekly meetings dealt with all NCA correspondence regarding parliamentary elections; advised localities on registration issues; systematically worked through Commons division lists on key votes to identify MPs who might be supported and others who were to be opposed; approached Chartist localities to suggest particular Chartists who might stand in their constituencies; administered a fund built up from donations and subscriptions, disbursing sums to local Chartist registration committees as appropriate. It was never intended that candidates had explicitly to declare themselves Chartists to receive support. Thus in February 1847 Colonel Perronet Thompson received a £5 donation towards registration expenses at Bradford. The NCREC did require, though, that candidates from outside the movement agree to support the implementation of the Charter in any parliamentary division.[24] It also mounted a brief campaign for repeal of the rating clauses of the 1832 Reform Act: even those holding property of the requisite value to confer the vote were disqualified if they were in arrears of rates. Only 38 MPs, however, supported Duncombe's parliamentary motion on the issue.[25]

Local registration committees harried or supported sitting MPs as necessary and saw to the detail of registration at constituency level. How effectively this was done it is impossible to judge. These committees were quick to publicise triumphs as, for example, when Deptford Chartists invited their local MP to attend a public meeting, to defend his Commons voting record, and predictably he failed to turn up. But the backroom work undertaken by such groups can only be guessed at. However, a letter detailing the *modus operandi* of a Liberal Reform Association in Rochdale provides some insight:

> When the time comes to see about the payment of rates, the Secretary goes to the Overseers' Books (as a ratepayer he can do this, & in the Townships in which he is not he gets someone else to do it if the Overseer be a Tory & refuse, but that is not our case) and copies the names of such of our friends as have not paid – he then calls upon the defaulters, persuades them to pay up – if too poor, he lends them money, but *always is repaid by them* – he also sees that the Registration Shilling is paid, and examines the rate Book to discover if any of our friends can be placed upon the register who have heretofore been omitted.[26]

It is unlikely that Chartist localities would have been so thorough and inconceivable that they could either pay a secretary £25 yearly for his troubles or retain a solicitor to mount challenges in the Revising Barrister's court, both of which the Rochdale RA did. The Chartist challenge at the general election of 1847 was better prepared than in 1841, but it was inevitably made more in hope than expectation. An early indicator, were it needed, was to be found in the Derby by-election on 16 June where McGrath made an impressive showing at the hustings; but when his Liberal opponent was declared elected and McGrath demanded a poll, the Mayor's instant riposte was: 'let me have your money then, I am entitled in fees to your share to the amount of £23 10s. Let me have your money before we proceed.' Amid scenes of 'great confusion' McGrath declined and the Mayor declared the Honourable Frederick Leveson-Gower, Liberal, elected.[27]

The following week the general election began in earnest. O'Connor called for 'a glorious month of resurrection … our SACRED MONTH – sacred not to idleness, but sacred to Labour in Freedom's cause'. Yet his own attitude to the election was studiously casual. One cannot but question the judgement of someone who spent most of July digging and manuring the Lowbands' estate 'for swedes and white turnips', he announced in the *Star*, rather than participate in the election. O'Connor appeared in few constituencies and did not attend even the great annual Blackstone Edge rally on 11 July, claiming that the organisers had failed to send a welcome party to collect him ('I had a right to expect the committee to send to me'). There was, however, a conspicuous exception, Norwich, where O'Connor made a special journey to support the candidate Chartists endorsed. He, however, withdrew without explanation shortly before O'Connor arrived. Feargus was not amused: 'this picking up and hawking about of candidates, upon the modest assurance that they will condescend to represent us, is positively a disgrace to our cause'. The incident

demonstrated the frailty of the NCREC's authority over the candidates it agreed
to support. Norwich Chartists had undertaken a full canvass of every ward and
their efforts seemed wasted until, ten days before the hustings, the National
Association's treasurer, William Lovett's friend John Humffreys Parry, arrived
to challenge the sitting Liberal and Tory candidates. The Chartists were sufficiently organised and confident to demand a poll, and, although Parry lost,
he polled 1,572 votes, trailing the Tory by only 155. Parry trimmed his support
for the Charter by advocating only triennial parliaments, but that he was the
Chartist candidate was never in doubt.[28]

The other seat Chartists felt most confident of winning was Halifax, where
Jones was their candidate. Anti-state church politics were an important factor
here. Halifax's radical dissenters formed a tactical alliance with the Chartists
to contest the two-member constituency against a Tory and a Whig–Liberal
(Chancellor of the Exchequer Sir Charles Wood). The contest revived memories of complete suffragism, for the dissenters' candidate (describing himself
as a 'Radical') was Edward Miall. So effective were Miall and Jones that Wood
was forced into running a joint campaign with the Conservative. In terms of
personal presentation there was no contest between the rival pairs of candidates.
'Miall was a splendid speaker, full of wit and humour, and a close reasoner', the
Chartist Ben Wilson recalled; 'Jones had a powerful voice with a musical ring;
he was the finest speaker I had ever heard.' However, there were tensions in
the radical–Chartist camp: Chartist exclusive dealing extended beyond simply
boycotting unsympathetic tradesmen to 'crowds of people congregating in
front of their shops and hooting their customers'. Eventually Miall's committee
issued a sharp notice that the election should be 'conducted in such a manner as
will least interrupt any social relationships ... good neighbourhood and perfect
political freedom'. Relationships were particularly soured by the sudden death
of a prominent Whig–Liberal employer while speaking at an election meeting
packed by Chartist hecklers. Wilson recalled that exclusive dealing made the
fortunes of several Halifax tradesmen and publicans for years to come; but
it was a delicate question whether Chartist tactics ultimately alienated more
voters than they secured. Miall came third by a margin of 158 votes, with Jones
a further 69 behind.[29]

Nine radical–Liberal candidates endorsed by the NCREC were elected.[30] At
Marylebone the approved candidate withdrew before the poll. Robert Owen,
without endorsement, took his place, lost convincingly at the hustings and
then polled just one vote. Unendorsed candidates supporting Chartism stood
at Northampton and Tavistock where Samuel Carter carried the hustings
along with Henry Vincent, even though the latter failed to turn up. However,
the greatest disappointment attached to the outcome of those elections where
Chartists, like Jones, won the hustings but went on to defeat at the poll: Thomas
Clark at Sheffield, McGrath at Derby, W. P. Roberts at Blackburn, John West at

Stockport and Vincent at Ipswich. As in 1841 there were some notable hustings performances. Harney sealed his reputation as a politician of substance at Tiverton, confronting the Foreign Secretary Lord Palmerston with a dissection of his foreign policy that forced Palmerston to improvise a lengthy and detailed rebuttal. Harney won the hustings but did not go to the poll, as was the case also with the Chartist challengers at Derby, Dudley, Greenwich, South Shields, Wigan, Greenock and Aberdeen. The last two were the only Scottish constituencies where there was any election activity. 'Where are the Chartist candidates for Scotland? What is Glasgow about?' asked the *Northern Star*: Dundee and Paisley Chartists tried but failed to find a qualified candidate; no other Scottish locality even involved itself in the election.[31]

One Chartist, however, *was* elected to Parliament in 1847: Feargus O'Connor, in Nottingham. Despite the volatility of Nottingham elections and his hustings victory at the 1846 by-election, this had not been predicted. At its final meeting before polling began, the NCREC noted 'the moral certainty of Mr. Ernest Jones's return', and voted further funds accordingly; informed of an 'increasing prospect' at Nottingham, it simply wrote back with the assurance 'of its best support'. Similarly it was not Nottingham but Halifax that the *Northern Star* had in its sights, devoting an entire editorial to the contest, something done for no other constituency. O'Connor barely campaigned (in contrast to Clark, Jones McGrath and Roberts, who removed to their constituencies some weeks before polling). Having issued an address as early as the first week of June, Feargus spent most of the ensuing seven weeks on land plan business, never addressing a meeting in the town until the night before the hustings.

The *Star* did not even send a reporter to cover Nottingham. The account printed in a hurriedly compiled late edition on 31 July was lifted entirely from *The Times*. Since voting was public, the relative standing of candidates could be calculated at regular intervals during polling. Two hours before voting closed, O'Connor had fewer votes than the other three candidates. He benefited, though, from a unique combination of factors. First his opponents were even more off-hand than he in their approach to the election: the two sitting Whig candidates neither canvassed nor spoke in the constituency before the hustings, while the Tory never turned up. Second, the bulk of O'Connor's support came from those who supported him along with the Tory. O'Connor attracted few disgruntled Whig voters and would clearly have lost had either a second Tory contested the election or a Whig withdrawn. Third, Nottingham's Chartists deployed experience accumulated from seven earlier parliamentary contests. Prompted by his 'little general', the local Chartist secretary James Sweet, O'Connor emphasised local issues and a trail of broken promises by local Whig MPs extending back to 1818. Finally, the absence of the Tory candidate (whose father was dying) gave O'Connor free rein to mould the anti-Whig position entirely to his own liking. The split between Peelites and protectionists that damaged Conservatism elsewhere hardly appeared. O'Connor espoused protectionist measures to assist the local framework-knitting industry and praised 'the great reformer' Sir Robert Peel, 'who had the daring and the boldness to grapple with truth'. Feargus did not so much win his seat as have it gifted to him by his opponents, but in the ensuing euphoria few cared or even noticed.[32]

The 1847 general election was important in providing a platform for Chartism to reassert its core political objectives and shake off too-close an identification between it and the land plan. O'Connor alone, pledging to 'struggle to make the Small Farm System a Government measure, according to the rules of the National Land Company', alluded to the plan by name in his election address. Other Chartist candidates adhered closely to a common programme, drawn up by the NCREC, which confined discussion of agrarian issues simply to 'an extension of the small proprietary system' and repeal of primogeniture and entail (legal reforms intended to free up the market for land). At the programme's heart was what the Chartist church pastor John McRae at Greenock referred to as 'the great Charter of your liberties', involving a pledge, if returned, to submit to re-election each year. Calls to separate Church and State, and for a voluntary system of education (as opposed to state subsidies paid mainly to Anglican schools) were aimed at nonconformist electors. Other measures included restoration of Church property to the purpose of poor relief; the abolition of the New Poor Law; the repeal of the game laws; the abolition of capital punishment; an extension of direct taxation and free trade; and opposition to British participation in 'all foreign wars, not rendered necessary for self defence, or the purposes of humanity'. Some, like Irishman John West at Stockport, also advocated self-government for Ireland.[33]

As always, there was also the opportunity to expose the intrinsic unfairness of the existing electoral system and frequent class discrimination in its administration. Even Whig newspapers felt unable to endorse the Mayor's decision at the Derby hustings that the vote was won by the Whig candidates. At Wolverhampton, Samuel Cooke was refused permission even to speak at the hustings without a surety to cover the returning officer's expenses. In Dudley an attempt was made to prevent Joseph Linney speaking unless he could prove he was qualified to sit as an MP. Tavistock's returning officer sought to limit those voting at the hustings to propertied electors only, until Carter the Chartist candidate forcibly intervened to point out that this was illegal. In Swansea the Chartist George Cudlippe mercilessly taunted the sole Liberal candidate at the hustings (returned unopposed for the district no less than six times, 1832–52), before concluding, 'I see this will be a one-sided Parliament, a rich man's Parliament.'[34]

The general election came at a crucial time for Chartism. Although the land plan had helped sustain it through the mid-1840s, the movement needed an opportunity to reaffirm its central purposes. Participation in the election provided this even when there was no Chartist to support. In Bath a determined effort was made to see off a Conservative challenge on the basis that isolated social reforms were no substitute for even a partial transfer of political power, to which the Liberal was committed. Colchester's NCA branch was revived to campaign for a Whig against a Tory who had vowed 'to defend the constitution against the attacks of Whigs, Radicals, Repealers, Chartists and Socialists'. In return for their support, Bury St Edmunds Chartists extracted a promise from the Whig to vote for a free pardon for Frost, Williams and Jones.[35]

However, O'Connor's success at Nottingham obscured the fact that the outcome of the 1847 election fell well below Chartists' expectations: 9 NCREC-approved Liberals were successful compared to the 6 claimed as 'Chartists' in 1841. But O'Connor had called for 20–30 'Duncombeite' MPs, of whom 12 would be avowed Chartists. In the event, the movement brought to the polls only 2 more candidates (8) than it had done at the 1841 general election; more critically, it had candidates at far fewer hustings (16 against 33). Chartism's depleted strength was particularly apparent in Scotland but by no means exclusively so: there were hustings challenges in six fewer English constituencies.[36]

The election also exposed tensions in the movement. Carlisle Chartists refused on principle to get involved in the election, much to the *Star*'s disgust. In Leeds, memories of the complete suffrage movement were very much alive and controversy dogged the endorsement of Joseph Sturge, despite 'his entire concurrence in every point contained in the People's Charter'. Bristol Chartists were criticised for supporting an anti-State Church candidate who favoured five points of the Charter but only triennial parliaments. Yet this was precisely the position of Muntz and Scholfield in Birmingham, widely seen as renegades for deserting the 1839 Convention yet endorsed by the NCREC. Even the *Northern Star* was ambivalent about exclusive dealing:

> The Electors themselves are harassed by the exclusive privilege they possess. All long for the BALLOT, many for the CHARTER. They look for this to screen them from the arrows of party hate – and so wretched is the system that numbers run away at an election time, others intentionally disqualify themselves, and many boldly refuse to vote at all, since they cannot do so with safety.[37]

The total funds raised by the NCREC paled by comparison to even a single week's income for the land plan. Its balance sheet for the election revealed that although 297 localities contributed, its total income was only £470 (compared to over £1,420 for the land plan in the week of publication alone); also that it was able to make direct contributions to only 7 constituency campaigns, averaging under £32 each. Expenditure at Nottingham was £95 but most of this was incurred retrospectively in the form of gifts to O'Connor's committeemen.[38]

There were criticisms that land plan members were apathetic about the election. Only in Leicester did the local NCA and the land plan branch combine to mount an election campaign, securing the nomination of their leader at the hustings. There was also an understandable reluctance on the part of many Chartists to be seen to take the electoral process too seriously. An element of this was evident in O'Connor's conduct and certainly in Vincent's. After his poor performance at Ipswich, Suffolk Chartists concluded that Vincent 'had deserted ... workingmen'. In Worcester, 'the Chartist candidate' Robert Hardy lost the election by 214 votes. In the half-admiring, half-critical words of a *Star* reporter, Hardy 'did not canvass a single elector, employ a single lawyer, or spend one shilling; he is not an eloquent speaker'.[39]

Nor was Chartism's new MP a particularly adept parliamentarian. This was of practical significance, for Duncombe, a chronic asthmatic, was seriously ill during the election and played little part in Westminster affairs for the next two years. O'Connor's presence in the Commons therefore had an even greater totemic value; but totemic rather than substantial is what it largely remained. He was seldom other than immersed in land plan business: his tendency to exaggerate not much to the fore when he described himself as 'Bailiff, Contractor, Architect, Engineer, Surveyor, Farmer, Dung-Maker, Cow and Pig Jobber, Milkman, Horse Jobber, and Member of Parliament'.[40] O'Connor lacked Duncombe's skill as a parliamentary operator, and was too much the individualist ever to attempt to form the 'Duncombeite' circle he had once argued was necessary. Indeed, his habit of sitting with Peel, Disraeli, the Marquis of Granby and other Tories symbolised his uneasy relationships not only with Whigs but with radical Liberals; and it ran contrary to the growing disposition of Chartists to make common cause with sympathetic Liberals.[41]

## Internationalism

Similarly symbolic was O'Connor's distance from the burgeoning internationalist dimension of Chartism. It had always been actively aware of continental radicalisms, especially in London where many European exiles made their homes. In 1844 Lovett had founded the short-lived Democratic Friends of All Nations, short-lived because a somewhat patronising inaugural 'Address to the Friends of Humanity and Justice among all Nations' warned sternly against 'outbreaks of violence'. European refugees, from the subject nations of the Austro-Hungarian and Russian empires especially, tended not to share Lovett's 'faith in the mental and moral combinations of men being able to achieve victories for humanity beyond the force of armies'. London's *émigré* associations declined to become involved and the organisation folded.[42] Something of its spirit was revived, however, in the People's International League (formed November 1847), though Lovett was only briefly involved, believing it to be too extreme. The League's council brought together several Chartists who were estranged from the NCA (Cooper, Parry, Vincent, W. J. Linton and James Watson) with NCREC-endorsed MPs. It was closely associated with the capital's Italian community, centred on Giuseppe Mazzini.[43]

However this social and political axis was atypical of Chartist internationalism. More characteristic was the 'No vote! No musket!!' campaign of 1846, when the possibility briefly arose of war with the United States (over the Oregon territory) and a Militia Bill was proposed in Parliament. The campaign mixed obvious self-interest with expressions of solidarity with the workers of the American republic. Incidentally it was almost the last political gasp of the National Association.[44] This campaign was transitory. The bedrock of Chartist internationalism was the Fraternal Democrats: larger, livelier and longer lived than any similar organisation, it attracted a broader membership reflecting mainstream Chartism and had a provincial dimension. It had emerged in 1845 and its membership overlapped the NCA's.

The range of Chartists involved was considerable: it included the NCA executive and land plan stalwarts Clark, Jones, and McGrath; also provincial leaders, like Macclesfield's John West, who formed a network through which pamphlets on international issues were disseminated outside London. The driving force was Harney, whose earlier exuberant reverence for the French Revolution had matured into an impassioned but disciplined commitment to the cause of universal brotherhood. Harney's links with London's Polish community extended back to the earliest days of the LDA, but the Fraternal Democrats' main affiliates were La Société Democratique Française and the cognate German association in the capital which actually included Dutch, Flemish, Russian, Scandinavian and Turkish members. After the Cracow insurgency of 1846, the Democratic Committee for the Regeneration of Poland emerged under the presidency, first, of McGrath and then of Jones. This effectively operated as a subsidiary of the Fraternal Democrats. Popular Russophobia guaranteed particular sympathy for Polish nationalism in Britain, and 'friends of Poland' were to be found in many Chartist localities. Even O'Connor was prevailed on to become the committee's (largely titular) treasurer.[45]

O'Connor contributed to the Fraternal Democrats mainly by giving Harney a free hand to develop the *Northern Star*'s foreign coverage and by occasional appearances at its larger meetings: 'I have invariably declared that I cared not where the country, what the colour, or which the creed, of the patriot was', he stated on one occasion, 'if he loved liberty and struggled for it, I would call him brother and take him by the hand.' This probably summarised the opinion of most Chartists; but so too did O'Connor's disinclination to exert much energy beyond the occasional amicable gesture. 'CHARTISTS MUST ADMIT OF NO FOREIGN QUESTION OR QUARRELS OR DISPUTES, BEING MIXED UP WITH YOUR CAUSE', he declaimed in one of his regular *Northern Star* letters;

'let Frenchmen work for France, Russians for Russia and Prussians for Prussia. I WILL WORK FOR HOME SWEET HOME.'[46]

In fairness to O'Connor, he wrote this in the midst of the general election, in which Chartism's opponents were none-too fastidious in distinguishing the movement from continental revolutions. O'Connor was not innately xeno-phobic: he travelled widely on the Continent and in 1845 wrote a series of substantial letters on peasant farming during a European tour. He did, however, share in the broad mood of anti-Semitism that manifestly disfigured English nineteenth-century radicalism. 'Jew' as a synonym for money-lender crops up in his 1844 book *The Employer and the Employed*, while in 1841, reviewing his record as MP for Cork (1832–35), O'Connor regretted nothing except voting to permit Jews to become MPs: 'not that I hate a Jew, but because I dread the influence of his money', O'Connor elaborated, 'I would now rather see the devil than a Jew walking into the House of Commons'.[47]

Many Chartists probably supposed that Jews sat in the Commons already: the Jewish financier featured routinely in radical demonising of 'old corrup-tion' earlier in the century, a political demonology that persisted into the Chartist movement. The great banner of the Wigan RA depicted O'Connor on one side and on the reverse 'the British Lion, rampant ... trampling Under foot Starvation Bastilles, Debts, Funds, [and] Jew Jobbers'. When Reginald Richardson contested the 1841 election in Perth he was cheered when he condemned his opponent 'because the Jews held his masters, the ministry, in bonds – because the Jews were fund-holders, stock-brokers, and loan-mongers'. John Campbell's widely admired book on the Corn Laws depicted 'the present iniquitous system' as built on laws 'enacted by landlords, parsons, Jews, bankers, brokers, manufacturers, merchants, lawyers, shopkeepers and others'; and unabashed anti-Semitism was readily apparent in the pages of the *Northern Liberator*.[48]

Chartist anti-Semitism was casual and economic rather than racialist or systemic. The most blatant anti-Semitism belonged to Chartism's earliest years, though occasional barbs about 'Jewocracy' and 'Jew Jobbers' persisted, espe-cially in Chartist fiction.[49] The broadly educative function of Chartism and the widened intellectual horizons of its members helped stem the worst excesses of anti-Semitic sentiment. Here the Fraternal Democrats played an important role. Their strong socialist leanings reinforced an economic perspective that did not hinge on the caricature of old corruption. This in itself diminished the scope to lampoon Jewry.

Meanwhile, among the German *émigrés* brought into the orbit of Chartism by the Fraternal Democrats were a number of secular Jews, notably Dr Charles Marx, 'a celebrated writer on political economy and social philosophy', commented the *Northern Star*.[50] Karl Marx, as he was soon better known, first visited Britain – and Harney – in 1845, then again in 1847. In 1846 he co-authored fulsome pieces for the *Star*, praising O'Connor and 'the only English paper worth reading for the continental democrats'. In November 1847 Marx spoke at the Fraternal Democrats' celebration of the 1830 Polish revolution, in German, but with a simultaneous translation greeted with 'tremendous cheering' for these sentiments: 'the Chartists of England were the real democrats ... the moment they carried the six points of that Charter, the road to liberty would be open to the whole world. Effect that grand object, then, you working men of England, and you will be hailed as the saviours of the whole human race.'[51]

It is important not to read back into that 1847 meeting a spurious significance based on the subsequent eminence of this speaker. At the time it was just one among many meetings involving Fraternal Democrats which heightened the awareness of London audiences, and a national Chartist readership, of political events in continental Europe. The Fraternal Democrats were essential, alongside the land plan and the 1847 general election, in reviving the movement after the precarious years of the mid-1840s. As the summer of 1847 drew to an end there was a strong sense within Chartism that it was poised for a major revival. Weekly sales of the *Northern Star*, which had slumped to 6,000 in 1846, now matched those of 1842.[52] O'Connor once again spoke of the need for a daily paper, this time to be called *Democrat*. Magnanimous in victory, he presented his Nottingham triumph as the movement's rather than his own and called 'for a reunion of all the dissevered elements of Chartism. The O'Briens, Lovetts, Vincents, Coopers, and all. Now is the time, if their honest fears have been dissipated, to return to the popular embrace and join in a national jubilee.' To a limited extent there was some *rapprochement*: O'Connor, Cooper, O'Brien and Vincent appeared together at a gala celebrating George Thompson's election, and the following February John Collins appeared on a general Chartist platform for the first time since 1842. As in 1841, it was agreed to test the new Parliament with a further Petition for the Charter to be submitted in May 1848: petition sheets were circulated from late August and plans laid for a new National Convention to oversee the campaign. Victorian parliamentary timetables, however, were relaxed and Parliament did not assemble until November. So O'Connor took the opportunity to organise a national tour, raising funds for the Convention and collecting Petition signatures, and to travel abroad for three weeks' holiday. He must have sensed a new mood in Chartism because he went to some lengths to detail his movements, 'lest a revolution should be at hand, and lest as in the Newport affair it might be supposed I have absconded to avoid it'. The same issue of the *Northern Star* reported reduced working hours and mill closures in Ashton-under-Lyne and discussions among Lancashire workers concerning what action to take in response to a slump in the industry's fortunes.[53]

## A quickening pulse

Economic vicissitude provided the final ingredient for a Chartist revival in 1847–48. Chartism's arguments carried greatest weight and attracted widest support in circumstances of economic misfortune. Trades in decline or under pressure from developing mass production were disproportionately represented in Chartist ranks, while the years of highest commodity prices were ones in which Chartist mobilisation peaked. Thus the years from 1838 to 1841, when the average price of home grown wheat per quarter never fell below 64s 4d (and 1842 when prices averaged 60s until that year's abundant harvest) were years when Chartism flourished. Average domestic wheat prices for 1843–45 did not exceed 51s 3d and an increase in 1846 still brought it only to 54s 8d. But in 1847 this important economic indicator reached 69s 9d, a price not exceeded since the portentous year of 1819. Commodity prices also leapt overall by around 12.5 per cent in 1847, to a level unequalled since 1841.[54]

Statistics can obscure important sectoral and regional variations, as well as the lived reality of human experience. So it is worth noting that the cotton industry was a heavy and early casualty of the downturn in the economy: nearly half of Manchester's factory labour force was on short-time or laid-off completely in March. Though the situation improved over the summer, it then soared in the autumn to the extent that barely a third were working full-time by November. Abundant American cotton harvests in the mid-1840s came to an abrupt end in 1845 and 1846, the latter coinciding with a downturn in demand for cotton goods. Bankruptcies in the cotton sector were high. These in turn helped reinforce a general commercial crisis in October 1847 which severely depleted Bank of England reserves, saw the bank rate leap from 5 to 8 per cent and the Government suspend the Bank Charter Act.[55]

The midlands textile districts were also badly hit. Poor relief expenditure in Leicester over the winter of 1847–48 exceeded 1842's. A Nottingham curate estimated in April 1848 that less than half the workmen in his parish had been employed full-time during the previous twelve months. Nottingham's workhouse was crammed beyond its official capacity and in addition to its 1,600 inmates several thousands more were receiving outdoor relief. London, largely insulated from the economic depression of 1838–42, felt that of 1847–48 especially severely. *The Times's* journalist Henry Reeve noted 'remarkable depression' in his diary as the old year ended: 'general illness; great mortality; innumerable failures; funds down to 76; want of money; no society at all'. Lower down the social scale the cabinetmakers' trade society spent more money on relief for unemployed members in 1847 than at any time since 1842; and its 1848 spending was higher than for any year since 1834.[56] On the other hand the woollen and linen industries buckled under the immediate impact of the October crisis, but were otherwise fairly buoyant. However, as

Halifax Chartist Ben Wilson later recalled, 'in this year flour was very dear, reaching the price of 5s. per stone, whilst trade was also very bad. This was the time to make politicians, as the easiest way to get to an Englishman's brains is through his stomach. It was said by its enemies that Chartism was dead and buried and would never rise again, but they were doomed to disappointment.'[57]

The pattern of activity Wilson went on to describe drew a careful contrast with 1839: there were no mass meetings or processions, but instead a purposeful buzz of lower level activity: '*The Northern Star* was their principal paper, and it was a common practice, particularly in villages, to meet at friends' houses and talk over political matters.' In an open letter to Chartism's 'old guards', 'an old pioneer' spoke of Chartism as 'a thousand times more fashionable' than it had been in the autumn of 1842, 'the country never was in such a state than it is now ... these are events favourable to the bringing forth of our claims for a full measure of social justice'.[58] In its first editorial of the New Year, the *Star* summarised the situation thus:

> Throughout England, lectures, public meetings, and assemblages of local delegates, attest that the 'dry bones' are once more quickening into life and action. The very numerously attended and enthusiastic meetings recently holden in the metropolis, exhibit a most hopeful sign of the times.[59]

The quickening pulse of the capital was a welcome development. Torpid in 1838–39 and only partially politicised in 1842, London was at last playing a part in Chartism commensurate with its great size.

Nationally, however, though the revival of Chartism's fortunes was plain to see, levels of activity thus far failed to match those of 1842. Since the NCREC made an appeal retrospectively to meet the costs of the 1847 election campaign, the balance sheet it published on 1 January 1848 provides a good guide to the relative strength of the movement. Of 297 localities contributing, only 6 were in Wales and 22 in Scotland. Lancashire, Cheshire and West Yorkshire were the regions of greatest density, with Manchester comfortably heading the table of donations (£42), trailed by London (£14) and Stockport (£10). Only two contributions were received from the Potteries. More money was raised by ex-patriot workers in Boulogne than in the entire Spen Valley of Yorkshire. Sheffield managed only 2s 6d, Trowbridge, Coventry and Sunderland nothing. There were new nodes of activity, notably Swindon, but they hardly compensated for ground lost.[60]

Only the land plan truly astonished observers that winter, despite the background blaring of O'Connor's dispute with Hobson and a spat with engineering unions which had intervened to prevent branches investing in the National Land and Labour Bank.[61] In August, the second land plan estate had opened at Lowbands. Preparations at both Snigs End and Minster Lovell were well advanced and negotiations progressing for the purchase of a fifth estate at Dodford, 12 miles south-west of Birmingham.

The opening of Lowbands coincided with the annual conference of the land plan at which it was agreed that O'Connor should be sole proprietor of the Bank. This followed legal advice that a joint stock company could not own the bank to which it mortgaged its property. Even by the standards of the Chartist land plan this was an unusual development; but Feargus was walking tall from his election victory and of subscriptions to the scheme there was seemingly no end. Weekly takings were routinely in excess of £1,000 and sometimes even £2,000. There were now 283 branches in England, 36 in Scotland, 10 in Wales and one each in Jersey, Rouen and Boulogne. In August the scheme boasted more than 40,000 shareholders; by February 1848 there were around 30,000 more, spurred to enrol by the conference's decision to close the company to new members on 31 December 1847.[62] The directors therefore launched a second company in January, but reactions to this proposal were equivocal. Some influential localities argued against it on the grounds that it breached conference decisions and that the resources did not exist to manage further expansion. This judgement was soon vindicated when the directors admitted that they did not know exactly how many subscribers there were.[63]

It is a moot point whether the land plan was now helping or hindering the re-growth of Chartism. There was, however, a clear leap in Chartist newspaper publishing: after the doldrums of 1845–46 when only 6 titles were published, there were 10 in 1847 and 20 in 1848. The new National Petition was often mentioned yet there was little sense that it lay at the heart of the movement. Early in January O'Connor cancelled a much-trumpeted tour of Scotland, pleading pressure of business, but also poor health, which for some weeks had rendered him 'utterly incapable of undertaking a journey' (he blamed influenza). It was hastily arranged therefore that McDouall should become the NCA representative in Scotland 'to forward the National Petition'. Similar appointments were made to north-east England, the midlands and the Pennines textile region, a belated and only partial reinstatement of the network of full-time missionaries the NCA employed earlier in the decade.

More encouraging was the close relationship English Chartists were building up with the Irish Confederation, a nationalist organisation which had seceded from O'Connell's Repeal Association shortly before his death in 1847. It was led by William Smith O'Brien, MP for County Limerick. Chartist attitudes were initially cool: Harney, for example, believed that O'Brien's circle desired merely 'an Irish middle-class supremacy dignified by a national flag'. In Ireland itself relations between the Chartist Irish Universal Suffrage Association and the Confederation were strained. Thomas Meagher, co-founder of the Confederation, boasted that he was no democrat; in May 1847 William Dyott, secretary of IUSA, resigned in frustration from the Dublin Confederate Club, alleging that voices like his were suppressed and accusing the broader non-O'Connellite Young Ireland movement of 'a spurious sort of Nationality, which expends itself in frothy abuse of England and unmeaning panegyric of ourselves'. O'Connor warmed to a similar theme, albeit with more restraint than Dyott, criticising prominent figures in Young Ireland and arguing that to repeal the Union without first enacting the Charter would merely mean a 'House of Landlords' sitting in Dublin.[64]

Dublin's discipline over Confederate clubs in England, however, was slender. Furthermore their social composition was anything but middle-class. The death of O'Connell in May 1847 had removed the fundamental obstacle to closer co-operation between British Chartists and Irish nationalists. Harney turned the *Northern Star* into the paper of record for English Confederates, especially their nine clubs in the capital, but also those in Barnsley, Birmingham, Liverpool, Manchester, Southampton, Stalybridge and Wolverhampton. Although he was English, the former NCA president James Leach contrived to represent Manchester at the Confederates' first annual conference in January 1848. He was well-received. Meanwhile in the Commons (where the number of Irish nationalists had nearly halved at the general election) O'Connor proved a valuable advocate for Irish issues, leading Meagher – 'although I am no Chartist' – publicly to thank him. The links between Chartism and Irish nationalism were further strengthened in February 1848 when the ultra-radical Young Irelander John Mitchel commenced a newspaper, the *United Irishman*, which circulated widely among English Chartists. The London-based Irish Democratic Confederate Club grew close to the Cripplegate branch of the land plan and boasted O'Connor as its president. Symbolically, on St Patrick's Day 1848, a working alliance between English Chartists and militant Irish nationalism was finally put in place at a mass rally in Manchester, attended by O'Connor, Meagher and other members of the Confederates' council. Henceforward Smith O'Brien would be closely identified with Chartism.[65]

Newspapers spoke facetiously of the 'nuptials of Chartism and Repeal'. However, with Ireland racked by the famine and European developments creating grave concern, the prospect of a Confederate–Chartist alliance was an alarming one for the Government. Intelligence suggested Confederalism was not merely froth and panegyric. Among the Liverpool Irish especially, elements of the violent and conspiratorial pre-famine protest movement the Ribbon Men still survived. English Confederates were drilling with pikes; some openly boasted of obtaining firearms.[66] Through the *Northern Star*, Harney and O'Connor consistently sought to promote Irish–Chartist solidarity by linking misgovernment in Ireland with an undemocratic Parliament in Westminster, arguing in particular that the famine was exacerbated by British misrule, 'evidence of their unfitness longer to continue its rulers'.[67]

It is a challenge for us to understand the depth of 'polite' English contempt for, and fear of, the Irish; but combined with apprehension about resurgent Chartism they formed a potent brew. What polite society knew of Chartism came largely through its newspapers and well-thumbed copies of Thomas Carlyle's 'glorious piece of work' *Chartism* (the description was John Stuart Mill's). It now re-read in a new and awful light chapter 4, and Carlyle's jeremiad on the 'crowds of miserable Irish [who] darken all our towns', 'sunk from decent manhood to squalid apehood ... the ready-made nucleus of degradation and disorder'.[68]

## The march of freedom

Lopsided thrones are creaking,
For 'loyalty' is dead;
And common sense is speaking
Of honesty instead.[69]

Even as they moved towards a conjunction, Chartists and Confederates were not poised to paralyse Britain. The catalyst which turned the spring and summer of 1848 into the most momentous few months in Victorian history was the overthrow of the French monarchy in late February. Ironically, this came soon after O'Connor had criticised Harney for devoting too much space to foreign news in the *Northern Star*. But Harney's judgement of *Star* readers was shrewd. He was nursing the paper's circulation back towards 1842 levels and as the political situation in France grew more serious its French coverage was read keenly.[70] The pace of change in Europe absorbed British observers of every political hue: in January there were anti-Austrian riots in Milan and an uprising against the King of Naples in Sicily. In the second week of February there was serious rioting in Munich; in the third, the French Government's attempts to suppress the reform movement led to massive crowd actions on the streets of Paris and large-scale desertions from the National Guard. On 24 February the Fraternal Democrats were holding their usual monthly meeting in Drury Lane, when 'suddenly the news from Paris was brought in. The effect was electrical. Frenchmen, Germans, Poles, Magyars sprang to their feet, embraced, shouted, and gesticulated with the wildest enthusiasm.' The news concerned the sacking of the Tuileries Palace and the abdication of Louis Philippe in favour of the infant Comte de Paris. The meeting abandoned, everyone crowded onto the streets, linked arms and marched to the offices nearby shared by the land plan with a Confederate club and the Westminster NCA. 'Another enthusiastic fraternisation took place, and great was the clinking of glasses that night in and around Soho and Leicester Square.' Meanwhile at Sadler's Wells Theatre, occupants of the cheapest seats, in the pit and gallery, forced the evening's performance to stop, calling for the *Marseillaise* to be played.[71]

The *Star* went to press on Friday, for publication the following day, just as the French monarchy was overthrown completely and the royal family and its ministers fled. As the first news of these events reached London by telegraph, Harney worked frantically to put out further editions. 'The Revolution has been accomplished' was the headline he chose. Half-a-century later the memory of reading this, and the following week's more-detailed coverage, was still green in the memory of one Barnsley man:

> Before I entered my teens I was a sympathetic Chartist, and early in my life read with avidity the pages of the 'Northern Star' ... One Sunday night I read, for a houseful of listeners, ten columns of the proceedings on the banks of the Seine which culminated in the deposition and flight of Louis Philippe, king of the French. Of course the Chartists in England and the Young Irish Repealers in the sister isle were jubilant, for they nursed the delusion that the revolutionary waves would soon beat up against the White Cliffs of Dover.[72]

The conclusion that revolution in Britain and Ireland was delusional seemed obvious in retrospect, but was widely held at the time, and not among Chartists and Irish Repealers alone. 'In the whole course of my life in this country I never recollect such a period of unrest and alarm', the Christian Socialist J. M. Ludlow declared in 1894. 'The French Revolution', wrote Sir Archibald Alison (Sheriff of Lanarkshire) 'suddenly changed everything. The Chartist leaders immediately saw that their time had at length come.' The novelist and barrister Thomas Hughes wrote: 'It is only by an effort that one can now realise the strain to which the nation was subjected during that winter and spring.'[73]

Popular reaction to the news from France was extraordinary, especially in London. It can be gauged, for example, by the decision of the Royal Victorian Theatre, in Lambeth's Waterloo Road, to concoct for the following week a play, *Vive la Liberté*, depicting (according to the playbill) 'two glorious days of the French Revolution! And the wonderful and rapid results of the Grand Struggle of the People in the cause of liberty, now engrossing the thought and conversation of all.' Every performance culminated in a rousing rendition of the *Marseillaise* by the cast and audience.[74] Scarcely less dramatic was the irruption of the Revolution into the best-selling serial novel of early 1848, *Mysteries of London*. George W. M. Reynolds, political adventurer and Grub Street entrepreneur, wrote and published this sprawling tale, whose multiple plots had enthralled readers in penny-a-week instalments for the past two years. By February 1848 the plot of *Mysteries* had reached 1846. But the issue of 4 March 1848 tore off at a tangent to narrate instead 'the grand and glorious struggle that has so lately taken place in the capital of France'. And it did so with an uncompromising endorsement of the use of political violence:

> It is a monstrous absurdity and a hideous mockery to prate of treason, and

sedition, and rebellion, when a people rises up in its might and its power to demand the privileges that are naturally its own. The *few* cannot possibly possess an inherent right to enslave the *many*; nor is the present generation to be bound by the enactments of the preceding one ... France has shown that when moral agitation fails, violence *must* be used; – and if freedom can be gained by the loss of a few drops of blood – why, then, those drops should be shed cheerfully.[75]

Chartists across the country were quick to congratulate the French people 'on the glorious triumph they have achieved by the Establishment of a REPUBLIC', in the words of the poster issued by the Swindon NCA. 'Throughout Europe the enslaved People are casting off the tyranny of ages', declared West Yorkshire delegates, in a summons to Peep Green, near Hartshead Moor, on 12 March: 'Men of Yorkshire! You are now suffering in connexion with your Countrymen from the oppressions of an Aristocratic Government ... Attend in countless numbers and make known your demands!' Such meetings were largely peaceable and never equalled the worst fears of the authorities: 5,000 attended Peep Green, and nothing in the language of the speakers was objectionable, the Home Office was informed; and at Swindon, a company town where the writ of the Great Western Railway ran large, only 400 were present and 'the inhabitants appeared to take very little interest in it', according to the Chief Constable. Perhaps more remarkable were the meetings Swindon Chartists organised in 7 neighbouring villages over the next 3 weeks.[76]

There were, however, two conspicuous exceptions to this pattern, Glasgow and London. On Glasgow Green demonstrations of the unemployed had been a familiar sight for some time. On 3 March McDouall addressed a demonstration there; then, two days later, events took an ugly turn and shops were pillaged during a march on the city centre, a development for which Glasgow's Chartists were widely but erroneously credited. Sir Archibald Alison arrived around 3.00 a.m. on 4 March and found 'the utmost consternation; the streets placarded with proclamations from the magistrates, and the respectable inhabitants in great numbers preparing to fly'. Two rioters were killed and two seriously injured in clashes with troops later that day, and cavalry had to rescue a detachment of army pensioners, deployed to help the police, from a crowd chanting 'blood for blood'.[77]

In London there were no fatalities but two extraordinary days of disturbances on successive Mondays, 6 and 13 March. It is debateable to what extent the first of these was genuinely a Chartist initiative. But perception is everything and 'Chartist' was what both newspapers and authority perceived it to be. The meeting on 6 March in Trafalgar Square was ostensibly a protest against income tax. It took place in a leadership vacuum, for Harney, Jones and McGrath had gone to Paris to present the NCA's fraternal greetings to the new French Government, while the rest of the executive was absorbed in land plan business. Charles Cochrane, an NCREC-approved parliamentary candidate who had narrowly lost Westminster in 1847, convened the meeting but withdrew when the Metropolitan Police pointed out that public demonstrations within a mile of the Houses of Parliament were prohibited when it was in session. But a substantial crowd, estimated at 10,000–15,000, gathered anyway. Cochrane's place as chairman was filled by Reynolds, his first public platform appearance since forsaking the temperance and anti-Corn Law movements.[78]

Joseph Williams, a south London baker and LDA veteran (arrested with Charles Neesom in January 1840) 'made a very violent speech and in speaking of the Government said that sooner or later the villains would repent'. A resolution was passed demanding the Government repeal income tax or 'resign the reins of power'. Reynolds closed proceedings by announcing the meeting would adjourn for one week and called for cheers 'for the brave Parisians, and the People's Charter'. There matters might have rested had fighting not broken out at the edge of the crowd, which escalated when large numbers of police intervened to stop it. An evening of rioting involving crowds in the low hundreds followed. Barricades were erected in the square, gentlemen's clubs in Pall Mall were stoned, shops looted and lamps broken outside Buckingham Palace. Two further days of sporadic rioting followed. It was a powerful lesson in how not to police a large and volatile crowd, and it was quickly heeded.[79]

Clearly the link with income tax was incidental. As we saw at the opening of this chapter, Peel's introduction of income tax had been welcomed by O'Connor and the *Star* as a progressive measure. A tax applicable only to incomes in excess of £150 was hardly of direct concern to workmen. The operative factors were a generalised anti-government sentiment, emboldened by events in Paris and embittered by memories of the previous year's economic crisis, the effects of which were still widely felt. Income tax in this context stood in for taxation generally. The NCA executive, taken completely by surprise by the events of 6 March, made sure Clark, Dixon, Jones and McGrath were on the platform at the following week's reconvened meeting. Reynolds summoned this to Kennington Common, south of the Thames, beyond the mile radius from Parliament and where the implications of any rioting would be less grievous. And so it proved: some 500 broke off from the crowd of 20,000 and looted shops in nearby Camberwell, but otherwise the event passed off peaceably. Income tax was largely eclipsed in the speeches by the cost of the monarchy (Reynolds), the Charter (Clark and Joseph Williams), the French republic, police brutality and the need for political unity (Jones), and 'a fair day's wages for a fair day's work' (Dixon and McGrath).[80]

The executive was hastily improvising to keep up with the popular mood, and keep up too with Reynolds whose entry into Chartism was as sudden and unheralded as the sacking of the Tuilleries in his *Mysteries*. Reynolds contrived to publish his Trafalgar Square speech through a further intervention in the novel's next instalment, adding for good measure his address to a public meeting convened by Chartism's metropolitan district council that same night. 'The events of this morning had thrown him amongst them', he had declared there, 'and he would now remain amongst them until their great object was accomplished.'[81] The executive was also improvising on broader issues, and its next action had enduring consequences. On 18 March it announced that the National Petition would be presented to Parliament on Monday 10 April, over a month earlier than originally indicated. The Convention, arrangements for which were already in hand, would gather on Tuesday 4 April. This was a significant departure from the previous National Petitions. The 1839 Convention convened four months before the Petition was finally presented, which it had delayed to maximise the signatures collected. The 1842 Convention assembled just three weeks prior to submission, but had been able to rely on a well-established network of Chartist localities, backed by the regional and national infrastructure of the NCA. Furthermore its members spent much of this time extending metropolitan support for the Petition. Preparation of the 1848 Petition, however, was abruptly truncated and its management largely left to chance. The Convention would meet less than a week before submission, while a financially embarrassed executive relied on a national branch infrastructure which (though expanding) far from equalled that of 1842, and on a slender complement of full-time agitators, most of whom had to divide their time with the land plan. In 1842 O'Connor, at the peak of his powers, had devoted himself full-time to the Charter; now, however, he was an MP and his preoccupation was the land plan. In the interval between the executive's announcement and the Convention's commencement, O'Connor appeared just once at a meeting outside London, a joint Confederacy–Chartist rally on Oldham Edge; he arrived late and left early.[82]

The leadership's judgement had been swayed, first, by the French Revolution and, second, by the events of 6 March. A London-based executive, supported by a London-based newspaper, largely inferred its understanding of the national mood from the febrile atmosphere in the capital, cross-referenced to the situation in Paris. Meetings to congratulate the nascent French republic, however numerous (and there *were* many) did not necessarily indicate that petition sheets were being filled or the country covered systematically. Indeed, coverage in the *Star* suggested rather that they were not. The 18 March issue, for example, carried reports of only one general Chartist meeting in Wales (Merthyr Tydfil), 2 in Scotland and 51 in England, a quarter of them in London. Even more indicative of Chartism's polarised state, land plan revenue acknowledged in this issue exceeded £770, while NCA national funds accrued £5 19s 2d.

All this might have mattered less had Chartism not deployed so emphatically such rhetoric as 'The coming struggle – the beginning of the end' (to quote the *Star's* lead editorial header of 18 March). The executive intended that

10 April should be a new high point of constitutional agitation, but it is less obvious whether they also hoped to trigger a disturbance so comprehensive that Chartists elsewhere would rise in response. Members espoused both positions at various points during the following three weeks. If disturbance was the objective, then it was another Peterloo that was contemplated. 'We dare the despicable Whigs to do their worst', the *Northern Star* proclaimed. O'Connor related melodramatically that he had received several warnings that his safety would be at risk if he accompanied the planned march to Westminster with the Petition; but if the procession was attacked, O'Connor asserted, all Britain and Ireland 'would receive the intelligence as the declaration of war'.[83]

On Sunday 9 April Feargus discretely made his will: two of his closest friends had written to him with last-minute appeals for caution. On the eve of the demonstration, Thomas Allsop (O'Connor's closest friend and the source of considerable financial advice and assistance) urged him to do 'nothing rashly … Precipitate nothing, yield nothing. Aim not alone to destroy the government, but to render a class government impossible. No hesitation, no rash impulse, no egotism; but an earnest, serious, unyielding progress. Nothing for self, nothing even for fame, present or posthumous. All for the cause.'[84] Duncombe warned O'Connor of 'the folly of jeopardising a good and just cause by extravagant language and foolish threats … [and] any rash collision with the authorities', concluding: 'Think! Think! Think! And remember – one false step may seal the fate of millions.'[85]

In an elaborate metaphor designed to avoid any charge of sedition, Ernest Jones likened the approaching demonstration to a journey 'on the high road into progression, but across the way class rule has built a stone wall of monopolies'. It was pointless for the people to tell it, 'you naughty wall, you ought to be lying low'. They should instead take pickaxes, mallets and crowbars 'and break the rotten barrier to atoms'. Jones concluded with a veiled reference to 'our leaders' who 'should not damp a fine enthusiasm'. In the same speech he also concurred with the republican sentiments of a London Chartist, the mesmerist William Vernon, who had voiced 'disgust' at petitioning for the Charter at all. 'He thought they should give the House of Commons just one hour to consider whether they would grant it or not. (Loud cheering.) … and if they said "no" they should retire to their district meetings and decide what they were to do the next day. (Loud cheers.)' Dixon and O'Connor attacked these sentiments but concentrated their fire on Vernon rather than Jones, and criticised the overt espousal of republicanism rather than threats of violence. The French Revolution continued to dominate foreign news. O'Connor knew that to be associated too closely with events in Paris would alienate middle-class support. But talk of violence, though it assumed greater menace in the light of continental developments, was of course no novelty. Only the week before O'Connor himself had declared on Oldham Edge that 'if there should come dark and black and sanguinary news from Ireland, he should not confine his defence of Ireland to the House of Commons'.[86]

Jones was to the fore in openly contemplating violence. Of his Halifax constituents, he claimed that 'to a man they were ready to fight. (Cheers.) If necessary, they were ready to rush down from the hills of Yorkshire to aid their brother patriots in London.' At the last session of the Convention before 10 April, he slightly trimmed his belligerence, if not his taste for melodrama, predicting that violence, if it occurred, would result from the authorities striking the first blow:

> If I were to be killed, or wounded, or arrested, the moment the intelligence arrived at Halifax the people would rise and disarm the troops – imprison the authorities – and 100,000 Yorkshiremen would march upon London (enthusiastic cheers). So help me God I will march in the first rank tomorrow, and if they attempt any violence, they shall not be 24 hours longer in the House of Commons.[87]

Rhetorical froth though this might have been, it was assiduously reported in the press: not only the *Northern Star* but both *The Times* and the *Morning Chronicle* published almost verbatim accounts of the Convention's proceedings. This unparalleled degree of interest reflected growing alarm in the capital as Monday drew near.

## Kennington Common

Examples of how apprehensive the public mood in London was are numerous. A visitor from Hampshire found 'all in commotion' on Saturday 8 April, with 'artillery and troops moving in all directions, in order to be prepared for the monster meeting of the rabble'. That morning the royal family left London for the Isle of Wight, at the Government's request, though Foreign Secretary Palmerston worried that the Solent might still not be wide enough to protect them, while his political opponents Graham and Peel grumbled that the evacuation looked like cowardice and would only encourage 'a sense of danger'.[88] Sunday was tense: William Gladstone noted in his diary that 'there was a new & sad intrusion in the thoughts of & in conversation about tomorrow'.[89] However, the Government's preparations were nothing if not thorough. It spent £1,500 on the installation of an electric telegraph link to the Home Office and to establish temporary connections to key provincial centres not yet served by the Electric Telegraph Company.[90] The capital's military establishment of around 3,300 troops was almost doubled. Troops were issued with 10 days' emergency rations (15 days' for those at the Tower of London). In the early hours of Monday morning, covertly to avoid creating undue alarm, 500 additional troops were moved into London, mainly to protect the South Western Railway Company's goods' station and depot at Nine Elms (which served the lines to the Solent ports); in addition 1,142 army pensioners were mobilised and secret orders were issued to light London's gas lamps early to assist security.[91]

At the British Museum, stones were carried to the roof ready to hurl at assailants and the Royal Engineers supervised the construction of barricades and booby traps (which included sawing through the joists of the staircase to the coin and medal room so that it would collapse under the weight of more than a few people). In all, 250 Museum staff and building workers were sworn in as special constables to support a makeshift temporary garrison of 59 regulars and 20 pensioners.[92] The British Museum's contingent of specials was merely a fraction of a total force of around 85,000. These included 1,857 coal-whippers (paid up to 3s for the employment they lost), railway servants, civil servants, university students, keepers at the Surrey Zoological Gardens and William Gladstone. 'There was scarcely a merchant, a banker, or shopkeeper, or clerk in London, except the very old, who did not take the oath and carry a truncheon, to crack the skull of a Chartist if it became necessary', recalled the author Charles Mackay. 'Almost every gentleman, servant, and shopkeeper' was sworn-in, according to the MP William Ewart, who also described how a retired general took command of the area round his home, drilled the special constables and organised them into geographical sections, with messengers to link them all.[93]

'There was more genuine alarm in London on that day than I ever remember', wrote a junior government minister. 'There was an appearance of the expecta-tion of some struggle or disastrous event', the Secretary of State for India, John Hobhouse, noted in his diary. The door to his home had been chalked with political graffiti over the weekend and Hobhouse was barely able to work for nervousness, 'thinking it by no means improbable that I should hear discharges of musketry or cannon from the other side of the river. Indeed the slamming of doors made me start once or twice.'[94] Clearly, the Government had prepared for a full-scale uprising. Yet this was not what the Chartist leadership had in mind. The containment of 'the monster meeting of the rabble' was effec-tively achieved through a simple stratagem. When Reynolds decided after the 6 March riots to reconvene the following week south of the river on Kennington Common, he unwittingly solved the hardest part of the challenge confronting the authorities on 10 April. As long as control of the bridges over the Thames was retained, the demonstration could be contained. So the second strategy, announced Friday 7 April, was to prohibit processions to Parliament.

The heavy and ostentatious police and military preparations possibly discouraged some from attending. They certainly unnerved many leading Chartists. On the Friday afternoon the Convention sent a deputation to assure the Home Office that the proposed procession to the Commons would be entirely peaceable. On the Saturday Harney discretely tried to persuade a handful of delegates that both procession and demonstration should be abandoned. The next day, O'Brien publicly announced his resignation from the Convention, citing its failure to recognise that the Government was too strong for the Chartists. Over dinner that night, Jones blurted out to a close friend (who immediately conveyed it to the Home Secretary) 'that the Chartist leaders were much subdued and frightened'.[95] However, thousands of rank-and-file Chartists turned out on Monday expecting to escort the Petition to Parliament. They assembled early that morning at one of four muster points and then marched en masse to Kennington. Chartist and Confederate Robert Crowe recalled: 'we marched over the bridges eight abreast, on our way to Kennington Common, but no sooner did the procession pass over than the police and soldiery took possession of the bridges, and for nearly two hours we were held as prisoners'.[96]

Kennington Common never matched the 400,000 O'Connor claimed for it or even the 250,000 the executive predicted. However, a crowd of some 150,000 assembled there, a turn-out large enough to require at least three stages from which speakers addressed them, with a fourth for the Irish Confederates. Assembling a crowd this large was a major piece of political theatre. The main procession departed from the Convention's headquarters, off Tottenham Court Road, just after 10.00 a.m. Its passage through the streets of the capital took nearly eighty minutes to reach the Common. At its head were two huge carriages: the first, which would later double as a rostrum, carried forty-eight of the delegates; the second, symbolically constructed from timber cut on the Lowbands land plan estate, was to carry the Petition. It was embellished with slogans: 'The Charter and the Six Points'; 'No Surrender'; 'Liberty is Worth Living For and Worth Dying For'; 'The Voice of the People is the Voice of God'; 'Who Would Be A Slave that Could Be Free?'; 'Onward We Conquer, Backward We Fall'; 'No Vote, No Muskets'. Five immense bales of paper containing the Petition were loaded onto the carriage at the land plan's offices. 'The crowds increasing at every step', the procession made its way to Blackfriars Bridge, a double-file of police in military order on each side of the street as it passed. 'The crowd continued to increase and hem in the vehicles on both sides; still, everything was well conducted', Mackay (a reporter for the *Illustrated London News*) noted. At the Elephant and Castle 'a new mass joined the rear of those who, walking eight abreast, had followed the train'.[97]

Mackay's account hardly reads like the first stage of a mass uprising. Indeed, shortly after arriving at Kennington, O'Connor and McGrath readily agreed with the Metropolitan Police Commissioner, Sir Richard Mayne, that the Petition would not be accompanied back across the Thames by the crowd, but transported in a fleet of hansom cabs. O'Connor then joined the principal rostrum from where he made an emotional yet uncharacteristically terse speech, which he rounded-off by saying: 'I come now to disperse you. You will not walk in procession. You must go peaceably to your homes.' The meeting duly dispersed. It was not popular with large sections of the crowd, many of whom blamed O'Connor personally. Unknown to them, he was unwell, 'suffering from severe bodily pain' and 'evidently exhausted from the effort of speaking'. The dispatch which a relieved Mayne sent to the Home Office, shortly after he spoke to O'Connor, said that he looked frightened; but in a private conversation that evening Mayne elaborated on this, relating that O'Connor was 'deadly pale – perspiration running down'. The following day Feargus was forced to miss both Convention and Parliament, complaining 'my chest is in great pain'. Ten turbulent years at Chartism's head were clearly taking their toll.[98]

# Chartist lives:
# William Cuffay

'From the moment that Mr O'Connor took his departure impatience and uproar began to manifest themselves in the meeting' observed *The Times* of Kennington Common on the afternoon of 10 April. There was chaos as McGrath, chairing proceedings, declared the meeting closed: a section of the crowd rushed the platform with such force that it moved several yards and the Convention delegates standing on it were thrown by the impact. Among them was William Cuffay, a London tailor and chair of the 'Demonstration Committee' that had organised both the procession that brought the petition to the common and that which was meant to return with it across the Thames to Parliament. The cancellation of the latter astonished Cuffay, who like everyone had been kept in ignorance of the executive's final intentions. Some in the crowd yelled to him, 'Come – we will lead if you will follow, come weal, come woe.' According to an eyewitness (probably Charles Mackay),

> Cuffay spoke in strong language against the dispersal of the meeting and contended that it would be time enough to evince their fear of the military when they met them face to face! He believed the whole Convention were a set of cowardly humbugs, and he would have nothing more to do with them. He then left the van, and got among the crowd, where he said that O'Connor

must have known all this before, and that he ought to have informed them of it, so that they might have conveyed the petition at once to the House of Commons without crossing the bridges. They had been completely caught in a trap.

In his novel *Alton Locke* Charles Kingsley, drawing perhaps on information from Robert Crowe, depicted Cuffay leaping from the platform exclaiming that the crowd had been 'humbugged and betrayed',[*] though in all probability Cuffay did not leap (both his legs and spine were deformed from birth). There was, however, no doubting his anger: he was among the most militant members of the Convention, uncomfortable at the entry into Chartism of middle-class careerists like Ernest Jones and George Reynolds. The latter had secured a place in the Convention as delegate for Derby, a town he had never visited before securing his nomination.

When delegates assembled on 4 April, Cuffay quickly punctured Reynolds's air of self-importance by moving his exclusion on the grounds that he was not a Chartist. He accused the executive of shrinking 'from its responsibility, now that things had come to a crisis', and publicly questioned the logic of its proposal to memorialise the Queen if Parliament rejected the petition: 'he should take the rejection as a declaration of war, and be prepared to go to war accordingly, and the Executive should be prepared to lead on to liberty or death'.[†]

Yet Cuffay was no bellicose hothead. There were few surer indications of the new mood of militancy in 1848 among London Chartists than Cuffay's stance. He had just turned 60 and, in the words of one who knew him well, was 'of mild demeanour and quiet manners'. He epitomised the backroom political activist, conscientious, industrious and seldom given to grand gestures. He helped form the London tailors' Chartist locality, was Westminster's representative on the metropolitan district council of the NCA from 1841, and its treasurer from 1842, and he had helped rescue the national executive when it faced crisis late in 1842. Cuffay was also a member of the committee that advised Duncombe in his parliamentary fight of 1845 against tightening the law of Master and Servant, and a co-organiser of the *soirée* in Duncombe's honour when he succeeded. He represented his trade on the fund-raising committee for a metropolitan trades' hall, sat on the NCREC, the executive of the National Anti-Militia Association and the Democratic Committee for Poland's Regeneration. He was an elected delegate to land plan conferences in 1845 and 1846. 'When hundreds of working men elected this man to audit the accounts of their benefit society', a tribute to Cuffay pointed out in 1849,

---

[*]    *The Times* and *Morning Chronicle*, 11 April 1848; *NS*, 15 April 1848; *Illustrated London News*, 15 April 1848; C. Kingsley, *Alton Locke* (1850), chapter 34.

[†]    *Morning Chronicle*, 7 April 1848; *NS*, 8 April 1848.

'they did so in the full belief of his trustworthiness, and he never gave them reason to repent of their choice.' He was trusted, too, with tasks of a delicate nature: when allegations were made against McDouall of mischievously giving false advice to Chartist prisoners in 1841, Cuffay was one of a small group asked to investigate.[*]

William Cuffay epitomised those trade unionists politicised by Chartism, as he explained in a speech urging the London tailors to adopt the 1842 Petition:

> As a working man, a tailor, and a Chartist, he would never shrink from the performance of any public duty which his fellow tradesmen and brother-slaves elected him to perform ... As a trades unionist he had exerted himself to the utmost on behalf of his order; but he was now convinced that the cause of their distress was higher than the tyranny of their employers – that they must put the axe to the root of the tree; and, sink or swim, he would stand like a man to the last, and if he died he would die like a martyr gloriously in the cause.[†]

His comment about 'brother-slaves' would have had a special resonance for his audience because Cuffay was of West Indian slave descent. Older listeners may also have recognised an allusion to the earlier black radical Robert Wedderburn, also a tailor, whose *Axe Laid to the Root* was one of the liveliest periodicals circulating London in 1817. Indeed, Cuffay's remarks echo the opening declaration of Wedderburn's *Axe*: 'I am a West Indian, a lover of liberty, and would dishonour human nature if I did not show myself a friend to the liberty of others.'[‡] Wedderburn's mother, an African, had been sold into slavery in Jamaica, and sold-on when she was five months' pregnant by her Scottish owner who happened also to be the unborn Robert's father. The circumstances of William Cuffay's birth were slightly more propitious, his disability aside. His father had been born into slavery on St Kitts, the son of an African slave. Less is known about his mother, except that she was heavily pregnant when she and her husband sailed from St Kitts in 1788. His Chartist colleagues understood William to have been born at sea, though in old age he said that he had been born in Chatham, the naval dockyard town where the family, emancipated from slavery by virtue of being in Britain, made their home. Cuffay's father enlisted as a cook in the Royal Navy and his mother largely raised him and his sister alone. His name was probably an anglicisation of the Twi name *Kofi*

---

[*]    T. Frost, *Forty Years' Recollections* (London, Sampson Low, 1880), p.150; *Reasoner*, 26 December 1846; *DLB*, vol.6; *NS*, 27 November 1841.

[†]    *NS*, 5 March 1842.

[‡]    *Axe Laid to the Root, or a Fatal Blow to the Oppressors*, 1 (November 1817), pp.8–9; for Wedderburn see *DLB* entry, vol.8, and *ODNB*.

for a male born on Friday.* It was variously spelt but he consistently used 'Cuffay'. How far he retained his parents' patois is hard to discern. Chartist reportage routinely smoothed out all indicators of accent from the words of those it quoted, while in a leaden satire for the Christmas issue of *Punch*, in 1848, the novelist William Thackeray gave the 'pore old blackymore rogue' an accent close to contemporary burlesque Cockney.† However, since Cuffay was literate, an avid reader and long-time resident of the capital, there is no reason to suppose that his accent was other than that of Londoners of his social class. Chartist reportage also ignored his ethnic origins and disability, in contrast to mainstream papers, for example the *Illustrated London News* (which referred to the 'comic Cuffey' and 'his nigger humour'), and the satirical magazines *Puppet Show* (in which Cuffay was depicted as a hunchbacked monkey with tailor's shears), *Man in the Moon* (a hen-pecked Cuffay bent almost double) and the egregious *Punch*.‡

With the important exception of anti-Semitism (see chapter 9 above), Chartism was rarely overtly racist. Even the hard-swearing John Campbell, one of the movement's least-savoury characters, refrained from committing to print his racist sentiments until after he had emigrated to the United States. There his *Negro-Mania* gave full rein to white-supremacist opinions, strikingly bigoted even by contemporary standards.§ Nor was Cuffay the only black person involved in Chartism, though he was the only one to play a leading role. Unemployed seamen David Duffy, 'a man of colour', and Benjamin 'Black Ben' Prophett, along with a Romany, Charles Lee, were among the small group arrested after the 13 March Kennington Common meeting.¶

Where Chartists were often equivocal in their attitudes to black people, however, was in the clumsy association of 'wage slavery' and 'white slavery' (factory labour) with chattel slavery in the Americas. One widely circulated tract asserted that 'the possession of the franchise is the only difference between a freeman and the Russian serf ... or the slave of South Carolina'. The British worker, Patrick Brewster claimed, was 'as much at the mercy of his Master, as

---

\*   *ODNB*. Twi is spoken in modern Ghana.

†   'The three Christmas waits', *Punch*, vol.14, 23 December 1848, pp.181–3; see also W. M. Thackeray, *Ballads and Other Contributions to 'Punch'* (Oxford, Oxford University Press, n.d.), pp.170–4.

‡   *Illustrated London News*, 22 April 1848; for *Puppet Show* and *Man in the Moon* see I. Haywood, 'Reynolds and the "Trafalgar Square revolution"', *Journal of Victorian Culture*, 7:1 (spring 2002), pp.32, 57–9; *Punch*, vol.14, pp.169, 173, 176, 181–3, and vol.15, pp.154–5, 160.

§   J. Campbell, *Negro-Mania: Being an Examination of the Falsely Assumed Equality of the Various Races of Men* (Philadelphia, PA, Campbell & Power, 1851).

¶   D. Goodway, *London Chartism, 1838–48* (Cambridge, Cambridge University Press, 1982), p.116.

if he was a Negro Slave'. The ever-excitable Ernest Jones could be relied on to push such an argument further: 'Am I not right, then, in saying that the fate of the English working man is worse than that of the Russian serf, the Hindoo pariah, or the negro slave? It has no parallel in times past or present. It is slavery in its worst, its most cruel aspect'.[*]

Against this it should be stressed that the Chartist press and platform consistently opposed chattel slavery. For example, an early issue of the Northern Star, reporting an atrocity at a plantation, enjoined its readers to register 'a vow in heaven, which you religiously resolve to keep, that these things shall not be'. Brewster allied himself with the radical American abolitionist John Anderson Collins, while the Scottish Chartist Circular eulogised the American anti-slavery agitator William Lloyd Garrison. Lovett, Vincent and their circle took anti-slavery issues very seriously indeed. Lovett was a council member of the Anti-Slavery League and he and Vincent appeared on platforms with Garrison and the great black American campaigner Frederick Douglass when they visited Britain in 1846. Garrison also lectured at the National Association's hall. A rare relaxed moment in Lovett's autobiography describes singing the Marseillaise, spirituals and anti-slavery songs with Douglass, Garrison and Vincent, around the piano at J.H.Parry's home.[†]

William Cuffay, however, was not of Lovett's circle and there is no evidence that he heard Douglass speak in 1846. Had he done so, he might have heard the escaped Maryland slave emphasise that 'there was no more similarity between slavery, as existing in the United States, and any institution in this country, than there was between light and darkness'.[‡] This makes Cuffay's use of the term 'brother slaves' in addressing London working men all the more poignant. He had to dig where he stood and carve out a political philosophy and career, on his own terms but within an over-arching context of British ignorance about slavery. Perhaps he knowingly flattered his audience's susceptibility; or, never having directly experienced slavery himself, Cuffay may even have shared his fellow-workers' perceptions.

The final stage in his politicisation, as it was for many in Chartist London, was the news from France in March 1848: 'We have arrived at a time when a league of kings is no longer to be dreaded', and he told the London demonstration 'to congratulate the heroic people of France'.

---

[*] Finsbury Tract Society, The Question 'What Is a Chartist?' Answered (1840), p.1; P.Brewster, Seven Chartist and Military Discourses (Paisley, self-published, 1843), p.75; E.Jones, Evenings with the People No. 1 (London, People's Paper, 1856), p.6.

[†] NS, 2 December 1837; Chartist Circular, 9 May 1840; R.Bradbury, 'Frederick Douglass and the Chartists', Colloquium (1995), pp.169–86; W.Lovett, The Life and Struggles of William Lovett (London, Trübner, 1876), pp.321–2.

[‡] Bristol Mercury, 29 August 1846, quoted in J.W.Blassingame (ed.), Frederick Douglass Papers (New Haven, CT, Yale Uuniversity Press, 1979), p.344.

We no longer fear the Russian bear, the Austrian spider, or the Prussian vulture. (Loud cheers.) The French have set us a glorious example, beating the strongest army in the world, and sending Louis Philippe forth a wandering vagabond on the face of the earth. (Great cheering.) Never despair of your rights. 'Look there', said the speaker. Pointing to a huge placard bearing the words, 'The Republic for France – the Charter for England'. (Rapturous cheering.) Ay! and if they refused us the Charter, we should then begin to think about a republic. (Great cheering.) ... Let them follow up this meeting, and the day was not far distant when the charter must become the law of the land. (Great cheering.)\*

Although Cuffay declared at Kennington Common that he would have no more to do with the Convention, he returned to it the following day. O'Connor communicated his apology for absence due to illness and sent a letter arguing that if the procession had proceeded 'the dogs of war would have been let loose, and this morning our cause would have been a laughing-stock'. Cuffay confined his contribution to relating that exclusive dealing was being organised by Lambeth Chartists against the shopkeepers who had served as special constables the previous day. That night he returned to his Soho garret home to an unexpected personal crisis. Cuffay had recently become unemployed. Like many skilled workers he prided himself on being the bread-winner and was reluctant for his wife, Mary, to work outside the home. But losing his job had forced a change of views and Mary had found work as a charwoman. However, as he later explained, 'at one of the houses where she had been in the habit of charring she was asked if she was the wife of Cuffay of the Convention? She said she was, and she was then informed that her services would not be required again.'†

Their predicament did not, however, make Cuffay a desperate man and he continued to adhere to a position of robust but constitutional agitation. *The Times*, which had once summed up London Chartism as 'the Black man and his party', had fixed Cuffay firmly in its sights from the moment the Convention began; nonetheless, it summarised his views on 10 April as insisting 'that the petition should have been accompanied by the people until opposed by the military, and then, on the ground that such opposition was illegal, should have been withdrawn altogether'.‡ This was not a solution to the Chartists' dilemma at Kennington Common, and would not necessarily have avoided violence; but it would arguably have defended the integrity of constitutional

---

\*   *NS*, 11 March 1848.
†   *The Times*, 12 and 13 April 1848.
‡   Ibid., 11 April 1848; for other *Times* coverage see, e.g. 8–10, 12–15, 17 April, 15 May, 1 June, 9, 21 August, 1, 23, 25–6, 28–30 September, 2–3 and 27 October 1848.

campaigning. Instead, as the next chapter relates, division and embarrassment were to become rife.

A fortnight later the Convention dissolved, to be replaced the following month by a National Assembly, whose main task was to compile and present a memorial to the Queen to dismiss the Government. Cuffay was dismissive of this tactic and therefore not among those elected. He was, however, appointed one of the commissioners assisting the executive in managing the movement under a new plan of organisation. But London Chartism was spiralling beyond the control of the constitutional leadership. In particular, a conspiracy to foment a general rising, to be signalled by co-ordinated arson attacks on key London buildings, was being devised by an 'Ulterior Committee' of Chartists and Confederates meeting at The Orange Tree public house near Holborn. Cuffay was not among the originators of the conspiracy and first attended the committee only on 4 August, but within eleven days he became its secretary.[*] He was unemployed and his wife was being refused work because of who he was. More than that, though, he was a committed Chartist of nearly a decade's standing. He believed that the Charter, and the Charter alone, could retrieve the country both from corrupt government and the precipice of economic and social crisis. Cuffay was by some distance the eldest of the conspirators, widely respected for his organisational experience and acumen, fair and thoughtful. His move to clandestine violence was made late in life and, we may assume, with a heavy heart.

By the summer of 1848 commitment to an uprising within London Chartism was extensive. The conspirators were emboldened by the restless state of Ireland: it meant, Cuffay believed, that 'we shall be able to master the police since the Soldiers were being drained away'. Back home he and Mary began casting bullets from old printers' type. At the Chartist class he led at the land plan offices in Soho, Cuffay demonstrated a pike and gave instructions on how to make cartridges and bullets. 'He also said that Ginger Beer Bottles filled full of nails and ragged pieces of Iron were good Things for Wives to throw out of the Windows while the Men were down in the streets fighting the Police', Charles Filden, one of Cuffay's class members, subsequently related in evidence against him. This was a murky world where all was not as it seemed. The commitment of Cuffay and his colleagues to the conspiracy was real enough but it was being monitored, even accelerated, by police informers. Filden later admitted that it was *he* who told Cuffay about the gingerbeer bottles (to be filled with gunpowder and bound with hemp dipped in turpentine), and that he had been a police informer 'for about 1 month' before that.[†] Cuffay was

---

[*]   Goodway, *London Chartism*, pp.94, 126–7.

[†]   TS, 11/138/380, *R* v. *Ritchie et al.*, case notes, fos 5–6, and evidence of Charles Filden, fos 32–3; and 11/139/381, prosecution brief, *R.* v. *Mullins*, evidence of Filden, fo.12.

arrested while at home with Mary on 18 August. He was fully expecting his arrest: as one of the constables recited the requisite formula concerning his rights, Cuffay interrupted him: 'Oh that's quite sufficient as I am a Chartist I understand it.'[*]

Cuffay struck a defiant pose in court: 'I demand a fair trial by a jury of my peers in accord with *Magna Carta*', he shouted as the jury was empanelled from an assembly of shopkeepers and professional men. He was refused. Given that the scope and character of the conspiracy had been established in the trials of other conspirators, who had preceded Cuffay, the outcome was hardly in doubt. 'It has not been a fair trial, and my request was not complied with to have a jury of my equals', argued Cuffay when brought up for sentencing, 'but the jury as it is I have no fault to find with; I daresay they have acted conscientiously.' Understandably, Cuffay was torn by conflicting emotions, referring bitterly to

> the great prejudice that has been raised against me in particular ... almost the whole press of this country, and even other countries, has been raising a prejudice against me. I have been taunted by the press, and it has tried to smother me with ridicule, and it has done everything in its power to crush me. I crave no pity. I ask no mercy ... the press has strongly excited the middle class against me; therefore I did not expect anything else except the verdict of guilty, right or wrong ... I have the fortitude to endure any punishment your lordship can inflict upon me. I know my cause is good, and I have a self-approving conscience that will bear me up against anything, and that would bear me up even to the scaffold; therefore I think I can endure any punishment proudly. I feel no disgrace at being called a felon.[†]

Cuffay was sentenced to transportation for life. The prisoner found guilty in the same court immediately before him was William Dowling, secretary of the Davis Confederate Club and a portrait artist and engraver. In their Newgate cell, Dowling sketched Cuffay's portrait, a lithograph of which was distributed through the land plan's head office. It consciously imitated the portraits – almost exclusively of middle-class leaders of the movement and other luminaries – given away with the *Star*. Sales of the print raised funds for Mary Cuffay; and it was the basis of the woodcut accompanying an affectionate tribute, published by Reynolds in 1850.[‡] By then Cuffay was in Tasmania. There was a distressing delay before Mary could join him because parole for Cuffay, promised even before he left Britain, was delayed without explanation for eighteen months. Mary was reduced to the workhouse before authority for

---

[*]   TS, 11/138/380, fo.18, and TS 11/139/381 fo.4, evidence of Sgt Thompson.

[†]   *Reports of State Trials* (London, HMSO, 1896), ns, vol.7, cols 471, 478, 480.

[‡]   National Portrait Gallery, London, catalogue no. NPG D13148; (T.M.Wheeler) 'William Cuffay', *Reynolds's Political Instructor*, 13 April 1850.

her to join her husband was finally granted. This she did in 1853, her passage funded by Chartist subscriptions.[*]

William Cuffay cut a quietly impressive figure in Tasmania. Once paroled he quickly found employment as a tailor. His application for a conditional pardon in 1855 was warmly supported by local character references. When all political prisoners were pardoned in 1856, he and Mary decided to stay. Almost immediately he became involved in a campaign against the state's law of Master and Servant, 'and being a fluent and an effective speaker, he was always popular with the working classes', the Hobart *Mercury* commented. He also took 'a prominent part in election matters, and went in strongly for the individual rights of man'. These comments were occasioned by Cuffay's death, aged 82, in 1870. He had died in the Brickfield Invalid Depot (equivalent to the sick ward of an English workhouse). Brickfield's superintendent described him as 'a quiet man and an inveterate reader'. Almost his last appearance on a political platform had been at a Hobart theatre in 1866 to oppose the state administration. 'I'm old, I'm poor, I'm out of work, and I'm in debt, and there-fore I have a right to complain', he declared to the audience, the members of which he addressed as his 'fellow-slaves'.[†]

---

[*]   *NS*, 21 December 1850; see G. J. Holyoake, *Sixty Years of an Agitator's Life*, vol. 2 (London, Fisher Unwin, 1900), p.3, for an alternative version that Mary was employed by Richard Cobden.

[†]   *Mercury*, 11 August 1870, quoted in A. Briggs, 'Chartists in Tasmania', *Bulletin of the Society for the Study of Labour History*, 3 (1961), p.7.

# CHAPTER TEN

# April 1848–1852:
# 'Decent revolutionaries'?

## After Kennington

On Thursday 13 April, a House of Commons' Committee reported on the mass petition O'Connor had presented three days earlier. At Kennington Common, O'Connor had claimed that it contained 5,700,000 signatures, which happened to be almost exactly double the size of the 1842 Petition. This figure had a spurious ring to it, even more so minutes later when Jones rounded it up to 6 million, the total that stuck in the public mind. Now, however, according to the committee, 13 clerks working for over 17 hours had calculated that total to be 1,975,496 signatures. Furthermore 'a large number' of signatures were written consecutively by the same hand, and 'a large number were those of persons who could not be supposed to have concurred in its [the petition's] prayer: among those were the names of Her Majesty, signed as Victoria Rex, the Duke of Wellington, Sir Robert Peel, &c., &c.'. The report continued that a 'large number' of additional signatures were evidently fictitious and numerous names were obscene. The committee did not give figures for these large numbers, even though its clerks had managed to calculate the overall total with a precision that was as spurious in its own way as O'Connor's and Jones's estimate. However it did, by way of further undermining confidence in the Petition, calculate that 8,200 signatures in every 100,000 were those of women.[1]

O'Connor made a frantic arithmetical calculation of the logistics of the committee's claim: the clerks must each have counted non-stop at an average rate of 150 names per minute. This was physically impossible, he declared, indicating that along with a motion to enact the Charter, of which he had already given notice for the following day, he would demand a committee of enquiry. Unfortunately O'Connor also conceded that he had no knowledge of the Petition's content, not a single sheet of which, he admitted, had he seen. Worse still, he alleged that any false names the petition contained would have been the work of government spies. Worst of all was O'Connor's response to comments (admittedly vehemently expressed and personal in nature) made by a member of the scrutiny committee, William Cripps. Feargus demanded 'personal satisfaction of him outside the House', which, as any gentleman knew, was a challenge to a duel. O'Connor then strode out. In his absence Cripps apologised for using un-parliamentary language and MPs voted formally to require O'Connor to return forthwith and resolve the matter.

Meanwhile, the ever-obliging Ernest Jones agreed to act as O'Connor's second and sped to the Commons with a written challenge for Cripps. When a Commons' messenger tracked him down at the *Northern Star*'s offices, Feargus refused to return. The House in turn, on a motion from Prime Minister Russell, agreed that O'Connor should be detained by the Sergeant at Arms and brought back to the House. In due course Feargus was escorted into the chamber, where Cripps repeated his apology. O'Connor made a blustering acceptance but, in a fit of pique, then withdrew the motion he had intended to move the next day: 'he would leave the merits of the petition between the government and the country, and between the government and those that had signed it'. There the matter formally rested. It was an extraordinary episode. The past twenty years had winessed a sea-change in public attitudes to duelling (it had, for example, been prohibited in the armed services in 1844). This all-too-public exposure of O'Connor's increasing tendency to act erratically – shortly afterwards he challenged another MP over remarks made in the same debate – was damaging. Far more significantly, O'Connor's petulance deprived Chartism of its only real chance of challenging the arithmetic of the committee, of mounting a reasoned defence of the Petition's irregularities (few petitions were without them, as the Commons was perfectly aware) or of expounding that even the Commons' revised figure was double the size of the British electorate and quadruple the total votes cast in the 1847 general election.[2]

Henceforward the integrity of the 1848 Petition hung round the neck of Chartism like the proverbial albatross, never to be cast off. This mattered intensely because the credibility of the movement was on trial. So too was the Government's capacity to handle political dissent. That it was Russell himself who moved that O'Connor be detained was replete with symbolism. His Government had directly co-ordinated the handling of the 10 April demonstration and, in modern parlance, had managed an effective media campaign belittling the Chartists. The special constables were represented to the nation as a classless army of patriotic redressers, even though the only workmen to volunteer in significant numbers without pressure from their employers were the coal whippers, paid by the Government for their trouble.

As controversy raged as to whether attendance on the Common was anything like the 250,000 the Chartists claimed for it, a freelance reporter working for *The Times* admitted that 'the Commissioners of Police on Monday evening last sent round to the papers a document marked *private*, requesting them to state that there were only 15,000 persons present at the meeting'.[3] Monday's evening papers, sent to press before that communication arrived, reported attendance at between 80,000 and 150,000. By contrast the next day's newspapers (except for the ruggedly independent *Morning Chronicle*) placed attendance between 10,000 and 30,000, *The Times* alone mentioning 50,000 as 'the most liberal estimate'.[4] The reputation of Sir George Grey, the Home Secretary, was considerably enhanced by the outcome of 10 April. That evening he entered the Commons and 'before he could say a word he was hailed by the loudest of cheers from all sides of the House, as if we owed our safety to him'.[5] Shrewdly, the Government chose that night to present its Crown and Government Security Bill to the Commons. It was a far-reaching measure that redefined and extended the offence of treason, including a new treasonable offence of 'open and advised speaking'. The Bill encountered negligible opposition and was law within twelve days. It was strange, William Cuffay would later remark, 'how anything to abridge the rights of the working classes can be passed in a few hours'.[6]

'Your Chartist is a very decent sort of revolutionary', mused the French composer Hector Berlioz, who was living in London and had attended Kennington Common; he added that Chartists knew 'as much about starting a riot as the Italians about writing a symphony'.[7] This was unfair, at least to the Chartists. In any case, riot was not directly what they had in mind. Twelve months earlier, Chartism had appeared to be both peripheral to mainstream politics and in decline. Over a hectic few months much of its early character as a mass platform agitation had been rebuilt, in the hope that sheer weight of numbers would either intimidate a complacent Government or finesse it into an ill-judged attack after the manner of Peterloo. Now Chartism had been found wanting. As *Papers for the People*, a new Christian Socialist journal, declared in its first issue of May 1848: 'The Chartists chose to stake their cause upon a display of physical force, and by a display of physical force they were overwhelmed. They made number their argument, and it recoiled upon themselves.'[8]

The Convention was left to fulminate against the unconstitutional actions of the Government in blocking the legitimate exercise of the right to present a petition, while the realisation dawned on delegates that the executive had unwittingly abetted matters by botching the petition. The revised timetable announced on 18 March had left insufficient time to collect, deliver and collate the signatures. Sheets totalling around 200,000 signatures were apparently still stacked in the NCA offices and an estimated 47,000 more had yet to arrive from Halifax (both these pieces of information were omitted from the *Star's* report). There was little appetite for the strategy that had previously been agreed should Parliament reject the petition – a National Assembly to prepare a memorial to the Queen. Some, like Cuffay, refused to be involved; O'Connor, who had supported the idea, now roundly condemned it. Delegates postponed the Assembly by a week and drew up the memorial for adoption at meetings over Easter weekend (22–23 April). 'These islands present the anomalous spectacle of a people starving in the midst of plenty', the memorial begun, and it concluded by praying that the Queen would dissolve Parliament, dismiss her ministers 'and call to your aid men who will make the People's Charter a cabinet measure'.[9] Then the Convention dissolved and delegates embarked on an intensive weekend of agitation.

In this they were hampered by lack of both time and funds (the Convention had been rescued from financial embarrassment only by an anonymous donation of £100, almost certainly O'Connor's). However, the movement they encountered was buoyant, even expanding. Chartism had colonised new centres and reasserted itself in old ones. Among the latter, dormant since 1839, were Buckley (north Wales), Cirencester and Devonport. Among the new localities were Beverley and Driffield in East Yorkshire, Dartford (Kent), High Wycombe (Buckinghamshire), and in Scotland St Andrews and Holytown (north of Motherwell). The near-saturation coverage the movement achieved in its early years meant that these new localities by their nature were small, but their existence is a useful barometer by which to assess Chartism in 1848. Furthermore, their commitment to Chartism did not stem from the land plan alone. The market town of Dartford, for example, established an NCA branch in 1848, mustered 935 signatures to the petition and engaged in a lively pamphlet war with opponents, yet it never hosted a land plan branch.[10] There were also encouraging signs of new blood in many localities. For example, both the Manchester and the Colchester branch of the NCA had an energetic teenage secretary. In Manchester William Chadwick was also prominent in organising the unemployed, while in Colchester Henry Clubb welded the region's Chartist localities and land plan branches into a single Essex and Suffolk Chartist Union.[11] Chartists may have been frustrated and dismayed by the events of 10 April but they were emphatically not defeated.

Naturally, however, localities old and new shared in the frustrations of Kennington Common. Archibald Alison reckoned that you could spot Glaswegian Chartists on 11 April simply from the depressed look on their faces.[12] There was frequent criticism of the executive's handling of matters and widespread scepticism about the proposed next stage of agitation. The National Assembly which gathered in London on May Day was a lacklustre affair. Ambitious proposals to make it a truly representative body with, for example, a third of its seats reserved for trade unions came to nothing. Of a theoretical complement of 100, only 54 delegates appeared. It 'was a total failure', Matthew Stevenson told his Bolton constituency; furthermore, 'there had been considerable division in the Assembly, and subsequently little business done. It had been ascertained, however, that there were not 5,000 enrolled Chartists.' By this he meant paid-up members of the NCA. Their number, at least since the 1842 peak of 50,000, was an issue about which the executive had long dissembled, though the paltry sums remitted to it (especially compared to the land plan's) provided a fair clue.[13]

Jones tried valiantly to infuse proceedings with a sense of purpose, emphasising that 'National Guards' were forming in Scottish towns, pledging their support 'should this Assembly declare itself a parliament'. Jones had been intoxicated by his reception over Easter when he had toured Scotland as the Convention's missionary. National Guards were indeed forming in Aberdeen, Dundee and Edinburgh, and the sentiments surrounding the new development were uncompromising. Edinburgh Chartist Donald Mackay (an old soldier) told a Dundee audience: 'It was absolutely necessary to overturn the Government, or in a short time they would all be starved – (loud applause). Moral Force was all humbug.' The self-styled 'Brigadier General' continued: 'Was Sir William Wallace a moral force man?'[14] But the National Guards' strength was barely a tithe of that which Jones had ascribed to them; moreover Mackay's sentiments were not shared by Scots at the Assembly. Nonetheless, they stringently criticised O'Connor and even favoured changing the name of the NCA in order to distance it from him.

They were not alone in expressing such sentiments. John Shaw (Tower Hamlets), for example, 'complained of the injury done to the cause by Mr. F. O'Connor, and said a body of staunch reformers were ready to start a paper in opposition to the *Northern Star* which would show up Mr. O'Connor in his true colours'. The Assembly did accomplish two practical tasks. First was a new plan of reorganisation based on the class-meeting format that many northern centres had favoured earlier in the decade, but whose 10 men to a class and 10 classes to a ward regularity looked to authority suspiciously like the cellular structure used by the United Irishmen in the 1790s. Second, the Assembly prepared for the election of a new executive plus a network of commissioners to proselytise in the absence of paid lecturers. The new executive emerged as O'Connor (president), Jones, Samuel Kydd (secretary), McDouall and John McCrae, a Chartist Church pastor and longstanding Ayrshire radical. Then, after two fractious weeks, the Assembly dissolved. The presentation of the memorial to the Queen was postponed indefinitely on the face-saving grounds that an audience could not be obtained. In the dissolution debate, a much sobered Jones sought to rally delegates with a measured speech arguing that 'they must start fresh from the fountain head of democracy' and praising the Assembly for maintaining Chartist unity. William Vernon rounded on him:

> There was no use blinking the fact, that a division existed among the Chartists as to the best means of obtaining their objects ... He did not understand Mr

E. Jones, when he talked about there being division but not disunion. He said that they were disunited. The 10th April was not a victory, as had been asserted, but a signal defeat ... There were many of them who did not believe that the Charter was to be got by petitioning and agitation ... in fact, they must fight for it.[15]

## Terror and alarm

Vernon was not alone in being impatient with the role of decent revolutionary. The context for the controversies that beset the Assembly was not simply one that revolved round O'Connor and 10 April. The situation in Ireland appeared heavy with insurgent menace; in Britain, Confederates and Chartists were moving into closer conjunction, while the mood of northern England especially was increasingly reminiscent of the truculence of 1838–39. Each of these needs brief consideration in turn.

The Irish 'revolution' of 1848 was a milk and water episode, ingloriously floundering after a week with a battle on 29 July between around 100 Confederates and 40 police, as histories never tire of relating, on a cabbage patch in Tipperary. This, however, should not obscure the extent to which the British Government felt menaced by the *potential* for an Irish rebellion. In response to intelligence indicating that funds, arms and an emigrant 'Irish Brigade' would arrive from America, ships were searched on entering British waters. Liverpool docks and Dublin Castle were directly linked by telegraph (the Government's use of this new technology was developing fast).[16] In the event, the enduring significance of the rising led by Smith O'Brien was one of intellectual example rather than practical inspiration. For large swathes of British Chartists in the summer of 1848, however, its leadership *was* inspirational. John Mitchel, editor of the *United Irishman*, attracted much attention, partly because his paper commanded ready sales among British Chartists but also because he was the first person to be charged under the new Crown and Government Security Act. He was arrested on 13 May and by the end of the month was *en route* to Australia and a fourteen-year sentence of transportation. Mitchel's fate leant much momentum to events in England. Although English Chartists were far from united around the issue, there were numerous demonstrations to express solidarity with Mitchel.

Bradford, where the convergence of Chartism and the Confederates was effectively total, was approaching open rebellion. The biggest headache for the authorities developed there and in London. The key personnel in the Bradford NCA were Irish. Two, George White, wool comber and intermittently professional Chartist, and shoemaker John W. Smyth, had made some impact on the national stage. Smyth was the local NCA secretary and was frequently returning to his native Limerick. White was on the stomp. 'Sick of coming to meetings and doing nothing' (he told a West Riding camp meeting in March), he was on the move all summer, usually in the company of Irish emissaries.[17]

Bradford's large Irish population was represented disproportionately in the declining trade of woolcombing. There, and in the wider region, 'Chartist scouts' watched police and troops, and National Guards drilled with pikes on the adjacent moors by night. On 19 May Bradford magistrates reported that police had effectively lost control of Adelaide Street, a Chartist stronghold in the heart of the town's Irish quarter. Four days later, when McDouall visited the town for a mass rally, 2,000 marched from Halifax to join Bradford's 10,000 in an extraordinary quasi-military display, with tricolours flying from pikestaffs and bands playing.[18]

With Bradford stiffened by 1,500 specials and 800 troops, a local manufacturer just back from abroad detected 'much fear and suspicion, and a bitter class feeling'. Even in somnolent York, 30 miles away, there was violence at a by-election (contested by Vincent) on 24 May, leading to rumours in its rural hinterland of a Chartist 'insurrection' in the city.[19]

An editorial in the *Halifax Guardian* of 27 May rounded on outsiders, like Richard Cobden, who underestimated the state of northern England:

> Mr. Cobden declares the Chartists to be a 'small, insignificant and powerless party'. There are a few people in Lancashire and Yorkshire who can tell him a different story … We are no Chartists … we have no wish to over-rate the numbers or import of the Chartist body. But men who muster in tens of thousands to demonstrate their attachment to a political principle are neither 'small' nor 'insignificant'.[20]

This editorial was written without the knowledge that, the same day in Dublin, Mitchel had been convicted of treason; or that Joe Grady, 'head man of the Irish Confederates of Bradford', was calling for 'Agitation' which 'more and more … will prevent the Govmt from sending any more Troops to Ireland, and if Mitchell is found Guilty the Revolution immediately commences in Ireland'. Metropolitan Police inspectors arrived next day in Bradford to advise local magistrates. Two days earlier police had briefly lost control of the neighbouring town of Bingley and a Chartist crowd had rescued two prisoners from police custody. This further focused the minds of Bradford's authorities and a plan was implemented to close down Chartist drilling and secure the intricate warren of courts and alleys around Adelaide Street.[21]

Their plan failed totally. What seemed like the entire population of the area streamed out of their homes to confront the police and specials or hurled missiles from their upper windows. The police retreated and crowds surged through the town, chanting and singing Chartist hymns. A second assault by the police in the afternoon succeeded only when reinforced by infantry and dragoons. A house-to-house search secured 2 pikes and resulted in 18 arrests.

The other location conspicuously supportive of Mitchel was, predictably, London where the intertwining of Chartists and Confederates mirrored the situation in Bradford. On 29 June there was a vast demonstration in Mitchel's support. Several thousand assembled on Clerkenwell Green and were drilled into marching formation by John Fussell, Joseph Williams and Daniel McCarthy. All three were old Chartist hands and close to the centre of the London movement. Fussell had played an important part among militant Chartists in Birmingham in 1839 (see chapter 3); LDA veteran Williams we glimpsed in chapter 9, supporting Reynolds at Trafalgar Square on 6 March; and Irish-born McCarthy was a stalwart in the city's boot and shoemakers' NCA locality. Converging at Finsbury Square with a similar crowd, led by Jones, McCrae and McDouall, from Stepney Green, the column marched on Trafalgar Square. 'It was increased by large numbers at every street – the party said, "Fall in", and the people did fall in, as they went along', *The Times* reported. It estimated the turn-out at 50,000 to 60,000 and, like many other observers, was struck by the discipline of the chanting crowd and its gradual and peaceable dispersal as it returned to Finsbury. A hard core of around 3,000, however, forcibly resisted police attempts to disperse them for several hours that night. The Government response to this was immediately to ban all meetings and marches as 'calculated to excite terror and alarm'.

Several nights of smaller disturbances in the Finsbury and Clerkenwell areas followed, during which troops were deployed; and police conduct gave rise to widespread criticism. For example, shoemaker John Leno, a recent idealistic recruit to Chartism and the very antithesis of a street 'rough', was 'discussing the Irish question' with a small crowd when a plainclothes constable 'commenced to belabour me with a truncheon ... till the blood fairly poured down my face'. *The Times* commented on 2 June: 'Chartism is neither dead nor sleeping. The snake was scotched not killed on the 10th of April. The advancing spring had brought with it warmth, vigour, and renovation.'[22] 'The government are now getting seriously uneasy about the Chartist manifestations in various parts of the country, especially in London', senior civil servant Charles Greville noted in his diary on 3 June; 'many who on the 10th of April went out as special Constables declare they would not do so again if another manifestation required it'.[23]

The following day witnessed the most serious of all the Mitchel demonstrations, at Bishop Bonner's Fields in Bethnal Green. The number of demonstrators involved in the main gathering was small – at most 8,000 – but its mood was confrontational. Ernest Jones called by on his way to the north, and pleaded with the crowd to show patience. He reminded them that Whit Monday (12 June) had been designated by the executive as a day for simultaneous meetings across Britain: this was not the time for precipitate action. Jones spoke to pacify the crowd but could not resist a poetic peroration: 'only preparation,

only organisation is wanted, and the Green Flag shall float over Downing Street
and St Stephens', that is, Parliament. With that he left to catch a train. As
the crowd began to disperse, matters spiralled out of control. One account of
events was that forty policemen, who had been stationed in a nearby church all
day, surged out into the street: many were drunk and all launched themselves
indiscriminately into the crowd. The more likely version is that a section of the
crowd, realising that police were inside the church, attacked it with bricks and
stones. But the net result was the same: reinforced by further detachments, the
police spread across Bethnal Green, forced their way into homes and beershops
and assaulted all who offered resistance. It was an ugly episode, only intelligible
in the context of the deep-rooted antipathy to the police, endemic in much of
the capital, with which Chartism coincided. Sunday 4 June was the day that
officers of the Metropolitan Police, stretched to the limit over more than a
week of violence, physically reciprocated that antipathy.[24] For the police the
immediate consequence was a large file of detailed complaints and another of
rather more anodyne testimonials.[25] For Jones the consequence (rather surprisingly, for he had frequently voiced far more bellicose sentiments) was his arrest
two days later. The Government decided to impose a blanket ban on all public
meetings in or near London on Whit Monday.[26]

Suddenly, Feargus O'Connor's 'victory' at Kennington Common in securing
the right to freedom of assembly did not look such a sham after all. It was the
events of Monday 12 June rather than of 10 April which proved the sterner
test of the Government's resolve and capacity to subdue discontent, and led
it to impose the most draconian legal and physical measures. Against a background of nervousness concerning the arrival on the Kent coast of a 'great
number of Foreigners' appearing 'to coincide with the views of the Chartists';
of pikes openly on sale at the Confederate Club based at the NCA's Soho
offices; and intelligence indicating Whit Monday was 'the day appointed for
disturbances', military mobilisation matched that of 10 April. Fewer special
constables, however, enlisted. Many specials, like William Gladstone, stayed
inside their shuttered homes awaiting the call. Magistrates dispersed across
the city at key points where troops and police were concentrated; arrangements
were made for courts to sit into the night; public establishments, including the
Bank, Royal Mint, workhouses and Waltham Abbey gunpowder mills, were
crammed with soldiers, and Parliament 'not only garrisoned but provisioned
as if for a siege'.[27]

The ramifications of Whit Monday spread nationwide in a way 10 April's
had not. The executive called for an exact attendance count to be taken at every
meeting, to efface the embarrassment of the Petition. The Government wanted
to face-down Chartism. Troop movements into major towns over the preceding
weekend so congested Crewe station, for example, that a serious train crash
occurred when a Whitsun excursion collided with a troop transport. Many

provincial magistrates took their cue from Westminster and sought to ban Chartist meetings. At Edinburgh a march through the city was prohibited and an alternative procession was forcibly dispersed by police and specials. In Liverpool a combined Chartist and Confederate rally was forced out of the town and had to meet on the sands in Bootle. Manchester's open-air rally was cancelled due to a heavy police presence and a meeting was held in a nearby music hall instead.[28]

In some quarters it was thought, both before and after the event, that Whit Monday was intended for a national uprising. This was, for instance, the claim of the usually well-informed Croydon Chartist Thomas Frost.[29] However all available evidence contradicts this. Firstly, the use of 'simultaneous meetings' was itself elastic. Some potentially major demonstrations, on Blackstone Edge on the Lancashire–Yorkshire border and on Glasgow Green, for example, were held on the Saturday or the Sunday rather than the Monday; on the Tuesday Isle of Wight Chartists, reinforced from London, staged a small demonstration at the gates of Osborne House, Queen Victoria's retreat. Prudently, perhaps, they claimed to be members of the Foresters' Friendly Society. Secondly, the Whitsun meetings lacked focus. Mobilising to re-enforce the righteousness of the Chartist cause was rather lost from sight. The Bradford assembly on Toftshaw Moor was a self-congratulatory affair, basking in the lustre of the events of 29 May: 'they had established a republic there', declared an exuberant George White to cheering crowds. Samuel Kydd's address to a 'great demonstration' in Nottingham marketplace was advertised as explaining 'the present position of the Country, and the high hopes which are entertained of speedily obtaining the "PEOPLE'S CHARTER"'. Attendance 'in your thousands' was enjoined for no other reason than to prove Cobden wrong in describing Chartists as an 'insignificant minority'.[30] O'Connor had been against the idea of simultaneous meetings from the outset and ostentatiously spent 12 June at the Snigs End land plan estate in Gloucestershire, welcoming the first allottees who arrived that day. (A grandchild of an original allottee, still living on the family plot in the 1960s, remembered being told how O'Connor was driven up from the Minster Lovell estate in an imposing carriage attended by postilions.)[31]

All speculation about revolutionary intent on 12 June therefore necessarily hinges on London where the solitary figure of Peter McDouall (all other members of the executive being out of the capital) was left to co-ordinate a monster demonstration in defiance of the Government's ban, provocatively convened on Bishop Bonner's Fields. A total of 1,500 foot and 100 mounted police greeted him on his arrival; 500 army pensioners waited in a nearby workhouse yard and 2 squadrons of cavalry were close at hand. McDouall asked a magistrate present if it was intended to put down the meeting. 'Yes, sir', came the reply. Disconsolately, McDouall then trudged round the field, telling knots of waiting demonstrators to go home; then, amid the increasingly heavy drizzle that matched the Chartists' mood, he left for the shelter of a beershop on Bethnal Green Road. The dreaded Chartist demonstration had ended not with plumes of smoke but in torrential rain, leaving *The Times* to comment on the curious spectacle of groups of policemen, 'ill-satisfied weavers; larking youngsters and sombre adults; [and] brawny Confederates', all sheltering together beneath the trees in Victoria Park.[32]

It was an epiphanic moment for McDouall who now determined that Chartists should be decent revolutionaries no longer. Now and only now did a serious Chartist conspiracy take shape. That afternoon in The Albion beershop, he chaired a large and disaffected group of London Chartists. They agreed to form a committee to 'appoint the day and hour when the final struggle is to take place'. The group included Greenwich Chartist George Davis, and a *Northern Star* reporter, both of whom immediately sent word to the Government of what was afoot. The files of the Home Office are littered with spies' correspondence, much of it from regular informers and of limited value. However, the reporter T. R. Reading seems to have contacted the Home Office just once before, with information about Beniowski and Taylor's intention to visit Newport in November 1839. It is a reasonable supposition that he was therefore not a professional informer but a committed Chartist opposed to conspiratorial violence and that his decision to inform indicated the gravity of what he had heard.[33]

The mood in The Albion was certainly ugly. Ernest Jones was not the only Chartist leader arrested. Fussell, Williams, Vernon and the latter's fellow-National Assembly delegate from Tower Hamlets Alexander Sharp had all been recently arrested. By Tuesday morning the conspirators were examining a map of the capital, selecting sites for barricades and public buildings to be fired. They had agreed that the following Sunday, 18 June, was the latest that the uprising should be staged. But then, inexplicably, McDouall missed their Tuesday evening meeting and sent word from himself and fellow-executive member John McCrae that all plans were to be abandoned.[34] Presumably the executive was worried about spies. And if he knew of the conspiracy, it is probable that O'Connor (now president of the executive and so titular as well as *de facto* head of Chartism for the first time) would have invoked all his authority to squash it.

For a few weeks there was a lull in the feverish round of meetings and processions. The sole exception to this was an elaborate funeral for an east London silk weaver who had succumbed to typhus but whose death, the coroner's jury insisted, was the result of injuries inflicted by police on 4 June. Both McDouall and McCrae spoke at his graveside. Considerable effort was devoted to the 'Liberty Fund', to defend Chartist prisoners and provide for their families. Fussell and Williams had 7 and 6 children respectively, the youngest in each family only a few months old; both men had been unemployed for some time. Jones had 3 children; Sharp had 2 and his wife was pregnant. The 4, plus Vernon and Frank Looney (secretary of the Davis Confederate Club which shared accommodation with the NCA) received 2-year sentences. Furthermore the list of Chartist prisoners grew rapidly, notably with the arrest on 16 July of McDouall, charged with seditious speech at Ashton-under-Lyne where he had declared that 'before the harvest is in, or very soon after, I will promise you shall have the six points of the charter, and something more'.[35]

Then, on 25 July, *habeas corpus* was suspended in Ireland, adding the power of indefinite detention without trial to the Government's armoury. This brought demonstrators and police once more to London's streets, especially two days later when news of Smith O'Brien's rebellion reached the capital. The following day Londoners heard that Patrick O'Higgins, leader of the Irish Chartists, had been arrested on charges of high treason. The conspiracy mooted but then abandoned at Whitsuntide now took renewed shape. This revived conspiracy lacked any direct link to the NCA executive, but George Davis continued to attend and reported regularly to the Home Office, along with a second informer, Clerkenwell carpenter Thomas Powell.[36] The group came together on 20 July and never comprised more than 30-40 delegates. Most of its business was conducted by an 'ulterior committee', whose size and membership varied; but it included five Irishmen, among them William Dowling, the Davis Conferderates' new secretary, and from 4 August William Cuffay. It is from 4 August also that spies' reports mention contact with the NCA executive's secretary Samuel Kydd, apparently facilitating contact with Manchester. Cuffay and the Irishman Daniel Donovan were the only NCA commissioners involved, Cuffay the only Convention delegate and south Londoner James Bassett the only National Assembly member. There was some talk of John Churchill, Finsbury's delegate to the Assembly, 'who was in France during the revolution of February last', joining the group in a leading role, but this did not come about.[37]

The committee's emissary to the provinces was William Lacey, whose letters to the committee mention contact with Birmingham, Leicester, Loughborough, Nottingham and particularly Manchester. Bradford and Liverpool seem also to have been part of the network. Each delegate regularly reported on the preparedness of his locality to rise, and a general feeling emerged that London could be stirred up at any time. The timing of a nationwide general rising would therefore coincide with Manchester making a move. It was uncertain if this would be Monday 14 August or the following night. Both nights delegates from across the capital gathered to await news; on the second Lacey arrived direct from the north and announced that 'the men of Manchester, Birmingham and Liverpool were up and doing or would be that night'. It was then agreed: '*tomorrow night the blow must be struck*'.[38] Armed bands were to muster at 8.00 p.m. at four strategic locations. Arson attacks would create confusion and signal that the insurgency had begun. The overall aim was not the direct overthrow of the Government: co-ordinated insurgency in major centres would require troops to be withdrawn from Ireland; it would intensify general discontent and thus ultimately might force a change of ministry to one inclined to reform.

Evidence for a general rising is uneven: but clearly not all the ulterior committee's talk was fantasy. During July the recruitment of Chartist National Guards had accelerated and their operations were anything but clandestine. At Hebden Bridge the local NCA went so far as to call on the national executive to be reconstituted as a national defence committee: 'all former agitations for the attainment of the People's Charter have failed in consequence of being based on moral arguments in opposition to an authority based on physical force'.[39] Accumulating Home Office intelligence suggested preparations for a rising were in hand, and that support in local communities was extensive. A report from Oldham noted with astonishment that 'a woman Mrs Theobald ... gave a Strong Recommendation to all Arm and enrol them selves as National Guards'. The report continued that gunpowder would be dispatched to Oldham in blacking, patent medicine and 'Pop Bottles'. Mrs Theobold was touring Lancashire and Cheshire delivering the same message, the first phase of a short but influential career as Chartism's only full-time female lecturer.[40]

After news of Smith O'Brien's rebellion reached Bolton, several hundred Chartists and Confederates gathered nightly on Bolton Moor for drill instruction in companies of 20–30, each directed by a 'wardsman'. At Hyde on 8 August, itinerant fire-brand George Mantle of Birmingham addressed a crowd estimated by police at 1,800: 'If you want the Charter you must arm yourselves and be prepared to take it by force for I can tell you that that the Tyrannical Government of this Country will never grant the Charter by Moral force.' When Mantle asked 'all of you that will join with me and are for fighting and putting down this Government signify the same by putting up your right hands', nearly everyone present complied.[41] In the midlands, on the other hand there was no evidence that Birmingham or anywhere else was 'up and doing', beyond rumours that the town houses of two local dignitaries were to be fired. Similarly, in Liverpool news of Smith O'Brien's defeat and the authorities' effective action combined to demoralise the Confederates. Bolton, too, it turned out, was quiescent.[42] Plans for the Manchester rising were shattered on the night of 15 August by simultaneous police raids on a range of Chartist and Confederate meetings. Among the twenty arrested were John Leach and, at the Ancoats' coffee house that was the conspiracy's regional headquarters, the Bradford Chartists George White and George Webber.[43]

The absence of the expected signal from Manchester left National Guards and other conspiratorial elements in the north confused and fractured. A force of armed Chartists set out from Oldham's Working Men's Hall in the early hours of Tuesday morning, met with a Royton contingent marching 'with pikes shouldered' and set off for Manchester apparently to fire buildings and assassinate selected magistrates. But the force was only seventy strong, and when confronted by police and cavalry 'the processionists dispersed and came back in twos and threes'.[44]

Ashton-under-Lyne's National Guard mobilised on the Monday night to rendezvous with contingents from Hyde, Stalybridge, Newton and Dukinfield. Alarmed by the pounding of hundreds of clogs on the pavements, the Chief Constable sent a mounted policeman for military assistance. He soon returned to say that colliers from a local pit had barricaded the road to the barracks. Following a confrontation with one Guards' detachment, a policeman was shot at point-blank range and in cold blood.[45] Meanwhile Hyde's Guards were systematically touring the town's mills, drawing boiler plugs just as in 1842. Challenged by a policeman they coolly responded: 'They're now all out, all over England, Ireland and Scotland, and before this time tomorrow we'll either make it better or worse.'[46]

Hyde was the only location where the Chartist rising of 1848 was characterised by neither rout nor tragedy. At Heywood, armed Chartists who had been up several nights practising arms drill were heard to complain on Wednesday 'that they had been waiting every night for an expected signal'. At Halifax, 'hundreds of men sat up with pikes in hand, ready to fight'. Bradford conspirators, likewise waiting on a signal from Manchester, prepared to rip up rail tracks, fracture gas pipes (to plunge the town into darkness) and storm the police station. On Tuesday the Bradford Chartist council sent John Smyth into Lancashire. He returned the following morning to tell a dejected meeting at Daley's beershop 'that all was broken up and come to an end'.[47] The following week police systematically raided the homes of Bradford's Confederate and Chartist 'Clubbists'. They searched the two shared rooms where Smyth lived but found nothing more incriminating than the NCA branch ledger. A revealing insight into Smyth's personal circumstances was that his home was completely empty, save for two beds and a box of books.[48]

In London the conspiracy ended in bathos. The eleven leading conspirators assembled at 5.00 p.m. on Wednesday 16 August in The Orange Tree pub, near Holborn, to make the final preparations ahead of the muster that night. They had been there scarcely an hour when police poured into the room and arrested them all. Later that evening another 300 police apprehended a second group at The Angel Tavern, south of the river. Silently but swiftly the news sped across the capital. At Seven Dials junction in Soho, one of the four muster points, around 150 men were clustering on the street-corners or fidgeting the final hours away in nearby pubs. 'A man approached a group at the corner of Great St Andrew Street, and spoke a few hurried words in a low voice ... the man moved quickly from one group to another, and as he left each the men composing it separated, some walking quietly away, and others entering the public-houses at the corner of the streets to communicate what they had heard'. Within minutes Seven Dials was almost deserted.[49]

## The beginning of an end

Six Orange Tree conspirators, as they quickly became known, were transported. Fifteen others received sentences of 18–24 months. McDouall was sentenced to 2 years in prison; George White, John Leach and John West for one; and young William Chadwick for 6 months. This does not indicate that Chadwick, Leach or West were implicated in the August conspiracy, but rather that late 1848 was a fertile climate in which to secure convictions of known Chartists, on charges ranging from seditious speech through armed drilling to attendance at unlawful meetings: forty-six from Lancashire alone appeared at assizes later in the year. Just as in 1839–40 and 1842, a policy of mass arrests backed up by inflated bail terms contained Chartism, regardless of whether cases reached court. As a weary Manchester Chartist observed, mass arrests 'depressed their spirits and exhausted their funds'. Exemplary sentences subdued Chartism but stopped someway short of creating martyrs. Even the death sentences on Smith O'Brien and Meagher were commuted to transportation the following year; so too was the death sentence on Joseph Radcliffe, a wheelwright and 'colonel' in Ashton's National Guard, who was convicted (on shaky evidence) of murdering the policeman there on 14 August. Six other sentences of transportation and eight spells in prison were handed down to political prisoners from Ashton. 'Discard all Association of this sort', the judge advised those receiving lesser sentences, 'you have an idea to benefit your selves by obtaining the People's Charter – Why the People's Charter? What would it signify to you if there was universal suffrage all over England?'[50] Their answer went unrecorded. The nine Ashton men who turned Queen's evidence were given assisted passages to Australia, with their families, partly as a reward and partly for their own safety. Clearly, community support for the conspirators ran deep.[51]

There was no hiding, however, the mood of confusion and defeat that characterised Chartism at the end of 1848. In those localities most involved in the August rising it took hold almost immediately. The usually excitable informer William Dawson (who had shadowed White across northern England that summer) reported from Bradford on 1 September that 'the system is dieing away fast … as the Chartism is all done away for the Present'. McDouall's two-year sentence, Dawson believed, 'hath damped all the spirits of the Chartist'. Two days later Dawson reported that all Bradford Chartists except one section had 'agreed to sceace and not to Carry on for they found as would be taken Prisoners'. All nine members of the dissenting section were rounded up by police the following day.[52] For James Taylor, a long-standing Ashton radical, the root of Chartism's predicament lay in having equated its aspiration to democracy with a requirement to be itself democratic:

> They were in times of excitement too eager to admit members regardless of their character or condition; this was the cause why Ashton had brought disgrace on the cause ... He had watched the democratic cause from the Blanketeering movement, the Peterloo massacre, and Reform agitation, until the present time, and was certain that this indiscriminate admission of members was a primary cause of their previous and present misfortunes.[53]

Philip McGrath offered a parallel analysis to Taylor's in the same *Northern Star* issue, comparing the cheerless autumn with the confidence of the preceding spring:

> Since then all had been one waste blank, one huge monument of misfortune ... Violent measures were not suited to the general constitution of the British mind ... Their object should be lectures, public meetings, and a proper direction of their moral power and by falling back on a legal system of organisation to recover that position which they had lost by want of prudence and common sense.

It was not, however, just the exposure of the August conspiracy that prompted such feelings: Chartists tended to explain that away as the work of *agents provocateurs* employed by a repressive regime to lead the despairing patriots astray. 'We live under Martial Law!' Harney was apt to claim, and he was prominent among those arguing that Thomas Powell bore prime responsibility for the Orange Tree conspiracy. Feargus O'Connor caught this mood perfectly through his generous contributions to the defence of Chartist prisoners, as well as through the presentation of engravings of Meagher, Mitchel and Smith O'Brien to *Northern Star* readers.[54]

Feelings of despair went much deeper. At the end of a bruising year it was unclear what Chartism had to offer anymore. O'Connor tried to fan the embers by offering himself for 're-election' at Nottingham. At the imitation hustings ceremony in the marketplace, the crowd stood in for the British people as a whole, exactly as O'Connor presented himself as 'the people's MP' and not Nottingham's alone. Lavishly reported in the *Star*, it was, however, a hollow exercise. Few Chartists were taken in by O'Connor's reiterated claims that 10 April had been a victory for the movement, still less that 'never did Chartism stand as high as after that meeting'.[55] The sense of despondency was palpable.

There was little elsewhere in Chartism to brighten the mood. While the political drama of 1848 unfolded, the fortunes of the land plan commenced a steep decline. O'Connor's response to the continued failure to secure its legal registration was to seek its enrolment under an Act of Parliament. He moved the first reading of a Bill for this purpose on 12 May, but the process was preempted by the House of Commons' decision on 23 May to establish a Select Committee on the scheme. The Committee was not inherently hostile to the plan, to Chartism or to O'Connor personally. Four of its sixteen members had been NCREC-endorsed candidates at the previous general election (including O'Connor himself) and two were Irish Repealers. Sitting twice weekly over two months they undertook a thorough examination of all aspects of the plan and called witnesses ranging from a Suffolk smallholder to the actuary to the National Debt, as well as O'Connor and land plan officials. Events that summer, plus the opening of the Snigs End and Minster Lovell estates (the latter renamed Charterville), enabled O'Connor to disguise the unfolding crisis.

The Select Committee's 390-page proceedings, published 1 August, did not make pretty reading. It went out of its way to exonerate O'Connor from any charge of personal dishonesty; in fact, he was shown to have subsidised the undertaking from his own pocket by as much as £3,400. The Committee could not be precise about the amount because, to quote its final conclusions, 'accounts have not been kept with strict regularity'. O'Connor widely publicised this exoneration, but drew less attention to the other conclusions (to which he had nonetheless assented): that the plan was definitely ineligible for registration as a friendly society; that its records were imperfectly kept and all but three of the quarterly balance sheets destroyed; and most damaging of all that it was 'an illegal scheme, and will not fulfil the expectations held out by the directors to the Shareholders'.[56]

Buried in 4,600 numbered paragraphs of evidence was yet more potentially damaging information. O'Connor had refused to be drawn about how long it would take to settle all shareholders, but the Government actuary's best estimate was 150 years.[57] Even this assumed that the £300 average cost to locate each smallholder so far would diminish and that allottees would henceforward pay an economic rent for the property they occupied. Much of the land plan's original promotional material, however, had stated that occupiers would have the freehold of their land. Furthermore, there were doubts as to whether a holding of 4, 3 or especially 2 acres could fully support the occupant's family and yield sufficient surplus to pay rent. To assess this, the Committee called to give evidence John Revans, a Jersey smallholder and former senior civil servant who had serviced Royal Commissions on both the Poor Law and the Irish Poor. 'I am quite confident they cannot maintain themselves; it will be a failure', Revans declared. The Committee's other expert agricultural witness, Suffolk smallholder and agricultural writer John Sillett, was far more sanguine. Subsequent experience would indeed show that 4-acre allotments, particularly if operated as market gardens rather than subsistence farms, were viable. But the evidence in 1848 was at best ambiguous, especially as it pitched Revans against Sillett who freely claimed O'Connor's 'excellent work on small farms' had inspired him to become a smallholder.[58]

Even accepting that the scheme was technically viable, however, there remained the problem of its infeasible magnitude and an official enquiry that uncovered multiple examples of mismanagement. No one was certain how many subscribers there were: 'the total number who have subscribed ... are [sic] said to be 70,000'. This the Committee accepted as a working estimate, though an alternative reading of the evidence provided by McGrath (interviewed in his capacity as director and financial secretary) suggests the figure may have been 87,000 or higher.[59] Unsurprisingly, the registration procedure as a joint stock company had been abandoned ('The number of names overcame us', a hapless clerk admitted); but there was limited evidence that the National Land Company's financial procedures would have withstood legal scrutiny had registration been achieved. Philip McGrath, for example, admitted paying £75, on O'Connor's verbal authority, to 1848 Convention delegates from subscriptions received, but had no notion if this was ever repaid. The *Northern Star's* printer acted as the plan's treasurer, but conceded that the only paperwork he ever kept were the revenues and expenditure columns that appeared in the newspaper.[60]

Some of the evidence probably impressed only those already critical of O'Connor – for example, the large sums paid into local bank accounts in his name, from which setting-up costs for the estates were then met, or paid direct to his friend Thomas Allsop to service mortgages or toward the purchase of further estates. Similarly, O'Connor was sole proprietor of the National Land & Labour Bank. Asked what the capital of this Bank consisted of, its manager flatly responded that 'it is principally made up of Mr. O'Connor's character and the money he has put in'.[61] This reply was unnerving from a legal point of view but the overwhelming majority of Chartists trusted Feargus unreservedly. It was that trust, born of a political solidarity incomprehensible to parliamentary politicians, that kept the land plan from sinking and taking O'Connor with it.

An eloquent illustration of this occurred at the trial of the Orange Tree conspirators, when defence counsel sought to discredit the informer Powell by calling a number of workmen to attest to his bad character. Cross-examining one, an unemployed sofa-maker, the Attorney-General teased him about his land plan membership. The response was sharp: 'I am a land plan member still ... I am not in the least shaken in it myself, for as much money as I can get I am prepared to pay in now – I consider as far as the press has gone they have misrepresented it altogether. I am satisfied with what money I have paid in.'[62]

This broadly summarised the attitude of the majority of the members in the autumn of 1848. Fed a carefully filleted diet of extracts from the parliamentary report in the *Northern Star* (and reassured by Feargus that the will he had made on 9 April left everything to trustees for the land plan), their attention now concentrated on getting all the shareholders located on the land. Subscriptions continued to be received from members anxious to complete their share payments and thus become eligible for future ballots. Relations between O'Connor and the membership began to break down seriously only the following winter. Neither subscriptions nor Land & Labour Bank investments were arriving in sufficient quantities to permit the purchase of further estates: indeed a substantial deposit was forfeited when O'Connor failed to raise sufficient money to complete the purchase, in February 1849, of a sixth estate. The fifth and final Chartist colony, Dodford, opened in July 1849 with little of the fanfare that had greeted the others. To avoid prosecution for running an illegal lottery, plots at Dodford were allocated to those land plan shareholders prepared to offer the largest additional payment towards the capital value of an allotment. Although agreed by a land conference the previous November, this totally negated the ethos of the plan. It also meant the new occupiers were uninhibited in criticising their properties.[63] Similarly demoralising were the attempts by the Company and its mortgagees to charge rent to allottees at the other estates, which led to sixty-eight eviction orders being served at Charterville in January 1850.

The final recommendation of the Select Committee was that, due to the large number of members involved and the honest intentions with which the National Land Company had been conducted, permission could be sought by the promoters to wind it up and be relieved from the personal liabilities to which they had 'incautiously subjected themselves'.[64] However, O'Connor had still not given up hope of securing joint stock company status. In January 1849 he began an eighteen-month legal action to secure registration without the requisite shareholders' register. The result was yet another frustrating ruling: a joint stock company had to operate for the profit and advantage of the shareholders; if the National Land Company provided freehold allotments then profit and advantage lay with the freeholders alone; but if it charged rent on allotments, that revenue could not be deemed profit since it must be devoted to the purchase of further land for unlocated members. Finally a petition to wind up the National Land Company was presented to Parliament in July 1850. Yet another year elapsed before the necessary Act was passed. Ironically, it began from the premiss that for the purposes of winding up the scheme should be deemed a joint stock company. Thereafter the affairs of the National Land Company were overseen by a manager appointed by the Court of Chancery.[65] Like Dickens's celebrated case of Jarndyce v. Jarndyce, the land plan dragged its weary length for seven more years, perennially hopeless. In all 234 allotments were made: the serviceable and attractive houses built on each of them bore continuing witness to Chartists' hunger for 'a new life, intense and unconfined' (the words of a Leicester house painter, associated with Thomas Cooper).[66]

Land and building societies were the paradigmatic voluntary associations of early Victorian England. The leviathan proportions of the land plan, as much as its association with Chartism, were its undoing. With hindsight, if the scheme had followed the principle of Bowkett building societies (see chapter 8 above) and developed a string of small societies, with clear limits on the membership of each, it might have met success. O'Connor's heroically flawed attempt to merge the ethos of working-class mutualism with the scope and ambition of a major commercial undertaking would prove a crippling embarrassment to the Chartist movement. This was beginning to become apparent when the 1848 land plan conference met at Birmingham in November, though it manifested itself chiefly in criticism of allottees who sub-let their land, and of profiteering in the sale of shares or rights of allotment. The conference was more significant for an emergency meeting tacked on to it to discuss the direction of Chartism generally. This had no constitutional status, comprising as it did only land plan delegates, but the NCA's situation was critical. With McDouall and Jones in prison and McCrae forced to return to Scotland because there were no funds to meet his expenses or salary, Samuel Kydd was the sole effective member of the executive. He guardedly referred to O'Connor (who had excused himself from attending) as being 'so occupied, that he could not devote much of his time to his duty as a member of the Executive'.

The situation was clearly untenable even had the movement been in good health, but of course it was not. 'Chartism had retrograded', Kydd told the meeting; it 'had foundered', said Taylor; 'their conduct had murdered Chartism', Mitchell of Rochdale concluded bluntly. The NCA had no funds with which to pay an executive, most of its income was devoted to paying an allowance to the wives of Jones and McDouall (the latter so impoverished that his 9-year-old daughter died while he was imprisoned). The ad hoc meeting assumed supervisory powers, decided the executive should in future be unpaid except for the secretary, and elected Kydd to that post at a weekly salary of £2. It summarily overturned the new organisational plan established by the National Assembly six months earlier: out went the cellular structure (which delegates believed appeared intrinsically conspiratorial in the eyes of the authorities) and out went the commissioners. A new executive was elected, comprising 8 London members, to conduct routine business, and 45 others representing major towns. The map of Chartist strength revealed by the distribution of those towns was revealingly skewed: 3 centres in Devon, for example, but only 2 (Leeds and Todmorden) in West Yorkshire, and Clitheroe and Preston from the north-west, but not Ashton or Stockport; 4 Scottish centres were represented and 2 Welsh.[67]

Also revealing was the programme the emergency meeting decreed that the NCA should pursue. There was an explicit rejection of close alignment with continental movements: 'exciting events abroad had brought many democrats to hasty conclusions', Kydd argued. There was a tacit endorsement, hardly surprising since all present were land plan activists, of greater emphasis on social issues. Several speakers argued for more overt involvement in education and propaganda, including establishing a 'central tract depot' to co-ordinate procuring and supplying inexpensive literature. Centralised management had been used to great effect by the ACLL which, for example, dispatched 9 million items from its Manchester depot in 1843 alone.[68] However, it had never been adopted by the NCA, possibly because printers, publishers and booksellers exercised considerable influence within Chartism. But lack of funds now meant that central co-ordination of promotional literature was still not adopted.

As the movement's sole paid worker, Kydd's schedule was frenetic. During the next seven weeks he undertook a national lecture tour and contested the West Riding by-election hustings, in addition to routine secretarial duties. His reports of the lecture tour contained revealing comments, for example about meetings far from full as well as those that met the once-universal standard of 'full to suffocation'; and after an evening spent in Halifax, Kydd ventured the conclusion that during the previous summer Chartism had 'swelled for a moment to an unnatural size'.[69]

O'Connor's perception of the situation differed sharply from the most active members'. He welcomed what he called the 'social turn' of the Birmingham conference: it was consistent with his own increasing emphasis on 'the Labour Question'. However, his prescription for the latter was limited: 'the Land Plan – which is the only possible social plan for the emancipation of Labour', combined with 'the vote to protect their inheritance'. He now proposed that a new convention should meet at Easter 1849, first, to draw-up a 'digest of the Labour Question' for presentation to mass open air meetings and, second, to supervise the presentation of further petitions to Parliament. Rather than a single national petition, each locality should organise its own using a prescribed text. O'Connor's suggestion flew in the face of the prevailing mood of the movement, but in a letter to 'All Who Live by Industry' he asserted: 'you cannot be guilty of a greater folly than that of protesting against petitioning'. O'Connor clung to the mass platform still.[70]

Abandon it, however, is what Chartists did. No convention met in 1849 and the local Chartist petitions finally presented in July 1849 numbered only 19 and totalled only 53,816 signatures. A Commons' motion in favour of the Charter was then defeated by 222 votes to 13, the smallest ever display of parliamentary support for Chartism.[71] A 'national delegate conference' did assemble in December 1849, but its twenty-three delegates met to debate whether the NCA title should be abandoned in favour of National Charter Union (they decided not) and to resume paying the executive (to which they agreed). Provincial representation was thin: even mighty West Yorkshire was absent.

Thus Chartism in 1849 was much like it had been at the beginning of 1847, effectively a pressure group with an adjunct land scheme. But now the land plan was ailing and a want of general direction everywhere apparent. 'We have now had ten years of Chartist organising, speech-making, petitioning, and suffering', wrote Harney in the first *Northern Star* of 1849, 'and how near are we to the enactment of the Charter?' In the same issue 'Eliza D.' of London wrote lamenting the state of female Chartism: 'A few months ago there flourished in this metropolis several female localities', she wrote. 'In vain I seek them now.' And the malaise, in her opinion, went further: the Victim Fund for prisoners' families was 'exhausted' and 'feebleness' apparent throughout the movement.[72]

No longer claiming the status of a mass platform agitation, Chartism struggled for primacy of place among a number of competing initiatives. Viewed collectively, Chartists were young in years and not prepared to blunt their considerable energies in pursuit of the unobtainable. This did not mean that their commitment to the principles embodied in the Charter dissolved: but there was an understandable drift towards the politics of the possible in preference to what increasingly looked like an agitational wilderness. The process is better encapsulated as *drift* rather than *shift*, because it was gradual, sometimes almost imperceptible. There was no clear point at which Chartists decided that their movement had failed and accordingly shifted their allegiances.

The NCA persisted for the next decade, but even a membership of 5,000 (which so dismayed the National Assembly in 1848) was never reached again: indeed by May 1850 it may have fallen as low as 500. 'I have not been supported in my endeavours to resuscitate the Chartist Movement,' Kydd complained when he resigned as the NCA's secretary in October 1849. He was disillusioned after spending 6 of his 11 months in office on the road, 4 without a salary. The weekly remittances to the NCA recorded in the *Northern Star*, he revealed, were primarily the takings from his lectures.[73]

In every respect, 1849 was not a happy year. In March the *Star* gave a very public airing to the differences between its proprietor and editor. O'Connor claimed that Harney covered foreign politics to the virtual exclusion of Chartist news. Harney's response was dignified and refrained from pointing out that very little 'Chartist Intelligence' was now sent to the paper.[74] Privately he was furious about 'O'Connor's villainous denunciation of our principles':

> The fact is he is a thorough aristocrat masquerading in the outward profession of democracy. More still; he is worse than an aristocrat, he has all the vulgarism, the money-grubbing (in spite of his boasting to the contrary) of a dirty bourgeois. But I believe the hour of his fall is at hand … James Leach, John West, and Geo. White, [are] imploring me to stand firm and save our cause … They cry that the hour has struck when the great, worst enemy of our cause must be overthrown.[75]

After O'Connor insisted on a right to censor all Harney's copy, the latter threatened to make their differences even more public. In consequence, not only did O'Connor back off suddenly, he also withdrew from almost all involvement in the paper for over a month.

This was but one example of his increasingly erratic behaviour. His stance regarding collaboration with radical liberals constantly shifted. In July he published a much-quoted open letter to Queen Victoria, addressed 'Well beloved cousin' and signed 'Feargus Rex by the Grace of the People'. Conceivably he meant this as a lampoon; some allowance may also have been made by sympathetic Chartists for the unspecified 'severe indisposition' he referred to suffering two weeks earlier; he also spoke of a pressing need for 'mental calm' and of being 'tortured with anxiety' lest he commit an indiscretion in Parliament that injured Chartism. His talent for controversy was no longer backed by the sure judgement of former years. A disastrous libel action against the *Nottingham Journal* cost him £2,000 and he was successfully sued for non-payment of fees by the barrister he had hired in 1848 to defend Williams, Sharp and Fussell.[76]

A bitter dispute also raged alleging preferential treatment of certain prisoners' families, and centred on White and McDouall, which effectively drove the latter from the movement. That summer cholera cut a swathe through London Chartism, carrying off, among others, the prisoners Sharp and Williams, as well as Henry Hetherington. To his death and funeral *Northern Star* gave fulsome coverage, signifying recognition on Harney's part that the time had come to make peace with Lovett's circle. O'Connor too was softening his stance: a few weeks later he went out of his way to praise Lovett's friend John Humffries Parry.[77] The immediate context of this, however, was O'Connor's unexpected shift to support the middle-class National Parliamentary and Financial Reform Association. Four months earlier O'Connor, likening it to the NCSU of 1842, threatened to withdraw from Chartism altogether if Chartists supported the NPFRA. Now he urged *Star* readers, 'in the name of honour, justice, patriotism, and the CHARTER, to join the new Parliamentary Reform Association, heart and soul'.[78]

O'Connor's switch stemmed partly from his wooing of Charles Gavan Duffy, an NPFRA admirer and leading figure in the recovery of Irish nationalism after the humiliation of 1848. In part O'Connor was also exploring avenues that might revivify Chartism. His search took him to Ireland in November 1849 and again in March 1850, to forge a working relationship with Irish nationalism. When Duffy's largely middle-class Irish Alliance proved unreceptive, O'Connor shifted his overtures to the Irish Democratic Association, whose occupational profile more closely mirrored that of Chartism. This met, albeit fleetingly, with more success and branches of the Association were formed in nine British centres, overlapping Chartism just as the earlier Confederate clubs had done. However, Irish nationalism after 1848 was no less given to sectarian shifts and rivalries than British Chartism in the same period: the Association proved ephemeral.[79]

The sectarian shifts within and around Chartism at this time were numerous and potentially bewildering.[80] However, it should first be stressed that, no less than during the movement's earlier history, Chartists by conviction rather than enrolment were still the norm. The financially beleaguered NCA remained at the movement's core but a proliferation of other bodies laying claim to the Chartist mantle underline these were troubled times. Not without a certain symbolism, the first of these, the People's Charter Union, emerged in the wake of the March 1848 demonstrations with an emphatic commitment to peace and legality in pursuit of the Charter. Thomas Cooper was its president and a number of ex-LWMA members (though not Lovett) were involved.[81] Lovett instead established the People's League, intended as a successor to the defunct National Association. It lasted eighteen months.[82]

That same spring Joseph Hume launched a campaign for 'the little charter': household suffrage, triennial Parliaments, equal electoral districts and the ballot. These in turn were the planks of the NPFRA's platform when it formed in January 1849.[83] In October Bronterre O'Brien launched his National Reform League, abetted by G.W.M.Reynolds, the popularity of which never matched its intellectual rigour, though alone of this clutch of radical grouplets it endured (until 1869).[84] In June 1850 a Scottish Democratic Association was formed that distanced Chartism there from the NCA. In August the NCA proposed a federation with the National Reform League and the Owenite Social Reform League to form a 'National Charter and Social Reform Union'. After six months of regular meetings to progress this, the proposal collapsed.[85] The Union's chief significance was the havoc it caused within the NCA. In March 1850 Clark and McGrath resigned from the executive to form the National Charter League, brazenly supported by O'Connor and more subtly by Lovett (though he never attended meetings, it occasionally met at his National Hall).[86] Clark and McGrath argued that Chartism should keep aloof from socialism and that co-operation with the NPFRA was necessary. The dispute between Clark and his former NCA colleagues generated some of the most abusive literature in the history of Chartism, no mean feat in a movement imploding under the weight of internal faction.[87]

The dispute also forced back to the surface Harney's deteriorated relationship with O'Connor. Though Feargus remained on the NCA executive he applauded Clark, whose pamphlet war was conducted from the land plan's offices. In May 1850 Harney announced he would leave the *Northern Star* in August. Since launching his cerebral monthly *Democratic Review* the previous June, Harney's journalistic heart had lain elsewhere than the *Star*, and in June 1850 he added a further weekly publication, the *Red Republican*. Harney took a dim view of

O'Connor's use of the *Star* to proselytise for both the NPFRA and the floundering land plan: his views on the encomia he was required to print when Peel died went unrecorded, likewise O'Connor's decision to add the deceased Prime Minister to the paper's portrait gallery.[88] The *Star's* readership was sharply declining: average weekly sales in 1850 hit a low of 5,000, below by 1,000 those in 1846, the worst previous year. *Reynolds's Political Instructor* easily outsold it, and in previously solid Chartist centres like Loughborough and Merthyr Tydfil the *Northern Star* mustered barely a dozen sales.[89] So rudderless was the paper that it is even unclear who edited it for the first eight months after Harney's departure. Presumably it was the Owenite and NAUT activist George Fleming, who officially became editor the following spring.

## The Charter in the early 1850s

'The Chartism of '51 is not that of '39 or '48', wrote Harney in April 1851. 'The outward and visible form of Chartism perished in 1848, or if ought remained, it was but a miserable wreck and remnant of its former strength … Defeated, disappointed of the political victory they had hoped for in 1848, the hard-working thinkers turned their attention to social questions.'[90] A number of reform agendas now competed for Chartists' energies, while municipal politics absorbed many. There could be no mistaking Chartism's 'social turn'. Even O'Connor had argued that 'the great, the paramount duty of a Chartist Parliament would be to see and know how to equalise taxation, and to decide upon a just and equitable distribution'. Furthermore, popular critical thinking about labour economics was encouraged by the recurrent emphasis that migration back to the land would 'thin the artificial labour market by employing thousands who are now destitute, and constituting an idle reserve to enable capitalists to live and make fortunes upon the reduction of wages'.[91] It was therefore a natural development for Chartism to engage more fully with social democratic ideas, a development encapsulated under the banner of 'The Charter and Something More', a play on the long-established O'Connorite slogan 'The Charter and nothing less'.[92]

This strand in Chartist thought developed naturally from the long-standing perception that measures proposed by existing radical MPs would be, to quote Harney, 'surface reforms [which] might take place without materially benefiting the proletarians'. They might include disestablishment of the Anglican Church, House of Lords' reform, reductions in the cost of monarchy and reforms in property law designed to free up the market in land. To the latter (increasingly emphasised by former ACLL leaders) Harney and his circle responded that nothing short of land nationalisation would suffice, an argument also made by O'Brien. Underpinning Harney's programme was a strong belief that 'the feudal lords are doomed – they are worn out, their race is run, and the hand-writing on the walls predicts their speedy extinction'. On the other hand 'the money-lords are full of life and energy' and the only effective prevention of their supplanting aristocracy was by agitating for *'the Charter and something more* – THE CHARTER, THE LAND, AND THE ORGANISATION OF LABOUR!'[93]

In the very first issue of the *Red Republican*, under this soon-familiar headline, Harney was confident enough to predict that this new strand within Chartism was approaching a position of ascendancy. It was 'whole hog' Chartism that, despite traditionally espousing 'the Charter and nothing less', proved most amenable to 'negotiating with the enemies of Democracy – the bourgeois liberals'. Chartism, Harney suggested, was divided into two irreconcilable parts: 'the Chartists and something more' and 'the Chartists, *or* something *less*'. Those who might still be termed 'Chartists pure and simple' had dwindled to the point of insignificance. 'In this life inertness is destruction. We must advance or retreat; the earth moves and so must the earth's children.'[94]

Harney's imagery was forceful, but in essence red republicanism rested on the supposition that 'the Charter and something more' would prove as compelling a rallying point as the European revolutions had in 1848. Then, as Gerald Massey described in his *Song of the Red Republican*, 'Our hopes ran mountains high, – we sung at heart, – wept tears of gladness'.[95] Now the mood was very different; moreover Chartism faced a leadership vacuum. Harney was well aware that he lacked leadership qualities: 'I am convinced', he had written in 1846, that were O'Connor 'thrown overboard we might go further and fare worse'. Sentiment guaranteed Feargus an honorary place at the head of Chartism, but he was absent more than he was present: 5 times in the 12 months from August 1850 he unexpectedly disappeared abroad, and he had a 6-week bout of unexplained illness in April and May. By August 1851 his 'enfeebled and shattered' state had become an open secret.[96]

The only event in prospect that might have re-ignited the flame was the release from prison of Ernest Jones on 9 July 1850. But the reception that greeted him was muted. In 1840–41 it had been O'Connor's good fortune to be in prison when Chartism was buoyant, and free prior to the death of any imprisoned Chartists. However, following the death of Williams and Sharp in 1849, London Chartists had little appetite for pomp and festivity, and Jones had to be content with a small *soirée* and tea-party. However, Halifax did him proud. If the dank odours of Tothill Fields Prison had dispelled Jones's enthusiasm for Chartism, then 'a grand jubilee' in the bracing Pennines' air restored it. He rose to the occasion with an almost messianic sense of purpose.[97]

With O'Connor increasingly marginal, it was Jones who sought to take his place, allied with Harney in the struggle to retain control of the NCA but largely eschewing 'The Charter and something more' in favour of a vision of a secularised millennium where the economy would rest on small farms and religion on the precepts of primitive Christianity. 'Christ was the first Chartist, and Democracy is the gospel carried into practice', he told Manchester's first open-air rally since 1848.[98] It was an astute reading of the popular mood, in which anti-clerical feeling was never far from the surface and which had yet to cast-off yearning for the pastoral of the Chartist land plan.

Jones was his own man, albeit thrown by circumstance into popular politics because his career at the bar was, for the time being anyway, beyond retrieval. The main attraction of the NCA for Jones did not lie in its adoption of 'The Charter and something more', and it certainly did not lie in its membership which, Clark had recently alleged, without contradiction, numbered only 500; rather, the attraction of the NCA derived from its claims to be the true custodian of the People's Charter. The National Charter League (with a membership only just in double figures) was content to get the Charter incrementally. Bronterre O'Brien's National Reform League was only incidentally Chartist and its reach did not extend much beyond Soho. The People's Charter Union had evolved into the National Newspaper Stamp Abolition Committee (and worked amicably with the NCA).[99]

Jones stuck with the NCA for want of another vehicle, but stick to it he did. Over the ensuing 6 months he took its membership back to nearly 2,000, though opponents pointed out with some acerbity that 'if any other party were to assume national authority, or claim to be the head of a National Movement, on such a slender basis, there is not a Democrat in the country who would not laugh to scorn such a preposterous assumption'.[100] It was a bumpy ride. Jones was unpopular among those who favoured 'The Charter or something less' rather than nothing at all, or among those he swept aside in his dash to become, as one east London locality put it, 'the would-be dictator of Chartism, Napoleon the Little'.[101]

Jones's second coming as a Chartist leader therefore split an already fractious movement further rather than helped heal it. A graphic illustration of this was the artificial life he gave to the National Charter League. In October 1850 O'Connor proposed a new convention to be held early in 1851, beyond London where the movement, he said pointedly, 'is a real one'. Jones and the NCA executive opposed this but an influential section of Manchester Chartists, urged on by the League and led by James Leach (founding president of the NCA in 1840 and a prisoner in 1842 and 1848–50), took up the call and convened a national conference in February. Now was the time, Leach argued, for 'a new organisation upon a more intelligent, tolerant and conciliatory basis'. The conference was farcical: only four delegates (apart from O'Connor, Clark and McGrath) attended: but Jones's vehemently personal criticisms, plus an ill-judged attempt to wreck a lecture organised by Leach a month earlier, effectively marked Manchester's divorce from the NCA. The Manchester CA roundly denounced metropolitan 'Communistic Chartism'. Soon Manchester Chartism was reduced to the merest shadow of its former self: even Leach now gave up politics.[102]

The collapse of the Manchester conference left the field open for the NCA to hold a convention in London on 31 March. This saw the completion of its move to 'The Charter and something more'. Jones was the presiding genius. A majority of the fifty-three remaining NCA localities sent delegates who put their hearts once more into drawing up a programme of agitation for Chartism. There was to be a further National Petition, adopted at simultaneous meetings across the country on a date to be announced. At the next general election a Chartist should be nominated at every hustings, and candidates should go to the poll in each constituency where a locality could mount a contest. Central funds would be used to underwrite campaigns in rural areas and among trade societies. All this was unexceptional (so long as the cost was not estimated and compared to the NCA's income). However, the 1851 programme speci-fied policies on which 'support of Chartist organisation [should] be solicited'. These were a fundamental departure. The unemployed were to be settled on the land via 'the restoration of poor, common, church and crown lands to the people' and a by programme of gradual land nationalisation through govern-ment purchase. Education should be secular, 'universal, gratuitous, and, to a certain extent, compulsory'. The law of Master and Servant would be set aside, and legal and financial assistance made available for producer co-operatives. Unemployment relief for those for whom work on the land could not be found would be universal and allowances paid to the elderly and sick, enabling them wherever possible to remain in their own homes or those of relatives. The National Debt would be gradually paid off. The army and the navy would be steadily diminished in size until reduced colonial commitments (and a new citizen militia) rendered them 'no longer requisite'; until then conditions of service in both would be more humane. Religious activity would be wholly disestablished. Taxation would be levied on land and accumulated wealth only.[103]

The 1851 programme was a vision for a humane society, albeit stronger on noble aspiration than detail for its implementation. But it signified little in practical terms. Its two architects quarrelled bitterly, partly because Jones was furious that Harney, and not he, acquired the *Northern Star* early in 1852, and partly, one suspects, because Jones was incapable of working with other independent-minded individuals. There never was another National Petition. Instead Jones called a conference at Manchester in May 1852 'to raise the Chartist cause once more'. It agreed to repeat the 1849 tactic of co-ordinating the presentation of separate petitions from each locality using a common text. But a derisory six localities sent delegates to this conference. The eight-man executive was halved (Jones, Gammage and Londoner James Finlen), with

William Grocott, formerly secretary to the Miners' Association, as secretary. The executive's members each embarked on an exhaustive tour, distributing printed collection sheets and moving adoption of this new petition at each place they visited. In his *History*, Gammage mentions around fifty specific meetings in the months that followed, plus an unspecified quantity of others, at all of which, apparently, petitions were adopted. But the total presented numbered no more than 20, their aggregate signatures – 11,834 – barely a fifth of the disappointing muster in 1849.[104]

Meanwhile the NCREC had sunk into debt-ridden oblivion. Only 7 constituencies were contested at the general election of July 1852: Chartists came bottom of the poll in 6 of them, including Halifax where Jones won just 37 votes. Gammage and Finlen were to have contested Exeter and Coventry, respectively, but abandoned even appearing at the hustings. Harney (having recently relaunched the *Northern Star* as the *Star of Freedom*, and being therefore much preoccupied) failed to win even the hustings at Bradford. His paper did not even mention the seventh constituency, Tavistock in Devon, where Samuel Carter (the Chartist who had contested the 1847 election there) *was* elected. However, it was a pyrrhic victory: Carter was unseated weeks later when it was shown that he did not meet the property qualification. O'Connor could not defend his Nottingham seat, for he had been committed to an asylum the month before having been declared insane.

The *Star of Freedom* closed on 27 November, 'a heavy blow and sore discouragement', observed 'An Old Chartist' in a valedictory letter to Harney. A few weeks previously another correspondent using the same name wrote from the north-east:

> In this locality, the very name Chartist has become a by-word and a reproach ... yet we are not without hope, I believe, Sir, that a real People's Party is now forming, which will secure the confidence of the great mass ... But you will say, what are we doing? I answer, we are forming ourselves into Local Societies, we are getting ourselves on the Register for Municipal Electors. We think this is a step in the right direction. It is true that we are not bawling and making a great noise, but we have begun to work.[105]

Henceforth, the history of Chartism would be no more than a multiplicity of small victories.

# CHAPTER ELEVEN

# Chartist lives: 'Ever present to the progressive mind'

### 'He lived and died for us'

O'Connor in decline was an embarrassment to many Chartists. In death he became a rallying point. His last years were bereft of dignity. Evidently deranged from February 1852 onwards, he was finally committed to an asylum by House of Commons' authorities in June after a minor assault on the Attorney-General. He had frequently claimed that devotion to Chartism had imperilled his health: the personal regimen he set himself in the decade from 1837 was certainly punishing. As early as January 1839 he had been laid low by a serious bronchial condition, possibly pleurisy, and he was similarly afflicted on several occasions in subsequent years. His demeanour at Kennington Common on 10 April 1848 was consistent with symptoms of an angina attack, doubtless induced by stress. Now, however, Feargus was diagnosed as suffering from general paralysis of the insane, the tertiary stage of syphilis. The link between his condition and syphilis was not fully known at the time and his insanity was widely ascribed to overwork and bitter disappointment at the desertion of the Chartist faithful. Robert Gammage, in his *History of the Chartist Movement* (an otherwise sustained assault on his almost every action) even went so far as to draw a parallel between O'Connor and Christ: 'one day "Hosanna"; the next "Crucify him"'.[1]

After three agonising years O'Connor died penniless. His sister Harriet, who nursed him at her home for the final fortnight of his life, 'had not money enough to bury the body' the coroner's inquest was informed. However, a public subscription was raised to provide a funeral that proved to be the last great Chartist demonstration on London's streets. By a bizarre coincidence, one Feargus himself might have relished, the name of the undertaker was Lovett. Processions of mourners formed in the City and Finsbury, converged with a further gathering in Bloomsbury and then walked to Notting Hill where the cortège assembled outside Harriet's neat terraced home. The mourners possibly exceeded 50,000; even *The Times*, no admirer of the deceased, estimated them to number between 30,000 and 40,000. 'He lived and died for us' read several of the banners accompanying his hearse to Kensal Green Cemetery.[2]

Yet in death O'Connor still contrived briefly to divide Chartism. Reynolds and Jones, in their capacities as rival newspaper owners rather than political leaders, competed with appeals for funds to erect a monument on his grave. Eventually an uneasy peace assured the placing of a modest monument at Kensal Green, while separate fund-raising erected a statue in Nottingham, 'a good likeness of him, in a standing position, about eight feet high', reported Ben Wilson, the old Halifax Chartist who made a pilgrimage to the site in 1883.[3] Feelings about Feargus were not infrequently ambivalent. Yet the Robert Gammage who momentarily caught the pathos of Feargus's situation at the close of his astonishing career was arguably a more faithful historian than the Gammage who diligently (as he saw it) chronicled O'Connor's every error. 'Few men have been worse maligned and less deserved it' wrote a Merthyr Tydfil radical in 1867.[4]

Occasional personal insights into the lives of old Chartists reveal that England's greatest Irishman continued to be revered. William Chadwick 'constantly' wore one of the medals issued to celebrate O'Connor's 1841 release from prison right up to his death in 1908. Prestwich Chartist William Grimshaw (elected a life member of his local Liberal Club in the 1880s, 'as a recognition of his services to the cause of Liberalism') hung a studio photograph of himself in Foresters' Friendly Society regalia, surrounded by *Northern Star* presentation portraits of Cobbett, Hunt and O'Connor, 'whom he was wont to call his "body guard"'.[5] A living memorial could be found in the myriad children given 'Feargus' as a first name, 316 of them discovered by the 1851 Census, 46 of whom had 'O'Connor' as their middle name.[6]

Two years before O'Connor's funeral, Ben Wilson had witnessed a possibly even greater assembly escort the coffin of 'the grand old man' of Halifax Chartism, Ben Rushton, weaver, popular preacher and treasurer of the West Yorkshire NCA council. Throughout the second half of the century, radical and local newspapers regularly reported the funerals of stalwart figures in whose public careers Chartism had been a central part. Men like James Maw of Middlesbrough, militant teetotaller and committeeman of the local Liberal Association, escorted to his grave with full honours by the combined membership of the town's temperance societies; but still 'his earliest and strongest speeches were delivered in connection with the Chartist movement' an obituary recorded.[7] For the funeral of Ernest Jones in 1869, the *lower* estimate of the attendance was 50,000.[8] This is plausible given, for example, that 40,000 turned out in 1864 in Rochdale to mourn Thomas Livesey, who had chaired the last NCA Convention in 1858. 'A diamond, though not highly polished,'

(John Bright's arch tribute), Livesey was widely regarded as the architect of Rochdale's incorporation.[9]

To emphasise those popular assemblies is, however, to present an unduly elegiac and somewhat unreliable portrait of Chartism in its final phase. Firstly, it is a prosaic point but nonetheless one worth making in this context, that not all Chartists made a good death. George White, for example, died in the workhouse. 'Believe me to be true to my principles to the last' he wrote shortly before he died, but the oral tradition that endured in Bradford was that he was 'a reight bugger' who was 'allus half-canned'.[10] Secondly, and more substantively, the dominant mode of Chartist discourse in this later period was neither mournful nor despairing but rather resilient and positive, not in the expectation of the imminent enactment of the Charter but on the principle that concerted action improved working lives. Of course, this attitude was not derived from Chartism alone, but those who had been involved in the movement took from it an energy and expertise that suffused a wide range of popular political and associational activities.

## Robert Carter and William Newton

Municipal politics was one such arena. For many Chartist activists local politics had been a focal point since the mid-1840s. The extent to which this was so varied widely between localities: the social composition of local electorates differed considerably; so too did the legal frameworks within which municipal politics was played out, both because bodies sharing responsibility for local governance proliferated and because of the widely varying terms of the improvement commissions, embodied under local acts, which were mainly responsible for many towns at this time. Significant local government challenges in Yorkshire were mounted in Bradford, Halifax, Leeds, Middlesbrough, Selby and Sheffield;[11] in Lancashire, in Bolton, Rochdale and pre-eminently Manchester and Salford;[12] and, in the midlands, Leicester, Nottingham and Arnold, and the Potteries.[13] Other examples of Chartist electoral success include Merthyr, Newport, Penzance, Glasgow and many other localities in Scotland.[14] It is inconceivable this brief list is exhaustive.

Municipal Chartism recorded some of its earliest notable victories in Leeds, as the career of Robert Meek Carter illustrates. As early as the autumn of 1838 the objective of Leeds Chartists was to 'make the Municipal Council of Leeds in miniature what we want the Commons House of Parliament to be'. Circumstances in the West Yorkshire town permitted Chartists to go some way towards achieving this. George White attempted to get Joshua Hobson elected to the Improvement Commission in 1840; Chartists were first elected in 1841; then, in 1842, by packing the nomination meeting, they succeeded in electing the whole Commission. The Commission was dissolved the following year and its powers transferred to the town council, and throughout the remainder of the 1840s there were notable Chartist successes in elections to that body and to the Leeds Poor Law Guardians, churchwardens and highway surveyors.[15]

Robert Meek Carter's entry into electoral politics was achieved through the latter. Though the lowest rung in the municipal ladder, highways boards were not without financial teeth or political significance. Chartist candidates were 'men who would look after the cleansing of the courts and alleys in which the poor resided, as well as repair the highways over which the horses of the manufacturers travelled', promised a campaigner in the Potteries in 1844. Carter joined a highway surveyors' board controlled by Chartists from 1843 into the mid-1850s, and on which ex-Chartists then sat among the controlling radical interest until this tier of local government was abolished in 1866. Carter's attitude to this lowly elected office indicated the actions of a Chartist conscience: 'the gentleman part of such bodies did not do the work and would not do the work. No, the work must be done by plain practical hardworking men like himself', he was quoted saying in 1854, adding that 'the barristers, the lawyers and the physicians were the worst attenders of any committee'.[16]

Robert Carter had been born in East Yorkshire in 1814, just as his father, a small farmer, underwent ruin in the depression that followed the Napoleonic Wars. So impoverished were the family that Robert received no formal education and was working as an agricultural labourer by the time he was 6. After ten years he migrated to Leeds to work, first, in a textile mill and then, from 1844, as a coal merchant's weighman. It was in Leeds that Carter acquired his education through attendance at adult Sunday school and night school, and developed a commitment to civic improvement and radical politics that stayed with him until his death in 1882. As well as belonging to the Owenite Leeds Redemption Society, he was on the committee and subsequently became president of the 'People's Mill', which evolved into the Leeds Co-operative Society. He was also a noted temperance advocate. Then, in 1852 he was one of the two last candidates, standing overtly as Chartists, elected to Leeds Council. Carter's habit of regularly putting money aside had allowed him to set up business as a coal merchant on his own account; subsequently he expanded into cloth finishing. Election to the Council exposed Carter to a broader political spectrum. Guardedly at first, he began to work with leading local Liberals, including James Marshall (MP for Leeds, 1847–52) and Edward Baines (MP, 1859–74), on a manhood suffrage agenda. Marshall's interest in moderate parliamentary reform was a matter of record (we saw in chapter 6 how he was involved in the LPRA), but throughout the 1840s Baines had been decidedly of the 'finality' school of opinion on the 1832 Act. From 1852 he began to moderate his position. It is important to register this because although men like Carter were sometimes criticised by fellow-Chartists for compromising with the middle classes, the making of compromises was not all one way.[17]

Carter's track record in local politics (he finally left the Leeds Council, of which he became an alderman, in 1874) recommended him to office in the 1860s in the Leeds Society for the Erection of Improved Dwellings, the local Mechanics' Institute, the Leeds Manhood Suffrage Association and the Leeds branch of the Reform Union. In 1866 he became a vice-president of the National Reform League. Two years later, following the Second Reform Act, he joined Baines as one of the Liberal MPs for Leeds. At Westminster he pursued, according to *The Times*, 'thoroughly Radical opinions', including legal protection for trade unions and the disestablishment of the Anglican Church. Carter was re-elected in 1874 but his parliamentary career was cut short by business failure and he resigned in 1876. Like many Chartists he made a restless radical even late in life: despite the humiliation of bankruptcy he returned to serve two more years on Leeds Council, proudly recording his occupation in the 1881 Census as 'Town Councillor & Cloth Finisher'. He died the following year.[18]

Carter's career was exceptional only in culminating at Westminster and (to a lesser extent) for its longevity. From the early 1850s there were ex-Chartist councillors without number. Some had been prominent in the movement, like John Collins in Birmingham; others remained dedicated 'grassroots' figures, like ironworks labourer John Anderson, formerly Middlesbrough NCA secretary and a town councillor in 1858–61, or William Gould of Merthyr Tydfil. The latter, an iron puddler turned grocer, served on Merthyr's Burial Board, as a Poor Law Guardian and on the Board of Health, in connection with which in 1872 he was still being disparaged as 'the Chartist lip'.[19] And of course only a minority of those who called themselves Chartists sought and attained elected office: the conscientious participant in municipal electoral processes, such as Ashton-under-Lyne's Richard Pilling, who 'exerted himself strenuously at election times in the Liberal interest', would have been more typical, though this facet of former Chartists' lives is seldom well documented.[20]

Municipal activities of the kind described here were the truest expression of Chartism's democratic aspirations, rather than Jones's isolated and unsuccessful forays as a Chartist candidate in Nottingham in parliamentary elections (1857 and 1859). Inevitably they involved an accommodation with liberalism. Yet this was not quite the betrayal of Chartist principle it might appear. Liberalism's version of popular constitutional reform was sufficiently close to that of Chartism, in language and content, for it to seem a natural conjunction. Both shared the genealogy of Protestant dissent, the revolutions of the seventeenth century and the radical patriotism of the eighteenth century. Factors that had kept Chartism and liberalism apart were the New Poor Law, Corn Law repeal and radical liberalism's exaggerated deference to free-market economics. In mid-Victorian England, however, the routine operation of the Poor Law mitigated against its most draconian intentions, and Corn Law repeal had been removed as an object of contention. In seeking to instate land reform in its place, Cobden and his allies chose a cause with which every Chartist concurred.

Free-market economics endured longer, but even here diminishing dogmatism in the third quarter of the century laid the grounds for a broadening progressive coalition.[21] In many localities, vigorous Chartist activity in the 1830s and 1840s contributed to the emergence of radical liberalism in the 1850s and 1860s. Conversely, localities where Chartism was weak tended to be those where subsequent liberalism inclined to orthodoxy.[22] Very soon, radical liberals would embrace Chartism and work it into their own pedigree. When George Thompson visited his old constituency for a reform demonstration in 1859, he declared to general applause: 'The Charter can stand by the Declaration of Independence in America, by Magna Charta, or the Bill of Rights.'[23]

Arresting visual evidence for this process can be found in a photograph of two leading members of Failsworth Liberal Club, proudly posing with Chartist pikes which the Club owned. One of those pictured, Councillor George Whitehead, was chairman of the Failsworth Urban District Council. Though published (in a Liberal Party bazaar souvenir) in 1913, it was probably taken in 1884, the year of the Third Reform Act and a Failsworth reform demonstration that reunited surviving veterans of Peterloo.[24] We have seen how in 1847, Chartism's NCREC had supported the election of 'Duncombeites', like George Thompson, in addition to avowed Chartist candidates. In 1841 the *Northern Star* had claimed 'as Chartists' the radical Liberal election successes at Rochdale and Oldham; on the same principle, Reginald Richardson widened the net of virtual Chartist MPs to include Coventry's William Williams: it was in support of the latter's successful campaign at the 1850 Lambeth by-election that the NCREC finally bankrupted itself. The heat generated in the quarrels that beset the NCA in the 1850s, along with Ernest Jones's skills as a self-publicist, diverted attention from the extent to which Chartists were prepared at the local level to sink their differences with progressive liberalism, remaining 'Chartist in principle' but 'willing to accept', as William Newton put it in 1852, 'a less[er] measure of reform'.[25]

At Tower Hamlets Newton's was one of the two most impressive challenges by Chartists at the 1852 general election; the other, as we saw in chapter 10, being Samuel Carter's at Tavistock. Carter's stated position was that 'if so instructed by his constituents, [he] would give the Charter his cordial support; but, in the absence of that authority would vote for an extension of the suffrage, the ballot, and triennial parliaments'.[26] William Newton, a foreman engineer until dismissed for trade union activities in 1848, was a decisive force in the emergence of the Amalgamated Society of Engineers in 1851. His political conviction was that 'the time had come when they should strike out onto a new and broader path'. He retained manhood suffrage and equal electoral districts in his manifesto, and pledged to present himself for re-election annually if returned to Westminster. Harney believed the return of 'Labour's candidate',

William Newton, 'would be a victory worth any labour, any sacrifice'.[27] Newton won the hustings but came bottom of the poll. However, his total of 1,095 votes was the highest ever for a Chartist parliamentary candidate other than O'Connor and Parry in 1847.

Newton then seriously canvassed the idea of a 'National Party' that would ally Chartists, trade unionists and Christian socialist co-operators, with manhood suffrage as its sole immediate objective. Supporters included the freethinker George Holyoake and the Chartist poets Leno and Massey. Newton still spoke of his 'love' for the Charter but conceded: 'I know that this proposal will be met by an outcry from some.'[28] And so it proved: Harney was quietly sceptical and Ernest Jones vocally so. Discouraged, Newton failed to progress the idea further, concentrating instead on the engineers' union and on parochial reform. Parishes were a keenly contested political arena in the 1850s and 1860s: parochial reform chimed-in well with Chartist sentiments, especially the rhetoric of anti-centralisation that was much evident in the land plan. Here was another cause in which Liberals and Chartists could comfortably co-operate.[29]

It was a further six years before Jones also concluded that incremental reform was preferable to the political wilderness. Until then, much of the energy Jones devoted to the remnants of formally organised Chartism tended to repel support rather than augment it. When the *Star of Freedom*, Harney's attempt to re-launch the *Northern Star*, foundered in November 1852, he faced an uncertain future. Whatever inclination Harney might still have had to remain in London and continue the wearying round of sectarian argument that now characterised metropolitan Chartism evaporated. On 28 November a joint meeting of Polish exiles and metropolitan democrats ended in a brawl as Jones loyalists opposed Harney's election to the chair. Soon Harney moved to Newcastle, working from 1854 on the *Northern Tribune*, a journal with a strong interest in foreign affairs and which in its domestic agenda exactly reflected the aims of Newton's aborted National Party. Holyoake, Kydd, Linton, Massey and Thomas Cooper were among the contributors, all of them part of the recent exodus from the NCA (Cooper had briefly rejoined in 1851).[30]

## Thomas Winters

Jones's relationships with the trades were no less tempestuous. The north-east pitmen's leader Martin Jude was another disenchanted NCA activist who wrote for *Northern Tribune*. Increasingly organised trades, if they expressed political inclinations at all, were moving towards liberalism. However, there was never a total rupture between Chartism and individual trade unionists, not least because the Charter retained a totemic status: 'Himself always the same, Times have changed' reads the gravestone (erected 1904) of one Kidderminster carpet weaver, Chartist and Liberal activist.[31]

In Scotland the participation of well-known Chartists in trade unionism continued for a generation. They included Allan McFadyen in the Glasgow textile trades, Duncan Robertson among the coal and ironstone miners and William Pattison, the steam engine maker who moved the adoption of the National Petition on Glasgow Green in March 1838, and led his union into the Amalgamated Society of Engineers in 1851. A number of Chartist activists assumed leadership or advisory roles in a wide range of East Anglian trade unions, including the engineers', the Amalgamated Society of Carpenters and Joiners, the Yarmouth seamen's movement and Joseph Arch's National Agricultural Labourers' Union.[32] Martin Jude continued as 'secretary to the miners', even when the unionisation of the north-east coalfield had crumbled. He was instrumental in reviving a regional pitmen's union from 1858. Joseph Linney, who took leading roles in the Staffordshire strikes of 1842 and the land plan in the Black Country, continued to play an active part in trades' agitations, for example against employers evading the Truck Acts. Subsequently Linney joined Wolverhampton's Liberal WMA.[33] On Teesside Chartists fought against Truck Acts offences and many switched to trade union activity in the 1850s. Halifax weaver Alexander Stradling, a leading local Chartist, was recruited by Rochdale carpet weavers to co-ordinate a strike in 1860, from which evolved a national union for the trade.[34]

Over-arching the activities of them all was W. P. Roberts (retained by almost every group of workers, unionised or not, needing representation in court) and, more sedately, Duncombe. The Finsbury MP maintained an active interest in trade union affairs until his death in 1861. In particular, Duncombe was the parliamentary spokesman for the National Association of United Trades, the formation of which under his presidency was noted in chapter 8. The unassuming heart of the NAUT, however, was its secretary Thomas Winters, formerly a Leicester framework glove knitter and Chartist.

The fortunes of the NAUT after 1848 mirrored those of Chartism as a whole. It relied heavily on the *Northern Star* to communicate with its affiliates. The quickening political pulse in 1847–48 prompted it to issue its own *Monthly Report*, followed in August 1848 by a lively weekly, the *Labour League*. This failed in May 1849. The NAUT then reverted to using the *Northern Star*, whose final editor, George Fleming, succeeded Duncombe as president in 1852 when the latter was too ill to continue. Fleming was a co-operator and Owenite of some distinction but he lacked the commanding presence in the labour movement enjoyed by Duncombe. His accession contributed to the erosion of the NAUT's breadth of appeal.

In 1856 Winters described the NAUT as consisting of 5,000–6,000 individuals, drawn from 'the wood trade, the iron trade, the salt trade, and the leather trade, and various other trades; I cannot call them all to mind ... dispersed over different parts of the country'.[35] It was Winters who held the NAUT together as an administrator, publicist and trade union adviser and arbitrator. His trade society had participated in the first mass Chartist demonstration in Leicester in November 1838 and Winters himself had been prominent in Thomas Cooper's 'Shakespearian Chartists'. When Cooper was tried, first for arson and then sedition after the 1842 Potteries riots, Winters led a defence committee raising funds and collecting evidence. It was he who kept Cooper's wife Susanna informed of events as they unfolded at the trials. Subsequently Winters played an important role in a series of industrial disputes in the Leicestershire glove-making industry, for which he was finally sacked in May 1844. It is unclear if he ever worked as a glover again, though he remained secretary of his union.[36]

In due course Winters devoted himself full-time to the NAUT and during its decline in the 1850s combined his duties as its secretary with those of 'Manager of a Working Men's Friendly Society'.[37] In this Winters was following a path well trodden by former Chartists, many of whom utilised networking and administrative skills acquired in the movement to build careers in life assurance and other mutualist organisations. Officially friendly societies tended to disdain associating closely with Chartism for fear of jeopardising their legal security; privately members frequently took a different perspective: 'both [are] aiming at the same end; viz., the social and intellectual improvement of man; the one trying to elevate his social, the other his political condition'. A number of Chartists, including Philip McGrath and John Leach were involved in the British Industry Life Assurance Society. Ruffy Ridley had founded the United Patriots' Benefit Society as early as 1843, advertising extensively in the Chartist press. Other associations with close Chartist links included a number of building, friendly and assurance societies, for example the British Prudential, the United Brothers, Finsbury Mutual Life, Integrity Life, the Labour League Industrial Provident Society and the Friend-in-Need, the largest of them all and referred to again below.[38] Winters did not specify which friendly society employed him but conceivably it was one of these.

Leadership of the only national co-ordinating body for trade unions was never less than demanding and the 1850s was a particularly challenging decade. The NAUT was a far cry from the organisation of around 50,000 members that briefly flourished in the late 1840s. It was not easy to create a united front among the trades and on its own admission NAUT encountered difficulties in 'inducing such a combination of trades, each having different pursuits, different rates of wages, and, at first sight, different interests, to unite in sufficiently large numbers to give these principles a fair trial'.[39] Under Winters' guidance, however, it was far from merely a tokenistic presence in mid-Victorian labour politics and survived into the 1860s.

Alongside O'Brien's National Reform League, the NAUT therefore has some claim to be considered the most enduring institutional expression of Chartism. In 1851–52 it became closely involved in a strike of the Wolverhampton Society

of Tin-Plate Workers, one of the critical trade disputes of the nineteenth
century. Three NAUT officials, including both Winters and London Chartist
Frederick Green (a morocco-leather finisher) were arrested for conspiracy
along with the union's leadership. Charges against Winters were dropped but
Green was among those imprisoned for three months in a disturbing shift
in the judicial interpretation of conspiracy. As the law stood after this case,
simply to offer advice to strikers or to attempt conciliation in a strike risked
indictment for conspiracy. Even more seriously, participation in a strike might
itself be construed as conspiracy. Supported first by the *Northern Star* and then
Harney's *Star of Freedom*, the NAUT reacted as vigorously as the prevailing
mood of labour politics permitted and presented a petition of nearly 80,000
signatures to Parliament asking for the law to be changed.

Ernest Jones's position, however, was one of implacable opposition: 'All
*trades'-unions are lamentable fallacies*.' Energies channelled into trade unionism
served only to divide labour and uphold the economic system: 'How foolish
and how vain are all unionistic attempts – how useless are co-operative efforts
– under the present governmental system of our nation'. There was a clear logic
to Jones's argument and earlier Chartists had voiced it, notably in 1839 (see
chapter 3 above). Then, however, the imminent overthrow of 'the governmental
system' had seemed possible. Herculean optimism was required to believe that
now. But Jones never consciously understated an argument, even claiming 'the
high paid Trades recruited the constabulary ranks of 1848'. There was no scope
for reconciliation between trade unionism and formally organised Chartism
under Jones's tutelage:

> Do we fight against class-government? Well, then? There is class-government
> in our own ranks, and we ought to fight against it, too. Do we fight against
> aristocratic privilege? Well, then – there is aristocratic privilege of the vilest
> die among the high-paid trades, and we ought to fight against it too ... THE
> ARISTOCRACY OF LABOUR MUST BE BROKEN DOWN, the same as an[y]
> other aristocracies.[40]

Chartist leaders had frequently resented trade union separatism; but as
recently as 1851, when Harney, Holyoake, O'Connor and Reynolds remained
on the NCA executive, criticism was tempered. 'There must not be two parties
in our ranks – the one struggling for *social rights*, the other for political power
– *we must* ALL *contend for* BOTH', they argued in *An Appeal for Joint Action
of All Sections of the Working Class*.[41] Trade unionism, however, was about
the politics of the possible. Winters and the NAUT drew up a parliamentary
Bill designed to neutralise the judicial interpretation of conspiracy in the
Wolverhampton case. Supported by the short-lived Conservative administration of 1852, the Bill weathered a particularly stormy spell in Westminster only
to fall in the Lords in June 1853. Whig–Liberal governments were suspicious

of trade unionism and it required the return of the Conservatives in 1858 to restore the legal landscape. A Bill 'to amend and explain' relevant legislation, presented by Duncombe, was passed with only minor amendment in 1859. As a precursor to the more important and enduring reforms of the 1870s, Duncombe's Act was, as it remains, something of a benchmark.[42]

The NAUT's other main sphere of activity in the 1850s was promoting arbitration and conciliation, a central part of its philosophy since its inception. Here, too, the NAUT and Winters laid a basis for significant subsequent development. The NAUT publicised and encouraged the establishment of arbitration boards in a variety of industries, and provided arbitration and conciliation advisers, often Winters himself, in hundreds of cases during the 1850s. Winters gave extensive oral and written evidence to parliamentary select committees on this issue in 1856 (as did William Newton) and in 1860. Winters freely conceded that the NAUT's membership had dropped to around 6,000, yet it is clear that these committees recognised, and indeed respected, the extent of the NAUT's experience in the industrial relations field. It provided arbitrators, for example, to a number of industrial disputes involving unions that were not affiliated to it. In evidence to the 1860 Select Committee, Winters was able to give details of more than 100 trade societies, plus 6 trade councils or delegate meetings (among them Glasgow and Manchester), who wanted to see 'equitable courts of conciliation' established. Winters lived to advise on a Bill with this objective which the Conservative Government supported in 1867. With the NAUT no more, his life took a last and unpredictable twist. Thanks to the discrete patronage of the Conservatives, exercised through the Commission of Works, Winters secured a job for the remainder of his life as gatekeeper at Brompton Cemetery in London's Fulham Road. He died in 1882.[43]

## John Frost

Like Ernest Jones's receipt of grants (1854 and 1859, totalling £75) from the Royal Literary Fund, the circumstances of Winters's retirement from labour politics signal something of the *rapprochement* that emerged between Chartists and the establishment in the second half of the century.[44] More substantial was the unconditional pardon, celebrating the conclusion of the Crimean War, offered in May 1856 to all transported political prisoners. Many, like William Cuffay and the other Newport leaders William Jones and Zephaniah Williams, decided to remain in Australia; but some, most notably Smith O'Brien and John Frost, returned. The long-anticipated return of the martyr of Newport to Britain throws an interesting light on the state of Chartism in the mid-1850s.

In 1854, reversing his sectarian zeal of two years earlier, Ernest Jones extended an olive branch to the trade union movement. He had shrewdly held back from calling a convention in 1853, but circumstances in 1854 were more propitious. A number of dormant Chartist localities fluttered into life with Britain's entry into the Crimean War against Russia, which also coincided with high bread prices. Russophobia was deep-seated in British radical politics and Chartists (most of whom had fêted Polish nationalist exiles, and a good few of whom shared David Urquhart's obsessive views of Tsarist ambitions) enthusiastically embraced the war. Jones, whose *People's Paper* had been pushing Urquhartite views since the previous year, was no exception. One practical consequence of this revival was Jones's decision in the month Britain entered the war to convene at Manchester not a convention but, underlining his new-found belief in the trade unions as instruments of political change, a 'Labour Parliament'. Little concrete came of this (except the formation of the assurance society United Brothers). Indeed by enthusiastically canvassing support for a new 'Mass Movement' Jones unwittingly further undermined the NCA which wilted in its shadow. The absence from Manchester of certain remaining areas of NCA strength, notably Halifax, indicated this.[45]

The 1854 'Labour Parliament', however, at least had the effect of stirring the embers of Chartism. The return of Frost two years later was a welcome fillip after the death of O'Connor and was widely heralded as a renaissance for the movement. At Newport and London the reception he met was tumultuous. Jones implausibly estimated the total crowd that turned out to witness events in London at a million. That figure can be safely dismissed, but *The Times* conceded that traffic in the capital was disrupted 'for several hours' and described how many more people gathered on Primrose Hill than the area set aside for the rally could hold, leading to half-an-hour of fighting among those fearful of not witnessing the proceedings.

Frost's speech was brief, measured and unapologetic. 'Forty years ago I became convinced that the miserable state of our country, and of its industrious inhabitants, was occasioned by the lawgiver – the corruption of the House of Commons ... The only remedy, as it then appeared to me, was to recur to the principles of our ancient constitution, which principles are embodied in what is now called the Charter.' So it was still, Frost maintained: 'Let us be cool, but determined, prudent, but fearless; giving up no principle, satisfied with no less than our due.' Jones spoke at greater length. He was appropriately laudatory of his distinguished fellow-speaker, but found the opportunity for self-promotion irresistible: 'He had ruined himself individually; he had sacrificed all the hopes of his life by his adherence to their cause, and he was ready, if need were, to offer up life itself for it.' Jones assiduously maintained the appearance of the gentleman leader, but it was more difficult to keep up the pretence there was much to lead. Even the official address he presented to Frost on behalf of London's Chartists spoke of the current context of 'reproach ... political apostasy and compromise'.[46]

Expectations of Frost were unfeasibly high: 'From you we expect much for the future ... assist us to gather up the scattered elements of our movement', declared 'the Democracy of Stalybridge'.[47] Frost's triumphant tour permitted Jones to cultivate, through the columns of the *People's Paper*, the appearance of a national movement; but it had little substance, as Frost soon realised. His preparedness to resume an active role in the movement, coupled with the extensive tour he undertook on his return, meant that his conclusions commanded reluctant respect. His view of Wales was especially dispirited: 'In all the mining districts of Wales', he wrote in 1857, 'among the scores of thousands that at one time took an active part in public meetings, it would at present be impossible to get a meeting ... there are at present no Chartists and no Chartist agitation'.[48]

Frost was exaggerating, but allowance should be made for the jaundiced view of a septuagenarian whose fifteen-year exile in Tasmania, it must have seemed, had been for nothing. Representatives from Montgomeryshire and Merthyr Tydfil attended the final Chartist conference in 1858. Llanidloes NCA sent 'the kind assurance of the faithful few' and a modest donation.[49] John Frost, however, held aloof and lent his support to none of the reform organisations of the next twenty years. He had announced that he would offer himself as a candidate for the Merthyr constituency at the general election of 1857, but for reasons that are unclear changed his mind.[50] He became absorbed in spiritualism, a common resort of radicals, to which Chartism contributed a number of practitioners.[51] Frost confined his platform appearances mainly to attacking penal policy and transportation, on which he also published. In his late eighties he contemplated writing an autobiography in serial format for the lively *Newcastle Weekly Chronicle* (the paper, more than any other, which consciously kept memories of Chartism green in the late nineteenth century and enjoyed sizeable sales beyond Tyneside as a result). But Frost wrote to the editor in December 1873 with news that he had suffered a fall, his memory was impaired ('but not as to past events') and his sight affected. None of the promised instalments were sent.[52] An autobiography, as Lovett's had demonstrated, can be a powerful means of fixing posterity's attention, but Frost's was not to be. He died, aged 92, in 1877.

## Thomas Martin Wheeler

When the final issue of the *Star of Freedom* appeared on 27 November 1852 it contained a 'For Sale' notice: Thomas Martin Wheeler, O'Connor's lieutenant in the development of the land plan, was advertising his O'Connorville cottage and plot. Wheeler was far from the first allottee to abandon the land. He had stuck at the cultivation of his 2 acres, although, as he reported to the land plan conference at Birmingham's Oddfellows' Hall in November 1848, 'depression in the condition of many of the allottees' was all-too evident. O'Connor's vision of the fecundity of the Chartist allotments came closest to realisation where market-garden techniques were used on the lighter soils of Gloucestershire and Worcestershire. Allottees who persisted with subsistence cultivation, especially on the heavy clays of O'Connorville and Charterville, had a raw time of it. A Charterville allottee, John Bennett, a former sailcloth weaver from Stockton-on-Tees, commented ruefully in 1868:

> Those that paid up a whole share got the first choice of an allotment. I paid up mine, £1. 7s. 6d. I got one in six months. I never would have if I had known what I do now. It has taken me 20 years to learn how a man can live without victuals, and I've just about come to it. Thousands paid up part of their share and lost it all, and I believe they were best off.[53]

Wheeler was used to abrupt changes of career direction, having been successively an apprentice woolcomber, baker, gardener, schoolmaster, London correspondent of the *Northern Star* (and also author of its remarkable serial novel *Sunshine and Shadow*), secretary of the NCA executive, land plan director and chief clerk of the National Land & Labour Bank. He would henceforth make a living as the manager of life-assurance schemes, initially the British Industry Society but from 1853 the Friend-in-Need Life & Sick Assurance Society, working alongside two other Chartists, his brother George and John Shaw (one of the August 1848 conspirators and imprisoned for two years). Wheeler master-minded the take-over of Thomas Clark's failed National Assurance Friendly Society in 1857. The combined body was among the most successful of the mid-Victorian mutuals, with 300 agencies and upwards of 1,000 full- and part-time staff.[54]

The consistent thread in Wheeler's life, however, was Chartism. Entering the movement from Owenism in 1839, he was a *Star* correspondent in 1840–43, a delegate to the council of the Metropolitan District NCA and also its secretary, NCA executive secretary 1842–46 (a job assumed in the difficult circumstances of Campbell's controversial departure), delegate to the NCSU conference in December 1842, auditor of the Victim Fund, secretary of the Newport Exiles' Restoration Committee, a member of the Fraternal Democrats and the Democratic Committee for the Regeneration of Poland, and a delegate to the 1848 National Convention and Assembly. Wheeler was also a member of the West London Anti-Enclosure Association, a lively group on Chartism's agrarian fringe. While at O'Connorville he was active on Rickmansworth local vestry, resumed work as a correspondent for the *Star*, was a delegate to the 1851 Convention, a member of the NCA executive, and a committee member of the National Loan Society (an abortive attempt to help secure the finances of the land plan). He was also secretary to the shareholders of Jones's *People's Paper* and occasionally its editor when Jones was touring the provinces. Wheeler's novel *The Light in the Gloom* was published in the paper in 1852.

Although working for the Friend-in-Need absorbed much of his time after 1853, Wheeler was committed to what remained of formally organised Chartism; but like so many Chartist stalwarts, his relationship with Ernest Jones, having begun warmly, deteriorated spectacularly. He remained loyal, however, to the *People's Paper* through the vicissitudes of the mid-1850s. It bumped along with a circulation about half that achieved by the *Northern Star* in even its leanest years. Although apt to pretend otherwise, Jones, unlike O'Connor before him, genuinely had no private resources with which to subsidise his paper or maintain the façade of disinterested gentleman leader. He had to borrow frequently to keep the paper afloat, being hit particularly by the final abolition of all Stamp Duty on newspapers in 1855, which brought down the prices of his rivals and sparked off a circulation war in which Jones could not afford to participate.

The affairs of the *People's Paper*, and with them Jones's relations with the wider movement, reached a nadir in 1858. Six years earlier, Jones had borrowed £50 from a commercial lender to keep the paper afloat, for which sum Wheeler agreed to be the surety. When Jones, having repaid just £10, defaulted on the debt it was Wheeler whom the company sued for the remainder (plus interest). In October 1858 Wheeler was thrown into debtors' prison because he could not pay. Wheeler's allies alleged that Jones tried to suppress news of what had happened and a committee of London Chartists was formed to raise the sum needed to free Wheeler. Ten years later the incident was still being bandied about as a means of compromising Jones's reputation.[55]

There was a crucial political context to this sorry episode. Just as Jones had shifted ground to seek trade union co-operation in 1854, so in 1857 he finally conceded that collaboration with middle-class radicals was not anathema. Defeat as a Chartist candidate at Nottingham in the March general election focused his mind. 'There can be no doubt', he wrote a month later, 'as to the wisdom of allying with the middle classes and their leaders if they offer such a measure of reform as we can be justified in accepting.'[56] With a convert's zeal, Jones rejected earlier shibboleths: 'We leave aside the beer-besotted and unthinking of the working classes', he wrote, calling on the Chartists to 'bury in oblivion the faults of the past on both sides; the want of faith shown by the middle classes in not making the Reform Bill the fulcrum to enfranchise the masses, and the deadly hatred of the working men to that great middle-class movement – the Repeal of the Corn Laws'.[57]

Though his conversion was sudden, his approach to building an alliance was both thoughtful and thorough. Proposing a Chartist conference the following February to launch a new movement, Jones encouraged debate and canvassed opinion both within and beyond Chartism. Compared to Chartist conferences earlier in the decade, the one that gathered in 1858 was well-attended: 49 delegates, representing 71 localities, included both William Newton and his close colleague from the Amalgamated Society of Engineers William Allen. The octogenarian Robert Owen also attended, but there were conspicuous absences. George Holyoake and Edward Hooson (leader of Manchester Chartism) were there, but almost every other figure of significance was not. Bright, Cobden, Charles Kingsley and Sir Joshua Walmsley (formerly president of the NPFRA) all resisted the opportunity to hear Jones concede that 'times altered'. He announced: 'They were not going to abandon the Charter but they were going to obtain what they could towards it, at the same time agitating for the whole six points.' To 'obtain what they could' the conference delegates agreed to the formation of a new body, the Political Reform League. A week later Joseph Sturge agreed to become its president. It seemed that the rupture regarding the NCSU in 1842 was finally ended. The NCA was effectively put into abeyance through the election of Jones as a one-man executive.[58]

Wheeler and a sizeable contingent of London Chartists reacted to this affront by establishing a new organisation to seize, as it were, the ark of the Chartist covenant from the NCA: the National Political Union for the Obtainment of the People's Charter.[59] It operated from the same address as the Integrity Life Assurance Society whose secretary ran its London branch. There were several other branches in the Manchester region. Wheeler was elected president and Leno printed its monthly journal, the *National Union*. Bronterre O'Brien was warmly supportive, as was G.W.M.Reynolds who for years had been conducting journalistic guerrilla warfare against Jones. Reynolds now alleged that Jones's loyalty to the Charter had been subverted by middle-class lucre.

The NPU attracted support and readers for its journal for two reasons. Firstly, it (in practice Wheeler) acted as advocate for land plan shareholders at the critical point of the National Land Company's final closure in 1858. Secondly, the NCA no longer existed in any meaningful sense. Since 1852 its primary purpose was as the vehicle for Jones's political career. Now its identity was merged into the PRL. Furthermore, the circulation of the *People's Paper* was declining. The month after the 1858 conference, Jones reduced it to six pages and launched an appeal to sustain it for the future. 'For God's sake send me something – anything – five, if you can … I am almost driven mad', he begged Robert Owen in June.[60] Soon afterwards he sold the paper to a well-heeled PRL member on the condition he retained control of two columns each week for PRL and Chartist matters, but the *People's Paper* did not last beyond September under its new owner. The NPU was left as the final and, it has to be said, forlorn custodian of the Charter. The PRL, too, did not last out the year. Jones was too gamey a personality for many middle-class reformers to feel comfortable around. However, his spadework in advance of its formation was significant, and the formation of a number of local manhood suffrage societies clearly owed something to the debate he engendered. To some extent, perhaps, so too did the Northern Reform Union, established in Newcastle's Chartist Hall in December 1857.[61]

Jones now directed his energies at editing a further weekly, the *Cabinet Newspaper: The Union of Classes and the Liberty of Man*. Despite its grandiloquent title, however, the paper was distinguished mainly for its sensationalist crime coverage (with a predilection for errant clergymen and 'the dirty blackguardism of the English aristocracy'). Its political coverage dived after the spring 1859 general election (when Jones again came bottom of the poll at Nottingham). It closed in February 1860.[62] To be fair to Jones, he was forced to neglect the paper to prepare for a serious libel action against Reynolds. This reached the courts in July 1859 and centred on a series of items published in *Reynolds's Newspaper*. The first of these, 'Political Renegadism: An Impudent and Notorious Turncoat', was a spirited attempt to bolster the reputation of the NPU by assaulting its chief adversary, Jones. It might well have passed for fair comment but subsequent articles accused Jones of pocketing money subscribed to keep the *People's Paper* afloat; of cynically inveigling his way into O'Connor's confidence and then caricaturing Feargus in his 1851–52 novel *De Brassier*; and (especially wounding) of being the purveyor of 'tenth-rate stump oratory'.[63]

Morally, the outcome of Jones's libel action was a resounding victory. He could show that the finances of the *People's Paper* were regularly audited and that the proceeds of appeals to readers had been used in good faith; he produced solid character witnesses; and he gave a good account of a conscientious Chartist career, complete with reference to O'Connor's warm endorsement of *De Brassier*. Reynolds's counsel never presented a defence, with the result that Jones left the court without 'a shadow of imputation' resting on him, in the words of the judge. But the award of a mere £2 damages and a printed apology was scarcely an emphatic endorsement. It was also of no financial consequence to the now-wealthy Reynolds. His failure to defend any of his claims about Jones's careerism betrayed as cynical a regard for Chartism as that which he alleged in his adversary. Even Wheeler's imprisonment for Jones's debt went unmentioned in court. However, the real casualty of all this was Chartism, exposed to the prurient gaze of an establishment press who sneered (as did the *Saturday Review*, for example) that the outcome reflected little credit on the half-million readers of *Reynolds's Newspaper*, for all of whom both Jones and Reynolds claimed the vote.[64]

In theory, the NCA persisted until 1860 when Jones, tidying away the loose ends of his Chartist career, abandoned journalism, resumed his legal practice and applied himself to a career in radical liberalism. It brought him to the cusp of winning a parliamentary seat when he unexpectedly died, the day after his fiftieth birthday, in 1869. Released from prison early in 1859, Wheeler returned to his work at the Friend-in-Need Assurance Society. Such as it was,

NPU business was covered in the Society's house journal. Wheeler died on 16 February 1862, aged 50. A heavy cold, contracted, it was said, during a nostalgic visit to O'Connorville earlier that winter, had developed into the bronchitis which killed him.[65]

## A comment by way of conclusion

There is a minor figure in Greek mythology called Procrustes. A notorious robber, his practice was to lure weary travellers into his wayside home, promising them a perfect bed for the night. If their length exceeded that of the bed, he cut short their limbs; if the bed proved longer, he stretched them to make them equal to it. Accounts of Chartism tend to define *the end* of the movement in a not dissimilar fashion, truncating or stretching their narratives to fit the Procrustean bed of the author's interpretation. Thus Chartism has variously been seen as disintegrating by 1842, or in the early 1840s, on 10 April 1848, after August 1848, in 1851 or 1858. History is seldom tidy: events, movements and organisations rarely come neatly packaged. The end of Chartism was especially untidy. The extent to which specifically Chartist activity was sustained varied widely between localities. A movement that unquestionably failed on its own terms succeeded in empowering many of its adherents to participate, often with marked effect, in a wide range of civic, political, educational and associational activities. This chapter has concentrated on political activities because Chartism (for all its compelling cultural dimensions) was nothing if not a political movement. Its emphasis has therefore been upon selected 'lower tier' Chartist leaders because it was at this level that the movement's enduring legacy was so vital. This is not to claim that questions of national leadership do not matter in the history of Chartism; but ultimately the movement succeeded and endured as far as it did despite, not because of, its national leaders. Hence this study's recurrent emphasis on those whose contribution to Chartism was largely unsung outside their particular locality or region. The previous chapter concluded that Chartism was a movement of small victories. It might also be characterised as having a multiplicity of small endings.

The first section of this chapter emphasised the perils of the elegiac mode. Blatant careerism, political charlatanry, and vapid oratory could all be found in Chartism, as we have seen, along with casual anti-Semitism and racism and personal dishonesty. There were serious systemic flaws too. O'Connor's alarm at the implications of the new move reflected a creditable concern that, above all, Chartism must remain united around the democratic and egalitarian vision of *The People's Charter*. Yet more than once in the movement's history, he and other Chartist leaders were confounded, even unnerved, when suddenly faced by truly mass political mobilisation: for example, in the north midlands and Pennine textile regions in August 1842 or in London in 1848. When he spoke of

Chartism having 'swelled for a moment to an unnatural size' in 1848, Samuel Kydd was reflecting a not uncommon view, born of a steady drift to respectability. A second systemic flaw concerned gender. For all that it mobilised women on a scale without precedent at the time, Chartism's internal culture was limited by this. A gradual transition from a movement that emphatically mobilised whole communities to one which increasingly espoused the male-breadwinner ideal and the politics of respectability closed-off opportunities for women's participation.

This is clear in a brief comparison of the 1839 and 1848 National Petitions. Where separately recorded, the female signatories in 1839 ranged from around 13 to 20 per cent. In 1848, by contrast, the House of Commons' Committee on Petitions (with no incentive to underestimate the figure since it saw women's signatures as discrediting Chartism) calculated the proportion to be 8 per cent. The diminution of women's roles in Chartism, and with it the stature of the movement itself, is tellingly evident in small details from the early 1850s: Abram Hanson continued to represent Elland at West Yorkshire delegate meetings, yet Elizabeth (whose politicisation is arguably the most striking feature of their Chartist life together) apparently did no more than send occasional donations to the 'Honesty Fund', to recompense O'Connor for his prodigious efforts in the Chartist cause.[66]

Chartism was celebrated in the later nineteenth century, however, for its manifest merits rather than deplored for its flaws. Chartism's vision of a more equitable society, where real gains in the quality of life in its every dimension would be realisable, was of enduring significance and a reference point for future generations, 'ever present to the progressive mind', in the words of the Durham miners' leader and 'Lib–Lab' MP John Wilson in 1910.[67] The sense that this was so is almost palpable by the 1880s, as Chartism was written into the genealogy of progressive politics. It is striking that the number of autobiographies published in the 1880s, and written by authors who foregrounded their involvement in Chartism, was double that of the previous decade; and, although the pool of potential authors was obviously diminishing, output in the next two decades persisted at around the same rate.[68]

With the acceleration of support for progressive politics in the late nineteenth century, there was also an increasing tendency for political groups and activists to claim kinship with Chartism. It should be said that there was also a tendency for Chartists to rewrite themselves into the free-trade tradition with rather more avidity than original relations with the ACLL strictly speaking permitted. William Chadwick's stock-in-trade emphasis on the evils of protectionism in the 1840s reflected this; so too did John Leno's autobiography, for all his leaning towards the socialism of William Morris.[69] However, the celebration of affinity from all points across the spectrum of progressive politics was genuine. William Morris's warm and thoughtful recognition of Leno was described in

the latter's 1892 autobiography as an 'oasis in the desert of an old man's life'.[70]
John Clifford, Fabian socialist and the most eminent figure in the English
Baptist Church at the turn of the century, emphasised his credentials as a boy
Chartist ('I was brought up to admire Will Lovett ... and to detest Feargus
O'Connor') when he became leader of the Christian Socialist League in 1894.[71]
But it was not the case that Lovettite 'moral force' credentials prevailed over
O'Connorite 'physical force' ones, as the Failsworth photograph (referred to
earlier) attests.

William Chadwick made no secret of his imprisonment for sedition in 1848,
yet built a career later in life from public speaking as 'Th' Owld Chartist' and
was much in demand by the Liberal Party. He also appeared at meetings
during the 1906 general election to support Will Thorne, a leading figure in the
(Social) Democratic Federation and foundation member of the Parliamentary
Labour Party. In 1896 leading Lancashire Liberals organised a testimonial to
Chadwick in recognition that he had 'devoted his life to advocacy of the principles of Liberalism & of Free Churchism'. When he died in 1908, the preface to
a booklet compiled in his memory was written by the chief agent of the Liberal
Party.[72] At the turn of the century, Richard Hawkin, a young activist in the
Independent Labour Party, maintained an extensive correspondence with the
elderly former York Chartist Thomas Rooke. Hawkin contemplated writing a
history of Chartism, as apparently did the Fabian socialist Graham Wallas.[73] In
1903 *Justice*, the paper of the Marxist-influenced Democratic Federation claimed
its members as 'the legitimate heirs and successors of the Chartists'.[74]

'In a few years more all the last pioneer Chartists will disappear, as the
Waterloo veterans have', the journal *Notes & Queries* observed in 1906, initiating a correspondence about who might be the last of them.[75] At the century's
turning there was an abiding sense that Chartism had been an epoch-defining
movement. It had moved society closer to the recognition of a profound truth,
that our essential humanity and dignity are protected and preserved only
where government answers not merely to the propertied and wealthy but to
all people.[76]

# Notes to the text

### Notes to Chapter 1: May–September 1838: 'I hold in my hand a charter – the people's charter'

1. The following account is based on (and, unless otherwise stated, direct quotations taken from) the *Scotch Reformers' Gazette* (26 May 1838), Birmingham Central Library (BCL), Lovett Collection, vol. 1, fos 181–7; supplementary details are drawn from A. Wilson, *The Chartist Movement in Scotland* (Manchester, Manchester University Press, 1970), pp. 48–52.

2. Banner slogans reported in *Northern Star* (*NS*), 2 June 1838, quoting the *Scots Times*.

3. R. Burns, *History of the Sufferings of the Church of Scotland from the Restoration to the Revolution* (Glasgow, Blackie, 1829), pp. 69–70.

4. For Wade see *Dictionary of Labour Biography* (*DLB*), vol. 11.

5. On newspaper prose style and audience response see C. Yelland, 'Speech and writing in the *Northern Star*', *Labour History Review*, 65:1 (2000), pp. 22–40, reprinted in S. Roberts (ed.), *The People's Charter* (London, Merlin, 2003).

6. E.g. 'I print, what, if circumstances had permitted, I should have spoken': R. Oastler, *Damnation! Eternal Damnation to the Fiend-begotten, 'Coarser Food' New Poor Law: A Speech by Richard Oastler* (London, Hetherington, 1837), p. 2.

7. *NS*, 2 June 1838; R. G. Gammage, *History of the Chartist Movement, 1837–54* (Newcastle, Browne, 1894), p. 21.

8. M. Chase, *Early Trade Unionism: Fraternity, Skill and the Politics of Labour* (Aldershot, Ashgate, 2000), p. 181.

9. E. Chadwick, *Report on the Sanitary Condition of the Labouring Population of Great Britain by Edwin Chadwick*, ed. M. Flinn (Edinburgh, Edinburgh University Press, 1965), p. 99; G. J. Harney writing in *NS*, 2 September 1843; J. C. Symons (Assistant Handloom Weavers' Commissioner, 1839), quoted in W. H. Fraser, *Conflict and Class: Scottish Workers, 1700–1838* (Edinburgh, Donald, 1988), p. 159.

10. E. King, *Strike of the Glasgow Weavers, 1787* (Glasgow, Glasgow Museums & Art Galleries, 1987), p. 29.

11. Fraser, *Conflict and Class*, p. 110; P. B. Ellis and S. Mac a'Ghobhainn, *The Scottish Insurrection of 1820* (London, Pluto, 1989), pp. 179–90; see also the account, apparently written by a participant, 'The pioneers: or, a tale of the radical rising at Strathaven in 1820', *Chartist Circular*, 21 and 28 May 1842.

12. M. Gebbie, *Sketches of the Town of Strathavon and Parish of Avondale* (Edinburgh, Menzies, 1880), p. 86. This banner was also borne at the Ayrshire county meeting at Kilmarnock in November 1819: A. Mackay, *History of Kilmarnock* (Kilmarnock,

Wilson, 1848), p. 210. A substantial remnant survives in the John Hastie Museum, Strathaven. Woven from cream silk, it was originally 1.8 metres square and included an embroidered Bible. Another flag, 'borne by our forefathers in the wars of the Covenant', was carried at a Chartist rally at Cumnock in 1840: *NS*, 17 October 1840; see also article on the Battle of Drumclog in *Chartist Circular*, 5 March 1842.

13. D. J. Moss, *Thomas Attwood: Biography of a Radical* (Montreal, McGill–Queen's University Press, 1990), p. 77.

14. 'One of no party', *Random Recollections of the House of Commons* (London, Smith Elder, 1836), p. 281. In essence, Attwood argued that gold and silver were commodities the value of which was subject to variations unrelated to the economy and hoarding, which exaggerated shifts in public confidence. A circulatory medium based on notes alone would permit the controlled expansion of money supply and the stimulation of demand: Moss, *Attwood*, esp. pp. 56–70.

15. *Birmingham Journal*, 23 December 1837.

16. 'The BPU radicals were steered, by their underlying philosophy, dangerously close to a theory of "virtual representation" of working-class interests by the middle-class': C. Behagg, 'An alliance with the middle class: the Birmingham Political Union and early Chartism', in J. Epstein and D. Thompson (eds), *Chartist Experience* (London, Macmillan, 1982), p. 74.

17. T. A. Devyr, *The Odd Book of the Nineteenth Century* (New York, Greenpoint, 1882), p. 160.

18. British Library (BL), Add. Mss 37,773, LWMA Minutes, vol. 1, fo. 107.

19. *Address to Reformers on the Forthcoming Elections* (1838), quoted in W. Lovett, *The Life and Struggles of William Lovett* (London, Trübner, 1876), p. 118.

20. *The People's Charter; Being the Outline of an Act to Promote the Just Representation of the People of Great Britain and Ireland in the Commons House of Parliament*, 3rd edn (London, Hetherington, 1838); the opening address was dated 8 May, when Lovett's text was approved by the LWMA. This is commonly assumed to indicate the publication date but for the delay in production see BL, Add. Mss 37,773, LWMA Minutes, vol. 1, fos 105–7.

21. For quickening interest in Magna Charta see: *John Bull's Mirror, or Corruption and Taxation Unmasked* (London, Johnston, ?1814); *Fairburn's Edition of Magna Charta, or the Great Charter of Liberties* (London, Fairburn, ?1817); *The Queen and Magna Charta; or, the Thing that John Signed* (London, Dolby, 1820); 'Magna Charta, or the Great Charter of Liberties', in *The Extraordinary Red Book* (London, Johnston, 1819), pp. xvii–xviii; see also J. A. Hone, *For the Cause of Truth: Radicalism in London, 1796–1821* (Oxford, Oxford University Press, 1982), p. 323.

22. *A Brief Account of the French Revolution of 1830 … to which is added an appendix, containing … the New Charter* (Glasgow, Ogle & M'Phun, 1830); *The New Charter, Humbly Addressed to the King and Both Houses of Parliament; Proposed as the Basis of a Constitution for the Government of Great Britain and Ireland, and as a Substitute for the Reform Bill* (London, Strange, 1831); *The People's Charter … giving a Condensed View of the Great Principles of Representative Government, and the Chief Objects of Reform* (London, Brooks, 1832).

23. A point made by George Howell in his unpublished history (1900) of the LWMA – edited by D. J. Rowe, as *A History of the Working Men's Association* (Newcastle upon Tyne, Graham, 1970), p. 87. There is no evidence to support Gammage's claim that O'Connell suggested the title: Gammage, *History*, p. 6. The extent of the LWMA's provincial correspondence is evident in its pamphlet *The Radical Reformers of England, Scotland, & Wales, to the Irish People* (London, Cleave, ?1838), pp. 6–8.

24. *The People's Charter*, pp. 2 and 4.
25. BCL, Lovett Collection, vol. 1, fo. 22, poster for public meeting at the Crown & Anchor Tavern, 28 February 1837, annotated by Lovett: 'the Prayer of this was the first of the People's Charter'.
26. Ibid., fo. 170, Lovett to Sharman Crawford (?3 June 1838). Place claimed, in an unpublished history of the LWMA, that he wrote most of the Charter: BL, Place Collection, Set 56, vol. 1, fos 8–9. In this, as in much else, he misled subsequent historians.
27. The following is based on a more-detailed account in Chase, *Early Trade Unionism*, pp. 182–4.
28. *NS*, 10 February 1838.
29. Ibid., 17 February 1838. Lovett clearly felt the publication of this letter was a defining moment in his career and reproduced it prominently in his *Life and Struggles*, pp. 159–62.
30. I. J. Prothero, 'London Chartism and the trades', *Economic History Review*, 24:2 (1971), p. 202; *Address and Rules of the Working Men's Association, for Benefiting Politically, Socially, and Morally, the Useful Classes* (London, 1836), copy in BL, Add. MSS 27,835, fos 257–50.
31. BCL, Lovett Collection, vol. 1, fo. 34A, Prospectus of the East London Democratic Association; see also J. Bennett, 'The London Democratic Association, 1837–41', in Epstein and Thompson (eds), *Chartist Experience*, pp. 87–119.
32. *London Democrat*, 18 May 1839.
33. *NS*, 21 December 1850.
34. Important correctives in terms of understanding metropolitan Chartism are I. J. Prothero, *Artisans and Politics* (Folkestone, Dawson, 1979), and D. Goodway, *London Chartism, 1838–48* (Cambridge, Cambridge University Press, 1982), to both of which the present author is indebted.
35. On the election see J. A. Epstein, *Lion of Freedom: Feargus O'Connor and the Chartist Movement, 1832–42* (London, Croom Helm, 1982), pp. 21–4; and S. A. Weaver, *John Fielden* (Oxford, Clarendon, 1987).
36. As late as 1913, a leading Oldham Liberal equated the Labour Party's role in the borough's 1911 by-election with O'Connor in 1835: A. Marcroft, *Landmarks of Liberalism* (Oldham, privately published, 1913), pp. 90–1.
37. *NS*, 26 June and 16 January 1841.
38. *Weekly Free Press*, 26 September 1829, quoted in J. Belchem, *'Orator' Hunt: Henry Hunt and English Working-Class Radicalism* (Oxford, Clarendon, 1985), pp. 198–9.
39. M. Bush, *The Casualties of Peterloo* (Lancaster, Carnegie, 2005); Labour History Archive and Study Centre (LHASC), Manchester, Vincent MSS 1/1/9, Vincent to J. Miniken, 18 August 1838.
40. O'Connor, Manchester speech, July 1835, quoted in Epstein, *Lion of Freedom*, pp. 23–4.
41. R. Balmforth, *Some Social and Political Pioneers of the Nineteenth Century* (London, Sonnenschein, 1902), p. 189; Balmforth's father was a Huddersfield handloom weaver and a supporter of O'Connor.
42. *Barnsley Times*, 27 May 1882.
43. Papers of General Francisco Burdett O'Connor, now in the possession of Eduardo Trigo O'Connor d'Arlach, Bolivia (hereafter, O'Connor d'Arlach Papers), letter to Frank O'Connor, 28 September 1843. O'Connor may have exaggerated the loss, but his personal finances by the mid-1830s were in considerable disarray. On this theme in political leadership see J. Belchem and J. Epstein, 'The nineteenth-century gentleman leader revisited', *Social History*, 22:2 (May 1997).

44. H. Southall, 'Agitate! Agitate! Organize! Political travellers and the construction of a national politics, 1839–80', *Transactions of the Institute of British Geographers*, ns, 21:1 (1996), pp. 178–82.

45. *NS*, 16 January 1841.

46. For his own account see *Bronterre's National Reformer*, 28 January 1837.

47. G. Claeys, 'A utopian tory revolutionary at Cambridge: the political ideas and schemes of James B. Bernard', *Historical Journal*, 25 (1982), pp. 583–603; Epstein, *Lion of Freedom*, pp. 42–8; BCL, Lovett Collection, vol. 1, fos 58–79.

48. Oastler, *Damnation!*, pp. 3–5.

49. J. H. Burland, 'Annals of Barnsley and its Environs', unpublished MS, Barnsley Central Library, Archives and Local Studies Section (hereafter, Burland), vol. 2 (1881), fo. 68. Burland based his account on a mixture of press reports and recollections. For a consistent, more detailed, contemporary account, see *Leeds Mercury*, 20 May 1837; also J. Knott, *Popular Opposition to the 1834 New Poor Law* (London, Croom Helm, 1986), pp. 113–22.

50. Burland, fo. 71. In understanding the development of *NS*, Epstein, *Lion of Freedom*, chap. 2, is invaluable; for Hobson see *DLB*, vol. 8.

51. M. Chase, 'Building circulation, building identity: engraved portraiture and the *Northern Star*', in J. Allen and O. R. Ashton (eds), *Papers for the People* (London, Merlin, 2005), pp. 25–53.

52. Gammage, *History*, p. 17.

53. Oastler, *Damnation!*, p. 4.

54. *Monthly Liberator*, 13 June 1838.

55. *Barnsley Chronicle*, 29 June 1889.

56. C. Driver, *Tory Radical: The Life of Richard Oastler* (New York, Oxford University Press, 1946), pp. 378f.

57. *NS*, 21 April 1838.

58. J. Jackson, *Demagogue Done Up: An Exposure of the Extreme Inconsistencies of Mr Feargus O'Connor* (Bradford, Wilkinson, 1844) p. 6; *NS*, 4 August and 8 September 1838.

59. *NS*, 30 June, 21 July and 18 August 1838.

60. For example: *NS*, 13 October; *The Times*, 26 December; and *Morning Post*, 29 December 1838; *Annual Register, or a View of the History and Politics of the Year of 1838* (London, Rivington, 1839), p. 310; J. Watkins, *Five Cardinal Points of the People's Charter* (Whitby, Forth, 1839), p. 35; West Yorkshire Archives Service (WYAS), Leeds, Harewood Papers. Lieutenancy Box 2, deposition of J. Glover, 26 July 1839; *Temperance Journal*, January 1840; O'Connell to D. Pigot, 30 September 1838, reprinted in *The Correspondence of Daniel O'Connell*, ed. M. R. O'Connell (Dublin, Blackwater, 1977), vol. 6, p. 185.

61. B. Wilson, *Struggles of an Old Chartist* (1887), reprinted in D. Vincent (ed.), *Testaments of Radicalism: Memoirs of Working-Class Politicians, 1790–1885* (London, Europa, 1977), pp. 209–10.

62. C. Feinstein, 'Pessimism perpetuated: real wages and the standard of living in Britain during and after the industrial revolution', *Journal of Economic History*, 58:3 (1998).

63. J. Leach, *Stubborn Facts from the Factories* (London, Ollivier, 1844), p. 11.

64. F. von Raumer, *England in 1841* (London, Lee, 1842), vol. 1, p. 106; E. Cook, *The Life of Florence Nightingale* (London, Macmillan, 1914), vol. 1, p. 80.

65. *People's Magazine*, April 1842.

66. A. B. Reach, *Manchester and the Textile Districts in 1849*, ed. C. Aspin (Helmshore, Helmshore Local History Society, 1972), p. 73.

67. *NS*, 3 May 1845; see also A. Peacock, *Bradford Chartism, 1838-40* (York, Borthwick Institute, 1969), pp. 42, 48.

68. *NS*, 16 June 1838.

*Notes to Chapter 2: October–December 1838: 'The people are up'*

1. *Leeds Times*, 20 October 1838.

2. *NS Extraordinary*, 16 October 1838.

3. Ibid.; M. Chase, *Early Trade Unionism: Fraternity, Skill and the Politics of Labour* (Aldershot, Ashgate, 2000), pp. 145, 157–8 and 163–4.

4. D. J. V. Jones, *Chartism and the Chartists* (London, Allen Lane, 1975), p. 103; for Vincent as a Chartist missionary see also H. Southall, 'Agitate! Agitate! Organize! Political travellers and the construction of a national politics, 1839–80', *Transactions of the Institute of British Geographers*, ns 21 (1996), pp. 182–3.

5. HO, 40/53, fos 937–44, J. Beecham to Vincent, 17 February 1839.

6. *NS*, 29 September 1838.

7. *Warwick Advertiser* and *NS*, 22 September 1838.

8. *Leeds Times*, 20 October 1838; J. C. F. Barnes, 'Popular protest and radical politics: Carlisle, 1790–1850', D.Phil. thesis, Lancaster University (1981), p. 328; *Essex and Suffolk Times* quoted in A. F. J. Brown, *Chartism in Essex and Suffolk* (Chelmsford, Essex County Records Office [CRO], 1982), p. 48; *North Staffordshire Mercury* quoted in R. Fyson, 'Chartism in north Staffordshire', D.Phil. thesis, Lancaster University (1999), p. 78; *True Scotsman*, 20 October 1838; *Bolton Free Press*, 12 September 1838; *Norfolk Chronicle*, 3 November 1838, quoted in J. K. Edwards, 'Chartism in Norwich', *Yorkshire Bulletin of Economic and Social Research* 19:2 (1967), p. 91.

9. Entries for Ashton: *Dictionary of Labour Biography* (*DLB*), vol. 3; Knight: ibid., vol. 9; George: ibid., vol. 10; Richardson: ibid., vol. 11; *NS*, 2 June (Elland) and 8 September (Stratford) 1838, 27 November 1847 (Smart); R. Fyson, 'Homage to John Richards', in O. Ashton, R. Fyson and S. Roberts (eds), *The Duties of Discontent: Essays for Dorothy Thompson* (London and New York, Mansell, 1995), pp. 71–96.

10. R. G. Gammage, *History of the Chartist Movement, 1837–54* (Newcastle, Browne, 1894), pp. 42–3; *NS*, 17 November 1838.

11. *NS*, 1 September 1838.

12. W. R. Ward (ed.), *Early Victorian Methodism* (Oxford, University of Durham Press, 1976), p. 51.

13. *NS*, 9 June 1838; Norwich speech quoted in H. Jephson, *The Platform: Its Rise and Progress* (London, Macmillan, 1892), vol. 2, p. 247; *Wigan Gazette*, 16 November 1838.

14. *NS*, 25 August 1838.

15. Ibid., 11 August 1838; D. Goodway, *London Chartism, 1838–48* (Cambridge, Cambridge University Press, 1982), pp. 24–5.

16. LHASC, Vincent MSS 1/1/10, Vincent to J. Miniken, 26 August 1838.

17. Ibid., Vincent to Miniken, 23 September 1838; Gammage, *History of the Chartist Movement*, p. 79; A. Randall, *Before the Luddites* (Cambridge, Cambridge University Press, 1991), pp. 149–86 and 278–82.

18. *Leeds Times*, 24 November 1838; R. Wells, 'Southern Chartism', *Rural History* 2:1 (1991), p. 39; W. Barnes, 'The Unioners', *Dorset County Chronicle*, 16 December 1838, reprinted in J. Draper, 'William Barnes and "The Unioners" in Dorset', *Southern History*, 22 (2000), pp. 209–10.

19. Roberts quoted by Draper, 'William Barnes', p. 216; BCL, Lovett Collection, vol. 1, fo. 291b, Vincent to Lovett, 16 November 1838.

20. T. Middleton, *History of Hyde and its Neighbourhood* (Hyde, Higham, 1932), p. 99; *Monthly Messenger*, 3 November 1838; R. B. Pugh, 'Chartism in Somerset and Wiltshire', in A. Briggs (ed.), *Chartist Studies* (London, Macmillan, 1959), p. 178; *NS*, 10 November 1838; W. Aitken, 'Remembrances and struggles of a working man for bread and liberty', quoted in R. G. Hall and S. Roberts (eds), *William Aitken* (Ashton-under-Lyne, Tameside Leisure Services, 1996), p. 30.

21. Gammage, *History*, pp. 94–5; for Gammage see *DLB*, vol. 6.

22. Barnes, 'Popular protest', p. 333; see also W. Farish, *Autobiography of William Farish* (privately published, 1889), p. 38; Home Office, 40/40, 23 November 1838, evidence of Foley and Stapledon; H. Goddard, *Memoirs of a Bow Street Runner* (London, Museum Press, 1956), p. 155; *Leeds Times*, 15 December 1838.

23. W. Wilks, *The Half Century: Its History, Political and Social* (London, Cash, 1853), p. 279; C. Dickens, *The Old Curiosity Shop* (1840–41), ch. 45.

24. Brown, *Chartism*, p. 75; M. S. Edwards, *Purge This Realm: A Life of Joseph Rayner Stephens* (London, Epworth, 1994), p. 58; Goddard, *Memoirs*, pp. 154–60.

25. L. Croft, *John Fielden's Todmorden* (Todmorden, Tygerfoot, 1994), pp. 43–8.

26. Goddard, *Memoirs*, pp. 158–60.

27. *NS*, 29 December 1838; Edwards, *Purge This Realm*, p. 60; Goddard, *Memoirs*, p 159; J. R. Stephens, *Political Preacher* (London, Whitaker, 1839), p. 13.

28. For O'Connor's earlier lukewarm view of the other points of the Charter see *NS*, 21 April 1838 and 16 January 1841.

29. *True Scotsman*, 17 November; *NS*, 10 November; *Nottingham Review*, 9 November 1838.

30. Data extrapolated from the Appendix to D. Thompson, *The Chartists: Popular Politics in the Industrial Revolution* (London, Temple Smith, 1984), pp. 341–68; for 1839 Thompson lists 109 female societies (all but 5 in localities with other recorded activity), 429 non-gender-specific associations and 208 localities with other Chartist activity, i.e. 642 places in all; data for 1830–32 taken from N. LoPatin, *Political Unions* (Basingstoke, Macmillan, 1999), pp. 103, 174–7, 179 and 182, and C. Flick, *Birmingham Political Union* (Folkestone, Dawson, 1978), pp. 185–6. LoPatin (p. 182) describes twenty-nine PUs as 'infrequent one-time meeting Unions'. None of these figures are completely accurate but they do permit useful broad comparison.

31. (W. Lovett) *Radical Reformers of England, Scotland, & Wales, to the Irish People* (London, Cleave, 1838); this is commonly supposed to have been published in 1841, but see discussion of it in *Leeds Times*, 3 November, and *True Scotsman*, 10 November 1838.

32. For Birmingham's FPU see H. Rogers, 'What right have women to interfere with politics?', in T. Ashplant and G. Smythe (eds), *Explorations in Cultural History* (London, Pluto, 2001).

33. Indeed a *Montrose Review* report on the Kerriemuir 'female union', quoted in *True Scotsman*, 22 December 1838, refers to 'the other political union'.

34. For a male Chartist's complaint about exactly this, see *Fleet Papers*, 9 April 1842.

35. BL, Add. Mss 34245A, fo. 341, Carlisle FRA to Lovett, 30 April 1830; Thompson, *Chartists*, Appendix.

36. J. Schwarzkopf, *Women in the Chartist Movement* (Basingstoke, Macmillan 1991), p. 239.

37. BL, Add. Mss 34245A, fo. 124, Vincent to Lovett, 13 March 1839; HO, 40/42/311, Mason to Home Office, 18 July 1839; and *NS*, 3 August 1839; *Charter*, 27 October 1839.

38. *True Scotsman*, 22 December 1838 (my emphasis).

39. Chase, *Early Trade Unionism*, p. 47.

40. See especially D.Thompson, 'Women and nineteenth-century radical politics: a lost dimension', in J.Mitchell and A.Oakley (eds), *Rights and Wrongs of Women* (Harmondsworth, 1976); A.Clark, *Struggle for the Breeches: Gender and the Making of the British Working Class* (London, Rivers Oram, 1995), pp.220–47; M.de Larrabeiti, 'Conspicuous before the world: the political rhetoric of the Chartist women', in E.J.Yeo (ed.), *Radical Femininity* (Manchester, MUP, 1998), pp.106–26; Rogers, 'What right have women to interfere in politics?'; and H.Rogers, *Authority, Authorship and the Radical Tradition in Nineteenth-Century England* (Aldershot, Ashgate, 2000), pp.80–123.

41. Stephens and Salt quoted in Rogers, *Authority*, p.89; Deegan, *NS*, 1 June 1839.

42. Clark, *Struggle*; also A.Clark, 'The rhetoric of Chartist domesticity: gender, language and class in the 1830s and 1840s', *Journal of British Studies*, 31:1 (1992), pp.62–88.

43. *Western Vindicator*, 23 February 1839.

44. *NS*, 8 December 1838.

45. *True Scotsman*, 24 November 1838; *Birmingham Journal*, 6 October 1838; the Birmingham FPU address is reprinted in Rogers, 'What right have women to interfere in politics?', pp.69–70, see also pp.76 and 78.

46. O.Ashton, '*Western Vindicator* and early Chartism', and W.H.Fraser, 'The Chartist press in Scotland', in J.Allen and O.Ashton (eds), *Papers for the People: A Study of the Chartist Press* (London, Merlin, 2005); J.Allen, '"A small drop of ink": Tyneside Chartism and the *Northern Liberator*', in O.Ashton, R.Fyson and S.Roberts (eds), *The Chartist Legacy* (Woodbridge, Suffolk, Merlin, 1999); see also R.Harrison, G.Woolven and R.Duncan (eds), *The Warwick Guide to British Labour Periodicals* (Brighton, Harvester, 1977), and A.Wilson, *The Chartist Movement in Scotland* (Manchester, Manchester University Press, 1970).

47. BL, Add. MSS 34245A, fo.82.

48. J.Burnett, *Useful Toil* (London, Allen Lane, 1974), p.308; B.Grime, *Memory Sketches* (Oldham, Hirst & Rennie, 1887), p.26; B.Brierley, *Home Memories and Recollections of a Life* (Manchester, Heywood, 1886), p.23; *NS*, 6 May 1838 and 6 May 1848; W.H.Challinor (ed.), 'Reminiscences of Thomas Dunning', *Transactions of the Lancashire and Cheshire Antiquarian Society*, 59 (1947), pp.112–13 and 121; W.Cudworth, *Rambles Round Great Horton* (Bradford, Brear, 1886), pp.27–8; J.A.Epstein, 'Feargus O'Connor and the *Northern Star*', *International Review of Social History*, 21 (1976), pp.74–6; B.Wilson, 'Struggles of an old Chartist' (1887), in D.Vincent (ed.), *Testaments of Radicalism: Memoirs of Working-Class Politicians* (London, Europa, 1977), p.206; T.Frost, *Forty Years' Recollections* (London, Sampson Low, 1880), pp.181–3.

49. W.H.Fraser, *Conflict and Class: Scottish Workers, 1700–1838* (Edinburgh, John Donald, 1988), p.110; P.B.Ellis and S.Mac a'Ghobhainn, *The Scottish Insurrection of 1820* (London, Pluto, 1989), pp.179–90; George: *DLB*, vol.10; Preston: ibid., vol.8.

50. *True Scotsman*, 24 November and 1 December 1838.

51. Quoted in Wilson, *Chartist Movement in Scotland*, p.61.

52. *NS*, 15 December, and *True Scotsman*, 22 December 1838; Wilson, *Chartist Movement in Scotland*, pp.62–3.

53. *Ayr Examiner* quoted in Wilson, *Chartist Movement in Scotland*, pp.63–4.

54. *NS*, 12 January 1839.

55. Letter to P.Fitzpatrick, 11 February 1839, reprinted in D.O'Connell, *The Correspondence of Daniel O'Connell*, ed. M.R.O'Connell, vol.6 (Dublin, Blackwater, 1977), p.216.

56. *Birmingham Journal*, 1 December 1839; see also 17 and 24 November.
57. For example Robert Lowery in his autobiography (1856–57), reprinted in B. Harrison and P. Hollis (eds), *Robert Lowery: Radical and Chartist* (London, Europa, 1979), p. 112.
58. *NS*, 17 November 1838.

### Notes to Chapter 3: January–July 1839: 'The People's Parliament'

1. *NS*, 2 February 1839; 'William Carpenter': *ODNB*; *Charter*, 15 March 1840.
2. 'Our position, principles and prospects', *Charter*, 27 January 1839.
3. *Operative*, 27 January 1839.
4. BL, Add. MSS 34245A, fos 11 and 240; C. Behagg, 'An alliance with the middle class: the BPU and early Chartism', in J. Epstein and D. Thompson (eds), *The Chartist Experience: Studies in Working-Class Radicalism and Culture, 1830–1860* (London, Macmillan, 1982), esp. pp. 73–9; *NS* 30 April 1839.
5. *Rules and Regulations of the General Convention of the Industrious Classes* (London, Northcott, 1839).
6. *National Instructor* 14 September 1850; *Charter*, 3 March 1839; *NS*, 15 June 1839; *Western Vindicator*, 23 February 1839.
7. See especially chapter 6 below for hostility between Chartism and ACLL.
8. National Archives, Kew, Home Office Papers (HO), 40/37, 3 February 1839; *NS*, 49 February 1839; J. Hawkes (trans.), *The London Journal of Flora Tristan* (London, Virago, 1982), p. 48; I. McCalman, 'Ultra-radicalism and convivial debating clubs in London, 1795–1838', *English Historical Review*, 102 (1987), pp. 309–33. On the Lumber Troop see J. Grant, *Sketches in London* (London, Tegg, 1838), pp. 89–128.
9. Anon, *The Critic in Parliament and in Public* ... (London, Bell, [1841]), pp. 186–7; Tristan, *London Journal*, p. 48; Fletcher quoted in J. Epstein, *The Lion of Freedom: Feargus O'Connor and the Chartist Movement* (London, Croom Helm, 1982), p. 140.
10. *Charter*, 17 February 1839; *Hansard*, vol. 45, 11 February 1839, col. 220.
11. HO, 40/37, fos 72ff., T. J. Mills to Home Office, 16 February 1839.
12. HO, 40/37, 4 February 1839; Bolton Central Library, Local Studies Library, Heywood Papers, ZHE 35/43, 20 January 1839, and ZHE 35/47, nd; Attwood quoted by G. J. Holyoake, *Life of Joseph Rayner Stephens* (London, Williams & Norgate, ?1881), p. 103; *London Dispatch*, 13 January 1839; *NS*, 5 January 1839; *Manchester and Salford Advertiser*, 12 January 1839, quoted in J. Baxter, 'Armed resistance and insurrection', *Our History*, 76 (1984), p. 14; *Leicestershire Mercury*, 9 February 1839, quoted by A. Little, 'Chartism and liberalism: popular politics in Leicestershire, 1842–74', D.Phil thesis, University of Manchester, 1991, p. 47.
13. *The Times*, 18 March, 2 April 1839; C. C. F. Greville, *The Greville Memoirs, 1814–60*, ed. L. Strachey and R. Fulford, vol. 4 (London, Macmillan, 1938), p. 117; W. Napier, *The Life and Opinions of General Sir Charles James Napier*, vol. 2 (London, Murray, 1857), pp. 5, 6 and 8.
14. R. Sykes, 'Physical-force Chartism: the cotton district and the Chartist crisis of 1839', *International Review of Social History*, 30 (1985), pp. 214–15; W. Cudworth, *Rambles Round Great Horton* (Bradford, Brear, 1886), p. 27; R. O. Heslop, 'A Chartist spear', *Monthly Chronicle of North-Country Lore and Legend*, vol. 3 (1889), pp. 148–50; J. E. Archer, *'By a Flash and a Scare'* (Oxford, Oxford University Press, 1990), p. 106; HO, 40/48, fo. 5.
15. (J. Hobson), 'Now then – heads of families!!', *A Copy of the Poll* ... (Huddersfield, Hobson, 1837), p. 23; *Address of the Radical Association of Colne*, 26 November 1838, reprinted in D. Thompson, *Early Chartists* (London, Macmillan, 1971), pp. 193–4; *NS*, 3 February 1839.

16. W. Benbow, *Grand National Holiday and Congress of the Productive Classes* (London, Benbow, 1832), p. 13; *DLB*, vol. 6 and *ODNB*.

17. *Charter*, 17 February 1839.

18. BL, Add. MSS 34245A, fo. 41; *NS*, 23 February.

19. BL, Add. MSS 34245A, fos 24, 102, 320 and 323.

20. It has been suggested the response rate to these questionnaires was poor, but this is purely conjectural: see D. J. Rowe, 'The Chartist Convention and the regions', *Economic History Review*, 2nd series, 20 (1969).

21. *Charter*, 26 February 1839; BL, Add. MSS 34245A, fos 61, 74f., 175 and 388, 34245B, fos 276f.

22. *Western Vindicator*, 30 March 1839; D. J. V. Jones, *The Last Rising: The Newport Insurrection of 1839* (Oxford, Clarendon, 1985), p. 65.

23. A. Wilson, *The Chartist Movement in Scotland* (Manchester, Manchester University Press, 1970), pp. 70–1; *NS*, 16 and 30 March 1839; BL, Add. MSS, fos 101, 145, 148, 162–3.

24. Vincent wrote up his travels each week for the *Western Vindicator*; they can also be read on the 'Vision of Britain' website: www.visionofbritain.org.uk/Travelers.

25. *Western Vindicator*, 23 March 1839.

26. Ibid., 9 March 1839; *NS*, 22 June 1839.

27. For Salt's jeremiads see BL, Add. MSS 34245A, fos 41 (17 February) and 102–10 (9 March); *NS*, 30 March 1839.

28. *NS*, 9 and 16 March 1839.

29. *Charter*, 24 March 1839; *NS*, 27 March 1839; *Morning Chronicle*, 19 March 1839.

30. W. A. Munford, *William Ewart MP, 1798–1865* (London, Grafton, 1960), p. 98; Wilson, *Chartist Movement in Scotland*, p. 74; *NS*, 29 June 1839. Craig polled 46 votes, the Conservative 1758 and the Whig–liberal 1296.

31. *Western Vindicator*, 30 March, 6 and 13 April 1839; *The Times*, 28 March and 3 April 1839.

32. *Monmouthshire Merlin*, 13 April 1839, cited in Jones, *Last Rising*, p. 70; *NS*, 6 April 1839, see also p. 83; HO, 40/44, fo. 260 (20 March 1839); *The Times*, 10 and 29 April, 8 May 1839.

33. *Poor Man's Guardian*, 11 April 1831. Manchester-born Macerone (sometime aide-de-camp to Napoleon's puppet king of Naples) lived in London at this time: see *ODNB* entry for Macerone.

34. R. J. Richardson, *The Right of Englishmen to Have Arms* (London, Cleave, 1839).

35. For comments on the magistracy during April and May 1839 see Napier, *Life*, pp. 7, 8, 11, 14, 15, 24, 28, 36 and 45; also HO, 40/43, fo. 342, 15 July 1839 and Napier's 23 May 1840 report on garrisoning in HO, 50/451.

36. Letter, 24 April 1839, quoted in Napier, *Life*, p. 16; see also pp. 8, 10, 13, 15, 17, 18, 21, 22, 24, 26 and 32.

37. Napier to Ross, 22 April, and to Fitzroy, 12 May, and journal entries for 5, 6 and 8 May, quoted in *Life*, pp. 15, 24, 25, 26 and 33.

38. Napier to Wemyss (commanding officer at Manchester), 22 April 1839, quoted in Napier, *Life*, p. 14.

39. Napier to Ross, 25 May 1839, and journal entry for 27 April, quoted in ibid., pp. 39 and 23.

40. HO, 40/50, fo. 40, Scolefield to Russell, 9 May 1839; Sykes, 'Physical-force Chartism', p. 216.

41. BL, Add. MSS 34245B, fo. 31, undated [June?] letter from Joseph Goulding, Shoreditch CA; on Goulding see D. Goodway, *London Chartism* (Cambridge, Cambridge University Press, 1982), p. 245, n77;

42. W. Lovett, *Life and Struggles of William Lovett* (London, Trübner, 1876), pp. 206–8; (W. Lovett), *Manifesto of the General Convention of the Industrious Classes* (London, Dyson, 1839), pp. 4–6.
43. *Manifesto*, pp. 7 and 8.
44. Barnsley, Bradford, Dewsbury, Halifax, Huddersfield, Leeds, Todmorden, Wakefield (all west Yorkshire), Ashton, Blackburn, Bolton, Bury, Colne, Manchester, Oldham, Rochdale, Wigan (Lancashire), Congleton, Hyde, Stockport (Cheshire), Bristol, Cirencester and Stroud (Gloucestershire), Bradford-on-Avon, Devizes, Trowbridge and Warminster (Wiltshire), plus Birmingham, Derby, Mansfield, Nottingham and Newcastle upon Tyne. Welsh towns covered were Monmouth, Newtown, Newport, Merthyr Tydfil and Pontypool. Scotland was ignored. A diluted version (without instructions regarding immediate arrests) was sent to Bath, Coventry, Leicester and Northampton. See the copy of the circular in HO, 41/13, fo. 260 (7 May 1839).
45. Fielden to the Convention, 1 May 1839, BL, Add. MSS 34245A, fo. 365.
46. *Western Vindicator*, 18 May 1839; *Charter*, 12 May 1839; *NS*, 11 May.
47. *The Times*, 3 and 6 May 1839; D. Williams, *John Frost: A Study in Chartism* (Cardiff, University of Wales, 1939), pp. 158–9; O. Ashton, 'Chartism in mid-Wales', *Montgomeryshire Collections*, 62:1 (1971), pp. 25–33.
48. *The Times*, 14 May 1839; Napier, *Life*, pp. 27–8; R. Fyson, 'Chartism in north Staffordshire', University of Lancaster D.Phil thesis (1999), pp. 106–7.
49. *The Times*, 13 May 1839; *NS*, 18 May 1839; A. R. Schoyen, *Chartist Challenge: A Portrait of George Julian Harney* (London, Heinemann, 1958), pp. 67–8.
50. *Western Vindicator*, 4 and 18 May 1839; Jones, *Last Rising*, p. 80.
51. *NS*, 4 May 1839; O'Brien quoted by Epstein, *Lion of Freedom*, p. 157.
52. *Birmingham Journal*, 6 April 1839.
53. Duddeston-cum-Nechells, address to Convention, 13 May 1839, BL, Add. MSS 34245A, fo. 442.
54. *NS*, 11 May 1839, Sykes, 'Physical-force Chartism', pp. 214 and 216.
55. Ibid., 18 May 1839; Napier, letters to Home Office and Sir Hew Ross, 25 May 1839, reprinted in *Life*, p. 39; see also pp. 35 and 37.
56. J. A. Epstein, 'Feargus O'Connor and the *Northern Star*', *International Review of Social History*, 21 (1976), pp. 69 and 96–7.
57. *Halifax Guardian*, 25 May 1839; *NS*, 25 May 1839; R. G. Gammage, *The History of the Chartist Movement, 1837–54* (Newcastle, Browne, 1894), pp. 113–22.
58. HO, 45/249A, fo. 120, Tower Armoury dispatch note, 25 May 1839.
59. A. Prentice, *The History of the Anti-Corn-Law League*, vol. 1 (London, Cash, 1853), pp. 214–18.
60. The Seditious Societies Amendment Act reduced from £20 to £5 the penalty for issuing a publication without the name and address of the printer; and henceforward only the government could initiate a prosecution. This has been spuriously hailed as evidence of an almost permissive attitude to Chartism on the part of the Government: see K. Judge, 'Early Chartist organization and the Convention of 1839', *International Review of Social History*, 20 (1975), p. 396; L. Radzinowicz, *A History of English Criminal Law*, vol. 4 (London, Stevens, 1968), p. 247.
61. *NS*, 22 June 1839.
62. Ibid., 15 June 1839; Benbow, *Grand National Holiday*, p. 14, see also p. 12; *Charter*, 14 July 1839, see also Schoyen, *Chartist Challenge*, p. 70; B. Harrison and P. Hollis (eds), *Robert Lowery: Radical and Chartist* (London, Europa, 1979), p. 142; *Operative*, 28 April 1839.

63. *NS*, 18 May 1839. On Chartist–trade union relations see M.Chase, *Early Trade Unionism* (Aldershot, Ashgate, 2000), pp.184–90.

64. Harrison and Hollis, *Robert Lowery*, p.142; *NS*, 6 and 27 July 1839; Epstein, *Lion of Freedom*, pp.167–8; BL, Add. MSS 34245B, fos 53–4.

65. *Birmingham Journal*, 21 September 1839.

66. C.Behagg, *Politics and Production in the Early Nineteenth Century* (London, Routledge, 1990), pp.201, 211–14.

67. *Bolton Free Press*, 13 July 1839; p.170; 'A member of the Northern Political Union', *State of the Question between the People, the Middle Classes, and the Aristocracy* (Newcastle, Northern Liberator Office, 1839), p.19; see also *NS*, 13 and 20 July 1839. For Cold Bath Fields see M.Chase, *'The People's Farm'* (Oxford, Clarendon, 1988), pp.161–2.

68. Taylor to Arthur, quoted in W. H. Fraser, *John Taylor, Chartist: Ayrshire Revolutionary* (Ayrshire Archaeological and Natural History Society, 2006), p.60.

69. Quoted in J. A. Langford, *Staffordshire and Warwickshire Past and Present* (London, Mackenzie, ?1870), vol.2, p.585.

70. *Charter*, 14 July 1839; National Archives, Kew, Treasury Solicitor's Papers (TS), 11/816, fo.114.

71. Lovett, *Life*, p.220; TS, 11/816, fo.116–18; Gammage, *History*, p.133.

72. *NS*, 6 July 1839; *State of the Question*, p.22; T. A. Devyr, *Odd Book of the Nineteenth Century* (Greenpoint, NY, 1882), p.177; HO, 40/43, fo.342 (15 July 1839); *Western Vindicator*, 13 July 1838; LHASC, Vincent MSS 1/1/19, Vincent to J.Miniken, 19 July 1839.

73. *The Times*, 18 July 1839.

74. *Hansard*, vol.49, 12 July 1839, cols 219–77; BCL, Lovett Collection, vol.2, fo.52; Harrison and Hollis, *Robert Lowery*, p.140.

75. BL, Add. MSS 34245B, fo.53; Goodway, *London Chartism*, p.262; R.Challinor, *A Radical Lawyer in Victorian England* (London, Tauris, 1990), pp.26–7; prosecution brief against Higgins, TS, 11/1030/4424; for the Binns' family and Samuel Cook, see *ODNB*; for James Williams see J.O.Baylen and N.J.Gossmann (eds), *A Biographical Dictionary of Modern British Radicals*, vol.1 (Hassocks, Harvester, 1979), pp.544–8; S.Roberts, *Radical Politicians and Poets in Early Victorian Britain* (Lampeter, Mellen, 1993), pp.14–15.

76. Lowery's autobiography is reprinted in Harrison and Hollis, *Robert Lowery*, pp.37–194. See also Epstein, *Lion of Freedom*, pp.171f. Direct quotations that follow are from *Charter*, 28 July 1839.

### Notes to Chapter 4: July–November 1839: 'Extreme excitement and apprehension'

1. This paragraph follows C.Behagg, *Politics and Production in the Early Nineteenth Century* (London, Routledge, 1990), pp.206–18, Wellington quoted p.217; C.C.F.Greville, *The Greville Memoirs, 1814–60*, ed. L.Strachey and R.Fulford, vol.4 (London, Macmillan, 1938), p.189.

2. 'State of the country', *Charter*, 28 July 1839; *The Times*, 22 July 1839; Henry Vincent: *ODNB* entry; W.H.Maehl, 'Chartist disturbances in northeastern England, 1839', *International Review of Social History*, 8(1963), pp.402–3.

3. *Charter*, 28 July 1839.

4. West Yorksire Archives Service (WYAS), Leeds, Harewood Papers, Lieutenancy Box 2, depositions of W.Egan and J.Glover, 26 July 1839.

5. Meetings of 'great numbers of people' were held to be illegal under common law if they exhibited 'such circumstances of terror as are calculated to excite alarm and

to endanger the public peace', a point emphasised by the Home Office in a circular of 3 June, see F.C. Mather, *Public Order in the Age of the Chartists* (Manchester, Manchester University Press, 1959), p.188.

6. Wales: Dowlais, Merthyr Tydfil and Pontypool; England: Ashton, Barnsley, Bath, Birmingham, Blackburn, Bolton, Bradford, Bristol, Bury, Cheltenham, Chester, Chorley, Cirencester, Darlington, Dewsbury, Halifax, Hull, Hyde, Leigh, London (St Pauls and Spitalfields), Loughborough, Manchester, Mansfield, Newcastle, Norwich (four different locations), Nottingham, Preston, Rochdale, Sheffield, Stockport, Stroud and Wigton.

7. C. Wilkins, *A History of Merthyr Tydfil* (Merthyr Tydfil, 1867), p.307; for a full analysis of Chartist church-going see E.J. Yeo, 'Christianity in Chartist struggle, 1838–42', *Past & Present*, 91 (1981), pp.109–39.

8. J.W. Whittaker, *Dr Whittaker's Sermon to the Chartists*, second edn (Blackburn, 1839), pp.16–17; I. Collingridge, *Outline of an Address to the Chartists* (East Dereham, Wigg, 1839), p.4; see also *The Times*, 9 September 1839 and W. Cobbett, *History of the Protestant Reformation*, first published 1824; E. Stanley, *Sermon Preached in Norwich Cathedral, on Sunday, August 18th, 1839* (London, Limbard, 1839), p.7; D.J.V. Jones, *The Last Rising: The Newport Insurrection of 1839* (Oxford, Clarendon, 1985), p.95; F. Close, *The Chartists' Visit to the Parish Church* (London, Hamilton, 1839), p.17; *Preston Chronicle*, 17 August 1839, quoted in Yeo, 'Christianity', p.134.

9. W. Brimelow, *Political and Parliamentary History of Bolton* (Bolton, Tillotson, 1882), p.367; W. Napier, *Life and Opinions of General Sir Charles James Napier* (London, Murray, 1857), vol.2, p.61.

10. Some estimates put peak sales as high as 60,000 copies. Average weekly sales for 1839, based on stamp returns, were 36,000 but this obviously masks wide variations. *NS*, 17 August 1839, claimed an average of 42,000 for the April–June quarter. In September O'Connor reported a weekly circulation of 48,000 (*NS*, 14 September 1839). Privately he claimed 43,000 (letter to Frank O'Connor, 28 September 1843, O'Connor d'Arlach Papers); see also J.A. Epstein, 'Feargus O'Connor and the Northern Star', *International Review of Social History*, 21 (1976), pp.69–70 and 96–7.

11. Broadside, *To the Middle-classes of the North of England* (Sunderland, Williams & Binns, [1839]), copy in HO, 40/42 fo.249, also printed in *Northern Liberator* 21 July 1839; see also T.A. Devyr, *The Odd Book of the Nineteenth Century* (New York, Greenpoint, 1882), pp.182–6 (Devyr claimed to have written the address).

12. Broadside, *To the Middle Classes of Darlington, and its Neighbourhood* (Darlington, Oliver, [1839]), copy in HO, 40/42, fo.361.

13. WYAS, Leeds, Harewood Papers, Lieutenancy Box 2, deposition of Marsden, 26 July 1839, and copy 'Address of the working men to the shopkeepers, butchers, &c., of the town of and neighbourhood of Bradford'.

14. R.J. Richardson, *To the Officers and Members of Trades' Unions* (Manchester, Willis, 1839); Bolton WMA, Placard, 'Appeal to the Trade Societies of Bolton', in HO, 40/43, 29 July 1839.

15. *Hansard*, vol.49, col.727–39; see also D. Foster, *The Rural Constabulary Act 1839* (London, Bedford Square Press, 1982).

16. Bolton WMA, *Appeal*; *Charter*, 28 July 1839; Richardson, *To the Officers and Members of Trades' Unions*.

17. Poster, 'General Strike!' (Newcastle, Bell, 7 August 1839) – copy in the Working-Class Movement Library, Salford: see its *Bulletin*, 3 (1993), p.26.

18. R.P. Hastings, *Chartism in the North Riding of Yorkshire and south Durham, 1838–48* (York, University of York, 2004), p.7.

19. See M.Chase, 'Chartism, 1838–58: responses in two Teesside towns', *Northern History* 24 (1988), pp.149–52. Quotations from HO, 40/42, fols 229 and 241, *Gateshead Observer*, 27 July 1839.

20. *Charter* 28 July 1839, quoting *Northern Liberator*; BL, Add. MSS 34245B, fo.126, Knox to the Convention.

21. BL, Add. MSS 34245B, fo.103, Bussey to Convention 5 August 1839; WYAS, Leeds, Harewood Papers, Lieutenancy Box 2, Thompson to Harewood, 9 July 1839.

22. BL, Add. MSS 34245B, fols 103–26; B.Harrison & P.Hollis (eds), *Robert Lowery: Radical and Chartist* (London, Europa, 1979), p.143; T.Clarke, 'Early Chartism in Scotland: a "moral force" movement?' in T.M.Devine (ed.), *Conflict and Stability in Scottish Society, 1700–1850* (Edinburgh, Donald, 1990), pp.106–21.

23. BL, Add. MSS 34245B, fos 114, 116–17 and 124.

24. *Charter*, 18 August, *NS*, 17, 24 and 31 August, *The Times*, 14 August 1839. Dukestown poster, Newport Museum and Art Gallery.

25. *Ashton Reporter*, 30 January 1869, which however misdated this incident to 1838.

26. *NS*, 3 August 1839; Harrison and Hollis, *Lowery*, pp.144–8.

27. *The Times*, 14 August 1839; *NS*, 3 April and 6 November 1841; K.Wilson, 'Chartism and the north-east miners', in R.W.Sturgess (ed.), *Pitmen, Viewers and Coalmasters* (Newcastle, Northeast Labour History Society, 1986), p.96.

28. *Charter*, 18 August 1839; *The Times*, 14 August 1839; J.Baxter, 'Early Chartism and labour class struggle, South Yorkshire, 1837–40', in S.Pollard and C.Holmes (eds), *Essays in the Economic and Social History of South Yorkshire* (Sheffield, South Yorkshire County Council, 1976), pp.135–72.

29. This account is based on Bolton Central Library, Local Studies Library, Heywood Papers, ZHE 35/61 – Alderman Heywood's 'authentic account'; *Bolton Chronicle* and *Bolton Free Press*, 17 August 1839; *Bolton Evening News*, 23 June 1874.

30. 'One of the people', writing in *National*, 29 June 1839; Lowery, *Carlisle Journal*, 13 July 1839, quoted in B.Harrison & P.Hollis, 'Chartism, Liberalism and the life of Robert Lowery', *English Historical Review*, 82 (1967), p.514; O'Connor, letter in *NS*, 15 September 1838.

31. *Charter*, 28 July 1839; Jones, *Last Rising*, pp.82, 93–4.

32. Burland, vol.2, fo.113.

33. J.Jackson, *Demagogue Done Up: An Exposure of the Extreme Inconsistencies of Mr Feargus O'Connor* (Bradford, Wilkinson, 1844), pp.3, 16; J.C.F.Barnes, 'Popular protest and radical politics: Carlisle, 1790–1850', D.Phil thesis, University of Lancaster (1981), p.342.

34. O'Connor speech to Convention quoted in *Charter*, 28 April 1839; 'To the working men of Bolton', *NS*, 17 August 1839.

35. Jackson, *Demagogue*, p.18.

36. W.M.Torrens, *Memoirs of the Rt Hon. William, Second Lord Melbourne*, vol.2 (London, Macmillan, 1878), pp.311–12; H.Martineau, *History of England during the Thirty Years' Peace, 1816–46*, vol.2 (London, Knight, 1850), p.413.

37. The Act and the three other police bills received Royal Assent on 26 and 27 August; news of Stephens's and McDouall's trials broke mainly through *NS*, 24 August 1839.

38. *NS*, 14 September; *Charter*, 15 September 1839. The Declaration was written by a German émigré lawyer and associate of Hetherington called Schroeder (*London Dispatch*, 18 August 1839).

39. *NS*, 24 August 1839; W.Thomson, 'Preface', *Chartist Circular*, 23 October 1841. See also Clarke, 'Early Chartism in Scotland'; A.Wilson, *The Chartist Movement in Scotland* (Manchester, Manchester University Press, 1970), pp.85–8.

40. HO, 40/44, fo.860.

41. *Western Vindicator*, 6 April 1839; *Monmouthshire Merlin*, 27 April 1839, quoted in Jones, *Last Rising*, p. 73, cf. pp. 93–4 and 118; *Charter*, 16 June 1839; poster quoted D. Williams, *John Frost: A Study in Chartism* (Cardiff, University of Wales, 1939), p. 169.

42. *NS*, 3 May 1845, reprinting *National Reformer*, 30 March 1845 (of which no copy survives). Ashton alleged Hill and O'Connor spoke before 6 October, specifically at the Bull & Mouth Hotel in Leeds, which Hill later denied; *National Reformer*, 19 April and 10 May 1845.

43. HO, 20/10, interviewed by W. J. Williams, 23 December 1840; W. Farish, *The Autobiography of William Farish* (self-published, 1889), p. 40.

44. Harrison and Hollis, *Lowery*, p. 155. In an earlier version, Ashton claimed that a rising was hatched by a group of delegates, Taylor prominent among them, who were antagonistic to O'Connor, see *NS*, 29 February 1840.

45. (A. Somerville), *Autobiography of a Working Man* (London, Gilpin, 1848), pp. 423–4 and 441–2, and *Cobdenic Policy: The Internal Enemy of England* (London, Hardwicke, 1854), pp. 28–30. For Somerville's anti-physical force writings see his *Warnings to the People on Street Warfare* (London, 1839), and advertisements in *NS*, 25 May and 1 June 1839.

46. See HO, 40/44 and National Archives, Kew, Metropolitan Police Papers (MEPO), 2/43; on Beniowski see P. Brock, 'Polish democrats and English radicals, 1832–62', *Journal of Modern History*, 25:2 (June 1953), pp. 146–7; and J. Bennett, 'The London Democratic Association', in J. Epstein and D. Thompson (eds), *The Chartist Experience: Studies in Working-Class Radicalism and Culture, 1830–1860* (London, Macmillan, 1982), pp. 87–119 and generally. Also *NS*, 30 August 1845 for disputes with other Polish émigrés and claims 'he had renounced his Democratic opinions, and passed over to the opposite camp'.

47. Published by George Crawshay as 'The Chartist correspondence' in *Free Press Serials*, 13 (January 1856) – hereafter 'Chartist correspondence' – quotation from anonymous letter of 22 September 1839, p. 1. Two letters in this collection (pp. 3–4) were sent by Taylor to Birmingham FPU secretary Mary Ann Groves, subsequently an Urquhart supporter. Ashton alleged Taylor had a five-week 'childish, criminal (not carnal) dalliance'; with her, *NS*, 29 February 1840.

48. Balliol College Library, David Urquhart Papers, Box 8, IEI, P. Taylor to anon (H. Cameron), 22 September 1839, cited in R. Fyson, 'Chartism in north Staffordshire', D. Phil thesis, University of Lancaster (1999), p. 114.

49. Urquhart to Willis, 19 December (1855?), 'Chartist correspondence', p. 19; D. Urquhart, *Recent Events in the East* quoted in *Northern Tribune*, 1:12 (December 1854), p. 390; Urquhart quoted in Gertrude Robinson, *David Urquhart* (Oxford, Blackwell, 1920) p. 89.

50. On Urquhartite suspicions of Beniowski see 'Chartist Correspondence', pp. 1–4 and D. Urquhart, 'Chartism: A Historical Retrospect', *Diplomatic Review*, 31:3 (July 1873), pp. 222–4.

51. W. Lovett, *Life and Struggles of William Lovett* (London, Trübner, 1876), pp. 239–40. Taylor gave his version to Lovett in a letter dated 10 June 1841, now in BCL, Lovett Papers, vol. 2, fo. 5.

52. *NS*, 2 November 1839; Harrison and Hollis, *Lowery*, p. 155; Devyr, *Odd Book*, pp. 194–7. For an account placing some weight on the Blakey correspondence see A. Peacock, *Bradford Chartism, 1838–40* (York, St Anthony's Press, 1969), p. 31.

53. During the Gordon Riots of 1780, 75 had been killed; at least 22 died at Newport: Jones, *Last Rising*, pp. 154–6. The section that follows is much indebted to Jones's work.

54. *NS*, 19 October 1839: announcement that Frost was to speak at the Halifax Theatre (with Bussey, O'Connor, Pitkethley and Taylor) on 21 October. Peacock, *Bradford Chartism*, p. 32 suggests this was a deliberate ruse to confuse the authorities as to the men's whereabouts; Lovett, *Life and Struggles*, p. 240.

55. HO, 40/44, fos 958–9, R. J. Edwards to Normanby, 6 November 1839; Letter to Taylor (13 November 1839), Durham University Library, Grey Papers, GRE/B102/7/4, reprinted in W. H. Fraser, *Dr John Taylor* (Ayrshire Archaeological & Natural History Society, 2006), p. 93.

56. Jones, *Last Rising*, p. 12.

57. J. Humphries, *The Man from the Alamo* (St Athan, Glyndwr, 2004) is a lively recreation of Rees' life, arguing he was the Rising's fourth key leader. For Samuel Shell see BCL, Lovett Collection, vol. 2, fo. 160.

58. Jones, *Last Rising*, pp. 98, 104–9, at 108.

59. Ibid., pp. 109–13; TS, 11/503, Homfray to Phillips, 2 November 1839.

60. George Sanger, *Sixty Years a Showman* (London, Pearson, 1910), p. 27; Hughes quoted in O. Jones, *Early Days of Sirhowy and Tredegar* (Tredegar Local History Society, 1969), p. 102; M. Ferriday quoted in Jones, *Last Rising*, p. 123.

61. Jones, *Last Rising*, pp. 136–40; Shell's letter, 'Sunday night, November 4th' first appeared in the *Monmouthshire Merlin*, 23 November 1839 and was widely reprinted, e.g. *NS*, 30 November 1839. Williams (*Frost*, p. 230) suggests it is inauthentic because of misdating and language use. But Shell was an articulate son of a radical father who had recently tried to persuade him to leave Chartism: the language is consistent with that context.

62. B. Reay, *Last Rising of the Agricultural Labourers* (Oxford, Clarendon, 1990).

63. Thomas Watkins quoted in Jones, *Last Rising*, p. 153; (E. Dowling), *Rise and Fall of Chartism in Monmouthshire* (London, Bailey, 1840), p. 43.

64. *Monmouthshire Merlin*, 16 November 1839, cited in I. Wilks, *South Wales and the Rising of 1839* (London, Croom Helm, 1984), p. 65; Jones, *Last Rising*, pp. 154–6, provides the most authoritative and sensitive analysis of casualties.

### Notes to Chapter 5: November 1839–January 1840: After Newport

1. (E. Dowling) *The Rise and Fall of Chartism in Monmouthshire* (London, Bailey, 1840), p. 46; HO, 40/47, Brewer to Bristol, 4 November 1839; anonymous resident quoted in D. J. V. Jones, *The Last Rising: The Newport Insurrection of 1839* (Oxford, Clarendon, 1985), p. 159.

2. D. Williams, *John Frost* (Cardiff, University of Wales, 1939), pp. 232–4; Jones, *Last Rising*, pp. 169–86; *Monmouthshire Merlin*, 5 November 1839; R. Challinor, *A Radical Lawyer in Victorian England* (London, Tauris, 1990), p. 43; *NS*, 30 November 1839.

3. Jones, *Last Rising*, pp. 185–7; Newport Museum and Art Gallery, Poster, 'Monmouthshire Special Commission, January, 1840: Sentences of the Prisoners' (Monmouth, Heath, 1840).

4. Durham University Library, Grey Papers, GRE/B102/7/4, letter to Taylor (London, 13 November 1839), reprinted in W. H. Fraser, *Dr John Taylor* (Ayrshire Archaeological & Natural History Society, 2006), p. 93.

5. *NS* and *True Scotsman*, 9 and 16 November; *Charter*, 10 and 17 November.

6. BCL, Lovett Collection, vol. 2, fo. 5; T. A. Devyr, *The Odd Book of the Nineteenth Century* (New York, Greenpoint, 1882), pp. 194–6; 'Yours devotedly' (13 November 1839) to Taylor, reprinted in Fraser, *Taylor*, p. 93.

7. W. Lovett, *Life and Struggles of William Lovett* (London, Trübner, 1876), pp. 239–40.

8. *NS*, 5 October 1839 and, for O'Connor's retrospective account, 3 May 1845; see also J. A. Epstein, *The Lion of Freedom: Feargus O'Connor and the Chartist Movement, 1832–42* (London, Croom Helm, 1982), pp. 198–200. The libel case was the culmination of extensive official scrutiny of *NS*; see e.g. HO, 73/52/61, 9 December 1837, and papers relating to *R. v. O'Connor* in TS, 11/813, fos 81–96, 11/814, fos 52–7 and 65–76, 11/817, no. 2694.

9. B. Harrison and P. Hollis (eds), *Robert Lowery: Radical and Chartist* (London, Europa, 1979), p. 155; and see above, chap. 4.

10. *NS*, 30 November 1839.

11. *True Scotsman*, 16 November 1839.

12. *NS* and *True Scotsman*, 23 November 1839.

13. C. C. F. Greville, *The Greville Memoirs, 1814–60*, ed. L. Strachey and R. Fulford, vol. 4 (London, Macmillan, 1938), p. 221.

14. *NS*, 7, 14 and 28 December 1839.

15. Letter to Taylor (13 November 1839), reprinted in Fraser, *Taylor*, p. 93.

16. Harrison and Hollis, *Lowery*, p. 156; HO, 40/43, Wemyss to Home Office, 12 November 1839, HO, 40/45, Phillips to Home Office, 16–19 November, inc., HO, 40/44, 16 November 1839 and HO, 65/10 fo. 23–4 (13 November 1839); J. C. F. Barnes, 'Popular protest and radical politics: Carlisle, 1790–1850', D.Phil thesis, University of Lancaster (1981), p. 346; *NS*, 2, 30 November, 7 and 14 December 1839.

17. WYAS, Bradford, DB3 C4/1; R. Holder, *Lines on Busy Peter's Escape from Bradford*. Bussey went to New York where he ran a boarding house. He remained in regular contact with Yorkshire Chartists, suggesting he had neither robbed the movement nor perhaps played the part of a coward. He returned to run a pub near Leeds in 1854. See also *Yorkshire Daily Observer*, 12 February 1902, and A. Peacock, *Bradford Chartism* (York, St Anthony's Press, 1969).

18. Taylor to 'My dear Mary Anne' (Groves), 8 December 1839, published in 'The Chartist correspondence', *Free Press Serials*, 13 (January 1856), pp. 3–4; original in Balliol College Library, Urquhart Bequest, 1E1, fos 15–16.

19. HO, 40/51 17 December; see also WYAS, Leeds, Harewood Papers, Lieutenancy Box 2, enclosure with letter of 19 December 1839 to Home Office; HO, 40/43, 12 November 1839; W. Napier, *Life and Opinions of General Sir Charles James Napier* (London, Murray, 1857), pp. 101–2.

20. *Regenerator*, 2 November 1839; Napier to Huband, (27) November 1839, to Home Office, 28 November, and journal entries for December, and 1, 2 and 4 January, quoted in *Napier*, pp. 92–3, 101 and 107; J. Baxter, 'Early Chartism and labour class struggle', in S. Pollard and C. Holmes (eds), *Essays in the Economic and Social History of South Yorkshire* (Sheffield, South Yorkshire County Council, 1976); Harewood Papers, Lieutenancy Box 2, enclosure with letter of 19 December.

21. *NS*, 7 December 1839.

22. Ibid., 3 May 1845; Harrison and Hollis, *Lowery*, p. 159.

23. J. Campbell, *Speeches of Lord John Campbell* (Edinburgh, Black, 1842), p. 485; M. S. Hardcastle, *Life of Lord Campbell*, vol. 2 (Edinburgh, Murray, 1881), p. 127; *NS*, 3 May 1845; see also Epstein, *Lion of Freedom*, p. 208.

24. *NS*, 6 May 1848; *National Instructor*, 25 May 1850; W. Thomasson, *O'Connorism and Democracy Inconsistent* (Newcastle, Tyne Mercury, 1844), p. 8.

25. *NS*, 11 January 1840; R. Sykes, 'Physical-force Chartism: the cotton district and the Chartist crisis of 1839', *International Review of Social History*, 30 (1985), p. 234; Napier, *Life*, p. 109; Devyr, *Odd Book*, pp. 204–7; *Leeds Mercury* and *Leeds Times*, 18 January 1840; *Halifax Guardian*, 18 January 1840.

26. Quotation from examination of Samuel Thompson, TS, 11/816/2688, also reproduced in D. Thompson, *Early Chartists* (London, Macmillan, 1971), pp. 270–9.

27. University of Leeds, Brotherton Library, Special Collections, 'Sexagenarian', 'Sheffield as it was: the Chartists and their attempt at revolution', undated (1872) cutting from the *Sheffield Daily Telegraph*; J. Baxter, 'The life and struggle of Samuel Holberry, physical force Chartist', in *Samuel Holberry: Sheffield's Revolutionary Democrat* (Sheffield, Holberry Society, 1978), pp. 7–21; Baxter, 'Early Chartism', pp. 149–52; TS, 11/816/2688, examinations of Foxhall and Thompson, reprinted in Thompson, *Early Chartists*, pp. 264–79; HO, 40/44, fo. 545.

28. *Morning Herald* and *Morning Post*, 16 January 1840. *Charter*, 19 and 26 January 1840.

29. TS, 11/18/2678; *NS*, 3 May 1845; J. Taylor, *The Coming Revolution* (Carlisle, Arthur, 1840), pp. 3 and 11.

30. For an authoritative account see Peacock, *Bradford Chartism*, pp. 39–43.

31. Committal hearing, *Leeds Times*, 15 February 1840.

32. Interview with W. J. Williams, HO, 20/10.

33. Williams, *John Frost*, p. 286; Lord Broughton (J. C. Hobhouse), *Recollections of a Long Life*, vol. 5 (London, Murray, 1911), p. 244; *Greville Memoirs*, vol. 4, pp. 233–5.

34. *NS*, 29 February 1840; Epstein, *Lion of Freedom*, pp. 208–9; A. Wilson, *The Chartist Movement in Scotland* (Manchester, Manchester University Press, 1970), pp. 106–7.

35. H. Martineau, *History of England during the Thirty Years' Peace, 1816–46*, vol. 2 (London, Knight, 1850), p. 413.

36. Hobhouse, *Recollections*, vol. 5, p. 244.

37. *NS*, 3 May 1845.

38. *John Bates of Queensbury: The Veteran Reformer. A Sketch of his Life* (Queensbury, Feather, 1895), pp. 5–6.

39. In the following paragraphs all un-attributed information is taken from *NS*, 28 September 1839–26 December 1840.

40. *NS*, 23 May 1840; J. Christodoulou, 'The Glasgow Universalist Church and Scottish radicalism', *Journal of Ecclesiastical History*, 43:4 (October 1992), pp. 608–23.

41. *True Scotsman*, 9 November 1839; Barnsley Central Library, Archives & Local Studies Section, unpublished MS by J. H. Burland, 'Annals of Barnsley and its environs', vol. 2 (1881), fo. 117; *Hymns to be Sung at the Bradford and Barnsley Chartist Camp Meeting* (Sheffield, Smith, 1839).

42. On this theme see E. Yeo, 'Culture and constraint in working-class movements, 1830–1855', in E. and S. Yeo (eds), *Popular Culture and Class Conflict* (Brighton, Harvester, 1981), pp. 155–86.

43. *NS*, 20 June 1840. Cromwell never visited Stockton but this was an understandably appealing myth.

44. *True Scotsman*, 22 February 1840; *NS*, 19 December 1840; for sales of the *Chartist Circular* in France see its 18 September 1841 issue.

45. *NS*, 16 November 1839. See also J. A. Epstein, *Radical Expression* (New York, Oxford University Press, 1994), pp. 147–65.

46. Sutton-in-Ashfield, see TS, 11/601, letter to T. Cooper, 16 May 1842; Barnsley, see Burland, 'Annals', vol. 2, p. 82. See also Wilson, *Chartist Movement in Scotland*, p. 201. Chartist amateur dramatics deserve further investigation, but see P. Pickering, *Chartism and the Chartists in Manchester and Salford* (London, Macmillan, 1995), pp. 186–7, and C. Barker, 'The Chartists, theatre reform and research', *Theatre Quarterly*, 1:4 (December 1971), pp. 3–10.

47. *Leeds Times*, 3 March 1838.

48. *McDouall's Chartist and Republican Journal*, 17 (24 July 1841); see also C. Turner, 'Politics in mechanics institutes, 1820–50: a study in conflict', D.Phil thesis, University of Leicester (1980), esp. p. 78.

49. *NS*, 9 May 1840 8 August 1840; *True Scotsman*, 29 February 1840.

50. 'Reform, by a Radical of the old school', *People's Magazine*, March 1841, pp. 88–9.

51. M. Tylecote, *Mechanics' Institutes of Lancashire and Yorkshire before 1851* (Manchester, Manchester University Press, 1957), 241.

52. *NS*, 3 October and 12 December 1840, 17 July 1841; A. Briggs, 'Industry and politics in early nineteenth-century Keighley', *Bradford Antiquary*, ns, 9 (1952), p. 314; HO, 107/2278, fos 495–6.

53. B. O'Brien, *Life and Character of Maxmilian Robespierre*, vol. 1 (London, Watson, 1838), p. 284; *True Scotsman* 22 February 1840; *NS*, 12 September, 29 August and 16 May 1840. On contemporary mutualism see S. Cordery, *British Friendly Societies, 1750–1914* (London, Palgrave, 2003).

54. *NS*, 5 January and 6 April 1839; *Charter*, 8 September 1839; see also M. Purvis, 'Co-operative retailing in England, 1835–50: developments beyond Rochdale', *Northern History*, 22 (1986), pp. 198–215; R. C. N. Thornes, 'Change and continuity in the development of co-operation, 1827–44', in S. Yeo (ed.), *New Views of Co-operation* (London, Routledge, 1988).

55. *NS*, 21 December and 1 August *Northern Liberator*, 7 September 1839.

56. *True Scotsman*, 22 February 1840.

57. For a contemporary tribute to *NS* temperance coverage see W. Farish, *Autobiography of William Farish* (self-published, 1889) p. 41; W. Hick, *Chartist Songs and Other Pieces* (Leeds, Hobson, 1840); *NS*, 3 April 1841.

58. *Essex & Suffolk Times*, 2 February 1838, quoted in A. F. J. Brown *Colchester, 1815–1914* (Chelmsford, Essex County Council, 1980), p. 112.

59. Pickering, *Chartism*, p. 186.

60. These are a few valedictions in personal letters to Thomas Cooper, seized by police when he was arrested in 1842 and preserved in TS, 11/600 and 601.

61. P. Pickering, 'Chartism and the "trade of agitation" in early Victorian Britain', *History*, 247 (June 1991), pp. 222–37.

62. *NS*, 25 July 1840; for a printed Chartist circuit plan on the Methodist model, see HO, 45/46 fo. 3; also E. Yeo, 'Practices and problems of Chartist democracy', in J. Epstein and D. Thompson (eds), *The Chartist Experience: Studies in Working-Class Radicalism and Culture, 1830–1860* (London, Macmillan, 1982), pp. 345–80.

63. H. Heavisides, *Centennial Edition of the Works of Henry Heavisides* (London, self-published, 1895), and *Gateshead Observer*, 27 July 1839; M. Fletcher, *Letters to the Inhabitants of Bury* (Bury, 1852), quoted in Thompson, *Early Chartists*, pp. 27–8.

64. This 'political emigration' (Harney's term in *Newcastle Weekly Chronicle*, 6 May 1882) included Devyr from Newcastle, Thornton from Halifax and a dozen Sheffield Chartists, among them the Convention delegate James Wolstenholme.

65. HO, 20/10, interview with Hutton by W. J. Williams.

66. *Parliamentary Papers*, 1840 (600) vol. 38, analysed in C. Godfrey, 'Chartist prisoners, 1839–41', *International Review of Social History*, 24 (1979), pp. 231–2. Professionals (including publishing) accounted for 21, shopkeepers and publicans 18; occupations of 58 prisoners were not given.

67. 'The reminiscences of Thomas Dunning', *Transactions of the Lancashire & Cheshire Antiquarian Society*, vol. 59 (1947), p. 119; *Bradford Observer*, 19 December and *Halifax Guardian*, 21 December 1839; see chapter 8 below on the sexual allegations.

68. 'James Williams', in G. Batho (ed.), *Durham Biographies, Volume 2* (Durham, Durham County Local History Society, 2002), p. 126; R. Peddie, *The Dungeon Harp*

(Edinburgh, self-published, 1844), p.17; *NS*, September 1840; Godfrey, 'Chartist prisoners', pp.217–21.

69. *Barclay Fox's Journal*, ed. R.L.Brett (London, Bell & Hyman, 1979), p.181; Frost's letter was reprinted in full in R.G.Gammage, *The History of the Chartist Movement, 1837–54* (Newcastle upon Tyne, Browne, 1894), pp.171–2.

### Notes to Chapter 6: February 1840–December 1841: 'The Charter and nothing less'

1. LHASC, Vincent Papers 1/1/24, Vincent to Miniken 5 March 1840.
2. *NS*, 21 December 1839; 11 April 1840; *Charter*, 23 February 1840; J.Burchardt, *The Allotment Movement in England, 1793–1873* (Woodbridge, Boydell & Brewer, 2002), pp.200–1.
3. J.Campbell, *An Examination of the Corn and Provision Laws* (Manchester, Heywood, 1841), pp.11, 70; for Campbell see P.A.Pickering, *Chartism and the Chartists in Manchester and Salford* (Basingstoke, Macmillan, 1995), esp. p.190.
4. HO, 45/50, fo.30, placard (May 1841).
5. Anon., *Memoranda of the Chartist Agitation in Dundee* (Dundee, Kidd, 1889), p.16; *Anti-Corn Law Circular* 25 March 1841; un-named workman quoted in D.J.V.Jones, *Chartism and the Chartists* (London, Allen Lane, 1975), p.126.
6. *NS*, 4 January, 18 and 25 April, 29 August 1840; *Charter*, 15 and 29 December 1839; D.Goodway, *London Chartism, 1838–48* (Cambridge, Cambridge University Press, 1982), pp.31, 38.
7. *NS*, 20 June 1840.
8. See T.M.Parssinen, 'Association, convention and anti-parliament', *English Historical Review*, 88 (July 1973), pp.504–33.
9. *Southern Star*, 23 February 1840.
10. LHASC, Vincent Papers 1/1/23(i), Vincent to Miniken 28 February 1840.
11. *NS*, 18 and 25 April, 2 May 1840; *Northern Liberator*, 21 March 1840.
12. *NS*, 18 and July 1840.
13. See the 'Aims and rules' of the NCA in ibid., 1 August 1840, reprinted in D.Thompson, *The Early Chartists* (London, Macmillan, 1971), pp.288–93, from which the unattributed quotations that follow are taken.
14. *NS*, 11 April 1840; on Leach see entry in *DLB*, vol.9, and Pickering, *Chartism and the Chartists*, esp. pp.198–9.
15. *NS*, 18 April 1840; HO, 45/258A, fo.21, NCA membership card; see also S.Roberts and D.Thompson, *Images of Chartism* (Woodbridge, Merlin, 1998), p.58.
16. Ibid., 11 December 1841 claimed 282 localities totalling 13,000 members; the higher figures relate to 1842, see *NS* 16 April 1842 and Jones, *Chartism and the Chartists*, pp.70–6.
17. A.Wilson, *The Chartist Movement in Scotland* (Manchester, Manchester University Press, 1970), p.91. *Chartist Circular* claimed an average weekly circulation of 40,000: see its 18 September 1841 issue. In total, 27 Chartist papers were published during some or all of 1839, but only 22 in 1840: calculation based on periodicals listed in O.R.Ashton, R.Fyson and S.Roberts (eds), *The Chartist Movement: A New Annotated Bibliography* (London, Mansell, 1995), pp.62–70.
18. BL, Place Newspaper Collection, set 56, copies of *Executive Journal of the National Charter Association*, issues 1–4 (16 October–6 November 1841).
19. *NS*, 7 March 1840; see also J.A.Epstein, *The Lion of Freedom: Feargus O'Connor and the Chartist Movement, 1832–42* (London, Croom Helm, 1982), pp.211–12 and 215–20.
20. *NS*, 21 March 1840.

21. Ibid., 25 April 1840.

22. Ibid., 23 May; *Yorkshire Gazette*, 25 May and 6 June 1840.

23. *NS*, 6 June 1840; O'Connor d'Arlach Papers, letter to Frank O'Connor, 20 September 1843; F. O'Connor, *Practical Work on the Management of Small Farms* (London, Cleave, 1843).

24. For example see *NS*, 23 May, 6 June, 11 and 18 July, 15, 22 and 29 August, 31 October 1840.

25. Ibid., 16 May 1840.

26. M. Chase, *'The People's Farm'* (Oxford, Clarendon, 1988), pp. 1–17, 136, 143–4, 178–9; and *DLB*, vols 8 and 10. For earlier Chartist interest in land reform see *Bronterre's National Reformer*, 15 January, 25 February and 4 March 1837; *Charter*, 1 December 1839; *Chartist Circular*, 21 December 1839; *London Democrat*, 18 May 1839; *London Dispatch*, 4 and 18 June 1837; *Northern Liberator*, 23 and 30 December 1837, 20 January, 7 and 14 April, 27 October 1838, 15 June, 6 and 13 July 1839; *NS*, 16 June and 18 October 1838, 25 April and 2 May 1840; *Operative*, 25 November 1838; Lowery, speech at Carlisle, *Carlisle Journal*, 27 October 1838, reprinted in B. Harrison and P. Hollis (eds), *Robert Lowery: Radical and Chartist* (London, Europa, 1979), pp. 223–7.

27. *NS*, 11 and 18 July 1840.

28. Cirencester 'Agrarian Company', *NS*, 29 August 1840; Christian Co-operative Joint Stock Company (Manchester), ibid., 26 September 1840; see also Pickering, *Chartism and the Chartists*, pp. 117–19.

29. *NS*, 31 October 1840; and see *DLB*, vol. 8.

30. F. O'Connor, *'The Land' the Only Remedy for National Poverty and Impending National Ruin* (Leeds, Hobson, 1842), p. 14.

31. Lovett and Collins to Normanby, 6 May 1840, quoted in W. Lovett, *The Life and Struggles of William Lovett* (London, Trübner, 1876), p. 235.

32. *NS*, 1 August 1840.

33. W. Lovett and J. Collins, *Chartism; A New Organization of the People* (London, Watson, Hetherington & Cleave, 1840), p. 1.

34. Ibid., pp. 7, 16 and 21.

35. Ibid., p. 24; J. Wiener, *William Lovett* (Manchester, Manchester University Press, 1989), pp. 80–4.

36. *To the Political and Social Reformers of the United Kingdom: An Address, by W. Lovett and others, in reference to the formation of a National Association of the United Kingdom*, reprinted in Lovett, *Life*, pp. 245–50; *NS*, 10 April 1841.

37. Lovett, *Life*, p. 243.

38. *NS*, 28 November 1840.

39. LHASC, Vincent Papers 1/1/36, Vincent to Miniken 5 October 1840.

40. H. Vincent et al., *Address to the Working Men of England, Scotland, and Wales* (London, Johnston, 1841–42); *ECC*, 9–11 (March–April 1841).

41. *NS*, 3 April 1841.

42. Ibid., 7 March 1846; similarly, T. Cooper, *The Life of Thomas Cooper, Written by Himself* (London, Hodder, 1872), p. 136.

43. *Leeds Times*, 8 June 1839; *NS*, 12 and 19 September 1840; see also J. F. C. Harrison, 'Chartism in Leeds', in A. Briggs (ed.), *Chartist Studies* (London, Macmillan, 1959), pp. 83–5; D. Fraser (ed.), *A History of Modern Leeds* (Manchester, Manchester University Press, 1980), pp. 284–5, and Epstein, *Lion of Freedom*, pp. 265–73.

44. *Leeds Times*, and *NS*, 23 January 1841; Smiles to O'Connell, 4 January, and Stansfield to O'Connell, 8 January 1841, reprinted in *The Correspondence of Daniel O'Connell*, ed. M. R. O'Connell, vol. 7 (Dublin, Blackwater, 1978), pp. 1 and 5.

45. *Leeds Times*, 23 January 1841.

46. Ibid., 23 October 1841.

47. M. Chase, 'Building identity, building circulation: engraved portraiture and the *Northern Star*', in J. Allen and O. Ashton (eds), *Papers for the People* (London, Merlin, 2005), pp. 32–3.

48. *NS*, 8 May 1841.

49. Ibid., 10–24 April, 1–15 May, 5 and 12 June 1841; Wiener, *Lovett*, p. 87.

50. Wiener, *Lovett*, p. 88; cf. Goodway, *London Chartism*, p. 41; D. Stack, 'William Lovett and the National Association', *Historical Journal*, 42:4 (1999), p. 1028.

51. Wilton Lodge Museum, Hawick, Sederunt Book for 1842.

52. W. J. Linton, *James Watson* (Manchester, Heywood, 1880), p. 50.

53. *NS*, 24 April 1841.

54. Ibid., 1 May 1841; see M. Chase, 'Chartism 1838–58: responses in two Teesside towns', *Northern History*, 24 (1988), pp. 146–71.

55. *Hansard*, vol. 58, 25 May 1841, cols 742ff.; *NS*, 5 June 1841.

56. *McDouall's Chartist & Republican Journal*, 12 June 1841, see also 19 June 1841 and the 'Address of the eighteen stonemasons', *ECC*, 24 (?June 1841).

57. 'One of no party', *Random Recollections of the House of Commons* (London, Smith Elder, 1836), p. 251.

58. *NS*, 5 June, and *McDouall's Chartist & Republican Journal*, 12 June 1841.

59. The adage is L. P. Hartley's, from the prologue to *The Go-Between* (1953). On the evolution of election procedures and their significance for the emergence of parties see P. Salmon, *Electoral Reform at Work: Local Politics and National Parties, 1832–41* (Woodbridge, Boydell & Brewer, 2002).

60. Unattributed quotations and information in the following paragraphs are from the Chartist press, checked against C. R. Dod, *Electoral Facts from 1832 to 1852* (London, Whitaker, 1852) and *McCalmont's Parliamentary Pollbook* (1879), enlarged and edited by J. Vincent and M. Stenton (Brighton, Harvester, 1971). I have followed McCalmont's practice of using 'Liberal' to designate candidates supportive of the Whig Government.

61. See Harrison & Hollis, *Lowery*, pp. 181–6.

62. For Brooker see his *Appeal to the British Nation … for the Repeal of the Poor Law Amendment Act* (Brighton, Andrews, 1840), *NS*, 1 September 1838 and 19 June 1841.

63. Northampton's plebeian electors were mainly surviving members of an unusually inclusive pre-1832 electorate. For a detailed analysis of this contest see J. A. Phillips, *The Great Reform Act in the Boroughs* (1992), pp. 169–70.

64. *NS*, 5–26 June, 3 and 10 July 1841; *McDouall's Chartist & Republican Journal*, 12–26 June and 10–24 July 1841; *Dundee Chronicle*, 9 July 1841 (cutting in 'Richardson's Works' scrapbook, Manchester Central Library, Local Studies Section).

65. HO, 45/102A, fo. 29, police report (June 1841).

66. Harrison and Hollis, *Lowery*, p. 185.

67. *NS* 3 July 1841; *The Speech Delivered by Mr William Dixon, the People's Candidate at the Nomination of Members* (Wigan, Ramsdale, 1841), p. 8; Derby Local Studies Library, MS BA/909/16186, item 9, Police report, 'Mr Martin's Language on Thursday the 3rd of June 1841'; W. E. Adams, *Memoirs of a Social Atom*, vol. 1 (London, Hutchinson, 1903), p. 183.

68. Harrison and Hollis, *Lowery*, p. 186.

69. *Newcastle Weekly Chronicle*, 27 August 1892; Epstein, *Lion of Freedom*, p. 285.

70. York City Library, Local Studies Section, 'Chartism MSS', Y342.42T, Rooke to R. Hawkin, 31 October 1901; *Yorkshire Gazette*, 28 August and 4 August 1841; *NS*,

4 September 1841 and 19 February 1842; O'Connor d'Arlach Papers, Feargus to Frank O'Connor, 28 September 1843.

71. 'Alfred' (S. H. G. Kydd), *History of the Factory Movement*, vol. 1 (London, Simpkin, 1857), pp. 235–54; *NS*, 8 May and 4 September 1841. This analysis follows P. Pickering's perceptive article, 'Class without words: symbolic communication in the Chartist movement', *Past & Present*, 112 (1986), esp. pp. 156–62.

## Notes to Chapter 7: 1842: 'Toasting muffins at a volcano'

1. Letter to G. Arbuthnot, 4 October 1841, quoted in D. Read, *Peel and the Victorians* (Oxford, Blackwell, 1987), p. 103; J. Sinclair, *National Education and Church Extension* (London, Rivington, 1849), p. 52.
2. Derby Local Studies Library, MS BA/909/16186, item 17, J. Bairstow, quoted in police report, 18 July 1841.
3. For a transcript of the Peel–Hobson interview see *The Ten Hours' Question: A Report Addressed to the Short Time Committees of the West Riding of Yorkshire* (London, Ollivier, 1842), pp. 4–15.
4. HO, 45/256, 22 February 1842; Read, *Peel*, pp. 108, 119, 120–1; entry for Daniel McNaughton: *ODNB*; *True Scotsman*, 13 June 1841.
5. Letter to A. W. Weston, 24 June 1841, reprinted in C. Taylor, *British and American Abolitionists* (Edinburgh, Edinburgh University Press, 1974), p. 154.
6. *Barclay Fox's Journal*, ed. R. L. Brett (London, Bell & Hyman, 1979), entry for 8 February 1842, p. 259.
7. Quoted in entry for Edward Miall: *ODNB*.
8. See A. Tyrell, *Joseph Sturge* (London, Croom, 1987).
9. *Nonconformist*, 3 and 17 November and 15 December 1841; A. Prentice, *History of the Anti-Corn-Law League* (London, Cash, 1853), p. 276.
10. W. Jones, *Chartism: Authentic Report of the Speech* (Liverpool, Stewart, 1841), p. 12; for Thorogood see A. F. J. Brown, *Chartism in Essex and Suffolk* (Chelmsford, Essex CRO, 1982), pp. 49 and 86–7; and *Address to All Rational Chartists and Rational Anti-Chartists by a Stranger* (London, 1840).
11. *Nonconformist*, 29 December 1841; A. Wilson, *The Chartist Movement in Scotland* (Manchester, Manchester University Press, 1970), p. 174; *NS*, 29 January 1842; *Reconciliation between the Middle and Labouring Classes* (Manchester, Heywood, 1842); TS, 11/600, Anon. to T. Cooper, 18 February 1842.
12. *ECC*, 59 (March 1842); *Nonconformist*, 22 December 1841, 26 January and 16 February 1842; *NS*, 19 February and 12 March 1842.
13. For example: *Leeds Times*, 1 October 1842; *Leicester Chronicle*, 1 January 1842; *NS*, 22 January 1842. The author was ACLL activist William Biggs: see A. T. Patterson, *Radical Leicester* (Leicester, Leicester University Press, 1975), pp. 326–7.
14. *Nonconformist*, 23 February 1842.
15. *ECC*, 58 (March 1842); *NS*, 26 March 1842.
16. *NS*, 2 April 1842.
17. Perronet Thompson differentiated 'sensible Chartists from the *unsensible*' in a letter of April 1841, quoted in M. J. Turner, 'Thomas Perronet Thompson, "sensible Chartism" and radical unity', *Albion*, 33:1 (spring 2001), pp. 63–4.
18. *NS*, 9 April; *Nonconformist*, 23 February 1842.
19. *NS*, 12 March and *Manchester Guardian*, 9 March 1842; see also E. Royle, *Chartism* (Harlow, Longman, 1996), pp. 108–10.
20. HO, 45/249C, fo. 25, report of Manchester Police Commissioner; Watkin to Cobden, quoted in N. McCord, *The Anti-Corn Law League* (London, Allen & Unwin, 1958), pp. 102–3.

21. *Nonconformist*, 16 March 1842. Bailey, Doyle, Murray and Scholefield were leading Manchester Chartists: see P. Pickering, *Chartism and the Chartists in Manchester and Salford* (Basingstoke, Macmillan, 1995) *passim*, and, for Scholefield, especially O. Ashton and P. Pickering, *Friends of the People* (London, Merlin, 2002), ch. 5.

22. See the important reassessment by P. Pickering and A. Tyrell, *The People's Bread* (London, Leicester University Press, 2000).

23. *NS*, 2 April 1842.

24. *Report of the Proceedings of the Conference of Delegates of the Middle and Working Classes, held at Birmingham* (London, Davis, 1842), pp. 29–30.

25. Ibid., pp. 55–6 and 62.

26. *Nonconformist*, 13 April 1842; *Report*, pp. 55 and 67.

27. Bright to Cobden, 10 April 1842, quoted in McCord, *Anti-Corn Law League*, p. 115.

28. *Report*, p. 76.

29. Brook, Burrows, Dewhirst, Hodgson and J. W. Smyth (all Bradford), Cook (Stroud), Linney (Eccles) and McCartney (Liverpool).

30. *NS*, 16, 30 April, 7 and 14 May, and *British Statesman* 15 May and 9 July 1842.

31. J. B. O'Brien, *Mr O'Brien's Vindication of His Conduct at the Late Birmingham Conference* (1842), quoted in A. Plummer, *Bronterre* (London, Allen & Unwin, 1971), p. 174.

32. G. Weerth, *A Young Revolutionary in Nineteenth-Century England* (Berlin, Seven Seas, 1971), pp. 106–7.

33. LHASC, Vincent Papers, 1/1/51, Vincent to Miniken, 30 July 1842.

34. T. Cooper to R. G. Gammage, 26 February 1855, printed in the latter's *History of the Chartist Movement, 1837–54* (Newcastle upon Tyne, Browne, 1894), pp. 404–10; Cooper: *DLB* entry, vol. 9.

35. D. M. MacRaild, *Irish Immigrants in Modern Britain, 1750–1922* (London, Macmillan, 1999), pp. 54–6.

36. B. Harrison & P. Hollis (eds), *Robert Lowery* (London, Europa, 1979), pp. 144–8.

37. D. Thompson, 'Ireland and the Irish in English radicalism before 1850', in J. Epstein and D. Thompson (eds), *The Chartist Experience: Working-Class Radicalism and Culture, 1830–1860* (London, Macmillan, 1982), p. 136; B. Reaney, 'Irish Chartists in Britain and Ireland', *Saothar*, 10 (1984), p. 98.

38. [P. O'Higgins], *Chartism and Repeal* (Dublin, Dyott, 1842), pp. 15–16.

39. 'The National Petition of the Industrious Classes', copy in BL, Add. MSS 27835, fo. 189.

40. *Chartist Circular*, 29 January 1842; *NS*, 15–29 January, 5, 19 and 26 February 1842; Wilson, *Chartist Movement in Scotland*, pp. 171–3.

41. O. Ashton, 'Chartism in mid-Wales', *Montgomeryshire Collections*, 62:1 (1971), pp. 39–43.

42. *Y Gofyniad Pabeth yw Siartist?* (Merthyr, John & Williams, 1840) and *Cyfieithad o Lythyr Diweddaf Mr. Feargus O'Connor* (Merthyr, John & Williams, 1840); *Udgorn Cymru* appeared fortnightly, March 1840–October 1842, the *Advocate* monthly, July 1840–April 1841.

43. HO, 45/265, fos 18–26; in June 1841 bullet moulds and a copy of Macerone's *Defensive Instructions*, hidden in a consignment of haberdashery, were intercepted in transit from Birmingham to a Pontypool address used (under an alias) by Black: HO, 45/49, fo. 6, T. J. Phillips (Newport) to MO, 7 June 1841.

44. *NS*, 23 April 1842; R. Wallace, *Organise! Organise! Organise! A Study of Reform Agitations in Wales, 1840–86* (Cardiff, University of Wales Press, 1991), p. 43; D. J. V. Jones, *The Last Rising* (Oxford, Oxford University Press, 1985), pp. 218–20.

45. *NS*, 16–30 April 1842: totals reported to the National Convention (1839 figure in brackets) Boston 1,400 (3,074); Colchester 2,250 (2,092); Ipswich 1,400 (7,312); King's Lynn 197 (550); Norwich 2,200 (6,646).

46. R. Wells, 'Southern Chartism', *Rural History*, 2:1 (1991), pp. 45–51; and cf. petition figures for Lewes of 1,100 (2,966); R. P. Hastings, *Chartism in the North Riding of Yorkshire and south Durham, 1838–48* (York, University of York, 2004), pp. 26–8.

47. *NS*, 13 November 1841 and 8 January 1848. Beesley was a pivotal figure in north Lancashire Chartism: W. Turner, 'The lion of north Lancashire', in A. Duckworth (ed.), *Aspects of Blackburn: Discovering Local History* (Barnsley, Wharncliffe, 1999), pp. 43–55; also chapter 8 this book.

48. *Hansard*, vol. 62, 2 May 1842, cols 1373–81, and *NS*, 16–30 April and 7 May 1842: totals reported to Parliament and/or the National Convention (1839 figure in brackets): Aberdeen 17,606 (8,116); Ashton-under-Lyne 14,200 (6,300); Banbury 4,000 (2,200); Barnsley 6,800 (3,645); Bolton 18,500 (16,600); Brighton 12,700 (8,000); Bristol 11,000 (8,160); Cheltenham 5,800 (1,720); Exeter 3,000 (2,560); Huddersfield 23,181 (19,432); Hull 7,400 (3,091); Leamington 1,800 (1,000); Leicester 18,000 (13,126); Liverpool 32,000 (20,689); Loughborough 7,600 (6,180); Merthyr Tydfil 21,934 (14,710); Oldham 21,800 (13,566); Plymouth 4,400 (2,250); Preston 24,000 (18,533); Rochdale 19,600 (9,050); Sheffield 27,200 (16,829); Shrewsbury 2,800 (850); Stalybridge 10,000 (4,863); Stockport (14,000 (10,781); Todmorden 8,400 (7,328); Tonbridge 2,000 (461); Warrington 4,200 (1,500); Wolverhampton 3,000 (1,960).

49. Calculations based on summary data from 1841 Census in B. R. Mitchell and P. Deane, *Abstract of British Historical Statisitics* (Cambridge, Cambridge University Press, 1962), pp. 12–13, and from electoral data in C. Rallings and M. Thrasher, *British Electoral Facts, 1832–1999* (Aldershot, Ashgate, 2000), p. 97.

50. *The Times*, 3 May 1842; *NS*, 16 April 1842; Duncombe lived in set F3 and Macaulay in E1: G. Doré and D. Jerrold, *London* (London, Harper, 1890, p. 84.

51. *The Times* and *Morning Chronicle*, 3 May 1842; *NS*, 7 May 1842; see P. Pickering, '"And your petitioners &c.": Chartist petitioning in popular politics, 1838–48', *English Historical Review*, 116 (April 2001), pp. 368–88.

52. *Hansard*, vol. 63, 3 May 1842, cols 31 and 51.

53. *Chartist Circular*, 14 May 1842; *NS*, 7 May 1842.

54. London School of Economics, Allsop Papers, Coll. Misc., 525/2, O'Connor to T. Allsop (n.d., but 1843); *NS*, 14 May 1842.

55. E.g. *NS*, 28 May 1842.

56. Beesley, letter to the editor, ibid., 30 April 1842.

57. TS, 11/601, J. Sweet to T. Cooper, enclosing Nottingham NCA handbill (n.d., but May 1841).

58. T. Cooper, *The Life of Thomas Cooper, Written by Himself* (London, Hodder, 1872), p. 157; TS, 11/601, letter to Susanna Cooper (n.d., but August 1842).

59. See R. Church, *Economic and Social Change in a Midland Town: Victorian Nottingham, 1815–1900* (London, Cass, 1966), pp. 141–3.

60. See M. Jenkins, *The General Strike of 1842* (London, Lawrence & Wishart, 1980). The interpretation here largely follows M. Chase, *Early Trade Unionism* (Aldershot, Ashgate, 2000), pp. 190–200, but places greater emphasis on the confrontational, as opposed to theatrical, nature of the strike-wave.

61. Cited in C. S. Parker, *Sir Robert Peel from His Private Papers*, vol. 2 (London, Murray, 1899), p. 541.

62. HO, 45/43, fo. 4; *McDouall's Chartist and Republican Journal*, 17 April 1841.

63. D. McNulty, 'Bristol trade unions in the Chartist years', in J. Rule (ed.), *British*

*Trade Unionism, 1750–1850* (London, Longman, 1988), p. 227; I. Prothero, 'London Chartism and the trades', *Economic History Review*, 24 (1971), p. 202; *NS*, 16 July, 20 and 27 August 1842; Thompson, *Chartists*, pp. 186, 193; Pickering, *Chartism*, pp. 61–2.

64. Quoted in D. J. V. Jones, *Chartism and the Chartists* (London, Allen Lane, 1975), p. 138.

65. *The Trial of Feargus O'Connor Esq. (Barrister-at-Law) and Fifty-Eight Others* (Manchester, Heywood, 1843), p. 98 (hereafter *Trial*).

66. Operative Stone Masons Fortnightly Returns 22 April – May 1841, quoted in C. Behagg, *Politics and Production in the Early Nineteenth Century* (London, Routledge, 1990), p. 109.

67. *ECC*, 62 (April 1842); G. Barnsby, *The Working-Class Movement in the Black Country, 1750–1867* (Wolverhampton, Integrated Publishing, 1977), pp. 103–10.

68. *North Staffordshire Mercury*, 23 July 1842, quoted by R. Fyson, 'The crisis of 1842', in Epstein and Thompson (eds), *Chartist Experience*, p. 198, to which this paragraph is particularly indebted.

69. *Manchester Guardian*, 23 July, and *NS*, 16 and 30 July 1842; Jenkins, *General Strike*, pp. 60–3.

70. HO, 45/263, fo. 36, placard, 'TOILING SLAVES, UNION IS STRENGTH'; Cooper, *Life*, p. 186.

71. *NS*, 20 August 1842.

72. On miners' pragmatic links to Chartism see, e.g., D. Phillips, 'Riots and public order in the Black Country', in R. Quinault and J. Stevenson (eds), *Popular Protest and Public Order* (London, Allen & Unwin, 1974), esp. pp. 153–8.

73. Chase, *Early Trade Unionism*, p. 201; *Trial*, p. 246.

74. McCord, *Anti-Corn Law League*, pp. 123–6; N. C. Edsall, *Richard Cobden* (Boston, MA, Harvard University Press, 1986), pp. 11–14; *NS*, 16 July 1842; *Quarterly Review*, 71 (December 1842), pp. 244–314; see also N. Gash, *Sir Robert Peel: The Life of Sir Robert Peel after 1830* (London, Longman, 1972), pp. 354–5.

75. HO, 45/249, fo. 121, 15 August.

76. *NS*, 5 March 1842.

77. *Trial*, pp. 17, 27 and 73; Jenkins, *General Strike*, pp. 64–6.

78. *Trial*, p. 28.

79. HO, 45/249, fo. 51, 8 August; A. Watkin, *The Diaries of Absalom Watkin*, ed. M. Goffin (Stroud, Sutton, 1993), p. 224, 9 August 1842; Jenkins, *General Strike*, pp. 72–5.

80. Pickering, *Chartism*, p. 70.

81. HO, 45/264, fos 102–4, enclosed with letter from Mayor of Hull to Home Office, 11 August 1842.

82. HO, 45/249, fo. 94; Watkin, *Diaries*, pp. 225–6.

83. Evidence of Bannister, *Trial*, pp. 76–80; HO, 45/249C, fo. 137.

84. HO, 45/244, fos 24 and 25 (14 and 12 August).

85. Stockport Central Library, Family and Local History Library, SH/11, 'Stockport Chartist Papers', unsigned note of meeting on Waterloo, 13 August, 8.00 p.m.; HO, 45/242, fo. 61.

86. HO, 45/264, fo. 49 (14 August 1842); *Bradford Observer*, quoted in D. Wright, *The Chartist Risings in Bradford* (Bradford, Bradford Libraries, 1987), p. 30.

87. HO, 45/249, fo. 121, 15 August; Tameside Local Studies Library (Ashton-under-Lyne) Broadsheets L322; Bolton Central Library Local Studies Section, Heywood Papers, ZHE 38/62, H. Heywood to R. Heywood, 24 August 1842 (referring to 'the last fortnight').

88. A.Campbell, *The Lanarkshire Miners: A Social History of Their Trade Unions* (Edinburgh, Donald, 1979), pp.250–2; L.C.Wright, *Scottish Chartism* (Edinburgh, Oliver, 1953), p.146; *NS*, 13 August 1842.

89. *NS*, 20 August 1842; Cooper, *Life*, pp.191–9; Fyson, 'Crisis of 1842', p.213.

90. HO, 45/264, fo.80; F.H.Grundy, *Pictures of the Past* (London, Griffith, 1879), p.98; F.Peel, *The Risings of the Luddites, Chartists & Plug-Drawers*, 3rd edn (Brighouse, Hartley, 1895), pp.333–4 and 338–9.

91. Grundy, *Pictures*, pp.103, 105; HO, 45/264, fos 171–5; *NS* and *Halifax Guardian*, 20 August 1842; M.Blatchford, *History of Halifax Industrial Society* (Halifax, Womersley, 1901), pp.29–30; B.Wilson, *Struggles of an Old Chartist* (1887), reprinted in D.Vincent (ed.), *Testaments of Radicalism: Memoirs of Working-Class Politicians, 1790–1885* (London, Europa, 1977), pp.200–1.

92. Wilson, *Struggles*, p.201.

93. *Bolton Free Press*, 20 August 1842; J.Lewis 'to the Committee meeting at Glossop', 16 August 1842, reprinted in *Trial*, p.149; Jenkins, *General Strike*, pp.150–9.

94. 'Stockport Chartist Papers', report from station master, 16 August 1842; Cooper, *Life*, p.206.

95. Cooper, *Life*, pp.208–11; *NS*, 20 August 1842; P.McDouall, *Letters to the Manchester Chartists* (Manchester, Leach, ?1843), p.9.

96. 'Stockport Chartist Papers', 'Sunday' (16 August).

97. HO, 45/266, fos 8 and 13; Campbell, *Lanarkshire Miners*, pp.250–2.

98. Quoted in Phillips, 'Riots and public order', p.155.

99. 'The executive committee of the National Chartist Association: To the People!!!', poster in HO, 45/249C, fo.218, MS copy in 45/249A, fo.171f. and reprint in *NS*, 20 August 1842.

100. *Derby & Chesterfield Reporter*, 25 August 1842 and *NS*, 27 August; Derby Local Studies Centre, scrapbook BA 900 WAL(14117), A.Wallis, 'Some reminiscences of old Derby'; West: *DLB* entry, vol.7.

101. HO, 45/266, fo.114, Dundee strike placard (19 August); 45/249, fo.233, Blackburn JPs; 45/242, fo.2, Mayor of Carlisle to Home Office; *NS*, 20 and 27 August 1842.

102. HO, 45/261, fo.71, transcript of Duddeston Row placard.

103. HO, 45/250, fo.95; *NS*, 27 August and 3 September 1842.

104. HO, 45/265, fo.38.

105. *NS*, 27 August and 3 September 1842; HO, 45/242 (Chard) and 262, fos 4–7.

106. Cooper, *Life*, pp.211–12; *NS*, 3 September 1842; A.Little, 'Chartism and liberalism: popular politics in Leicestershire, 1842–74', D.Phil thesis, University of Manchester (1991), p.71.

107. J.A.Epstein, 'Feargus O'Connor and the Northern Star', *International Review of Social History*, 21 (1976), pp.91–2; *Evening Star*, 23 August 1842.

108. HO, 45/254, Mayor of Nottingham to Home Office, fos 13 and 22; see also R.Church, *Economic and Social Change*, pp.143–4.

109. M.Winstanley, 'Oldham radicalism and the origins of popular liberalism', *Historical Journal*, 36:3 (1993), p.636; *NS*, 20 August 1842 (third edition, reprinted in early editions the following week).

110. J.C.F.Barnes, 'Popular protest and radical politics: Carlisle, 1790–1850', D.Phil thesis, University of Lancaster (1981), pp.355–6; HO 45/262 fo.4.

111. HO, 45/249C, fo.287, and 45/244, fos 150–1.

112. HO, 45/264, fos 181, 184, 191, 214, 217 and 223.

113. HO, 45/249, fo.233, and 45/265, fos 50 and 52.

114. Little, 'Chartism and liberalism', p.67; HO, 45/242, 18 September (Macclesfield's Mayor to Home Office); Watkin, *Diaries*, p.229, entry for 1–30 September.

115. The Home Office under Graham spent a monthly average of £3.24 on domestic espionage, compared to £25.69 under Normanby and £40.68 under Russell.
116. 'Stockport Chartist Papers', letter from T. Stringer, 15 August; Gash, *Peel*, p. 344.
117. C. S. Parker, *Life and Letters of Sir John Graham*, vol. 1 (London, Murray, 1907), pp. 323–4; Gash, *Peel*, pp. 344–5.
118. Sinclair, *National Education*, pp. 57 (30 August) and 75 (7 September 1842); see also introduction to this chapter and W. B. Stephens, *Education, Literacy and Society* (Manchester, Manchester University Press, 1987), pp. 132–3.
119. University of Leeds, Brotherton Library, Special Collections, MS 739/6, 3 September 1842; MS 739/1, 16 August 1842; MS 739/5, 'Thursday' (18 August 1842).
120. J. Lawson, *Letters to the Young on Progress in Pudsey* (Stannington, Birdsall, 1887), p. 132.
121. I borrow this notion (via Fyson, 'Crisis of 1842', p. 216) from A. J. P. Taylor, *The Course of German History*, rev. edn (London, Methuen, 1961), p. 69.
122. HO, 45/266, fos 258–9, deposition of Hannam.
123. HO, 45/41, Napier to Phillips 11 August 1841; HO, 50/451, 23 May 1840 (Napier's report on barracks under his command).
124. HO, 45/264, fos 195–8 and 480.
125. H. M. Boot, *The Commercial Crisis of 1847* (Hull, Hull University Press, 1984), p. 77; BL, 695.L.14 (76), poster, 24 September 1842.
126. Copy in HO, 45/249C, fos 325 and 333.
127. Jenkins, *General Strike*, p. 218; *Leeds Mercury*, 3 and 10 September 1842; Pilling: *DNB* entry, vol. 6.
128. *Council of the National Complete Suffrage Union, to Political Reformers of All Shades of Opinion* (Trueman, Birmingham, 1842), reprinted in Lovett, *Life*, pp. 276–82.
129. *NS*, 17 September and 19 November 1842.
130. Tailor William Blackwood, in a speech at Coalbrookdale, HO, 45/258A, fo. 40 (police report, 23 May).
131. HO, 45/265, fo. 60, 29 August 1842.
132. Lovett, *Life*, pp. 282–3.
133. Cooper, *Life*, p. 221; *NS*, 3, 17 and 24 December 1842.
134. Following account based on Cooper, *Life*, pp. 221–7; Lovett, *Life*, pp. 283–5; Tyrell, *Sturge*, pp. 129–31; *Nonconformist*, 28 and 31 December and 4 January 1843; and *NS*, 31 December 1842 and 7 January 1843.
135. S. Hobhouse, *Joseph Sturge* (London, Dent, 1919), p. 78; Cooper, *Life*, p. 224.

### Notes to Chapter 8: 1843–46: Doldrums years

1. TS, 11/600, White to Cooper, (n.d., but July 1842).
2. *Brighton Gazette*, 8 December 1842, quoted by R. Wells, 'Southern Chartism', *Rural History*, 2:1, p. 48; *NS*, 3 and 17 September 1842; A. Plummer, *Bronterre* (London, Allen & Unwin, 1971), p. 177; R. Fyson, 'Bronterre O'Brien: a Chartist in the Isle of Man, 1844–47', *Isle of Man Natural History and Antiquarian Society Proceedings*, 10:4 (1998), pp. 393–400.
3. *NS*, 10 December 1842, 4 February 1843; P. Storey, entry for James Williams in *Biographical Dictionary of Modern British Radicals* (Hassocks, Harvester, 1979), pp. 544–8; S. Roberts, *Radical Politicians and Poets in Early Victorian Britain* (Lampeter, Mellen, 1993), pp. 50–4 and 110.
4. TS, 11/601, Mead to Cooper, (n.d. but July 1842).
5. LHASC, Miniken Papers, 1/1/50, Vincent to Miniken, 13 July 1842; *The Times*, 20 May 1844; W. Dorling, *Henry Vincent* (London, Clarke, 1879), pp. 33–40. Perronet Thompson equalled Vincent's number of unsuccessful challenges but was

also elected an MP on two occasions: *McCalmont's Parliamentary Poll Book*, ed. M. Stenton and J. Vincent (Brighton, Harvester, 1971).

6. *ECC*, 62 (?April 1842); TS, 11/601, White to Cooper, 12 July 1842.
7. *NS*, 3 September, 29 October and 19 November 1842.
8. Main quotation from *NS*, 10 December 1842, see also 26 November, 3, 17 and 24 December 1842; *British Statesman*, 19, 26 November and 3 December 1842; see also E. Yeo, 'Practices and problems of Chartist democracy', in J. Epstein and D. Thompson (eds), *Chartist Experience* (London, Macmillan, 1982), p. 357.
9. *NS*, 7 January 1842.
10. Ibid., 28 January and 4 February 1843.
11. Ibid., 4 February 1843; J. A. Epstein, 'Feargus O'Connor and the Northern Star', *International Review of Social History*, 21 (1976), pp. 92 and 97.
12. *NS* 12 August 1843; F. O'Connor, *A Letter from Feargus O'Connor, Esq., to the Reverend William Hill* (London, Cleave, 1843); W. Hill, *A Scabbard for Feargus O'Connor's Sword* (Hull, Johnson, 1844); see Hill's periodical, *Lifeboat* (December 1843–January 1844).
13. F. C. Mather, 'The Government and the Chartists', in A. Briggs (ed.), *Chartist Studies* (Macmillan, 1959), pp. 390–3.
14. Pollock to Graham, 9 October 1842, quoted in Mather, 'Government and the Chartists', pp. 391–2.
15. BL, Peel Papers, Add. Mss 40436, fo. 93, 10 March 1843, quoted in J. A. Epstein, *The Lion of Freedom: Feargus O'Connor and the Chartist Movement, 1832–42* (London, Croom Helm, 1982), p. 301.
16. Calculations based on O. Ashton et al., *The Chartist Movement: A New Annotated Bibliography* (London, Mansell, 1995), pp. 64–70; *ECC*, 153 [January 1843]. None of the Scottish papers cited here surface in W. H. Fraser's survey, 'The Chartist press in Scotland', in J. Allen and O. Ashton (eds), *Papers for the People* (London, Merlin, 2005), pp. 82–105.
17. *NS*, 3, 17 June, 2, and 9 September 1843, 24 March 1849; O. Ashton, 'Chartism in mid-Wales', *Montgomeryshire Collections*, 62:1 (1971), p. 43.
18. M. Chase, 'Chartism, 1838–58: responses in two Teesside towns', *Northern History*, 24 (1988), p. 162; *NS*, 2 September 1843.
19. O'Connor sold large numbers of membership cards on such occasions but apparently added to reported totals the quantities he left behind for his hosts to sell: *Lifeboat*, 30 December 1843, *National Reformer*, 16 January 1847, A. Wilson, *The Chartist Movement in Scotland* (Manchester, Manchester University Press, 1970), p. 206.
20. R. Challinor and B. Ripley, *The Miners' Association* (London, Lawrence & Wishart, 1968); R. Colls, *Pitmen of the Northern Coalfield* (Manchester, Manchester University Press, 1987), pp. 281–301; M. Chase, *Early Trade Unionism* (Aldershot, Ashgate, 2000), pp. 205–7, 224 n. 6.
21. Chase, *Early Trade Unionism*, pp. 205–6; Challinor and Ripley, *Miners' Association*, p. 62.
22. The English collieries' workforce was approximately 103,000 in 1841: see J. Benson, *British Coalminers in the Nineteenth Century* (London, Longman, 1989), p. 217. Scottish membership of MAGBI peaked around 6,000 and the union failed completely in Wales, see Chase, *Early Trade Unionism*, pp. 206 and 224 n. 6.
23. HO, 45/348, fo. 2; *NS*, 30 September 1843.
24. Mines agent to Earl Fitzwilliam, 22 April 1844, quoted in Challinor and Ripley, *Miners' Association*, p. 163.
25. *Newcastle Journal*, 22 June 1844, quoted in Colls, *Pitmen*, p. 300.
26. Challinor and Ripley, *Miners' Association*, p. 241.

27. D.R.Green, *From Artisans to Paupers* (Aldershot, Scolar, 1995), pp.99-100; R.Gurnham, *200 Years: The Hosiery Unions, 1776-1976* (Leicester, NUHKW, 1976), pp.15 and 19; A.Little, 'Chartism and liberalism: popular politics in Leicestershire, 1842-74', D.Phil thesis, University of Manchester (1991), pp.79-127.

28. T.Koditschek, *Class Formation and Urban Industrial Society: Bradford, 1750-1850* (Cambridge, Cambridge University Press, 1990), p.481; D.McNulty, 'Bristol trade unions in the Chartist years', in J.Rule (ed.), *British Trade Unionism, 1750-1850* (Harlow, Longman, 1988), p.239; C.Behagg, *Politics and Production in the Early Nineteenth Century* (London, Routledge, 1990), p.115. Mason introduced Cooper to Chartism, see the illuminating vignette in *Life of Thomas Cooper, Written by Himself* (London, Hodder, 1872), pp.135-7.

29. W.H.Fraser, *Trade Unions and Society* (London, Macmillan, 1974), p.43; R.G.Gammage, *History of the Chartist Movement, 1837-54* (Newcastle upon Tyne, Browne, 1894), pp.251-2; National Association for the Promotion of Social Science, *Trade Societies and Strikes* (London, Parker, 1860), p.542.

30. J.B.Jefferys, *The Story of the Engineers* (London, Lawrence & Wishart, 1945), p.25; P.Pickering, *Chartism and the Chartists in Manchester and Salford* (Basingstoke, Macmillan, 1995), p.238; A.F.J.Brown, *Chartism in Essex and Suffolk* (Chelmsford, Essex CRO, 1982), p.74; D.Goodway, *London Chartism* (Cambridge, Cambridge University Press, 1982), p.165 and 173; I.J.Prothero, 'London Chartism and the trades', *Economic History Review*, 24 (1971), pp.212-13.

31. *NS*, 30 December 1843.

32. Ibid., 5 December 1846 and 28 October 1843; McNulty, 'Bristol trade unions', 229-32; Chase, *Early Trade Unionism*, pp.208 and 224 n.9.

33. S.Pollard, *History of Labour in Sheffield* (Liverpool, Liverpool University Press, 1959), pp.74-5; *NS*, 9 and 16 November 1844.

34. For the history of the NAUT see Chase, *Early Trade Unionism*, *passim*; Prothero, 'London Chartism and the trades', pp.213-19; Goodway, *London Chartism*, *passim*.

35. Wheeler: *DLB* entry, vol.6.

36. *NS*, 16 September 1843,

37. Yeo, 'Practices and problems', pp.357-8; *Letter from Mr. Lovett to Messrs. Donaldson and Mason ...* (London, Hetherington, 1843), pp.2 and 4.

38. *NS*, 29 April 1843; apart from internal evidence, the claim that Wheeler wrote much of *Practical Work* was made by W.Stevens, *A Memoir of Thomas Martin Wheeler* (London, Leno, 1862), p.25.

39. E.Royle, *Robert Owen and the Commencement of the Millennium* (Manchester, Manchester University Press, 1998).

40. M.Chase, 'We wish only to work for ourselves: the Chartist land plan', in M.Chase and I.Dyck (eds), *Living and Learning* (Aldershot, Scolar, 1996), pp.139-40.

41. Quoted by J.A.Phillips, *The Great Reform Bill in the Boroughs* (Oxford, Clarendon, 1992), pp.155-6; on the congruence of Owenism and Chartism see E.Royle, 'Chartists and Owenites - many parts but one body', *Labour History Review*, 65:1 (Spring 2000).

42. *NS*, 8 April 1843.

43. J.F.C.Harrison, *Robert Owen and the Owenites* (London, Routledge, 1969), pp.59-60.

44. F.O'Connor, *Practical Work upon the Management of Small Farms* (seventh edition, Manchester, Heywood, 1847), pp.40-1.

45. *NS*, 2 September 1843; *The Poor Man's Guardian and Repealer's Friend*, 1 (3 June 1843).

46. Quotation from *NS*, 27 April 1844; Registration – 25 May, 22 June, 10, 17 August, 7 September and 12 October 1844; McDouall, 6 April and 18 May 1844; National Hall 15 June; O'Brien and Vincent, 29 June; Moir, 29 June and 13 July.

47. Quotation from *NS*, 6 June 1844; White, 25 May; Liverpool 27 July; NCA 18 May.

48. A. Marcroft, *Landmarks of Liberalism* (Oldham, privately published, 1913), p. 101, but cf. J. Vernon, *Politics and the People* (Cambridge, Cambridge University Press, 1993), p. 223.

49. *NS*, 15 June 1844. He had been injured at Frome, Somerset, the previous July when the floor of an upper room in which he was speaking collapsed, *NS*, 29 July 1843.

50. Ibid., 10 August 1844; cf Gammage, *History*, pp. 253–5.

51. *NS*, 19 October and 30 November 1844, 5 April 1845.

52. Ibid., 9 November 1844; see also 26 October and 2 November.

53. For detailed analysis of the ideology of the land plan see Chase, 'We wish only to work for ourselves'.

54. *NS*, 28 December 1844; C. C. F. Greville, *The Greville Memoirs, 1814–60*, ed. L. Strachey and R. Fulford, vol. 5 (London, Macmillan, 1938), p. 183.

55. Peel to Queen Victoria, 29 March 1842, quoted in Goodway, *London Chartism*, p. 56; *NS*, 7 March and 11 July, *The Times*, 9 and 13 July 1846.

56. *Morning Star*, 1 February 1845.

57. *NS*, 3 May 1845.

58. Ibid., 26 April 1845.

59. Ibid., 1 February 1845.

60. Ibid., 8 and 15 February 1845, see also 16 and 23 November 1844.

61. Ibid., 3 May 1845, reprinting *National Reformer* of 30 March 1845.

62. *NS*, 10 May 1845.

63. The exact number of subscribers was never clear: see chapter 10 below.

64. *NS*, 7 June, 23 August, 30 December 1845; Chase, 'We wish only to work for ourselves', pp. 142–3.

65. The best account is Yeo, 'Practices and problems', pp. 366–74 to which the ensuing two paragraphs are indebted.

66. *National Reformer*, 14 November 1846, 6 February, 1 and 15 May 1847. For Bowkett societies see M. Chase, 'Out of radicalism: the mid-Victorian Freehold Land Movement', *English Historical Review*, 106 (April 1991), p. 323; and S. Newens, 'Thomas Edward Bowkett', *History Workshop Journal*, 9 (1980), pp. 143–8.

67. *NS*, 11 January, 15 and 22 November, 20 December 1845; *Chartist Co-operative Land Society: Important Meeting of Members Resident in the West Riding* (Huddersfield, Brown, 1845).

68. *NS*, 14 March, 18 April 1846. The best source for detailed information about the Chartist estates remains A. M. Hadfield, *The Chartist Land Company* (Newton Abbot, David & Charles, 1970).

69. *NS*, 23 May, 13 June, 11 July 1846, Hadfield, *Chartist Land Company*, p. 96.

70. M. Chase, 'The concept of jubilee', *Past & Present*, 129 (1990), pp. 132–47.

71. *NS*, 22 August 1845.

### Notes to Chapter 9: July 1846–April 1848: 'A time to make men politicians'

1. R. Stewart, *The Politics of Protection* (Cambridge, Cambridge University Press, 1971), p. 41.

2. R. Q. Gray, *The Factory Question and Industrial England, 1830–60* (Cambridge, Cambridge University Press, 1996), pp. 36, 171.

3. *NS*, 4 July 1846; C. F. Henningsen, *Sixty Years Hence* (London, Newby, 1847), 3 vols; M. Chase, 'Building identity, building circulation', in J. Allen and O. Ashton (eds), *Papers for the People* (London, Merlin, 2005), p. 44.

4. G. S. Jones, 'Rethinking Chartism', in his *Languages of Class* (Cambridge, Cambridge University Press, 1983), esp. pp. 175-8; there is a briefer version of this seminal essay in J. Epstein and D. Thompson (eds), *The Chartist Experience: Studies in Working-Class Radicalism and Culture, 1830-1860* (London, Macmillan, 1982); see also B. Hilton, 'Peel: a reappraisal', *Historical Journal*, 22:3 (1979), esp. p. 614.

5. Feargus to Frank O'Connor, '28 September' (completed 14 December) 1843, O'Connor d'Arlach Papers; all unattributed quotations in this and the following paragraphs are from this source.

6. See J. Dunkerley, 'Francisco Burdett O'Connor', in his *Warriors and Scribes: Essays on the History and Politics of Latin America* (London, Verso, 2000), pp. 145-67.

7. *Hansard*, vol. 48, 28 February 1845, cols 154-5.

8. Goldsmiths' Library, University of London (Senate House), 'Cuttings from the *Manchester Examiner* of Hobson's letters on the land scheme of Feargus O'Connor'; R. G. Gammage, *History of the Chartist Movement, 1837-54* (Newcastle upon Tyne, Browne, 1894), pp. 287f.; *DLB*, vol. 8; *NS*, 26 June, 6 November to 11 December 1847.

9. London School of Economics, Allsop Collection, Coll. Misc. 525/2, fo. 10, O'Connor to T. Allsop 25 June (1847); *NS*, 13 June 1846 and 13 November 1847.

10. T. Cooper, *Two Orations Against Taking Away Human Life Under Any Circumstances* (1846), cited in S. Roberts, 'Thomas Cooper: radical and poet, c. 1830-60', M. Litt thesis, Birmingham University (1986), p. 148; *NS*, 21 February, 11 April and 20 June 1846; *Lloyd's Weekly London Newspaper*, 28 June 1846.

11. *NS*, 20 June, 8 and 22 August 1846.

12. Explored by M. Taylor, *Ernest Jones, Chartism, and the Romance of Politics, 1819-1869* (Oxford, Oxford University Press, 2003), pp. 79-83, and A. Janowitz, *Lyric and Labour in the Romantic Tradition* (Cambridge, Cambridge University Press, 1998), pp. 159-94.

13. T. Cooper, *Life of Thomas Cooper* (London, Hodder, 1872), p. 273; *NS*, 20 September-13 December 1845 and 28 April 1848; T. Cooper, *Purgatory of Suicides* (London, How, 1845).

14. Taylor, *Ernest Jones*, pp. 66, 69, 77-8.

15. *Labourer*, January (1847), title page. G. Airey, 'Fergus O'Connor, Ernest Jones and the *Labourer*', in J. Allen and O. Ashton (eds), *Papers for the People* (London, Merlin, 2005), pp. 106-28.

16. *NS*, 1, 8 and 29 May 1847.

17. *Cooper's Journal*, 17 January 1850.

18. *NS*, 19 December 1846.

19. Ibid., 3 April 1847; *Labourer*, vol. 1 (1847), p. 45.

20. 'You mean he was an Owenite; all for equality, and community of goods, and that kind of absurdity?' 'No, no! John Barton was no fool.' E. Gaskell, *Mary Barton: A Tale of Manchester Life* (first published 1848), chap. 37.

21. *Labourer*, vol. 2 (1847), p. 181; *NS*, 19 December 1846, 20 February 1847.

22. *NS*, 28 December 1844, 27 December 1845, 7 March, 4-18 July, 8 and 15 August 1846.

23. Ibid., 8 August, 12-26 September 1846.

24. Ibid., 13 and 20 February, 6 March 1846.

25. *Hansard*, vol. 90, 23 February 1847, col. 406.

26. *NS*, 24 April 1847; J. Bright to G. Crosfield, quoted by H. Hanham, *Nineteenth-*

*Century Constitution* (Cambridge, Cambridge University Press, 1969), p. 242. For a detailed study of registration as a live political issue at this time see J. Prest, *Politics in the Age of Cobden* (London, Macmillan, 1977).

27. *The Times*, 17 June; *NS*, 19 June; *Derby Mercury*, 23 June 1847.

28. *NS*, 3–17 July 1847; *Norfolk Chronicle*, 24 July 1847; J. K. Edwards, 'Chartism in Norwich', *Yorkshire Bulletin of Economic and Social Research*, 19:2 (1967), pp. 85–100.

29. B. Wilson, *Struggles of an Old Chartist* (1887), reprinted in D. Vincent (ed.), *Testaments of Radicalism* (London, Europa, 1977), p. 205; T. Iwama, 'The middle class in Halifax, 1780–1850', D.Phil thesis, University of Leeds (1983), pp. 196–204.

30. Muntz and Scholefield (Birmingham), Bowring (Bolton), Thompson (Bradford), Duncombe and Wakley (Finsbury), John Williams (Macclesfield), George Thompson (Tower Hamlets), Crawford (Rochdale).

31. Quotation from *NS*, 17 July 1847;

32. *NS*, 31 July and 7 August 1847; C. Binder, 'The Nottingham electorate and the election of the Chartist, Feargus O'Connor, in 1847', *Transactions of the Thoroton Society*, 107 (2003), pp. 145–62; R. Church, *Economic and Social Change in a Midland Town: Victorian Nottingham, 1815–1900* (London, Cass, 1966), pp. 144–5.

33. *NS*, 5 June, 3 and 31 July 1847; West: *DLB* entry, vol. 7.

34. *NS*, 31 July, *Derby Mercury*, 4 August 1847; G. Barnsby, *Working Class Movement in the Black Country, 1750–1867* (Wolverhampton, Integrated, 1972), pp. 128–33; *Plymouth & Devonport Weekly Journal*, 5 August 1847; R. Wallace, *Organise! Organise! Organise! A Study of Reform Agitations in Wales, 1840–86* (Cardiff, Uuniversity of Wales Press, 1991), p. 45.

35. R. S. Neale, *Bath* (London, RKP, 1981), pp. 376–7; A. F. J. Brown, *Chartism in Essex and Suffolk* (Chelmsford, Essex CRO, 1982), p. 78.

36. See chapter 6, this book.

37. *NS*, 17 July and 7 August 1847.

38. Ibid., 7 August 1847 and 1 January 1848.

39. A. T. Patterson, *Radical Leicester* (Leicester, Leicester University Press, 1975), p. 346; Brown, *Chartism in Essex and Suffolk*, pp. 78–9; *NS*, 7 August.

40. *NS*, 23 October 1847.

41. O'Connor's habit of sitting 'on the foremost seat of opposition' is widely attested: G. Weerth, *A Young Revolutionary in Nineteenth-Century England* (Berlin, Seven Seas, 1971), p. 169; *Daily News*, 9 December 1847; Lord Stanley, diary entry for 23 March 1849, reprinted in J. Vincent (ed.), *Disraeli, Derby and the Conservative Party* (Hassocks, Harvester, 1978), p. 2.

42. W. Lovett, *The Life and Struggles of William Lovett* (London, Trübner, 1876), pp. 307–8; J. Wiener, *William Lovett* (Manchester, Manchester University Press, 1989), pp. 110–11.

43. *Address of the Council of the People's International League* (London, Palmer, 1847), p. 3; *Report of a Public Meeting … to Explain the Principles and Objects of the People's International League* (London, People's International League, 1847), pp. 3–4.

44. Lovett, *Life*, pp. 312–19; D. Goodway, *London Chartism* (Cambridge, Cambridge University Press, 1982), p. 56.

45. H. Weisser, *British Working-Class Movements and Europe, 1815–48* (Manchester, Manchester University Press, 1975), pp. 140–4; A. R. Schoyen, *The Chartist Challenge: A Portrait of George Julian Harney* (London, Heinemann, 1958), pp. 138–40.

46. *NS*, 26 September 1846, 24 July 1847.

47. F. O'Connor, *The Employer and the Employed* (London, McGowan, 1845), pp. 29, 42; *NS*, 16 January 1841.

48. *NS*, 22 August 1840; Manchester Central Library, Local Studies Section, BR/ F942.081/RiI, unsourced, undated press cutting in 'Richardson's Works'; J.Campbell, *Examination of the Corn and Provision Laws*, 2nd edn (Manchester, Heywood, ?1842), p.11; *Northern Liberator*, 6 April 1839, 7 November 1840; 'A Tyne Chartist', *The Way to Universal Suffrage* (Newcastle, Northern Liberator, 1839), pp.28–9. See also, I.Haywood, *Chartist Fiction*, vol.1: *Sunshine and Shadow* (Aldershot, Ashgate, 1999), pp.8–9, 15–16.

49. E.g. T.M.Wheeler, 'Sunshine and shadow', *NS*, 26 May 1849 (and see Haywood, *Chartist Fiction*, pp.71, 90); and E.Jones, 'Woman's wrongs', *Notes to the People*, vol.2 (1852), p.651; see also I.Haywood, *Chartist Fiction*, vol.2: *Ernest Jones, Women's Wrongs* (Aldershot, Ashgate, 2001), p.49.

50. *NS*, 4 December 1847.

51. Ibid., 18 and 25 July 1846, 4 December 1847.

52. J.A.Epstein, 'Feargus O'Connor and the Northern Star', *International Review of Social History*, 21 (1976), p.97. Average weekly sales in both 1842 and 1847 were 8,700 but these figures obscure wide variations. On 4 September the paper said it was planning for a circulation increase of 4,000.

53. *NS*, 7 August and 4 September 1847; G.J.Barnsby, *Birmingham Working People* (Wolverhampton, Integrated, 1989), p.105.

54. B.R.Mitchell, *Abstract of British Historical Statistics* (Cambridge, Cambridge University Press, 1962), pp.418 and 470; H.M.Boot, *Commercial Crisis of 1847* (Hull, Hull University Press, 1984), p.77. A quarter was a capacity measure equal to 64 gallons, approximately 291 litres.

55. Boot, *Commercial Crisis of 1847*, pp.34, 51–2.

56. *Memoirs of the Life and the Correspondence of Henry Reeve*, ed. J.K.Laughton, vol.1 (London, Longmans, 1898), p.190; E.P.Thompson and E.Yeo, *The Unknown Mayhew* (Harmondsworth, Penguin, 1973), pp.435–8; see also Goodway, *London Chartism*, pp.68–9, 227.

57. Boot, *Commercial Crisis*, p.39; Wilson, 'Struggles', p.206.

58. Wilson, 'Struggles', p.206; *NS*, 27 November 1847.

59. *NS*, 1 January 1848.

60. Ibid.

61. Ibid., 18 September, 4, 11 December 1847, 8 January 1848.

62. Ibid., 31 July, 7 August, 28 August (H.Gracchus, 'Lowbands'), 4 September, 11 December 1847.

63. Ibid., 15, 22 January, 15 February 1848.

64. (W.H.Dyott) *Reasons for Seceding from the Seceders by an Ex-Member of the Irish Confederation* (Dublin, Dyott, 1847), pp.9 and 17; *NS*, 8 August 1846, 1 and 22 January 1848.

65. *NS*, 22, 29 January, 19 February, 25 March 1847; Goodway, *London Chartism*, pp.64–7; J.Treble, 'The Irish agitation', in J.T.Ward (ed.), *Popular Movements* (London, Macmillan, 1970), pp.174–7.

66. *Douglas Jerrold's Weekly Newspaper*, 1 April 1848; J.Belchem, 'Liverpool in the year of revolution', in J.Belchem (ed.), *Popular Politics, Riot and Labour: Essays in Liverpool History* (Liverpool, Liverpool University Press, 1992), pp.75–8.

67. T.Brotherstone and L.Leicester, 'Chartism, the great hunger, and the "hugest question"', in T.Brotherstone, A.Clark and K.Whelan (eds), *These Fissured Isles: Ireland, Scotland and the Making of Modern Britain, 1798–1848* (Edinburgh, Donald, 2005), pp.195–218; *NS*, 1 January 1848.

68. T.Carlyle, 'Chartism', *Selected Essays*, ed. I.Campbell (London, Dent, 1972), pp.182–3; National Library of Scotland, MS 618, fo.191r, J.S.Mill to T.Carlyle, 1839.

69. E. Jones, *The March of Freedom*, NS, 18 March 1848; see *Labourer*, vol. 3 (March 1848), pp. 100f.

70. O'Connor to Harney, 4 and 6 January (1848), reprinted in *The Harney Papers*, ed. F. G. Black and R. M. Black (Assen, Van Gorcum, 1969), pp. 61–2; NS, 26 February 1848.

71. T. Frost, *Forty Years' Recollections* (London, Sampson Low, 1880), pp. 128–9; Schoyen, *Chartist Challenge*, p. 159.

72. J. Kavanagh, 'A Barnsley man's autobiography', *Barnsley Chronicle*, 9 June 1900.

73. Ludlow, unpublished lecture notes, quoted by J. F. C. Harrison, *History of the Working Men's College* (London, RKP, 1954); A. Alison, *Some Account of My Life and Writings*, vol. 1 (Edinburgh, Blackwood, 1883), p. 572; Hughes quoted in *Charles Kingsley: His Letters and Memories of His Life*, ed. F. E. Kingsley, vol. 1 (London, King, 1877), p. 161.

74. M. Brodie, 'Free trade and cheap theatre', *Social History*, 28:3 (October 2003), p. 357.

75. G. W. M. Reynolds, *Mysteries of London*, vol. 4 (ns, vol. 2), no. 77 (4 March) 1848, p. 199 (ch. 157); see also I. Haywood, *The Revolution in Popular Literature* (Cambridge, Cambridge University Press, 2004), pp. 177–9.

76. HO, 45/2410/3, fos 403–5, 4 March 1848; and 2410/5, fos 849 and 853, 12 March; R. Pugh, 'Chartism in Somerset and Wiltshire', in A. Briggs (ed.), *Chartist Studies* (London, Macmillan, 1959), p. 215.

77. Alison, *Some Account*, pp. 573, 575; *The Times*, 7 August 1848; A. Wilson, *The Chartist Movement in Scotland* (Manchester, Manchester University Press, 1970), pp. 218–19.

78. P. Pickering and A. Tyrell, *The People's Bread: A History of the Anti-Corn Law League* (London, Leicester University Press, 2000), p. 170. There is a burgeoning literature on Reynolds but the best introduction remains the entry in *DLB*, vol. 3; see also I. Haywood, 'Reynolds and the "Trafalgar Square revolution"', *Journal of Victorian Culture*, 7:1 (spring, 2002), pp. 23–59.

79. MEPO, 2/64, 6 March 1848, report of Haynes; Goodway, *London Chartism*, pp. 71, 112–14.

80. NS, 18 March ignored income tax altogether in its report, but Reynolds and McGrath alluded to it in passing according to the *Morning Chronicle*, 14 March 1848; see also Goodway, *London Chartism*, pp. 71–2, 114–16.

81. Reynolds, *Mysteries*, vol. 4 (ns vol. 2), no. 78 (11 March) 1848, p. 202; NS, 11 March 1848.

82. NS, 25 March 1848.

83. NS, 11 March, 1 April 1848; see also W. Stevens, *Memoir of T. M. Wheeler* (London, Leno, 1862), p. 42.

84. Stevens, *Memoir*, p. 42; T. Allsop to O'Connor, 9 April 1848, quoted in Allsop's *ODNB* entry. Allsop's papers passed at his death to G. J. Holyoake, author of the 1885 *Dictionary of National Biography* essay on Allsop, and this letter was subsequently lost; see also G. J. Holyoake, *Life of Joseph Rayner Stephens* (London, Williams, 1881), pp. 189–90.

85. Duncombe to O'Connor, 6 April 1848, quoted in T. H. Duncombe (ed.), *Life and Correspondence of Thomas Slingsby Duncombe*, vol. 1 (London, Hurst, 1868), p. 275.

86. NS, 25 March and 1 April 1848.

87. Ibid., 8 April 1848; *Morning Chronicle*, 10 April 1848.

88. *The Diary of Colonel Peter Hawker*, vol. 2 (London, Longmans, 1893), p. 286; J. Saville, *1848: The British State and the Chartist Movement* (Cambridge, Cambridge

University Press, 1987), p. 105; C. C. F. Greville, *The Greville Memoirs, 1814–60*, ed. by L. Strachey and R. Fulford, vol. 6 (London, Macmillan, 1938), pp. 47–8.

89. *The Gladstone Diaries*, ed. M. R. D. Foot and H. C. G. Matthew, vol. 4: *1848–54* (Oxford, Oxford University Press, 1974), p. 23.

90. HO, 45/2410/1, fo. 270; and 45/2410/4, fos 844–90.

91. National Archives, Kew, War Office Papers (WO), 30/111, memos 8, 9 April, and telegraph 8.00 a.m., 10 April 1848; Goodway, *London Chartism*, pp. 134–6.

92. E. Miller, *That Noble Cabinet* (London, Deutsch, 1973), pp. 167–72; W. A. Munford, *Edward Edwards* (London, Library Association, 1963), pp. 52–3.

93. HO, 45/2410/1, fo. 277f, payments to coal-whippers; C. Mackay, *Forty Years' Recollections* (London, Chapman, 1877), p. 54; W. A. Munford, *William Ewart* (London, Grafton, 1960), pp. 174–5.

94. *Letters of the Rt Hon. George Cornewall Lewis*, ed. G. F. Lewis (London, Longmans, 1870), p. 172; Lord Broughton (J. C. Hobhouse), *Recollections of a Long Life* (London, Murray, 1911), pp. 214–15.

95. HO, 45/2410/4, fo. 68, 7 April 1848; *NS*, 2 February 1850; *The Times*, 10 April 1848; G. Grey to Russell, 9 April 1848, quoted in S. Walpole, *Life of Lord John Russell*, vol. 2 (London, Longman, 1889), p. 69; and see Taylor, *Ernest Jones*, p. 108.

96. R. Crowe, *Reminiscences of Robert Crowe, the Octogenarian Tailor* (New York, 1901), p. 9.

97. Mackay, *Forty Years*, pp. 55–7. The contentious issue of how many attended on 10 April is carefully analysed in Goodway, *London Chartism*, pp. 136–42.

98. HO, 45/2410/1, fo. 453, Mayne to HO, '1/4 to 12: Kennington'; George Howard, diary entry for 10 April, quoted in D. D. Olien, *Morpeth: A Victorian Public Career* (Washington, DC, University Press of America, 1983), p. 329; *NS*, 15 April 1848.

### Notes to Chapter 10: April 1848–52: 'Decent revolutionaries'?

1. This account is based on *The Times*, 14 April, *NS*, 15 and 22 April, *Hansard*, vol. 98, cols 284–301 and *National Instructor*, 5 October 1850; see also P. Pickering, '"And your petitioners &c": Chartist petitioning in popular politics', *English Historical Review*, 466 (April 2001), pp. 383–6.

2. Cripps's Cirencester constituents explained that they copied out names because a lack of printed sheets meant that most signatures were submitted on slips of paper: *NS*, 29 April 1848. Many argued that large numbers of petitioners could not write, others that some signatories were afraid to identify themselves and used pseudonyms instead.

3. *NS*, 22 April 1848.

4. D. Goodway, *London Chartism, 1838–48* (Cambridge, Cambridge University Press, 1982), pp. 136–42.

5. Lord Broughton (J. C. Hobhouse), *Recollections of a Long Life* (London, Murray, 1911), p. 214.

6. *Reports of State Trials* (London, HMSO, 1896), ns vol. 7, col. 480.

7. D. Cairns, *Berlioz: Servitude and Greatness* (London, Allen Lane, 1999), p. 412.

8. *Papers for the People*, 6 May 1848.

9. *The Times*, 15 April and *NS*, 15 April (3rd edn) 1848.

10. *NS*, 22 April and 1 July 1848; HO, 45/2410/3, fo. 318, 4 April (High Wycombe); and 45/2410/4, fo. 920 (Buckley); (A. Applegarth) *A Letter on Chartism* (Dartford, Reeves, 1848), p. 6; Council of the Dartford NCA, *Reply to a Letter on Chartism* (Dartford, Reeves, 1848); D. Thompson, *Chartists* (London, Temple Smith, 1984), Appendix.

11. Chadwick: *DLB*, vol. 7; Clubb: A. F. J. Brown, *Chartism in Essex and Suffolk*

(Chelmsford, Essex CRO, 1982), p. 81, and Anon., *History of the Philadelphian Bible-Christian Church* (Philadelphia, PA, Lippincott, 1922), pp. 67–89.

12. A. Alison, *Some Account of My Life*, vol. 1 (Edinburgh, Blackwood, 1883), p. 580.
13. *Bolton Chronicle*, 20 May 1848. The best account of the Assembly remains R. G. Gammage, *History of the Chartist Movement, 1837–54* (Newcastle upon Tyne, Browne, 1894), pp. 324–30.
14. *Memoranda of the Chartist Agitation in Dundee* (Dundee, Kidd, 1889), p. 75; A. Wilson, *The Chartist Movement in Scotland* (Manchester, Manchester University Press, 1970), pp. 225–32.
15. *NS*, 6 and 20 May 1848.
16. J. Belchem, 'Britishness, the United Kingdom and the revolutions of 1848', *Labour History Review*, 64:2 (1999), p. 147.
17. *Bradford Observer*, 16 March 1848; HO, 45/2410/3, fo. 997.
18. HO, 45/2410/5, fos 1002 and 1017–23; see also D. Wright, *The Chartist Risings in Bradford* (Bradford, Bradford Libraries, 1987), pp. 45–50.
19. T. W. Reid, *The Life of the Right Honourable William Edward Forster* (London, Chapman, 1888), p. 138; A. Peacock, 'Chartism in York', *York History*, 3 (1976), pp. 142–3.
20. *Halifax Guardian*, 27 May 1848.
21. HO, 45/2410/5, fos 1038 and 1048.
22. Goodway, *London Chartism*, pp. 81–3, 117–19, at 81; J. B. Leno, *The Aftermath* (London, Reeves, 1892), pp. 57–8; *The Times*, 2 June 1848; Leno: *DLB*, vol. 11.
23. C. C. F. Greville, *The Greville Memoirs, 1814–60*, ed. L. Strachey and R. Fulford, vol. 6 (London, Macmillan, 1938), p. 73.
24. *NS*, 15 July 1848; Goodway, *London Chartism*, pp. 83–5, 119–22.
25. MEPO, 2/66 and 2/67.
26. TS, 11/136, fo. 91.
27. MEPO, 2/43 (Aliens file), 7 June 1848; *The Times*, 14 June 1848; *The Gladstone Diaries*, ed. M. R. D. Foot and H. C. G. Matthew, vol. 4: *1848–54* (Oxford, Oxford University Press, 1974), p. 42; T. Hughes quoted in F. E. Kingsley (ed.), *Charles Kingsley*, vol. 1 (London, King, 1877), p. 161.
28. Wilson, *Chartist Movement in Scotland*, pp. 231–2; *NS*, 17 June 1848.
29. T. Frost, *Forty Years' Recollections* (London, Sampson Low, 1880), p. 152.
30. HO, 2410/3, 13 June (Isle of Wight), and fo. 103B (Nottingham poster, 7 June); White quoted in *Manchester Observer*, 13 June; see also HO, 2410/5, fo. 534.
31. A. M. Hadfield, *The Chartist Land Company* (Newton Abbot, David & Charles, 1970), p. 190.
32. *Greville Memoirs*, vol. 6, p. 77; *The Times*, 13 June; *NS*, 17 June 1848.
33. HO, 45/2410/2, information of Davis, 12 and 14 June, and Reading, 12 June; Goodway, *London Chartism*, pp. 88 and 264.
34. Goodway, *London Chartism*, pp. 86–9.
35. *NS*, 1, 22 July 1848; *The Authentic Report of the Trial of Doctor Peter McDouall* (Manchester, Heywood, 1848), p. 1.
36. This paragraph is indebted to Goodway's meticulous reconstruction in *London Chartism*.
37. TS, 11/141/388, fo. 248.
38. TS, 11/138/380, fo. 3.
39. *NS*, 22 July 1848.
40. HO, 45/2410/3, fo. 972; *Manchester Guardian*, 2, 5, 12 August 1848; for Theobald's later career see, e.g., *NS*, 23 September 1848, 3 February 1849; also J. Schwartzkopf, *Women in the Chartist Movement* (London, Macmillan, 1991), pp. 237–8.

41. *Bolton Chronicle*, 29 July 1848; HO, 45/2410/3, fo. 284.
42. *The Times*, 18 August 1848; J. Belchem, 'Liverpool in the year of revolution', in J. Belchem (ed.), *Popular Politics, Riot and Labour* (Liverpool, Liverpool University Press, 1992), p. 92.
43. *The Times*, 17–19 August 1848; see also J. Belchem, '1848: Feargus O'Connor and the collapse of the mass platform', in J. Epstein and D. Thompson (eds), *Chartist Experience* (London, Macmillan, 1982), pp. 298–9.
44. F. C. Mather, *Public Order in the Age of the Chartists* (Manchester, Manchester University Press, 1959), p. 24; A. Marcroft, *Landmarks of Liberalism* (Oldham, Wildgoose, 1913), p. 104 (Marcroft misdates the episode to 1 May).
45. HO, 45/2410/2, fo. 302; *The Times*, 17 and 18 August, 1848; R. G. Hall, 'Work, class and politics in Ashton-under-Lyne 1830–1860', D. Phil thesis, Vanderbilt University (1991), pp. 224–6; H. Davies, 'A shot in the dark', in S. A. Harrop and E. A. Rose (eds), *Victorian Ashton* (Ashton, Tameside Libraries, 1974), pp. 16–28.
46. HO, 48/40, deposition of Thomas Brown, quoted in Mather, *Public Order*, p. 25.
47. *The Times*, 19 August 1848; HO, 45/2410/5, fo. 1132; *Halifax Guardian*, 19 August 1848; Belchem, '1848', pp. 298–9.
48. *The Times*, 25 August; *NS*, 30 December 1848.
49. Frost, *Forty Years*, pp. 164–5.
50. *NS*, 11 November 1848; Ashton quotation from Davies, 'Shot in the dark', p. 27.
51. P. Gregory, 'The exile of Thomas Winterbottom', quoted by *Chartist Ancestors* at www.chartists.net/Prosecution-witnesses; see also Davies, 'Shot in the dark', p. 25.
52. HO, 45/2410/3, fo. 1014.
53. *NS*, 11 November 1848; for other ramifications in Ashton, see R. G. Hall, 'A united people', *Journal of Social History*, 38 (fall 2004), pp. 194–5.
54. *NS*, 17 June, 19 August–9 September 1848.
55. Ibid., 9 and 23 September 1848.
56. Select Committee on the National Land Company (SCNLC), *Parliamentary Papers* (Reports from Committees), Session 1847–48 (398), vol. 19, Sixth Report, p. iii.
57. Ibid., Third Report, para. 2454, and Fifth Report, para. 4541; M. Chase, 'We wish only to work for ourselves', in M. Chase and I. Dyck (eds), *Living and Learning* (Aldershot, Scolar, 1996), p. 134, erroneously gives a figure of 115 years.
58. M. Chase, 'Wholesome object lessons: the Chartist land plan in retrospect', *English Historical Review*, 475 (2003), pp. 59–85, Sillett quotation at 63.
59. Quotation from SCNLC, Fifth Report, paras 4416, 4445 and 4468; for a possibly higher figure compare First Report, para. 58, and Second Report, para. 1218.
60. SCNLC, First Report, paras 186, 768–90, and Second Report, paras 1829–30.
61. Ibid., Second Report, para. 1842, and Third Report, para. 2175.
62. TS, 11/140/387, fos 79–80, evidence of D. Burn.
63. *NS*, 4 and 11 November 1848, 23 June and 7 July 1849; D. Poole, *The Last Chartist Land Settlement: Great Dodford, 1849* (Dodford, self-published, 1999), pp. 10–11.
64. SCNLC, Sixth Report, p. iii.
65. The land plan's history after 1848 awaits a legal historian of uncommon enthusiasm, but meanwhile see Hadfield, *Chartist Land Company*, pp. 68–86.
66. W. Whitmore, 'Respite hours', *Firstlings* (London, Chapman, 1852), p. 28. All five estates survive and the National Trust preserves the last unmodernised holding at Dodford.
67. *NS*, 11 and 18 November 1848.
68. P. Pickering and A. Tyrell, *The People's Bread: A History of the Anti-Corn Law League* (London, Leicester University Press, 2000), pp. 22–5.

69. *NS*, 23 December 1848.
70. For an opposing interpretation see Belchem, '1848'; quotations from *NS*, 18 and 25 November 1848.
71. *NS*, 7 July 1849; *Companion to the Almanac and Year-book of General Information for 1850* (London, Knight, 1849), p. 224.
72. *NS*, 6 January 1849.
73. Ibid., 27 October 1849 and 11 May 1850.
74. Ibid., 17–31 March 1849.
75. Letter to F. Engels, 19 March 1848, reprinted in *The Harney Papers*, ed. F. G. and R. M. Black (Assen, Van Gorcum, 1969), p. 149.
76. *NS*, 14 and 28 July, 10 November–8 December 1849, 30 November 1850.
77. Ibid., 25 August–6 October 1849.
78. Ibid., 26 May and 13 October 1849.
79. P. Pickering, 'Repeal and the suffrage: Feargus O'Connor's Irish "mission"', 1849–50', in O. Ashton, R. Fyson and S. F. Roberts (eds), *The Chartist Legacy* (Woodbridge, Merlin, 1999), pp. 119–46.
80. There is no detailed history, but see R. G. Gammage, *The History of the Chartist Movement, 1837–54* (Newcastle upon Tyne, Browne, 1894), pp. 18–20 and 347f.; D. J. V. Jones, *Chartism and the Chartists* (London, Allen Lane, 1975), pp. 169–81; E. Royle, *Chartism*, 3rd edn (London, Longmans, 1996), pp. 47–52.
81. C. D. Collet, *A History of the Taxes on Knowledge*, abridged edn (London, Watts, 1933), p. 43.
82. J. Wiener, *William Lovett* (Manchester, Manchester University Press, 1989), pp. 116–17; W. Lovett, *The Life and Struggles of William Lovett* (London, Trübner, 1876), pp. 335–49.
83. N. C. Edsall, 'A failed national movement: the Parliamentary and Financial Reform Association', *Bulletin of the Institute of Historical Research*, 49 (1976), pp. 108–31.
84. *Social Reformer*, 20 October 1849; A. Plummer, *Bronterre* (London, Allen & Unwin, 1971).
85. *NS*, 3 August 1850 to 8 February 1851; Gammage, *History*, p. 356.
86. *NS*, 6 April to 7 December 1850; Thomas Clark: *DLB*, vol. 6.
87. T. Clark, *A Letter Addressed to G. W. M. Reynolds ... together with copious extracts from his most indecent writings* (London, Clark, 1850); T. Clark, *Reflections Upon Past Policy ... also a Letter Condemnatory of Private Assassination, as recommended by Mr. G. J. Harney* (London, Boonham, 1850); (G. J. Harney) 'Review of a renegade's revelations', *Democratic Review* (July 1850), p. 33.
88. *NS*, 6 and 13 July 1850.
89. J. A. Epstein, 'O'Connor and the Northern Star', *International Review of Social History*, 21 (1976), p. 97; J. Ginswick (ed.), *Labour and the Poor in England and Wales, 1849–51*, vol. 2 (London, Cass, 1983), pp. 59–60; A. Little, 'Chartism and liberalism: popular politics in Leicestershire, 1842–74', D.Phil thesis, University of Manchester (1991), p. 209.
90. *Friend of the People*, 19 April 1851.
91. *NS*, 18 November and 12 August 1848; for the 'macroeconomics' of the land plan see Chase, 'We wish only to work for ourselves'.
92. *Democratic Review*, February 1850; *Red Republican*, 22 June 1850.
93. *Democratic Review*, February 1850.
94. *Red Republican*, 22 June 1850.
95. *Cooper's Journal*, 15 June 1850, reprinted as *The Red Banner* in *NS*, 13 July 1850, and on the verso of the title of the collected issues of *Red Republican*.

96. Harney to Engels, 30 March 1846, reprinted in *Harney Papers*, p. 242; *NS*, 3 August, 5 October, 2 November 1850, 3, 10, 24 May and 23 August 1851.

97. *NS*, 13, 20 July 1850; M. Taylor, *Ernest Jones, Chartism, and the Romance of Politics, 1819–1869* (Oxford, Oxford University Press, 2003), pp. 130–6.

98. *NS*, 26 October 1850; Taylor, *Jones*, pp. 140–3.

99. *NS*, 11 May 1850 and 1 March 1851; Collet, *Taxes on Knowledge*, pp. 46–9.

100. *NS*, 4 January 1851.

101. *Star of Freedom*, 26 June 1852.

102. *NS*, 12 October 1850–8 February 1851, quotation from 1 February; J. Belchem, 'Chartism and the trades', *English Historical Review*, 98 (1983), pp. 585–6; M. Hewitt, *The Emergence of Stability in an Industrial City: Manchester, 1832–67* (Aldershot, Scolar, 1996), pp. 250–2.

103. *Friend of the People*, 12 April; *NS*, 5–19 April; *The Times*, 22 and 23 April 1851.

104. *NCA Fund Ten Shillings Collection Sheet* (1852), copy in Tameside Local Studies Library, Ashton-under-Lyne, Tameside Broadsheets, L322; Gammage, *History*, pp. 386–7, 390–4; *Companion to the Almanac and Year-Book of General Information for 1853* (London, Knight, 1852), p. 232.

105. *Star of Freedom*, 25 September and 27 November 1852.

### Notes to Chapter 11: Chartist lives: 'Ever present to the progressive mind'

1. R. G. Gammage, *History of the Chartist Movement, 1837–54* (Newcastle upon Tyne, Browne, 1894), p. 390; L. M. Geary, 'O'Connorite Bedlam', *Medical History*, 34 (1990), pp. 125–43.

2. *The Times*, 4 and 11 September; *Reynolds's Newspaper*, 16 September 1848.

3. B. Wilson, *Struggles of an Old Chartist* (1887), reprinted in D. Vincent (ed.), *Testaments of Radicalism* (London, Europa, 1977), p. 222; P. Pickering, 'Chartist rites of passage', in P. Pickering and A. Tyrell (eds), *Contested Sites* (Aldershot, Ashgate, 2004), pp. 101–26.

4. C. Wilkins, *History of Merthyr Tydfil* (Merthyr Tydfil, 1867), p. 308.

5. T. P. Newbould, *Pages from a Life of Strife* (London, Palmer, n.d. [?1911]), p. 33; R. J. Broughton, 'The Chartist hero of Prestwich', *East Lancashire Review*, vol. 2 (1891), p. 162.

6. A critical contextual point is that the 1851 Census lists only seven English-born men born before 1837 and named Feargus.

7. (Middlesbrough) *Daily Gazette*, 22 September 1875; see also *DLB*, vol. 10.

8. *The Times*, 27 January 1869; see also M. Taylor, *Ernest Jones* (Oxford, OUP, 2003), pp. 1, 5–6, 251–4.

9. M. R. Lahee, *Life and Times of the Late Alderman Livesey* (Manchester, Heywood, 1865), J. Garrard, *Leadership and Power in Victorian Industrial Towns* (Manchester, Manchester University Press, 1983), pp. 35, 129 …

10. Quoted in S. Roberts, *Radical Politicians and Poets in Early Victorian Britain* (Lampeter, Mellen, 1993), p. 32.

11. *NS*, 1, 8 November 1851; A. Elliott, 'Municipal government in Bradford', in D. Fraser (ed.), *Municipal Reform and the Industrial City* (Leicester, Leicester University Press, 1982); Wilson, *Struggles*, pp. 203–4, 208; M. Chase, 'Chartism, 1838–58', *Northern History*, 24 (1988), pp. 156, 166; *NS*, 9 April 1842; S. Pollard, *History of Labour in Sheffield* (Liverpool, Liverpool University Press, 1959), pp. 48–9.

12. Garrard, *Leadership and Power*, pp. 118, 168, 208; P. A. Pickering, *Chartism and the Chartists in Manchester and Salford* (Basingstoke, Macmillan, 1995), pp. 73–85.

13. A. Little, 'Chartism and liberalism: popular politics in Leicestershire, 1842–74',

D.Phil thesis, University of Manchester (1991), pp. 289–94; R.Church, *Economic and Social Change in a Midland Town: Victorian Nottingham, 1815–1900* (London, Cass, 1966), pp. 152, 155–6; R.Fyson, 'Chartism in north Staffordshire', D.Phil thesis, University of Lancaster (1999), pp. 319–39; Jeremiah Yates: *DLB*, vol. 9.

14. D.J.V.Jones, *Chartism and the Chartists* (London, Allen Lane, 1975), p. 93.

15. *Leeds Times*, 13 October 1838; D.Fraser, 'Politics and society in the mid-nineteenth century', in D.Fraser (ed.), *History of Modern Leeds* (Manchester, MUP, 1980), pp. 286f; see also D.Fraser, *Urban Politics in Victorian England* (Leicester, Leicester University Press, 1976).

16. *North Staffordshire Mercury*, 30 March 1844, quoted in Fyson, 'Chartism', p. 321; *Leeds Mercury*, 1 April 1854, quoted in Fraser, *Politics and Society*, p. 107.

17. G.J.Holyoake, *Jubilee History of the Leeds Industrial Co-operative Society* (Leeds, LICS, 1897), p. 249; C.Godfrey, *Chartist Lives* (New York, Garland, 1987), pp. 475–6.

18. *The Times*, 11 August 1882; RG, 12/4539, 1881 Census, fo. 133.

19. R.Wallace, *Organise! Organise! Organise! A Study of Reform Agitations in Wales, 1840–86* (Cardiff, University of Wales Press, 1991), pp. 97–8; A.V.John, 'The Chartist endurance', *Morgannwg*, 15 (1971), pp. 36–44.

20. *Ashton Reporter*, 5 December 1874.

21. M.Finn, *After Chartism: Class and Nation in English Radical Politics, 1848–74* (Cambridge, Cambridge University Press, 1993).

22. See K.Tiller, 'Working-class attitudes and organisation in three industrial towns, 1850–75', D.Phil thesis, University of Birmingham (1975); see also her 'Late Chartism: Halifax, 1847–58', in J.Epstein and D.Thompson (eds), *The Chartist Experience: Working-Class Radicalism and Culture, 1830–1860* (London, Macmillan, 1982); B.Lancaster, *Radicalism, Co-operation and Socialism: Leicester Working-class Politics* (Leicester, Leicester University Press, 1987), pp. 76–84; on Rochdale, see J.Vincent, *The Formation of the Liberal Party* (London, Constable, 1966), p. 111.

23. *East London Observer*, 12 March 1859, quoted by J.Vernon, *Politics and the People* (Cambridge, Cambridge University Press, 1993), p. 321.

24. A.Marcroft, *Landmarks of Local Liberalism (Oldham Liberal Bazaar Souvenir)* (Oldham, Wildgoose, 1913), p. 103; D.Ball, *The Story of Failsworth* (Oldham, Failsworth UDC, 1973), p. 91; S.Schofield, *Short Stories about Failsworth Folk* (Blackpool, Union, 1905), p. 64.

25. *Star and National Trades' Journal*, 3 April 1852.

26. Statement in *Dod's Parliamentary Companion*, 2nd edn (1852), quoted in M.Stenton, *Who's Who of British Members of Parliament*, vol. 1: *1832–85* (Hassocks, Harvester, 1976), p. 68.

27. *Star and National Trades' Journal*, 3, 17 and 24 April; *Star of Freedom*, 8 May 1852; see also *DNB*, vol. 2.

28. *Star of Freedom*, 11 November 1852; A.R.Schoyen, *The Chartist Challenge: A Portrait of George Julian Harney* (London, Heinemann, 1958), pp. 225–8.

29. M.Taylor, *The Decline of British Radicalism, 1847–60* (Oxford, Clarendon, 1995), pp. 87–93; Vernon, *Politics and the People*, pp. 202–3.

30. Schoyen, *Chartist Challenge*, pp. 230–1; *Northern Tribune*, vol. 1 (1854), title page and contents.

31. L.D.Smith, *Carpet Weavers and Carpet Masters* (Kidderminster, Tompkinson, 1986), p. 251.

32. A.F.J.Brown, *Chartism in Essex and Suffolk* (Chelmsford, Essex CRO, 1982), pp. 83–4, 119–21; A.Wilson, *The Chartist Movement in Scotland* (Manchester, Manchester University Press, 1970), pp. 256–7.

33. B. Rees, 'Lost years: Northumberland miners, 1844–62', *North-East Labour History*, 19 (1985); Pickering, *Chartism and the Chartists*, p. 200.

34. Chase, 'Chartism, 1838–58', pp. 166–7; *Halifax Courier*, 3 May; *Halifax Guardian*, 3 March and 28 April 1860.

35. *Parliamentary Papers* (Reports from Committees), Session 1856 (343), vol. 13: Select Committee on Masters and Operatives (Equitable Councils of Conciliation), qq. 2–4.

36. *NS*, 3 and 17 September 1842, 22 October 1842, 21 and 28 December 1844, 18 January and 29 November 1845.

37. *Parliamentary Papers* (Reports from Committees), Session 1860 (307), vol. 22, Select Committee on Masters and Operatives, q. 249.

38. 'Censor', 'Rechabitism *versus* Chartism', *ECC*, 56 (February 1842); T. Frost, *Reminiscences of a Country Journalist* (London, Ward, 1886), pp. 94–5; M. Hewitt, *Emergence of Stability in the Industrial City* (Aldershot, Ashgate, 1996), p. 260; S. Cordery, *British Friendly Societies, 1750–1914* (London, Palgrave, 2003), pp. 58–9; W. Stevens, *Memoir of Thomas Martin Wheeler* (London, Leno, 1862), pp. 62–70, 78–86; I. Prothero, *Radical Artisans in England and France, 1830–70* (Cambridge, Cambridge University Press, 1997), pp. 151–5.

39. Monthly Report of the NAUT, 1 December 1847.

40. *Notes to the People*, vol. 2, p. 976 (March) and p. 862 (February 1852).

41. Copy in the Howell Collection, Bishopsgate Institute, London.

42. M. Chase, *Early Trade Unionism* (Aldershot, Ashgate, 2000), pp. 211–14.

43. 1856 Select Committee on Masters and Operatives (Equitable Councils of Conciliation), qq. 1–511 and Appendix 1, pp. 255–6; 1860 Select Committee on Masters and Operatives, qq. 249–385 and Appendix 3, pp. 103–7; Chase, *Early Trade Unionism*, p. 214; W. H. Fraser, *Trade Unions and Society* (London, Macmillan, 1974), p. 109; M. Curthoys, *Governments, Labour and the Law in Mid-Victorian Britain* (Oxford, Oxford University Press, 2004), p. 241.

44. T. W. Porter, 'Ernest Jones and the Royal Literary Fund', *Labour History Review*, 57:3 (1992), pp. 84–94; other recipients included Massey and Cooper.

45. Tiller, 'Late Chartism', pp. 328–9.

46. *The Times*, 16 September 1856.

47. *The Democracy of Stalybridge to John Frost, Esq.* (1856), copy in Tameside Local Studies Library, Ashton-under-Lyne, Tameside Broadsheets, L322.

48. *People's Paper*, 14 November 1857.

49. Ibid., 12 and 26 December 1857; Wallace, *Organise!*, pp. 94–5.

50. *Peoples's Paper*, 12 December; *The Times*, 29 December 1856.

51. D. Williams, *John Frost* (Cardiff, University of Wales Press, 1939), p. 321; L. Barrow, *Independent Spirits* (London, RKP, 1986).

52. Letter to the editor, *The Times*, 17 June 1857; J. Frost, *Horrors of Convict Life* (London, Holyoake, 1856); letter to W. E. Adams, 15 December 1877, reprinted in the latter's *Memoirs of a Social Atom* (London, Hutcheson, 1903), pp. 201–2.

53. *Parliamentary Papers* (Reports from Commissioners), Session 1868–69, vol. 13, Second Report of the Commissioners on the Employment of Children, Young Persons, and Women in Agriculture, Appendix, part 1, p. 349.

54. T. M. Wheeler, *Lost Money Found* (London, Friend-in-Need, 1861), p. 13; for details of Wheeler's life see especially Stevens, *Memoir* and *DLB*, vol. 6.

55. Stevens, *Memoir*, p. 76; *National Union*, November and 4 December 1858; Taylor, *Ernest Jones*, pp. 162, 242.

56. Quoted in J. Saville, *Ernest Jones: Chartist* (London, Lawrence & Wishart, 1952), pp. 62–3.

57. *People's Paper*, 4 September 1858.
58. Ibid., 13 and 27 February 1858; Taylor, *Ernest Jones*, pp. 183–5; Saville, *Ernest Jones*, pp. 63–5, 68–9.
59. *National Union*, May 1858.
60. Co-operative College, Manchester, Owen Papers, Jones to R. Owen, 3 June 1858.
61. F. E. Gillespie, *Labor and Politics in England, 1850–67* (Chicago, Duke University Press, 1926), pp. 164–7; J. Allen, 'Resurrecting Jerusalem', in J. Allen and O. Ashton (eds), *Papers for the People* (London, Merlin, 2005), pp. 169–70, 175–83.
62. *Cabinet Newspaper*, 18 December 1858, quoted in Taylor, *Ernest Jones*, p. 172; see also pp. 165, 188, 190, 192.
63. *Reynolds's Newspaper*, 5 September 1858; *The Times*, 11 July 1859; Taylor, *Ernest Jones*, pp. 187–90.
64. *The Times*, 11 July 1859; Taylor, *Ernest Jones*, p. 190.
65. *Friend in Need Journal*, 2:3 (March 1862), pp. 33–7; Stevens, *Memoir*, p. 89.
66. *NS*, 28 December 1850; and see above (pp. 22–9) on Abram and Elizabeth Hanson.
67. J. Wilson, *Memories of a Labour Leader* (London, Fisher Unwin, 1910), p. 30.
68. Calculations based on J. Burnett, D. Vincent and D. Mayall, *Autobiography of the Working Class: An Annotated Critical Bibliography*, vols 1 and 3 (Brighton, Harvester, 1984 and 1989), as follows: 1870s (8); 1880s (16); 1890s (13); 1900s (13).
69. J. B. Leno, *Aftermath* (London, Reeves, 1892), pp. 18–19; see also E. F. Biagini, 'Popular liberals, Gladstonian finance and the debate on taxation, 1860–74', in E. F. Biagini and A. J. Reid, *Currents of Radicalism* (Cambridge, Cambridge University Press, 1991), p. 136.
70. Leno, *Aftermath*, p. 81.
71. Quoted in P. d'A. Jones, *The Christian Socialist Revival, 1877–1914* (Princeton, NJ, Princeton University Press, 1968), p. 343.
72. *DLB*, vol. 7; P. Clarke, *Lancashire and the New Liberalism* (Cambridge, Cambridge University Press, 1971), pp. 33–4; Newbould, *Pages from a Life of Strife*, pp. vii–xiii.
73. York City Library, Local Studies Section, 'Chartism MSS etc.', Y342.42; G. J. Harney to F. Engels, 24 February 1893, reprinted in *The Harney Papers*, ed. F. G. Black and R. M. Black (Assen, Van Gorcum, 1969), pp. 347–8.
74. *Justice*, 1 August 1903, quoted by M. Bevir, 'Republicanism, socialism and democracy', in D. Nash and A. Taylor (eds), *Republicanism in Victorian Society* (Stroud, Sutton, 2000), p. 77.
75. *Notes & Queries*, 9th series, vol. 9 (1902), p. 144; see also pp. 86 and 251. The 'last Chartist' was almost certainly Henry Clubb, former secretary of Colchester WMA and Michigan State senator, who died in 1921: see Anon., *History of the Philadelphian Bible-Christian Church* (Philadelphia, PA, Lippincott, 1922), pp. 67–89.
76. I have adapted this sentence from Robert F. Kennedy's speech at the University of Capetown, 6 June 1966, accessed via www.jfklibrary.org.

# Money, prices and wages: a note

In the pre-decimal sterling currency there were 12 pence in one shilling and 20 shillings in one pound; thus there were 240 pence in each pound. The abbreviation for a shilling was 's' and for a penny 'd' (from the Latin *denarius*). Prices were written in the form of, for example, £3 17s 6d (= £3.88).

Calculating equivalent values for money in past times and the present is not an exact science. Very broadly, £1 in 1839 had the purchasing power of about £59 at 2001 prices, a calculation based on a long-term price index.[*] However, £1 a week was considered a typical wage for a skilled artisan such as a tailor in 1839. A coal miner or adult male spinner working in a cotton factory could expect to earn maybe 5 shillings more, an agricultural labourer 4–5 shillings less and a handloom weaver often even less than that .

The reader should note that these wages were paid for a long working week (typically 69 hours for male factory workers), and that both prices and wages would vary widely between years and, even, seasons and regions. Overall, wage earners' average real incomes underwent modest growth in the mid-1830s, but then fell back in 1838–42. Recovery thereafter was modest. Sustained standard of living benefits from industrialisation were not really apparent until the 1850s.[†]

[*]   *Inflation: The Value of the Pound, 1750–2001*, House of Commons Library Research Paper 02/44 (London, Stationery Office, 2002).

[†]   C. Feinstein, 'Pessimism perpetuated: real wages and the standard of living in Britain during and after the industrial revolution', *Journal of Economic History*, 58:3 (1998).

# A note on sources
# and further reading

Readers needing detailed bibliographical information in addition to the sources and books cited in the notes should consult the two bibliographies devoted to Chartism: J. F. C. Harrison and D. Thompson, *A Bibliography of the Chartist Movement* (Hassocks, Harvester, 1978) and O. Ashton, R. Fyson and S. Roberts (eds), *The Chartist Movement: A New Annotated Bibliography* (London, Mansell, 1995). More recent publications in the field are listed in the annual bibliographies that appear in the journal *Labour History Review*.

For those wishing to read more extensively, the literature is abundant. Dorothy Thompson's *The Chartists: Popular Politics in the Industrial Revolution* (London, Temple Smith, 1984) distils a lifetime's wisdom and research, and is indispensable. In a field where local studies once dominated, several other books are outstanding: Paul Pickering's *Chartism and the Chartists in Manchester and Salford* (Basingstoke, Macmillan, 1995); David Goodway's seminal *London Chartism, 1838–48* (Cambridge, Cambridge University Press, 1982); John Saville's *1848: The British State and the Chartist Movement* (Cambridge, Cambridge University Press, 1987), which extends Goodway's insights into the events of 1848 on a national scale; and D. J. V. Jones's *The Last Rising: The Newport Insurrection of 1839* (Oxford, Oxford University Press, 1985) a monument of scholarship unlikely ever to be surpassed. *Ernest Jones, Chartism, and the Romance of Politics, 1819–1869* (Oxford, Oxford University Press, 2003), by Miles Taylor, and *The Lion of Freedom: Feargus O'Connor and the Chartist Movement, 1832–42* (London, Croom Helm, 1982), by James Epstein, are the two most thorough and perceptive biographical studies of Chartists; and, despite its age, *The Chartist Challenge: A Portrait of George Julian Harney* (London, Heinemann, 1958), by A. R. Schoyen, still has a good deal to offer a modern reader.

There are several important essay collections: Asa Briggs (ed.), *Chartist Studies* (London, Macmillan, 1959), contains much that is still of value; but the key collection is that edited by James Epstein and Dorothy Thompson: *The Chartist Experience: Studies in Working-Class Radicalism and Culture, 1830–60*

(London, Macmillan, 1982); the volume also contains an abridged version of Gareth Stedman Jones's powerful essay 'Rethinking Chartism', which appears in full in his *Languages of Class* (Cambridge, Cambridge University Press, 1983). More recent essay collections are: Owen Ashton, Robert Fyson and Stephen Roberts (eds), *The Chartist Legacy* (Woodbridge, Merlin, 1999); and Stephen Roberts (ed.), *The People's Charter: Democratic Agitation in Early Victorian Britain* (London, Merlin, 2003).

Robert Gammage knew almost all the leading figures of the later years of Chartism. Although he had a good few axes to grind, he wrote the appealing and very detailed *History of the Chartist Movement, 1837–54* (1854), a work that continues to command attention. The slightly revised edition of 1894 was twice republished in 1969, by Augustus Kelley (New York), with an excellent Introduction by John Saville, and by Merlin (London), the latter reissued in 2006. Finally, a wide range of writings by other Chartists can be found in the contemporary pamphlets collected in the six invaluable volumes edited by Gregory Claeys: *The Chartist Movement in Britain, 1838–50* (London, Pickering & Chatto, 2001).

# Index

Note: 'n.' after a page reference indicates the number of a note on that page